Educational Media and Technology Yearbook

EDUCATIONAL MEDIA AND TECHNOLOGY YEARBOOK

Mary Ann Fitzgerald, Michael Orey, and Robert Maribe Branch, Editors

2002 VOLUME 27

Published in Cooperation with the
ERIC® Clearinghouse on Information & Technology
and the
Association for Educational Communications
and Technology

2002
Libraries Unlimited
A Division of Greenwood Pubishing Group
Englewood, Colorado

Libraries Unlimited
A Division of Greenwood Publishing Group, Inc.
P.O. Box 6633
Englewood, CO 80155-6633
1-800-237-6124
www.lu.com

Suggested cataloging supplied by Libraries Unlimited:

Educational media and technology yearbook. — Englewood, CO : Libraries Unlimited,
    A Division of Greenwood Publishing Group, Inc., 1985-
    v.-
    Annual
    2002- vol. 27-
    "Published in cooperation with the ERIC® Clearinghouse on Information and
Technology and the Association for Educational Communications and Technology"
    Continues: Educational media yearbook.
    ISBN 1-56308-910-6

    1. Educational technology -- United States -- Yearbook. 2. Instructional materials
centers -- United States-- Yearbook. 3. Instructional materials personnel -- United States
-- Yearbook. I. Fitzgerald, Mary Ann, ed. II. Orey, Michael, ed. III. Branch, Robert
Maribe, ed. IV. ERIC® Clearinghouse on Information and Technology. V. Association
for Educational Communications and Technology.

LB 1028.3.E372   2002   370.778   2002

Contents

Standards

Part Two
TECHNOLOGY CENTERS AND INSTITUTES
FOR LEARNING

Part Three
SCHOOL AND LIBRARY MEDIA

Part Four
LEADERSHIP PROFILES

Part Five
ORGANIZATIONS AND ASSOCIATIONS

Part Six
GRADUATE PROGRAMS

Part Seven
MEDIAGRAPHY
Print and Nonprint Resources

Preface

The purpose of the 27th volume of the *Educational Media and Technology Yearbook* is to explore current developments in the field of instructional technology as of early 2002. In the year 2001, we noted several trends in the field, some new and others continuing from recent years. The international surge toward online education, or "e-learning," continues to gain momentum. Instructional technology projects and initiatives continue to emphasize the themes of collaboration and integration. The interdisciplinary nature of this field seems to be broadening, and the borders that define instructional technology, information science, educational media, and information technology are becoming increasingly blurred. Among K–12 and higher education leaders, tension between the standards reform movement and the constructivist philosophy remains an issue for debate, and this debate has many implications for our field. In broader contexts, experiential education seems to be gaining importance, and designers are applying emerging technologies to create learning environments that simulate authentic situations. Finally, over the last few years we have witnessed a changing of the guard as many prominent leaders in the field of instructional technology retired. These developments and trends are represented in the *Yearbook* in the form of research studies, descriptive reports, and conceptual pieces with a solid scholarly foundation.

The audience for the *Yearbook* consists of media and technology professionals in K–12 schools, higher education, and business. Topics of interest to professionals practicing in these areas are broad, as the table of contents demonstrates. The theme unifying each of the chapters to follow is the use of technology to enable or enhance education. Forms of technology represented in this volume vary from traditional tools, such as the book, to the latest advancements in digital technology, whereas areas of education encompass wide-ranging situations involving learning and teaching.

As in prior volumes, the assumptions underlying the chapters presented here are as follows:

- Technology represents tools that act as extensions of the educator.

- Media serve as delivery systems for educational communications.

- Technology is *not* restricted to machines and hardware, but includes techniques and procedures derived from scientific research about ways to promote change in human performance.

- The fundamental tenet is that educational media and technology should be used to

    achieve authentic learning objectives,

    situate learning tasks,

    negotiate the complexities of guided learning,

    facilitate the construction of knowledge,

    support skill acquisition, and

    manage diversity.

The *Educational Media and Technology Yearbook* has become a standard reference in many libraries and professional collections. Examined in relation to its companion volumes of the past, it provides a valuable historical record of current ideas and developments in the field. Part 1, "Trends and Issues," presents chapters that develop the current themes listed above. Part 2, "Technology Centers and Institutes for Learning," includes reports from several research laboratories where exciting projects are unfolding. Part 3, "School and Library Media," concentrates on chapters of special relevance to K–12 education, school learning resources, and school library media centers. In part 4, "Leadership Profiles," the authors provide biographical sketches of the careers of instructional technology leaders. Part 5, "Organizations and Associations," and part 6, "Graduate Programs," are, respectively, directories of instructional technology-related organizations and institutes of higher learning offering degrees in related fields. Part 7, "Mediagraphy," presents an annotated listing of selected current publications related to the field.

The editors of the *Yearbook* invite media and technology professionals to submit manuscripts for consideration for publication. Contact Mary Ann Fitzgerald (mfitzger@coe.uga.edu) for submission guidelines.

Mary Ann Fitzgerald

Robert Branch, Michael Orey, and Tom Reeves each contributed ideas to this preface.

Contributors to
Educational Media and Technology Yearbook 2002

Yvonne Belanger
Ask ERIC
621 Skytop Road, Suite 160
Syracuse, NY 13244

Elizabeth Bennett
Associate Professor
Department of Media & Instructional
    Technology
State University of West Georgia
Carrollton, GA 30118
ekirby@westga.edu

Lisa Boes
Graduate School of Education,
Harvard University
5 Webster Avenue
Cambridge MA 02141
617-492-7231
boesli@gse.harvard.edu

Robert Maribe Branch
Professor and Department Head
Department of Instructional Technology
University of Georgia
604 Aderhold Hall
Athens, GA 30602
rbranch@coe.uga.edu

Jonathan Brinkerhoff
Division of Psychology in Education
Arizona State University
5622 South Rocky Point Road
Tempe, AZ 85283
jbrinker@asu.edu

Kathy Brock
Assistant Professor
Department of Media & Instructional
    Technology
State University of West Georgia
Carrollton, GA 30118
Kbrock@westga.edu

John K. Burton
Professor
Instructional Technology
Virginia Tech
220 War Memorial Hall
Blacksburg, VA 24061-0313
jburton@vt.edu

Rhoda Lintz Casey

Shu-Hsien Chen
Assistant Professor
Graduate School of Library and
    Information Studies
Queens College
City University of New York
65-30 Kissena Boulevard
Flushing, NY 11367
SHCMCHEN@aol.com

Leslie Cole
Editorial Assistant
Educational Media & Technology
    Yearbook
604 Aderhold Hall
Athens, GA 30602

Walter Dick
Professor Emeritus
Instructional Systems Design
Florida State University
117 Walnut Street
Brookville, PA 15825
wdick@mailer.fsu.edu

Rodney Earle
McKay School of Education
Brigham Young University
MCKB 210Q
Provo, UT 84602
Rodney_earle@byu.edu

James B. Ellsworth
Professor of Online Education
U.S. Naval War College
P.O. Box 5162
Newport, RI 02841-0102
JBElsworth@aol.com

Donald P. Ely
Professor Emeritus
Instructional Design, Development and
    Evaluation
Syracuse University
704 Hamilton Parkway
DeWitt, NY 13214
dely@ericir.syr.edu

John D. Emerson
Professor of Mathematics and Computer
    Science
Middlebury College
Department of Mathematics and Computer
    Science
Warner Hall
Middlebury, VT 05753
802-443-5589
jemerson@midd-unix.middlebury.edu

Linda Esser
School of Information Science & Learning
    Technologies
University of Missouri-Columbia
221B Townsend Hall
Columbia, MO 65211

Mary Ann Fitzgerald
Assistant Professor
Department of Instructional Technology
University of Georgia
604 Aderhold Hall
Athens, GA 30602
mfitzger@coe.uga.edu

Vicki Gregory
Professor and Director
School of Library and Information Science
University of South Florida
Tampa, Florida 33620
VLGAMPA@aol.com;
gregory@luna.cas.usf.edu

Kent L. Gustafson
Instructional Technology
The University of Georgia
604 Aderhold Hall
Athens, GA 30602
kgustafs@coe.uga.edu

James Klein
Division of Psychology in Education
Arizona State University
Tempe, AZ 85287-0611

Carol Koroghlanian
Foundations of Education Department
University of Wisconsin-Eau Claire
621 Farr Court
Eau Claire, WI 54701
koroghcm@uwec.edu

Ann Kwinn
Project Manager/Design Manager
MOHR Learning
11338 Moorpark Street
North Hollywood, CA 91602

Kim Kyung-Sun
School of Information Science & Learning
    Technologies
University of Missouri-Columbia
221B Townsend Hall
Columbia, MO 65211

Yuliang Liu
Instructional Technology
Department of Educational Leadership
Southern Illinois University Edwardsville
Edwardsville, Illinois 62026-1125
Office Phone: (618) 650-3293
Fax: (618) 650-3359
E-mail: yliu@siue.edu
URL: http://www.siue.edu/~yliu/

Barbara B. Lockee
Associate Professor
Instructional Technology
Virginia Tech
220 War Memorial Hall
Blacksburg, VA 24061-0313

Carrie A. Lowe

Emily Marsh
College of Information Studies
University of Maryland
4111M Hornbake Library, South Wing
College Park, MD 20742
emarsh@wam.umd.edu

Robbie McClintock
Institute for Learning Technologies
Teachers College, Columbia University
525 West 120th St.
New York, NY 10027
romz@columbia.edu

Michael Molenda
Associate Professor
Instructional Systems Technology
Indiana University
Education 2234
Bloomington, IN 47405
molenda@indiana.edu

D. Michael Moore
Professor
Instructional Technology
Virginia Tech
2502 Manchester Street
Blacksburg, VA 24060
moorem@vt.edu

Joi Moore
Assistant Professor
School of Information Science & Learning
    Technologies
University of Missouri-Columbia
221B Townsend Hall
Columbia, MO 65211
Moorejoi@missouri.edu

Frederick Mosteller
Professor Emeritus, Department of
    Statistics
Harvard University
Science Center 610
One Oxford Street
Cambridge, MA 02138

Michael Orey
Associate Professor
Department of Instructional Technology
University of Georgia
604 Aderhold Hall
Athens, GA 30602
morey@coe.uga.edu

Tjeerd Plomp
Department of Curriculum Development
    & Implementation
University of Twente
P.O. Box 217
7500 AE Enschede
Netherlands
Tel:+31-53-489 3595
Fax:+31-53-489 3759
E-mail: plomp@edte.utwente.nl

Thomas C. Reeves
Instructional Technology
The University of Georgia
604 Aderhold Hall
Athens, GA 30602
treeves@coe.uga.edu

Rita Richey
Professor
Instructional Technology
Wayne State University
13101 Vernon
Huntington Woods, MI 48070
rrichey@coe.wayne.edu

James D. Russell
Professor
Dept. of Curriculum & Instruction
Purdue University
1442 LAEB
W. Lafayette, IN 47907-1442

Shayne Russell

Michael Sullivan
Executive Director
Agency for Instructional Technology
P.O. Box A
Bloomington, IN 47402-0120

Lajeanne Thomas
Louisiana Technical University
P.O. Box 3161 TS
Ruston, LA 71272

Robert Tinker
The Concord Consortium, Inc.
37 Thoreau Street
Concord, MA 01742
(978) 369-4367v
bob@concord.org

Part One
Trends and Issues

Introduction

The primary focus of this yearbook is to identify trends and issues in the field of instructional technology, to document the normal ebb and flow of ideas, concepts, theories and applications that are a part of the nature of this field. This book is no different in that regard from its 26 predecessors. We try to capture the essence of the field, taken as a snapshot for this year. Unlike past volumes, we chose to include two subsections of the "Trends and Issues" part. The first subsection is ERIC Digests, which are reprints of ERIC reports available on the Internet. These reports help point to trends in the field. Other trends across all fields of education are standardization, testing, and accountability. We have included a subsection on a variety of standards that emerged during the past couple of years.

For those readers who are interested in finding out what the field of instructional technology is all about, we suggest that you take a look at Don Ely's digest, "A Dozen Frequently Asked Questions." This chapter will give you a sense of the field, and the Klein, Brinkerhoff, and Koroghlanian chapter will give you additional insight. Finally, we suggest you take a look at the Molenda and Sullivan chapter to get a sense of what is happening in the field.

As with the past several volumes, Michael Molenda, along with colleagues, takes the pulse of the field. In this issue, he and Michael Sullivan have taken up the task again, with a possibly misleading subtitle, "Hitting the Plateau." They look at higher education, K–12 education, and corporate training. In the face of the claim that e-learning is the next "killer app" for the Internet (a claim made by John Chambers, the chief executive officer of Cisco Systems), Molenda and Sullivan point to the previous killer apps of film, radio, and television and point out that they never met the expectations of the "cheerleaders" of that time.

Two of our chapters reflect the movement of Internet learning. The Moore, Lockee, and Burton chapter describes a master's program in instructional technology at Virginia Tech. The Liu chapter describes a study regarding computer-mediated communication, a topic that has increased in importance as a result of the e-learning movement.

The Emerson, Boes, and Mosteller chapter asks us to think about the importance of critical thinking across many fields of study. Whereas others push for the technologies of delivery and still others focus on content, this chapter focuses on how to get people to become better thinkers in various content areas, without regard to delivery platform. This piece balances nicely with the other chapters.

The Belanger and Ellsworth chapters look at technology proliferation and change. As the Molenda and Sullivan article noted, technology infrastructure has hit a plateau with some schools going so far as to equip all their students with laptops, but it has stabilized as change theory would suggest. So these two chapters afford further study for those interested in that portion of the Molenda and Sullivan chapter.

We conclude the ERIC Digests section with two chapters on the role of school library media specialists and librarians. Because school media is a large part of the field of instructional technology, it is important to include that representation.

Finally, we conclude part 1 with a section on standards. The first chapter describes those technology competencies we should expect of students in the K–12 schools, as well as the competencies we expect of the teachers in the schools. The second chapter focuses on standards or competencies for people who work in the field. The last chapter focuses on accreditation standards for departments that train people to work in the field.

You are welcome to submit work for this yearbook for consideration in future volumes. Please direct any comments, questions, and suggestions about the selection process to the senior editor.

Michael Orey

Issues and Trends in Instructional Technology
Hitting the Plateau

Michael Molenda
Indiana University

Michael Sullivan
Agency for Instructional Technology

The new millennium dawned on January 1, 2001, bright with the promise of dazzling prospects for instructional technology (IT). The year 2000 was a watershed year, in which information technology became ubiquitous in schools and colleges, and many dreamed that our world would truly be transformed. Not yet. Instead, the economy faltered and companies offering free computers and free software disappeared, along with companies offering free delivery of their free lunch. "Dot-com" became a term of derision rather than a promise of wealth. The once fashionable quest for "eyeballs"* looked like the Crusades of the Middle Ages—extremely questionable as a long-term plan.

As if joining a parade, schools cut back their high-tech investments, signaling their all-too-familiar budget struggles. Many universities scaled back their distance education business plans to stanch the flow of red ink. Corporate educators began to realize that the Internet was not some fantastic new form of collective intelligence but rather a distribution system—one that had some cost advantages but also some practical limitations.

In all sectors of education, signals appeared indicating that the seemingly inexorable upward curve of computer-based technology adoption was reaching a plateau. This suggests that we may actually be seeing the emergence of an **S**-shaped adoption curve, generally characteristic of the diffusion of innovations. This should not be surprising, but it always seems to come as a shock to the new-media enthusiasts of each generation that: "Pretty soon, all lectures will be replaced by radio . . . no, television . . . no, teaching machines . . . no, computers . . ."

As in previous reviews (Molenda, Russell, and Smaldino 1998; Molenda and Sullivan 2000; Molenda and Harris 2001), we have monitored developments in the three broad sectors in which instructional technology is employed—corporate training, higher education, and K–12 education—and report the status and trends in each sector. In the background of these different sectors, though, is a common technological and social environment. These technological and sociopolitical forces tend to be the "drivers" of change in education and training, so we begin with an overview of technological and societal trends that appear to have the greatest potential to affect developments in instructional technology.

---

*"Eyeballs" is a reference to the "business plans" of the high-flying Web portals such as Yahoo! They were (and are) selling advertising space on their portal, with advertising rates being based on how many "eyeballs" are attracted to their portal; that is, how many "hits" per day they receive. The weakness of this business plan is apparent if one calculates how much advertising revenue would be needed for the dot-com company to actually make a profit, then calculate how many "eyeballs" would have to be attracted to those advertising rates. It works out that every human alive would have to "hit" that portal more than once every day.

TECHNOLOGY TRENDS IN GENERAL

Hardware Hiatus

The quest for ever-greater bandwidth—the holy grail of telecommunications—faltered along with many other hardware trends. Warnings about the downside of digital subscriber lines (DSL) and the cost of cable modems spooked a public already uncertain about the technological future. Total expenditures for telecommunications actually *decreased* from $860 billion in the first quarter of 2000 to $837 billion in the first quarter of 2001 (Intelect 2001a). In addition, expenditures for personal computers (PCs) and peripherals experienced a similar decrease; from $20 billion in the first quarter of 2000 to $16 billion in the first quarter of 2001 (Intelect 2001b). In fact, PC sales actually declined for the first time in the information age and were predicted to sink 6 percent from 2000 to 2001 (Ewalt 2001). Fewer new generation machines could translate into less demand for the high bandwidth to feed those machines.

Everything Going Wireless

One of the most notable trends in information technology is toward wireless computing. Handheld devices capable of remotely accessing banks of data are already transforming the practice in professions, from medicine to firefighting. Some see wireless computing as the path to "ubiquitous computing," particularly on college campuses. A market forecast predicts that "61.5 million people will be using wireless devices to access the Internet in 2003, up from 7.4 million in the U.S. today." (Software & Information Industry Association 2000). This prediction, written in 1999, seems overly optimistic only two years later. The trend toward wireless communication is advancing, but there are still significant barriers ahead, particularly cost barriers, especially for education institutions.

Obsolescence of Older Media

CD-ROM

It has long been predicted that digital video disc (DVD) drives would replace CD-ROM drives in computers and that the DVD would become the medium of choice for educational materials. Certainly DVD sales have increased, but virtually all of the sales have been for entertainment products. At the same time, CD-ROM sales have fallen. In that most new DVD drives will support CD-ROMs, there is no particular technology-based reason for this fall-off. What is becoming increasingly obvious is that the Internet is diluting the demand for off-the-shelf media. Consumers and suppliers are beginning to view software as a service rather than a product.

Textbooks

On the other hand, the long-predicted demise of the textbook has not yet occurred. More e-textbooks are being published, with a tenfold increase in titles published between 2000 and 2001. But market demand remains weak. Hardware is one problem: There is not yet an accepted standard for a compact reader, and students resist textbooks that tie them to their computer. Software is another problem: Again, standards are lacking and users have difficulty accessing materials and navigating within the e-books. Further, most e-textbooks do not yet incorporate the multimedia features, such as animation, that would make them qualitatively superior to printed texts (Blumenstyk 2001).

Software Standards: Reusable Learning Objects Becoming Practical

Spurred by the capabilities of the Internet, a critical need has emerged to become more efficient in the design and production of digital media. At universities, in the military, and in corporate training designers are seeking a shortcut to converting tens of thousands of hours of course material to online formats. The key to this problem is to create reusable learning objects: "small (relative to the size of an entire course) instructional components that can be reused a number of times in different learning contexts" (Wiley 2001, 4). The next challenge is to code the learning objects digitally so that they will transfer to and run on your own organization's learning management system, WebCT, for example.

Several international efforts are underway to establish standards, or open specifications, for the technical building blocks of online learning. One effort is led by the IMS Global Learning Consortium, Inc., which has produced the IMS Meta-data Specification. (Meta-data are the labels that are put on learning objects, enabling these objects to be stored and retrieved efficiently as building blocks.) The IMS specification, in turn, has been incorporated into the Sharable Courseware Object Reference Model (SCORM), developed by the Advanced Distributed Learning (ADL) Co-Laboratory. In 2001, the ADL Co-Lab released version 1.1 of the SCORM and demonstrated the ability to create learning objects in real time and then load them and run them on a wide range of platforms (ADL Co-Lab 2001). Thus, standards for interoperability actually exist.

SOCIOPOLITICAL FORCES

Decentralization and Privatization of K–12 Education

Charter Schools

More than 1,800 charter schools operated in the 2000–2001 school year, an increase of 53 percent from the prior year (Hance 2001). Although for-profit schools often get more press, the largest of these, Edison Schools, manages only 113 schools and is struggling to maintain some of those (Branch 2001, 10). Certainly the decentralization movement has continued, but the privatization movement has slowed somewhat. Vouchers continue to be the lightning rod of the privatization movement, and setbacks in Cleveland and Milwaukee, coupled with the failure of the Bush administration to enact federal legislation in that area, may signal a hiatus for the voucher movement.

Virtual Schools

The onset of virtual schools has not yet had a noticeable impact on the predominance of traditional public schools. To date, as many public efforts as private ones have been established to serve this still emerging market. There is one new player entering the marketplace that could have an impact. K12, an organization led by William Bennett and funded in part by Knowledge Universe Learning Group, intends to offer a full K–12 curriculum online and has applied to operate at least one charter school, www.k12.com.

Resistance to Productivity Moves in Education

As has occurred throughout the history of education, new technological developments suggest ways to reorganize the delivery of education to become more cost-effective. School and college faculty have traditionally resisted such reorganization when it threatens their core values or basic work processes. That cycle is being repeated with the growth of interest in Internet-based delivery. An example at the K–12 level is the Virtual High School (VHS), a project funded by the U.S. Department of Education to provide online courses and assess their effectiveness. The VHS sets a number of quality criteria, including that all participating teachers must complete a 26-week online professional development course to prepare them to develop an online course. It also requires close monitoring of students and small class sizes. VHS is now working with the National Education Association on criteria for judging the quality of courses. These criteria will, of course, include student–teacher ratios and teacher qualifications (Electronic Education Report 2001a). All these require-ments tend to reinforce existing patterns of staffing and compensation, causing overall costs to *increase* at a time when costs are already increasing at rates greater than inflation.

Digital Divides

The original digital divide referred to the disparity in Internet access between the wealthy and the poor. This still exists. Households with incomes over $75,000 are 20 times more likely to have access to the Internet than those at lower income levels, and they are nine times more likely to have computers at home (Puma, Chaplin, and Pape 2000). Other divides, however, have also emerged. There is a large urban–rural gap, a male–female gap, and other gaps in most categories tracked by educators. These gaps are examined below in the K–12 section and collectively comprise the digital divides.

National Standards and Assessment

The U.S. federal government has a National Educational Technology Plan (U.S. Department of Education 2000). Its first goal is to make access to technology universal, and its second is that "All teachers will use technology effectively to help students achieve high academic standards." The plan itself seems to interpret this to mean the design and use of a rich learning environment. Unfortunately, in practice, the concept of "high academic stan-dards," is often interpreted in terms of content mastery, which is translated as performance on standardized tests. As states implement plans to enforce "standards," the emphasis on standardized testing increases. Among educators this trend is largely regarded as perni-cious, as "teaching to the test," which tends to suck the life out of lessons. To the extent that technology use is associated with teaching to the test, it will suffer the disdain of a large seg-ment of educators.

RATE OF ADOPTION OF DIFFERENT FORMS OF TECHNOLOGY

As a framework for our observations within each sector, we have chosen several broad issues that cut across sectors and have been of perennial interest in the literature of in-structional technology: rate of adoption of different forms of technology for delivery of in-struction, institutional constraints on acceptance of instructional technology, and challenges to existing paradigms.

Classroom Instruction

Face-to-face classroom instruction is still the most universally applied format of training, being used in 96 percent of companies (Industry report 2000: The methods 2000), up 6 percent since the previous year. In terms of the percentage of time spent in training, classroom instruction stands at about 80 percent overall, indicating an *increase* of about 10 percent in the past four years (Van Buren 2001, 16).

Traditional Classroom Media

Print materials—manuals and workbooks—remain high in popularity, being used at 85 percent of companies, rising 10 percent over the previous year (Industry report 2000: The methods 2000).

Videotapes are used at 79 percent of companies; this is a decrease from a high of 92 percent in 1995, but the number has held steady over the past four years. The use of slides and overhead transparencies has not been tracked consistently over the years, but these media formats seem to be receding slowly, as computer-based display media replace them. The use of games and simulations (non-computer-based) has declined markedly, from 63 to 28 percent since the mid-1990s, but has held steady for the past four years (Industry report 2000: The methods 2000).

Telecommunications Media

Videoconferences distributed via satellite or cable are used for training at about 23 percent of all companies, but they are not used for a large proportion of training time, except in the military services. They tend to be used for special purposes, such as the rollout of new products or new tools at companies with widely scattered locations. Desktop computer-based streaming video is used at about 7 percent of companies (Industry report 2000: The methods 2000).

Computer-Based Media

Computer-based delivery systems have made gradual advances in the past decade. In the early 1990s, this meant delivery via floppy disk or local area network (LAN); more recently, this means delivery via CD-ROM, the Internet, or an intranet. About 75 percent of all companies report using CD-ROM-based instruction, and 51 percent use Internet or intranet delivery (Industry report 2000: The methods 2000).

However, taken together, these computer-mediated delivery systems account for only about 8 percent of all time spent in training—surprisingly, a small *decrease* from the high point of 9 percent in reported in 1998 (Van Buren 2001, 16). If the American Society for Training and Development (ASTD) findings are a valid indicator, the growth rate seems to have reached a plateau. Perhaps because of the amount of advertising and public relations pumped into high-tech advocacy, this plateau effect seems to have gone largely unnoticed. In any event, the growth curve appears to be more of a straight upward diagonal than an **S** shape.

Issue 2: Constraints on Acceptance and Use of Technology

This leveling off in the growth of computer-based media may indicate that corporations are still experimenting to find the proper fit of technological delivery within their toolkit, or it may reflect some hesitancy on the part of trainees and training managers. Researchers at ASTD contacted some of the companies that reported declines in the use of e-learning. Several managers reported that they faced declining enrollments in e-learning courses as a result of negative experiences of learners in e-learning courses (Van Buren 2001, 17). This finding is supported by a study of 700 learners in 30 different e-learning courses. The study found that learners who reported negative previous experiences with e-learning were significantly less likely to take future e-learning courses offered to them (The Masie Center 2001, 6).

In a survey conducted in the United Kingdom, involving over 400 training and human resources professionals, the participants were asked about their *own* experiences with computer-based or online learning. When asked to describe their experiences in a few words, the most frequent responses were "convenient" and "flexible." However, next in frequency was "lonely." Only about one third of professionals used positive terms, such as "interesting" and "quick," with about as many respondents characterizing e-learning as "boring" and "slow" (Pickles 2001, 3). If the decision makers themselves harbor such mixed feelings about e-learning, one might expect their support to be less than passionate.

Issue 3: Challenges to Existing Paradigms

Blended Training

In everyday discussion, we tend to yield to the temptation to classify learning events into discrete categories: classroom, online, self-directed, action learning, and so on. In fact, though, corporate training programs are changing to consist more of hybrids: face-to-face classroom plus Web-based discussions; satellite video plus small-group interactions at remote sites; or on-job action learning plus mentoring via the Internet. The idea of combining conventional and online methods is coming to be recognized as a third path, referred to as *blended training.* A survey of e-learning vendors and industry professionals predicted that there will be "more emphasis on 'blended solutions' based on the realization that e-learning does not address all learning needs" (Schelin 2001, 28).

Reusable Learning Objects

Both training managers and the vendors of prepackaged training materials have a huge stake in the movement to develop technical standards for digital learning courseware. Currently, a company that has several thousand hours of analog material and wants to convert that material to an online format faces a daunting challenge. If those courses had been created with tools that were compliant with widely accepted standards, it would be relatively easy to find the needed text, images, and simulations and incorporate them into new lessons, regardless of the learning management software being used. This could be the most promising contribution to productivity in instructional design since the ADDIE model. At the moment, though, whose standards will become universal is still being debated (Lifelong Learning Market Report 2001).

HIGHER EDUCATION

Issue 1: Use of Technology-Based Media for Delivery of Instruction

Classroom Media

One of the hallmarks of instructional technology in higher education at this time is the uneasy coexistence of the whole panoply of analog media (slides, videocassettes, films, CDs, etc.) with the expanding array of digital (computer-based) media. Both classes of media are characterized by a multitude of incompatible formats and conflicting standards. In the typical college or university, one finds that most instructors still tend to rely on the older, more familiar media formats, such as overhead projection, slides, and video. A lot of capital and human resources are tied up in acquiring, maintaining, and moving around the hardware needed for this format. Even more time and effort is expended in development projects to produce new customized software in the analog formats. Typically, the output of such projects is too specialized to be adopted—or even to be adapted by other instructors. Therefore, such projects are both expensive and have little impact (South and Monson 2001).

At the same time, college and university media managers are struggling to meet the demand for more computer-based infrastructure. The hardware must be upgraded constantly, and so, too, does software, which becomes obsolete at a dizzying pace. The capital and human costs of this proliferation of media formats and the attendant complexities of working in this environment tend to put instructional technology people on the hit lists of both faculty and administration.

The way out of this dilemma being chosen by many institutions is to gradually reduce support for analog media and to shift to a policy of producing future materials in digital format. Further, the digital formats are standardized to increase compatibility across departments, even to the point of imagining a single database for all the university's instructional media. Such standardization would finally make possible the use of reusable learning objects, thus introducing the possibility of actually reducing the cost of providing instructional media as needed by faculty.

In fact, though, there is evidence that the pace of faculty adoption of computer-based media may be slowing. Prior to 2000 there appears to have been a fairly steady pace of adoption of Internet-based innovations, such as incorporating Internet resources into courses and establishing a Web page for each course. But since then, the pace may have slowed. The Campus Computing Project (2000) reports that the percentage of courses using Internet resources rose each year between 1997 and 1999 by 10 percent, 8 percent, and 6 percent, respectively. Then, between 1999 and 2000 it rose by only 4 percent. The comparable figures for Web pages are 5 percent, 9 percent, 6 percent, and 3 percent. This points to a possible plateau effect in adoption—long before reaching universality. For Internet resources, the adoption plateau will be approximately 45 percent and for Web pages approximately 35 percent.

For other sorts of computer-based technologies, such as computer simulations and computer presentation media, a plateau effect is also visible, with computer simulation adoption lingering around 15 percent since the mid-1990s, and presentation media stalling out at around 45 percent of all courses (Green 2000).

So, in the higher education sector we appear to be seeing the emergence of an S-shaped adoption curve that is characteristic of innovation adoption generally.

Distance Education

The "land rush" mentality continues to impel administrators to worry about positioning their institutions in the distance education (DE) marketplace. In the 2001 EDUCAUSE survey of information technology officers, distance education was ranked first among issues with "potential for explosive strategic impact" (Lembke and Rudy 2001). This frenzy is disproportional to the economic payoffs. It is widely accepted that most traditional colleges and universities are losing money on their DE operations.

The number of institutions actually offering DE courses and programs is difficult to pin down precisely. The last scientific survey was conducted by the U.S. Department of Education for the 1997–98 academic year. One source of estimates is an annual survey by Market Data Retrieval (MDR). Their most recent survey indicates that the number of post-secondary institutions offering courses leading to accredited degrees grew rapidly between 1999 and 2000 but plateaued between 2000 and 2001, settling at about 30 percent of all two- and four-year colleges and universities in the United States (Jecusco 2001). The most authoritative catalog of DE courses, *Peterson's Guide to Distance Learning Programs, 2001* (2000), contains listings for more than 1,000 institutions; this is congruent with the MDR reports. Of course, the offering of distance programs varies greatly by type of institution. Although relatively fewer community colleges or small liberal arts colleges offer such programs, about 80 percent of four-year public universities do offer distance programs, with the proportion rising to nearly 90 percent for larger institutions.

Although the number of institutions may have leveled off, the number of courses and programs appears to be growing. That is, the growth is coming not from new institutions entering the marketplace but new courses and programs being offered. Further, the growth is coming in courses offered wholly or in part via the Internet. Courses offered via one-way or two-way video have remained stable.

Because geographic boundaries are irrelevant to online learning, higher education institutions are being driven to think in terms of capturing a share of the national—or even global—market. It is not clear yet, though, what a successful business model might be for "dual mode" institutions—that is, institutions that offer both traditional residential programs and distance programs. Distance-only universities, such as the Open University in

Britain and Jones International University in the United States, which were accredited to offer degrees in 1999, have demonstrated a successful model for that type of institution. But the jury is out on how traditional universities can make the transition.

The period of 2000 to 2001 was marked by a welter of consortium-building. Many universities were concluding that only by sharing the up-front costs, such as course development and marketing, could their DE programs hope to be economically competitive. Many consortia have been formed on a statewide basis; in fact, 35 such consortia had been formed by 2001, including Illinois Virtual Campus, Kentucky Virtual University, and SUNY Learning Network. Others have been formed on a regional basis, Southern Regional Electronic Campus and Western Governors University, the best known. Others aim to forge alliances among peer institutions—universities with common interests, including National Technological University, Universitas 21, Alliance of Four, Jesuit Distance Education Network, and Associated Colleges of the South, Fathom.

In many cases, these consortia serve primarily as portals, offering a single front door to courses and degrees at many different institutions, emphasizing the marketing function. In other cases, there is an intent to create a new degree-granting entity, such as Western Governors University, or Cardean University, which was established by Unext.com, pooling resources from Columbia Business School, Stanford University, University of Chicago, Carnegie Mellon University, and London School of Economics. Even such widely publicized efforts as Western Governors and Cardean still enroll only a few hundred students in degree programs. Whether there exists a large market for degrees from new universities remains to be seen.

Some large, "brand-name" universities are exploring a third path; University of Maryland, New York University, and Columbia University, for example, have formed for-profit subsidiaries to offer online degree programs. The idea is an attempt to exploit their intellectual capital without diluting the brand name value of the residential university. In addition to the courseware offered by higher education institutions, there are major offerings available from for-profit organizations, such as University of Phoenix, Nova Southeastern University, and Jones International University.

The long-term viability of any of these ventures depends on whether the ideas on which they were founded can be translated into a successful business model. The key to profitability is providing quality education while reducing labor costs. The dual-mode universities have little hope of reaping huge profits because they are already saddled with an existing conventional faculty, who expect to be compensated at their usual rate whether they are doing face-to-face or online work. A partial solution is to use regular faculty to design the courses and less expensive adjunct faculty to do the day-to-day teaching. This eventually raises the question of the comparability of quality.

Another approach is to automate more of the day-to-day interaction in the online course. Cardean University hopes to combine both approaches. Experience to date, though, is that the up-front development costs for truly interactive software are beyond the means of most institutions. Many doubt whether Cardean can ever recoup the tens of millions of dollars they have invested in course development. As mentioned earlier, if more of the developed materials could be recycled in other courses or sold to other organizations in the form of reusable learning objects, development costs might some day be reduced.

Issue 2: Constraints on Acceptance and Use of Technology

Faculty Acceptance

Incremental growth in faculty use of media continues, although perhaps at a reduced rate of growth, as indicated in the Campus Computing Project (2000) report cited earlier. For most faculty users, media are still incorporated in their teaching in supplementary ways. That is, technology is used to the extent that it is consistent with conventional roles;

face-to-face courses are designed to be teacher dependent. However, there is a growing array of success stories of large-scale projects to provide technology enriched, learner-centered environments. A good example is the Math Emporium at Virginia Tech—a facility housing 500 computer stations arranged in study pods of six, providing students with round-the-clock access to a wide range of software and human assistance. In the Math Emporium, students can take advantage of the diagnostic quizzes, an electronic hyperlinked textbook, and interactive self-paced tutorials. There are also many tutors in the emporium to give students personal help when they do not understand the tutorials or quizzes. The evidence indicates that student performance and satisfaction have risen while Mathematics department costs have fallen (Twigg 1999).

Faculty acceptance of technology is also being affected by their involvement in distance education, and about 10 percent of all faculty members now teach or have taught distance courses (National Education Association, 2000). Because most DE courses are taught by the same faculty who teach face-to-face courses, the faculty tend to carry their DE habits over into the conventional classroom. Course Web pages, links to Internet resources, team work spaces, and e-mail correspondence turn out to be just as valuable for face-to-face classes as they are for DE classes.

Funding Infrastructure and Support

Colleges and universities continue to struggle to pay for their information technology infrastructure. In the 2000–2001 academic year, information technology costs rose 13 percent over the previous year, while overall expenditures rose only about 3 percent (Olsen 2001). The budget squeeze impacts more severely at smaller colleges that are already struggling to survive in the competitive American higher education marketplace. Many institutions have not yet made structural changes to their budgets to account for information technology expenditures, instead improvising from year to year, using "budget dust" left over from other accounts to take care of technology needs (Phipps and Wellman 2001). One possible strategy is to off-load part of the hardware cost onto students by requiring them to provide their own computers. So far, this has not proven to be an easy answer because it raises many administrative and marketing problems. Most colleges have found that they can't require students to bring their own laptops without offering a subsidy. It turns out to be easier to provide ample computer lab facilities. Hence, only about 5 percent of colleges require students to provide their own hardware, with the rate of increase remaining quite flat (Olsen 2001).

As wireless technology develops, there is some hope that wireless systems might some day replace wired systems, at lower overall cost. As of 2000, only about 5 percent of college campuses were fully wireless. Some colleges have found that the cost of setting up wireless networks would be far more expensive than conventional wired networks. One of the sales features of wireless networks is the notion of "ubiquitous computing"—being able to be plugged in all the time, from anywhere. But ubiquitous access could well be a mixed blessing educationally. One study found that online access was an advantage as long as students remained focused on class activity, but many didn't. In general, students who spent more time browsing while in class had poorer grades (Carlson 2001). In Japan, where the great majority of students access their e-mail through handheld devices, instructors are already reporting that e-mailing and Web surfing is a major distraction in class.

Retaining the necessary staff to take care of the infrastructure is part of the struggle. Information technology staffing showed up as one of the top two concerns of respondents to the 2001 EDUCAUSE survey (Lembke and Rudy 2001). In the Campus Computing Project annual survey (2000), the top two issues identified by respondents were "retaining current information technology personnel" and "helping information technology personnel stay current."

It has taken a few years for the realization to dawn, but many colleges and universities are coming to understand that their technology investments are unlikely to have an impact on improved teaching and learning until they actively support faculty utilization. A new enterprise is emerging: the Teaching, Learning, and Technology Center (TLTC). Hundreds of universities now support a one-stop shopping center where faculty can go to get help preparing technology-based instruction. Typically, according to Long (2001), these TLTCs combine the services of information technology support and faculty development, sometimes adding the library. The TLTC is yet another cost of the high-tech enterprise, one that is often overlooked in the accounting.

Issue 3: Challenges to Existing Paradigms

The Faculty and the Traditional Classroom Paradigm

Plenty of evidence exists that educational institutions are investing more in technology. There is not a lot of evidence that this investment is yielding greater productivity. In the business sector, such investments took a decade to yield results, but they eventually did. However, the crucial factor was facing the necessity to undergo re-engineering of business processes for greater efficiency. That has not happened yet at most colleges and universities. The case is stated clearly by Saba (2001): "[I]f we follow the road where technology is used to reduce the cost of education and speed up time-to-degree for students, while making education more personal, it might succeed." That success, however, "does not depend on better technology or better instruction by faculty alone, but depends on the massive reorganization of the university." The economic problem is that most distance education and other technology-based instruction continues to follow the traditional labor-intensive paradigm of 25 students engaged with a professor, who plays the roles of subject-matter expert, designer, lecturer, orchestrater of all activities, giver of feedback, and evaluator. There's no way to obtain more than marginal efficiency improvements under those rules.

Changing the paradigm in ways that would affect the roles of faculty would not be popular. In fact, faculty groups have clearly spoken out about the need to carry over traditional practices into distance education. Resolutions to that effect were passed at the American Federation of Teachers and National Education Association conventions in the summer of 2000 and also by the Nova Scotia Teachers Union more recently (Carr 2001). But the tools for restructuring the teaching-learning paradigm are now at hand; successful models are readily available. The Open University has successfully served more than 12,000 students per year in an online course. The University of Illinois has tripled enrollment in its foreign language courses without adding faculty by relying heavily on a new software program that automates grading of homework exercises and quizzes. Virginia Tech has lowered costs while increasing enrollments and student success in mathematics with its lab-based Math Emporium.

Reusable Learning Objects

As previously discussed, in regard to classroom media and corporate training, the development of standards around reusable learning objects would usher in a paradigm shift in course design. Instead of creating everything from scratch, designers would select elements from vast repositories of text, images, audio and video clips, and simulations, thus reducing cycle time and labor by quantum leaps (Gnagni 2001).

K–12 EDUCATION

Issue 1: Use of Technology-Based Media for Delivery of Instruction

Traditional Audiovisual Media

Patterns of use are difficult to determine because analog media have disappeared from the radar charts of agencies collecting information. Although we are certain that not all VCRs and overhead projectors have been thrown in the trash, we are also fairly certain that neither administrators nor vendors demonstrate much interest in such established items. Our own sampling of practice indicates that regional service agencies (RESAs), local education agencies (LEAs), and even individual school buildings still maintain collections of analog media and experience some demand for such products. Video use in schools is overwhelmingly supplemental. Certain topics lend themselves to video presentations, and teachers continue to use video and print materials for health topics, career counseling, and other specific issues. Public Broadcasting Service (PBS) documentaries and feature films are also used rather commonly, although the instructional intent is often nebulous.

Overall, approximately $10 billion is spent annually on instructional materials used in schools. A hidden factor in this figure is that teachers themselves spend about 13 percent of that amount from their own private funds. A recent estimate is that teachers spend $437 of their personal funds per year to buy materials for their classes (Hance 2001).

Computer-Based Media

The popular measure of success for technology in schools has become Internet access. By the fall of 2000, 98 percent of all U.S. public schools were connected to the Internet (Cattagni and Westat 2001). Similarly, virtually all schools have some computers on the premises. Victory has been declared.

On the other hand, spending for instructional technology in U.S. schools actually dropped from $6.7 billion in 1998–1999 to $5.6 billion in 1999–2000 (Quality Education Data 2001), while overall expenditures for education grew. E-rate reimbursements and other federal and state programs provided a substantial share of these billions, which leads to the inference that state and local commitments to instructional technology are fairly shallow.

Teacher Computer Use

In our previous annual overviews, we have documented the relatively low rate at which teachers actually employ computers in day-to-day practice. A recent illustration is the finding of a NetDay survey (2001) that indicates that only 20 percent of teachers used the Internet to communicate with parents, and only 18 percent posted lesson plans online. In fact, among teachers who have Internet access, 60 percent said they spent less than 30 minutes online each day (which is less than the average user). As access to computer facilities has grown, usage has grown incrementally. However, this increase does not diminish the generalization that computers have so far made minimal impact on teacher practice. The reasons are many and well covered in the literature. One new insight is provided by Becker and Riel (2000) who categorized teachers according to their level of professional engagement. They found that those categorized as the least professionally engaged tended to be more transmission oriented in their teaching philosophy (as opposed to a more constructivist posture) and were far less likely to use computers in learner-centered ways (i.e., group work, projects, or active, cognitively challenging pedagogy).

Student Computer Use

The apparent ubiquitous state of Internet access is offset somewhat by the 37 percent of classrooms not connected to the Internet (Education Week 2001, 51) and the ratio of students to Internet connected computer, estimated to be about eight to one (Education Week 2001, 49). This would imply that the typical student is able to access the Internet no more than one period per day. In fact, a recent poll of students found that the average student used school computers one hour or less per week versus five hours on home computers. Among those who attended so-called high-tech schools, only 23 percent used computers at least five hours per week in school (Harris Interactive 2001, 4). This may not be a serious problem for students in that only 7 percent said computer use was extremely important to how well they do in school (Harris Interactive 2001, 14).

The issue of usage is colored by what has been labeled the digital divide. It was fashionable even a few years ago to document the differences in spending between schools with many low-income students and schools with few of these students. The E-Rate program and other programs have poured vast sums of money into all schools, but particularly schools with large populations of low-income students. With hardware disparities diminishing, the issue now has been refocused to reflect "inequities [that] involve not so much access to computers, but the way computers are used to educate children" (Education Week 2001, 10). The issues creating the chasms would appear to be the traditional ones of racial inequality, gender, language group discrimination, and other such factors that go beyond mere economic differences.

Issue 2: Constraints on Acceptance and Use of Technology

Staff Development

Perhaps because of the success in equipping and wiring schools, there is currently more public attention focused on professional development. The need is indicated in survey responses that show that a majority of teachers had neither changed the way they teach because of Internet access nor were under pressure by administrators to do so (Electronic School 2001). There is widespread agreement that training in technology use is a necessary, but frequently lacking, element in the equation. Schwab and Foa (2001) summed it up well: "[T]here are still many more thousands of teachers who, while they know how to do word processing or even search the Internet, don't have the slightest clue how to truly integrate technology into their teaching. The problem for educators nationwide is how to scale up effective training to reach tens of thousands of teachers quickly."

Lending urgency to in-service technology training is the finding that it is the single most critical factor associated with improving student achievement when using technology in instruction (CEO Forum 2001, 9). Despite the demonstrable need, the latest indication is that only 8 percent of technology expenditures are directed toward professional staff development (Topics in Education Group 2001).

Preservice Training

Recently degreed teachers who are entering the profession from schools of teacher education do seem to be better prepared. Teachers with three or fewer years of teaching experience were more likely to feel well prepared than teachers with 20 or more years of experience (31 percent vs. 19 percent; National Center for Education Statistics 2000, 75). Further, new national standards for technology skills for teachers, promulgated by the International Society for Technology in Education (ISTE) in 2000, are expected to have an influence on preservice training in the future. As in-service teachers retire or leave the profession and are replaced by recently graduated teachers, technological literacy is expected to rise. However, the larger question of whether this knowledge will lead to better performance in the classroom is still very much open.

Technology Support

Survey data gathered by Becker and his colleagues show that teacher use of technology is highly correlated with level of support at the building level (Ronnkvist, Dexter, and Anderson 2000). Support entails a wide range of services: facilities, presence of a support staff, personal help and guidance, professional development, and professional incentives. All of these services are problematic. One recent indicator is that 46 percent of surveyed teachers said that their schools lack technical support to help when there are problems (NetDay 2001). This reliability or dependability factor is seldom pointed out when identifying factors impeding the use of technology, but field experience indicates that teachers are loath to base lessons on technology that may not work when needed. We anticipate technology support to be the next major issue identified after staff development is fully addressed.

Outdated Hardware

Schools, like colleges and universities, are struggling with the challenge of acquiring and maintaining an information technology infrastructure. Some of this is attributable to the "one time purchase" mentality. In fact, initial purchase costs represent only about one quarter of the total cost of ownership, and districts, like colleges, are ill prepared for the long-term costs involved with maintaining and replacing computer equipment (Fitzgerald 1999).

Curricular Match

The dependence on the Internet for instruction has been a mixed blessing for educators. The conventional wisdom continues to be that Internet-delivered content is free and valuable. Indeed, we have seen the demise of most fee-based instructional services. Unfortunately, though, the dot-com crash of 2000 led to the disappearance of many educationally valuable content sites on the Web (Hoch 2001). Even casual observers are aware that much of the Web is a quagmire of advertising, pornography, politically inspired commentary, and sophomoric humor. Hence, the challenge for schools is not in acquiring computers or obtaining connections but in finding meaningful and useful content or instruction. Education journals supply regular lists of suitable sites for educators, but the issue of teacher time is a major factor restricting usage. The few dependable continuing sites receive regular and constant use. Among the 25 most popular children's Web sites as of March, 2000, were PBS Online, Discovery Online, Thinkquest.org, The Smithsonian Institution, and The Official Home of *Sesame Street*. None of the other 20 sites indicated any educational content (American Library Association 2000).

Of course there are still vendors supplying software for lease or purchase. The consolidation movement has continued, and a few large conglomerates control much of the instructional content business. Few of the software companies report being profitable. For example, Riverdeep Interactive Learning, American Education, Heartsoft Inc., and Lightspan all reported net losses, ranging from $250,000 to $18 million, in the first quarter of 2001 (Electronic Education Report 2001b). The entire educational software market shriveled by over 22 percent in one year and is now a rather paltry $454.6 million. The K–12 institutional market is certainly a very small part of this.

Issue 3: Challenges to Existing Paradigms

Homeschooling

The dominant paradigm for schooling in the United States has, for almost 200 years, been going to a public (or, to a lesser extent, a private) school. But homeschooling has emerged as an increasingly popular alternative. How popular it is is difficult to determine. Homeschoolers win national spelling bees and attract the popular press, but there are no reliable sources of data. Estimates of students being homeschooled vary widely, and the expected emergence of technology-based schools has not really occurred. William Bennett's "K12," as previously mentioned, will target homeschoolers and will again test the thesis that there are hundreds of thousands of homeschooled students waiting for a technology-based education.

CONCLUSIONS

What is becoming clear is that we are experiencing déjà vu regarding educators' responses to today's new media, comparable to the patterns of previous media, such as film, radio, and television. The new medium emerges with great fanfare. Public pressure builds to employ it in education. Schools and colleges acquire the hardware needed to enter the game. Software lags behind. Instructor adoption lags even further behind, but it eventually grows to substantial proportions before plateauing; however, it never reaches the levels predicted by the cheerleaders.

We know that hardware penetration is a necessary, but not sufficient, condition for productive use of technology in instruction. The key stakeholders decide how quickly and to what extent new technologies are adopted. We know that different stakeholders move at different rates in the various public and private sectors. Their decisions depend greatly on their perception of the personal advantage offered by the new technology as well as their organizations' demands on them to find ways of making their practice more productive.

These organizational dynamics, explained in greater detail in Molenda and Sullivan (2000), go far toward explaining the variations in rate and extent of use of technology in different sectors.

REFERENCES

ADL Co-Lab. (2001, June 6). *ADL Plugfest 4 proves e-learning specifications work.* News release. [Online]. Available: http://www.adlnet.org/. (Accessed June 7, 2001).

American Library Association. (2000). *50+ great web sites for parents and kids.* American Library Association. [Online]. Available: http://www.ala.org/parentspage/greatsites/50.html. (Accessed November 27, 2001).

Becker, H. J., and Riel, M. M. (2000). *Teacher professional engagement and constructivist-compatible computer use.* Irvine, CA: Center for Research on Information Technology and Organizations, University of California, Irvine and University of Minnesota.

Blumenstyk, G. (2001, May 18). Publishers promote e-textbooks, but many students and professors are skeptical. *Chronicle of Higher Education,* A35–A36.

Branch, A. (2001, June). The News Connection: Edison Schools struggle in New York and San Francisco. *Curriculum Administrator* 37:6, 10–11.

The Campus Computing Project. (2000, October). *The 2000 National Survey of Information Technology in Higher Education: Struggling with IT staffing.* [Online]. Available: http://www.campuscomputing.net. (Accessed April 19, 2001).

Carlson, S. (2001, April 21). Wireless technology is a double-edged sword, researchers conclude. *Chronicle of Higher Education,* A55.

Carr, S. (2001, May 29). A teachers' union in Canada seeks more control over distance education. *Chronicle of Higher Education.* [Online]. Available: http://chronicle.com/free/2001/05 /2001052902u.htm. (Accessed May 29, 2001).

Cattagni, A., and Westat, E. F. (2001). *Internet access in U.S. public schools and classrooms: 1994–2000.* NCES 2001-071. Washington DC: U.S. Department of Education, National Center for Education Statistics.

CEO Forum. (2001). *Education technology must be included in comprehensive education legislation.* Washington DC: CEO Forum on Education and Technology.

Education Week. (2001, May 10). Technology Counts 2001: The new divides. *Education Week* XX:35.

Electronic Education Report. (2001a, June 6). NEA working on criteria that will judge quality of on-line learning. *Electronic Education Report* 8:11, 3.

———. (2001b, May 23). Financial briefs. *Electronic Education Report* 8:10, 8.

Electronic School. (2001, June). Teachers aren't using the Internet, survey finds. *Electronic School,* 10–11.

Ewalt, D. M. (2001, June 8). PC industry's first decline predicted. *Information Week.* [Online.] Available: http://www.informationweek.com/story/IWK20010608S0003. (Accessed June 14, 2001).

Fitzgerald, S. (1999). Technology's real costs. *Electronic School,* September 1999. [Online]. Available: http://www.electronic-school.com/1999909/0999sbot.html. (Accessed July 9, 2000).

Gnagni, S. (2001, February). Building blocks: How the standards movement plans to revolutionize electronic learning. *University Business.* [Online]. Available: http://www.universitybusiness.com. (Accessed June 12, 2001).

Green, K. C. (2000). *Campus computing, 2000.* Conference presentation. [Online]. Available: http://www.campuscomputing.net/archive/Green-CC2000.PDF. (Accessed June 1, 2001).

Hance, M. (2001, January). Top twenty trends in K–12 schools. *DataPoints.* [Online.] Available: http://www.schooldata.com/datapoint59.html. (Accessed March 15, 2001).

Harris Interactive. (2001). *Education Week/Market Data Retrieval/Harris Poll of Students and Technology.* [Online.] Available: http://www.edweek.org/sreports/tc01/35survey.pdf. (Accessed June 6, 2001).

Hoch, F. (2001, May). Trends 2000 wrapup. *Upgrade,* 11.

Industry report 2000: The methods. (2000, October). *Training,* 57–63.

Intelect. (2001a). Telecom. [Online.] Available: http://www.intelectmt.com/corp/intelectmt/tele /tele_index.htm. (Accessed June 14, 2001).

———. (2001b). PCs and peripherals. [Online.] Available: http://www.intelectmt.com/corp/intelectmt/pcs /pc_index.htm. (Accessed June 14, 2001).

Jecusco, C. (2001, January). Internet infiltrates college campuses. *Datapoints.*

Lembke, R., and Rudy, J. (2001). *Second annual EDUCAUSE Survey identifies key IT issues.* [Online]. Available: http://www.educause.edu/issues/survey2001/report.asp. (Accessed June 8, 2001).

Lifelong Learning Market Report. (2001). *E-learning standards push evident in news from Training 2001 Conference in Atlanta.* News release. [Online]. Available: http://www.simbanet.com/press /headlines/llmr_03.21.html. (Accessed March 26, 2001).

Long, P. D. (2001, June). Trends: technology support trio. *Syllabus,* 8.

The Masie Center. (2001). *E-learning: "If e build it, will they come?"* Alexandria, VA: American Society for Training & Development.

Molenda, M., and Harris, P. (2001). Issues and trends in instructional technology. In R. M. Branch and M. A. Fitzgerald (eds.), *Educational media and technology yearbook 2001: Volume 26.* Englewood, CO: Libraries Unlimited.

Molenda, M., Russell, J., and Smaldino, S. (1998). Trends in media and technology in education and training. In R. M. Branch, and M. A. Fitzgerald (eds.), *Educational media and technology yearbook 1998: Volume 23.* Englewood, CO: Libraries Unlimited.

Molenda, M., and Sullivan, M. (2000). Issues and trends in instructional technology. In R. M. Branch and M. A. Fitzgerald (eds.), *Educational Media and Technology Yearbook 2000: Volume 25.* Englewood, CO: Libraries Unlimited.

National Center for Education Statistics (NCES). (2000). Teacher use of computers and the Internet in public schools. *Education Statistics Quarterly: Summer 2000.* Washington, DC: U.S. Department of Education.

National Education Association (NEA). (2000). A survey of traditional and distance learning higher education members. Washington, DC: National Education Association.

NetDay. (2001). 84% of teachers say Internet improves quality of education. News Release. [Online.] Available: http://www.netday.org/news_survey.htm. (Accessed April 6, 2001).

Olsen, F. (2001, April 20). Survey finds another increase in campus spending on information technology. *Chronicle of Higher Education*, A53.

Peterson's Guide to Distance Learning Programs, 2001. (2000). Lawrenceville, NJ: Peterson's.

Phipps, R. A., and Wellman, J. V. (2001, April). *Funding the "Infostructure."* Indianapolis, IN: Lumina Foundation.

Pickles, T. (2001). *Training trends 2001.* Training ZONE Ltd. [Online]. Available: http://www.trainingzone.co.uk. (Accessed March 3, 2001).

Puma, M. J., Chaplin, D. D., and Pape, A. D. (2000). *E-Rate and the digital divide: A preliminary analysis from the integrated studies of educational technology.* Washington DC: U.S. Department of Education, Planning and Evaluation Service.

Quality Education Data. (2001). *QED's Technology Purchasing Forecast, 2000–2001. 6th Edition.* Denver, CO: Quality Education Data.

Ronnkvist, A., Dexter, S. L., and Anderson, R. E. (2000*). Technology support: Its depth, breadth and impact in America's schools.* Irvine, CA: Center for Research on Information Technology and Organizations, University of California, Irvine and University of Minnesota.

Saba, F. (2001). Why distance education will fail and harm higher education. Distance-Educator.com. [Online]. Available. http://www.distance-educator.com/horizonlive/saba_presentation.pdf. (Accessed April 10, 2001).

Schelin, E. (2001, April). E-learning beyond the hype. *E-learning*, 26–28.

Schwab, R. L., and Foa, L. J. (2001, April). Integrating technologies throughout our schools. *Phi Delta Kappan* 82:8, 620.

Software & Information Industry Association (SIIA). (2000). *Trends shaping the digital economy, Part 1: Software as a service.* [Online.] Available: http://www.trendsreport.net/software/5.html. (Accessed May 10, 2001).

South, J. B., and Monson, D. W. (2001). A university-wide system for creating, capturing, and delivering learning objects. In Wiley, D. A., II (ed.), *The instructional use of learning objects.* Bloomington IN: Agency for Instructional Technology and Association for Educational Communications and Technology.

Topics in Education Group. (2001, May). *Reaching the Classroom Through the Internet* 1:3, 3.

Twigg, C. A. (1999). *Improving learning & reducing costs: Redesigning large-enrollment courses.* Troy, NY: Center for Academic Transformation, Renssaelaer Polytechnic Institute.

U.S. Department of Education. (2000). *E-learning, putting a world-class education at the fingertips of all children: The National Educational Technology Plan.* Washington DC: .U.S Department of Education, Office of Educational Technology.

Van Buren, M. E. (2001). *The 2001 ASTD State of the Industry Report.* Alexandria, VA: American Society for Training & Development.

Wiley, D. A., II. (2001). Connecting learning objects to instructional design theory: A definition, a metaphor, and a taxonomy. In Wiley, D. A., II (ed.), *The instructional use of learning objects.* Bloomington IN: Agency for Instructional Technology and Association for Educational Communications and Technology.

The Foundations of Educational Technology

James D. Klein

Jonathan Brinkerhoff
Division of Psychology in Education
Arizona State University

Carol Koroghlanian
Foundations of Education Department
University of Wisconsin-Eau Claire

ABSTRACT

The purpose of this paper is to present the results of a study conducted to determine the optimal instructional content and delivery method for the course "The Foundations of Educational Technology." The study also examined feelings about using the Internet to deliver the course. Implications for teaching an introductory course aimed at providing students with knowledge about our field are provided.

THE FOUNDATIONS OF EDUCATIONAL TECHNOLOGY

Many graduate programs in educational technology offer an introductory course aimed at providing students with knowledge about the field. Typically, this course provides entry-level master's and doctoral students with their first exposure to both historical and recent developments in the field (Pershing et al. 2000; Reiser et al. 1999).

The Educational Technology program at Arizona State University (ASU) has offered a course called "The Foundations of Educational Technology" since 1970. The course has evolved over the past 30 years from a survey of the product development cycle to an examination of the accomplishments and issues in the field.

Recently, we conducted a study to determine the optimal instructional content and delivery method for The Foundations of Educational Technology course at ASU. The study also examined feelings about using the Internet to deliver the course.

The study was prompted in part by the results of a focus group consisting of students, graduates, and faculty of ASU's Educational Technology program and employers that hire the program graduates. This focus group indicated that "knowledge about the field" and "technical literacy" were among the essential skills and knowledge a student should possess upon graduation from the program. Another impetus for our study was the recent merger of the Educational Technology program and the Educational Media and Computers program at ASU, which arose from the desire to combine two courses about the field into one course.

The purpose of our study was to answer the following questions:

- What is the optimal instructional content for a foundations course in educational technology?

- What is the optimal delivery method for a foundations course in educational technology?

- What feelings do respondents have about the use of the Internet for a foundations course in educational technology?

METHOD

Methods and techniques for our study followed suggestions provided by Allison Rossett (1987) in her book *Training Needs Assessment.*

Data Sources

Extant Data

We collected extant data to identify the content and topics most frequently covered in foundations or introductory survey courses in educational technology. These data were obtained by examining syllabi for graduate-level courses taught at the following institutions: Arizona State University, Florida State University, University of Georgia, Indiana University, San Diego State University, and Syracuse University.

Current Students

We contacted 35 students enrolled in our educational technology program about participating in the study. Twenty-three students responded to the request, indicating a 66 percent response rate. The majority of these participants were female (74 percent), between 23 and 30 years old (52 percent), and were enrolled in the master's degree program (87 percent) in educational technology at ASU. Most rated their level of computer skill as either intermediate (48 percent) or advanced (39 percent). Nine current students indicated previous experience with courses delivered via the Internet.

Graduates

We also contacted 10 graduates of our program about participating in the study. Eight graduates responded to the request, indicating an 80 percent response rate. The majority were female (75 percent), more than 31 years old (88 percent), and held a master's degree in educational technology (88 percent). Most rated their level of computer skill as intermediate (50 percent) or advanced (50 percent). Three graduates indicated previous experience with courses delivered via the Internet.

Faculty

We contacted 10 individuals with a faculty position at Educational Technology or Instructional Design and Technology programs throughout the United States to request their participation in the study. Nine faculty responded to the request, indicating a 90 percent response rate. The majority of these faculty were male (78 percent) and more than 41 years old (88 percent). Six faculty indicated that they had previously taught a course on the foundations of educational technology, and three faculty indicated experience teaching courses delivered via the Internet.

Instruments

Each respondent group (students, graduates, faculty) completed a survey developed to address issues related to content, delivery method, and use of the Internet for a foundations course in educational technology. These surveys were designed to collect specific information from each respondent group. Items related to content were written based on a document analysis of the book *Instructional Technology: Past, Present and Future,* by Gary Anglin (1995). We developed an initial content topic list using the section headings from this book. Next, the list was expanded to include other topics that appeared in at least two of the course syllabi that we had collected. Respondents were asked to identify the topics that should be included in a foundations course from a list of 18 possible topics. Items related to delivery provided a list of five possible methods and asked respondents to indicate the optimal delivery method for a foundations course. Items related to feelings about use of the Internet asked respondents to indicate whether required use of this medium would encourage or discourage faculty–student interaction and help or hinder learning. We also collected data on participant demographics and experience with the Internet and related technology.

Results

Optimal Content

A major purpose of our study was to identify the optimal instructional content for a foundations course in educational technology. We examined the syllabi from the six graduate programs listed previously to identify the topics most frequently covered in these courses (see Table 1). We found that (1) topics related to the definitions of educational technology and instructional design models were included in all six of the courses; (2) topics related to the history of educational technology and professional competencies and issues were included in five of the courses; (3) topics on evaluation, instructional theory, learning theory, and trends in educational technology were covered in four of the courses; (4) topics related to innovation and change, needs assessment, and performance technology were included in three of the courses; and (5) topics about adoption and diffusion, distance education, Gagne's events of instruction, instructional message design, and media research were covered in two of the courses.

Table 1: Topics Covered by Two or More Courses

TOPIC	FREQUENCY
Definitions of educational technology	6
Instructional design models	6
History of educational technology	5
Professional competencies and issues	5
Evaluation	4
Instructional theory	4
Learning theory	4
Trends in educational technology	4
Innovation and change	3
Needs assessment	3
Performance technology	3
Adoption and diffusion	2
Distance education	2
Gagne's events of instruction	2
Instructional message design	2
Media research	2

We also asked graduates and faculty to identify the optimal topics that should be included in a Foundations of Educational Technology course (see Table 2, page 22). Eight graduates and seven faculty responded to items on optimal topics. Topics selected by approximately half or more graduates and faculty include definitions of educational technology (100 percent), instructional design models (93 percent), trends in educational technology (93 percent), history of educational technology (80 percent), needs assessment (73 percent), instructional theory (53 percent), professional competencies and issues (53 percent), adoption and diffusion (47 percent), and evaluation (47 percent).

Table 2: Optimal Course Topics Identified by Graduates and Faculty

COURSE TOPIC	GRADUATES	FACULTY	TOTAL
Definitions of EDT	8 (100%)	7 (100%)	15 (100%)
Instructional Design Models	8 (100%)	6 (86%)	14 (93%)
Trends in EDT	7 (88%)	7 (100%)	14 (93%)
History of EDT	6 (75%)	6 (86%)	12 (80%)
Needs assessment	6 (75%)	5 (71%)	11 (73%)
Instructional theory	5 (63%)	3 (43%)	8 (53%)
Professional competencies	5 (63%)	3 (43%)	8 (53%)
Adoption and diffusion	3 (38%)	4 (57%)	7 (47%)
Evaluation	3 (38%)	4 (57%)	7 (47%)
Learning theory	2 (25%)	4 (57%)	6 (40%)
Media research	2 (25%)	4 (57%)	6 (40%)
Distance education	4 (50%)	2 (28%)	6 (40%)
Gagne's events of instruction	4 (50%)	2 (28%)	6 (40%)
Media selection	4 (50%)	1 (14%)	5 (33%)

Note: EDT = Educational Technology.

We also examined the data on optimal course topics separately for graduates and faculty. Topics identified by half or more graduates, but not by half or more faculty, were instructional theory (63 percent), professional competencies and issues (63 percent), distance education (50 percent), Gagne's events of instruction (50 percent), and media selection (50 percent). Topics identified by half or more faculty, but not by half or more graduates, were adoption and diffusion (57 percent), evaluation (57 percent), learning theory (57 percent), and media research (57 percent).

It is interesting to note that two faculty declined to respond to the items regarding optimal course content. One questioned whether the foundations of educational technology should be taught as a distinct course. The other indicated that topics could not be identified without knowledge of the objectives of the course.

Optimal Delivery Methods

Another purpose of our study was to identify the optimal delivery methods for an educational technology foundations course. Respondents were asked to indicate the optimal delivery method from a list of five possible methods (see Table 3).

Twenty-one students responded to the items on optimal delivery method. Seven students (33 percent) indicated that the course should be delivered using entirely face-to-face classroom activities. Six students (28 percent) responded that face-to-face classroom activities with online readings and assignments would be the optimal delivery method. Four students (20 percent) indicated that the course should be delivered using half online activities and half face-to-face classroom activities. Four others (20 percent) responded that a course emphasizing online instruction with classroom meetings would be optimal. None of the students indicated that the course should be delivered entirely online.

Table 3: Optimal Delivery Methods Identified by Students, Graduates, and Faculty

COURSE DELIVERY METHOD	STUDENTS	GRADUATES	FACULTY	TOTAL
Entirely face-to-face classroom activities	7 (33%)	0 (0%)	2 (28%)	9 (25%)
Emphasize face-to face classroom activities with online readings and assignments	6 (28%)	5 (63%)	3 (43%)	14 (38%)
Half online activities and half classroom activities	4 (20%)	1 (12%)	1 (14%)	6 (16%)
Emphasize online activities with class-room meetings	4 (20%)	1 (12%)	0 (0%)	5 (14%)
Entirely online (class never meets face to face)	0 (0%)	0 (0%)	0 (0%)	0 (0%)
Other	0 (0%)	1 (12%)	1 (14%)	2 (5%)

Eight graduates answered the items concerning optimal course delivery method. Five graduates (63 percent) indicated that face-to-face classroom activities with online readings and assignments would be an optimal delivery method. One graduate indicated that the course should be taught using half online activities and half face-to-face classroom activities, and another stated a preference for online instruction with classroom meetings. In addition, one other graduate responded that one third of the course should be online. None of the graduates indicated that the course should be delivered entirely online.

Seven faculty answered the items concerning optimal course delivery method. Three faculty (43 percent) responded that face-to-face classroom activities with online readings and assignments would be the optimal delivery method. Two others (28 percent) indicated that the course should be delivered using entirely face-to-face classroom activities. Another faculty member indicated that the course should be taught using half online activities and half face-to-face classroom activities. The other faculty respondent included a statement that the class should be Web supported, but the level to which the class should be online depended on the goals of the course. None of the faculty indicated that the course should be delivered entirely online.

Feelings About Use of the Internet

The final purpose of our study was to determine how students, graduates, and faculty felt about using the Internet for a foundations course in educational technology. Items related to feelings about use of the Internet asked respondents to indicate whether required use of this medium would encourage or discourage faculty–student interaction and help or hinder learning (see Table 4).

Twenty-three students completed the items concerning feelings about required use of the Internet for the course. Results include the following: (1) fourteen students (61 percent) indicated that the Internet would discourage faculty–student contact; (2) thirteen students (57 percent) responded that Internet use would discourage student-to-student contact; (3) eleven students (48 percent) felt that the Internet would prevent some students from succeeding in the course, and (4) six students (26 percent) felt that Internet use would create a hardship for some students and put an unfair emphasis on computer literacy instead of course content. However, eleven students (48 percent) thought that required use of the Internet for the course would help them stay current with technology, and six students (26 percent) felt that Internet use would prepare them for the job market.

Eight graduates completed the items concerning feelings about required use of the Internet for the course. Seven graduates (88 percent) indicated that Internet use would help students stay current with technology, and five graduates (63 percent) felt that such a requirement would prepare students for the job market. However, four graduates (50 percent) thought it would prevent some students from succeeding in the course, and three graduates (38 percent) indicated that required Internet use would discourage faculty-to-student and student-to-student contact.

Seven faculty responded to the items concerning feelings about required Internet use. Five faculty (71 percent) indicated that it would help students stay current with technology and prepare them for the job market. However, four faculty (57 percent) indicated that required Internet use would discourage faculty-to-student and student-to-student contact.

Table 4: Participants' Feelings Toward Use of the Internet

	STUDENTS	GRADUATES	FACULTY	TOTAL
In your opinion, required use of the Internet for the course would do the following:				
Help students stay current with technology	11 (48%)	7 (88%)	5 (71%)	23 (61%)
Prepare students for the job market	6 (26%)	5 (63%)	5 (71%)	14 (37%)
Encourage faculty–student contact	4 (17%)	2 (25%)	2 (28%)	8 (21%)
Encourage student–student contact	4 (17%)	2 (25%)	1 (14%)	7 (18%)
Discourage faculty–student contact	14 (61%)	3 (38%)	4 (57%)	21 (55%)
Discourage student–student contact	13 (57%)	3 (38%)	4 (57%)	19 (50%)
Prevent some students from succeeding in this class	11 (48%)	4 (50%)	3 (43%)	18 (47%)
Create a hardship for students	6 (26%)	3 (38%)	3 (43%)	12 (32%)
Put an unfair emphasis on computer literacy	6 (26%)	2 (25%)	0 (0%)	8 (21%)
Be inappropriate for this course content	0 (0%)	1 (13%)	2 (28%)	3 (8%)

Implications

The results of our study are currently being used to revise the foundations course at Arizona State University. For example, although 93 percent of respondents to our survey indicated that trends in educational technology should be covered in a foundations course, our course has not focused much on recent trends in the field. The course has traditionally included topics such as definitions and history of the field, instructional design models, and needs assessment. We have revised the course to give students an opportunity to learn more about contemporary issues such as performance technology and constructivism (Reiser and Ely 1997). In fact, we have renamed the course from The Foundations of Educational Technology to Foundations and Issues in Educational Technology to reflect an increased focus on trends in the field.

We have also revised the course to include some online delivery of course materials. Our study revealed that a majority of students, graduates, and faculty who responded to our survey favored some form of online delivery for the course. However, a majority also indicated that requiring students to use the Internet for the course would discourage faculty-to-student and student-to-student contact and would prevent some students from succeeding in the course. Based on the results of this study, we continue to emphasize face-to-face classroom instruction, but students now have online access to course objectives, assignments, and readings.

CONCLUSION

We believe that this study provides some implications for others who teach an introductory course aimed at providing students with knowledge about the field of educational technology. Our study indicates some optimal instructional content and delivery strategies for a foundations course; it also suggests some feelings about the use of the Internet for such a course. Readers should note that we sampled a small number of students and graduates of our Educational Technology program and a small number of faculty from other programs. We encourage others to collect data to determine the optimal instructional content and delivery method for their own course on the foundations of educational technology.

REFERENCES

Anglin, G. (1995). *Instructional technology: Past, present and future* (2d ed.). Englewood, CO: Libraries Unlimited.

Pershing, J. A., Molenda, M. H., Paulus, T., Lee, L.H.J., and Hixon, E. (2000). Letters home: The meaning of instructional technology. *TechTrends,* 44:1, 31–38.

Reiser, R., Davidson-Shivers, G., Anglin, G., Lowther, D., Rasmussen, K., and Richey, R. (1999, February). *Trends and issues in instructional design and technology: What shall be taught and how shall we teach it?* Symposium presented at the annual meeting of the Association for Educational Communications and Technology, Houston, TX.

Reiser, R. A., and Ely, D. P. (1997). The field of educational technology as reflected through its definitions. *Educational Technology Research and Development,* 45:3, 63–72.

Rossett, A. (1987). *Training needs assessment.* Englewood Cliffs, NJ: Educational Technology Publications.

Developing and Delivering an On-line Master's Program in Instructional Technology

D. Michael Moore
Barbara B. Lockee
John K. Burton
Virginia Tech

Within the Commonwealth of Virginia and throughout the nation, there is an urgent need for increased teacher competence for the integration of instructional technologies into the teaching-learning process. In a June 1996 document, the task force charged with developing the Technology Standards for Instructional Personnel, based on Virginia's revised Standards of Learning, acknowledged these needs in sections 22.1–22.16 of the *Code of Virginia:*

> The task force quickly realized that serious inequalities exist in the ability of schools to provide instruction to enable students to use technology for effective problem solving and productivity. These inequalities can be linked to two main causes: The lack of access to adequate equipment, and the lack of training for teachers, which must be addressed as technology standards are implemented.

As a land grant institution, Virginia Tech has an obligation to the citizens of Virginia to ensure that K–12 teachers are prepared to address the Standards of Learning in the area of instructional technology. Although Virginia Tech has one of the strongest graduate programs in instructional technology in the country, practicing teachers at the remote locations seldom have opportunities to pursue coursework at Virginia Tech. Professional and personal obligations make it difficult to commute to classes or engage in graduate work altogether. Offering an instructional technology master's program through distance delivery allows students who would not otherwise attend Virginia Tech to benefit from the programs we offer.

In this context, a field-based master's program in instructional technology was developed and delivered through distance learning technologies to practicing teachers working in the K–12 environment. The primary delivery mode was Web-based instruction, with a few supplemental face-to-face meetings. This program (Cycle One) was started at the three locations (Southwest Virginia Graduate Center, 30 students; Franklin County School District, 20 students; and at the Northern Virginia Graduate Center, 30 students) in the fall of 1998. Because of the interest in and success of the first cycle, a second cycle was started in the fall of 2000 at three additional sites (Roanoke area, 40 students; Tidewater area, 40 students; and Southwest Virginia Graduate Center, 20 students). These students were recruited and admitted to the off-campus Masters/Educational Specialist program at Virginia Tech.

A cohort model focusing on the integration of technology in curriculum, instruction, and assessment was used. The program centered on the development of communities of learners within and between the participating school divisions. Program design emphasized teacher inquiry into how various technologies can assist the learning process. All projects were based on questions, concerns, and curiosities generated by the needs of the teachers, their students, and their schools. The program focused on identifying successful practices that can be imported or exported to complement existing practices. Such a field-based program accommodated the individual technology needs of the teachers, instructing them to use the technologies available at their site while exposing them to new developments in the field and providing them with the information needed to pursue additional funding for technology. Teachers were introduced to a wide range of current technologies to facilitate instructional events and activities. Training included work on Macintosh and Windows platforms and provided hands-on experiences with appropriate instructional software and hardware. They evaluated the utility of the software as it applies to different levels of learner needs. Also, they extended their knowledge of classroom activities related to the use of computers and other technologies in which the K–12 student is the end user. Thus, the outcomes of the proposed master's program included the integration of instructional technology by both teachers and students

Through a variety of experiences and technologies, we have provided opportunities for (a) active learning; (b) interactive communications; (c) self-directed, self-paced learning; (d) computer literacy integrated with content; (e) electronic access to course material and supplemental resources; and (f) electronic access to course information, announcements, and news. Table 1 provides a listing of instructional delivery strategies and their approximate percentage of usage in the Instructional Technology MAsters (ITMA) program.

Table 1: Strategies/Media Used in the Instructional Technology Masters (ITMA) Program

STRATEGIES/MEDIA USED	PERCENTAGE OF PROGRAM
Web-based instruction	90
Week-long, on-campus summer courses	5
Individual computer-based instruction	5

We have modified existing courses and created new ones to take advantage of distance learning technologies available at Virginia Tech and the remote sites. For example, we have provided access to online course materials and resources through Web sites, ongoing online access to course instructors and other students through e-mail and listservs, and opportunities for electronic project submission and feedback.

More important, we are teaching K–12 teachers to plan and deliver activities that achieve the *same* set of outcomes. We assess their ability to achieve these outcomes by assessing their ability to meet the specific outcomes delineated by the Virginia Standards of Learning for Instructional Personnel, as cited in the *Code of Virginia,* which include the following:

- Operate a computer system and use software.
- Apply knowledge of terms associated with educational computing and technology.
- Apply productivity tools for professional use.
- Use electronic technologies to access and exchange information.
- Identify, locate, evaluate, and use appropriate instructional technology-based resources (hardware and software) to support Standards of Learning, and other instructional objectives.

- Use educational technologies for data collection, information management, problem solving, decision making, communications, and presentations within the curriculum.

- Plan and implement lessons and strategies that integrate technology to meet the diverse needs of learners in a variety of educational settings.

- Demonstrate knowledge of ethical and legal issues relating to the use of technology.

Additional outcomes of the master's program are required by our Instructional Technology program and are outlined in the following list of competencies, adapted from competencies outlined by the Association of Educational Communications and Technology, the major professional organization in the field of instructional technology:

- Design: Candidates demonstrate the knowledge, skills, and dispositions to design conditions for learning by applying principles of instructional systems design, message design, instructional strategies, and learner characteristics.

- Development: Demonstrating knowledge, skills and dispositions to develop instructional materials and experiences using print, audiovisual, computer-based, and integrated technologies.

- Evaluation: Candidates demonstrate knowledge, skills, and dispositions to evaluate the adequacy of instruction and learning by applying principles, theories, and research related to problem analysis, criterion-referenced measurement, formative and summative evaluation, and long-range planning.

- Management: Candidates demonstrate knowledge, skills, and dispositions to plan, organize, coordinate, and supervise instructional technology by applying principles, theories, and research related to project, resource, delivery system, and information management.

- Utilization: Candidates demonstrate the knowledge, skills, and dispositions to use processes and resources for learning by applying principles, theories, and research related to media utilization, diffusion, implementations, and policy making. (Association for Educational Communications and Technology 2000)

The students in the ITMA program received instructional support through a variety of channels. First, the cohort groups were intentionally located near an educational facility equipped with hardware and software and Internet access. In two of the three cohort locations, those facilities were graduate centers in which Virginia Tech has a presence in terms of programming and staff. The third facility in Rocky Mount, Virginia, is a technology-intensive middle school, which our program has permission to use for laboratory access. The facilities were used for several purposes: First, some ITMA program instruction required hands-on approaches to teaching and learning, so the facilities were used for face-to-face sessions with the distance students. Also, some of the modules required the use of high-end computer equipment that the students likely did not have in their own schools, such as digital video-editing technology. We used the facilities to house such equipment so students could access it conveniently to do coursework. We also offered weekly open lab hours, so students could meet and work together if they so desired. During the open lab time, we provided a lab assistant to make sure the facility was open and that the equipment was functioning properly.

A virtual resource that the students had available was perhaps one of the strongest components of our program—the IT Studio. The Studio was a "help" Web site located within the body of our ITMA program Web site. Through the Studio, students could get several types of assistance. First, if they had technology-related questions, they could e-mail their questions and problems to itstudio@vt.edu and would receive a response within 24 hours from our graduate assistant (hired specifically to provide technological support to the students and program faculty). Other forms of assistance were available as well. There were links to tutorials that addressed program-related skills, such as building Web sites and using online quizzing tools. Also, there was a list of frequently asked questions (FAQs) and a link to the latest program-related news (registration info, course calendars, etc.). There was a link to download various tools that were necessary or helpful, such as the latest browsers, plug-ins, freeware, and so on. A student discussion forum, called IT Talk, was also available through the Studio. Most students, however, used the program's listserv to communicate with each other and the program coordinator when they wanted to interact as a group. Finally, there was a link from the IT Studio to the students' electronic portfolios so that they could publicly display their work, as well as refer to their colleagues' work for ideas, suggestions, and so on.

The ITMA students had a variety of support services available to them in addition to instructional support. Two graduate students provided extensive support to the ITMA program and were vital to its operation. First, we had a position provided by the Provost to serve as the ITMA Program Coordinator. This graduate assistant was a doctoral student in our campus-based IT program and worked with students on many program-related issues, such as registration, tuition waivers (Virginia's teachers receive a reduction in tuition), course calendar questions, and the many other logistical issues that arise in distance-delivered programs.

The graduate school worked with instructional technology program faculty to coordinate the admissions process. Our graduate program coordinator, who met with each cohort group and each individual student to determine an appropriate plan of study, managed course advising. Student records were managed by our departmental graduate records staff person who works directly with the instructional technology faculty.

The course registration process evolved over the past three years from a manual procedure, managed by the ITMA Program Coordinator to an electronic process that was introduced and is currently managed by the Associate Director for Support Services in the university's Institute for Distance and Distributed Learning. Registration, billing, and payment options for distance learning students in the ITMA program were the same as for students on campus.

Many of the program's localized support services were funded by the Provost through Virginia Tech's Center for Innovation in Learning (CIL). The ITMA program received CIL program development grants for three consecutive years for the purpose of designing the distance instructional technology program and getting it off the ground. The program currently serves as a model for other curricular departments that seek to establish distance-delivered programs with strong support services.

PROGRAM FUNDING

During the development phase of the project (Fall 1997 through Summer 1998), the instructional technology faculty group received $21,000 from a university incentive grant and $26,000 from the Department of Teaching and Learning to support the costs of course development. During the academic year of 1998–1999, we received $67,000 from a university incentive grant and $20,000 from the department to cover implementation expenses. Also, the Department and the College of Human Resources provided $48,000 in funding to instructional technology faculty during the summer of 1999 to continue course development. These resources funded salaries for graduate student development assistance. Also, in the spring of 1999, Virginia Tech's Institute for Distance and Distributed Learning (IDDL) provided $24,000 for equipment and software needed to support the ITMA program.

During the academic year of 1999–2000, the ITMA program received $57,000 from a university incentive grant and approximately $20,000 from the department to support expenses. Again, during the summer of 2000, faculty were assisted with continuing development efforts by the department, college, and university through the allocation of $27,000 for summer buyout time (department and college), $5,000 for a faculty incentive grant, and $3,400 for equipment and student wage support. Finally, since the beginning of ITMA program planning (Fall 1997), the College has also allocated a postdoctoral position to the instructional technology group to support the development and implementation of the distance program. This allocation represents approximately $55,000 in funding per year, totaling $165,000 to date. The position has been assigned to the ITMA program once more for the upcoming three-year cycle.

The projected revenues for the first year were $57, 960 (70 students at $828 per year tuition). With attrition of 60 students, the projected revenues for the second year were $49,680 (60 students at $828 per year tuition). Assuming attrition to 50 students in the first ITMA group and beginning a second group of 100 in Fall 2000, the projected revenues for the third year are $124,200 (150 students at $828 per year tuition). Actual expenses, disregarding development costs, have stayed close to $60,000 a year. This amount includes support for two graduate students, travel costs to sites for faculty and graduate assistants, site personnel wages, and operational expenses, such as telephone, postage, and software and hardware purchases.

LESSONS LEARNED

Designing and implementing distance-delivered courses and programs requires a tremendous amount of time, resources, and personnel. Being instructional technology professionals, our group was likely more prepared than most to deal with the instructional design and development issues that are inherent in what we do. However, it is safe to say that we learned a great deal along the way that we hope will inform our own practice and contribute to the knowledge base of our field.

The first iteration of program design emerged in rapid prototype fashion, as we designed and created course materials just in time for their implementation in the program sequence. Although we were able to take a deep breath and revise the second phase, ITMA2, based on our initial experiences, we found (as does anyone in instructional technology) that the process is never done. As soon as a module was implemented, we immediately began compiling necessary changes and recommendations for the next iteration. Also, basic technological change mandates the need for ongoing revision. Server updates and transitions, as well as Web course development software were factors that had major impacts on our implementation and support strategies. Whoever said, "the only thing constant is change" could easily have been referring to distance-delivered instruction.

Design issues soon became apparent, above and beyond the concern for order, interface, and organization. Design lessons that were learned included the discovery (no surprise) that the instructional design was more important than the technology used. For, example, "high touch" courses had to be significantly modified to address the "lowest common denominator" in terms of student knowledge of the technology, the equipment available, and Internet access. Student support became a major variable on par with the course content development and the student use of the delivery system. It was realized that the course planning had to include real-time assistance to students, technology support, and major logistical support including program maintenance, class registration, advisement, grading of assignments, and so on. Additional outside support was found to be needed from the university in terms of credit options, tuition adjustments, payment of fees, and length of class restrictions.

We learned that a distance-delivered program requires not just simple cooperation among program faculty but a true team-based, integrated approach to program development and implementation. We began the first cycle with little coordination among ourselves, designing and implementing modules rather independently. It was soon discovered that we needed program consistency in the format, interface, instructions, and the "feel" of courses because of apparent student confusion about procedures and expectations. It was also soon determined, again not surprisingly, that the order of the courses affected the content and design of other subsequent courses. We quickly learned that we were each encountering the same problems and challenges that could be remedied by applying a more centralized, team-oriented approach.

It is commonly assumed that the role of a faculty member changes when he or she becomes a distance educator. This holds true for students also. We learned quickly, as did many students, that all students were not suitable distance learners. Some students were not motivated, some were easily distracted and needed more structure (as in a regular classroom), and others were not particularly good at managing their learning and instructional time. We found that some students had the perception when beginning an online class that these types of classes would be easier than regular on-campus classes. In addition, students soon found that they had to trade some level of access to an instructor for the advantage of their personal learning time convenience. We have also learned that interaction is important but that the interaction does not necessarily have to be with the instructor. We have become more efficient designers in terms of facilitating learning while maintaining our traditional workload and responsibilities at a Research One institution.

Finally, the question of quality is often a concern for all stakeholders in the delivery and consumption of distance programs. Upon completion of our first online degree program, we are convinced that we have been able to maintain the same high quality of the learning experiences that we design and develop for face-to-face delivery. The key to our success, we believe, is that the undertaking of this effort has consistently been an integral part of our instructional portfolio, not an additional project tacked on to everything else that we do. The benefits of engaging in the delivery of our distance program is that it has informed our efforts as instructional technologists and as educators of instructional technologists and that it has allowed us to contribute to the fields of distance education and instructional technology.

REFERENCES

Association for Educational Communications and Technology. (2000). NCATE Program Standards: Initial and Advanced Programs for Educational Communications and Technology. [Online]. Available: http://www.aect.org/Affiliates/National/Standards.pdf (Accessed October 12, 2001).

The Impacts of Frequency
and Duration of Messaging on Relational Development
in Computer-mediated Communication
An Exploratory Study[1]

Y. Liu

Department of Educational Leadership
Southern Illinois University–Edwardsville

ABSTRACT

Contrary to previous computer-mediated communication (CMC) research, this exploratory study indicates that CMC is a viable mode of social-emotion-oriented communication. In this study, the impacts of frequency and duration of messaging on relational development in CMC were investigated. Undergraduate participants were randomly assigned to each of the four experimental groups. For a period of two weeks participants monitored discussion lists that differed in frequency and duration of messaging. ANOVA results indicated that duration and frequency had significant main effects on relational development in CMC environments. No interaction effects were found. The results of this study not only theoretically support the social-emotion-oriented model in CMC but also lay foundations for further research in many popular types of interactive CMC environments, including e-learning, e-commerce, and e-health.

Relational development, as one of the early and major topics within social psychology, refers to the process of interpersonal relationship development by which people employ all available information to attract and maintain personal relationships. There has been much research regarding relational development in face-to-face (FtF) environments. According to Burgoon and Hale (1987), relational development in FtF environments includes eight independent major themes: immediacy/affection, similarity/depth, receptivity/trust, composure, formality, dominance, equality, and task orientation.[2] Recent FtF research (Krauss and Fussell 1996) has consistently indicated that both nonverbal cues and verbal cues jointly affect the process of the above aspects of relational development.

In recent decades, CMC has emerged as a new communication format. Because CMC is an "altered state of communication" (Vallee, Johansen, and Sprangler 1975, 12), this type of communication may be different from communication in other settings. CMC may "change the psychology and sociology of the communication process itself" (Turoff 1978, 10), including many aspects of interpersonal relationship development. Thus, similar to FtF environments, relational development has recently become an important topic in CMC research (Walther 1992).

Since Walther's (1992) pioneering work in relational development in CMC research, there has been increasing literature in this area (Parks and Floyd 1996; Walther 1996). This study is intended to supplement and extend the research by (1) offering theoretical support for the social-emotion-oriented nature of CMC and (2) laying the foundation for research in many interactive CMC environments, including e-learning, e-commerce, and e-health. Specifically, this experimental study is designed to explore how the two nonverbal cues—frequency (e.g., number) and duration (e.g., length) of messaging—affect relational development in asynchronous CMC environments.

Recent CMC research indicates that there have been two dominant research models in CMC: the task-oriented model and the social-emotion-oriented model (for detailed information, please refer to Liu and Ginther's paper, 1999a). According to the task-oriented model (e.g., Short, Williams, and Christie 1976), the CMC environment is restricted in terms of nonverbal cues; therefore, CMC tends to be tasked oriented, depersonalized, and inhibitive of relational development between CMC users. However, contrary to the task-oriented model, Walther (1992) proposed the Social Information Processing Model to explain how interpersonal relationships could be established in CMC environments. Specifically, this model explains how CMC users process social information using various media in CMC and FtF environments, as well as the effects of such information on relational development.

Most prior CMC research tended to be consistent with the model of the task-oriented communication and seldom dealt with CMC's emotional content because of the lack of nonverbal cues within the CMC context (Connolly, Jessup, and Valacich 1990; Hiltz, Johnson, and Turoff 1986). However, a few recent studies have identified the existence of certain nonverbal cues in CMC and have investigated how users are involved in social-emotion-oriented communication (Breazeale 1999; Halbert 1999; Jacobson 1999; Lea and Spears 1991; Parks and Floyd 1996; Rice and Love 1987; Utz 2000; Walther 1995; Walther, Anderson, and Park 1994; Wright 1999).

Other studies found that CMC users are involved in both task-oriented communication and social-emotion-oriented communication (Tangmanee 1999). Even so, compared with research within the task-oriented model, there have been very few studies related to the social-emotion-oriented model in CMC (Liu and Ginther 1999b). A few studies investigated the effects of certain nonverbal cues on social emotional development, such as temporal aspects (Hesse, Werner, and Altman 1988; Walther and Tidwell 1995), primacy and recency effects (Rintel and Pittam 1997), pictographs or typographic marks and emoticons (Asteroff 1987; Reid 1995; Thompsen and Foulger 1996). However, there is no published literature regarding the effects of frequency and duration on social and relational development in CMC (Liu 2000).

In FtF environments, frequency and duration of speech have generally been considered good predictors of an individual's participation and relational development in a group interaction. Persons with a high frequency of verbal responses are perceived as being competent and having greater participation, whereas persons with a low frequency of verbal responses are perceived as incompetent and having less participation (Willard and Strodtbeck 1972). Similarly, persons with shorter duration verbal responses are perceived as incompetent and lacking confidence, whereas persons with longer duration verbal responses are perceived as competent and confident (Koomen and Sagel 1977).

Are the effects of frequency and duration of messaging in CMC the same as those in FtF environments? Some CMC researchers have predicted that frequency and duration of messaging in CMC are two important aspects of CMC information communication (Rice and Love 1987) and that these two variables are highly correlated with the degree of one's participation and relational development in group communication (Hiltz and Turoff 1978). Thus, based on these predictions, at least three hypotheses can be derived regarding relational development in CMC:

> *Hypothesis 1:* High frequency and long duration of messaging will result in a higher mean score on a relational communication questionnaire, whereas low frequency and short duration of messaging will result in a lower mean score on a relational communication questionnaire in CMC.

> *Hypothesis 2:* High frequency of messaging will result in a higher mean score on a relational communication questionnaire, whereas low frequency of messaging will result in a lower mean score on a relational communication questionnaire in CMC.

Hypothesis 3: Long duration of messaging will result in a higher mean score on a relational communication questionnaire, whereas short duration of messaging will result in a lower mean score on a relational communication questionnaire in CMC.

In addition, according to Walther's (1992) Social Information Processing Model described previously, CMC users can, over time, form and develop relationships with their partners through both verbal and nonverbal cues in CMC. Thus, a fourth hypothesis can be derived from this model.

Hypothesis 4: The mean scores for relationship development at Time 2 will be higher than those at Time 1 on a relational communication questionnaire in CMC.

METHOD

Participants

One hundred and sixteen undergraduate volunteers (male = 33 and female = 83) were initially recruited from 11 psychology summer courses at a southern university in the United States in 1999. Immediately after the experimenter's (the author's) classroom presentation, the students were shown a prerecorded five-minute video about experimental instructions. Then, volunteers were asked to complete consent forms and demographic surveys. Participants were equally divided among the four groups and were randomly assigned to each of the four experimental groups. Eighty-three (male = 24 and female = 59) participants were used for final statistical analyses, with two groups each having a total of 20, one group having 21, and one group having 22.[3] In addition, in the final analysis, each group had an almost equivalent ratio of males and females (each group involved six males).

Definitions of Independent Variables

To clearly define the independent variables, two separate pilot studies were conducted in several Internet discussion lists to determine typical frequency and duration of messaging. First, frequency of messaging was based on the number of messages sent to each discussion list per week and was divided into high frequency and low frequency. According to the results of the first pilot study, high frequency was defined as a minimum of five messages per week, and low frequency was defined as two or fewer messages per week. Messages were sent to subjects only during the weekdays, not on Saturday or Sunday. In the high-frequency condition, each message was separated by about 24 hours; in the low-frequency condition, each message was separated by about 48 hours. Second, duration of messaging was based on the length of a message sent to the discussion list by each of the four discussants. Duration of messaging was divided into long messages and short messages. According to the results of the second pilot study and the American Psychological Association criteria (1994) for a long quotation, a long message was defined to include a minimum of 40 words per message, and a short message was defined to include a maximum of 20 words.

Design

This quasi-experimental factorial design involved two independent variables: frequency and duration of messaging. Each of these independent variables had two treatment levels. This resulted in a 2 (high frequency versus low frequency) x 2 (long duration versus short duration) factorial design. There were four treatment combinations. These four combinations were respectively described as Condition 1 (long duration and high frequency), Condition 2 (short duration and low frequency), Condition 3 (long duration and low frequency), and Condition 4 (short duration and high frequency). In addition, according to the Social Information Processing Model in CMC (Walther, 1992), interpersonal relationships develop over time. Therefore, a time factor was used as a repeated variable in this design, with the dependent variable being measured on two occasions during the study.

Discussion Lists

The experimenter enrolled each of the subjects in one of the four discussion list groups. Each discussion list group was moderated by the experimenter, which meant that all electronic submissions from participants to each group were under the control of the experimenter. To control the influence of the message content, each member of each group was a "lurker" (i.e., the subjects monitored but were not allowed to directly participate in the discussion on the lists). The fundamental role of each subject was to read and review the discussion list messages.

Instruments

In this study, both impression development (which will be reported elsewhere) and relational development were measured separately. Burgoon and Hale's (1987) Relational Communication Questionnaire[4] was selected to measure relational development in this study because it has been extensively used in FtF research for more than 10 years and because it has been used in CMC research in recent years (Walther 1997; Walther and Burgoon 1992; Walther and Tidwell 1995). This questionnaire includes eight scales and 41 items: (1) Immediacy/Affection (nine items; e.g., "intensely involve in conversion"); (2) Similarity/Depth (five items; e.g., "make feel similar"); (3) Receptivity/Trust (six items; e.g., "willing to listen"); (4) Composure (five items; e.g., "calm and poised"); (5) Formality (three items; e.g., "make interaction formal"); (6) Dominance (six items; e.g., "try to control the interaction"); (7) Equality (three items; e.g., "want to cooperate"); and (8) Task Orientation (four items; e.g., "is very work-oriented").

These scales have seven-interval Likert-type items each. The seven intervals include *strongly agree, agree, agree somewhat, neutral or unsure, disagree somewhat, disagree,* and *strongly disagree.* The score of each item ranges from one to seven points, with some items reverse scored. The calculation method for each scale was to add the sum of the points of all the items belonging to that scale, then divided by the number of items. Higher scores represent greater immediacy, similarity, receptivity, composure, formality, dominance, equality, and task orientation. According to Burgoon and Hale (1987), the values of the internal reliability for the eight scales range from 0.76 to 0.86, respectively. To investigate the construct validity of this questionnaire, Burgoon and Hale conducted exploratory oblique and orthogonal factor analyses, as well as confirmatory factor analysis for three experiments. All these analyses supported the division of the instrument into the eight scales.

Experimental Instructions

Participants received experimental training, which described their role as both a member of their respective discussion list and a subject for this study. In addition to a copy of the written experimental instructions, each subject saw a five-minute prerecorded video describing experimental instructions. Specifically, subjects were told that they would be required (a) to read all messages generated on their discussion list at least once a day, Monday through Friday; (b) to not to discuss the experimental task with any participants or nonparticipants (to check whether participants did interact outside of the discussion lists, a simple two-item survey was administered at the end of the experiment, via e-mail. If any participant discussed the experiment task with anyone during the experiment, he or she was eliminated from the final analysis); (c) to reply immediately to the list with key ideas about each message, with the original message included in the reply (These key ideas could be several words and were intended to verify whether each participant had read each message on the list. If a participant did not send key ideas within 24 hours of receiving a message on the discussion list, he or she was reminded via e-mail to read the unread messages on the list. If a subject had to be reminded more than two times, he or she was removed from further participation in the study); (d) to complete the instrument on Saturdays during the first and the second experimental weeks; and (e) to complete a two-item survey on Sunday during the second week.

Experimental Stimulus

Initially, to control the content validity of the discussion topic in this study, the experimenter attempted to involve the participants in a neutral discussion topic, such as statistics. But it was soon predicted that this type of topic would hardly stimulate participants' interest. Therefore, the experimenter chose another potentially interesting topic for participants at that time. This topic was the Littleton, Colorado, school shootings that occurred on April 20, 1999. Each of the four discussion lists discussed this same topic. Each discussion list had four members that, for purposes of this study, were referred to as discussants. Essentially, the subjects in this study were told that they were lurking on a discussion list with four active members.

An experimental assistant helped the experimenter to select and adapt the messages that were later provided to each subject in their discussion list group. The experimenter and the assistant selected a minimum of 40 archived actual messages about the Colorado school shooting from an existing discussion list. These messages were messages that were posted to the CNN Web site at http://community.cnn.com/ on April 21, 1999. The detailed prescripting procedure is described as follows.

1. The experimenter and the assistant identified four members of the discussion list in the CNN Web site at the http://community.cnn.com/ to serve as model discussants. Each of the four selected list members was chosen because they tended to produce long-duration messages of high frequency. Ten messages produced by each of the four list members were selected for later presentation to each of the four subjects in the long duration/high frequency condition of this study.

2. The 40 messages selected to represent the long duration/high frequency message condition were then reviewed and modified to produce the messages for the other three experimental conditions. For the short duration/high frequency messaging condition, the 40 messages of the long duration/high frequency condition were reduced in length for the short duration/high frequency condition. This reduction in length was done in such a manner as to maintain the syntax, grammar, vocabulary, and essential meaning of the original messages.

3. The 16 messages for the long duration/low frequency condition were selected from the 40 messages selected for the long duration/high frequency condition. These messages were selected so that the thread of the discussion was maintained. Similarly, the 16 messages for the short duration/low frequency condition were selected from the 40 selected for the short duration/high frequency condition.

To control the influence of the content in list messages during the experiment, the contents of all list messages were prescribed, were embedded in an ongoing dialogue, and were designed to be as neutral as possible. Specifically, all list messages were selected or modified to contain (a) no typing or spelling errors, (b) no "flaming" language or personal attacks, and (c) no obscene language.

During the treatment phase of this study, the experimenter sent the selected messages to each respective experimental discussion list with the subject header in each message as "Littleton, School Shootings." For Conditions 1 and 4, each message was sent on Monday through Friday mornings, for Conditions 2 and 3, each message was sent in the mornings on Monday and Wednesday. For each subject-discussant, a separate e-mail account was established, so the messages appeared to the subjects to be generated by four separate individuals. Verification comments made by each subject were sent to the list but intercepted by the list moderator (the experimenter) and not distributed to list members.

Administration of the Dependent Measure

The Relational Communication Questionnaire was administered to participants on two occasions via e-mail: once on Friday afternoon of the first experimental week and once on Friday afternoon of the second experimental week. This time frame was similar to several previous studies about relational development in CMC (Walther and Burgoon 1992; Walther and Tidwell 1995). Participants in each of the four experimental groups were told to rate only one of the four designated discussants and to e-mail their responses back to the experimenter within 24 hours after receiving the instruments.

RESULTS

Preliminary statistical (t and X^2) results of demographic variables indicated that there were no significant differences among the four experimental groups in terms of participants' characteristics. In addition, statistical assumptions were checked before statistical analysis, and results indicated that all relational scores at Time 1 and Time 2 were normally distributed and none of the ANOVA assumptions were violated.[5] Generally, the results of relational scores are mixed. Specifically, only some hypotheses related to relational scores at both Time 1 and Time 2 were supported. The ANOVA results for the eight relational scores at Time 1 and Time 2 are presented in Tables 1 through 16 in the next few pages, respectively.

First, Tables 1 through 16 all indicate that there were no interaction effects between duration and frequency on all eight relational scores: immediacy/affection ($\alpha > .05$), similarity/depth ($\alpha > .05$), receptivity/trust ($\alpha > .05$), composure ($\alpha > .05$), formality ($\alpha > .05$), dominance ($\alpha > .05$), equality ($\alpha > .05$), and task orientation ($\alpha > .05$) at Time 1 and Time 2. Therefore, Hypothesis 1 was not supported.

Second, Tables 1 through 16 indicate that frequency had significant main effects on such relational scores: similarity/depth ($F_{(1, 82)} = 4.09, \alpha < .05$), composure ($F_{(1, 82)} = 6.99, \alpha < .05$), formality ($F_{(1, 82)} = 6.52, \alpha < .05$), dominance ($F_{(1, 82)} = 5.67, \alpha < .05$), equality ($F_{(1, 82)} = 6.80, \alpha < .05$), and task orientation ($F_{(1, 82)} = 6.77, \alpha < .05$), as well as immediacy/affection ($F_{(1, 82)} = 7.37, \alpha < .01$) and receptivity ($F_{(1, 82)} = 9.07, \alpha < .01$) at Time 1; immediacy/affection ($F_{(1, 82)} = 6.30, \alpha < .05$), composure ($F_{(1, 82)} = 5.62, \alpha < .05$), and equality ($F_{(1, 82)} = 4.82, \alpha < .05$), as well as formality ($F_{(1, 82)} = 9.92, \alpha < .01$), dominance ($F_{(1, 82)} = 10.58, \alpha < .01$), and task orientation ($F_{(1, 82)} = 10.24, \alpha < .05$). Therefore, Hypothesis 2 was supported for all relational scores at Time 1 and supported for some relational scores at Time 2. In addition, the values of ω^2 (estimation of the strength of association between the independent variables and dependent variables) in Tables 1 through 16 indicate that there was a medium association between frequency and immediacy/affection scores ($\omega^2 = .069$), between frequency and receptivity/trust scores ($\omega^2 = .090$), between frequency and composure scores ($\omega^2 = .067$), between frequency and formality scores ($\omega^2 = .062$), and between frequency and equality scores ($\omega^2 = .061$) at Time 1, as well as between frequency and formality scores ($\omega^2 = .094$); there was also a medium association between frequency and dominance scores ($\omega^2 = .100$) at Time 2.

Similarly, Tables 1 through 16 indicate that duration had significant main effects on such relational scores: immediacy/affection ($F_{(1, 82)} = 5.20$, $\alpha < .05$), as well as similarity/depth ($F_{(1, 82)} = 7.43$, $\alpha < .01$), dominance ($F_{(1, 82)} = 10.88$, $\alpha < .01$), and equality ($F_{(1, 82)} = 7.14$, $\alpha < .01$) at Time 1; immediacy/affection ($F_{(1, 82)} = 4.03$, $\alpha < .05$), receptivity/trust ($F_{(1, 82)} = 6.70$, $\alpha < .05$), composure ($F_{(1, 82)} = 6.43$, $\alpha < .05$), formality ($F_{(1, 82)} = 4.90$, $\alpha < .05$), dominance ($F_{(1, 82)} = 4.67$, $\alpha < .05$), and task orientation ($F_{(1, 82)} = 5.89$, $\alpha < .05$), as well as similarity/depth ($F_{(1, 82)} = 7.68$, $\alpha < .01$) and equality ($F_{(1, 82)} = 7.75$, $\alpha < .01$) at Time 2. Therefore, Hypothesis 3 was supported for some relational scores at Time 1 and supported for all relational scores at Time 2. In addition, the values of ω^2 in Tables 1 through 8 indicate that there was a medium association between duration and similarity/depth scores ($\omega^2 = .070$), between duration and dominance scores ($\omega^2 = .102$), and between duration and equality scores ($\omega^2 = .065$) at Time 1, as well as between duration and similarity/depth scores ($\omega^2 = .075$), between duration and receptivity/trust scores ($\omega^2 = .065$), between duration and equality scores ($\omega^2 = .073$), and between duration and task orientation ($\omega^2 = .051$) at Time 2.

Table 1: Analysis of Variance for Immediacy/Affection Scores at Time 1 ($N = 83$)

Source	*df*	*SS*	*MS*	*F*	ω^2
Duration	1	4.52	4.52	5.20*	.046
Frequency	1	6.40	6.40	7.37**	.069
Duration * Frequency	1	.15	.15	.17	
Error	79	68.65	.87		
Total	82	79.72			

Note. $^*p < .05$. $^{**}p < .01$.

Table 2: Analysis of Variance for Immediacy/Affection Scores at Time 2 ($N = 83$)

Source	*df*	*SS*	*MS*	*F*	ω^2
Duration	1	3.96	3.96	4.03*	.034
Frequency	1	6.18	6.18	6.30*	.059
Duration * Frequency	1	.10	.10	.10	
Error	79	77.56	.98		
Total	82	87.80			

Note. $^*p < .05$.

Table 3: Analysis of Variance for Similarity/Depth Scores at Time 1 ($N = 83$)

Source	df	SS	MS	F	ω^2
Duration	1	8.87	8.87	7.43**	.070
Frequency	1	4.88	4.88	4.09*	.034
Duration * Frequency	1	.71	.71	.59	
Error	79	94.29	1.19		
Total	82	108.75			

Note. $^*p < .05.$ $^{**}p < .01.$

Table 4: Analysis of Variance for Similarity/Depth Scores at Time 2 ($N = 83$)

Source	df	SS	MS	F	ω^2
Duration	1	11.84	11.84	7.68**	.075
Frequency	1	2.29	2.29	1.49	.069
Duration * Frequency	1	.01	.01	.06	
Error	79	121.77	1.54		
Total	82	135.91			

Note. $^{**}p < .01.$

Table 5: Analysis of Variance for Receptivity/Trust Scores at Time 1 ($N = 83$)

Source	df	SS	MS	F	ω^2
Duration	1	.55	.55	.82	
Frequency	1	6.10	6.10	9.07**	.090
Duration * Frequency	1	.17	.17	.26	
Error	79	53.14	.67		
Total	82	59.96			

Note. $^{**}p < .01.$

Table 6: Analysis of Variance for Receptivity/Trust Scores at Time 2 ($N = 83$)

Source	df	SS	MS	F	ω^2
Duration	1	5.52	5.52	6.70*	.065
Frequency	1	2.78	2.78	3.47	
Duration * Frequency	1	.75	.75	.93	
Error	79	63.23	.80		
Total	82	72.28			

Note. *$p < .05$.

Table 7: Analysis of Variance for Composure Scores at Time 1 ($N = 83$)

Source	df	SS	MS	F	ω^2
Duration	1	2.45	2.45	1.84	
Frequency	1	9.30	9.30	6.99*	.067
Duration * Frequency	1	.75	.75	.56	
Error	79	105.11	1.33		
Total	82	117.61			

Note. *$p < .05$.

Table 8: Analysis of Variance for Composure Scores at Time 2 ($N = 83$)

Source	df	SS	MS	F	ω^2
Duration	1	6.80	6.80	6.43*	.059
Frequency	1	5.94	5.94	5.62*	.050
Duration * Frequency	1	.64	.64	.60	
Error	79	83.43	1.06		
Total	82	96.81			

Note. *$p < .05$.

Table 9: Analysis of Variance for Formality Scores at Time 1 ($N = 83$)

Source	df	SS	MS	F	ω^2
Duration	1	3.13	3.13	2.15	
Frequency	1	9.50	9.50	6.52*	.062
Duration * Frequency	1	.85	.85	.58	
Error	79	115.20	1.46		
Total	82	128.68			

Note. $^*p < .05.$

Table 10: Analysis of Variance for Formality Scores at Time 2 ($N = 83$)

Source	df	SS	MS	F	ω^2
Duration	1	7.42	7.42	4.90*	.041
Frequency	1	15.02	15.02	9.92**	.094
Duration * Frequency	1	.37	.37	.25	
Error	79	119.62	1.51		
Total	82	142.43			

Note. $^*p < .05.$ $^{**}p < .01.$

Table 11: Analysis of Variance for Dominance Scores at Time 1 ($N = 83$)

Source	df	SS	MS	F	ω^2
Duration	1	6.53	6.53	10.88**	.102
Frequency	1	3.40	3.40	5.67*	.048
Duration * Frequency	1	0.003	0.003	.04	
Error	79	47.41	.60		
Total	82	57.34			

Note. $^*p < .05.$ $^{**}p < .01.$

Table 12: Analysis of Variance for Dominance Scores at Time 2 ($N = 83$)

Source	df	SS	MS	F	ω^2
Duration	1	2.70	2.70	4.67*	.039
Frequency	1	6.11	6.11	10.58**	.100
Duration * Frequency	1	.13	.13	.23	
Error	79	45.60	.58		
Total	82	54.54			

Note. $^*p < .05.$ $^{**}p < .01.$

Table 13: Analysis of Variance for Equality Scores at Time 1 ($N = 83$)

Source	df	SS	MS	F	ω^2
Duration	1	13.16	13.16	7.14**	.065
Frequency	1	12.52	12.52	6.80*	.061
Duration * Frequency	1	1.52	1.52	.83	
Error	79	145.51	1.84		
Total	82	172.71			

Note. $^*p < .05.$ $^{**}p < .01.$

Table 14: Analysis of Variance for Equality Scores at Time 2 ($N = 83$)

Source	df	SS	MS	F	ω^2
Duration	1	14.20	14.20	7.75**	.073
Frequency	1	8.83	8.83	4.82*	.041
Duration * Frequency	1	.58	.58	.32	
Error	79	144.67	1.83		
Total	82	168.28			

Note. $^*p < .05.$ $^{**}p < .01.$

Table 15: Analysis of Variance for Task Orientation Scores at Time 1 ($N = 83$)

Source	df	SS	MS	F	ω^2
Duration	1	3.77	3.77	2.85	
Frequency	1	8.95	8.95	6.77*	.003
Duration * Frequency	1	.14	.14	.11	
Error	79	104.48	1.32		
Total	82	797.64			

Note. *$p < .05$.

Table 16: Analysis of Variance for Task Orientation Scores at Time 2 ($N = 83$)

Source	df	SS	MS	F	ω^2
Duration	1	6.41	6.41	5.89*	.051
Frequency	1	11.15	11.15	10.24**	.096
Duration * Frequency	1	.01	.01	.06	
Error	79	86.04	1.09		
Total	82	103.61			

Note. *$p < .05$ ** $p < .01$.

Third, because no interaction effects on relational scores were found between fre-quency and duration of messaging, the results of the Bonferroni multiple comparisons at Time 1 were conducted and are presented to compare the relational scores across the groups in Tables 17 and 18. Table 17 indicates that at Time 1 there were significant differences be-tween the group of short duration/low frequency and the group of long duration/high fre-quency in terms of receptivity/trust scores, composure scores, formality scores, and task orientation scores ($\alpha < .05$); there were very significant differences between the group of short duration/low frequency and the group of long duration/high frequency in terms of immediacy/affection scores, similarity scores, dominance scores, and equality scores ($\alpha < .01$). In addition, Table 18 indicates that at Time 2 there were significant differences between the group of short duration/low frequency and the group of long duration/high fre-quency in terms of immediacy/affection scores, similarity/depth scores, receptivity scores, and composure scores ($\alpha < .05$); there were very significant differences between the group of short duration/low frequency and the group of long duration/high frequency in terms of formality scores, dominance scores, equality scores, and task orientation scores ($\alpha < .01$). However, at both Time 1 and Time 2, there were no significant differences between other groups in terms of any of the eight relational scores ($\alpha > .05$).

Table 17: Mean Differences of Bonferroni Multiple Comparisons Among Eight Relational Scores at Time 1 (N=83)

(I)	(J)	(I-J) Immediacy	(I-J) Similarity	(I-J) Receptivity	(I-J) Composure	(I-J) Formality	(I-J) Dominance	(I-J) Equality	(I-J) Task Orientation
1	2	1.02**	1.14**	.71*	1.01*	1.07*	.97**	1.57**	1.08*
	3	.47	.30	.63	.86	.88	.44	.51	.74
	4	.38	.47	.25	.53	.59	.60	.53	.51
2	1	-1.02**	-1.14**	-.71*	-1.01*	-1.07*	-.97**	-1.57**	-1.08*
	3	-.55	-.84	.00	-.15	-.19	-.52	-1.07	-.34
	4	-.64	-.67	-.45	-.48	-.48	-.37	-1.05	-.57
3	1	-.47	-.30	-.63	-.86	-.88	-.44	-.51	-.74
	2	.55	.84	.00	.15	.19	.53	1.07	.34
	4	.00	.17	-.38	-.32	-.29	.16	.00	-.23
4	1	-.38	-.47	-.26	-.53	-.59	-.60	-.53	-.51
	2	.64	.67	.45	.48	.48	.37	1.05	.57
	3	.00	-.17	.38	.32	.29	-.16	.00	.23

Note. Group 1 (long duration/high frequency), Group 2 (short duration/low frequency), Group 3 (long duration/low frequency), and Group 4 (short duration/high frequency), respectively.

$*p < .05.$ $** P < .01.$

Table 18: Mean Differences of Bonferroni Multiple Comparisons Among Eight Relational Scores at Time 2 ($N = 83$)

(I)	(J)	(I-J) Immediacy	(I-J) Similarity	(I-J) Receptivity	(I-J) Composure	(I-J) Formality	(I-J) Dominance	(I-J) Equality	(I-J) Task Orientation
1	2	.98*	1.09*	.88*	1.11*	1.45**	.90**	1.48**	1.29**
	3	.48	.27	.56	.71	.99	.62	.82	.68
	4	.37	.69	.71	.75	.73	.44	.99	.50
2	1	-.98*	-1.09*	-.88*	-1.11*	-1.45**	-.90**	-1.48**	-1.29**
	3	-.51	-.82	-.33	-.40	-.47	-.28	-.66	-.61
	4	-.62	.40	-.18	-.36	-.72	-.46	-.49	-.79
3	1	-.48	-.27	-.56	-.71	-.99	-.62	-.82	-.68
	2	.51	.82	.33	.40	.47	.28	.66	.61
	4	-.11	.42	.15	.00	-.25	-.18	.17	-.18
4	1	-.37	-.69	-.71	-.75	-.73	-.44	-.99	-.50
	2	.62	.40	.18	.36	.72	.46	.49	.79
	3	.11	-.42	-.15	.00	.25	.18	-.18	.18

Note. 1 = Group 1 (long duration/high frequency), 2 = Group 2 (short duration/low frequency), 3 = Group 3 (long duration/low frequency), and 4 = Group 4 (short duration/high frequency), respectively.
* $p < .05.$ ** $p < .01.$

Finally, all paired *t* tests in all four groups were conducted, and results indicated no significant differences in terms of eight relational scores between Time 1 and Time 2 in any of the above four experimental groups ($\alpha > .05$). Therefore, Hypothesis 4 was not supported.

DISCUSSION

Contrary to prior CMC research emphasizing comparison studies between CMC and FtF environments, this experimental study took another quite different research methodology, which emphasized the effects of two nonverbal cues on relational development in CMC environments. Specifically, this laboratory study explored the effects of frequency and duration of messaging on different aspects of relational development in CMC. Generally, the results in this study are mixed. Specifically, two hypotheses (Hypotheses 2 and 3) were supported, whereas two others (Hypotheses 1 and 4) were not. As stated previously, there were no interaction effects between duration and frequency on relational scores in CMC. However, frequency and duration both had significant main effects on relational scores in CMC. Therefore, the main effects of frequency and duration on relational scores in CMC are discussed below.

First, contrary to the expectations, Hypothesis 1 was not supported. That is, there were no interaction effects between duration and frequency of messaging on any of the eight relational scores in CMC. This result was different from the results in previous FtF studies (Koomen and Sagel 1977) and previous predictions in CMC environments (Hiltz and Turoff 1978; Rice and Love 1987). According to Rice and Love and Hiltz and Turoff, duration and frequency of messaging in CMC, similar to duration and latency of verbal response in FtF, should have significant interaction effects predicting an individual's participation in CMC. These researchers also maintained that long duration and high frequency are related to greater perceived sociability and leadership in relational development in CMC environments.

Second, Hypothesis 2 was supported. Frequency of messaging had significant main effects on relational scores in CMC. That is, high frequency in CMC resulted in higher scores than low frequency in all eight relational scores at Time 1 and in some relational scores at Time 2. This result was well demonstrated in Groups 1 (long duration/high frequency) and 2 (short duration/low frequency; see Tables 9 and 18). Group 1 involved high frequency and developed higher relational scores than Group 2, which involved low frequency. This result was in agreement with the results in some previous studies in FtF environments (Willard and Strodtbeck 1972). Therefore, it appears that frequency of messaging is an important factor in CMC and may have similar effects on relational development in both FtF and CMC environments. So, frequency of messaging may be a good predictor of an individual's participation and some aspects of relational development in CMC group interaction. Specifically, CMC users with high frequency may be perceived as being more developed and as having greater participation, whereas those with low frequency may be perceived as less developed and as having less participation in CMC.

Third, Hypothesis 3 was supported. Duration of messaging had significant main effects on relational scores in CMC. That is, longer duration in CMC resulted in higher scores than shorter duration in some relational scores at Time 1 and in all eight relational scores at Time 2. This result was also well demonstrated in Groups 1 (long duration/high frequency) and 2 (short duration/low frequency; see Tables 9 and 18). Group 1 involved long duration and developed higher relational scores than did Group 2, which involved short duration. This result was in agreement with the results in some previous studies in FtF environments (Koomen and Sagel 1977). Therefore, it appears that duration of messaging is also an important factor in CMC and may have similar effects on some aspects of relational development in both FtF and CMC environments. So, duration of messaging is also a good predictor of an individual's participation and relational development in CMC group interaction. Specifically, CMC users with shorter duration may be perceived as less developed and lacking confidence, whereas persons with longer duration may be perceived as more developed and confident.

In all, Hypotheses 2 and 4 support the predictions of Hiltz and Turoff (1978) and Rice and Love (1987), who maintained that frequency and duration of messaging have similar effects in both FtF and CMC environments and that both are important predictors of a CMC user's participation in group communication. In addition, these results partially support Walther's (1992) Social Information Processing Model. According to Walther, CMC users can process all relational cues available and social identity using various media to present and solicit their relational behaviors. Specifically, in relation to this study, CMC users can manipulate nonverbal cues, such as duration and frequency of messaging, to more favorably present their behaviors and to achieve better relational development with their partners.

Fourth, contrary to the expectations, Hypothesis 4 was not supported. That is, the statistical results of all relational scores did not significantly increase from the end of the first week to the end of the second week. This finding seems not to support Walther's (1992) initial hypothesis of gradual relational development in CMC. According to Walther, CMC users can gradually develop relationships with their own partners over time. However, in this study, although visual presentation showed that the means at Time 2 were all higher than the means at Time 1, no significant differences were found in terms of all eight relational scores between the two occasions in all four experimental groups.

In all, there may be several major reasons why the present study fails to completely support Rice and Love's (1987) and Hiltz and Turoff's (1978) predictions of the interaction effects and Walther's (1992) hypothesis of gradual relational development over time in CMC. These may include, are not limited to the following:

> *Experimental duration.* This study only involved a period of two weeks, whereas most prior studies used a longer period of time, such as five weeks.
>
> *Participants as observers.* Participants in this study were only allowed to be lurkers rather than participants, wheras most prior studies allowed participants to participate actively in the list discussions.
>
> *Composition of participants.* There was an imbalance toward females in the subject pool in this study, whereas most prior studies did not involve such a high percentage of females.
>
> *Experimental tasks.* This study only involved one task, whereas most prior studies used more tasks for participants to discuss with each other. In addition, this study involved an emotional topic to stimulate the participants' interests.
>
> *Research type.* This study only involved the manipulation of two independent variables in CMC environments, whereas most prior studies involved the comparison of FtF and CMC environments.
>
> *Characteristics of participants.* This study involved participants mostly having CMC experiences, whereas most prior studies used participants with no CMC experience.
>
> *Other relevant factors.* These may include group sizes and language styles.

Finally, as CMC is becoming more widely used, there is an urgent need to study the affects of interactive CMC, such as e-commerce, e-learning, and e-health. Based on the findings in this experimental study and Walther's (1992) Social Information Processing

Model in CMC, the following recommendations are proposed for future research in different interactive CMC environments:

1. Investigating the effects of frequency and duration of messaging in interactive CMC discussion in different areas, such as education, work, commerce, or health.

2. Extending the experimental duration to longer periods so that participants can have enough time to develop impressions and relations.

3. Adding more discussion topics in CMC so that participants will not become bored in the experiment.

4. Increasing participants' duration of messaging in extended periods of communication.

5. Using participants from a variety of settings, including educational, industrial, organizational, and personal communications.

6. Recruiting a more balanced group of males and females in the subject pool.

CONCLUSION

Although the findings in this experimental study are preliminary, and further study is needed in interactive CMC environments with different samples, the initial results are promising. The results indicate that frequency and duration of messaging are potentially important variables in CMC relational development; high frequency and long duration can help CMC users achieve more developed relationships with their CMC partners. This conclusion is in contrast to the task-oriented model of CMC discussed previously. The author agrees with this conclusion because it can help explain many CMC phenomena. Therefore, the present study generally supports one of CMC's two major theoretical models—the social-emotion-oriented model in CMC environments described previously. CMC users may control the frequency and duration of messaging to achieve more developed relationships with their partners in various CMC environments. In addition, the results in this study have laid the foundation for future research in many popular types of interactive CMC environments, including e-learning, e-commerce, and e-health.

NOTES

1. This study was a portion of the author's doctoral dissertation in 2000. The author extends his gratitude to the valuable advice and comments from Drs. Dean Ginther and Paul Zelhart, who are both professors of Psychology at Texas A&M University–Commerce.

2. These themes are described in the "Instruments" section of this paper. For detailed information regarding these themes, please refer to Burgoon and Hale's paper in 1987.

3. Of the 116 participants, 33 were excluded from final analysis because of the participants' violation of the experimental instructions. Specifically, 30 participants violated (b) and 3 violated (c) in the "Experimental Instruction" section of this paper.

4. The author extends his gratitude to Dr. Judee Burgoon's permission to use her Relational Communicational Questionnaire in this study.

5. The Levene's test from SPSS 10.0 indicated no severe departure from homogeneity across the groups. The boxplot tests from SPSS 10.0 also indicated no severe departure from multivariate normality observed across the groups.

REFERENCES

American Psychological Association. (1994). *Publication manual of the American Psychological Association* (4th ed.). Washington, DC: Author.

Asteroff, J. F. (1987). *Paralanguage in electronic mail: A case study.* Unpublished doctoral dissertation, Columbia University.

Breazeale, S. C. (1999). A meeting of minds: The alumni-l listserv(r) (administrators, computer mediated communication, professional community). *Dissertation Abstracts International,* 60:04, AAT 9928286.

Burgoon, J. K., and Hale, J. L. (1987). Validation and measurement of the fundamental themes of relational communication. *Communication Monographs,* 54, 19–41.

Connolly, T., Jessup, L. M., and Valacich, J. S. (1990). Effects of anonymity and evaluative tone on idea generation in computer-mediated groups. *Management Science,* 36:6, 689–703.

Halbert, C. L. (1999). The presentation of self in computer-mediated communication: managing and challenging gender identity (impression management, chatrooms). *Dissertation Abstracts International,* 60:08, AAT 9943012.

Hesse, B. W., Werner, C. M., and Altman, I. (1988). Temporal aspects of computer-mediated communication. *Computers in Human Behavior,* 4, 147–165.

Hiltz, S. R., Johnson, K, and Turoff, M. (1986). Experiments in group decision making: Communication process and outcome in face-to-face versus computerized conferences. *Human Communication Research,* 13, 225–252.

Hiltz, S. R., and Turoff, M. (1978). *The network nation.* Reading, MA: Addison-Wesley.

Jacobson, D. (1999). Impression formation in cyberspace: Online expectations and offline experiences in text-based virtual communities. *Journal of Computer-Mediated Communication* 5:1. [Online]. Available: http://www.ascusc.org/jcmc/vol5/issue1/jacobson.html.

Koomen, W., and Sagel, P. K. (1977). The prediction of participation in two-person groups. *Sociometry,* 40:4, 369–373.

Krauss, R. M., and Fussell, S. R. (1996). Social psychological models of interpersonal communication. In E. T. Higgins and A. W. Kruglanski (eds.), *Social psychology: Handbook of basic principles.* New York: The Guilford Press.

Lea, M., and Spears, R. (1991). Computer-mediated communication, deindividualization and group decision-making. *International Journal of Man-Machine Studies,* 34, 283–301.

Liu, Y. (2000). The effects of nonverbal cues on impression formation in computer-mediated communication: An exploratory study. *Dissertation Abstracts International,* 61:4, AAT 9965844.

Liu, Y., and Ginther, D. (1999a). *A comparison of task-oriented model and social-emotion-oriented model in computer-mediated communication.* Paper presented at the annual meeting of the Southwestern Psychological Association, Albuquerque, NM. (ERIC Document Reproduction Service Number ED 437 924)

———. (1999b). *How to achieve a better impression in computer-mediated communication.* Information Resources (IRO 19863), Commerce, Texas (ERIC Document Reproduction Service Number ED 437 035)

Parks, M. R., and Floyd, K. (1996). Making friends in cyberspace. *Journal of Communication,* 46:1, 80–97.

Reid, E. (1995). Virtual worlds: Culture and imagination. In S. G. Jones (ed.), *Cybersociety: Computer-mediated communication and community.* Thousand Oaks, CA: Sage.

Rice, R. E., and Love, G. (1987). Electronic emotion: Socioemotional content in a computer-mediated communication network. *Communication Research,* 14, 85–108.

Rintel, E. S., and Pittam, J. (1997). Strangers in a strange land: Interaction management on Internet relay chat. Human *Communication Research,* 23:4, 507–534.

Short, J. S., Williams, E., and Christie, B. (1976). *The social psychology of telecommunications.* London: John Wiley.

Tangmanee, C. (1999). The use of computer-mediated communication systems by programmers. *Dissertation Abstracts_International,* 60:08, AAT 9940573.

Thompsen, P. A., and Foulger, D. A. (1996). Effects of pictographs and quoting on flaming in electronic mail. *Computers in Human Behavior,* 12:2, 225–243.

Turoff, M. (1978). The EIES experience: Electronic information exchange system. *Bulletin of the American Society for Information Science,* 4:5, 9–10.

Utz, S. (2000). Social information processing in MUDs: The development of friendships in virtual worlds. *Journal of Online Behavior,* 1:1. [Online]. Available: http://www.behavior.net/JOB /v1n1/utz.html.

Vallee, J., Johansen, R., and Sprangler, K. (1975). The computer conference: An altered state of communication? *The Futurist,* 9:3, 116–121.

Walther, J. B. (1992). Interpersonal effects in computer-mediated interaction: A relational perspective. *Communication Research,* 19:1, 52–90.

———. (1995). Relational aspects of computer-mediated communication: Experimental observations over time. *Organizational Science,* 6:2, 186–203.

———. (1996). Computer-mediated communication: Impersonal, interpersonal, and hyperpersonal interaction. *Communication Research,* 23:1, 3–43.

———. (1997). Group and interpersonal effects in international computer-mediated collaboration. *Human Communication Research,* 23:3, 342–369.

Walther, J. B., and Burgoon, J. K. (1992). Relational communication in computer-mediated interaction. *Human Communication Research,* 19:1, 50–88.

Walther, J. B., and Tidwell, L. C. (1995). Nonverbal cues in computer-mediated communication, and the effect of chronemics on relational communication. *Journal of Organizational Computing,* 5:4, 355–378.

Walther, J. B., Anderson, J. F., and Park, D. W. (1994). Interpersonal effects in computer-mediated interaction: A meta-analysis of social and antisocial communication. *Communication Research,* 21:4, 460–487.

Willard, D., and Strodtbeck, F. (1972). Latency of verbal response and participation in small groups. Sociometry, 35:1, 161–175.

Wright, K. B. (1999). Computer-mediated social support, older adults, and coping. *Dissertation Abstracts International,* 60:01, AAT 9918762.

Critical Thinking in College Students
Critical Issues in Empirical Research

John D. Emerson
Department of Mathematics and Computer Science
Middlebury College

Lisa Boes
Graduate School of Education
Harvard University

Frederick Mosteller
Professor Emeritus, Department of Statistics
Harvard University

INTRODUCTION

Critical thinking is a prominent goal for students in the nation's schools, and college teachers also want their students to think deeply and rigorously. To succeed, students must learn substantial sets of material. But college teachers do not view the mastery of facts and the "surface learning" of information presented in lectures or textbooks as sufficient for success in college-level courses. In most if not all disciplines, critical thinking (CT) requires the deep learning expected at the college level.

Robert Ennis offers a concise definition of CT: *Critical thinking is reasonable reflective thinking focused on what to believe or do* (1987, 10). By *reasonable,* Ennis means "using reason," rather than "not extreme."

The phrase *critical thinking* may connote a process that seems destructive (in the sense of finding fault), but the negative aspects of CT are not primary. Healthy skepticism and a questioning attitude underlie CT, but CT also deals with synthesizing and with developing new insights. CT is a creative process that sometimes devises new solutions to thorny problems and thus expands knowledge. The critical thinker *does* as well as criticizes.

New technologies—especially computers, the Internet, the World Wide Web, and multimedia—support college teaching in many ways (Emerson and Mosteller 1998a, 1998b). Teachers who use technology in their courses search for ways to strengthen their students' thinking skills by involving students more actively in the learning process.

This paper focuses primarily on critical thinking in college students, but occasionally it draws on research from schools. It provides brief summaries of the skills and dispositions that define critical thinking and of some standardized tests of CT. It reviews some findings from empirical research about CT. Three important review articles about CT research contribute much to this section, and we supplement findings from these reports with discussions of further recent empirical work.

The paper then turns to controversies in the community of researchers on CT. For example, some experts believe that CT is a general construct that can be taught in a stand-alone course. Others believe that CT necessarily occurs within a context or a discipline; they believe instruction should be integrated within discipline-based courses. Experts disagree on whether and how instruction in CT can enable learners to transfer their capacities for CT to new contexts and content areas.

We offer practical advice for college teachers about supporting and teaching CT, and we present conclusions and recommendations.

CHARACTERIZING AND EVALUATING CRITICAL THINKING

Although education researchers and philosophers have long debated the definition and the characteristics of critical thinking, they generally agree about the meaning of CT in teaching practice. CT is thinking that uses most of the skills from five broad areas: interpretation, analysis, evaluation, research, and self-regulation. To engage successfully in CT requires not only the requisite skills but also the disposition to use these skills in addressing problems. An effective critical thinker is disposed to be inquisitive and open-minded and is willing to use evidence and reasoning to adjust beliefs, reach conclusions, and make decisions.

Critical Thinking Skills and Dispositions

To arrive at a useful and detailed characterization of critical thinking, we examined several formulations from researchers in CT, identified component skills within their conceptualizations, and grouped the skills into six broad categories. Table 1, page 54, summarizes this work and attributes the skills to researchers who have used them in characterizing CT.

This summary table suggests that a critical thinker benefits by adopting the skills and the mind-set of a scholar. Teaching someone to be successful in critical thinking amounts to teaching him or her to assume the role and the perspective of a researcher.

Not everyone who thinks critically can design elaborate investigations and carry them out; this is rarely realistic for our students—or even for us. But we do want critical thinkers to engage in *exploration*. A critical thinker can and should often be active in gathering information and data pertaining to a particular question. He or she must also learn to analyze and interpret data and make valid inferences from it. Searching for, assembling, interpreting, and synthesizing relevant information is likely to make one more willing to question assumptions and to adjust one's views.

Assessment Instruments

A college teacher organizes lectures and instructional materials for a course and decides what he or she hopes students will learn. Usually the teacher also needs to evaluate student learning and must therefore decide how to measure learning outcomes. This assessment may use short-answer questions, essay questions, oral evaluation, student portfolios, or independent projects. The content addressed in the evaluation may closely follow what the teacher presented or what was in assigned readings and homework, or it may address new contexts and thus require creativity by students in transferring their learning. The evaluation of learning not only gives information needed by the teacher that goes beyond grading student performance but also aids the teacher in developing strategies for teaching improvement. Whatever choices are made for learning assessment, evaluation of student learning is essential for teaching and its improvement.

Assessing CT poses a special challenge because CT is, by definition, a broad and general construct. Investigators design standardized tests to assess the level of mastery of CT and its component skills. Usually the contexts chosen for teaching CT skills will not coincide with those used in a standardized test for CT. Therefore, an important consideration is transferability of skills to new settings. A mismatch often exists between what is taught in CT instruction and what is measured using general CT test instruments.

Researchers have developed several standardized tests of critical thinking—widely marketed tests that provide norms for assessment comparisons. The initial work was informed by the development of IQ tests early in the twentieth century. By 1941, Goodwin Watson and Edward Glaser had developed a version of their Test of Critical Thinking, a multiple-choice test still widely used today (Glaser 1941).

Table 1: Qualities and Capabilities of Critical Thinkers

Dispositions	Engage problems with inquisitiveness and reflective skepticism (Ennis; McPeck) Value making accurate judgments about specific things in everyday life using available evidence (Glaser) Be open-minded and willing to revise thinking (Ennis; Glaser; Norris)
Interpretation	Recognize and define problems (Glaser) Identify assumptions, reasons, and conclusions (Ennis)
Analysis	Examine data and other forms of evidence (Glaser) Offer reasonable hypotheses (Norris, Ennis) Make sound inferences (Norris; Hagedorn et al.)
Evaluation	Appraise evidence and the credibility of sources (Glaser; Ennis) Judge the quality of an argument, including the acceptability of its reasons, assumptions, and evidence (Ennis; Norris; Hagedorn et al.) Evaluate and synthesize information (Paul) Draw warranted conclusions and generalizations (Glaser; Ennis; Hagedorn et al., Facione)
Research	Gather and use pertinent information and data (Glaser; Ennis) Design investigations to produce reliable observations (Ennis, Norris) Create alternative explanations, models, or theories (Norris)
Self-regulation	Test the conclusions at which one has arrived (Ennis; Glaser; Paul) Think critically about one's own thinking to make it better (Norris; Facione; Paul)

Sources: Ennis (1993, 180); Facione (1990a, 3–4, 1990b, 7); Glaser (1941, 6); Hagedorn et al., 1999, 265–266); McPeck (1981, 5–14); Norris (1985, 40, 44); Paul (1987, 140)

Purposes of CT Tests

Robert Ennis lists seven major purposes for tests of critical thinking: (1) diagnosing the levels of students' CT, (2) giving feedback to students about their CT prowess, (3) motivating students to be better at CT, (4) informing teachers about their success in teaching students to think critically, (5) doing research about CT instructional questions and issues, (6) providing help in deciding whether a student should undertake further education, and (7) giving information to hold schools accountable for their students' CT (Ennis 1993, 180).

Ennis characterizes the last two purposes as having high stakes, and he cautions that many standardized test are not suitable for these purposes.

Overview of Six Standardized Tests

Table 2, page 56, summarizes six standardized tests that have been used both for research about CT and for assessment of CT skills and dispositions. One test, the Ennis-Weir Critical Thinking Essay Test (EWCTET), uses an essay format, and another, the Reflective Judgment Interview (RJI), uses structured interviews to address problems having no clear right answers. Because of its unique focus on ill-structured problems, we provide additional background on the Reflective Judgment Model and the related test instrument.

The Reflective Judgment Model describes seven developmental stages for belief structures when the thinker is faced with ambiguity and ill-defined problems (King, Wood, and Mines 1990, 171). These stages of intellectual maturity are characterized in part by beliefs about how certain knowledge is

1. absolutely certain; knowledge is gained from authorities and needs no justification;

2. absolutely certain but not immediately available;

3. temporarily uncertain; knowledge is gained both from authorities and from personal biases;

4. acceptance of uncertainty as essential part of all knowledge; the individual is the only judge of his or her personal truths;

5. knowledge claims are subjective evaluations of reality; there is no objective reality;

6. beliefs are justified as plausible opinions, using generalized rules of evidence; and

7. objective knowledge; beliefs are reflective judgments grounded in critical inquiry and evaluations of evidence. They are fallible and subject to revision.

Table 2: Tests of Critical Thinking

	Format and Background	Remarks
Watson-Glaser Critical Thinking Appraisal (WGCTA)	80-item short-answer test, 40 minutes Two forms for pretest/posttest application Developed by Goodwin Watson and Edward Glaser Originally developed in 1941 (Glazer 1941) Current version 1980	Relatively free of school-subject content; "everyday life" focus Five sections address: inference, recognition of assumptions, deduction, interpretation, evaluation of arguments Test used most widely for research purposes (McMillan 1987; and Tsui 1998)
Cornell Critical Thinking Test (CCTT)	Level X (grades 5–14) and Level Z (advanced high school, college, other adults); Level Z—52 multiple-choice items; 50 minutes; developed by Ennis and Millman (1971, 1985)	Seven areas of CT covered: induction, credibility, prediction and experimental planning, fallacies, deduction, definitions and assumptions, and identification.
Ennis-Weir Critical Thinking Essay Test (EWCTET)	Analyze a "letter to the editor" with eight numbered paragraphs, respond with essay Evaluate each paragraph and justify evaluation 40 minutes Developed by Robert Ennis and Eric Weir (1985)	Purpose: evaluate ability to appraise an argument and to formulate a written argument in response Scoring addresses: getting the point, seeing reasons and assumptions, stating one's point, offering good reasons, seeing other possibilities, irrelevance; over generalization, and several others (Norris and Ennis 1989, 80–84)
California Critical Thinking Skills Test (CalCTST)	34-question multiple-choice test, 45 minutes Two forms for pretest/posttest application Developed by Peter Facione (1990b) for use in California State University and Community College System (1992) Current version 1998	Follows recommendations of 1987–1989 Delphi Panel of American Philosophical Association (Facione 1990a) Panel identified six cognitive skills as central to CT: interpretation, analysis, evaluation, explanation, inference, and self-regulation. Five subtests address five of the six skills but not self-regulation or "meta-cognition" (Facione 1990b)
California Critical Thinking Disposition Inventory (CCTDI)	75 items; for each item the respondent indicates degree of agreement or disagreement; a six-point Likert scale; 15–20 minutes Developed by Pete Facione and Noreen Facione Current version 1992 (Facione and Facione 1992)	Dispositions identified by 1987–1989 Delphi Panel Tests dispositions (not skills or knowledge) on seven scales: truth-seeking, open-mindedness, analyticity, systematicity, self-confidence, inquisitiveness, and maturity Example item: "It's easy for me to organize my thoughts."
The Reflective Judgment Interview (RJI)	Four ill-structured problems that invite self-doubt about one's current understanding Two contradictory points of view presented Trained interviewer probes and elicits responses	Assesses stages of intellectual development as identified in the RJM (Kitchener and King 1981; King and Kitchener 1994) Problems used: how the Egyptian pyramids were built; the objectivity of news reporting; how human beings were created; and the safety of chemical additives in food

Kitchner and King devised a semistructured test instrument, the Reflective Judgment Inteview, to assess one's ability to use reflective judgment in facing ambiguity (Kitchener and King 1981; King and Kitchener 1994, chapter 5).

FINDINGS FROM EMPIRICAL RESEARCH

Throughout most of the twentieth century, empirical research has addressed various claims about critical thinking, what affects it, how to teach it, and how to measure it. This section reviews some of these claims and identifies empirical research findings that support them.

Three Reviews: McMillan 1987; Tsui 1998; and Bangert-Drowns and Bankert 1990

McMillan (1987) and Tsui (1998) each review literature on college students' critical thinking. McMillan uses 27 empirical studies published between 1950 and 1985. Tsui builds on McMillan's work to include 62 studies, extending the literature review through 1997. Their findings reveal that developing CT remains a central goal of American higher education. It is also a goal for school education and is repeatedly mentioned as a requirement for democracy in the United States.

McMillan (1987) and Tsui (1998) both examine three types of educational interventions designed to promote CT: (1) specific instructional techniques within courses, (2) individual courses devoted to CT, and (3) general programs or curricula having a duration one year or more, including the entire college experience. Because of the similarities in these two reviews and their findings, we discuss them together.

Specific Instructional Techniques

The majority of studies McMillan and Tsui review address the use of specific instructional variables. These studies examine pedagogical approaches, such as methods of clarifying values, individually paced instruction, class discussion, and interactive use of computer simulation. Some studies identify interventions that seem to aid CT, for example, courses emphasizing problem solving and uses of peer-to-peer interaction (Tsui 1998, 7).

Tsui contributes a study of this type herself, using a national sample of 24,837 students from over 392 four-year colleges and universities (Tsui 1999). She reports that writing assignments and instructor feedback on such work positively affect students' self-reports of the development of their CT skills, just as they strengthen writing skills.

Courses and Programs

The second category of intervention McMillan and Tsui examine consists of specific courses or educational programs. These interventions include both instructional units on CT within disciplinary courses and general courses in informal logic, argumentation, debate, problem solving, or CT skills. The study findings are mixed; the use of intact groups instead of random assignment of students to treatment, the influence of individual instructors, and factors specific to individual colleges provide plausible rival hypotheses for the findings (McMillan 1987, 8). Sometimes the choice of analysis may also influence the strength of findings.

An example illustrates the empirical research about instruction aimed at improving CT. Facione (1990b) reports on a study at California State University at Fullerton, done in the 1989–1990 academic year. It uses the California Critical Thinking Skills Test (CalCTST) in a paired pretest-posttest design to assess how much is learned in a college course on CT. In one part of Facione's study, 262 students achieve a pre-test mean of 15.9 and a post-test mean of 17.4; the 1.5-point improvement on the 34-question test is statistically highly significant, though small in magnitude. In another part of the study, independent groups of students have test averages that differ by approximately one point, again in a direction showing improvement after taking the course.

Although significant in a statistical sense, these gains of 1 or 1.5 points from an entire college course addressing CT are not important practically. What teachers taught in many of the courses may not reflect well the CT skills measured by the CalCTST. A standardized test of general CT skills, no matter how well constructed, may not measure the particular skills taught in a college course.

Facione believes that students taking the pre-test were more strongly motivated than when taking the post-test. The post-test occurred near the end of the term when students were completing papers and preparing for final exams. The teachers told their students that the testing supported a research program and that results on the CalCTST would not affect final course grades. Facione excludes from the analyses his own two course sections, which showed an average gain of five points. He instead told his students that the CalCTST was serving as the final exam in his course. Whether the impressive gain for Facione's students derives in part from his skill in teaching CT, from student motivation to do well on the exam, or from some combination of these and other factors is not answerable. But the results suggest possibilities for extending this kind of research.

Sustained Curricula

A few studies reviewed by McMillan and by Tsui focus on programs or curricula that engage students over one or more years of college. One such intervention is a one-year program designed to enhance CT of freshmen (Tomlinson-Keasey and Eisert 1978; see also McMillan 1987, 8). Using a locally developed instrument to evaluate CT gains from the ADAPT program (Accent on Developing Abstract Processes of Thought), the investigators report a very substantial effect size—nearly 1.2 (103). A comprehensive and intensive effort to improve CT throughout the curriculum at Alverno College also gives statistically significant gains in CT as measured by the WGCTA (Mentkowski and Doherty 1984). McMillan characterizes the Alverno College program as "perhaps the best example of an entire college devoted to teaching and measuring critical thinking" (McMillan 1987, 9).

Although practical realities mean that long-term studies often lack control groups or use nonequivalent groups, this research provides preliminary findings that merit attention. At least some programs that focus heavily on enhancing CT in college students do meet with success that is measurable by a general test of CT. Studies that focus on curricula report that the greatest gains in CT occur at colleges offering integrative coursework such as that provided in interdisciplinary courses and in some liberal arts curricula (Tsui 1998, 9).

A Meta-Analysis

Bangert-Drowns and Bankert report a formal meta-analysis that synthesizes the results of explicit instruction to improve CT (1990). They use studies of instruction at all levels, not just the college level. To be included in the meta-analysis an investigation needed to compare the performance of two groups of students on some measure of CT. The investigators located 20 studies, including 19 doctoral dissertations, suitable for the meta-analysis. Ten of the studies use the Watson-Glaser Critical Thinking Appraisal (WGCTA), and five use the Cornell Critical Thinking Test (CCTT).

Unlike both McMillan and Tsui, Bangert-Drowns and Bankert (1990) report findings consistently favoring programs that use explicit instructional methods, such as class discussion of CT or adoption of new instructional materials. Findings from 18 of the 20 studies favor CT instruction, and 8 of these are statistically significant. The average improvement attributable to CT instruction has an effect size of 0.37. It is particularly notable that the effect size for elementary and junior high school students is 0.50 standard deviations, whereas for high school and college students it is 0.21 standard deviations (7). Gains in general CT skills seem to come most readily in school-age children, and gains in CT skills come more slowly after the first year of college.

As Students Mature, Critical Thinking Improves (But More Slowly)

That CT abilities improve with age is well documented. Some gains in critical thinking abilities are a consequence of natural maturation, and these gains should be distinguished from those resulting from educational programs and instructional interventions (Tsui 1998, 6; McMillan 1987, 9). With its focus on seven developmental stages of "knowing," the Reflective Judgment Model (RJM) lends itself naturally to examining the development of thinking abilities over time.

King and Kitchener provide a detailed report of a 10-year longitudinal study of 80 individuals from 1977 to 1987 (1994, chapter 6; see also Kitchener et al. 1989). The original participants included 20 high school juniors, 40 college juniors, and 20 third-year doctoral students, all attending schools and colleges in the Minneapolis area. The students took a battery of six standardized tests, including the RJI on four occasions: in 1977, 1979, 1983, and 1987. In the last testing, 53 of 80 students participated, a 66 percent follow-up rate.

Without exception, the reflective judgment scores improved over time for the high school juniors and the college juniors. With the advanced doctoral students, the scores increased between 1977 and 1979 and leveled off thereafter. The gains over 10 years, measured as effect sizes, are approximately 5.1 standard deviations for high school juniors, 1.9 standard deviations for college juniors, and 0.6 standard deviations for doctoral students (see King and Kitchener 1994, 133). As younger students with less educational training, the high school juniors give the greatest gains in the test scores of reflective CT about ill-posed problems. The variability in the test scores generally increases over time for each group, and higher levels of education are associated with greater variation in test scores.

By comparing members of the group of high school juniors (in 1977), who either never entered college or who had entered but had not completed a degree, with group members of similar ages who had earned a bachelor's degree by 1983, King and Kitchener separate education effects from maturation effects on growth in RJI scores. The mean growth in RJI for the first group is 1.65 developmental stages, whereas the mean growth for the second group is 2.30; the completion of college gives a statistically significant benefit (Kitchener et al. 1989, 85).

The reports by King and Kitchener suggest that gains in reflective judgment, a rather sophisticated CT skill, can be substantial during the high school and college years, but further gains taper off with advanced graduate study years. This study and other empirical research support what may seem self-evident to most teachers: Improved CT skills come with chronological age. The finding appears to extend from grade school through graduate school, but we uncovered no evidence about growth in CT in older adults.

Going to College Improves Critical Thinking

Empirical research demonstrates that students' critical thinking ability improves while in college, even without special training in CT (Dressel and Mayhew 1954; McMillan 1987; Pascarella 1989; Pascarella et al. 1996). For example, Robert Mines and his colleagues (Mines, King, Hood, and Wood 1990) study 100 college students in three groups: 20 freshmen, 40 seniors, and 40 graduate students who had completed one or more years of graduate study. The groups are balanced for gender and for academic area (mathematical sciences or social sciences). Mines and his colleagues administer three tests to all the students—WGCTA, CCTT (Form Z), and RJI. They find that, without exception, the overall scores from each measure increased with educational level. From her review of this study and others, Tsui (1998, 5) concludes that, "Generally speaking, research reveals more years of education is associated with higher scores on tests for critical thinking."

The research findings typically indicate that college students make their greatest gains in CT during the freshman year (Tsui 1998, 6). Dressel and Mayhew (1954) report on studies of gains in CT for a total of 3,100 freshmen students in several groups at multiple universities. In nearly all groups, they identify freshman-year gains with an effect size of about a half standard deviation unit (or more).

Ernest Pascarella (1989) studies a matched sample of 47 students (30 attended college and 17 did not attend college). He reports that freshman-year college attendance leads to a gain on the WGCTA—an effect size of 0.44 standard deviation units. Tsui (1998) identifies this study by Pascarella as the only one she found that compares a college group with a non-college-attending group. Pascarella, Bohr, Nora, and Terenzini report end-of-freshmen-year gains for full-time students of 0.41 standard deviation units on the College Assessment of Academic Proficiency (1996, 167). Freshmen year gains in general CT consistently appear to be about one-half standard deviation, or nearly 20 percentile points.

The greater gains for freshmen may reflect the impact of their courses, the immediate benefits of a college environment (compared with a high school environment) in promoting an intellectual agenda both within and beyond classrooms, the high motivational levels of many students as they begin college, the developmental stages of 18-year-olds, or (likely) some combination of these factors and others. Tsui urges research to address the question, "Why do subsequent college years fail to rival freshmen year in its efficacy to enhance students' critical thinking?" (1998, 7).

Impact of Academic Factors

Lehman and Nisbett (1990) report a longitudinal investigation of the effects of undergraduate study on inductive reasoning requiring the use of statistical skills and methodological principles, and on reasoning about problems in conditional (if-then) logic. Students who majored in the natural sciences and humanities improve substantially in conditional reasoning, but students from the social sciences and psychology do not. Students in the sciences tend to take more mathematics courses—courses that treat conditional reasoning when they present deductive arguments and proofs. By also reporting gains in general verbal reasoning scores, which are slightly positive but not statistically significant, Lehman and Nesbitt support their belief that the gains in specific areas of CT are attributable in part to educational programs and not only to chronological maturity.

Impact of Non-Academic Factors

The sources of gains in CT skills during the college years are not limited to academic factors; additional factors, such as residential setting and out-of-classroom experiences, influence students' CT (Terenzini et al. 1995; Pascarella 1989; see also Tsui 1999). Pascarella and Tarenzini (1991) review research findings about the impact of many aspects of college on students. They suggest that the total level of engagement in the academic and social systems of the institution may be more important than the impact of any one academic or nonacademic experience on general cognitive outcomes such as CT.

Tsui (2000) examines qualitative empirical data gathered at four strategically chosen case study sites to explore differential effects of diverse campus cultures on students' self-reported assessment of their CT. Intensive interviews of five students, five faculty members, and one administrator at each of the four universities provide her raw material. Tsui asks how differences in campus cultures relate to the average institutional growth in CT, derived by using data from a national sample of college students through the Cooperative Institutional Research Program (CIRP).

Three elements associated with campus culture seem to support the development of students' CT skills:

1. Emphasis on an enhanced epistemological orientation (e.g., where students learn primarily from cooperative exploration of knowledge rather than from knowledge transmittal)

2. An ability to instill responsibility and self-reflection in students

3. Success in fostering social and political awareness in college students

Campus culture is a "potent and pervasive force that shapes actions and outcomes"—including CT outcomes (Tsui 2000, 428).

Hagedorn et al. assess the impact of the average CT level for an institution's entering first-year class on an individual's CT development. They compare gains in CT tests taken when students first arrive at college, at the end of the first year, and at the end of the third year (1999, 268).

The average level of student body CT gives statistically significant but modest positive effects on the gains in CT skills of individual students at the end of the first year in college. Comparing the gains from attending the institution with the highest (versus the lowest) student body CT level, students in the first group answer between 3.7 and 5.7 more questions correctly on a 32-question test. After three years, however, there is no further statistically significant effect from the institutional CT context (Hagedorn et al. 1999, 276–277).

SOME CRITICAL ISSUES FOR CRITICAL THINKING

Our understanding of critical thinking—its meaning, assessment, and improvement—benefits from lively debates among experts whose views and perspectives can be sharply divergent.

Is CT Necessarily Context-Specific?

The availability of college courses to teach CT and standardized tests to assess CT skills suggest that CT is a general construct that transcends context and discipline. The CT skills outlined in Table 1 make sense in many settings—in both academic and everyday contexts. For example, Ennis' (1989, p. 4) view that "critical thinking is reasonable reflective thinking focused on what to believe or do" makes sense when answering questions such as whether unanticipated tax revenues should be used to retire public debt; what model automobile to purchase for the family; or how political decisions made in the two World Wars influence current events in the Balkans.

Deanne Kuhn reports that most educators today believe that CT skills must be taught in a specific subject-matter context, although she does not argue for or against that position (1999, 17). John McPeck articulates this popular view; he believes that courses in CT and tests of CT place too much emphasis on "argument analysis" and "everyday reasoning" (1984). He believes that, for reasoning about everyday problems, "our quandary is seldom about validity, and almost always about the truth of complex information, concepts, and propositions. We are not analyzing arguments so much as data, information, and putative facts" (1984, 36). Although McPeck may be overstating his point that the challenge for everyday problems is "seldom about validity," his emphasis on the challenges in getting good and relevant data and information about a problem is well placed.

McPeck emphasizes the importance of knowledge and understanding in the disciplines; he believes that their improvement is tied to improvement in CT. He believes that CT is not a content-free general ability and that we should be skeptical about educational programs that assume that it is (1985, 299; see also McPeck 1992 for a general review). To develop CT abilities of students working in the disciplines, McPeck recommends giving "philosophy of" literature and material in various courses and disciplines (1985, 307–308).

Other experts believe that, just as general skills and techniques for good writing can be taught, so too can the skills that constitute CT. Robert Ennis argues that general CT skills transcend subjects and disciplines (1989, 1990, 1992).

Vincent Ruggiero (1988) challenges McPeck's position that it is impossible to conceive of CT as a generalized skill. He suggests, "the best evidence that McPeck is mistaken lies in the fact that numerous other skills—from writing and speaking to typing and driving a car—are subject-specific yet are taught in special courses" (1988, 10–11). That writing and speaking depend in part on effective thinking lends support to Ruggiero's position.

How and by How Much Does Critical Thinking Differ Across Disciplines?

If critical thinking is at least somewhat context-specific, differences in CT across the disciplines deserve careful study. Several investigations have helped reveal the nature of these differences.

Examining National Standards Documents for School Subjects

Robert Marzano (1998) reasons that similarities and differences in thinking and reasoning skills across disciplines should be evident in formal statements of national standards for education in the schools. His empirical analysis relies on a detailed and comprehensive review of standards documents for 11 subject areas and for a 12th area, "the world of work." In the subjects of science, English, and the workplace, more than one standards documents is used so that altogether he examines 17 documents (1998, 269).

Marzano and his colleagues searched these documents for thinking and reasoning skills that were stated either explicitly or implicitly. They cataloged every skill found, and they recorded the source and page numbers along with whether the reference was explicit or implied. Among many general thinking and reasoning skills, the investigators identified six that were mentioned in a majority of the 12 subject areas:

1. Utilizes mental processes that are based on identifying similarities and differences (mentioned in all 12 areas)

2. Applies problem-solving and troubleshooting techniques (10 areas)

3. Understands and applies basic principles of argumentation (10 areas)

4. Applies decision-making techniques (nine areas)

5. Understands and applies basic principles of hypothesis testing and scientific inquiry (seven areas)

6. Understands and applies basic principles of logic and reasoning (six areas)

Marzano uses the data to investigate which of the six CT skills are most important in the various subject areas. For example, he reports that "similarities and differences" (skill 1) is dominant in the foreign languages, important in English language arts, and has a rather modest role in mathematics, whereas problem solving (skill 2) is strongly represented in mathematics and is not mentioned at all in English language arts or foreign languages (1998, 271).

Marzano stresses that all six skills are represented in half or more of the 12 areas studied. His chief finding is that, "The debate over the existence of a set of general thinking and reasoning processes that cut across multiple content areas has been settled if one accepts the recommendations made in the various standards documents and (this) analysis of those documents" (1998, 272). He believes that his research provides strong evidence for general CT skills across disciplines.

Disciplinary Differences in Faculty Goals for Teaching

Melissa Eljamal and her colleagues (Eljamal et al. 1998) analyze both interview data (69 faculty members at eight colleges) and survey data (2,105 faculty members at 267 colleges) to investigate how faculty goals for effective thinking differ across disciplines. Their term *effective thinking* is broad in that it includes classification, logical/deductive reasoning, problem solving, synthetic thinking, creative thinking, as well as critical/analytical thinking. The interviews and the survey address faculty goals for introductory college courses in the mid- and late 1980s.

The authors report that CT and analytical thinking goals are most frequently mentioned among the effective thinking goals in every discipline except mathematics, where statements using the phrase *problem solving* are often mentioned. Mathematicians use the phrase *critical thinking* only rarely; some might use it to describe the process of discovering a theorem, a task that beginners in mathematics find very difficult. As commonly understood by mathematics teachers in the schools and at the first-year college level, problem solving is not the same as critical thinking, and often problem solving uses little CT. Much mathematics teaching is aimed at teaching techniques and algebra skills, and students work many fairly routine problems to master these techniques and skills. In this setting, the critical thinking associated with assessing assumptions and hypotheses, critiquing the deductive process, and developing creative insights takes a backseat.

The investigation of the detailed responses by faculty reveals differences across the disciplines in the meanings of phrases such as *critical thinking*. For example, teachers of composition and literature use *critical thinking* to describe finding deeper meanings in essays and passages and also to describe the ability to judge a work critically and evaluate its quality. Faculty in literature and history often link critical thinking with the development of basic reading and writing skills. Humanities faculty tend to link synthesis with critical thinking and analytical thinking. Social scientists and statisticians use critical thinking as the ability to evaluate data and information to ensure its objectivity and to differentiate fact from fallacy. In contrast, faculty in the sciences and fine arts rarely mention the connection between basic skills and CT.

Faculty members also differ across disciplines in their perceptions of how to develop CT skills and of which other skills enhance their development (Eljamal et al. 1998, 143). But in general, faculty members strongly identify content knowledge as an integral part of the development of thinking skills (144). Eljamal and her colleagues interpret this finding as suggesting that effective thinking is domain specific.

Because the disciplines emphasize different aspects of effective thinking skills, Eljamel and her colleagues believe that one should include a broad range of general educational experiences in an undergraduate program (1998, 145). They also recognize benefits to faculty members in learning the varied views of their colleagues across the disciplines about how to promote effective thinking. For example, faculty workshops can help participants learn how other colleagues integrate thinking in their courses, and thus how to strengthen their own contributions to the students' entire educational program. The authors conclude that an understanding of the varied disciplinary approaches to instilling effective thinking may help faculty members improve their own approaches and thus lend greater coherence to the general education program (1998, 146).

Can Computers Aid Critical Thinking?

Teachers have long used computer programs to support student learning. Software can offer tutorials on factual material and drills in algebra skills. It can automate the creation of graphical displays and provide the results of complex mathematical or statistical calculations almost instantly. It can search millions of Web sites and provide convenient access to those identified by the search engine as relevant to a query. But most of these computer applications seem more relevant to surface learning than to critical thinking and deep learning because they often address information transfer more than interpretation and synthesis.

Cheryl Cohn (1999) uses a computer simulation program with teams of four students to aid them in developing their problem-solving skills and critical thinking skills in a macroeconomics course. She reports that the final term papers on the current state of the U.S. economy are better and have deeper insights for those students who worked cooperatively on the simulation projects than for her previous students. Over 90 percent of her students strongly agree that their CT skills have improved, and most believe that simulation was a key factor in their successes (54).

Marie Abate (1994) reports on her development of a software program that educates pharmacology students to evaluate and interpret published drug studies. Her students succeed in learning specialized skills for critically evaluating drug efficacy studies, with the computer tutorial as their only teacher.

A Controlled Experiment in Information Science

Clive Cochrane had been using conventional seminars in his second-year undergraduate Information Society module for discussing controversial issues in information science. Faced with increasing enrollments, Cochrane and his colleagues adopted a computer-mediated conferencing system that supports focused dialogue by the students using a simple graphical interface (Newman et al. 1997). Their project evaluates learning technologies in a group learning setting as a way to promote deep learning and critical thinking.

The investigators report on a controlled experiment at Queen's University Belfast that compares the efficacy of face-to-face seminars with group seminars that rely on the computer conferencing system. For each of three seminar groups, one half of the seminars met face-to-face, and the other half used the conferencing system. Thus, each seminar group served as its own control, but the groups differed as to which seminars were face to face and which relied on conferencing.

The study used two instruments for evaluating and comparing the critical thinking that emerged from the two treatments. One instrument used student questionnaires designed to assess student development in each of five stages of CT: (1) problem identification, (2) problem definition, (3) problem exploration, (4) problem applicability, and (5) problem integration (Newman et al. 1997, 490). The other instrument used a systematic assessment of transcripts of face-to-face seminars and of the conferencing messages; this assessment led to quantitative and technical indicators of the depth of CT (Newman et al. 1997, 491).

Both analyses show evidence of similar amounts of critical thinking in face-to-face encounters and in computer conference discussions, but some subtle differences emerged. The second analysis (of CT content) shows a modest but statistically significant advantage for the computer conferencing. Each of the teaching treatments seems to give benefits for CT. Face-to-face seminars are better for creative problem exploration and idea generation, and computer conferencing supports more effectively the later CT stages of linking ideas, interpretation, and problem integration (Newman et al. 1997, 492–493).

Taking Stock

College teachers identify general skills of CT used in many disciplines and in real-world problems. Yet many teachers believe that CT skills are best taught in a particular subject-matter domain.

Empirical research may never resolve the debate between those who believe that many CT skills transcend content areas and those who believe these skills are domain specific. Marzano's (1998) findings establish that faculty members across disciplines use a common language when identifying important CT skills. But Marzano also reports that the relative emphasis on the different CT skills varies considerably among disciplines. Eljamal and her colleagues (1998) find evidence that, even when using the same language across disciplines, the precise meanings faculty members attach to the language can differ.

In a practical sense, general skills for critical thinking do exist. Examples of such skills include identifying assumptions used in an argument, detecting potential sources of bias in evidence presented, using rules of deductive reasoning correctly, synthesizing information from multiple sources, and designing empirical investigations to address new questions raised. Research based on the Reflective Judgment Model shows that the self-conscious monitoring of one's own use of these skills—for example, searching for potential biases—helps improve CT (Kronholm 1996). But domain-specific subject-matter knowledge, including accurate information and good data, is essential for CT in most complex problems. College teachers should see valuable truths in both positions and teach accordingly.

Computers can aid the development of critical thinking skills. Some computer software (e.g., software for simulation and graphical display) aids students in understanding relationships in complex systems. Other software (e.g., conferencing systems and data analysis programs) supports active student involvement in their learning, and this involvement in turn strengthens CT. With the rapid pace of technological change, empirical research needs to identify the kinds of computing environments that are most promising in their support of CT.

STRATEGIES FOR TEACHING CRITICAL THINKING

Teaching CT presents many challenges for college teachers, and one of the greatest is to help students learn to confront ill-structured problems. Martha Kronholm addresses this challenge by combining elements from the two views about teaching CT.

An Experiment in Teaching Reflective Judgment

Kronholm (1996) gives CT instruction within college science courses to improve students' reflective judgment skills. She carried out a controlled experiment on 80 students in a one-semester general studies course on environmental issues. The treatment section of the course helped students examine their own epistemic perspectives as they confronted controversial issues and ill-structured problems.

Kronholm uses an instructional model she had developed—the Reflective Judgment-Developmental Instructional Model—to aid students in moving up the seven levels of the RJM. Her formal training enables Kronholm to recognize the level at which each student is performing. She questions the students to provoke group discussion and help them raise their cognitive performance by one level at a time.

Kronholm randomly selected three groups of 26, 26, and 28 students at Southern Illinois University from a volunteer group of 334 students enrolled in either of two general science courses, GE 110 Earth Science or GE 221 Living in the Environment (1996, 213–214). Students in the treatment group ($n = 28$) had enrolled in GE 221, and students in the two control groups ($n = 26$ for each) came from both courses. The research uses a pre-test-post-test design, and all the students thus took the RJI twice. Kronholm conducted and taped all interviews, and two certified RJI raters analyzed and scored these verbal responses.

The average gain for the treatment group is about three tenths of one stage in the seven-stage model. This gain score on the RJI for the treatment group is approximately one standard deviation greater than for the two control groups. Kronholm reports, "For the first time in reflective judgment research, a purposefully structured one-semester intervention resulted in epistemic development" (1996, 217). Kronholm's incorporation of CT instruction in a general science course appears effective in helping students develop their reflective judgment skills for ill-posed problems. The evidence from this experiment suggests that students can successfully transfer these skills from the science course to the areas covered on the RJI.

Strategies for Developing Critical Thinking Skills

The research literature offers a variety of specific techniques and devices for aiding the growth of various CT skills. We illustrate these with a few examples, and we do not review the supporting empirical evidence. Among the strategies thought to be effective are demanding active student involvement in their learning (Tsui 1998, 1999); getting students to speak out loud about their thinking (Stice 1987); using student debate (Allen et al. 1999); and replacing short-answer tests with essay tests (Scouller 1998).

To these teaching tools, we add one that we have not seen in the recent literature on teaching CT at the college level: involve students in evaluation of their work.

The evaluation and grading of one's own work may be an effective, even ideal, way to lead students to think about their own thinking—that is, to be self-regulating in their thinking. Asking students to evaluate essays they have written, using a list selected from the CT skills in Table 1, seems both practical and instructive. It also forces them to be active participants in their learning.

One of the authors asks students in a first-year seminar to exchange drafts of short papers and to provide their critiques to the author. Although students are at first reluctant to criticize work by their friends, some help from the instructor and practice in offering suggestions in a positive way reduces their resistance. Once students accept the idea that the first draft is not the last, they appreciate a process that positively supports their own best efforts at improving the next draft.

Bill Nave investigates the role of critical assessment by elementary school students in grades three through five of their own and each other's writing assignments (2000, 31–32, 124–135). Teachers show the students how papers written by students the year before were graded in the statewide exams. Working with small groups of students, the teachers help students to evaluate their own work. Nave reports that in some schools in Maine this approach to teaching writing achieves marked success. By learning to evaluate their own writing and the writing of their peers, school children practice critical thinking, and they improve their writing. Similar practices deserve investigation at the college level for the enhancement of CT, and learning to evaluate the work of one's peers need not be reserved for writing assignments. Understanding what excellent work is can help a person produce it.

Strategies for Teaching Transfer to Other Domains

John McPeck believes that students should study CT by being immersed in the challenging problems of the various disciplines (1985, 296, 307). Effective thinking differs from one discipline to the next, and McPeck does not believe that CT skills can transfer across disciplines because he believes CT skills rely on the intellectual tools of the disciplines.

Diane Halpern believes that the transfer of CT skills to general settings is "the most important of the outcome measures" (Halpern 1993, 250). She reviews literature on transfer and concludes that students can learn CT in ways that promote its transfer to everyday problems (see Lehman and Nisbett 1990; Halpern 1993, 249–250; Halpern 1998, 449).

To investigate whether transfer takes place, Lehman and Nisbett (1990) called students at home several months after completing their course work and asked questions to assess their retention and application of CT skills—for example, understanding regression to the mean and recognizing the need for large sample sizes. The students demonstrated that they had learned these concepts and could use them in everyday problems.

Halpern (1998) believes that four factors are the key to successful transfer: (1) disposition that prepares students for "effortful" cognitive work, (2) instruction in skills of CT, (3) training in the structural aspects of problems, and (4) a metacognitive aspect that promotes monitoring progress toward a cognitive goal. In particular, Halpern shares the views of King, Kitchener, and their colleagues (King and Kitchener 1994; King, Wood, and Mines 1990; Kitchener and King 1981; Kitchener et al. 1989) that conscious attention to one's own thinking—self-regulation—is important for success in tackling complex problems.

Other experts, including Robert Ennis, also believe that students can learn to transfer CT skills (Ennis 1989, 1990). Robert Sternberg asserts that "the only way to insure the transfer of training from thinking-skills programs to everyday lives is to teach for that transfer" (1985, 280). One of the authors received similar advice in a course about teaching mathematics in 1937—long before the flurry of papers in the 1980s about whether CT skills are general and transferable. He believes that this advice served well his teaching of statistics courses over many decades.

Discussions of everyday policy issues, such as whether to require state inspections and emissions tests of automobiles or whether to have a death penalty, hold special interest for students. Students with experience in using CT skills in environmental science, for example, may not see how those skills relate to these practical problems or to others. Teachers can help their students learn to transfer CT by providing examples of such transfers, revealing the structures and other features that problems have in common, reflecting with students in a self-conscious way about the transfer process, and inviting them to practice in making transfers to new problems.

DISCUSSION AND RECOMMENDATIONS

Both sides of the debate about general CT skills versus subject-specific skills have something to offer college teachers. First, CT can and should be taught within subject areas, to enable students to use specific knowledge, understanding, and skills as they develop their CT abilities. Second, many CT skills and dispositions are general and transcend disciplinary boundaries.

College teachers should experiment with ways for encouraging students to reflect consciously about their own thinking in their courses. A science teacher can draw attention to those aspects of a line of inquiry that make deductions from theoretical assumptions; the teacher can contrast this process with a development grounded in empirical investigation that proceeds inductively. A sociology professor can end a complex development with a reflective discussion that begins, "Let's review the logic and knowledge sources that led to the conclusions we just reached." Intellectual controversy provides a special opportunity to compare and contrast the sources of evidence and the methods of analysis that support (or refute) opposing positions.

The lessons of empirical research reveal that a general course in CT, often given in the freshmen year of college, may lead to gains—albeit modest gains—for CT (McMillan 1987; Tsui 1998; Tomlinson-Keasey and Eisert 1978; Mentkowski and Doherty 1984; Facione 1990b). We know also that the largest gains for CT from the college experience come during the first year. Perhaps there is an effective limit to what general instruction in CT can accomplish. If we believe that CT is substantially context specific and depends on knowledge of subject matter, then further gains in the CT skills needed for addressing increasingly complex problems may benefit from teaching CT in subject area settings.

The problems and issues of our time are far more complex than the illustrative problems used in a general course in CT. For example, both public and private institutions are asked to address the question of whether to continue or terminate considerations of race in college admissions and the awarding of financial aid. Few people are free from opinions about this question, yet to examine it and its many facets using empirical evidence and critical thought is an imposing task.

This topic illustrates that a real-world issue could demand the attention of much of an entire college course. A freshman seminar in probability or an introductory statistics course is useful for examining this issue, but we also need other material and concepts. Higher-level courses in sociology, political science, and ethics can address the question in ways that would advance students' thinking about this complex social issue. Given its interdisciplinary nature, the question about racial considerations in admissions and financial aid is one that invites integration of material from each discipline mentioned. It is likely to sustain student interest, and its use as illustration may give students valuable experience in dealing publicly with a sensitive issue. It poses a considerable challenge for critical thinkers.

ACKNOWLEDGMENTS

We thank Barbara Hofer for providing useful references and Marie Emerson for her advice about legislation in California. Lincoln Moses gave valuable advice on an earlier draft. This work was funded by a grant from the Andrew W. Mellon Foundation to the American Academy of Arts and Sciences in support of its program, Initiatives for Children.

APPENDIX: SOURCE MATERIALS

We began a systematic investigation of college-level CT by searching electronic library databases, including ERIC (Educational Resources Information Center), PsychInfo, Social Science Citation Index, and the Harvard University Libraries Catalog.

From the lists the searches produced, and from the references in articles already identified, we selected books and articles addressing one or more of these areas: definitions of CT, assessing CT at the college level, methods or programs for enhancing CT skills, review articles, and empirical research about CT in college students. We gave special attention to reports that presented original empirical research findings about CT and about how to teach it.

We photocopied 140 articles or book chapters, and one of the authors read and abstracted approximately 122 of these using three-page forms that we designed for that purpose. The authors of this report each read and independently abstracted those articles thought to be most useful and important to our work.

REFERENCES

Abate, Marie A. (1994). *Development of a computer system to educate students to evaluate and interpret published drug studies.* (ERIC Report ED 416 823) Fund for the Improvement of Postsecondary Education (ED); Washington, DC.

Allen, Mike, Sandra Berkowitz, Steve Hunt, and Allen Louden. (1999). A meta-analysis of the impact of forensics and communication education on critical thinking. *Communication Education*: 48, 18–30.

Bangert-Drowns, Robert L., and Esther Bankert. (1990). *Meta-analysis of effects of explicit instruction for critical thinking.* (ERIC Report ED 328 614) Paper presented at the annual meeting of the American Educational Research Association (Boston, MA).

Cohn, Cheryl L. (1999). Cooperative learning in a macroeconomics course: A team simulation. *College Teaching* 47, 51–54.

Dressel, Paul L., and Lewis B. Mayhew. (1954) *General education: Explorations in evaluation.* Westport, CT: Greenwood.

Eljamal, Milissa H., Sally Sharp, Joan Stark, Gertrude L. Arnold, and Malcolm A. Lowther. (1998). Listening for disciplinary differences in faculty goals for effective thinking. *The Journal for General Education* 47, 115–148.

Emerson, John D., and Frederick Mosteller. (1998a). Interactive multimedia for college teaching. Part I: A ten-year review of reviews. In Robert M. Branch and Mary Ann Fitzgerald (eds.), *Educational Media and Technology Yearbook 1998.* Englewood, CO: Libraries Unlimited.

———. (1998b). Interactive multimedia for college teaching. Part II: Lessons from research in the sciences. In Robert M. Branch and Mary Ann Fitzgerald (eds.), *Educational Media and Technology Yearbook 1998.* Englewood, CO: Libraries Unlimited.

Ennis, Robert H. (1987). A taxonomy of critical thinking dispositions and abilities. In Joan B. Baron and Robert J. Sternberg (eds.), *Teaching thinking skills: Theory and practice.* New York: W. H. Freeman.

———. (1989). Critical thinking and subject specificity: Clarification and needed research. *Educational Researcher* 18 (3), 4–10.

———. (1990). The extent to which critical thinking is subject-specific: Further clarification. *Educational Researcher* 19 (4), 13–16.

———. (1992). Conflicting views on teaching critical reasoning. In Richard A. Talaska (ed.), *Critical reasoning in Contemporary culture.* Albany: State University of New York Press.

———. (1993). Critical thinking assessment. *Theory Into Practice* 32, 179–186.

Ennis, Robert H., and Jason Millman. (1971). *Cornell Critical Thinking Test Manual.* Urbana: Critical Thinking Project, University of Illinois.

———. (1985). *Cornell critical thinking test.* Pacific Grove, CA: Midwest Publications.

Ennis, Robert H., and Eric Weir. (1985). *The Ennis-Weir Critical thinking essay test.* Pacific Grove, CA: Midwest Publications.

Facione, Peter A. (1990a). *Critical thinking: A statement of expert consensus for purposes of educational assessment and instruction.* Research findings and recommendations. (ERIC Report ED 315 423) American Philosophical Association (Newark, DE).

———. (1990b). *The California critical thinking skills test—college level. Technical Report #1. Experimental validation and content validity.* (ERIC Report ED 327 549) American Philosophical Association (Newark, DE).

———. (1992/1998). *California critical thinking skills test, forms A and B.* Millbrae, CA: The California Academic Press.

Facione, Peter A., and Noreen C. Facione. (1992). *California critical thinking disposition inventory.* Millbrae, CA: The California Academic Press.

Facione, Peter A., Carol A. Sanchez, Norene C. Facione, and Joanne Gainen. (1995). The disposition toward critical thinking. *The Journal of General Education* 44, 1–25.

Glaser, Edward M. (1941). *An experiment in the development of critical thinking.* New York: Columbia University.

Hagedorn, Linda S. Ernest T. Pascarella, Marcia Edison, John Braxton, Amaury Nora, and Patrick Terenzini. (1999). Institutional context and the development of critical thinking: A research note. *The Review of Higher Education* 22, 265–285.

Halpern, Diane F. (1993). Assessing the effectiveness of critical-thinking instruction. *The Journal of General Education* 42, 238–254.

————. (1998). Teaching critical thinking for transfer across domains. *American Psychologist* 53, 449–455.

King, Patricia M., and Karen S. Kitchener. (1994). *Developing reflective judgment: Understanding and promoting intellectual growth and critical thinking in adolescents and adults.* San Francisco: Jossey-Bass.

King, Patricia M., Philip K. Wood, and Robert A. Mines. (1990). Critical thinking among college and graduate students. *The Review of Higher Education* 13, 167–186.

Kitchener, Karen S., and Patricia M. King. (1981). Reflective judgment: Concepts of justification and their relationship to age and education. *Journal of Applied Developmental Psychology* 2, 89–116.

Kitchener, Karen S., Patricia M. King, Phillip K. Wood, and Mark L. Davison. (1989). Consistency and sequentiality in development of reflective judgment: A six-year longitudinal study. *Journal of Applied Developmental Psychology,* 10, 73–95.

Kronholm, Martha M. (1996). The impact of developmental instruction on reflective judgment. *The Review of Higher Education* 19, 199–225.

Kuhn, Deanna (1999). A developmental model of critical thinking. *Educational Researcher* 28, 16–26.

Lehman, Darrin R., and Richard E. Nisbett. (1990). A longitudinal study of the effects of undergraduate training on reasoning. *Developmental Psychology* 26, 952–960.

Marzano, Robert J. (1998). What are the general skills of thinking and reasoning and how do you teach them? *The Clearing House* 71, 268–273.

McMillan, James H. (1987). Enhancing college students' critical thinking: A review of studies. *Research in Higher Education* 26, 3–19.

McPeck, John E. (1981). *Critical thinking and education.* New York: St. Martin's Press.

————. (1984). Stalking beasts, but swatting flies: The teaching of critical thinking. *Canadian Journal of Education* 9, 28–44.

————. (1985). Critical thinking and the "trivial pursuit" theory of knowledge. *Teaching Philosophy* 8, 295–308.

————. (1992). Teaching critical reasoning through the disciplines: Content versus process. In Richard A.Talaska (ed.), *Critical reasoning in contemporary culture.* Albany: State University of New York Press.

Mentkowski, Marcia, and Austin Doherty. (1984). Abilities that last a lifetime: Outcomes of the Alverno experiment. *AAHE Bulletin* 36, 5–14.

Mines, Robert A., Patricia M. King, Albert B. Hood, and Phillip K. Wood. (1990). Stages of intellectual development and associated critical thinking skills in college students. *Journal of College Student Development* 31, 538–547.

Nave, Bill (2000). *Among critical friends: A study of critical friends groups in three Maine schools.* Unpublished doctoral dissertation, Graduate School of Education of Harvard University, Cambridge, Massachusetts.

Newman, D. R., Chris Johnson, Brian Webb, and Clive Cochrane. (1997). Evaluating the quality of learning in computer supported co-operative learning. *Journal of the American Society for Information Science* 48, 484–495.

Norris, Stephen (1985, May). Synthesis of research on critical thinking. *Educational Leadership,* 40–45.

Norris, Stephen, and Robert Ennis. (1989). *Evaluating critical thinking.* Pacific Grove, CA: Critical Thinking Press and Software.

Pascarella, Ernest T. (1989). The development of critical thinking: Does college make a difference? *Journal of College Student Development* 30, 19–26.

Pascarella, Ernest T., Louise Bohr, Amaury Nora, and Patrick T. Terenzini. (1996). Is differential exposure to college linked to the development of critical thinking? *Research in Higher Education* 37, 159–174.

Pascarella, Ernest T., and Patrick T. Terenzini. (1991). *How college affects students*. San Francisco: Jossey-Bass.

Paul, Richard. (1987). Dialogical thinking: Critical thought essential to acquisition of rational knowledge and passions. In Joan B. Baron and Robert J. Sternberg (eds.), *Teaching thinking skills*. New York: W. H. Freeman.

Ruggiero, Vincent R. (1988). *Teaching thinking across the curriculum*. New York: Harper & Row.

Scouller, Karen (1998). The influence of assessment method on students' learning approaches: Multiple choice questions examination versus assignment essay. *Higher Education* 35, 453–472.

Sternberg, Robert J. (1985, December). Teaching critical thinking, Part 2: Possible solutions. *Phi Delta Kappan*, 277–281.

Stice, James E. (1987). Learning how to think: Being earnest is important, but it's not enough. In James E. Stice (ed.), *Developing critical thinking and problem-solving abilities*. San Francisco: Jossey-Bass.

Terenzini, Patrick T., Leonard Springer, Ernest T. Pascarella, and Amaury Nora. (1995). Influence affecting the development of students' critical thinking skills. *Research in Higher Education, 36*, 23–39.

Tomlinson-Keasey, Carol A., and Debra C. Eisert. (1978). Can doing promote thinking in the college classroom? *Journal of College Student Personnel* 19, 99–105.

Tsui, Lisa (1998). A review of research on critical thinking. Paper presented at the annual meeting of the Association for the Study of Higher Education, Miami, Florida.

———. (1999). Courses and instruction affecting critical thinking. *Research in Higher Education* 40, 185–200.

———. (2000). Effects of campus culture on students' critical thinking. *Review of Higher Education* 23, 421–441.

Watson-Glaser Critical Thinking Appraisal. (1980). San Antonio, TX: The Psychological Corporation.

ERIC Digests

The Field of Educational Technology
Update 2000. A Dozen Frequently Asked Questions

Donald P. Ely

Educational technology is a term widely used in the field of education (and other areas), but it is often used with different meanings. The word technology is used by some to mean hardware—the devices that deliver information and serve as tools to accomplish a task—but those working in the field use technology to refer to a systematic process of solving problems by scientific means. Hence, educational technology properly refers to a particular approach to achieving the ends of education. Instructional technology refers to the use of such technological processes specifically for teaching and learning.

Other terms, such as instructional development or educational media, which refer to particular parts of the field, are also used by some to refer to the field as a whole.

The purpose of this digest is to provide background information and sources that help one to understand the concept of educational technology. This digest should serve as a "pathfinder" to relevant and timely publications that view the field from a variety of perspectives.

1. WHAT IS EDUCATIONAL TECHNOLOGY?

The most recent definition of the field (which uses the term, instructional technology) has been published by the Association for Educational Communications and Technology (AECT): Instructional Technology is the theory and practice of design, development, utilization, management, and evaluation of processes and resources for learning.

The complete definition, with its rationale, is presented in the AECT publication:

- Seels, B. B., and Richey, R. C. (1994). Instructional technology: The definition and domains of the field. Washington, DC: Association for Educational Communications and Technology.

An overview of the field can be found in:

- Gagne, R. M. (Ed.). (1987). Instructional technology: Foundations. Hillsdale, NJ: Lawrence Erlbaum.

- Anglin, G. J. (Ed.). (1995). Instructional technology: Past, present, & future (2nd ed.). Englewood, CO: Libraries Unlimited.

2. WHAT ARE THE ROOTS OF EDUCATIONAL TECHNOLOGY?

The field is essentially a twentieth-century movement with the major developments occurring during and immediately after World War II. What began with an emphasis on audiovisual communications media gradually became focused on the systematic development of teaching and learning procedures which were based in behavioral psychology. Currently, major contributing fields are cognitive psychology, social psychology, psychometrics, perception psychology, and management. The basic history of the field was written by Saettler.

- Saettler, P. E. (1990). The evolution of American educational technology. Englewood, CO: Libraries Unlimited.

A briefer history may be found in:

- Reiser, R. (1987). Instructional technology: A history. In Robert M. Gagne (Ed.), Instructional technology: Foundations. (pp. 11–48). Hillsdale, NJ: Lawrence Erlbaum.

3. WHAT IS A GOOD SOURCE OF RESEARCH FINDINGS?

- Thompson, A., Simonson, M., and Hargrave, C. (1996). Educational technology: A review of the research. 2nd ed. Washington, DC: Association for Educational Communications and Technology.
- Jonassen, D. H. (Ed.). (1996). Handbook of research for educational communications and technology. New York: Macmillan Library Reference.

4. WHAT DO EDUCATIONAL TECHNOLOGISTS DO?

Most educational technologists carry out one or a few of the functions performed in the field. For example, some design instruction, some produce instructional materials, and others manage instructional computing services or learning resources collections. The competencies for instructional development specialists and material design and production specialists are published in:

- Richey, R., and Fields, D. (Eds.). (In press). Instructional design competencies: Essential and advanced professional standards. Syracuse, NY: ERIC Clearinghouse on Information & Technology

In the area of instructional design, the paper by M. Tessmer and J. Wedman, "The practice of instructional design: A survey of what designers do, don't do, an why they don't do it" is helpful. (See ERIC document Reproduction Service No. ED 404 712)

5. WHERE ARE EDUCATIONAL TECHNOLOGISTS EMPLOYED?

Until recently, most educational technologists were employed in schools and colleges as directors of resource centers and developers of curriculum materials. Many are still employed in such positions, but increasing numbers are being employed by training agencies in business, industry, government, the military, and the health professions. Colleges and universities employ individuals who are involved in instructional improvement programs that use a variety of technologies.

6. WHERE DO EDUCATIONAL TECHNOLOGISTS OBTAIN PROFESSIONAL EDUCATION?

Professional programs are offered mostly at the graduate level, although there are a few two-year postsecondary programs in junior and community colleges. Lists of programs are found in:

- Branch, R. M., and Minor, B. B. (Eds.). (1999). Graduate programs in instructional technology (pp. 154–196) In Robert M. Branch and Mary Ann Fitzgerald (Eds.). (1999). Educational media and technology yearbook. Englewood, CO: Libraries Unlimited.
- Johnson, J. K. (Ed.). (1995). Degree curricula in educational communications and technology: A descriptive directory (5th ed.). Washington, DC: Association for Educational Communications and Technology.

7. WHAT FIELDS OFFER GOOD PREPARATION FOR EDUCATIONAL TECHNOLOGY?

Many people enter the field following an undergraduate program in teacher education. More people come from the basic disciplines of the arts and sciences—English, sociology, communications, psychology, the physical sciences, and mathematics. Although there seldom are prerequisites for study in the field, persons who have good preparation in psychology and mathematics seem to have a head start. Formal course work and experience in human relations are helpful.

8. WHAT ARE THE MAJOR PROFESSIONAL ORGRANIZATIONS?

In the United States, most educational technologists would be a member of one or more of the following associations:

- American Educational Research Association (AERA) 1230 17th Street, NW, Washington, DC 20036-3078

- American Society for Training & Development (ASTD) 1640 King Street, Box 1443, Alexandria, VA 22313

- Association for Educational Communications & Technology (AECT) 1800 North Stonelake Drive, Bloomington, IN 47404, http://www.aect.org

- International Society for Performance Improvement (ISPI) 1300 L Street NW, Suite 1250, Washington, DC 20005

- International Society for Technology in Education (ISTE) 1787 Agate Street, Eugene, OR 97403-1923

- Society for Applied Learning Technology (SALT) 50 Culpeper Street, Warrenton, VA 20186

Major organizations in other parts of the world include:

- Association for Media & Technology in Education in Canada (AMTEC)
  3-1750 The Queensway, Suite 1318
  Etobicoke, Ontario M9C 5H5, Canada

- Association for Learning Technology (ALT)
  Headington Hill Hall
  Oxford OX3 0BP
  United Kingdom
  http://www.alt.ac.uk

9. WHAT PUBLICATIONS TO EDUCATIONAL TECHNOLOGISTS READ?

The most frequently read journals include:

- British Journal of Educational Technology, published by Blackwell Publishers Limited, 108 Cowley Road, Oxford OX4 1FH, United Kingdom

- Learning and Leading with Technology, published by ISTE, 1787 Agate Street, Eugene, OR 97403-1923.

- Innovations in Education and Training International, published by AETT, Kogan Page Ltd., 120 Pentonville Road, London N1 9JN, United Kingdom

- Educational Technology, published by Educational Technology Publications, 700 Palisade Avenue, Englewood Cliffs, NJ 07632

- Educational Technology Research and Development, published by AECT. 1800 North Stonelake Drive, Bloomington, IN 47404

- Journal of Research on Computing in Education, published by ISTE. 1787 Agate Street, Eugene, OR 97403-1923

- TechTrends, published by AECT. 1800 North Stonelake Drive, Bloomington, IN 47404

10. WHAT ARE THE COMPREHENSIVE REFERENCES FOR THE FIELD?

There is one major encyclopedia:

- Plomp, T., and Ely, D. P. (Eds.). (1996). The international encyclopedia of educational technology. 2nd ed. New York: Elsevier Science.

There is one major yearbook which offers articles on current issues and extensive lists of people, organizations, literature, and other resources:

- Branch, R. M., and Fitzgerald, M. A. (Eds.). (2000). Educational media and technology yearbook. Englewood, CO: Libraries Unlimited.

11. WHAT TEXTBOOKS ARE COMMONLY USED?

There are dozens of books used in educational technology courses. Selection of titles depends upon the content of the course, the primary audience, and the instructor's objectives. General textbooks that have been used in a variety of courses are:

- Heinich, R., Molenda, M., Russell, J., and Smaldino, S. (1999). Instructional media and technologies for learning (6th ed.). New York: Macmillan.

- Dick, W., and Carey, L. (1996). The systematic design of instruction (4th ed.). Harper Collins College. Glenview, IL: Scott, Foresman.

12. WHERE CAN MORE SPECIFIC INFORMATION ABOUT EDUCATIONAL TECHNOLOGY BE FOUND?

The ERIC (Educational Resources Information Center) system sponsored by the U.S. Department of Education has been selecting documents on educational technology since 1966 and indexing articles from key journals since 1969. Abstracts of the documents can be found in:

- Resources in Education, published monthly by the U.S. Government Printing Office and available in more than 3,500 libraries throughout the world.

Selected articles which have been indexed from educational technology journals are listed in:

- Current Index to Journals in Education, found in many libraries or available from Oryx Press, 4041 North Central at Indian School Road, Suite 700, Phoenix, AZ 85012-3397. (800-279-6799)

ERIC Database. Computer searching of the ERIC database is available in many academic and some public libraries. The ERIC database can also be searched over the Internet and on some commercial networks. Specific questions can be addressed to:

- ERIC Clearinghouse on Information & Technology (ERIC/IT)
  621 Skytop Road, Suite 160
  Syracuse University, Syracuse, NY 13244-5290
  (315) 443-3640; (800) 464-9107
  http://ericir.syr.edu/ithome
  e-mail: eric@ericir.syr.edu

There are World Wide Web sites that focus on discussion of issues in educational technology. The addresses are:

http://www.aect.org/

http://h-net.msu.edu/~edweb

http://www.askeric.org

The ERIC/IT Clearinghouse has a publications list of monographs and digests about current issues and developments in the field and publishes a newsletter, ERIC/IT Update, twice each year. Both items are available without charge.

Laptop Computers in the K–12 Classroom

Yvonne Belanger

INTRODUCTION

Over the past decade, many schools have investigated the educational possibilities of mobile computing. More recently, an increasing number of K–12 schools are implementing the use of laptop computers. Improvements in portable computing technology and examples of successful pilot programs using laptops and other portables have inspired many K–12 schools to consider laptops for their students.

EMERGENCE OF LAPTOPS IN SCHOOLS

Organized laptop programs in higher education date as far back as 1988 when Drew University in Madison, New Jersey, began providing notebook computers (paid for from tuition) to all incoming freshmen. Now more than 50 post-secondary institutions worldwide require at least some of their students to use laptops (Brown 1999). Throughout the 1990s, a number of private schools in the United States and abroad began requiring ownership of laptops. In 1996, inspired by the successful use of laptops in Australian schools, the Microsoft Corporation and Toshiba began one of the most high-profile programs now underway, currently known as Microsoft's Anytime Anywhere Learning (AAL) Program (Healey 1999). Technology corporations, such as NetSchools (http://www.studypro.com/), NoteSys Inc. (http://www.notesys.com/), Apple (http://www.apple.com/education/), and others are promoting the use of laptops in K–12 education, providing hardware packages for schools, and in some cases, software and technical support as well.

TRANSITION TO LAPTOPS

How are schools integrating laptops into their technology infrastructure? Microsoft commissioned an ongoing study of Anytime Anywhere Learning, published as the Rockman Report. In their study, Rockman et al. (1998) identified five models of laptop use currently in place at the K–12 level:

- Concentrated—each student has his or her own laptop for use at home or in school
- Class set—a school-purchased classroom set is shared among teachers
- Dispersed—in any given classroom, there are students with and without laptops
- Desktop—each classroom is permanently assigned a few laptops for students to share
- Mixed—some combination of the above models

Each model has potential advantages, either in terms of instructional benefits, ease of implementation, or savings. In the concentrated model, teachers are free to integrate technology fully into instruction as well as assignments, since all students have access to a computer for homework, study, and projects. In the class set and dispersed models, teachers are free to integrate laptops during the school day; however, there may still be students within the same class who lack access to a computer in the home, so integration options are more limited. In the desktop model, although the computers are owned and maintained by the school, a student working on a computer-based project during the school day might be allowed to take the laptop home to complete their work. Also, teachers are better able to reconfigure their classroom setup to suit their technology integration needs. Laptops can also take the place of desktops in a traditional lab setting. For example, the Cuba-Rushford School District in Allegheny County, New York, created a 70-computer laptop lab. These computers are available for checkout to their middle and high school students. For many schools, the primary advantage of laptops over desktops is in creating opportunities for all students to have access to a computer both during and outside of the school day.

PORTABLE ALTERNATIVES

Traditional laptops are not the only portable computers appearing in elementary and secondary institutions. Some schools uncomfortable with the high cost of laptops have explored the advantages of lower-priced portables designed for K–12 students. The AlphaSmart and DreamWriter, for example, make it possible to provide each student with a rechargeable portable that can be used for word processing or keyboarding instruction at a fraction of the cost of a traditional laptop. Some mini-portables do more than word processing. Casio's Cassiopeia Computer Extender, for example, includes the graphing program Maple as well as Geometer's Sketchpad, a dynamic geometry program. This mini-portable can therefore be used in math and science instruction at the high school level. In addition to scaled-down portables, manufacturers are also designing full-scale laptops with younger students in mind. The StudyPro, for example, is a durable infrared wireless laptop with few moving parts marketed specifically for K–12 use. Also, Apple's AirPort wireless network hub is another wireless technology designed to meet the needs of laptop schools. With wireless networks, schools can allow multiple users to share a single network connection, as well as avoid some of the hassle and expense of physical cabling.

CLASSROOM EXPERIENCES

Educators who work with laptops have begun to explore their unique advantages. The 1999 Laptop Learning Challenge sponsored by Toshiba and the National Science Teacher's Association (http://www.nsta.org/programs/laptop/index.htm) recently recognized innovative uses of laptops in K–12 mathematics and science education. Some award-winning ideas showed students using laptops to facilitate group work, to analyze data immediately during a lab exercise, or to conduct scientific investigations in the field rather than in the classroom. Evaluators of the Copernicus Project, a multi-district laptop pilot program in Seattle, Washington, found laptops to be especially suited for writing activities, student projects, and presentations (Fouts and Stuen 1997). Other uses for laptops include creating spreadsheets to solve math homework problems; creating book reports that inspire student creativity with presentation software such as PowerPoint or HyperStudio; or having students routinely hand in assignments via floppy disk or connect to the school network and save their work to a central file server for the teacher to review, add comments, and leave for the student to retrieve.

DOES RESEARCH SUPPORT THE USE OF LAPTOPS?

Several studies suggest educational benefits related to laptop use. Specific benefits noted include increased student motivation (Gardner 1994, Rockman et al. 1998), a shift toward more student-centered classroom environments (Stevenson 1998; Rockman et al. 1998), and better school attendance than students not using laptops (Stevenson 1998). In his study of a laptop pilot program in Beaufort, South Carolina, Stevenson (1998) also reported that students with laptops demonstrated a "sustained level of academic achievement" during their middle school years, as opposed to students not using laptops who tended to decline during this same period. He also noted that these academic benefits were most significant in at-risk student populations.

In their study of laptop use in middle school science classrooms, Fisher and Stolarchuk (1998) found that those laptop classrooms in which skills and the process of inquiry were emphasized had the most positive impact on student learning and attitudes. According to Rockman, a majority of teachers in laptop schools reported an increase in both cooperative learning and project-based instruction. Other research has not supported the educational benefits of laptop use.

Gardner et al. (1993) found that the impact of laptops after one year was "at best marginal" on achievement in mathematics, science, and writing. Also, Fisher and Stolarchuk (1998) reported a more positive relationship between laptops and student attitudes than between laptops and academic achievement. Research into the educational use of laptops has only begun; relatively few K–12 schools have had laptops in place long enough to generate longitudinal studies of their impact on student achievement. It remains to be seen what additional research will reveal about the long-term impact of laptops on student achievement and outcomes.

EQUITY CONTROVERSY

With growing concern over equity in access to technology, laptop programs have become increasingly attractive. Whether through leasing programs, purchasing refurbished hardware, or obtaining technology grants, many schools hope to reduce their student-to-computer ratio by considering some form of laptop program. Critics point out the possibilities of theft, vandalism, and accidental damage. Newer "student-friendly" laptop models address some of these issues; not only are they more durable, but some have included theft-deterrent technology as well.

However, despite the creative educational possibilities of laptops and promise of equitable access for all students, added costs in the form of hardware, network costs, technical support considerations, and faculty training remain the greatest obstacles. The presence of laptops in a school does not necessarily imply student ownership; however, some schools are advocating or requiring student purchase or rental. Partnerships between schools, nonprofit organizations, and corporations can defray costs, but ultimately parents share the expense with schools that hope to put a laptop in the hands of every child (Wishengrad 1999). For this reason, there is concern among some that laptop programs may worsen technology inequities among students for families who are unable to assume these costs (Jameson 1999). The controversy over laptops is not limited to issues of equity and cost, however; the Texas Board of Education recently made headlines by suggesting the state replace all textbooks with CD-ROMS and fund a laptop leasing program for all 3.9 million students with the estimated $1.8 billion in savings over six years (Mendels 1998). Despite these issues, many educators hoping to bring the benefits of educational technology to more students continue to look for creative ways to overcome these obstacles.

SUMMARY

The future of mobile computing in K–12 education is still uncertain. Laptops may never become as common in classrooms as hand-held calculators. Solutions for issues of cost, technical support needs, security, and equitable access are challenging for many schools. Many schools with laptops, however, remain positive and enthusiastic about the changes observed and benefits their students derive from access to portable computers. Although many laptop programs are young and studies are still in progress, research has shown educational benefits from the use of laptops, particularly with respect to increasing student motivation and creating more student-centered classrooms. Continuing improvements in student portable computing technology as well as models of successful programs may make laptops an increasingly attractive option for K–12 educators and technology planners.

BIBLIOGRAPHY AND FURTHER READING

Baldwin, F. (1999). Taking the classroom home. Appalachia, 32(1), 10–15. (EJ 586 599)

Brown, R. (1999). Notebook colleges and universities. [Online]. Available: http://www.acck.edu /~arayb/NoteBookList.html

Buchanan, L. (1998). Three portable options: AlphaSmart, DreamWriter, Apple eMate. Multimedia Schools, 5(1), 36–38, 40, 42–43. (EJ 558 547)

Fisher, D., and Stolarchuk, E. (1998). The effect of using laptop computers on achievement, attitude to science and classroom environment in science. Proceedings Western Australian Institute for Educational Research Forum 1998. [Online]. Available: http://cleo.murdoch.edu.au/waier /forums/1998/fisher.html

Fouts, J. T., and Stuen, C. (1997). Copernicus project: Learning with laptops: Year 1 Evaluation Report. (ED 416 847)

Gardner, J. (1994). Personal portable computers and the curriculum. Edinburgh, Scotland: Scottish Council for Research in Education. (ED 369 388)

Gardner, J., et al. (1993). The impact of high access to computers on learning. Journal of Computer Assisted Learning, 9(1), 2–16.

Gold, R. A. (1999). Leadership, learning, and laptops: How one district brought everyone on board. Multimedia Schools, 6(4), 32–36.

Gottfried, J., & McFeely, M.G. (1997–1998, Dec-Jan). Learning all over the place: Integrating laptop computers into the classroom. Learning and Leading with Technology, 25(4), 6–12. (EJ 557 248)

Hardy, L. (1999). Lap of luxury: School laptop programs raise issues of equity. The American School Board Journal, 186(3), A33–A35.

Healey, T. (1999). Notebook programs pave the way to student-centered learning. T.H.E. Journal, 26(9), 14.

Jameson, R. (1999). Equity and access to educational technology. Thrust for Educational Leadership, 28(4), 28–31.

Jenny, F. J. (1998) The information technology initiative at Grove City college: Four Years Later. Proceedings of the Association of Small Computer Users in Education Summer Conference. (ED 425 718)

The Laptop College. (1999, Spring). Learning technologies report [Online]. Available: http://thenode.org/ltreport/issues.cfm

Mendels, P. (1998, May 20). Texas weighs the value of laptops vs. textbooks. The New York Times.

O'Donovan, E. (1999). Mobile Computing Grows Up. Technology & Learning, 19(8), 53–56.

Rockman, et al. (1998). Powerful tools for schooling: Second year study of the laptop program. Rockman, et al: San Francisco, CA. [Online]. Available: http://www.rockman.com/projects /laptop/ (Accessed November 27, 2001).

Stevenson, K. R. (1998). Evaluation report-Year 2: Schoolbook laptop project. Beaufort County School District: Beaufort, S.C. [Online]. Available: http://www.beaufort.k12.sc.us/district /ltopeval.html

———. (1999, April). Learning by laptop. School Administrator, 56(4), 18–21.

Stoll, M. (1998, June 9). Lessons on laptops. Christian Science Monitor.

Wishengrad, R. (1999). Are paper textbooks ready to fold? The Education Digest, 64(6), 57–61.

A Survey of Educational Change Models

James B. Ellsworth

(This Digest is based on *Surviving Change: A Survey of Educational Change Models* by James B. Ellsworth 2000.)

Change isn't new, and neither is its study. We have a rich set of frameworks, solidly grounded in empirical studies and practical applications. Most contributions may be classified under a set of major perspectives, or "models" of change. These perspectives are prevalent in the research, and combine to yield a 360 degree view of the change process. In each case, one author or group of authors is selected as the epitome of that perspective. A small group of studies from disciplines outside educational change (in some cases outside education) also contribute to key concepts not found elsewhere in the literature.

Everett Rogers, one of the "elder statesmen" of change research, notes that change is a specialized instance of the general communication model (Rogers 1995, 5–6). Ellsworth (2000) expands on this notion to create a framework that organizes these perspectives to make the literature more accessible to the practitioner.

The change framework might be summarized as follows: a change agent wishes to communicate an innovation to an intended adopter. This is accomplished using a change process, which establishes a channel through the change environment. However, this environment also contains resistance that can disrupt the change process or distort how the innovation appears to the intended adopter. By uniting these tactics in a systemic strategy, we improve our chances of effective, lasting change.

PUTTING IT ALL TOGETHER

Change efforts should employ a systemic understanding of the context in which we undertake them. Nevertheless, depending on the circumstance, or as the implementation effort progresses, it may be most effective to focus interventions on a particular component of the framework at a time.

Anyone trying to improve schools (teachers, principals, students, district administrators, consultants, parents, community leaders, or government representatives) may look to The New Meaning of Educational Change (Fullan and Stiegelbauer 1991) to decide where to start (or to stop an inappropriate change).

From there, Systemic Change in Education (Reigeluth and Garfinkle 1994), considers the system being changed, and assumptions about the nature of that system (its purpose, members, how it works, its governing constraints and so forth). Question those assumptions to see whether they still hold true. Look inside the system to understand its subsystems or stakeholders and how they relate to one another and to the system as a whole. Look outside the system too, to know how other systems (like business or higher education) are interrelated with it, and how it (and these other systems) in turn relates to the larger systems of community, nation, or human society. The new understanding may illuminate current goals for the proposed innovation, (or concerns for the change you are resisting) and may indicate some specific emerging issues.

This understanding is crucial for diagnosing the system's needs, and how an innovation serves or impedes them. The Change Agent's Guide (Havelock and Zlotolow 1995) helps to guide and plan future efforts. The Guide serves as a checklist to ensure that the right resources are acquired at the proper time. The Guide also helps to conduct and assess a trial of the innovation in a way that is relevant and understandable to stakeholders. It extends implementation both in and around the system and helps to prepare others within the system to recognize when it is time to change again.

At some point one must commit to a plan, and act. The Concerns-Based Adoption Model [CBAM] (Hall and Hord 1987) provides tools to "keep a finger on the pulse" of change and to collect the information needed. This model's guidelines help readers to understand the different concerns stakeholders experience as change progresses. This will help readers to design and enact interventions when they will be most effective.

Even the most effective change effort usually encounters some resistance. Strategies for Planned Change (Zaltman and Duncan 1977) can help narrow down the cause(s) of resistance. Perhaps some stakeholders see the innovation as eroding their status. Possibly others would like to adopt the innovation, but lack the knowledge or skills to do so. Opposition may come from entrenched values and beliefs, or from lack of confidence that the system is capable of successful change.

One way to approach such obstacles is to modify or adapt the innovation's attributes. Even if the actual innovation cannot be altered, it may be possible to change the perceptions of the innovation among stakeholders. For example, instead of competing with them, perhaps it is more appropriately seen as a tool that will help others achieve appropriate goals. Whether one modifies the attributes or merely their perceptions, Diffusion of Innovations (Rogers 1995) identifies the ones that are generally most influential, and will help readers select an approach.

Other obstacles may arise from the environment in which change is implemented. The "Conditions for Change" (Ely 1990) can help you address those deficiencies. Possibly a clearer statement of commitment by top leaders (or more evident leadership by example) is needed. Or maybe more opportunity for professional development is required, to help the stakeholders learn how to use their new tool(s).

Change models are frequently interrelated. For example, when modifying innovation attributes pursuant to Rogers (1995), one might make a component checklist (see Hall and Hord 1987) to avoid accidental elimination of a critical part of the innovation. When assessing the presence or absence of the conditions for change (Ely 1990), verify that the systemic conditions mentioned in Reigeluth and Garfinkle (1994) are present as well. While using the Concerns-Based Adoption Model (Hall and Hord 1987) to design interventions aimed at stakeholders at a particular level of use or stage of concern, consider the psychological barriers to change presented by Zaltman and Duncan (1977).

READING OUT, REACHING ACROSS

Much useful knowledge of the change process comes from other fields as well—particularly the business-inspired domains of Human Performance Technology (HPT) and Human Resource Development (HRD). Include these other knowledge bases as an involvement with educational change grows.

Reach out to other disciplines to share experiences and to benefit from theirs. Reach across to other stakeholders, to build the sense of community and shared purpose necessary for the changes that must lie ahead. The road won't always be easy and everyone won't always agree which path to take when the road forks but with mutual respect, honest work, and the understanding that we all have to live with the results, we can get where we need to go.

SUCEEDING SYSTEMATICALLY

The lessons of the classical change models are as valid today—and just as essential for the change agent to master—as they have ever been. Yet a single innovation (like a new technology or teaching philosophy) that is foreign to the rest of the system may be rejected, like an incompatible organ transplant is rejected by a living system. Success depends on a coordinated "bundle" of innovations—generally affecting several groups of stake-holders—that results in a coherent system after implementation.

These are exciting times to be a part of education. They are not without conflict, but conflict is what we make of it. Its Chinese ideogram contains two characters: one is "danger" and the other "hidden opportunity." We choose which aspect of conflict—and of change—we emphasize.

RESOURCES

Craig, R. (1996). *The ASTD training and development handbook: A guide to human resource development*. New York: McGraw-Hill.

Ellsworth, J. B. (2000). *Surviving change: A survey of educational change models*. Syracuse, NY: ERIC Clearinghouse on Information and Technology. (ED number pending, IR020063)

Ely, D. (1990). *Conditions that facilitate the implementation of educational technology innovations. Journal of Research on Computing in Education*, 23(2), 298–305. (EJ 421 756)

Fullan, M., and Stiegelbauer, S. (1991). *The new meaning of educational change*. New York: Teachers College Press. (ED 354 588)

Hall, G., and Hord, S. (1987). *Change in schools: Facilitating the process*. Albany, NY: State University of New York Press. (ED 332 261)

Havelock, R., and Zlotolow, S. (1995). *The change agent's guide*, (2nd ed.). Englewood Cliffs, NJ: Educational Technology Publications. (ED 381 886)

Reigeluth, C., and Garfinkle, R. (1994). *Systemic change in education*. Englewood Cliffs, NJ: Educational Technology Publications. (ED 367 055)

Rogers, E.M. (1995). *Diffusion of innovations*, (4th ed.). New York: The Free Press.

Stolovitch, H., and Keeps, E. (1999). *Handbook of human performance technology: A comprehensive guide for analyzing and solving performance problems in organizations*. San Francisco, CA: Jossey-Bass/Pfeiffer.

Zaltman, G., and Duncan, R. (1977). *Strategies for planned change*. New York: John Wiley and Sons.

The Roles and Responsibilities of Library and Information Professionals in the Twenty-first Century

Carrie A. Lowe

Librarians are the original information specialists in society, and library media specialists fill that position in K–12 schools. This is underscored in the AASL/AECT monograph Information Power: "The mission of the library media program is to ensure that students and staff are effective users of ideas and information." (ALA 1988, 1; AASLA 1998, 6)

In this Digest, we will explore the expanding role of and endless opportunities for the library media specialist in an increasingly complex and technologically challenging world.

TECHNOLOGY AND OPPORTUNITY

Technology is primarily a tool; a tool that extends our abilities. What kinds of technology tools will be available to schools in 20 years? Some trends appear clear—we will have more connectivity and technology that is more customized to individuals. Technology will be integrated seamlessly—processing tools will be connected to communications tools will be connected to information tools—with common access mechanisms and interfaces. Clearly, future technology will present a special challenge and opportunity for education.

Library media specialists are part of the solution. As noted, librarians are the original information specialists. We call this "the information perspective," and it means that library media specialists look at curriculum, assignments, and learning in terms of the information resources, processes, and technologies required for student success. From early on, library media professionals have tried to teach students that when they have an assignment to complete, they should consider the information resources they need and then use the appropriate access technology to find that resource and information.

Library media specialists have been pioneers in the area of teaching information skills and integrating technology skills into the information problem-solving process. One of the most popular approaches to integrated information and technology skills is the Big6™ approach, developed by Mike Eisenberg and Bob Berkowitz (1988). The Big6 and other models of the information process (such as those by Kuhlthau 1993; Stripling and Pitts 1988; and Pappas and Tepe 1995) define the path that students take to solve information problems. When the focus is on the intellectual endeavor—the problem-solving aspects of learning—technology assumes its rightful place as a tool; a means that is used to get to where we want to be, rather than the answer itself.

CHALLENGES FOR LIBRARY MEDIA SPECIALISTS

Gary Hartzell, professor of education at the University of Nebraska, refers to library media specialists as "invisible" professionals (1997). He argues that in many school districts, library media specialists are routinely excluded from decisions affecting technology, curriculum, and resources at the school and district level. He also points to the widespread trend of cutting library budgets and, in some cases, library media positions to ease school financial problems.

According to Hartzell, teachers and administrators are not aware of the valuable contributions that library media specialists can make to the school. Hartzell points out that no course in any major school of education in this country focuses on the use of library and information in learning and teaching; in almost all teacher training programs, there is little mention of the roles of the library media program and the library and information professional at all. The library media specialists compound this problem by failing to promote themselves to fellow educators and school administration in communicating the nature and role of library and information work to others.

Library media specialists must do a better job of clearly and loudly articulating their roles in preparing students for the information- and technology-rich workplace of the future. It is essential that library media specialists commit themselves to the ideas central to the profession that defines their roles as information specialists and educators helping students to achieve information literacy.

GUIDING PRINCIPLES

The core set of beliefs and practices guiding library and information professionals provide the conceptual understandings needed for the future.

Principle One: School libraries don't have walls.

This idea draws from the belief that "library" is not a place; rather, library is everywhere. Within the school, this means that library media specialists must not be cloistered within the walls of the library and within the constraints of scheduled library time. Beyond the school, students will need to make the skills typically associated with "library" a part of their everyday lives. One such skill is information problem-solving.

Principle Two: Library and information professionals must be flexible.

In the opening chapter of *Information Power: Building Partnerships for Learning*, the authors describe the vision of the library media specialist in the information-rich society of the future. In their view, library media specialists of the future will need to wear a wide variety of professional hats. These responsibilities can be broken into four broad categories—teacher, instructional partner, information specialist, and program administrator (AASLA 1998).

Principle Three: Ensure that students are effective users of ideas and information.

This principle describes the central vision of Information Power. This is also one of the central tenants of the library profession. Additionally, it highlights the most important and enduring role that the library media specialist plays within the school—that of the provider of information services and skills instruction. It is important that all members of the school community understand that the library media specialist is uniquely qualified and valuable within the school to provide essential information literacy instruction and valuable information services.

Principle Four: Information is everywhere, essential, central.

This principle relates directly to the first principle. Just as school libraries do not have walls, information resources are everywhere, both inside and outside the library. This idea indicates the need for students to master the information literacy skills they need in everyday life. The idea that information is everywhere is the basis of the idea of information literacy (Spitzer, Eisenberg and Lowe 1998).

INFORMATION POWER: LESSONS AND LEGACY

In 1988, the American Association of School Librarians published its standards monograph *Information Power*. This publication, along with its extremely significant follow-up published in 1998, provide a road map to guide educators into the next century. This publication underscores the importance of the role of the library media specialist in producing well-rounded, information literate students.

Information Power does more than offer an inspiring vision of the future of library media specialists in the school. The authors of *Information Power* provide standards for information literacy learning, as well as indicators for each standard. These standards create goals for all educators.

CHANGE AND THE LIBRARY MEDIA SPECIALIST

The changing role of technology in education will increase opportunity for information literacy educators. As technology becomes more prevalent in learning and teaching, there is even greater need for information, library, and technology work in schools. This is a role that librarians can and must assume to create information-literate students.

The word "disintermediation" is batted around quite a bit in reference to future technologies. Disintermediation is the idea that as technology becomes more advanced, users will no longer require assistance to use it (Gillian 1996). The development of the WWW has told a very different story. We have seen a staggering rise in the use of question-and-answer services (such as AskERIC) in the past five years. As the Web becomes larger and more tangled, users need help finding what they want. This is where information and technology specialists step in.

THE INFORMATION AND TECHNOLOGY TEAM

Of course, the roles and responsibilities that members of the school faculty currently assume will change in the future. It will become increasingly important that faculty members and administrators collaborate to ensure the successful integration of technology. One way this can occur is through the formation of an information and technology team, composed of technology teachers, library and information professionals, and key administrators. These team members bring together the political muscle, technical savvy, and information literacy expertise to ensure that all students get the information literacy instruction they need.

The work of the information and technology team goes beyond creating technology-rich learning environments for students, although this is one of their most important tasks. Great teams have a close relationship with classroom teachers and administration, and their responsibilities affect every aspect of the school. They provide a technical support system by coordinating tech services and resources and coordinating purchasing decisions. In terms of curriculum, the team oversees the information and technology literacy program and ensures it is implemented as part of the classroom curriculum. An active, dynamic information and technology team is an integral part of the school; it is the right arm of overburdened administrators and teachers.

WHERE DO WE GO FROM HERE?

We have outlined some of the important thinking on the role of information technology in the school of the future, and more importantly, the leadership role that educators must assume to ensure students receive the education they need. But how can we begin to make this vision a reality? There are a few steps that each one of us can take now to create the promising future that we envision for ourselves.

- The first step is to learn and absorb. All library media specialists should read and learn about information literacy and pass that knowledge on to their colleagues.

- Library media specialists need to become actively involved in the information and technology program. Other teachers, administrators, and parents need to become aware of the importance of library media efforts in helping students learn essential skills.

- Assume an active role in decision-making and planning. Become involved with your school's technology committee, and come to meetings with your own vision of what the school's technology policy should be. Take advantage of leadership opportunities.

These efforts are not optional. As educators, it is our responsibility to prepare our students with the skills and understanding they will need to live in such a world. Clearly, this will require high-quality library and information technology programs meeting students' needs in physical schools or in whatever electronic, networked, virtual learning environment they might find themselves.

SOURCES

American Association of School Librarians and Association for Educational Communications and Technology (1988). *Information power*. Chicago: American Association of School Librarians.

American Association of School Librarians and Association for Educational Communications and Technology (1998). *Information power: Building partnerships for learning*. Chicago: American Association of School Librarians.

American Library Association Presidential Committee on Information Literacy. (1989). *Final Report*. Chicago: Author. (ED 316 074)

Caffarella, E. (1998). The new information literacy standards for student learning: Where do they fit with other content standards? (ED 421 076).

Eisenberg, M. B., and Berkowitz, R. E. (1988). *Curriculum initiative: An agenda and strategy for library media programs*. Greenwich, CT: Ablex.

Gillian, A. (1996). Disintermediation: A disaster or a discipline? In: Online Information 96. Proceedings of the International Online Information Meeting (20th, Olympia 2, London, England, United Kingdom, December 3–5, 1996). (ED 411 809)

Hartzell, G. (1997). The invisible school librarian: Why other educators are blind to your value. *School Library Journal*, 43(11), 24–29.

Haycock, K. (Ed.). (1998). *Foundations for effective school library media programs*. Englewood, CO: Libraries Unlimited. (ED 428 776)

Kuhlthau, C. (1993). *Seeking meaning: A process approach to library and information services*. Greenwich, CT: Ablex.

Lighthall, L., Ed.; Haycock, K., Ed. (1997). Information Rich but Knowledge Poor? Emerging Issues for Schools and Libraries Worldwide. Research and Professional Papers Presented at the Annual Conference of the International Association of School Librarianship Held in Conjunction with the Association for Teacher-Librarianship in Canada (26th, Vancouver, British Columbia, Canada, July 6–11, 1997). (ED 412 942)

Pappas, M., and Tepe, A. (1995). Preparing the information educator for the future. *School Library Media Annual (SLMA)*, 13, 37–44.

Spitzer, K. (1999). Information literacy: Facing the challenge. *Book Report* 18(1), 28–28. (EJ 589 883)

Spitzer, K., Eisenberg, M. B., and Lowe, C. A. (1998). *Information literacy: Essential skills for the information age*. Syracuse, NY: ERIC Clearinghouse on Information & Technology.

Stripling, B., and Pitts, J. (1988). *Brainstorms and blueprints: Teaching library research as a thinking process*. Littleton, CO: Libraries Unlimited.

Teachers and Librarians
Collaborative Relationships

Shayne Russell

INTRODUCTION

Since the early 1980s, library literature has examined progress toward establishing successful collaborative relationships between classroom teachers and library media specialists. In 1989, Berkowitz and Eisenberg acknowledged the gap between the library media specialist's potential as a curriculum consultant in theory and in practice, noting that library media specialists' interest in being involved in curriculum dates back to the 1950s. Assignments developed in partnership between teachers and library media specialists are known to be more "authentic"—exhibiting a higher degree of meaning and significance (Gross and Kientz 1999). When not guided in the use of a process, students tend to approach research as though there is only one right answer, and fail to learn how to use information to construct their own meaning (Kuhlthau 1995). This ability to construct meaning is at the heart of information literacy, which collectively describes the skills students will need to cope in a complex world with access to an ever-increasing wealth of information.

The results of a study by the Library Service Center of the Colorado State Library offer the most recent support for library media specialists and teachers working collaboratively. The study concludes that test scores increase as school librarians spend more time collaborating with and providing training to teachers, providing input into curricula, and managing information technology for the school (Manzo 2000). A significant number of prior studies also indicate a positive relationship between the library media program and academic achievement. Didier (1984) examines 38 of these studies, including Gaver's (1963) study of the impact of elementary library service on test scores; Greve's (1974) research on the effect of library service on the academic achievement of high school seniors; and Snider's (1965) investigation of the relationship between college success and knowledge of information skills.

COLLABORATION DEFINED

Collaboration is based on shared goals, a shared vision, and a climate of trust and respect (Muronago and Harada 1999). Each partner fulfills a carefully defined role; comprehensive planning is required; leadership, resources, risk, and control are shared; and the working relationship extends over a relatively long period of time (Callison 1999). The teacher brings to the partnership knowledge of the strengths, weaknesses, attitudes and interests of the students, and of the content to be taught. The media specialist adds a thorough understanding of information skills and methods to integrate them, helping the teacher to develop resource-based units that broaden the use of resources and promote information literacy (Doiron and Davies 1998). Additional benefits include more effective use of both resources and teaching time, integration of educational technologies, and a reduced teacher/student ratio (Doiron and Davies 1998). Teachers with experience in collaborative planning and teaching view the role of the library media specialist more positively and welcome continued collaboration. Participants believe that the results of the collaboration are more powerful and significant than the results of their individual efforts (Friend and Cook 1996).

CONDITIONS FAVORABLE TO COLLABORATIVE PARTNERSHIPS ADMINISTRATIVE FACTORS

Studies of successful collaborative partnerships have helped us to learn more about the factors conducive to this type of relationship. A recognized barrier to successful collaboration is lack of time (Bishop and Larimer 1999). Library media specialists with flexible schedules are able to devote more time to planning and working with teachers (Callison 1999). While media specialists on a fixed schedule spend up to five minutes planning with a teacher, a media specialist on a flexible schedule spends more than 30 minutes (Haycock 1998). Media specialists with flexible schedules also develop four and one-half times as many integrated units of study than do those on fixed schedules, as well as teaching more information skills lessons integrated with classroom instruction (Tallman and van Deusen 1994). Scheduling common planning time for teachers and media specialists also promotes collaboration. The greatest amount of collaboration occurs when the media specialist has a flexible schedule and team planning is encouraged by the principal (Tallman and van Deusen 1994).

Several Canadian studies have shown that principals have a better understanding of the school library program and view it more positively than do classroom teachers (Oberg 1995). Their critical role in promoting collaborative relationships goes beyond scheduling. Principal support includes working directly with teachers to develop their understanding of the role of the library. This is accomplished through staff inservices, featuring library activities in staff meetings, stating expectations of teachers regarding library use both during the hiring process and afterwards, and serving as a role model by effectively using the library and its information literacy program (Oberg 1995). Administrators who ask how teachers are using the resources of the media center and the expertise of the library media specialist create an atmosphere where collaboration is more likely to occur (Bishop and Larimer 1999).

INTERPERSONAL FACTORS

Successful collaboration involves changing both the attitudes toward and expectations of the role of the library media specialist (Wolcott 1996). Research shows that most students, teachers, and administrators don't perceive library media specialists and media centers as integral to their own success (Hartzell 1997). Library media specialists are often viewed as storytellers and providers of resources rather than co-teachers who share common goals (Bishop and Larimer 1999). It is up to the library media specialist to take steps to change this by serving on curriculum committees, attending planning meetings, and sharing ideas for integrating the media center into the curriculum (Bishop and Larimer 1999).

Likewise, teachers need help to make the transition from independent teaching to collaboration. The library media specialist can help facilitate this change by acting as the change agent, innovator, opinion leader and/or monitor (Haycock 1999). The qualities of a library media specialist most often mentioned in discussions of collaboration are initiative, confidence, communication skills, leadership qualities, and, above all, the willingness to take risks. Library media specialists must assume partnership and look for opportunities to plan with teachers, rather than waiting to be asked (Callison 1999). Effective social skills are necessary to realizing the vision of collaboration set forth in *Information Power: Building Partnerships for Learning* (AASLA 1998). Indeed, cognitive styles have been examined, and library media specialists defined as "field-dependent" were found to engage more frequently in collaborative efforts with classroom teachers regardless of time and resource limitations (Montgomery 1991). Field-dependent library media specialists were characterized by their interest in people, use of others as a source of reinforcement, focus on socially oriented subject matter, and preference for working with others. Less outgoing library media specialists should note that in the collaborative relationship, both leadership, and risk are shared.

CONTINUED COMMITMENT TO THE GOAL

Haycock (1999) notes that collaborative program planning and team teaching are complex evolutionary changes which require time—perhaps two to five years—to reach effective levels. In the case of library media specialist/teacher collaboration, the transition has been slow. Although library literature reflects more than two decades of interest in collaborative planning, and library media specialists are well-trained to perform in this capacity, there are still fewer examples of instructional partnerships than might be expected (Haycock 1999). However, commitment to the goal remains strong. The term "collaboration" is one of the most frequently used terms in *Information Power: Building Partnerships for Learning* (Callison 1999). "Instructional consultant" has been upgraded to instructional and curriculum "partner," reflecting a collaborative relationship where the teacher and library media specialist are viewed as equal contributors (Muronago and Harada 1999). The future of the library media program will be shaped by the vision for a student-centered library media program described in this revised document. This vision for the future is based on three central ideas, which suggest a framework to support the authentic student learning that is the goal of the successful, student-centered library media program. These central ideas are collaboration, leadership, and technology.

REFERENCES AND SUGGESTED READINGS

American Association of School Librarians and Association for Educational Communications and Technology. (1998). *Information power: Building partnerships for learning*. Chicago: Author.

Berkowitz, R., and Eisenberg, M. B. (1989). The curriculum roles and responsibilities of library media specialists. *ERIC Digest*. Syracuse, NY: ERIC Clearinghouse on Information & Technology. (ED 308 880)

Bishop, K., and Larimer, N. (1999, October). Literacy through collaboration. *Teacher Librarian*, 27(1), 15–20.

Callison, D. (1999, January). Keywords in instruction: Collaboration. *School Library Media Activities Monthly*, 15(5), 38–40.

Didier, E. K. (1984). Research on the impact of school library media programs on student achievement: Implications for school library media professionals, (ED 279 340). In MacDonald, F. B. (Ed.), *The emerging school library media program* (pp. 25–44). Englewood, CO: Libraries Unlimited.

Doiron, R., and Davies, J. (1998). *Partners in learning: Students, teachers, and the school library*. Englewood, CO: Libraries Unlimited. (ED 417 721)

Friend, M., and Cook, L. (1996). *Interactions: Collaborative skills for school professionals*. (2nd ed.). White Plains, NY: Longman. (ED 340 688)

Garland, K. (1995). The information search process: A study of elements associated with meaningful research tasks. *School Libraries Worldwide*, 1(1), 41–53. (EJ 516 594)

Gaver, M. V. (1963). *Effectiveness of centralized library service in elementary schools*. (2nd ed.). New Brunswick, NJ: Rutgers University Press.

Greve, C. L. (1974). The relationship of the availability of libraries to the academic achievement of Iowa high school seniors. (Doctoral dissertation, University of Denver, 1974).

Gross, J., and Kientz, S. (1999, October). Developing information literacy: Collaborating for authentic learning. *Teacher Librarian*, 27(1), 21–25.

Hartzell, G. (1997). The invisible school librarian. *School Library Journal*, 43(11), 24–29. (EJ 554 171)

Haycock, K. (1998, May). Collaborative cultures, team planning and flexible scheduling. *Emergency Librarian*, 25(5), 28. (EJ 570 639)

———. (1999, March). Fostering collaboration, leadership and information literacy: Common behaviors of uncommon principals and faculties. *NASSP Bulletin*, 83(605), 82–87. (EJ 585 580)

Kuhlthau, C. C. (1995). The process of learning from information. *School Libraries Worldwide*, 1(1), 1–12. (EJ 503 404)

Lance, K. C. (1994, May). The impact of school library media centers on academic achievement. *ERIC Digest*. Syracuse, NY: ERIC Clearinghouse on Information & Technology. (ED 372 759)

Manzo, K. K. (2000, March 22). Study shows rise in test scores tied to school library resources. *Education Week on the Web*. [Online]. Available: http://www.edweek.org/ew/ewstory.cfm?slug=28libe .h19 [2000, August].

McGregor, J. (1994). Analysis of thinking in the research process. *School Libraries in Canada*, 14(2), 4–7.

Montgomery, P. (1991). Cognitive style and the level of cooperation between the library media specialist and classroom teacher. *School Library Media Quarterly*, 19(3), 185–191. (EJ 428 857)

Muronago, K., and Harada, V. (1999, October). Building teaching partnerships: The art of collaboration. *Teacher Librarian*, 27(1), 9–14.

Oberg, D. (1995). *Principal support: What does it mean to teacher-librarians?* [Online]. Available: http://www.ualberta.ca/~doberg/prcsup.htm [2000, August].

Snider, F. E. (1965). The relationship of library ability to performance in college. (Doctoral dissertation, University of Illinois, 1965).

Tallman, J. I., and van Deusen, J. D. (1994). Collaborative unit planning: Schedule, time and participants. *School Library Media Quarterly*, 23(1), 33–37. (EJ 493 343)

———. (1994). The impact of scheduling on curriculum consultation and information skills instruction. *School Library Media Quarterly*, 23(1), 17–25. (EJ 493 341)

Wolcott, L. (1996). Planning with teachers: Practical approaches to collaboration. *Emergency Librarian*, 23(3), 8. (EJ 518 337)

Standards

ISTE National Educational Technology Standards (NETS)
Educational Technology Expectations for Students and Teachers

Lajeane Thomas
Louisiana Tech University

INTRODUCTION

A challenge facing America's schools is the empowerment of all children to function effectively in the future; a future marked increasingly by change, information growth, and evolving technologies. Technology is a powerful tool with enormous potential for paving high-speed highways from our outdated educational system to a system capable of providing learning opportunities for all children—a system that will better serve the needs of twentieth century work, communications, learning, and life. Through its NETS Project the International Society for Technology in Education (ISTE) is encouraging educational leaders to provide learning opportunities that produce technology capable students.

To live, learn, and work successfully in an increasingly complex and information-rich society, students must use technology effectively. Within a sound educational setting, technology can enable students to become:

- Capable information technology users

- Information seekers, analyzers, and evaluators

- Problem solvers and decision-makers

- Creative and effective users of productivity tools

- Communicators, collaborators, publishers, and producers

- Informed, responsible, and contributing citizens.

(International Society for Technology in Education 1998a)

Corporate America and the public at large have begun to recognize the potential of technology to change education, to improve learning, and to become a powerful catalyst in promotion of the learning, communications, and life skills necessary for economic survival in today's world. The CEO Forum in *From Pillars to Progress* stated:

To thrive in today's world and tomorrow's workplace, American students must learn how to learn, learn how to think, and have a solid understanding of how technology works and what it can do (CEO Forum 1997).

Societal change historically produces widespread change in education. Unleashing the power of technology for learning, information exchange, productivity, communication, and collaboration in our schools has the potential to affect profound changes in how teachers facilitate learning, how students contribute to the learning process, how knowledge is demonstrated, and even the venues in which learning takes place (Thomas and Knezek 1999).

A major challenge for educational leaders is to map a course that takes advantage of this power to improve learning. It is critical that educational leaders embark on a journey toward reshaping our educational system to take advantage of the available technologies that are rapidly becoming integral to success in our information-oriented society. Educational technology standards for students, and for teachers who prepare those students, can contribute significantly to defining expectations for preparing a new, technology-capable generation of education professionals, prepared workers, and lifelong learners.

STANDARDS DEVELOPMENT

Standards development, growing out of the overall education reform movement, has defined expectations for navigating the route to systemic reform of the educational system. In the past decade, professional education organizations supporting each major curriculum area have developed national standards, setting the nation on a course of school improvement by focusing on high standards for student performance. This includes the development of local, state, and national standards and plans for achieving the outlined goals. A major leadership focus for the ISTE organization has been development of National Educational Technology Standards (NETS).

The academic standards developed by America's leading professional education associations reflected research and national consensus on what students should know and be able to do to demonstrate their mastery of subject matter. However, these content standards, though rich in their treatment of the subject matter, did not adequately address the powerful ways to use technology to apply subject matter knowledge in authentic contexts, to solve problems, to make decisions, to exchange information, and to communicate. ISTE contends that in a modern educational system, "knowing" content information is not a sufficient end in itself—that application of the knowledge to construct new understandings, solve problems, make decisions, develop products, and communicate ideas is essential for every student's education.

Experience has proven that technology applied effectively can support the learning environment in powerful ways that restructure the essence and depth of the learning experience. The resulting "new" learning environments are fertile ground for the facilitation of higher order thinking, informed decision making, problem solving, communication of ideas, and creativity. Therefore, ISTE embarked on a journey to develop educational technology standards for students that could be interwoven with the content standards and resources. The NETS Project has provided opportunities for stakeholders in grades PreK through 12 and higher education to come to national consensus on what students, teachers, technology leaders, and education administrators should know about and be able to do with technology to improve learning and define the role of technology in schools, including the conditions necessary to ensure that the potential gains from the use of educational technology are achieved. The NETS for students were released in 1998, with an update in 2000, (ISTE 2000a) and have been widely used across the United States.

CONNECTING CURRICULUM AND TECHNOLOGY

ISTE recognized that development of the student standards was not, in itself, enough to support integration of the standards in practice. It was important to demonstrate how the academic content standards and technology standards could be interwoven in practice. Therefore, the NETS Project gathered teachers at all grade ranges and in the subject areas of mathematics, science, social studies, English, reading, and foreign languages, plus representatives from the corresponding professional organizations for those subject areas, to develop model lessons, thematic units, and resources to support integration of technology and curriculum in grades PreK through 12 learning experiences. In November 1999, the NETS Project released the document, "NETS for Students: Connecting Curriculum and Technology" and posted all activities and resources from that document on the Web (http://cnets.iste .org).

Of course, the effectiveness of the standards to facilitate change in an educational setting depends a great deal on the readiness of the teachers and the educational system to support the use of technology to create and maintain these rich environments for learning. ISTE, through its NETS Project, is committed to providing both the roadmap for instructing students, teachers, and administrators in the effective use of technology and the resources for supporting our educational system as the technology is integrated across the curricular landscape.

The NETS for Students

In June 1998, ISTE released an initial set of national educational technology standards for grades PreK through 12 students. The document was produced through the NETS Project, with support from the U.S. Department of Education, NASA, the Santa Monica-based Milken Exchange on Education Technology, and Apple Computer, Inc.

The *National Educational Technology Standards for Students* (International Society for Technology in Education 1998a) document included learning standards and student performance indicators designed to focus on using technology to extend "knowing content" to include "application of the content knowledge in the context of learning, living, and working in our world." The document includes standards describing which technology skills should be interwoven in the curricular fabric of our schools; how technology-literate students at four grade ranges within the learning development continuum demonstrate those skills; when such skills should be taught; and how the power of technology can be focused to help our children become more successful learners, information users, communicators, and workers.

The NETS document represents responses to proposed educational technology standards from many groups and individuals across the nation who participated in conference sessions, technology forum meetings, Internet dialogue, or individually (by submitting surveys). The complete document is available in PDF and other formats at http://cnets.iste.org.

The *NETS for Students* standards include three major components:

1. technology foundation standards for students,

2. profiles of technology literate students, and

3. examples and scenarios describing how the standards and performances are exhibited in classroom practice.

The *NETS for Students* document is organized around six standards. Accompanying each standard are indicators providing a general description of what performance is expected of the students. Standards within each category are to be introduced, reinforced, and mastered by students.

Technology Foundation Standards for Students

1. Basic operations and concepts

1.1 Students demonstrate a sound understanding of the nature and operation of technology systems.

1.2 Students are proficient in the use of technology.

2. **Social, ethical, and human issues**

   2.1   Students understand the ethical, cultural, and societal issues related to technology.

   2.2   Students practice responsible use of technology systems, information, and software.

   2.3   Students develop positive attitudes toward technology uses that support lifelong learning, collaboration, personal pursuits, and productivity.

3. **Technology productivity tools**

   3.1   Students use technology tools to enhance learning, increase productivity, and promote creativity.

   3.2   Students use productivity tools to collaborate in constructing technology-enhanced models, preparing publications, and producing other creative works.

4. **Technology communications tools**

   4.1   Students use telecommunications to collaborate, publish, and interact with peers, experts, and other audiences.

   4.2   Students use a variety of media and formats to communicate information and ideas effectively to multiple audiences.

5. **Technology research tools**

   5.1   Students use technology to locate, evaluate, and collect information from a variety of sources.

   5.2   Students use technology tools to process data and report results.

   5.3   Students evaluate and select new information resources and technological innovations based on the appropriateness to specific tasks.

6. **Technology problem-solving and decision-making tools**

   6.1   Students use technology resources for solving problems and making informed decisions.

   6.2   Students employ technology in the development of strategies for solving problems in the real world. (International Society for Technology in Education 1998a)

Profiles of Technology Literate Students

A major component of the NETS Project is the development of a set of profiles describing the technology competence students should exhibit upon completion of the following grade ranges: PreK–2, grades 3–5, grades 6–8, grades 9–12. These profiles include performance tasks demonstrating achievement of the *NETS for Students*. The profiles are based on the assumption that technology skills are developed through coordinated activities that support learning throughout a student's educational experiences. The skills will be introduced, reinforced, and finally mastered and thus integrated into an individual's personal learning and social framework. The performance tasks represent essential, realistic, and attainable aims for lifelong learning. They encourage learners—including the teachers—to employ learning strategies that unleash the power of technology to reach beyond "knowing" facts, to experiencing, exploring, constructing knowledge, applying reasoning skills, and communicating results. The performance profiles for each grade range are included in the following:

**Profile for Technology Literate Students
Grades PreK–2**

All students should have opportunities to demonstrate the following performances. At the end of each task statement, the number within the parentheses denotes the standards category (1–6) being addressed. Prior to completion of grade 2 students will:

1. Use input devices (e.g., mouse, keyboard, remote control) and output devices (e.g., monitor, printer) to successfully operate computers, VCRs, audiotapes, telephones, and other technologies. (Standard 1)

2. Use a variety of media and technology resources for directed and independent learning activities. (1, 3)

3. Communicate about technology using developmentally appropriate and accurate terminology. (1)

4. Use developmentally appropriate multimedia resources (e.g., interactive books, educational software, elementary multimedia encyclopedias) to support learning. (1)

5. Work cooperatively and collaboratively with peers, family members, and others when using technology in the classroom. (2)

6. Demonstrate positive social and ethical behaviors when using technology. (2)

7. Practice responsible use of technology systems and software. (2)

8. Create developmentally appropriate multimedia products with support from teachers, family members, or student partners. (3)

9. Use technology resources (e.g., puzzles, logical thinking programs, writing tools, digital cameras, drawing tools) for problem solving, communication, and illustration of thoughts, ideas, and stories. (3, 4, 5, 6)

10. Gather information and communicate with others using telecommunications, with support from teachers, family members, or student partners. (4)

**Profile for Technology Literate Students
Grades 3–5**

All students should have opportunities to demonstrate the following performances. Prior to completion of grade 5, students will:

1. Use keyboards and other common input and output devices (including adaptive devices when necessary) efficiently and effectively. (1)

2. Discuss common uses of technology in daily life and advantages and disadvantages those uses provide. (1, 2)

3. Discuss basic issues related to responsible use of technology and information and describe personal consequences of inappropriate use. (2)

4. Use general-purpose productivity tools and peripherals to support personal productivity, to remediate skill deficits, and to facilitate learning throughout the curriculum. (3)

5. Use technology tools (e.g., multimedia authoring, presentation, Web tools, digital cameras, scanners) for individual and collaborative writing, communication, and publishing activities to create knowledge products for audiences inside and outside the classroom. (3, 4)

6. Use telecommunications efficiently and effectively to access remote information, communicate with others in support of direct and independent learning, and pursue personal interests. (4)

7. Use telecommunications and online resources (e.g., e-mail, online discussions, Web environments) to participate in collaborative problem-solving activities for the purpose of developing solutions or products for audiences inside and outside the classroom. (4, 5)

8. Use technology resources (e.g., calculators, probes, videos, educational software) for problem-solving, self-directed learning, and extended learning activities. (5, 6)

9. Determine when technology is useful and select the appropriate tool(s) and technology resources to address a variety of tasks and problems. (5, 6)

10. Evaluate the accuracy, relevance, appropriateness, comprehensiveness, and bias of electronic information sources. (6)

Profile for Technology Literate Students
Grades 6–8

All students should have opportunities to demonstrate the following performances. Prior to completion of grade 8 students will:

1. Apply strategies for identifying and solving routine hardware and software problems that occur during everyday use. (1)

2. Demonstrate knowledge of current changes in information technologies and the effect those changes have on the workplace and society. (2)

3. Exhibit legal and ethical behaviors when using information and technology, and discuss consequences of misuse. (2)

4. Use content-specific tools, software and simulations (e.g., environmental probes, graphing calculators, exploratory environments, Web tools) to support learning and research. (3, 5)

5. Apply productivity/multimedia tools and peripherals to support personal productivity, group collaboration, and learning throughout the curriculum. (3, 6)

6. Design, develop, publish and present products (e.g., Web pages, videotapes) using technology resources that demonstrate and communicate curriculum concepts to audiences inside and outside the classroom. (4, 5, 6)

7. Collaborate with peers, experts, and others using telecommunications and collaborative tools to investigate curriculum-related problems, issues, and information, and to develop solutions or products for audiences inside and outside the classroom. (4, 5)

8. Select and use appropriate tools and technology resources to accomplish a variety of tasks and solve problems. (5, 6)

9. Demonstrate an understanding of concepts underlying hardware, software, and connectivity, and of practical applications to learning and problem solving. (1, 6)

10. Research and evaluate the accuracy, relevance, appropriateness, comprehensiveness, and bias of electronic information sources concerning real-world problems. (2, 5, 6)

Profiles for Technology Literate Students
Grades 9–12

All students should have opportunities to demonstrate the following performances. Prior to completion of grade 12 students will:

1. Identify capabilities and limitations of contemporary and emerging technology resources and assess the potential of these systems and services to address personal, lifelong learning, and workplace needs. (2)

2. Make informed choices among technology systems, resources, and services. (1, 2)

3. Analyze advantages and disadvantages of widespread use and reliance on technology in the workplace and in society as a whole. (2)

4. Demonstrate and advocate legal and ethical behaviors among peers, family, and community regarding the use of technology and information. (2)

5. Use technology tools and resources for managing and communicating personal/professional information (e.g., finances, schedules, addresses, purchases, correspondence). (3, 4)

6. Evaluate technology-based options, including distance and distributed education, for lifelong learning. (5)

7. Routinely and efficiently use online information resources to meet needs for collaboration, research, publications, communications, and productivity. (4, 5, 6)

8. Select and apply technology tools for research, information analysis, problem solving, and decision-making in content learning. (4, 5)

9. Investigate and apply expert systems, intelligent agents, and simulations in real-world situations. (3, 5, 6)

10. Collaborate with peers, experts, and others to contribute to a content-related knowledge base by using technology to compile, synthesize, produce, and disseminate information, models, and other creative works. (4, 5, 6) (International Society for Technology in Education 1998a)

These standards, performance indicators, and profiles have been used widely since their release. States and districts across the nation have adapted, adopted, and correlated the standards, using them to influence the quality of experiences with technology provided to the students in our PreK through 12 schools.

The *NETS for Students* provided the foundation for development of the teacher, technology leader, and education administrator standards. Each set of new standards has been developed to support the systemic improvement of learning for the K–12 student. Once the *NETS for Students* was developed, it provided the definition for development of additional standards and resources for supporting the implementation of the student standards.

The NETS for Teachers

In June 2000, the *National Educational Technology Standards (NETS) for Teachers* (1998b) document was released. Each standard was supported by related performance indicators and profiles describing what the teacher should know about and be able to do with technology. There are six standards categories with two to five related performance indicators describing what the teacher or candidate should know about or be able to do with technology to meet the standard.

ISTE National Educational Technology Standards (NETS) and Performance Indicators for Teachers

All classroom teachers should be prepared to meet the following standards and performance indicators.

I.   Technology Operations and Concepts: Teachers demonstrate a sound understanding of technology operations and concepts. Teachers:

    A.   demonstrate introductory knowledge, skills, and understanding of concepts related to technology (as described in the *ISTE National Educational Technology Standards for Students*).

    B.   demonstrate continual growth in technology knowledge and skills to stay abreast of current and emerging technologies.

II.   Planning and Designing Learning Environments and Experiences: Teachers plan and design effective learning environments and experiences supported by technology. Teachers:

    A.   design developmentally appropriate learning opportunities that apply technology-enhanced instructional strategies to support the diverse needs of learners.

    B.   apply current research on teaching and learning with technology when planning learning environments and experiences.

    C.   identify and locate technology resources and evaluate them for accuracy and suitability.

    D.   plan for the management of technology resources within the context of learning activities.

    E.   plan strategies to manage student learning in a technology-enhanced environment.

III.   Teaching, Learning, and the Curriculum: Teachers implement curriculum plans that include methods and strategies for applying technology to maximize student learning. Teachers:

    A.   facilitate technology-enhanced experiences that address content standards and student technology standards.

    B.   use technology to support learner-centered strategies that address the diverse needs of students.

    C.   apply technology to develop students' higher order skills and creativity.

    D.   manage student learning activities in a technology-enhanced environment.

IV.   Assessment and Evaluation: Teachers apply technology to facilitate a variety of effective assessment and evaluation strategies. Teachers:

    A.   apply technology in assessing student learning of subject matter using a variety of assessment techniques.

    B.   use technology resources to collect and analyze data, interpret results, and communicate findings to improve instructional practice and maximize student learning.

    C.   apply multiple methods of evaluation to determine students' appropriate use of technology resources for learning, communication, and productivity.

V.   Productivity and Professional Practice: Teachers use technology to enhance their productivity and professional practice. Teachers:

    A.   use technology resources to engage in ongoing professional development and lifelong learning.

    B.   continually evaluate and reflect on professional practice to make informed decisions regarding the use of technology in support of student learning.

    C.   apply technology to increase productivity.

    D.   use technology to communicate and collaborate with peers, parents, and the larger community in order to nurture student learning.

VI.   Social, Ethical, Legal, and Human Issues: Teachers understand the social, ethical, legal, and human issues surrounding the use of technology in PreK–12 schools and apply that understanding in practice. Teachers:

    A.   model and teach legal and ethical practice related to technology use.

    B.   apply technology resources to enable and empower learners with diverse backgrounds, characteristics, and abilities.

    C.   identify and use technology resources that affirm diversity.

    D.   promote safe and healthy use of technology resources.

    E.   facilitate equitable access to technology resources for all students. (International Society for Technology in Education 2000b)

Also included in the *NETS for Teachers* document are performance profiles identifying specific performance tasks expected at four developmental levels in a teacher's preparation for effective technology use. These profiles are aimed primarily at guiding the preparation of new teachers to use technology, but they have powerful implications for planning professional development for in-service teachers, as well.

Also included in the document are expectations for meeting essential conditions that support the preparation of teachers to use technology. A combination of essential conditions is required for classroom teachers to create learning environments conducive to powerful uses of technology. The most effective learning environments meld traditional approaches and new approaches to facilitate learning of relevant content while addressing individual needs. For these new learning environments to develop, certain prerequisite factors or essential conditions must be present in every phase of an aspiring teacher's education—in the university's general education programs, in the chosen major, in teacher preparation programs, and at the school sites hosting student teachers and interns. Teachers and teacher educators cannot be expected to put into practice what they have learned about how to use technology without the presence of these essential conditions in their job environment. The following elements are necessary to be in place at the university, the college or school of education, and the school site:

Shared Vision—There is proactive leadership and administrative support from the entire system.

Access—Educators have access to current technologies, software, and telecommunications networks.

Skilled Educators—Educators are skilled in the use of technology for learning.

Professional Development—Educators have consistent access to professional development in support of technology use in teaching and learning.

Technical Assistance—Educators have technical assistance for maintaining and using the technology.

Content Standards and Curriculum Resources—Educators are knowledgeable in their subject matter and current in the content standards and teaching methodologies in their discipline.

Student-Centered Teaching—Teaching in all settings encompasses student-centered approaches to learning.

Assessment—There is continuous assessment of the effectiveness of technology for learning.

Community Support—The community and school partners provide expertise, support, and resources.

Support Policies—School and university policies, financing, and rewards structures are in place to support technology in learning. (International Society for Technology in Education 2000b)

ISTE/NCATE Standards for Educational Computing and Technology Leadership

The ISTE Accreditation and Professional Standards Committee has developed accreditation standards for teacher preparation programs for specialization in educational computing and technology. The technology specialization guidelines have been adopted by the National Council for Accreditation of Teacher Education (NCATE) and are currently being used in evaluation of teacher preparation programs for accreditation.

ISTE/NCATE accreditation standards for programs in educational technology include the following:

- ISTE/NCATE Educational Computing and Technology Literacy Standards—initial endorsement program to prepare teachers of educational technology literacy or campus leaders who support teachers' integration of technology in the classrooms
- ISTE/NCATE Educational Computing and Technology Leadership Standards—advanced program to prepare district, state, or regional educational technology coordinators
- ISTE/NCATE Educational Computing and Technology Secondary Computer Science Education Standards—initial endorsement or degree programs to prepare secondary teachers of computer science

These sets of standards were initially developed in 1991 and have been revised every five years. The ISTE/NCATE standards in Educational Computing and Technology are being revised this year and will be presented by ISTE to NCATE's Specialty Area Studies Board (SASB) in October 2001. For the current approved standards, see the NCATE Web site (http://www.ncate.org) or the ISTE site (http://www.iste.org).

Technology Standards for School Administrators (TSSA)

Leadership for educational technology in schools encompasses many other roles beyond the specific specialists in educational technology named above. Educational leaders such as superintendents, assistant superintendents, principals, and district program coordinators play critical roles in the total scheme of technology support, planning, administration, and implementation. Technology standards for educational leaders can map the route leading to a destination of strong support for integration of technology throughout the educational system. To this end, a number of organizations and entities have formed a collaborative for the expressed purpose of defining standards for school administrators. The collaborative for Technology Standards for School Administrators (TSSA Collaborative) began a year-long project in October 2000 to facilitate a national consensus and documentation of what school administrators should know about and be able to do to lead effective implementation of technology in PreK–12 education. Ultimately, it is the intent of the TSSA Collaborative to publish a set of foundation technology standards appropriate for all PreK–12 administrators and specific sets of technology standards beyond the foundations for

1. the superintendency and cabinet-level leaders,
2. building-level leaders, and
3. district-level leaders for curriculum and special programs.

With the value of standards for students and teachers established by the NETS Project, the TSSA Collaborative's emphasis on administrator standards addresses the leadership piece—important to ensuring high levels of learning for students and efficient operations of schools. Members of the TSSA Collaborative include the National Association of Elementary School Principals, National Association of Secondary School Principals, National School Board Association, International Society for Technology in Education, Consortium for School Networking, North Central Regional Technology Consortium at the North Central Regional Education Laboratory, Southern Regional Educational Board, Kentucky Department of Education, Mississippi Department of Education, University of North Carolina Principals' Executive Program, and Western Michigan University College of Education.

Based on its success with the NETS Project, the ISTE was requested by the Collaborative to manage this inclusive and broad-based standards development initiative. Contact information for project leaders and a current draft of *Technology Standards for School Administrators* are available online at http://www.iste.org. Final release of the standards is slated for fall of 2001.

NETS PROJECT PARTNERSHIP

Joining ISTE as project partners in developing technology standards for PreK–12 and teacher education are organizations representing major professional education groups in the United States. Each partner organization provides leadership to a broad spectrum of educators and includes members throughout the nation. Each of the partner organizations brings unique strengths to the project. The NETS partner organizations include the following:

- American Federation of Teachers (AFT)
- American Association of School Librarians (AASL), a division of the American Library Association (ALA)
- Association for Supervision and Curriculum Development (ASCD)
- Council of Chief State School Officers (CCSSO)
- Council for Exceptional Children (CEC)
- International Society for Technology in Education (ISTE)
- National Association of Elementary School Principals (NAESP)
- National Association of Secondary School Principals (NASSP)
- National Education Association (NEA)
- National Foundation for the Improvement of Education (NFIE)
- National School Boards Association's Education Technology Programs (NSBA-ITTE)
- Software and Internet Industry Association (SIIA)

An important strength of the NETS Project is the participation of representatives from the major curriculum organizations. The curriculum liaisons from each subject area participated in the writing teams responsible for linking the technology standards with the standards from their organization's academic subject area. These curriculum liaisons participated in work sessions designed to identify standards relating specifically to each curriculum area and to build interdisciplinary connections among the curricular areas. Joining the NETS Partnership are representatives from the following:

- American Council on the Teaching of Foreign Languages (ACTFL)
- International Reading Association (IRA)
- National Council for the Social Studies (NCSS)
- National Council for the Teachers of English (NCTE)
- National Council of Teachers of Mathematics (NCTM)
- National Science Teachers Association (NSTA)

Providing additional support for NETS development projects are Apple, Inc.; Milken Exchange on Education Technology; National Aeronautics and Space Administration (NASA); U.S. Department of Education; Intel Corporation; NASA Classroom of the Future; National Council for Accreditation of Teacher Education; North Central Regional Educational Laboratory; Classroom Connect; Knowvation, Inc.; The Learning Company; Microsoft Corporation; Semiconductor Industry Association; Public Broadcasting Services; T.H.E. Institute; Teacher Universe; and Cascio, Inc.

Without the support from the NETS and PT3 (Preparing Tomorrow's Teachers to Use Technology) partners and contributors, this standards development could not have been accomplished. Bringing together educational, governmental, corporate entities and community representatives for development and feedback on these standards has supported widespread dissemination, adoption, and acceptance of these standards.

CONCLUSION

Traditional educational practices can no longer provide students with all the necessary skills for economic survival in today's workplace. Students must be given opportunities to apply strategies for solving problems and to use appropriate tools for learning, collaborating, and communicating. Today's learning environments must incorporate strategies and tools that will prepare students for their futures. As districts attempt to navigate the road from traditional to enriched educational opportunities, there exists no single method for solving the problems of all schools that find their system in need of fundamental transformation. Each school must set a destination and develop its own route for reaching that goal. Educational technology expectations can serve as a powerful catalyst for school reform as each school embarks on its particular journey. And the NETS for students and teachers can serve as guidelines and milestones for measuring progress in reaching the destination of improved learning for all students.

Those planning the itinerary for travel from traditional schooling to schools that serve the needs of modern society will find that taking advantage of the advances in technology can indeed pave the road to improved education for tomorrow's students and unleash the potential of technology for supporting fundamental transformation of teaching and learning.

REFERENCES

CEO Forum. (1997). From *Pillars to Progress.* (Accessed October 12, 2001).

International Society for Technology in Education. (1998a). *National educational technology standards for students*. Eugene, OR: International Society for Technology in Education.

———. (1998b). *National educational technology standards for teachers*. Eugene, OR: International Society for Technology in Education.

Thomas, L., and Knezek, D. (1999). National educational technology standards. *Educational Leadership*, 56:5, 27.

ABOUT THE AUTHOR

Lajeane Thomas, Ed.D., serves as Director of the ISTE NETS Project, as Chair of the ISTE Accreditation and Standards Committee, and as a member of the Specialty Areas Studies Board of the NCATE. She has been a Professor of Educational Technology in the Curriculum, Instruction, and Leadership at Louisiana Tech University for 21 years and is a former ISTE President. (e-mail: lthomas@latech.edu)

NOTE

The International Society for Technology in Education (ISTE) is a nonprofit professional organization with a worldwide membership of technology-using educators. ISTE is dedicated to the improvement of education through the integration of technology and curriculum. ISTE's role is leadership—to provide its members with information, networking opportunities, and guidance as they face the challenge of incorporating computers, the Internet, and other new technologies in their schools. For additional information, see the ISTE Web site at http://www.iste.org.

The ibstpi Competency Standards
Development, Definition, and Use

Rita C. Richey
Professor, Instructional Technology
Wayne State University
and
Vice President, Research and Development
International Board of Standards for Training, Performance, and Instruction

The International Board of Standards for Training, Performance and Instruction[1] (ibstpi) is a professional organization serving the instructional design, training, and performance improvement communities. It contributes through research, publications, and conferences, and especially through the construction and validation of job-specific standards in the form of competencies and performance statements. Most notably, it has published competencies for instructional designers, instructors, and training managers (*Instructional Design Competencies* 1986; Hutchison, Shepherd, and Stein 1988; *Training Manager Competencies* 1989; *Instructor Competencies: The Standards—Vol. II* 1992; Richey, Fields, and Foxon 2001; Richey, Foxon, and Roberts forthcoming). These standards have been adopted and used by an array of public and private organizations. They also serve as the basis for certification programs established by organizations for internal use, as well as for industry-wide use. This chapter describes the ibstpi competency development process, two sets of ibstpi competency standards, and ways in which the standards can be used.

COMPETENCE AND THE IBSTPI COMPETENCY DEVELOPMENT MODEL

Competence and Competencies

There are differing views of the nature of a competency and its relationship to professional competence itself. Parry (1998) cited the tendency for many to mistake competencies for personality traits or characteristics, or for styles and values. Lucia and Lepsinger (1999), on the other hand, see personal characteristics and aptitudes as foundational to skill and knowledge demonstration. It is generally agreed, however, that whereas competence is the state of being well qualified, competency statements are descriptions of the critical ways in which such competence is demonstrated. Competencies are innately behavioral and positivistic in nature, even though most professionals are fundamentally interested in underlying competence. Spencer and Spencer (1993) portray competency as either core or surface entities, with skills and knowledge being surface variables that are easier to develop than core characteristics such as attitudes.

Ibstpi defines a competency as:

> a knowledge, skill, or attitude that enables one to effectively perform the activities of a given occupation or function to the standards expected in employment. (Richey, Fields, and Foxon 2001, p. 8)

The ibstpi competencies are statements of behavior—not personality traits or beliefs—but they do often reflect attitudes. Ibstpi competencies are correlated with performance on a job and are typically measured against commonly accepted standards. Moreover, there is an implication that the ibstpi competencies can be developed through training.

Competency Development

The construction of a valid set of competency standards is a large-scale research and development process. With respect to the ibstpi standards, each recent project has involved concentrated work by a research team, involvement of the entire board, and input from hundreds of practitioners and academics representing organizations worldwide. The generic ibstpi competency development model is shown in Figure 1.

A particular set of competencies relates to a general job role, such as that of instructional designer. The role definition is typically a preliminary step to competency definition. (Sometimes, as with the newly revised training manager standards, this process involves input from the field.) Competencies totally unrelated to actual jobs are typically impossible to use effectively. Job roles, however, can be defined generically, or they can be customized to reflect a given work context (Lucia and Lepsinger 1999).

Job roles must be interpreted in detail to facilitate competency definition. Specific job behaviors must be identified. In addition, the performance and ethical standards and values commonly used in the field to evaluate such behaviors must also be determined. Finally, one must clarify a vision of the field. This vision may be the result of interpretations of current research and emerging trends, or it may be the result of societal or business pressures. Job behaviors, vision, and standards provide the major input into the identification and validation of the knowledge, skills, and attitudes critical to a particular job role.

Structurally, the ibstpi competency model consists of three components—domains, competencies, and performance statements. Competency statements in the ibstpi format are short, general descriptions of complex efforts. One example would be "Communicate effectively in visual, oral, and written form." In this, and all other competencies, additional detail is needed to more fully explain what is entailed in the activity. These explanations are provided via performance statements. A full demonstration of a given competency would then consist of a series of more specific behaviors. For example, the communication competency identified above is partially supported by the performance statement "Deliver presentations that effectively engage and communicate." Competencies and performance statements are structurally the same, differing only in the level of behavior specificity. Performance statements are not, however, simply process or task descriptions.

Even though competencies are general, they can, nonetheless, be categorized into even larger domains of activity. This competency modeling tactic is recommended by Spencer and Spencer (1993). The ibstpi instructional designer competencies, for example, are clustered into domains that, by and large, follow a systematic design approach—planning and analysis, design and development, implementation and management. In addition, there is an initial professional foundations domain. These domains facilitate competency summaries and theme identification, even as the performance statements facilitate detailed analysis. All levels—domain, competency, and performance statement—can be used in program design.

The ibstpi competency development model provides overall direction for its competency development process. In actual operation, there are four major phases used in ibstpi's current competency definition and updating processes, each of which is fundamentally an empirical procedure. The phases are

- Identification of Foundational Research,
- Competency Drafting,
- Competency Validation, and
- Rewriting.

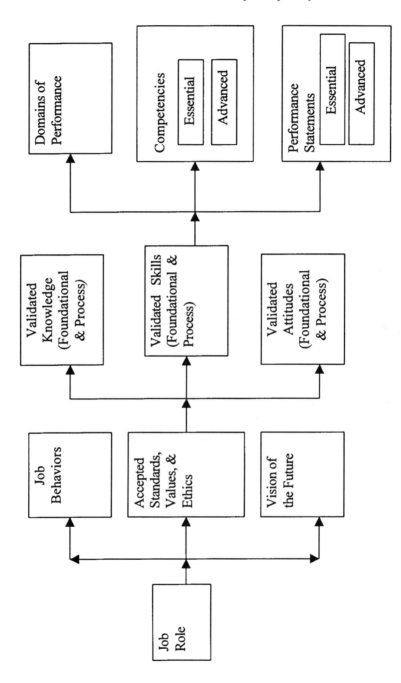

Figure 1. The Generic ibstpi Competency Development Model

Ibstpi competencies are based on research foundations, varying in terms of the particular topic. In the case of competency updates, the original set (which was rooted in a research base as well) also serves as a starting point. This serves as the first step in establishing content validity for the standards. Basic premises and tentative assumptions are then articulated and agreed upon. Finally, a base list of competencies is developed, using these sources of information. This list serves as the starting point for a new development process.

The ibstpi board of directors serves as an expert focus group that analyzes and debates the base list. Competencies and performance statements are rewritten by persons with particular expertise in a given area. The new list is analyzed, debated, and rewritten several times to reflect the evolving input and to establish format consistency.

Once a list is established that has full board approval, the formal content validation process begins. Typically, this is a survey research effort to establish the extent to which each competency and performance statement is critical in the workplace. (With the case of the 2,000 instructional designer competencies, however, the level of required designer expertise was also determined in this phase.) These instruments are administered to a volunteer sample of several hundred practitioners and academics in diverse geographical locations and work environments.

The final competency list is then modified to reflect the input of the validation group. Competencies or performance statements without a high degree of support are removed, and new statements that have been generated and supported substantially are added. If respondents offer conflicting opinions, the Board makes the ultimate decision based on its collective experience and vision. Ultimately, the Board approves a final set of competency standards.

Underlying Assumptions

Each set of competencies is predicated, using a set of assumptions; however, there are certain assumptions that transcend each competency development effort. The first of these is that each set of standards is directed toward persons who demonstrate those competencies on the job, regardless of their job title or training or the focus of a particular organization or industry. However, the competencies can be customized to meet the unique characteristics of a particular organization. One obvious type of customization is to adapt to the particular job titles used in an organization because there is little job title standardization in this field. This is particularly true of the title *training manager,* where organizations use a wide variety of terms for this function. It is also true of titles given to persons who teach in online environments around the world.

A second general assumption is that it is recognized that few persons, regardless of their levels of expertise, demonstrate all competencies of a given role in one job. The intent of the standards development process is to be comprehensive and generic, covering the entire field, rather than establishing the dimensions of any particular job. Consequently, a specific position with a given organization may relate to only a portion of the competencies. To some extent, the many variations in jobs may reflect the emergence of areas of specialization in the field. In other cases, the variations may be more indicative of particular emphases that naturally occur in some work environments. In still other situations, the variations may reflect geographical or cultural diversity.

Finally, it should be clear that the ibstpi competency standards define the manner in which practice should occur. As such, they reflect societal and disciplinary values and ethics, as well as visions of good practice. Dick, Watson, and Kaufman (1981) contrasted two approaches to competency development—a consensus model that emphasized the "what is" and the model-building approach that focused on "what should be." Although to a great extent the ibstpi instructional design ID competencies represent a blend of these two approaches, the dominant orientation is the more idealized stance. There is a conscious effort to capture trends and anticipate the needs of the future. The goal is to establish standards for expert behavior that will advance the field. The difficult part of the task is to create competencies that are not only idealistic in nature but are still practical and useable in actual work environments.

THE IBSTPI COMPETENCY STANDARDS

Three sets of competencies have been developed, and two—instructional designer and training manager—have been recently revised. The third—instructor—is currently undergoing revision and an expanded set of these competencies will address the role of the online instructor and facilitator.[2] The two completed sets of standards will be discussed here.

The Instructional Designer Competency Standards

There are 23 newly updated ibstpi ID competencies. These competencies are clustered into four general domains and are supported by 122 performance statements. The competencies are listed in Figure 2, page 116. (See Richey, Fields, and Foxon 2001 for a listing of the performance statements and a full discussion of the standards.) In each of the four domains there are specific skills and knowledge that every instructional designer is expected to master (labeled as "essential"), as well as skills and knowledge that only the most experienced and expert designers would be expected to master (labeled as "advanced").

The ID competencies do more than describe designers' skills and knowledge. They describe job requirements and provide guidance for those entering the field as well as for veterans seeking professional updating and improvement. They can even suggest the parameters of specialty areas. The 2000 ibstpi ID standards have been analyzed in terms of four such ID specialists:

- The Analyst—specializing in performance analysis and training needs assessment;

- The Evaluator—specializing in various forms of evaluation and assessment, but especially transfer and impact evaluation;

- The E-learning Specialist—specializing in development of multimedia and electronic learning products, particularly Web-based learning; and

- The Project Manger—specializing in managing internal designers, external designers, or both, on one or several projects.

Increased use of ID specialists can also be attributed to the globalization of companies and, as a consequence, the exponential increase in the number of persons to be trained. In some organizations, it is not unusual for tens of thousands of people located in more than a dozen countries to require the same training. In such cases teams of individuals specializing in certain aspects of ID, rather than individual designer, are employed. The new competencies accommodate such practice.

Figure 2. The 2000 ibstpi Instructional Designer Competencies ©

PROFESSIONAL FOUNDATIONS

1. Communicate effectively in visual, oral, and written form. (Essential)
2. Apply current research and theory to the practice of instructional design. (Advanced)
3. Update and improve one's knowledge, skills, and attitudes pertaining to instructional design and related fields. (Essential)
4. Apply fundamental research skills to instructional design projects. (Advanced)
5. Identify and resolve ethical and legal implications of design in the work place. (Advanced)

PLANNING AND ANALYSIS

6. Conduct a needs assessment. (Essential)
7. Design a curriculum or program. (Essential)
8. Select and use a variety of techniques for determining instructional content. (Essential)
9. Identify and describe target population characteristics. (Essential)
10. Analyze the characteristics of the environment. (Essential)
11. Analyze the characteristics of existing and emerging technologies and their use in an instructional environment. (Essential)
12. Reflect upon the elements of a situation before finalizing design solutions and strategies. (Essential)

DESIGN AND DEVELOPMENT

13. Select, modify, or create a design and development model appropriate for a given project. (Advanced)
14. Select and use a variety of techniques to define and sequence the instructional content and strategies. (Essential)
15. Select or modify existing instructional materials. (Essential)
16. Develop instructional materials. (Essential)
17. Design instruction that reflects an understanding of the diversity of learners and groups of learners. (Essential)
18. Evaluate and assess instruction and its impact. (Essential)

IMPLEMENTATION AND MANAGEMENT

19. Plan and manage instructional design projects. (Advanced)
20. Promote collaboration, partnerships and relationships among the participants in a design project. (Advanced)
21. Apply business skills to managing instructional design. (Advanced)
22. Design instructional management systems. (Advanced)
23. Provide for the effective implementation of instructional products and programs. (Essential)

The Training Manager Competency Standards

Today, the bulk of training activity takes place in private and public sector environments. Managers of this function are now likely to be assigned to their positions on a full-time basis, especially in larger organizations. They are integral parts of the organization's management team. They must have business acumen, whether they have instructional design expertise or not. The new training manager competencies reflect these new demands. These new standards include 14 competency statements (listed in Figure 3) and 88 performance statements,[3] which are categorized into four domains.

Unlike that of instructional designers, training manager specialization is dependent more on the type of department in which one is employed than on any other factor. The demands and expectations of training managers of one-person shops differ from those of the managers working in large organizations, as well as differing from those who work primarily with outsourced providers.

Figure 3. The 2002 Training Manager Competencies ©

PROFESSIONAL FOUNDATIONS

1. Communicate effectively in written, oral, and visual form.
2. Comply with established ethical and legal standards.
3. Maintain networks to advocate for and support the training and performance function.
4. Update and improve professional and business knowledge, skills, and attitudes.

PERFORMANCE ANALYSIS AND PLANNING

5. Develop and monitor a strategic plan.
6. Use performance analysis to improve the organization.
7. Plan and promote organizational change.

DESIGN AND DEVELOPMENT

8. Ensure the application of instructional design principles.
9. Use technology to enhance the training function.
10. Evaluate training and performance interventions.

LEADERSHIP AND MANAGEMENT

11. Apply leadership skills to the training function.
12. Apply management skills to the training function.
13. Apply business skills to the training function.
14. Apply knowledge management principles.

COMPETENCY USES AND ISSUES

There are at least four categories of professionals who can use competencies in their work. These are working practitioners, managers, academics, and professional development suppliers. Each is likely to approach the competencies with differing needs and consequently use them in a unique manner. The practitioners may use them for benchmarking, the managers for human resource functions and for leading projects, the academics and consultants for curriculum development and program accreditation.

A topic related to competency standards of recurring interest is that of professional certification. This is not an issue without controversy. Nonetheless, it is one that has again aroused new interest. Professional certification has been defined as a voluntary process by which a professional association or organization measures and reports on the degree of competence of individual practitioners (Gilley, Geis, and Seyfer 1987). The intent of certification is to inform the public that individuals who have achieved certification have demonstrated a particular degree of knowledge and skill. It offers title protection because only those who are certified may use a particular title. It is one method of protecting the public (Browning, Bugbee, and Mullins 1996). Functionally, professional certification constitutes a formal and public definition of a profession.

When considering the prospect of professional certification for instructional design, training, or performance improvement personnel, several issues need to be explored. First, who is being certified? It is clear from recent ibstpi competency development projects that there is no longer just one concept of most work roles. Designers vary based on expertise and experience. Training managers vary by organization. All often vary by geographical location. Should certification processes and criteria differ as well? Although many welcome certification as a way of upgrading the field, others feel threatened by the prospect. Some academics have questioned the value of certification, not only because of potential conflicts with graduate degrees in the field but also because of technical reservations dealing with testing and measurement procedures. They posit that testing abstracted from actual skill demonstration is of only minimal value, and portfolios of work are difficult to assemble given the nature of much practice. Finally, no certification process can be instituted without costs, either to the organization or to the individual. Who has the responsibility for shouldering these costs? All of these issues have yet to be resolved, even though certification is proceeding on many fronts.

CONCLUSION

It is difficult to project the nature of the future changes in the field other than anticipating a continuation of current trends. Technology will undoubtedly advance to an even greater extent. Work settings will probably become even more complex. Globalization will likely be seen as routine. However, other societal changes—changes that are less easy to predict—will take place and will impact this field, even as they impact other disciplines and professions. In the meantime, the Board is meeting these challenges by continuing to revise and expand their sets of competency standards.

Although previous ibstpi standards have stood the test of time for more than a decade, it may be likely that more frequent revisions will be demanded in the future to keep pace with rapid changes in the fields and organizations we serve. It is also possible that the new competency standards will need to be more complex to match the more sophisticated work environment. They may require standards subcategories, as is the case with the current development of online instructor competencies, and entirely new domains of standards may be devised to meet the needs of the instructional design, training, and performance improvement communities.

NOTES

1.   The ibstpi Board grew from the work of the Joint Certification Task Force, which was composed of the Association for Educational Communications and Technology (AECT) and the National Society for Performance and Instruction (NSPI, now the International Society for Performance Improvement, ISPI). Created in 1977, the Joint Task Force included over 30 professional practitioners and academics with expertise in various facets of training, performance, and instruction. The Task Force reorganized itself in 1983 to avoid conflicts of interest with its parent organizations. This action was taken with the approval and encouragement of the Boards of Directors of NSPI, AECT, and the Division of Instructional Development within AECT. Today, the Board consists of 15 professionals, selected to be broadly representative of the communities it serves. Members are from universities, government, large businesses, and consulting firms in Australia, Canada, England, Norway, and The Netherlands, as well as the United States. Ibstpi's work is described at http://www.ibstpi.org

2.   It is anticipated that this expansion and revision project will be completed 2002 and the resulting publications will be completed in 2003. Negotiations are underway relating to the certification of online instructors. The current instructor standards can be found on the ibstpi Web site (www.ibstpi.org). They are currently being used as the basis of the Certified Technical Trainer program administered by The Chauncey Group, a subsidiary of Educational Testing Service. For further information see http://www.chauncey.com.

3.   The performance statements, a full discussion of the training manager's job, specialization areas, applications and uses of the competencies, and the competency validation process are described in *Training Manager Competencies: The Standards* (2d ed.). The ERIC® Clearinghouse on Information & Technology will publish this book. It is anticipated in 2002.

REFERENCES

Browning, A. H, Bugbee, A. C., and Mullins, M. A., eds. (1996). *Certification: A NOCA handbook.* The National Organization for Competency Assurance: Washington, DC.

Dick, W., Watson, K., and Kaufman, R. (1981). Deriving competencies: Consensus versus model building. *Educational Researcher,* 10:10, 5–10.

Gilley, J., Geis, G., and Seyfer, C. (1987). Let's talk certification: Questions and answers for the profession about the profession. *Performance and Instruction,* 26:2.

Hutchison, C., Shepherd, J., and Stein, F. (1988). *Instructor competencies: The standards—Vol. I.* Chicago: International Board of Standards for Training, Performance and Instruction.

Instructional design competencies: The standards. (1986). Batavia, IL: International Board of Standards for Training, Performance and Instruction.

Instructor competencies: The standards—Vol. II. (1992). Batavia, IL: International Board of Standards for Training, Performance and Instruction.

Lucia, A. D., and Lepsinger, R. (1999). *The art and science of competency models: Pinpointing critical success factors in organizations.* San Francisco: Jossey-Bass/Pfeiffer.

Parry, S. B. (June, 1998). Just what is a competency? (And why should you care?). *Training,* 35:6, 58–64.

Richey, R. C., Fields, D. F., and Foxon, M. (2001). *Instructional design competencies: The standards* (3d ed.). Syracuse, NY: ERIC Clearinghouse on Information and Technology.

Richey, R. C., Foxon, M., and Roberts, R. (forthcoming). *Training manager competencies: The standards* (2d ed.). Syracuse, NY: ERIC Clearinghouse on Information and Technology.

Spencer, L. M., and Spencer, S. M. (1993). *Competence at work: Models for superior performance.* New York: John Wiley.

Training manager competencies: The standards. (1989). Batavia, IL: International Board of Standards for Training, Performance and Instruction.

AECT Accreditation Standards
Guidelines for the Quality Preparation of
Education Technology Professionals

Rodney S. Earle
Brigham Young University

This chapter provides an overview of the long-term partnership that the Association for Educational Communications and Technology (AECT) has enjoyed with national accreditation through the National Council for Accreditation of Teacher Education (NCATE). It also outlines the review processes to be followed by institutions applying for accreditation and then describes the newly revised and approved performance-based standards developed by AECT.

AN OVERVIEW OF THE
AECT/NCATE PARTNERSHIP [1]

Looking Back

From its early history as part of the National Education Association (NEA), the AECT has been a pioneer, not only in the field of technology but also in the relatively recent area of national accreditation for teacher education. Since its inception, AECT has been concerned with the development of competent teachers and qualified media and technology personnel. Efforts to influence the quality of teacher preparation began in earnest with AECT's establishment of task forces in 1971 to study certification and accreditation guidelines for educational media professionals (Bergeson 1973). The significant documents that resulted from this intensive three-year research study solidified the AECT's alliance with the NCATE, resulting in AECT's admission to constituent membership in that council in 1980—one of only three professional associations at that time to enjoy this affiliation with NCATE. This valuable partnership has flourished over the years. For example, at first AECT was responsible for reviewing the technology aspects of *every* teacher education program in the nation—a formidable task. In 1994, the AECT worked closely with NCATE to merge our basic media and technology guidelines into the general NCATE standards, which now expect institutions to provide adequate access to computers and other technologies and also expect university faculty, classroom teachers, and students to be able to use them successfully. Our current focus is on the accreditation of programs preparing professionals in the field of educational communications and instructional technologies (ECIT).

Looking Around

Many reports, some quite critical of American education, have consistently concluded that competent classroom teachers are essential for providing quality educational opportunities for all children. Senator Jeff Bingaman, a member of the U.S. Senate's Labor and Human Resources Committee, advocates raising standards for teachers as a national imperative.

The continued health and strength of our nation depends on our country's ability to improve the education of our young people. Integral to that is the strength and ability of our nation's teaching force. Teaching is among our most important professions and we should do all that we can to elevate it.

America needs teachers who are highly knowledgeable and competent in their subject and who are able to teach effectively. We need the best and the brightest. What can we do to raise the standard for all teachers? (Bingaman 1998, 1)

The 1996 report of the National Commissions on Teaching and America's Future, *What Matters Most: Teaching for America's Future*, indicated that, if schools of education are serious about preparing teachers, they should take the necessary steps to become accredited. In reflecting further on this report, Linda Darling-Hammond (1996) concluded:

Our highest priority must be to reach agreement on what teachers should know and be able to do in order to help students succeed. Unaddressed for decades, this task has recently been completed by three professional bodies: the National Council for Accreditation of Teacher Education (NCATE), the Interstate New Teacher Assessment and Support Consortium (INTASC), and the National Board for Professional Teaching Standards (the National Board). Their combined efforts to set standards for teacher, education, beginning teacher licensing, and advanced certification outline a continuum of teacher development throughout the career and offer the most powerful tools we have for reaching and rejuvenating the soul of the profession. (196)

So, what is involved in professional accreditation? What is NCATE? What are its purposes? Is there a value-added component to NCATE recognition? What is the AECT/NCATE partnership? What are the new AECT performance-based standards?

Professional Accreditation

Accreditation is the process of accountability by which an institution is recognized by the profession as meeting national standards for the content and operation of its teacher education program as well as for the performance of its candidates. In our world of fast-paced societal developments, rapid advances in technology, and shrinking political, economic, and cultural boundaries, we voice increasing anxieties about the preparation of America's youth and their survival in a competitive world. Is it any wonder, then, that we ask more of our schools? Why shouldn't we have the same trust in our teachers that we have placed in our doctors, scientists, and engineers? Is it because we know that this latter group of professionals has completed rigorous educational programs that have received an important academic seal of approval—accreditation by a recognized professional authority? States also promote quality assurance in these fields by only licensing graduates from accredited programs. Not so with teachers. Accreditation is not always a prerequisite for teacher licensure. Why should we expect less from teacher preparation programs than from other professional schools? Wouldn't such a system promote public confidence in our educational practitioners?

Accreditation is important because it (a) assures the public that institutions have met rigorous standards; (b) establishes common professional standards for preparation of teachers and other school personnel; (c) encourages excellence in curriculum, student performances, faculty, and resources in college and university units of education; (d) links national standards for teacher preparation with national standards for students; (e) ensures adequate resources to prepare quality personnel to improve students' learning; and (f) includes institutions in the profession's newly emerging quality-assurance system.

NCATE and Its Purposes

NCATE, formed in 1954, is a nongovernmental, nonprofit coalition of 33 national education organizations and members of the public—allied to advance quality in teacher preparation and teaching. NCATE accredits schools, colleges, and departments of education that produce America's teachers and other education specialists. This council is the sole education accrediting body recognized by the U.S. Department of Education and the Council for Higher Education Accreditation.

NCATE, as all professional accrediting bodies, derives its strength and legitimacy from the profession and the public it serves. That is why these 33 organizations representing those who teach in and operate PreK–12 schools, those who educate these teachers, and those public members who are committed to quality in education, work with NCATE to improve the quality of teachers for the benefit of our nation's children. NCATE is committed to working with its institutions to gather evidence that these teacher candidates are competent, caring, and well qualified as they move into the nation's schools.

NCATE, by way of its mission is to improve teacher preparation through the professional accreditation of colleges and universities that prepare teachers, acts as a lever for reform of colleges of education and serves as the mechanism that provides accountability to the public—especially the children whose lives are shaped in part by the quality of their teachers.

To promote high standards, NCATE

- sets and applies national standards for teacher preparation programs,

- encourages teacher preparation programs to reflect the latest knowledge and best practices,

- requires teacher education institutions to provide the necessary resources to provide the best preparation possible for the country's classroom professionals, and

- provides a seal of approval to those programs and institutions that meet its high standards.

Accreditation by NCATE is a voluntary process undertaken by those institutions that care enough about the quality of teacher education to commit to meeting NCATE's rigorous standards. NCATE currently accredits more than 500 institutions that prepare two thirds of the nation's teachers. Yet, there are about 1,200 institutions involved in teacher education. Where are the rest? Let me restate the challenge to institutions from the National Commission: If your institution is serious about preparing teachers, then take the necessary steps to become accredited.

Although the state has authority over all professional schools that prepare members of the professions that the state licenses, including schools of education, through the years, states have come to rely on national professional accrediting associations to carry out the state's responsibility for oversight of schools of medicine, law, and architecture, to name a few. In similar fashion, many states have begun to delegate the job of reviewing teacher preparation institutions to NCATE. Although the states retain their authority over professional schools, they see national professional accrediting associations that have the expertise to carefully review programs as resources that raise the quality of professional preparation. Increasingly, states look to NCATE to help them review teacher education programs. This allows states to place a greater focus on licensing. To date, 46 states have joined in partnership with NCATE to strengthen teacher preparation, program approval, and national accreditation.

NCATE is working with these states to raise standards for teacher preparation programs by developing partnership agreements to conduct joint reviews of schools of education; discussions are also underway with other states. The agreements are designed to mesh state and national professional expectations, eliminate duplication of effort on the part of the institution and the states, and save time and resources. In partnership states, institutions can gain state approval and NCATE accreditation simultaneously with a single process. The state decides the type of partnership it desires with NCATE. Although a few states use NCATE accreditation as a condition for state approval, accreditation in most partnership states is voluntary.

Benefits and Value-Added Aspects of NCATE Accreditation

There appear to be three major benefits for accredited institutions. First, NCATE is the teaching profession's stamp of approval. The institution gains the status and recognition that come with national professional accreditation and can market its school of education accordingly. Second, NCATE accreditation is a signal that the institution has met or exceeded professional standards of quality, created *by* the teaching profession and *for* the benefit of the nation's schoolchildren. Third, NCATE provides a framework for institutional planning, management, and evaluation. The standards are a tool that administrators and faculty find useful in carrying out the essential functions of managing programs within the professional education unit.

Institutions with NCATE accreditation add value to their candidates' education. NCATE-accredited colleges of education produce proportionately more qualified teachers than unaccredited institutions. *The Academic Quality of Prospective Teachers,* a recent study by Educational Testing Service (ETS; 1999), showed that graduates of NCATE-accredited teacher preparation programs pass ETS content examinations (e.g., PRAXIS II) for teacher licensing at a higher rate than do graduates of unaccredited colleges. In fact, teacher candidates who attend NCATE-accredited institutions boost their chances of passing the examinations by nearly 10 percent.

The AECT/NCATE Partnership

One of the most important outcomes of the 1986 NCATE redesign is that affiliated professional organizations are now responsible for individually guiding the review of their professional programs. To establish eligibility for initial accreditation evaluation by NCATE, an institution submits a preconditions report, which addresses a variety of areas ranging from governance to curriculum. One of those preconditions requires the institution to submit program review documentation for specific programs for which there are NCATE approved standards. As part of the NCATE review process, the role of the professional organization is to focus on the program review documentation. This documentation is, in effect, a description of the programs that prepare personnel in specialized fields and includes performances required of candidates as well as evidence of achievement of those performances. The continuing accreditation process is implemented every five years after initial accreditation and requires institutions to demonstrate ongoing compliance with NCATE standards and to address previously noted weaknesses.

The AECT Accreditation Committee trains and appoints qualified AECT members to review program review documentation of ECIT programs seeking accreditation. After NCATE receives the preconditions report, the program review documentation is separated and sent to the respective professional affiliates. In the case of AECT, the ECIT program reports are sent to the program review coordinator, who then distributes copies to three program reviewers who independently evaluate the strengths and weaknesses of the program. These reviewers also determine whether the program is in compliance with the standards. These individuals work alone, unaware of others reviewing the same program. This process ensures confidentiality and anonymity. After the three reviews are returned, the coordinator cross-checks the reviewer evaluations for consistency and consensus. The current level of consistency among the three reviewers is approximately 80 percent. Any institution that fails to provide sufficient information may be asked to resubmit the program review documentation or additional materials. After the coordinator ascertains compliance, a report of findings is sent to NCATE. These materials are used later by an NCATE on-site evaluation team from the Board of Examiners, which ultimately reports to the NCATE Unit Accreditation Board its evaluation of program/institutional compliance with NCATE standards.

AECT is responsible for reviewing two types of programs: initial programs in ECIT and advanced programs in ECIT. Authors of the earlier guidelines chose to use the term *media and technology,* whereas the newer term *educational communications and instructional technologies* reflects a broader representation of the field. This umbrella term provides for programs as diverse as multimedia, distance learning, computer technologies, instructional design, and library science.

Initial ECIT programs are defined as those that represent initial entry into the field. They are rooted in design and practice and, perhaps, could be likened to the knowledge, comprehension, and application stages of Bloom's taxonomy. Advanced ECIT programs are defined as those that represent additional study in the field. They emphasize theory, research, and higher-level management processes and, perhaps, could be likened to the analysis, synthesis, and evaluation stages of Bloom's taxonomy. For example, a baccalaureate or master's program that prepares individuals for either initial school certification or entry-level positions in business or industry may be considered an initial ECIT program. A graduate program (usually at the specialist or doctoral level) that advances knowledge and skills beyond the entry level for the profession constitutes an advanced ECIT program. Currently, ECIT initial programs are typically certification, licensure, or master's degree programs. It is anticipated that advanced candidates will also be able to demonstrate the competencies outlined in the initial program.

Looking Ahead

In looking ahead to the twenty-first century, NCATE, in its vision of performance-based accreditation, has moved forward in the development of standards and assessments that focus on teacher performance. Accreditation decisions will focus increasingly on the performance of the institution and its candidates and less on input and process measures. More emphasis will be placed on the quality of candidate work, subject matter knowledge, and demonstrated teaching skills. This focus on outcomes is a dramatic change and promises to provide more information to the public and the profession about the quality of teachers and other education personnel prepared by accredited institutions. "This information will be used to redesign and strengthen programs so that the nation's schoolchildren will reap the benefits of learning from better-qualified and more knowledgeable teachers" (Wise 1998).

In conjunction with this new perspective on accreditation, the AECT Accreditation Committee has revised the 1994 guidelines, developing new performance standards that are more directly linked with the knowledge base of our field (Seels and Richey 1994). These new standards were approved by the AECT Board in July 2000, and by NCATE in October 2000. This recently approved revision is available on the AECT Web site (http://www.aect .org). The Committee encourages ongoing input from technology professionals.

THE NEW AECT PERFORMANCE-BASED STANDARDS

The Knowledge Base for the Revised Standards[2]

The new AECT standards have been developed within the context of several years of effort to define the field of educational technology and to specify the knowledge base for the field. The general curriculum overview is based on *Instructional Technology: The Definition and Domains of the Field* (Seels and Richey 1994) and *The Knowledge Base of*

Instructional Technology: A Critical Examination (Richey et al. 1993). The *Instructional Technology* document provides a definition of the field and describes the domains and sub-domains of the field. The *Knowledge Base* document provides an in-depth examination of the knowledge base for each domain.

The standards are significantly changed from earlier versions that were based on roles and functions of instructional technology professionals. The new standards as well as the following definition of instructional technology prepared by the AECT Definitions and Terminology Committee are grounded in the research and theory of the field as described in the knowledge base of the field.

> Instructional Technology is the theory and practice of design, development, utilization, management, and evaluation of processes and resources for learning. . . . The words Instructional Technology in the definition mean a discipline devoted to techniques or ways to make learning more efficient based on theory but theory in its broadest sense, not just scientific theory. . . . Theory consists of concepts, constructs, principles, and propositions that serve as the body of knowledge. Practice is the application of that knowledge to solve problems. Practice can also contribute to the knowledge base through information gained from experience. . . . Design, development, utilization, management, and evaluation . . . refer to both areas of the knowledge base and to functions performed by professionals in the field. . . . Processes are a series of operations or activities directed towards a particular result. . . . Resources are sources of support for learning, including support systems and instructional materials and environments. . . . The purpose of instructional technology is to affect and effect learning. (Seels and Richey 1994, 1–9)

The knowledge base for the field is divided into five interrelated domains: design, development, utilization, management, and evaluation as shown in Figure 1, page 126 (Seels and Richey 1994, 21). Within each domain there are sub-domains that serve to describe each domain. For example, evaluation is divided into problem analysis, criterion-referenced measurement, formative evaluation, and summative evaluation.

The relationship among the domains shown in Figure 1 is not linear but synergistic. Although research may focus on one specific domain or sub-domain, practice, in reality, combines functions in all or several domains.

> For example, a practitioner working in the development domain uses theory from the design domain, such as instructional systems design theory and message design theory. A practitioner working in the design domain uses theory about media characteristics from the development and utilization domains and theory about problem analysis and measurement from the evaluation domain. (Seels and Richey 1994, 25)

Each domain also contributes to the other domains as well as to the research and theory shared by the domains.

> An example of shared theory is theory about feedback which is used in some way by each of the domains. Feedback can be included in both an instructional strategy and message design. Feedback loops are used in management systems, and evaluation provides feedback. (Seels and Richey 1994, 25–26)

The Definition and Terminology Committee has provided descriptions for each of the domains as well as for each of the sub-domains of the knowledge base.

Figure 1. Domains of the Field

Design refers to the process of specifying conditions for learning. . . . Development refers to the process of translating the design specifications into physical form. . . . Utilization refers to the use of processes and resources for learning. . . . Management refers to processes for controlling instructional technology. . . . Evaluation is the process for determining the adequacy of instruction. (Seels and Richey 1994, 24–43)

Standards for Initial Programs

The five standards represent the domains of the field. Supporting explanations and definitions are provided for each standard. In addition, for each standard, performance indicators are included in the full document but are not listed here. It is understood that programs, by their individual nature and focus, will vary in their concentration on each of the domains. The intent of the standards is to provide the maximum degree of flexibility enabling institutions to develop soundly conceived and defined programs.

Standard 1: Design

Candidates demonstrate the knowledge, skills, and dispositions to design conditions for learning by applying principles of instructional systems design, message design, instructional strategies, and learner characteristics.

Supporting explanations for design. "Design is the process of specifying conditions for learning" (Seels and Richey 1994, 30). The domain of design includes four sub-domains of theory and practice: Instructional Systems, Message Design, Instructional Strategies, and Learner Characteristics.

"Instructional Systems Design (ISD) is an organized procedure that includes the steps of analyzing, designing, developing, implementing, and evaluating instruction"(Seels and Richey 1994, 31). Within the application of this definition, *design* is interpreted at both a macro- and micro-level in that it describes the systems approach and is a step within the systems approach. The importance of process, as opposed to product, is emphasized in ISD. The following elements are included:

Analyzing: the process of defining what is to be learned and the context in which it is to be learned

Designing: the process of specifying how it is to be learned

Developing: the process of authoring and producing the instructional materials

Implementing: the process of actually using the materials and strategies in context

Evaluating: the process of determining the adequacy of the instruction

"Message design involves planning for the manipulation of the physical form of the message" (Seels and Richey 1994, 31). Message design is embedded within learning theories (cognitive, psychomotor, behavioral, perceptual, affective, constructivist) in the application of known principles of attention, perception, and retention, which are intended to communicate with the learner. This sub-domain is specific to both the medium selected and the learning task.

"Instructional strategies are specifications for selecting and sequencing events and activities within a lesson" (Seels and Richey 1994, 31). In practice, instructional strategies interact with learning situations. Instructional models often describe the results of these interactions. The appropriate selection of instructional strategies and instructional models depends on the learning situation (including learner characteristics), the nature of the content, and the type of learner objective.

"Learner characteristics are those facets of the learner's experiential background that impact the effectiveness of a learning process" (Seels and Richey 1994, 32). Learner characteristics impact specific components of instruction during the selection and implementation of instructional strategies. For example, motivation research influences the selection and implementation of instructional strategies based on identified learner characteristics. Learner characteristics interact with instructional strategies, the learning situation, and the nature of the content.

Standard 2: Development

Candidates demonstrate the knowledge, skills, and dispositions to develop instructional materials and experiences using print, audiovisual, computer-based, and integrated technologies.

Supporting explanations for development. "Development is the process of translating the design specifications into physical form" (Seels and Richey 1994, 35). The domain of development includes four sub-domains: Print Technologies, Audiovisual Technologies, Computer-Based Technologies, and Integrated Technologies. Development is tied to other areas of theory, research, design, evaluation, utilization, and management.

"Print technologies are ways to produce or deliver materials, such as books and static visual materials, primarily through mechanical or photographic printing processes" (Seels and Richey 1994, 37). Print technologies include verbal text materials and visual materials, namely, text, graphic and photographic representation and reproduction. Print and visual materials provide a foundation for the development and utilization of the majority of other instructional materials.

"Audiovisual technologies are ways to produce or deliver materials by using mechanical devices or electronic machines to present auditory and visual messages" (Seels and Richey 1994, 38). Audiovisual technologies are generally linear in nature, represent real and abstract ideas, and allow for learner interactivity dependent on teacher application.

"Computer-based technologies are ways to produce or deliver materials using microprocessor-based resources" (Seels and Richey 1994, 39). Computer-based technologies represent electronically stored information in the form of digital data. Examples include computer-based instruction(CBI), computer-assisted instruction (CAI), computer-managed instruction (CMI), telecommunications, electronic communications, and global resource /reference access.

"Integrated technologies are ways to produce and deliver materials which encompass several forms of media under the control of a computer" (Seels and Richey 1994, 40). Integrated technologies are typically hypermedia environments that allow for (a) various levels of learner control, (b) high levels of interactivity, and (c) the creation of integrated audio, video, and graphic environments. Examples include hypermedia authoring and telecommunications tools such as electronic mail and the World Wide Web.

Standard 3: Utilization

Candidates demonstrate the knowledge, skills, and dispositions to use processes and resources for learning by applying principles and theories of media utilization, diffusion, implementation, and policy making.

Supporting explanations for utilization. "Utilization is the act of using processes and resources for learning" (Seels and Richey 1994, 46). This domain involves matching learners with specific materials and activities, preparing learners for interacting with those materials, providing guidance during engagement, providing assessment of the results, and incorporating this usage into the continuing procedures of the organization.

"Media utilization is the systematic use of resources for learning" (Seels and Richey 1994, 46). Utilization is the decision-making process of implementation based on instructional design specifications.

"Diffusion of innovations is the process of communicating through planned strategies for the purpose of gaining adoption" (Seels and Richey 1994, 46). With an ultimate goal of bringing about change, the process includes stages such as awareness, interest, trial, and adoption.

"Implementation is using instructional materials or strategies in real (not simulated) settings. Institutionalization is the continuing, routine use of the instructional innovation in the structure and culture of an organization" (Seels and Richey 1994, 47). The purpose of implementation is to facilitate appropriate use of the innovation by individuals in the organization. The goal of institutionalization is to integrate the innovation within the structure and behavior of the organization.

"Policies and regulations are the rules and actions of society (or its surrogates) that affect the diffusion and use of Instructional Technology" (Seels and Richey 1994, 47). This includes such areas as Web-based instruction, instructional and community television, copyright law, standards for equipment and programs, use policies, and the creation of a system that supports the effective and ethical utilization of instructional technology products and processes.

Standard 4: Management

Candidates demonstrate knowledge, skills, and dispositions to plan, organize, coordinate, and supervise instructional technology by applying principles of project, resource, delivery system, and information management.

Supporting explanations for management. "Management involves controlling Instructional Technology through planning, organizing, coordinating, and supervising" (Seels and Richey 1994, 49). The domain of management includes four sub-domains of theory and practice: Project Management, Resource Management, Delivery System Management, and Information Management. Within each of these sub-domains, there is a common set of tasks to be accomplished: organization must be assured, personnel hired and supervised, funds planned and accounted for, facilities developed and maintained, and short- and long-term goals established. A manager is a leader who motivates, directs, coaches, supports, monitors performance, delegates, and communicates.

"Project management involves planning, monitoring, and controlling instructional design and development projects" (Seels and Richey 1994, 50). Project managers negotiate, budget, install information-monitoring systems, and evaluate progress.

"Resource management involves planning, monitoring, and controlling resource support systems and services" (Seels and Richey 1994, 51). This includes documentation of cost effectiveness and justification of effectiveness or efficiency for learning as well as the resources of personnel, budget, supplies, time, facilities, and instructional resources.

"Delivery system management involves planning, monitoring and controlling 'the method by which distribution of instructional materials is organized' . . . [It is] a combination of medium and method of usage that is employed to present instructional information to a learner" (Seels and Richey 1994, 51). This includes attention to hardware and software requirements, technical support for the users and developers, and process issues such as guidelines for designers, instructors, and ECIT support personnel.

"Information management involves planning, monitoring, and controlling the storage, transfer, or processing of information in order to provide resources for learning" (Seels and Richey 1994, 51). Information is available in many formats and candidates must be able to access and utilize a variety of information sources for their professional benefit and the benefit of their future learners.

Standard 5: Evaluation

Candidates demonstrate knowledge, skills, and dispositions to evaluate the adequacy of instruction and learning by applying principles of problem analysis, criterion-referenced measurement, formative and summative evaluation, and long-range planning.

Supporting explanations for evaluation. "Evaluation is the process of determining the adequacy of instruction and learning" (Seels and Richey 1994, 54). ECIT candidates demonstrate their understanding of the domain of evaluation through a variety of activities including problem analysis, criterion-referenced measurement, formative evaluation, and summative evaluation.

"Problem analysis involves determining the nature and parameters of the problem by using information-gathering and decision-making strategies" (Seels and Richey 1994, 56). ECIT candidates exhibit technology competencies defined in the knowledge base. Candidates collect, analyze, and interpret data to modify and improve instruction and ECIT projects.

"Criterion-referenced measurement involves techniques for determining learner mastery of pre-specified content" (Seels and Richey 1994, 56). ECIT candidates utilize criterion-referenced performance indicators in the assessment of instruction and ECIT projects.

"Formative evaluation involves gathering information on adequacy and using this information as a basis for further development. Summative evaluation involves gathering information on adequacy and using this information to make decisions about utilization" (Seels and Richey 1994, 57). ECIT candidates integrate formative and summative evaluation strategies and analyses into the development and modification of instruction, ECIT projects, and ECIT programs.

"Long-range planning that focuses on the organization as a whole is strategic planning. . . . Long-range is usually defined as a future period of about three to five years or longer. During strategic planning, managers are trying to decide in the present what must be done to ensure organizational success in the future" (Certo et al. 1990, 168). ECIT candidates demonstrate formal efforts to address the future of this highly dynamic field including the systematic review and implementation of current ECIT developments and innovations.

Standards for Advanced Programs

These standards for accrediting advanced programs in ECIT are built on the same definitions and domains as the standards for initial programs. Notice that the advanced standards also concentrate on the candidate's preparation in research, application of theory, and theory development within the field. Differences in expectations (from the initial standards) are obvious in the performances indicative of each stand. These may be viewed in the full document at http://www.aect.org.

Standard 1: Design

Candidates demonstrate the knowledge, skills, and dispositions to design conditions for learning by applying principles, theories, and research associated with instructional systems design, message design, instructional strategies, and learner characteristics.

Standard 2: Development

Candidates demonstrate the knowledge, skills, and dispositions to develop instructional resources and experiences by applying principles, theories, and research related to print, audiovisual, computer-based, and integrated technologies.

Standard 3: Utilization

Candidates demonstrate the knowledge, skills, and dispositions to use processes and resources for learning by applying principles, theories, and research related to media utilization, diffusion, implementation, and policy making.

Standard 4: Management

Candidates demonstrate knowledge, skills, and dispositions to plan, organize, coordinate, and supervise instructional technology by applying principles, theories, and research related to project, resource, delivery system, and information management.

Standard 5: Evaluation

Candidates demonstrate knowledge, skills, and dispositions to evaluate the adequacy of instruction and learning by applying principles, theories, and research related to problem analysis, criterion-referenced measurement, formative and summative evaluation, and long-range planning.

HOW IS PERFORMANCE-BASED PROGRAM REVIEW DIFFERENT FROM THE PREVIOUS AECT PROGRAM REVIEW?

The revised AECT standards represent a new approach to program review in NCATE's accreditation system. Three statements express the paradigm shift found in the new standards and program review. First, the standards describe what ECIT candidates should know and be able to do so that students learn. This contrasts with the previous course-based approach in which guidelines described what should be covered in courses and experiences in the program. Second, the evidence used for decisions about "national recognition" of programs is from assessments and evaluations of candidate proficiencies in relation to those standards. This contrasts with evidence, under the previous course-based approach, that described where particular material is covered in the syllabi and courses. Third, it is the responsibility of program faculty to make the case that candidates completing ECIT preparation programs are meeting the standards and to demonstrate how well candidates are meeting them.

WHAT SHOULD BE INCLUDED IN A SUBMISSION OF PERFORMANCE-BASED PROGRAM EVIDENCE?

The program report for an ECIT program must include a statement of context for the program along with information demonstrating candidate knowledge and skills relating to the AECT standards.

Context Statement

This statement creates an opportunity for the institution to provide background information that will assist reviewers' understanding of the candidate proficiency information. It should include the following:

- The conceptual framework for the program.

- Basic factual information about the program.

- Courses and experiences. (*Do not submit syllabi*, as previously requested. The title, description, objectives, and candidate tasks of each course would be sufficient. Web site addresses may be included with detailed syllabi. This information should explain how the candidates are provided opportunities to learn and practice the knowledge and skills contained in the AECT standards. You may submit this information in narrative or table format.)

- Description of the basis for faculty judgment that candidates are prepared to assume their professional responsibilities. (*Do not submit faculty vitae,* as previously requested. A summary including names, rank, tenure status, degrees, areas of specialization, and course responsibilities would be sufficient. Web site addresses may be included with detailed vitae. A table is attached for your convenience.)

- Descriptions of the specialized technology facilities, equipment, and nonfaculty staff.

- Descriptions of internships, practica, field, and clinical experiences.

- Relevant policies and practices affecting the institution's ECIT preparation, including any unique state requirements that may impinge on implementation of the AECT standards or on candidate performances, with an explanation of how the unit accommodates differences between NCATE and state standards.

- The program's own evaluation of its strengths, candidate proficiencies, and overall performance in relation to its mission and goals and in the context of the AECT standards.

- An overview of the program's assessment plan as a context for the performance evidence/data.

- Quality assurance processes used for ECIT preparation.

Performance Evidence

The performance evidence can be submitted as a narrative (each standard as a heading with the data and information in paragraph form) or in a matrix format (one column for the standard and one for the data)—*as long as the report connects performance data with each standard*. The following also must be performed:

- Candidate proficiency data from multiple sources must be aggregated and interpreted. Reviewers need to understand what the data say about the proficiencies of candidates through overall, summary descriptions.

- The relationship of the data to the program's goals and objectives must be articulated.

- The rubrics or criteria used to evaluate candidates' proficiency levels must be described.

- A few samples of candidate work representing the program's assessment criteria, some of which illustrate work at different levels of performance as defined by the institution, must be included.

CLARIFICATION OF APPROPRIATE NCATE STANDARDS

There are four sets of NCATE-approved specialty association standards related in some way to technology. The standards were created by the following associations:

- International Technology Education Association/Council on Technology Teacher Education (ITEA/CTTE)

- International Society for Technology in Education (ISTE)

- American Association of School Librarians (AASL)

- Association for Educational Communications and Technology (AECT)

The following guidelines are intended to help institutions decide which set of standards is appropriate for a particular program:

- Use ITEA/CTTE for programs preparing teachers for technology education that focuses on human innovations in communications, construction, manufacturing, and transportation (formerly known as vocational education programs).

- Use ISTE for endorsement programs preparing teachers of computer literacy and applications and endorsement/degree programs for secondary computer science teachers.

- Use AECT or AASL (or both, if you seek dual accreditation) for programs preparing school library media specialists.

- Use AECT for programs preparing educational personnel for positions in the broader arena of educational communications and instructional technology in areas such as K–12 education, higher education, business, industry, military services, government, and health/community services.

- Use either AECT or ISTE (or both, if you seek dual accreditation) for programs preparing K–12 technology leaders, technology specialists, and technology coordinators at the state, district, or building levels.

CONCLUSION

Members of the Accreditation Committee, in an attempt to be responsive to the profession, have initiated workshops to assist institutional representatives in the preparation of quality program review documentation. All institutions preparing for an NCATE review will be contacted by mail or e-mail and given the opportunity to take part in these workshops that will be held in conjunction with AECT's national conventions. In addition, periodic program reviewer training workshops will be scheduled at AECT conventions to increase the pool of qualified reviewers. All interested individuals should contact the committee chair, currently Kay Persichitte at the University of Northern Colorado at Greeley at persi@edtech.unco.edu.

AECT is a committed partner with NCATE in its belief that every child in America has the right to be taught by a well-prepared, qualified teacher. AECT, always a strong proponent of accreditation and licensure, has been a strong ally and supporter of NCATE for over 30 years. In recent action, AECT's Board of Directors reaffirmed its commitment to, partnership with, and acknowledgement of NCATE as *the* national organization that authorizes and accredits the professional programs that produce America's teachers and other education specialists. We call upon all such programs to seek national accreditation.

ACKNOWLEDGMENTS

The author acknowledges use of a variety of sources for this article in addition to the listed references: personal knowledge of the NCATE process, AECT standards documents, NCATE news releases, NCATE informational publications, and NCATE minutes, position papers, and board agenda notebooks.

NOTES

1. This introductory overview of AECT and NCATE has been used with permission from R. S. Earle. (2000), AECT and NCATE: A partnership for quality teaching through accreditation. *TechTrends*, 44:(3, 53–57.

2. This section and the sections containing the standards and the program report are used with permission from R. S. Earle, ed. (2000), *Standards for the accreditation of programs in educational communications and technology (ECIT)*. Washington DC: Association for Educational Communications and Technology.

REFERENCES

Bergeson, C. O. (1973). Accreditation of educational media personnel: A developmental look. *Audiovisual Instruction*, 19:3, 29.

Bingaman, J. (1998). Reviewing standards for teachers: An imperative. *Quality Teaching*. Washington DC: National Council for Accreditation of Teacher Education.

Certo, S. C., Husted, S. W., Douglas, M. E., and Hartl, R. J. (1990). *Business* (3d ed.). Boston: Allyn & Bacon.

Darling-Hammond, L. (1996). What matters most: A competent teacher for each child. *Phi Delta Kappa*, 78:3, 193–200.

Earle, R. S. (2000). AECT and NCATE: A partnership for quality teaching. *TechTrends*, 44:3, 53–57.

Earle, R. S., ed. (2000). *Standards for the accreditation of programs in educational communications and technology (ECIT)*. Washington DC: Association for Educational Communications and Technology.

Educational Testing Service. (1999). *The academic quality of prospective teachers*. Princeton, NJ.

Richey, R. C., Caffarella, E. P., Ely, D. P., Molenda, M., Seels, B., and Simonson, M. R. (1993, January). *The knowledge base of instructional technology: A critical examination*. Paper presented at the Annual Convention of the Association for Educational Communications and Technology, New Orleans.

Seels, B., and Richey, R. (1994). *Instructional technology: The definition and domains of the field*. Washington DC: Association for Educational Communicators and Technology.

What matters most: Teaching for America's future. (1996). New York: National Commission on Teaching and America's Future.

Wise, A. E. (1998). Accreditation and the profession. *Quality Teaching*, 8:1, 3.

ABOUT THE AUTHOR

Rodney S. Earle, professor of teacher education in the McKay School of Education at Brigham Young University in Provo, Utah, is AECT's liaison with NCATE and senior editor of the AECT standards. A past chair of AECT's Accreditation Committee, he has served as chair of NCATE's Specialty Area Studies Board and as a member of NCATE's Executive Board. He is currently a member of NCATE's State Partnership Board and the Coalition of Organizations for the Professional Preparation of Educators. Feel free to contact him at rodney_earle@byu.edu.

Part Two
Technology Centers and Institutes for Learning

Introduction

This section profiles centers and institutes that carry out extensive research and development in the field of instructional technology. A rationale for this section is that a large amount of the research dollars that are spent in our field are spent by these institutes. Therefore, if you want to get a sense for the kinds of important research and development that is occurring in the field, then a peek at the work being done in these centers and institutes provides that insight.

In the *Educational Media and Technology Yearbook,* Volume 25, we featured the Learning and Performance Support Lab at the University of Georgia and the Center for Technology Innovation in Education at the University of Missouri–Columbia. This time, we have chosen to feature the Concord Consortium and the Institute for Learning Technology at Columbia University. Both of these organizations are exciting to read about, and both are working hard to use media and technology to transform the teaching and learning experiences for many people.

The Concord Consortium is actively engaged in the kinds of research and development that have been a focus of the field for the past couple of years. They have worked on tools for learning that can be used in a problem- or projected-based approach in the classroom. Their hope is to transform learning from the acquisition of knowledge to the building of powerful mental models through the use of tools as scaffolding agents. Their work has revolved around some powerful tools, such as Probeware, Oslet, and Biologica. They have also begun to carefully examine online learning—a trend that is found throughout this book.

The Institute for Learning Technology at Columbia University is also interested in transforming the teaching and learning process, and their approach is to focus their work on real learners in real schools (primarily inner city schools in New York City). Their approach is more systemic in that they not only focus on the building of tools and teaching teachers how to use them, but they also focus on curricular integration and other large-scale political issues affecting the integration of technology and innovation into the schools. The idea that an entire institute is devoted to educational change for those who particularly need the change is refreshing, and the institute is doing it in a large-scale systemic way. They try to reach every level of an organization, from policy makers to individual learners to families to teachers to administrators.

You are welcome to nominate institutes or centers to be featured in this section. We are planning on featuring the Learning Technology Center at Vanderbilt and the Center for Highly Interactive Computing at the University of Michigan in subsequent volumes. Please direct any comments, questions, and suggestions about the selection process to the senior editor.

Michael Orey

The Concord Consortium, Inc.
Implementing the Educational Promise of Technology

Robert Tinker
President of the Concord Consortium, Inc.

WHO WE ARE

The Concord Consortium is a nonprofit corporation created in 1995 to improve education through innovative research, development, and implementations that exploit the educational potential of new technologies. We are interested in combining research with services that stimulate needed change in schools and informal settings, particularly those serving less-advantaged learners. A common thread of technology, innovation, social need, and potential impact runs through all of our work. To be able to generate innovations and support their implementation, we have assembled a creative staff with a variety of specialties, giving us the capacity to undertake large, complex projects requiring interdisciplinary teams.

The greatest impacts of information technologies on education will come through new technological tools, new distribution mechanisms, online courses, and innovative curricula that use these technologies. The Concord Consortium maintains ongoing programs in each of these areas.

TOOLS, MODELS, AND HYPERMODELS

In spite of the accelerating school acquisition of computers and networking, we have yet to see the revolution they could cause in learning. Information technologies have transformed the commercial sector, changing job functions, flattening hierarchies, and improving productivity. In contrast, education is largely unchanged by information technologies and primarily uses them to make slight improvements in current practices. We are, nevertheless, overdue for a surge in education performance driven by technology, as soon as educators are willing to make the necessary structural changes. Software tools are at the root of the transformation of business and hold the key to breakthroughs in education as well. To explore the transformational potential of powerful software tools, we are developing some important new modeling and computational applications and a unique architecture for these tools that we call hypermodels.

Software tools are general-purpose, flexible applications that users can apply to their specific interests and needs. In business, spreadsheets, presentation software, and communication tools have empowered workers to make decisions and marshal resources, and this has reduced the need for bureaucracy. Design tools have sped the development of new devices and software, increasing productivity. In education, tool applications have long been recognized as a major stimulus to increases in learning and productivity in all disciplines (Tinker and Papert 1989; Tinker 1990).

The probeware we have been developing for two decades is an example of an innovative technology-enabled educational tool. Probe software can access sensors and display data from them in real time, using a variety of representations. Over 40 kinds of sensors are currently marketed to education, allowing students to measure a wide range of inputs, including temperature, light, position, speed, acceleration, pH, dissolved oxygen, heart rate,

ECG, EEG, and much more. Probeware is an ideal general-purpose tool for student explorations in support of math, science, and technology (Tinker 1996).

We continue to improve probeware to make it more flexible and less expensive. We have pioneered the use of probes with inexpensive handheld computers[1] (Tinker and Krajcik 2001) and are now exploring the value of wireless networking between handhelds equipped with probes.[2] We are also working on "smart probes" that contain small computers that simplify their use.[3] One experimental probe we have developed has such sensitive inputs that a wide range of sensors can be directly attached to it, making it possible for students to build their own probes. The use of this probe would increase the range of projects students could undertake, increase their understanding, and save the cost of purchasing specialized probes.

The word *model* is used in many different and contradictory ways. We use the term to refer to a flexible program that incorporates approximations to some aspects of reality. This makes models a specialized kind of tool of particular interest to educators because students can, through exploration, construct their own understanding about the aspects of the real world that are captured in the model (Gobert and Buckley 2000). The software must be sufficiently flexible to allow students to learn about the model through exercising various options.[4] The model must also be sufficiently accurate so that the mental model that students construct through exploration is accurate and useful (Gobert 2000). No model will be completely accurate, so part of the instructional strategy used with the model must address epistemology, specifically, the strengths and limitations of the model and the validity of the conclusions drawn from the model (Gobert and Schwarz 2001).

Models based on fundamental concepts give students a new way to learn the interrelations between ideas, a way that is at the same time more profound and simpler.[5] To understand how this is possible, consider kinetic molecular theory, a topic commonly taught in middle school science. The usual approach is to introduce a series of postulates and then assert without proof that these postulates predict the gas laws. This approach leaves most students quite perplexed and gives them an inaccurate view of the theories, laws, and conduct of science.

A better alternative is to use a molecular dynamics model that connects the atomic and molecular interactions to the gas laws.[6] An excellent model can be built with Oslet, a general molecular dynamics engine under construction at the Concord Consortium.[7] Using this model, students can learn, through inquiry-based explorations, the relationships between pressure, temperature, and volume. The gas laws are obvious consequences of this system, as are phase change, latent heat, crystal structure, and much more. By going deeper into the underlying forces and using a model to connect these to macroscopic properties, students can understand many diverse topics that otherwise appear unrelated. This approach makes these topics easier to learn and more memorable. It also gives students more insight into the unity of science and its underlying principles.

Without computational modeling tools, the only way to relate atomic forces to emergent properties is through statistical mechanics. Molecular dynamics provides an alternative approach that is accessible to far younger students. The kinds of gains that are possible with a molecular dynamics model can be repeated in many areas of science, mathematics, and technology education and at all levels, K–12 and undergraduate. A few dozen tools of the depth of Oslet could address most topics in science, math, engineering, and technology education.

For example, BioLogica[8] is another modeling environment we have under development that simulates genetics at the molecular, genome, and individual level. When it has a planned population level and random mutation, BioLogica will be able to model selection and evolution as well.

Models and open-ended tools such as probeware could be the basis of a breakthrough in student learning because they provide an alternative and more accessible way of understanding abstract concepts. Instead of using complex formal methods, student understanding of fundamental ideas can be gained by interacting with a suitable tool or model. Deeper learning accessible to more students can be expected in all the sciences, mathematics, technical fields, quantitative social sciences, and business. Genetics, macroeconomics, chemical reactions, evolution, space shots, fire fighting, the stock market, global warming, epidemics, urban planning, and much more can be better understood through guided exploration of a model than by reading about them or trying to understand them through mathematics. Substantial gains in depth and breadth of understanding is possible from an approach based on tools and models (Tinker and Horwitz 2000).

Tool Scaffolding

Tools and powerful models have proven hard to use in education. Makers of educational tools have always had a problem: Do you produce a simplified version for the beginning learner or one with every conceivable feature for the expert? The stripped-down version is hard to sell because some other tool will have more features and get a better reputation. On the other hand, a full-featured tool is hard for teachers and students to master.

To make tools more effective in education, software designers often incorporate pedagogical strategies into the tool. One form of this is "scaffolding," a variety of helping strategies that fade away as the user becomes more expert. Context-sensitive help, an assistant-in-a-window, and tutorials are other strategies to address this problem.

We have developed an alternative design for educational tools that separates the tool from the pedagogical software. Using this architecture, the tool has no pedagogical strategy built into it. Instead, it has "hooks" to a second application that is designed for controlling tools to achieve learning objectives. We have built such a control program called Pedagogica. The combination of Pedagogica with a tool or model creates what we call a hypermodel, illustrated in Figure 1 (Horwitz 1996; Horwitz and Christie 1999).

Figure 1. A Hypermodel is a combination of a tool and Pedagogica, a control application. Pedagogica reads scripts written in EASL and produces student assessment data.

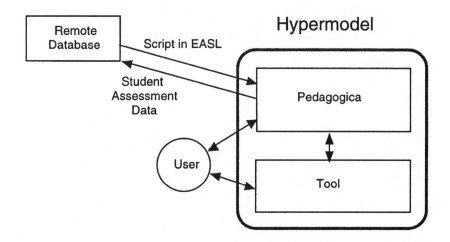

Pedagogica executes a script, written in EASL,[9] that controls how many of a model's options the user sees, sets the model's initial conditions, senses what users do with the model, and interacts directly with the user. By changing the script, Pedagogica can provide help, scaffolding, or the full-featured tool. Because the script can be changed over the Internet in real time, the educational strategy is not fixed and can be changed to adapt to the needs of the curriculum and the learning styles of students.

One of the benefits of a tool like Pedagogica is that it can provide embedded assessment. The script that controls what material is presented needs to make judgements about what to present. This requires assessment of student learning that can be embedded in the tasks. For example, consider the script that is used with a model of atoms in a box to teach that pressure and temperature are proportional under some conditions. The script can observe whether a student has considered enough conditions to make this prediction. It can suggest new conditions and then observe what generalizations the student makes. Watching and guiding this kind of problem solving will give the software detailed data on what the student knows and can do. These data are essential for the software to provide useful guidance, but they also provide invaluable assessment data. The software can tell what a student has done, how long it took, how many blind alleys were pursued, and how persistent these errors were.

NEW DISTRIBUTION MECHANISMS

In spite of their value, software tools are under-used in education. This is because of a number of factors, including the lack of funding for their development, the difficulty of marketing and maintaining them, their cost, and the difficulty of implementing them well. Current grant and commercial distribution arrangements are failing to provide the most useful kinds of educational software: large-scale tools with supporting educational materials.

Open source provides an alternative.[10] As in the case of Linux,[11] open source development of educational tools could unleash programming talent worldwide that no grant or company could afford. An online community could not only generate exciting new tools but also support them with continual improvements and fixes as new hardware and operating environments evolve. The open source community could also provide the related curriculum materials, professional development, and other resources needed for tool adoption and dissemination. An international educational open source movement could unleash the kind of global creativity that has created and expanded open source software for business. We hope to stimulate the development of the open source software tools needed in education.

A major structural change in education will be needed to take advantage of hypermodels based on fundamental ideas. Teachers will be needed who have a deeper understanding of their subjects and who know how to teach these concepts with the appropriate use of educational technologies. Educators at all levels will have to adjust to the increased learning that is possible, including the test makers, standards setters, colleges, and schools of education. Online courses for teachers and trainers can be an important teacher professional development vehicle. Online courses for students can accelerate change by disseminating improved materials and techniques while also creating competition that can stimulate change.

ONLINE COURSES

Since its inception, the Concord Consortium has been studying and improving online courses (Tinker and Haavind 1997).[12] We have found that effective online courses are able to engage learners at a distance in collaborative, activity-based learning, in small groups guided by trained facilitators. The best approaches use asynchronous, two-way technologies that rely on carefully designed activities, good evaluation strategies, and communities of learners facilitated by online discussions. They also take advantage of the computer for simulations, models, data collection, calculations, mentoring, and creations as appropriate. Well-designed online courses are at least as good as face-to-face courses and are usually more inclusive and better designed.[13]

We developed our methodology with the INTEC (International Netcourse Teacher Enhancement Coalition) project, a three-year teacher enhancement project that focused on the use of inquiry as a teaching strategy for mathematics and science at the secondary level.[14] We developed a rich, yearlong course that reached over 800 teachers. The course included new content and technologies in support of inquiry. Although large numbers of teachers were involved, the 20-person moderated discussion group was central to our design. Consequently, we needed to develop a way to train facilitators, first face to face and later entirely online. This online facilitator training has been an important success and has led to a popular book, *Facilitating Online Courses* (Collison et al. 2000).

Secondary education has lagged behind colleges and universities in using online courses because few schools have the incentives or resources to offer courses. Postsecondary institutions have strong financial incentives to increase income from tuition from distant students. In contrast, high schools are chartered to serve a community and cannot increase their income by enrolling students from other districts.

The answer for secondary education is to form cooperatives of schools to share expertise and online courses. This is the core idea in our Virtual High School (VHS) project that currently involves 200 schools.[15] We use the methodology developed in the INTEC project to teach teachers online to create and offer online courses. Each school that offers a course section can enroll 20 of their students in any of the 150 courses offered. Through almost five years of operation, we have demonstrated how such a cooperative can work. We have learned how to prepare teachers to offer online courses, how to keep standards high, and how to handle all the problems of scheduling, registration, orientation, and accreditation.

One of the most exciting current developments in teacher professional development is the use of interactive video case studies in online courses. The technology is nearing the capacity to handle video on demand, at least in short segments. This allows us to imagine that large numbers of videos of exemplary teaching could be made widely available. Online video case studies can be made highly interactive by linking them to lesson plans, typical student work, relevant standards and assessments, background content, expert commentary, teacher reflection, and moderated online discussion groups. As appropriate to the topics, there will be links to relevant tools, simulations, and implementation guidance. At any point, the user could stop, replay, jump ahead, or dive into the rich surrounding content.

We have begun to explore these ideas in a project funded by the Department of Education called Seeing Math.[16] With our partner TeachScape,[17] we are producing online case studies and short courses for teachers focused on grade four and five mathematics. We are hopeful that this project will demonstrate the power of interactive video case studies and short courses that use them.

The methodology for moderated asynchronous online courses with video has very broad applicability. Online courses using this design are less expensive than face-to-face instruction, more convenient, and able to reach learners anywhere and anytime. We currently are using them to extend the reach of a state-funded academy for math and science and to share the insights of the Center for Innovative Learning Technologies with graduate faculty in schools of education.

To share this methodology, we are offering "metacourses," online courses about online courses. For example, in the VHS course we have developed two metacourses that are central to the success of the project. The first is a yearlong, 125-hour course about designing, creating, and offering a VHS course. The second is a one-semester course on how to offer an online course. As part of a different project, we have developed Moving Out of the Middle, a popular course on facilitating online courses.

INNOVATIVE CURRICULA

The Concord Consortium sees many opportunities to use the power of technology to improve what is taught and to teach important but difficult concepts far earlier that previously thought possible. We are experimenting in several different curriculum areas including those described in the following sections:

Sustainable Development Education

We have a major project underway to explore ways of incorporating across the curriculum topics related to sustainable development. This involves students in thinking about the future, understanding their use of resources, and planning communities for sustainability. In conjunction with Cobb County Public Schools, we have developed technology-rich materials and online teacher professional workshops to address these complex ideas.[18]

The Macro-Micro Connection

Understanding the connections between the atomic-level interactions and macroscopic phenomena are central to much of physical science, chemistry, modern biology, and engineering. In spite of their centrality, these connections are ignored or poorly taught at the precollege level. We are developing dynamic modeling software and associated curriculum materials that permit students to learn these connections through exploration of highly visual models.

Genetics

The multiple levels of Mendellian genetics have proven hard for students to understand. We have developed and field tested a hypermodel environment that allows students to explore the relationships between DNA, genes, and phenotypes. We plan to expand this to include a population level and random mutations that can model evolution.

Flows

The idea that fluids and energy can flow is very hard for students to understand. By using new probes and visualizations we have developed ways to help learners understand temperature, heat flow, and related thermal phenomena. We are also exploring student understanding of flows in the mantle and atmosphere and models that help clarify how all these flows are related.

Middle School Science

We are using new probeware capacities to address the more difficult learning challenges of middle school science. The basic ideas of energy transformations and Newtonian dynamics are part of the middle school standards but often ignored or poorly taught. Using a new generation of sensitive probes and models we hope to come up with new approaches that are both feasible and powerful.

CONCLUSION

Information technologies have the potential of stimulating an educational revolution as they continue to drop in price, reshape society, and create new learning opportunities. Learners everywhere of all ages could be using information technologies to learn more and to realize their potential more fully. Before this can happen, there is a need for hardware and software that is better adapted to the needs of learners, for creative educational materials and strategies that take advantage of the power of technology, and for careful research that determines the value of these innovations. The Concord Consortium is pursuing all of these areas.

NOTES

1. http://www.concord.org/library/1999fall/untestedground.html

2. http://www.concord.org/library/1999fall/palm-computer.html

3. http://www.concord.org/library/2000fall/beam.html

4. http://www.concord.org/library/1998spring/smarterprobes.html

5. http://www.concord.org/library/2000winter/comp-models.html

6. http://www.concord.org/library/2000winter/atomic-scale.html

7. http://www.concord.org/%7Ebarbara/workbenchcc/workbench_index.html

8. http://www.concord.org/biologica/

9. EASL stands for Educational Application Scripting Language.

10. http://www.concord.org/library/1999spring/freeandopen.html

11. The best history of open source is "Open Sources: Voices from the Open Source Revolution" available online at http://www.oreilly.com/catalog/opensources/book/toc.html

12. http://www.concord.org/library/1997spring/profdev.html

13. http://vhs.concord.org/Pages/About+Us-Project+Evaluation

14. http://intec.concord.org/

15. http://vhs.concord.org

16. http://www.concord.org/seeing_math/

17. TeachScape will market the fully interactive version. See http://teachscape.com

18. http://csf.concord.org/esf/

REFERENCES

Collison, G., Elbaum, B., Haavind, S., and Tinker, R. (2000). *Facilitating online learning: Effective strategies for moderators*. Madison, WI: Atwood Publishing.

Gobert, J. (2000). A typology of models for plate tectonics: Inferential power and barriers to understanding. *International Journal of Science Education, 22*:9, 937–977.

Gobert, J., and Buckley, B. (2000). Special issue editorial: Introduction to model-based teaching and learning. *International Journal of Science Education, 22*:9, 891–894.

Gobert, J., and Schwarz, C. (2001). *The role of students' epistemologies in learning with models*. Center for Innovative Learning Technologies Seed Grant; Awarded December, 2000.

Horwitz, P. (1996). Linking models to data: Hypermodels for science education. *The High School Journal, 79*:2, 148–156.

Horwitz, P., and Christie, M. (1999). Hypermodels: Embedding curriculum and assessment in computer-based manipulatives. *Journal of Education,* 181:2, 1–23.

Tinker, R. (1990). Computer based tools: Rhyme and reason. In E. F. Redish and J. S. Risley (eds.), *Computers in physics education.* Reading, MA: Addison-Wesley.

Tinker, R., ed. (1996). *Microcomputer-based labs: educational research and standards.* Berlin: Springer-Verlag.

Tinker, R., and Haavind, S. (1997) Netcourses and Netseminars: Current practice and new designs. *Journal of Science Education and Technology,* 5:3, 217–224.

Tinker, R., and Horwitz, P. (2000). *Modeling across the curriculum.* IERI Planning Grant (NSF#REC-0089198) funded by the National Science Foundation.

Tinker, R., and Krajcik, J., eds. (2001). *Portable technologies: Science learning in context.* New York: Kluwer Academic/Plenum Publishers.

Tinker, R., and Papert, S. (1989). Tools for science education. In J. Ellis (ed.), *Information technology & science education.* Columbus, OH: AETS.

Relevance and Scale
Challenges to the Institute for Learning Technologies

Robbie McClintock
Director, Institute for Learning Technologies
Teachers College, Columbia University

At the turn of the century, a new strategic context for educational policy and practice emerged. Government, corporations, and philanthropies are investing substantial resources, opening access to information and research for broad use in schools, colleges, and universities, and through libraries and other cultural and public service institutions. These large initiatives, together with secondary public and private funding, will invest many billions of dollars in information technology and its cultural uses over the coming decade. To achieve the educational and cultural potential of such investment, educators need to step to the forefront of the effort, asserting leadership and taking responsibility for initiative.

In the twenty-first century, information and knowledge will arbitrate the fate of both individuals and institutions, and, more than ever, an enlightened citizenry will need to be intellectually empowered to provide for the common good. New communications technologies are facilitating once hard to practice pedagogies—learning by doing, inquiry-based education, project methods, autonomous study; in short, educators' great humanistic hopes and unfulfilled progressive aspirations. These have been the aspirations of the enlightenment tradition and the Institute for Learning Technologies (ILT) believes that in the twenty-first century Teachers College and Columbia University should and will be at the vanguard of their historical fulfillment. Toward this end, the Institute seeks to advance four basic objectives:

- **Technology configuration**—ILT seeks to configure advanced technologies in everyday educational settings, especially inner-city schools, to support constructivist curricula and pedagogies.

- **Curriculum innovation**—ILT acts to promote the reconfiguration of knowledge into an integrated, comprehensive resource, open to all, for bringing ideas and understanding to bear in the conduct of life.

- **Professional development**—ILT works to help teachers adapt to a setting in which students will exert substantial control over their educational work and have direct electronic access to all the resources of their culture and in which teachers will exercise influence primarily by posing powerful questions and by guiding student inquiry toward the frontiers of knowledge, understanding, and reflective practice.

- **Policy formation**—ILT aims to sustain public policy initiatives that rally broad coalitions of interested parties from academe, government, and industry committed to transforming education through the astute use of information and communications technologies.

This mission is stable. How we pursue it is not. During the period of 2001 through 2002, the Institute is going through a reexamination of our operational objectives, seeking greater relevance to work more effectively in a context in which the scale of initiative rapidly escalates.

During the 1990s the long-range transformation of education was in a nascent stage. Technologies were immature and the infrastructure available in schools was insufficient. How educators could use a good infrastructure to support educational reform and improvement was not clear. The situation called for limited, exploratory projects. Accordingly, ILT's operational objectives concentrated on funding and implementing multischool exploratory research and demonstration projects linking classrooms through school local area networks (LANs) to the Internet via high-speed connections and working with teachers and students to develop effective ways to improve educational experience through the use of these resources. Through these projects, ILT has pioneered in finding ways to bring higher education, with its deep cultural resources, into fuller interaction with students in our schools.

Our emergent project-based experience began in 1990–1991 when the Dalton Technology Project began—a four-year, multimillion-dollar effort to integrate networked multimedia resources throughout the educational work of a leading independent school in New York City. Subsequently, this project, which centered in an elite private school, led to a series of efforts in inner-city public schools. In 1994, ILT won funding for the Harlem Environmental Access Project, a two-year collaboration with the Environmental Defense Fund and five inner-city schools, supported by the Telecommunications and Information Infrastructure Assistance Program. Shortly thereafter, ILT developed the Living Schoolbook Project, a three-year collaboration with the Syracuse School of Education, involving the five schools, plus two more in New York City and more in Syracuse and its environs, subsidized by NYNEX (now Verizon, via Bell Atlantic) and the New York State Science and Technology Foundation. In 1996–1997, ILT conducted the Reinventing Libraries Project, a pilot program to redefine the role that school libraries can play in sustaining the curriculum with advanced media resources, sponsored by the IBM Corporation. In 1996, ILT designed the Eiffel Project and has managed it in partnership with the Center for Collaborative Education on behalf of the New York City Board of Education, funded through a five-year $7.8 million U.S. Department of Education Challenge Grant for Technology in Education. This project uses advanced media to support small schools reform in approximately 70 New York City schools and community-based organizations (CBOs).

These projects have provided ILT with a useful core of experience with attempts to use new media as transformative forces in education. With respect to technology configuration, we have learned that it is possible to get a lot of equipment operational in schools and community organizations, but it is a challenge to reach the point where it becomes integral to the educational work taking place, not merely an appliqué on the surface of existing educational arrangements. With respect to curriculum innovation, we found a vast range of possibilities hindered by some fundamental tensions that arise within the classroom, where the standards movement and high-stakes testing push teachers and students to concentrate on a much more narrow agenda while networked, interactive technologies open the potential discourse to greater diversity in depth. With respect to professional development, we are ever more mindful of the time constraints that bind teachers and the importance of reaching a point where the technology ceases to be an added object of professional development, a further demand on time, and becomes instead a means of efficient action and professional development; one that loosens the constraints under which teachers work. With respect to policy formation, we are increasingly aware that the educational potentialities of information technologies cannot be achieved by working within the school building and school day alone, for the technology is most beneficial when it operates as a linking empowerment permitting home, community, and school to interact in support of each person's cultural and civic aspirations.

Relative to what can and should be, ILT's exploratory projects, along with all others that we have seen, are far from having demonstrated the actual fulfillment of the educational possibilities that people expect educational technologies to enable. Despite this lack of fulfillment, the current juncture is such that we must rethink our course substantially. In essence, the situation in the world of practice is changing very rapidly, and the role that demonstration projects in one or a few schools may perform is fast disappearing. It is not that school-based action and innovation is becoming unimportant; it is all the more so, but not as privileged demonstrations but as part and parcel of the responsibility, incumbent on every school, to provide the best possible educational experiences for its students. Ready or not, full-scale implementation of information and communications technologies is coming to all levels of education, to every school, to each home, throughout the whole community. With that full-scale implementation, everyone needs to exercise great effort and imagination to make it work well. In this context, however, with educational technology becoming pervasive, the scale of the action and innovation in which groups such as ILT operate greatly grows, and the character of our work needs to change in response.

Contemplate the indicators of change in the technological context embedded in our recent experience working in New York City schools. In the spring of 1996, ILT wrote the proposal for the Eiffel Project as a break-the-mold challenge grant, setting for the project what—to our surprise—turned out to be rather modest infrastructure goals. Between 1996 and 2001, the project proposed to install T1 lines into approximately 70 participating schools and CBOs, with that connectivity to be distributed to classrooms via school-wide LANs, with workstations for the teacher and for students in small groups of five or so in participating classes. Our primary purposes concerned the educational uses of this infrastructure, especially the curriculum changes it made possible and the professional development challenges that came with the feasibility of different curricular and pedagogical arrangements.

Although achieving the substantive deepening of curricula and supporting teachers effectively has proven to be difficult under urban school conditions, movement toward the transformation of technological infrastructures has accelerated far beyond our expectations in 1996. In our field of experience, the actual situation in each school varies considerably according to the complex realities of people and their spaces, but our project approximated its infrastructure model faster than expected. About midway in the project, a variant of the model became the official objective of the New York City school system, and incorporation of the technology into the system has taken on a life of its own quite independent of demonstration projects such as Eiffel.

Now, full-scale technology deployment is near at hand. In the context of the startling rise of the Internet, the public and its leaders have made some important inferences from the numerous demonstration projects in the schools during the 1990s. They infer that the massive deployment of information and communications technologies is quite feasible. They also infer that the educational benefits of digital technologies are not fully realizable without its full-scale, pervasive deployment. In addition, in places such as New York City, where few expect public education to flourish under a regimen of business as usual, there is a readiness to try aggressive interventions. Hence, as the Eiffel Project is ending, the New York City Board of Education is setting its sights on a startling extension of basic technology goals in the expectation that it may thus turn a faltering system into one that again becomes capable of exemplary achievement.

Toward this end, at the start of 2001 the Board publicized an ambitious request, which sought partners for a pervasive, citywide effort to

- Architect, build, implement, and maintain an Internet portal for the entire Board of Education community.

- Develop and execute a plan for deploying Internet or computing appliances and Internet connections (for use both at school and home) to students, teachers, and other members of the BOE [board of education] community, including training.

- Implement a revenue-generating business model to help finance the development of this portal as well as the procurement and deployment of Internet appliances and connections. (New York City Board of Education 2001).

With this request, New York City is seeking thorough educational improvement, system wide, through the full-scale deployment of educational technology in home, school, and community. The project aims to equip and engage each student and teacher in the system with anytime, anyplace connectivity to the Internet and to provide via the Board portal for all the cultural and pedagogical resources to support all educational needs of the entire citywide public school community—more than 1.1 million students, more than 80,000 teachers and staff, and approximately 2.2 million parents, guardians, and caregivers. This project aims to use information and communications technologies as essential resources in the full education of each child, reforming the process of student learning by accomplishing important goals. Toward this end, the project will

- Provide access to the Internet to drastically increase student exploration of the educational resources of the Internet, thereby empowering students to enhance their learning abilities and better prepare themselves for school-based instruction. Students' learning abilities will be greatly accelerated by the vast educational resources and numerous opportunities presented on the Internet, such as search engines, electronic libraries, multi-media presentations, live performances or lectures, and current advances in scientific research.

- Place Internet technology firmly in the hands of all students, teachers and administrators to allow the Board to better facilitate collaborative work and research by both students and teachers.

- Connect both students and teachers to the Internet inside and outside classroom settings, improving teachers' ability to facilitate instruction to meet the needs of the varying learning styles and paces of their students, therefore allowing immediate implementation of teaching standards in a technological environment.

- Encourage increased interactivity and communication within the Board of Education's learning communities through the use of e-mail, Web pages, and electronic bulletin boards. The portal will also enable stronger ties between parents, teachers, students, administrators, and corporate partners.

- Allow for the rapid dissemination of current and future BOE information and relevant content quickly and easily. (New York City Board of Education 2001)

In May 2001 the Board received approximately a dozen responses from coalitions of powerful potential partners, and these are under evaluation now with the intention that work on the project will start before the year is over and unfold through this decade into a basic transformation of how public education works.

New York City's project includes a radical method of financing, which may or may not succeed, and if it does not, the move to full-scale deployment of educational technology throughout the city will be delayed. Yet it is a fair probability that during the first decade of the twenty-first century, system-wide initiatives like the one New York has proposed will start to be implemented the world around, drastically changing the scale of work with technology and education. This prospect poses a significant challenge for innovative groups such as the Institute for Learning Technologies. Groups such as ILT, which could take on large projects such as Eiffel, more or less sufficient for the task, are completely incommensurate with the scale of innovation that is beginning to unfold. The Board portal will encompass a comprehensive digital library and set of knowledge tools, providing a school community of more than 1.1 million children, ages 5 through 18, and more than 80,000 teachers and staff, along with the entire constituency of both groups, with all the educational resources it might need. Costs will be in the several hundred millions. This scale of innovation is simply incommensurate with the scale of action in which groups such as ILT can engage. What, then, if anything, should be the prospective role of ILT in the ensuing efforts to integrate digital technologies into educational practice?

ILT is in the midst of considering this question. With respect to our internal organization, different members of our group have interests in diverse possible answers. At this point, it is premature to say that here is what we intend to do in answer to the question. Instead, what follows constitutes some reflections within our process of examining it. In examining this problem of scale, let us set aside for now the four specific components of ILT's stable mission—technology configuration, curriculum innovation, professional development, and policy formation. To know what we can and should do in each of these areas, we may need to look behind them, so to speak, to find what will be at issue as whole school systems shift their entire operation to a primary base in information and communications technologies.

Fundamental changes bring more than new ways of achieving established purposes. In addition, fundamental changes act to transform the established purposes. It is important for different groups to attempt to explain those transformations of purpose and to elucidate the significance of those transformations for practical work in the field. Prospectively, it will not be evident which group has it right, but over time, some interpretations of the transformation will wax in influence, while others will wane. Through this interaction between alternative interpretations, over time, a new consensus about controlling purposes may emerge. From its outset, ILT has advanced basic views about the purposes of education and the significance of new media for them. An element of our work, as the scale of technology and education initiatives expands, may involve an effort to chart how changing technologies affect the controlling purposes of the system.

Consider an example. Through much of its work, ILT has tried to call attention to the fact that students are the primary recipients of investment in information and communications technologies in education. We think that equipping students with powerful tools may establish the material conditions for significant pedagogical changes, namely a wholesale change from a pedagogy of instruction to one of construction. Currently, the dominant educational activity in schools consists of instruction. Modern school systems have been built as large-scale systems for the delivery of instruction. Throughout the twentieth century, educational research concentrated on improving the methods of instruction, and the lesson, in one or another variant, has served as the primary opportunity for teachers to impart instruction to the young. Instruction locates the educative agency in the teacher and the formal curriculum and characterizes education as a causally effective transmission from the instructor to the learner, a receptive student. This teacher-centered quality in instruction is captured well in the following definition of instructional method by an influential theorist—instructional methods consist in "the provision of cognitive processes or strategies that are necessary for learning but which students cannot or will not provide for themselves" (Clark 1994, 27; cf. Clark and Estes 1999, 10). Most educational effort deployed in the twentieth century implements this idea that schools must use instruction to provide the input necessary for learning that students cannot or will not provide for themselves.

The deployment of digital technologies in education does not change greatly the amount or power of the instruction that schools and teachers can deliver to students. Lesson planning is a well-developed tradition, and the school has long optimized its schedule to permit the delivery of many lessons to its pupils. Online libraries of teacher-reviewed lesson plans may marginally improve the average quality of lessons delivered across the curriculum in the aggregate of the classrooms around the world. But the promise of educational technology lies neither in increasing the amount of instruction delivered nor in making it significantly more effective in transmitting knowledge, skill, and value to the receptive student. Students, not teachers, are the primary users of information and communications technologies in education. For each agent in a classroom providing what students cannot or will not provide for themselves, there are approximately 25 agents providing what students can and will provide for themselves. Educational technology primarily alters the capacities of this latter, student-driven, educative agency. If instruction denotes input needed for learning that students cannot and will not provide, construction denotes activities that students can and will provide, and construction in this sense is not a constant but a very significant variable. What students can and will provide themselves can greatly increase with improved guidance, resources, feedback, and stimulation.

Great educators have always worked by driving, challenging, and moving students to test and expand what they can and will provide for themselves. We remember and love, not those teachers who taught us the most, but those associated with our own awakenings to intellectual efficacy; those who conspired in our taking possession of our own education; those who triggered sustained independent effort, who provoked our resistance, who demanded our taking responsibility for our learning, our capacities, and our convictions. As digital technologies empower students to become more effective in their educative role, so the role of teachers, as they work within the system, changes. Teachers, working as Socratic subversives, have always conspired with students, within the interstices of instruction, to see how far the students can carry their learning. And within a system optimized for construction the best way to expand what students can and will do for themselves will be to put powerful questions to them, to confront them with the Socratic awakening that they know they do not know, and to equip them with powerful resources for pursuing knowledge in response.

Initiatives such as that underway in New York City are transformative because they depart fundamentally from the past premise of instructional primacy:

> To date, the Board has focused its efforts on ways to integrate new computer and information technology in the classroom by using a teacher-and-school directed model for technology integration. Using this approach, teachers and administrators have decided how and when students should have access to computer technology for educational use. Further, they have largely determined the pace of student learning about the educational resources available on the Internet and how such resources could be best used to promote high levels of academic achievement. With this initiative, the Board seeks a new paradigm for student use of information technology, whereby students can help integrate the use of technology into their learning through their self-guided exploration, study and review of the Internet's educational content. The end result of this initiative is to advance the Board's goal of creating a more technologically proficient community that will maximize the learning environment of teachers, students and citizens. (New York City Board of Education 2001)

Thus, the change in scale is also a transformation of type. Study—what students can and will do for themselves—will be a concern at least as large as that of instruction—what students cannot and will not do for themselves. And the role of teachers will be not only that of instructor, planning and delivering lessons, but equally, perhaps predominantly, that of educator, putting and pursuing questions in the company of others.

In this transformation, we are beginning to see a role that the Institute for Learning Technologies can develop, commensurate with our scale and our commitment to fundamental change in education. In the midst of transformative change, assumptions about evaluation and educational research, along with much else about education, must come into question. Educators have developed practices of summative and formative evaluation, along with much of the structure of educational research, to assess whether innovations, large and small, are sound and worthwhile. Predominantly, this research and assessment proceeds via one or another means of comparing the cost of a specific incremental change with the associated benefit that derives from it. At ILT, we are beginning to contemplate the problem of research and evaluation in which the link between before and after may not permit direct comparison. This work may lead us beyond summative and formative evaluation, introducing a third type—transformative evaluation.

Methods of research appropriate in times of incremental change may not work in the midst of transformative change. The shift from incremental to transformative change in historical situations is like a change of state in physics, most familiar when water boils. Methodologically, the assumptions on which educational research and evaluation has rested are akin to the observational expectations associated with heating liquid water—as one adds (or subtracts) increments of heat to the water one should observe a direct correlation with increases or decreases in its temperature. Of course, as the temperature of the water reaches the boiling point, this correlation breaks down and during a latency period added heat seems to do nothing, with the temperature staying steady and anecdotal evidence occurring to observers in the form of visual reports, suggesting that the water is becoming more active, as if it is beginning to stir itself in randomly distributed places. Further input of heat continues to leave the temperature steady, while the water starts to boil, with steam vapor escaping subsequently at a rate commensurate with the input of heat.

People have considerable experience with a change of state in boiling water, in both the laboratory and mundane life. Hence, the characteristics of the changed state, that is steam, are generally familiar, easy to anticipate before a particular pot of water may begin to boil. A historical transformation, which we experience taking place in our collective present, differs significantly, for we do not know much about the changed state that will follow from the transformation. In a transformative situation, neither formative nor summative evaluation is particularly feasible. In a transformative situation, what people need instead is transformative evaluation that tries to identify and understand the essential characteristics of the condition that the transformation is ushering in. The claim above, suggesting that pervasive use of information technologies will create a change in the role of the teacher from the planner of lessons to the putter of questions, might be taken as an initial hypothesis in such an effort at transformative evaluation. Our current questioning, as the scale of work with technology and education mounts, aims at developing procedures for generating, testing, and disseminating in useful ways, a transformative evaluation of the full-scale implementation of information and communications technologies in education. In the future, we would like to be an active center for the transformative evaluation of an emergent technology-based system of educational work.

CONCLUSION

In sum then, we anticipate continuing to develop projects at a scale commensurate with our size, within the context of full-scale, system-wide implementation of technology in education. In ILT's projects, we will continue to devote attention to the areas of technology configuration, curriculum innovation, professional development, and policy formation. Our aim in these will no longer be to demonstrate interesting possibilities but rather to describe and analyze how the emerging educational practices differ from the characteristics of the status quo ante. It is meaningless to compare two different states to each other, seeking to declare one better, more effective, more efficient than the other. They are different.

What we need to know are the defining characteristics of the new state. We need to discover what range of conditions are possible within it and what options we have for bringing the better conditions within that new state to fulfillment. Toward this end, ILT will continue to work in New York City schools and communities in pursuit of this knowledge.

REFERENCES

Clark, R. E. (1994). Media will never influence learning. *Educational Technology Research and Development,* 42:2, 27.

Clark, R. E., and Estes, F. (1999). The development of authentic educational technologies. *Educational Technology*, XXXIX:2, 10.New York City Board of Education. (2001). Educational Portal and Internet Appliance/Computer Laptops (REQUEST FOR PROPOSAL: Serial No. RFP # 1B548). [Online]. Available: http://www.nycenet.edu/whatsnew/rfp/RFP1B548.htm (Accessed June 9, 2001).

Part Three
School and Library Media

Introduction

In the year 2001, several themes were prominent in the landscape of the school library media profession. Intellectual property rights and educational reform have been featured in legislative action over the past year, and both movements have important implications for school library media specialists. A national shortage of library media specialists continues, as it likely will for years to come. In response, many library education programs are mounting distance learning initiatives. The 2000 census revealed increasing diversity in the American ethnic makeup, a trend that has important implications for educational materials. Technology continued to stride forward, producing a world in which every person, institution, and corporate entity wants an identity on the World Wide Web. Although it seemed that professionals everywhere were caught up in the urgent need to produce electronic materials, it is important to pause and consider the quality and implications of the materials that are now so easily and quickly produced. In this atmosphere, information literacy continued to be of vital importance as educators strove to enhance the information skills of their students. These disparate but current trends all have a powerful influence on the way that media centers operate, and their very disparity reflect the varied nature of the roles of the media specialist. The chapters in this section touch upon each of these important trends.

The past 18 months have been marked by increasing controversy in the area of intellectual property and copyright. The Napster Web site, which before court action allowed millions of Internet users to share digitized music without purchasing it, stimulated debate between people who felt that users should be able to take advantage of the ability of sharing intellectual property when technology enables it and producers who naturally want to protect their commercial rights. Although unrelated to the Napster case at the surface level, the Uniform Computer Information Transactions Act (UCITA) movement shares this same idea with the Napster case. If adopted by each of the 50 states, UCITA will allow software producers substantially greater ability to protect their copyrights, possibly to the detriment of practices that were considered fair use by educational entities in the past. In her chapter "The Uniform Computer Information Transactions Act (UCITA): More Critical for Educators Than Copyright Law?" Vicki Gregory describes the proposed law and explores its implications for libraries.

Kathy Brock and Elizabeth Bennett explore another legal trend in their chapter "Redefining Professional Growth: New Attitudes, New Tools." Focusing on the case of state-level educational reform in Georgia, they consider controversial, mandated reform from the practical and constructive perspective of professional development. Many Georgia reforms initiated in 2000 focused on the improvement of the teaching force. Although many teachers felt singled out unfairly as a cause of Georgia's educational problems, mandates encouraging a more capable teaching force can be seen as a positive influence. Brock and Bennett explore the effects of this legislation on the school library media community, where the abandonment of state standards for media programs has caused library media specialists to find alternative, powerful strategies for supporting their programs.

Shu-Hsien Lai Chen discusses another important national trend in her chapter "Diversity in School Library Media Center Resources." Census figures from the year 2000 indicate a rapidly growing degree of diversity in the United States, especially among Hispanic people. During the past decade, the ethnic and cultural makeup of American demographics shifted dramatically from a two-race configuration in many parts of the country to a multiethnic one. For the most part, schools have been concerned about serving the linguistic needs of students who speak English as a second language, if at all. Chen argues that school library media programs must likewise respond by increasing the diversity of their collections to reflect the cultural and ethnic makeup of the school. This position, long espoused by the American Library Association, is now more important than ever, and media specialists must reconsider it in light of new demographics. Chen discusses the many issues revolving around multicultural materials, suggests strategies for improving school library collections, and provides a bibliography of helpful materials.

While Chen explores children's literature from a critical stance, focusing on thematic material found in texts, Marsh turns to digital images in her chapter "Image-Text Relationships in Web Pages." Her research is based on a theory rooted in visual literacy: That the juxtaposition of text and images in a medium can present a powerful message through the combination of meaning they provide. This chapter reminds media specialists of the importance of examining the combination of text and images in materials they select, as well as in materials they produce for students and teachers to consume. Marsh explores Web images of particular interest to K–12 communities, providing a framework to examine these figures critically. As our technological ability to include images as a common part of most types of communication increases, such consideration is warranted and important. The ability to decode nontextual images is an important part of information literacy, and Marsh's framework describes much of the sublingual information that images can produce.

Along the lines of professional development, another important continuing trend is the national shortage of media specialists. In response to this shortage, many graduate programs have initiated distance learning initiatives to help reach potential media specialists who may have difficulty accessing required course work in the traditional manner. By now, several programs have existed long enough for efficacy data to have accumulated. One finding of many studies has been that distance education typically produces a high dropout rate, ranging from 40 to 60 percent. In a climate of shortages, this problem is one that library educators particularly want to avoid. In "Aiming for Effective Student Learning in Web-Based Courses: Insights from Student Experiences," by Joi L. Moore, Kyung-Sun Kim, and Linda R. Esser, the authors explore a distance library education course through the eyes of the students, focusing on their attitudes. The results of their study are instructive for all library educators who provide distance education or for those considering doing so.

The authors of these chapters were invited to write for the *Yearbook* on the basis of presentations made at important professional and research conferences during the past year. These chapters represent research and thinking that together exemplify the important trends and developments in the library media field this year. We hope that readers will find information to inform their practice within them.

Mary Ann Fitzgerald

The Uniform Computer Information Transactions Act (UCITA)
More Critical for Educators Than Copyright Law?

Vicki L. Gregory
School of Library and Information Science
University of South Florida

The personal computer and Internet revolution of the past dozen years or so has exponentially increased the dependence of scholars and teachers on electronic resources. This new and essentially universal "fact of life" means that educators of all types in all countries and at all levels must become aware of and understand the different legal environment in which they now must function. In the past perhaps the most important way in which scholarship was juristically impacted was through the application of the concepts and law of copyright to the works examined and used by scholars. This obvious concern arose almost from the time of the introduction of the printing process in the fifteenth century, which revolutionized Western thought and learning by making practically obtainable by means of a mass duplication process of printing the intellectual works that had previously been available only through the laborious and self-limiting process of hand-copying in the dusty scriptoria of monastic institutions. But the printing process was always circumscribed to a significant degree by the physical limitations that the medium of paper and the physical form of the book itself imposed. Although much cheaper than a hand copy, books nevertheless always presented a production and reproduction cost that imposed practical limits of which the copyright concept could take advantage in meeting its stated goal of protecting and encouraging intellectual activity.

The new electronic environment changes this to a great degree, making copying not only easy but essentially unlimited in scope and much more difficult to trace and police through the traditional copyright law concepts. How to address this problem has been a considerable matter of concern to publishers and writers, and in response has come the proposed Uniform Computer Information Transactions Act (UCITA), which presents critical legal/legislative issues of which educators must become cognizant. When and if UCITA becomes law in any particular state, it will likely become a major concern for scholars in that state when dealing with electronic resources for their teaching and research.

Information technology currently accounts for more than one third of the annual economic growth in the United States and by almost any measure is the most rapidly expanding component of our economy. The U.S. Department of Commerce (1999) predicts that by 2006 almost half the workforce will be employed by industries that are either major producers or intensive users of information technology and services. Education is already at the forefront of this development.

In theory, UCITA seems to be a good idea. Seen as a good-faith attempt to provide clear, consistent and uniform rules governing the intangible aspects of transactions involving computers, UCITA would codify and standardize a portion of the "crazy quilt" of contract laws that presently vary from state to state concerning the use of electronic resources.[1] The effect and efficacy of signed licenses, shrink-wrapped licenses, and click-through licenses respecting software, databases, and Web sites is more a question of the accident of location than the application of a clear and coherent body of applicable law. But like many a good idea gone awry, scholars and educators must be aware that UCITA contains far too many provisions that could adversely impact educators as they go about their business of accessing electronic resources for both research and classroom use. The impact on librarians, library users, and the general public will be enormous and in the opinion of many, highly detrimental (American Library Association 2001). UCITA has passed in the legislatures of Virginia and of Maryland (in the latter case where it became effective on October 1, 2000) and is expected to be introduced into as many as 20 state legislatures during their 2001 sessions. Thus, it is important for educators to recognize the potential problems that UCITA could pose respecting the use of electronic materials.

WHAT IS UCITA?

UCITA (2000) is a proposed uniform law that was approved and recommended for adoption by the states in July 1999 (with amendments approved in August 2000 by the National Conference of Commissioners on Uniform State Laws [NCCUSL]) as an appropriate and uniform method for state law to deal with software and database licensing issues. The proposed law would cover contracts involving computer software, documentation, databases, Web sites, e-books, digital movies, and digital sound recordings.

UCITA is not universally loved even by those who advocate a greater degree of uniformity in state laws, especially those governing business and commercial matters among the various states. Its current form actually grew out of a failed attempt to propose many of its terms and provisions as a new article (to be designated "UCC2B") intended for inclusion in Article 2, as Chapter B thereof, the Uniform Commercial Code (1998). The Uniform Commercial Code (UCC) is generally recognized as among the most successful and among the most universally adopted of the many uniform laws that have been proposed over the years with the intent of facilitating interstate commerce and improving the predictability of laws among the states. (Some form of the UCC is law in every state of the United States except Louisiana.) Possibly concerned with introducing too much of an element of disuniformity in the UCC, and because of the opposition of a significant number of its members, the American Law Institute withdrew its consideration of the amendment, and UCC2B was reconceived by its proponents as a stand-alone law and renamed UCITA. A proposed uniform law must be adopted by each state legislature before it becomes law in that state.

Like most commercial law statutes, UCITA presents the reader with a detailed, complex and somewhat convoluted document. Because it plows a lot of new ground, this detailed approach also means that there will come into existence—with UCITA's adoption—many new provisions of law that will not have been previously construed by any court, guaranteeing that such provisions will therefore have to be hashed out in the courts over the years as cases and controversies involving the application of the new law arise. Even something as seemingly basic as the scope of UCITA is presently the subject of a range of often-conflicting interpretations. In addition, many of the perceived potential problems with the areas covered by UCITA that will be discussed below are not necessarily inherent in the text of the proposed law itself but derive rather from various UCITA provisions that appear to legitimize (and perhaps legalize) a number of objectionable contract clauses that many software providers have been habitually inserting into their license agreements, providing those clauses and their advocates with a potentially strong legal footing that they have not heretofore enjoyed.

Computer Information is the proverbial middle name of UCITA, and the proposed act defines computer information very broadly: "information in electronic form which is obtained through the use of a computer or which is in a form capable of being processed by a computer"(Uniform Computer Information Transactions Act 2000, Section 102 a). With the current trends in publishing involving the provision of more materials in electronic form, clearly UCITA is going to apply to an increasing proportion of the new acquisitions of all types made by libraries and by extension thus to materials used by scholars and educators. For example, before the advent of e-books, it might have appeared to many that the computer information concept would likely wind up applying mostly to reference works and journal literature. However, the new materials are proliferating rapidly, and every day more books are becoming available as e-books, and this suggests that the problem will become much broader that had been assumed. It is clear that in the near future, textbooks used by students may be available only as e-books, a form that may be preferred by the students of the digital generation now beginning to come of age.

Extrapolating from the above-quoted definition contained in the proposed law to the field of library acquisitions, UCITA applies to a library's contracts to license or buy software, its contracts to create computer programs or computer games, its contracts for online access to databases, and its contracts to distribute information over the Internet. The relevance of the new law to librarians and educators is obvious.

Since the early 1980s, software and electronic information providers and publishers of lengthy printed materials have sealed the disks or other media on which their products are contained with printed materials purporting to contain the binding terms of the contractual relationship between seller and library in respect of the materials in question. Typically, the provisions contained in these materials are quite one-sided, attempt to push all responsibilities on to the purchaser, and on their face are stated to be deemed irrevocably accepted by the purchaser through the action of breaking the seal or the wrapper in which the disks or other media containing the product are packaged. Fortunately, the ability of publishers to enforce all of these so-called "shrink-wrap" contract terms has at least been questionable in many states, with court decisions coming down in favor of each side, depending on a variety of circumstances (Gregory 2001, 121–122).

COPYRIGTHT LAW VERSUS LICENSING ISSUES

Educators have found it necessary to become at least noddingly familiar with the copyright laws in respect to issues involving the activities of classroom copying, use of reserve materials, handling of audiovisual materials, and research copying. Educators and scholars have enjoyed a privileged status under the copyright laws and have been able to freely borrow materials from a library or receive materials on interlibrary loan through application of the "first sale" doctrine of the copyright law. Under the first sale doctrine, a person who legitimately owns a copy of a work (i.e., one who has purchased the work or otherwise acquired ownership of the work with the permission of the copyright holder) has the full authority under the copyright law to "sell or otherwise dispose of the possession of that copy" (U.S. Code Title 17 Section 109a). This is one of the main legal premises that allows libraries to lend the materials they acquire for their collections and thus function as they traditionally have and still do today. Thus, if a particular transfer of intellectual property is deemed to be a sale, then the owner of the copyright will have lost all control over that particular copy of the work. This is in stark contrast to the situation in which the copyright owner does not sell, but rather licenses a work, meaning that the owner of the copyright enters into a contractual agreement with another party regarding the use of the work, not its ownership. This is the crux of the matter when it comes to software and electronic resource licensing.

Enter UCITA, which defines a license as a

> contract that authorizes access to, or use, distribution, performance, modification, or reproduction of, information or informational rights, but expressly limits the access or uses authorized or expressly grants fewer than all rights in the information, whether or not the transferee has title to a licensed copy.
> (Uniform Computer Transactions Act, Section 102a)

Under a licensing agreement, the work has not been sold. Instead, mere permission to use the work, within whatever conditions or guidelines may be set forth or defined in the license, has been established. It is in these situations where UCITA's provisions may come into play in a negative way for educators and library users.

Assuming that one accepts the premise that copyright laws are still important to ensure the advancement of knowledge, whether through journals or other means of distribution, licensing issues may fast become the most important legal overlay to the provision of digital information. That is, the application of statutory commercial contract law governing the relationship of particular parties to particular contracts, as opposed to the statutory law principles promulgated in respect of the relations between the producers and users of copyrighted works generally, may become more important even than changes in copyright law. Although copyright law and the limitations imposed contractually through licensing both often share a common goal of protecting intellectual property, there are important distinctions in how these two legal constructs go about accomplishing their respective purposes. First, it must be remembered that copyright laws are federal laws that apply equally to everyone in the United States. By contrast, licensing and contracts apply on an individual basis, subject to the contract law of the state that has jurisdiction over the particular contract. Thus, these contracts may be seen as "market driven," as opposed to having a basis in federal law. Therein lies a potential snare for educational and research use of electronic materials.

William Arms summarizes the situation as it applies to electronic materials:

> The doctrine of first sale and the right of fair use do not transfer easily to digital libraries. While the first-sale doctrine can be applied to physical media that stores electronic materials, such as CD-ROMS, there is no parallel for information that is delivered over networks. The guidelines for fair use are equally hard to translate from physical media to the online world. This uncertainty was one of the things that led to a series of attempts to rewrite copyright law, both in the United States and internationally. (2000, 118)

This uncertainty in the applicability of the copyright law also provides a basis for the aggressive efforts by software publishers to seek passage of UCITA in the various states. The tension is obvious: Publishers and manufacturers of software want to tighten restrictions, and users of the new electronic world of information feel the need to possess the same level of access and rights to use information that they have enjoyed in the print world.

The following is a quotation from the *SCOTIS Newsletter,* which is published by the Standing Committee on Technology and Information Systems of the American Bar Association:

> Generally, UCITA lends weight to the argument that a "license" is fundamentally different from sale of a copy and that "licensees" aren't entitled to the same intellectual property rights. Libraries are concerned about losing rights to lend digital works freely and to archive them for future generations. Businesses could find transfer restrictions particularly problematic in a merger or acquisition. Software developers fear being sued for making new products that work with others. For consumers, the greatest concern is that transfer restrictions could eliminate or burden the second-hand market for digital books and for cars, computers, and other goods with significant computer programs in them. (2000, paragraph 14)

The thought of an automobile (or a refrigerator, for that matter) as a subject affected by UCITA should not necessarily come as a surprise given the ubiquity of miniaturized processors in many of the items and appliances of day to day life, but it illustrates the potential depth of the problems suggested.

Of course, it should be noted that UCITA applies to both licensed and purchased computer materials, but as more electronic materials merely are being licensed rather than being sold, the emphasis in this paper is on licensed resources.

FAIR USE IMPLICATIONS OF UCITA

In general, UCITA was developed to regulate business-to-business transactions in tangible goods. However, contract law increasingly impacts the everyday consumer of computer information and products as well as business and library users.

Concerns for copyright versus contract law include such things as a small (or large) business owner, an educator, and a consumer who use the same software or digital information may be subject to the same license restrictions, even though the ways and purposes for which they are using the software or information may be very different. Copyright laws have always made fair use exceptions for nonprofit educational and research use, to name just a few exceptional areas. An educator has the right to photocopy an article or a portion of a book for research or educational purposes, or a reviewer or scholar has the right to quote short passages in a review or in teaching or research activities. Opponents of UCITA fear the extinction of such fair use rights under UCITA. Librarians and educators should also fear contract clauses that prohibit lending materials or that prohibit activities or uses that libraries may make in preservation efforts. Lending and preservation efforts by libraries are extremely important for library users if they are to acquire materials for research and educational purposes without having to use those materials in a pay for view environment.

If one of the results of enactment of UCITA is that fair use becomes a thing of the past for electronic materials, this will definitely impair the ability of libraries to provide electronic resources to their users and impair the ability of educators to use electronic materials in their teaching and research. In many ways, without the availability of fair use, there may be little reason for the existence of the library. Looking down the road, if everyone must purchase materials on a sort of pay-per-view basis, the whole traditional function of the library as a middle layer between publishers and users vanishes—and providing access to resources on a purely pay-per-view basis would likely be beyond the financial capacity of most school, academic, and public libraries.

One of many criticisms of UCITA is that the proposal would allow software companies to restrict information about their product. Section 102a(19) provides:

> "Contractual Use Term" means an enforceable term that defines or limits use, disclosure of, or access to licensed information or informational rights, including a term that defines the scope of a license. (Uniform Computer Information Transaction Act 2000)

Several companies do this currently as part of their present licensing agreements, but UCITA would give this practice a solid legal grounding. For example, UCITA would let companies prohibit publication of criticism of their product by inserting a clause in the licensing agreement to the effect that, "The customer will not publish reviews of the product without prior consent from ABC Software Company." Many educators and librarians are rankled by the thought that they might not be legally able to write or access product reviews because of this kind of restriction.

Another major cause for concern is UCITA's provision for significant "self-help" to deal with suspected license violation. Not only might your software or databases lawfully be disabled under UCITA, but the self-help provisions might also open up the real possibility for security violations from hackers as vendors build "backdoors" or "trapdoors" into their software, which would allow them to activate their self-help provisions. Such devices are notorious as possible avenues for hackers to break into computer systems.

Distance education via the Web is another complicating factor for many educators. Restrictive licenses could make some electronic resources effectively unavailable to a growing segment of the student population who may never actually set foot on the campus. Many librarians are today busy building digital and virtual libraries intended to make resources much more widely available, but they are running into what seem like concrete barricades in the twin forms of copyright and licensing restrictions. UCITA will only make this worse.

Opponents of UCITA are beginning to lobby for anti-UCITA bills to be passed in several state legislatures. Last year Iowa passed a law intended to protect its citizens from the effects of UCITA after it became law in Virginia and Maryland, responding to the fear that once UCITA became effective in any state its provisions might carry over to other states through so-called choice of law provisions in the license agreement itself. Although this Iowa law will expire by its own terms in July 2001, it presently appears likely that it will be extended for at least another year. Anti-UCITA legislation has also been introduced in the North Dakota and Oregon legislatures, and there is a credible likelihood of one being introduced this year in New York.

A recommendation in a policy paper by EDUCAUSE states that

> As UCITA is debated at the state level, the higher ed community and others concerned with the effect of UCITA on traditional copyright notions might consider attempting to ensure that UCITA's broad enabling of contracts and license restrictions does not in fact lead to contracts which are completely at odds with the fundamental public policies reflected by the doctrines of fair use and first sale. (2000 5)

This is the heart of the matter. The doctrines of fair use and first sale were developed out of the notions and public policy decisions that gave rise to the copyright concept and laws in the first place. Turning over these concepts to the not so tender mercies of lawyers drafting licensing agreements naturally tending to favor their software publisher clients is something that UCITA at heart effectively promotes and almost unabashedly sets out to accomplish. Viewed from this angle, it is easy to see that UCITA itself should be seen as clearly at odds with the fundamental public policy expressed in the copyright laws. For educators, as the importance of copyright recedes, UCITA will become the critical battleground.

CONCLUSION

There are many reasons why educators and librarians should oppose UCITA when it is introduced in their respective state legislatures. Many of the current practices that we take for granted in the fields of education and librarianship could conceivably vanish almost overnight, making the provision of educational materials considerably more expensive for institutions, individual students, or both.

Widespread adoption of UCITA will certainly also create new layers of costly procedures for libraries in the United States as more time and money will necessarily be needed to educate library staff, negotiate licenses, track use of materials, and investigate the status of materials donated to libraries. Because UCITA's provisions more or less by default favor licensors, libraries (and businesses) will be finding themselves having to negotiate from a weaker position and will need to conduct expensive reviews of all their shrink-wrapped licenses.

NOTES

1.   The two states, Virginia and Maryland, that have passed UCITA already have differences in the law, so it is unlikely that UCITA provisions will actually be identical if passed by all states.

REFERENCES

American Library Association. (2001). *UCITA (Uniform Computer Information Transactions Act) concerns for librarians and the general public.* [Online]. Available: http://www.ala.org/washoff /ucita/

Arms, W. Y. (2000). *Digital libraries.* Cambridge, MA: MIT Press.

EDUCAUSE. (2000, April). *Uniform Computer Information Transactions Act (UCITA).* [Online]. Available: http://www.educause.edu/policy/ucita.pdf

Gregory, V. L. (2001). Problems presented by the new state Uniform Computer Information Transactions Act (UCITA) Respecting the Use of Electronic Resources. In H. A. Thompson (ed.), *Crossing the divide: Proceedings of the Tenth National Conference of the Association of College and Research Libraries.* Chicago: Association of College and Research Libraries, a Division of ALA.

Standing Committee on Technology and Information Systems of the American Bar Association. (2000, April/May). Spotlight on UCITA. *SCOTIS Newsletter,* 1:5. [Online]. Available: http://wwwabanet. org/scotis/vol1no5.html#article3

Uniform Commercial Code, Article 2B. (1998). [Online]. Available: http://www.law.uh.edu/ucc2b/

Uniform Computer Information Transaction Act. (2000). [Online]. Available: http://www.law.upenn .edu/bil/ulc/ucita/ucita92900.pdf

United States Code, Title 17, section 109(a).

United States Department of Commerce. (1999). *The emerging digital economy report II, executive summary.* [Online]. Available: http://www.ecommerce.gov/ede/summary.html

Redefining Professional Growth
New Attitudes, New Tools—A Case Study

Kathy Brock
Elizabeth Bennett
Department of Media and Instructional Technology
State University of West Georgia

Commitment to lifelong learning and ongoing professional development has always characterized the school library media (SLM) profession. Traditionally, the school library media specialist (SLMS) relied on "learning experiences . . . designed and delivered by colleges and universities, professional associations, regional and state agencies, or private consultants" (American Association of School Librarians & Association for Educational Communications and Technology 1988, 60–61) for continuing professional growth. This model typified a top–down approach in which SLMSs were the recipients of updated information about policy changes, new programs, and other trends and issues. They marked their calendars for annual professional conferences, watched their mail for printed updates from state or regional program administrators, and eagerly awaited new issues of their favorite professional journals.

New SLM standards place a renewed emphasis on continuing professional growth and expanding its definition. In the latest version of *Information Power: Building Partnerships for Learning* (American Association of School Librarians & Association for Educational Communications and Technology 1998), references to professional growth are pervasive and interwoven throughout the fabric of the document. In *Library Media Standards* developed by the National Board for Professional Teaching Standards (NBPTS), 4 of the 10 standards address how SLMSs grow as professionals:

> Standard VII: Reflective practice—Accomplished library media specialists engage in reflective practice to increase their effectiveness.

> Standard VIII: Professional growth—Accomplished library media specialists model a strong commitment to lifelong learning and to their profession.

> Standard IX: Ethics, equity, and diversity—Accomplished library media specialists uphold professional ethics and promote equity and diversity.

> Standard X: Leadership, advocacy, and community partnerships—Accomplished library media specialists advocate for the library media program, involving the greater community. (National Board for Professional Teaching Standards 2001, 5)

These standards not only recognize traditional concepts of professional development such as lifelong learning but also expand the definition to include reflective practice and proactive advocacy. Just as "authentic learning for today's student is not bound by the textbook, the classroom, the library media center, or the school" (American Association of School Librarians & Association for Educational Communications and Technology 1998, 122), professional growth for SLMSs has extended beyond the confines of organized courses, conferences, and publications.

Today's professional growth model employs a constructivist approach in which SLMSs examine their own programs and practices as well as the improvement goals of their schools and use what they learn to provide focus for their personal growth agendas.

They use networking abilities, knowledge of information sources, and communication tools to pursue learning goals, improve services, and advocate at all levels for policies and resources that positively impact media programs. No longer simply the recipients of staff development limited by predetermined objectives, SLMSs now have the opportunity to direct their own professional growth and shape the future of their programs. However, their success will depend on their understanding of the new model, willingness to accept responsibility, and participation in individual and group initiatives. The remainder of this chapter explores activities and tools used by SLMSs in Georgia to embrace this expanded role.

A CONTEXT FOR CHANGE

The recent history of SLM programs in Georgia may be typical of that in other states and regions. The decade of the 1990s began with a strong infrastructure for leadership of SLM programs at the school district and state levels. An extensive Georgia Department of Education (GDOE) leadership staff worked with regional committees to develop SLM components, such as program standards, guaranteed personnel and materials funding, SLMS role description and evaluation instrument, a training module for SLM paraprofessionals, facilities and technical consultation, and statewide licensing agreements for instructional videos and computer software. GDOE also coordinated legislative advocacy efforts and provided professional development opportunities in the form of regional workshops, state conferences, and video training resources and teleconferences. Communication with building level SLMSs and local implementation of programs was facilitated by the designation of an SLM contact person for every school district and the distribution of a monthly newsletter.

Recent policy shifts emphasizing local decision making, site-based management, cost cutting, and administrative downsizing at the state level and in some school districts have resulted in an altered administrative structure with reduced state and regional program responsibility. In this emerging context, individual SLMSs and professional media organizations have informally assumed many of the roles previously performed by state and district media administrators. Aided by technology-based communication and information retrieval tools, an informal infrastructure has evolved for identifying questions and topics of concern, researching and clarifying related issues and implications, formulating responses, developing and implementing plans, and evaluating results. Through this collaboration, Georgia media professionals in diverse job settings and geographical locations have tackled multiple concerns, not only improving SLM programs but also enhancing their own professional growth.

TRACKING AND INFLUENCING POLICY

In the past, changes in policy impacting SLM programs took place infrequently, involved much formalized discussion, and were explained to district and building SLMSs through GDOE-led workshops and print publications. A massive education act (Georgia HB1187, the A+ Education Reform Bill, available at http://www.ganet.org/services/leg /ShowBillPre.cgi?year=1999&filename=1999/HB1187) proposed by Governor Roy Barnes and passed during the 2000 session of the Georgia Legislature significantly impacted SLM and other educational programs and sounded a wake-up call for practitioners. Program standards were abolished, certification and recertification rules revised, staffing policies modified, and new agencies for accountability and technology created; however, traditional means of disseminating information about the changes and their implications were not used. Instead, state professional associations monitored and provided daily legislative updates on organizational Web pages, issues of concern were identified and discussed on listservs, and questions and recommendations for action were directed through e-mail campaigns to state officials. Finally, original and revised implementation guidelines were detailed on agency Web sites.

Recertification policy emerged as one area of concern in the new education package. The legislation mandated that all certified personnel teach a minimum of five full days per year in the classroom. Discussions on the Georgia Media Listserv revealed a lack of clarity and consistency in how this rule would be applied to SLMSs because their role involves collaborative teaching in the media center but not dedicated teaching in the classroom. Individual SLMSs and state professional association leaders shared this information with agency decision makers through meetings and e-mails, working to increase recognition and understanding of the SLMS's instructional role. Ultimately, the rule was redefined to exclude SLMSs from this requirement, and the revised interpretation was posted on the agency Web site.

Regional accrediting agency standards assumed new importance as a result of the A+ Reform Act. Although the Southern Association of Colleges and Schools (SACS) had always helped to guarantee strong SLM programs in Georgia, the abolition of state program standards made SACS standards even more crucial. With increased interest and listserv discussion came recognition that SACS standards were undergoing more frequent revision and that drafts were now available on Web sites soliciting e-mail input. Recent issues for discussion and change include required clerical and professional positions, required number of books and periodicals, and minimum certification requirements for elementary SLMSs (http://www.sacs.org).

GUARANTEEING RESOURCES

As a result of changes in organizational structure, responsibility for clarifying needs and for monitoring and influencing budget requests has also shifted to a grassroots level. K–12 participation in Georgia Library Learning Online (GALILEO), a state subscription database service for multiple user groups, was recently threatened because of the erroneous assumption that schools were provided database access through public library participation agreements. This assumption was discovered by individual SLMSs monitoring the online monthly Georgia Board of Education (GBOE) meeting agenda and minutes. Extensive discussion on the Georgia Media listserv led to state professional organization lobbying and massive e-mail campaigns targeting the governor, the state school superintendent, and GBOE members. Subsequently, support for K–12 GALILEO was reinstated and secured.

State funding for SLM materials based on student enrollment is guaranteed to every Georgia public school district, and the A+ Education Reform Act required that 90 percent of this allotment must be spent at the school where the funding was earned. However, information about exact funding amounts, how they are determined, and how they can be spent has not always been made available to building-level SLMSs. These questions have resurfaced annually in discussions on the Georgia Media listserv. Now concerned SLMSs are directed by listserv colleagues to links on the GDOE Web page, where they can view specific school allotments for media materials and personnel and obtain the other information of interest.

ALIGNING INFORMATION LITERACY SKILLS TO STATE CURRICULUM STANDARDS

During the 1990s, Georgia SLMSs embraced cooperative teaching of information literacy skills (ILS) within the K–12 curriculum but did so without a state-adopted skills framework. Although curriculum standards for all subject areas were revised under GDOE leadership, ILS standards were not targeted for inclusion. Individual SLMSs, armed with their new editions of *Information Power* (American Library Association & Association for

Educational Communications & Technology 1998), advocated through listservs and at conferences for the development of ILS standards.

In 1998, Georgia Library Media Association (GLMA) leaders, with GDOE assistance, planned the SLM Summer Leadership Institute to address this need. The Institute was publicized statewide through the Georgia Media listserv, e-mail, and direct mailings to schools. Participation was open to any SLMS willing to volunteer three days of summer vacation time. Attendees identified ILSs within the newly revised Georgia Quality Core Curriculum (QCC), developed a skills framework, and produced an alignment document that would support cooperative planning by teachers and SLMSs. Four Summer Institutes have been held to date. Each year ILS standards for an additional curricular subject area were developed, and the resulting draft documents were posted online for input. The current document is available on the Georgia Learning Connection (GLC) Web site (http://www.g.c.k12.ga.us). In response to SLMS' requests, a Media Skills Checklist was also developed at the 2000 Institute. This document, still in draft form, is available at http://www.ccps.ga.net/media/media_skills_checklist1.htm.

ENGAGING IN PROFESSIONAL DEVELOPMENT

When individual SLMSs reflect on their own practice, identify professional development needs, and discuss them with peers, the result may be a personal quest for information or a product or class developed to meet jointly held goals. The evolution of Internet and other telecommunications tools, such as two-way video teleconferencing, has transformed the nature of staff development activities from occasional face-to-face conferences to daily, technology-facilitated interactions. It has erased geographical and time limitations, creating a virtual community to inform, nurture, and support previously isolated SLMSs.

In pre-Internet days, SLMSs relied on monthly or quarterly print publications to provide professional information with content determined by editorial boards. They attempted to answer specific questions by consulting indexes and searching for relevant full-text documents authored by experts. Now a quick search of a listserv archive, a query e-mailed to vendors or colleagues, exploration of online full-text databases, or perusal of commercial Web sites can yield focused, instant answers. If an SLMS wants ideas for primary school reading promotion, a short post on LM_NET or the Georgia Media listserv will bring from practitioners suggestions and recommended Web sites for viewing. If cataloging questions are causing confusion, an SLMS can solicit advice online from colleagues or consult Web-based resources such as the MARC Standards site from the Library of Congress (http://www.loc.gov/marc/) or commercial sites including MARC Tag of the Month (http://www.tagofthemonth.com).

More than a decade ago, the GDOE produced an SLMS handbook containing information on roles and responsibilities, preparation and certification, standards and policies, services and resources, professional organizations, and facilities. By the mid-1990s, the SLMS role outlined in the handbook failed to adequately describe current practitioner responsibilities. SLMSs throughout the state used electronic communications including video teleconferencing and e-mail to discuss and draft a revised roles document. Subsequently, SLMSs clamored for an updated edition of the entire handbook, but downsizing at GDOE prevented this from occurring. Participants at the 2000 GLMA Summer Leadership Institute adopted this project, revising and updating the handbook content. Association leaders continued the editing process and placed the resulting draft online (http://www.ccps.ga.net/media/You%20Are%20the%20Key/index.htm) for input, continuous updating, and use by practitioners.

Sometimes needs that emerge from informal professional discussion lead to the development of a traditional in-service or course. In Georgia, a program called InTech provides training in classroom integration of technology for teachers, SLMSs, and other educators. Media professionals from different school districts working together at a GLMA

Summer Leadership Institute identified additional technology training needs specifically for SLMSs and proposed a course to meet those needs. Following the Summer Institute, the group continued to communicate via video teleconferencing and e-mail to develop the course curriculum. InTech for Media Specialists received endorsement and is now offered through the state's Educational Technology Training Centers.

AN EMERGING MODEL FOR PROFESSIONAL GROWTH

Examination of SLMSs' professional practices and of the environment in which they have developed reinforces the concept that professional growth is no longer bound by traditional means of development and delivery. The old model characterized by external leadership, predetermined objectives, and one-way communication has given way to an emphasis on grassroots responsibility, collaboratively identified needs, and technology-assisted interactions. Figure 1 is an initial attempt to describe this emerging model.

Figure 1. Professional Growth Model for SLMSs.

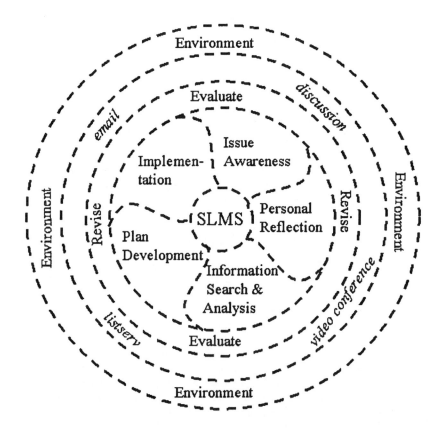

Professional growth begins with the individual SLMS, shown at the center of the model. The SLMS becomes aware of issues, needs, and concerns that arise in the local SLM center or are discussed on state or national listservs. Personal reflection provides focus and leads to the formulation of specific questions related to the impact of the issue on local SLM programs. These questions are explored and clarified through information search and retrieval using a variety of resources including online indexes and databases as well as informal discussions. Results are analyzed, and a plan for action is developed. The plan may include development of a lobbying initiative to influence policy or secure resources, a framework to integrate ILSs into curriculum content, or professional development activities to address identified needs. Although the plan was not initiated by external agencies, their endorsement or support may be sought to lend credibility and provide needed resources during the implementation phase. Evaluation and revision take place in each stage of the model. In addition, the curved, broken lines imply that information may flow back and forth between the various stages.

The two outer rings of the model emphasize the crucial role of communication and context. New technologies such as listservs, e-mail, and video teleconferencing provide the communication tools that make the emergence of the new model possible. They allow information to flow from the environment to the SLMS and, more important, from the SLMS to the environment, enriching each stage of the professional growth process. The new media connect each SLMS to the larger environment outside the school setting where trends develop, policies are formulated, programs are funded, and new resources emerge. Technology-based communication tools transform SLMSs from passive recipients to active instigators, able to influence the forces that impact them and their programs.

REFERENCES

American Association of School Librarians & Association for Educational Communications and Technology. (1988). *Information power: Guidelines for school library media programs.* Chicago: American Library Association & Association for Educational Communications and Technology.

———. (1998). *Information power: Building partnerships for learning.* Chicago: American Library Association & Association for Educational Communications and Technology.

National Board for Professional Teaching Standards. (2001). *Library media standards.* Arlington, VA: National Board for Professional Teaching Standards.

Diversity in
School Library Media Center Resources

Shu-Hsien Lai Chen, Ed.D.
Western Kentucky University

INTRODUCTION

In the past decade, we have seen a tremendous increase in school children from different ethnic, cultural, and linguistic backgrounds. A recent report by the U.S. Census Bureau indicates that the trend of demographic change is continuing. While the white population has gradually declined, the population of other nonwhite groups is on the rise, with Latinos gaining the most (U.S. Bureau of Census 2001). It is projected that by 2020, nearly half of children enrolled in U.S. schools will come from nonwhite ethnic groups.

Indeed, the United States has become a multiethnic, multicultural, and multilingual nation, comprising many groups holding different beliefs, values, and attitudes. Facing a classroom of children speaking several languages, educators can no longer ignore the special needs of a diverse student population and simply assume that these students can quickly assimilate into the American mainstream. When living and learning in this diverse society, all children should be able to see themselves reflected in the school curriculum and library programs so that they can develop a sense of identity, belonging, and pride. School library media specialists, as teachers and information specialists, need to ask themselves whether they provide adequate library resources and services that reflect the multiple groups and perspectives embodied in the student population. They must consider diversity in students' backgrounds when planning library programs and cooperative instruction with teachers.

Ethnic groups have always played a very important role in our national population, and their importance will likely increase in the future given the current demographic trends. Numerous outstanding men and women from these groups have made an indelible mark on American history with their contributions and accomplishments. No doubt, children are our future. Today's children in class are tomorrow's leaders in society. These children could be white, black, Asian, Latino, or those from any other ethnic or cultural group. Regardless, they need an equal opportunity to access information and to use quality library resources and services at school. Because information is power—power to lead them toward success first at school, then in society at large—the special library needs of these groups can no longer be overlooked. We hope to see more confident and successful students when they hear a stronger voice and see a more powerful image with which they can identify in the school curriculum and library programs.

This chapter discusses the importance of serving diverse student populations, with a focus on providing quality library resources and services for their varied needs, abilities, and interests. Next, evaluation and selection of multicultural resources will be addressed. A sample of selected outstanding authors and illustrators from four major ethnic groups will be discussed. Finally, the chapter delineates the active role that teachers and media specialists should play in serving students from different ethnic, cultural, or linguistic backgrounds.

DIVERSITY

The American Library Association (ALA) has long been a strong advocate of diversity in library resources and services. The mission of the ALA is to provide the highest quality library and information services for all people. In its statement of 1986, "Access to Resources and Services in the School Library Media Program," the ALA has maintained that diverse points of view and the linguistic pluralism of the community should be reflected in school library media collections (American Library Association 1986; Van Orden 1995). Throughout the recommendations made in 2000 by the ALA in its Congress for Professional Education, diversity in lingual, ethnic, and cultural aspects has been highly stressed as an important element both in the knowledge base of professionals and day to day work of library staff (American Library Association 2000b). Furthermore, the ALA is actively promoting equal access to information for all people through libraries and is encouraging development of unique library services for diverse populations (American Library Association 2000a).

What is diversity? It simply means difference (*American Heritage College Dictionary* 1993). Diversity is neither affirmative action nor equal employment opportunity. It is not deficiency or preferential treatment (Brown, Snedeker, and Sykes 1997). It is the "broad combination of peoples of different races, nationalities, ages, religions, and classes" (Carter, et al. 1982, 49). Diversity is the ways that people differ from each other in cultural, functional, and historical backgrounds (Pollar and Gonzalez 1994). The concept of diversity recognizes that individuals possess special or distinctive characteristics. Thus, it is "inclusive and is supposed to help everyone learn about each other's culture, language, values, and ideas" (Martinez 1997, 32). Diversity refers not only to ethnicity, race, language, and culture, however; it applies also to age, gender equity, social class, physical or mental disability, sexual orientation, and family structure (American Library Association 2000a).

In this chapter, discussion of diversity in the school library media center is limited to print resources by or about the following four major ethnic groups within the United States: African Americans, Asian Americans, Latino Americans, and Native Americans. Certainly, literature about and by Jewish Americans, Appalachian Americans, the elderly, the homeless, people with exceptionalities, or any other group is equally important, as every culture or group has its own unique place on library shelves. The reasons for the limited inclusion are twofold. First is the limited scope of this chapter. Second is the fact that these four major groups will make up the majority of Americans by the year 2050 (American Library Association 2000a).

CHANGING NATURE OF AMERICAN DEMOGRAPHICS

The white population has always been in the majority in our nation, so school curriculum has traditionally been oriented toward middle-class white children. During the period of 1890 to 1920, the first wave of American immigration came mostly from Europeans countries: Germany, Poland, Ireland, Hungary, and Russia. Only recently have immigrants come predominantly from Asia, Mexico, and Central American countries (Booth 1998). At the present time, 10 percent of the total U.S. population is foreign born (*A Melting Pot for the 21st Century* 1999). As the increase of ethnic population continues so too does the diversity in schools. In 1998, 37 percent of public school students enrolled in grades 1–12 were from ethnic groups, representing an increase of 15 percent from 1972 (National Center for Education Statistics 2001a). In 1999–2000, ethnic students increased to 38 percent of the total public school student population of 46.9 million, including 17.2 percent black students and 15.6 percent of Hispanics (National Center for Education Statistics 2001b).

The projected population in 2010 of children and young adults from birth to 24 indicates that of the total, white will represent 61.3 percent, Hispanic 17.3 percent, and black 16.1 percent, with the remaining 7.4 percent of Native Americans and Asian Americans combined (U.S. Department of Education, 2001). In California's Orange County schools, Latinos are now the largest ethnic group, constituting 42.3 percent of the total student population, with white students at 40.8 percent and Asian students third at 12.1 percent (Gale 2001).

As the American demographic landscape changes dramatically, a need exists to re-examine and refocus the special needs of diverse students in schools. Public education has always been considered an institution of American democracy, an enabler of the American dream, and it should always remain so. When many public schools such as those located in Atlanta, Los Angeles, and New York have over 100 countries represented in their student bodies, mainstream-based curriculum and resources can no longer adequately serve the academic and social needs of all students.

NEEDS FOR MULTICULTURAL RESOURCES

The need to belong to a common group is very strong for children in schools. Simply put, children want to fit in. They want to know that they are a part of the larger class and school community and that they are accepted.

Sense of Belonging and Self-Worth

In his hierarchy of needs, psychologist Abraham Maslow lists five human needs in a pyramid: biological, safety, love and friendship, self-worth, and self-actualization (Campbell 2000). Biological needs such as food, shelter, and air are at the base of the pyramid, whereas self-actualization occupies the top. The pyramid clearly illustrates that the need of self-actualization comes after self-worth, which is built upon the needs for love and friendship (i.e., need of belonging in a group and need of giving and receiving love). In applying this model of human needs to a school environment, it is evident that children feel a sense of pride, self-worth, and self-esteem only after their need of belonging is met. Without a sense of belonging and a sense of self-worth, children will not perform at their optimum.

Including multicultural resources in the school library media center is a key avenue for demonstrating that children of diverse groups are welcomed and valued as part of school programs. School library media specialists, as caring and supportive professionals, can work to create a positive and friendly climate in the media center to help children realize their sense of belonging and self-worth. Campbell (2000) states, "Students strengthen their sense of self-worth when they receive recognition, approval, appreciation, and respect from their peers. A human relations approach to multicultural education uses lessons to promote inclusion and acceptance of all students" (165).

Understanding Self and Others

All good literature gives readers satisfaction, entertainment, or information. Outstanding multicultural resources serve young readers in the same way. Multiple perspectives portrayed in books expand children's minds and vision, develop their critical views about various events, and broaden their awareness of the nation and the world. Well-written multicultural literature enables readers to feel and experience vicariously as if they were the characters of books. The emotional state that occurs when readers are deeply involved in books builds children's compassion for characters, develops their empathy for them, and sharpens their perception and sensitivity toward other ethnic or cultural groups. Multicultural literature speaks directly to children's minds and hearts; in addition, it validates their own feelings, experiences, and their own culture (Temple et al. 1998). Fiction, picture books, biographies, and informational books also help children better understand themselves, which in turn helps them understand others. Thus, multicultural literature serves as a mirror for children to see themselves, their people, and their culture.

Some people, including children and adults, may not have opportunities to know people who are ethnically or culturally different, or they may feel inhibited or uncomfortable interacting with them. In this regard, multicultural literature can serve as a bridge to bring readers and people from different groups together. Multicultural books create a non-threatening atmosphere for readers to meet other ethnic groups. They allow readers to explore deeply the thoughts, feelings, attitudes, and beliefs of diverse groups. Thus, throughout pages after pages of reading, children are able to gradually acquaint themselves with other ethnic groups, who otherwise may be beyond the physical and cultural worlds of young readers.

Multicultural literature thus provides a window into a totally new world to children. Understanding of and empathy toward people who are different in ethnicity, beliefs, customs, or value systems is a prerequisite for mutual respect and understanding among diverse groups. Mutual respect and understanding is not only important among the diverse groups on a national level, but also it is crucial on the international level. As the globalization of trade becomes more prevalent, the world economy is more dependent than ever on the successful interactions between many countries and peoples. Children can benefit from multicultural literature in understanding themselves, their cultures, and their countries, and other members of the world community.

Equal Access to Information

All students need information to learn and grow. Information need is especially critical for culturally and linguistically diverse students as they try to fit into schools, gain language skills, and learn their own as well as American mainstream culture. Currently, the ALA denotes five action areas: diversity, education and continuous learning, equity of access, intellectual freedom, and twenty-first century literacy (American Library Association 2000a). These five areas are closely related to one another, with the attainment of one area affecting the effectiveness of the others. In particular, a diverse student population requires the need for diverse library resources and equal information access for them.

In 1983, in the report of the Task Force on Library and Information Services to Cultural Minorities, the ALA proclaimed a need for serving culturally diverse groups (American Library Association 1986). Library media centers must assume a new and unique role in integrating cultural differences within the community; furthermore, these centers can assist cultural minorities in becoming equal participants in society through equal access to information (Beilke and Sciara 1986). Equity of information access for a diverse student population is a critical issue for school library media centers. Like those in the majority, ethnic students should have unrestricted access to school media centers that contain a broad range of ideas and viewpoints, library media resources that have been carefully selected, and assistance of library professionals who do not practice censorship.

Access to information can be viewed intellectually as well as physically. Intellectual access refers to "the freedom to read, the right to have available information on all subjects and points of view, the right to express ideas and the right and opportunity to acquire the skills necessary to locate and critically evaluate information" (Snyder 1992, 157). For ethnically and culturally diverse students, intellectual access includes the right to significant resources that portray their groups in a positive way and that describe the contributions and accomplishments of their group to American life. As it is a powerful vehicle to influence people's beliefs and change their attitudes, multicultural literature should be an important part of the library collection. Thus, the school media center must provide a culturally rich and resources rich environment, enabling students to learn intercultural skills that they can hope to use first in schools, and later in the workplace.

Physical access to information means providing students with information literacy skills to locate and retrieve information without unnecessary library regulations, language barriers, labeled collections, age or grade restrictions, improper collections, inadequate facilities or staff, or restricted shelves (Snyder 1992). Physical access is as important and fundamental as intellectual access. Many culturally or linguistically diverse students may have limited English proficiency, particularly the new immigrant students. Without proper guidance, they may find that a lack of knowledge in using the media center translates into both intellectual and physical access barriers. A few signs in students' native languages, posted in the media center and around the school, can ease to some degree uncertainty or anxiety of non-English speaking students. Seeing familiar written symbols will likely connect them faster to a new library, a new school, and a new country.

SELECTION AND EVALUATION OF MULTICULTURAL RESOURCES

Based on the degree of cultural elements included in books, multicultural resources generally are divided into three types: culturally neutral books, culturally generic books, and culturally specific books (Temple et al.1998). Culturally neutral books have themes not specifically identifiable or related to any particular cultural group. These books do not focus on the unique needs or characteristics of any ethnic group, nor do they portray any aspect of an ethnicity or culture. For example, a book that contains illustrations of children of several ethnic groups playing together on the playground is neutral. Diversity in this book is incidentally depicted. Culturally generic books feature ethnic characters, yet contain a general American theme or story line. The issue of whether the characters belong to any particular group is irrelevant in this type of book. Culturally specific books accurately portray the experiences, lives, customs, and beliefs of one particular group. The cultural details and nuances in these books convey authenticity with respect to that group. Among the three types, culturally specific books tend to evoke empathy in readers' hearts and exert influence in their perspectives. Nevertheless, all three types are useful resources for library media centers, as they all contribute to readers' awareness and understanding of their own as well as other cultures.

Selection Criteria

All good literature is characterized by an accurate description of settings, strong and believable characters, engaging and convincing plots, meaningful and universal themes, and the skillful use of language. Quality multicultural books for children and young adults are no exception. They not only must reach the general standards for good literature but also must meet a specific set of criteria for evaluating multicultural books. The following criteria are used frequently in evaluating multicultural literature (Pang et al. 1998; Temple et al. 1998; Totten, Garner, and Brown 1996; Van Orden 2000; Yokota 1993):

1. Is the portrayal of cultures and cultural details accurate?

2. Are historical facts or events correctly presented?

3. Is the use of native language or dialogue authentic?

4. Are characters portrayed positively, neither glamorized nor simplified?

5. Are illustrations accurate and true to cultural groups?

Accurate cultural portrayal implies that "issues are represented in ways that reflect the values and beliefs of the culture" (Yokota 1993, 188). Cultural details must be depicted in depth so that readers from a specific cultural group feel pride or joy in seeing themselves, their people, and their culture reflected in the authors' descriptions or artists' illustrations. One excellent example of culture accuracy is *Dragonwings*, in which Laurence Yep (1975) uncannily depicts the thoughts, beliefs, and values held by the Chinese families being left behind in Canton while the men went to the Golden Mountain searching for gold.

Accuracy in a history text can't be overemphasized. Correctness in historical background for multicultural literature is equally important. Some authors create historical fiction based on family tales; others conduct research to ensure the accuracy of historical facts. In *Roll of Thunder, Hear My Cry*, Mildred D. Taylor (1976) used family stories to portray an unfair society existing in Mississippi during the Depression era.

One technique used by authors of multicultural literature is to insert dialect or mother tongue of book characters, thus adding an authentic flavor to their works. The language used by the characters should reflect a natural communication style typical of the character's cultural groups at a particular place during a certain period of time. Use of phrases, terminology, or linguistic etiquette should demonstrate appropriate differences in age, gender, class, or educational level of the characters. *Scorpions*, by Walter Dean Myers (1988), has a vivid dialogue between a teenage African American boy and his younger sister at their home. The words and expressions used by them are those that readers can often hear in ethnic African American conversation today.

The characters in multicultural books should be portrayed positively and accurately as real humans with feelings, disappointments, hopes, goals, and aspirations. Both heroes and villains must be true to life. Caution should be taken to watch out for biographies that over-glamorize or oversimplify historical figures or contemporary political leaders. People of all ethnic or cultural groups should be treated with respect and dignity. Diversity doesn't mean difference only among ethnic or cultural groups; it also exists within each major ethnic group. As Bowie (1992) pointed out, there is no such a thing as single "black experience" because African Americans live various kinds of lives and differ in their perceptions of life and the world around them (27). One large ethnic group could consist of many smaller groups. For instance, Asian Americans include Americans of Chinese, Japanese, Korean, Filipino, Malay, and Vietnamese descent. Each group has its own traits. For this reason, ethnic groups should not be conveniently lumped together, with the assumption that they possess a set of common characteristics. Therefore, individuals within an identical ethnic group need to be portrayed in multiple dimensions without stereotyping.

Because illustrations are an important and essential part of books, they must be appropriate without distortions or stereotypes. *The Five Chinese Brothers* (Bishop and Wiese 1938) and *The Story of Little Black Sambo* (Bannerman 1951) present negative and stereotyped images of Chinese and blacks, respectively. In *The Five Chinese Brothers*, all people in the village look identical and with yellow skin, and *The Story of Little Black Sambo* depicts stereotyped images of blacks. Illustrations should reflect diversity and individuality among a cultural group. Illustrations of a racial group should not be exaggerated in facial or physical features such as the drawing of overly slanted eyes in Asian American literature. When Commodore Perry landed in Japan in the nineteenth century asking for trade, the caricature of the western as drawn by the reluctant Japanese is an example of unflattering portrayal of one race by another (Blumberg 1985).

Individuality, Authenticity, and Sensitivity

Clearly, a need exists for high quality multicultural resources to help children develop an understanding of other cultures. Before 1965, children's literature was dominated primarily by mainstream culture, the so-called all white world of children's literature reflecting white, middle-class children (Larrick 1965). Often nonmainstream culture was portrayed in patronizing, condescending, or unfavorable manners. To prevent collecting unworthy reading materials in schools, teachers and media specialists must evaluate multicultural books with keen and discerning eyes. They must first scrutinize stereotyping in depicting and illustrating cultural groups or settings.

By overlooking diversity and individuality within a group, an author or illustrator can easily assign a single set of attributes to all members of an ethnic group. As a result, stereotyped images are created. As discussed previously, several books including *The Five Chinese Brothers* and *The Story of Little Black Sambo* have such a fallacy. It is important to watch out for stereotypes simply because "Children are not prepared to value the multicultural characters of society when they are surrounded with literature that either presents minorities stereotypically or invisibly by omitting them completely" (Latimer 1976).

In addition to avoiding stereotypes, authenticity and sensitivity are two other criteria used to evaluate multicultural resources. Authenticity refers to accuracy, truthfulness, and details in portraying cultures, their people, and their specific issues and problems. When authors and illustrators are members of a cultural group, they are more likely to write authentically with an insider's perspective, with accurate cultural details and nuances (Yokota 1993). Mildred Taylor, Laurence Yep, Gary Soto, and Josesph Bruchac are examples of such authors from the four major ethnic groups.

When authors and illustrators are not from that specific cultural group, they write from an outsider's point of view. Their interpretations of ethnic experiences can be accurate, but often these interpretations may lack the unique color, flavor, and sound of the culture. Nevertheless, such an outsider could write like a member of the group if he or she conducts extensive research and has personal and in-depth experience obtained by living within the culture. Arnold Adoff and Paul Goble are Jewish American and British American, respectively, but their works reflect accurately the true voice of African Americans and Native Americans.

Sensitivity is another area that must be emphasized in evaluating multicultural resources. Whether an author or illustrator is sensitive determines the interpretation and representation of a culture and its members. Sensitive authors and illustrators observe with a keen eye and a sharp ear and then write or illustrate with a sympathetic heart. They portray cultural groups with empathy, and their works demonstrate their close observation of and deep involvement with a cultural group. Insensitivity on the part of an author or illustrator can show in many ways: distortion of historical facts, omission of historical events, the unintentional use of degrading language, and disrespectful writing about ethnic groups. One positive example is Allen Say's *Grandfather's Journey* (1993), which depicts with great sensitivity the protagonist's homesickness as he lives in two worlds. The text and illustrations are authentic and true to Japan and the United States. In addition, the feeling of homesickness does not degrade into sentimentality. This book can resonate with readers who have similar experiences of leaving their homeland to live in another culture.

BUILDING A BALANCED COLLECTION

The first and foremost mission of the school library media center is to support the school curriculum. As student populations become more diverse, multicultural education has become an important agenda in education. A balanced collection of multicultural resources is a necessity in schools to support multicultural education. Thus, the collection will be defined as the multicultural resources housed in the media center plus the books available for use in classrooms.

Guidelines for Collection Development

Organizing and obtaining a suitable library collection for a school serving diverse groups can be a challenge. First, the collection must reflect all the major cultural groups represented in a student body. The purchase of multicultural books should be oriented toward the special needs and interests of the ethnic groups within the school. Beyond that, all students should be acquainted with the rich diversity of cultures existing now in the nation and the world. In working on a library media center policy for collection development, a multicultural component must be included (Sharp 1992). The Dallas (Texas) Independent School District, for example, has specific guidelines for multicultural books in its selection policy (as cited in Van Orden 2000, 29–30):

1. Books and other materials should accurately portray the perspectives, attitudes, and feelings of ethnic groups.

2. Fictional works should have strong ethnic characters.

3. Books should describe settings and experiences with which all students can identify and yet accurately reflect various ethnic cultures and lifestyles.

4. The protagonists in books with ethnic themes should have ethnic characteristics but should face conflicts and problems that are universal to all cultures and groups.

5. The illustrations in books should be accurate, ethnically sensitive, and technically well done.

6. Ethnic materials should not contain racist concepts, cliches, phrases, or words.

7. Factual materials should be historically accurate.

8. Multiethnic resources and basal textbooks should discuss major events and documents related to ethnic history.

Genres of Multicultural Resources

To serve diverse groups, the school library media center needs an adequate collection as well as sufficient resources for cultural or ethnic groups represented within the student body. Even if the school has a more homogeneous population, a library media program, with multicultural elements, is highly desirable. As discussed earlier, children can benefit from multicultural resources in knowing themselves and others. Our nation has become a society of cultural pluralism; hardly anyone can live or work in isolation within one's own cultural or ethnic group anymore.

What types of resources should be included in multicultural collections for school library media centers? Multicultural resources are inclusive and should contain many literary genres: folklore, picture books, poetry, realistic fiction, historical fiction, biography, and informational books. Norton (1998, 2001) has suggested using similar categories of resources for studying multicultural literature. Her five-phase study model begins with the traditional literature, then moves on with historical nonfiction, historical fiction, and finally ends with contemporary literature.

Folklore embodies a set of beliefs and values of a cultural group, carried originally in oral form, from one generation to another. It is a valuable part of the literary and cultural heritage of any group. As mentioned previously, Norton (1998) maintains that study of various cultures begins with the oral tradition of the people—folk tales, fables, myths, and legends—as well as the history of the people. Folklore is powerful literature and should be read by everyone. Poetry illustrates distinctive linguistic sounds, patterns, and characteristics of a language, and it also includes nursery rhymes and folk songs popular among children. Outstanding picture books about ethnic groups and by ethnic authors are an invaluable component of a multicultural collection.

Biographies and historical books of ethnic and cultural groups are also crucial parts of a multicultural collection. Biographies can inspire children to achieve and succeed and illustrate good role models for students from the same ethnic group. Historical books teach children the joys and woes, struggles and triumphs of their ethnic group in history. By being aware of their history, children can relate the present to the past and connect it to the future. Bowie (1992) emphasized that the resources in the media center should include enough examples of African Americans' accomplishments for teachers to integrate them into all areas of curriculum. Her statement can be expanded to include the accomplishments of all other ethnic groups. She cautioned that teachers should encourage African American students to explore the lives of scientists, educators, artists, and political leaders, not just the lives of glittering stars in sports and entertainment. By the same token, other ethnic students should read and explore great people in all walks of life.

A well-written fiction work has the magic to transport readers into another place or time period and transform them into book characters as they experience emotional ups and downs. Multicultural literature could appeal particularly to certain young adults. The motifs or themes portrayed in books, such as loneliness, isolation, fear of rejection, troubles of fitting into larger society, and generational differences, are similar to what young adults experience as they make the transition from childhood to adulthood (Nilsen and Donelson 2001).

Language

To provide quality library services to ethnic groups, library collections must contain adequate information on major ethnic and cultural groups. In this regard, materials written in English are not the only appropriate resources for a multicultural collection. The media center can also provide books in languages other than English. Students with limited English proficiency or non-English speaking students have a right to information in their native languages (Dame 1993). If the only information available to them is written in a language that they cannot read, then these students are denied equal access to information. Furthermore, these students, with emotionally strong ties to their native lands, might like to see images and read stories in their native languages in the context of their own cultures (Dame 1993). Through these materials, they can also understand and appreciate the ethnicity, heritage, roots, and accomplishments of their people. As they gradually acquire English language skills, reading materials appropriate to their reading and interest level should be made available. Thus, there is a real need for acquiring foreign-language and bilingual materials.

Inclusion of materials in foreign languages has long been a policy of the ALA. In its 1986 statement "Access to Resources and Services in the School Library Media Program," the ALA clearly indicates

> While English is, by history and tradition, the customary language of the United States, the language in use in any given community may vary. Schools serving communities in which other languages are used make efforts to accommodate the needs of students for whom English is a second language. To support these efforts, and to ensure equal access to resources and services, the school library media program provides resources which reflect the linguistic pluralism of the community. (Van Orden 1995, 357)

To summarize, multicultural resources are used to support learning and teaching. Given the cultural pluralism of American society and the increasing numbers of ethnic students in American schools, multicultural education has become a new force in education. To implement such a curriculum in schools, one necessary component is inclusion of multicultural resources as part of the school library media collection.

ROLES OF MEDIA SPECIALISTS AND TEACHERS
AND THEIR COLLABORATION

As a teacher and information specialist, the media specialist should first select quality multicultural resources for the library media center. Limited knowledge or experiences on the part of the media specialist may hinder such selection and therefore become a barrier to children's information access. To select and use materials properly, media specialists need to be familiar with quality multicultural resources by reading a wide variety of ethnic literature. Reading professional literature, attending conferences, and seeking continuing education opportunities can also help media specialists keep abreast of ideas and trends in the field. Additionally, media specialists should perceive the needs and interests of their students and teachers and the current status of existing ethnic resources in their schools. If necessary, the media specialist can conduct a needs assessment or a preference survey to pinpoint areas of strength and weakness in the collection. Media specialists must provide adequate multicultural resources for integration into the curriculum and overcome their own personal bias for a particular belief or viewpoint. Beyond that, they should provide sufficient resources for pleasure reading.

Media specialists also need to play an active role as an advocate of information literacy and as a guardian of information access equity (Dame 1993). They must remove existing barriers to information access and information literacy, including English language literacy. Dame points out, "Library materials available to English dominant students should be accessible to linguistically and culturally diverse students. All students have the right to receive full service from the librarian and to become fully information literate" (viii). The final goal for these students as well as their peers is to attain the nine information literacy standards emphasized in Information Power (American Association of School Librarians, 1998).

Merely acquiring and placing quality multicultural resources in the media center will not automatically attract students into the media center to use them. It is necessary to use reading motivational techniques to increase students' awareness and interest. Promotion of multicultural resources is a necessity. Media specialists can give book talks, form a book club, put up displays around cultural or ethnic themes, or invite guest speakers from ethnic groups. Outstanding individuals from diverse backgrounds serve as role models to inspire students to emulate and achieve.

Like media specialists, teachers become familiar with others' perspectives by reading multicultural literature and professional literature. They too need to understand multiple and diverse viewpoints before they are able to help students understand multiculturalism (Temple et al. 1998). For children and adults alike, reading is an important means to enhance the understanding of multiple perspectives existing in the world. Reading multicultural children's literature allows teachers to see a child's world in other cultures, yet reading adult books provides teachers with more in-depth insight into ethnic cultures and issues. When sharing and discussing books with children, teachers' deeper insight will enable them to better understand students' various backgrounds. Understanding and familiarity with children's multicultural literature is a must for teachers.

Teachers can share multicultural literature with their students. Reading aloud, giving book talks, and holding literary discussions in an informal setting are several methods to encourage reading interests. When students are at ease and open, they tend to share their ideas and beliefs of a cultural group. Like media specialists, teachers should only introduce quality multicultural literature without being influenced by their personal views, bias, or stereotypes. Teachers need to share multicultural literature with an open mind.

Research indicates that children obtain most of their reading materials from the school library media center. Often their choices of reading materials are determined by their peers, teachers, and media specialists. Needless to say, the collaboration between teachers and media specialists is crucial in influencing children's reading interest in multicultural literature. Media specialists can render valuable services and create partnership with teachers. By working together, teachers and media specialists can provide materials, plan cooperative instructional units, design curriculum together, keep informed of new trends, research, workshops, and articles (Dame 1993).

For students whose first language is not English, more assistance is often needed in using the media center and improving their literacy and literary skills. Media specialists and teachers are likely the most important adults to help them gain such skills. Because students can relate better to teachers who have similar cultural backgrounds, teachers and media specialists should increase their own understanding of various cultural groups by broad reading themselves. With a cross-cultural understanding, their instruction will be much more effective and meaningful to their diverse student groups.

SAMPLE OF OUTSTANDING AUTHORS AND ILLUSTRATORS OF MULTICULTURAL LITERATURE

In the past three decades, we have seen more outstanding multicultural literature for children and young adults than ever before. In the broad sense, multicultural literature refers to literature portraying all ethnic or cultural groups living within the United States, as well as international literature. At the present time, the four major ethnic groups have occupied a more prominent spot in multicultural literature for children and young adults, although there also exists outstanding literature about Jewish Americans, Appalachian Americans, and other European Americans.

Multicultural literature, however, is not limited to literature by and about ethnic and cultural groups. Instead, it also represents the works that depict people who are physically disabled, mentally challenged, and those who have an alternative lifestyle or family structure. Works regarding social diversity, gender equity, or age difference also fall under the umbrella of multicultural literature. Nevertheless, as stated above, for this chapter, the scope of multicultural literature will include only the works by and about the four major ethnic groups.

Many multicultural picture books, fiction books, and informational books have been recognized and given prestigious literary awards. Several Caldecott Medal winners and Newbery Medal winners portray ethnic groups. A few examples of Caldecott winners include *Mufaro's Beautiful Daughters: An African Tale* (Steptoe 1987)*; Lon Po Po: A Red-Riding Hood Story from China* (Young 1989); and *Grandfather's Journey* (Say 1993). Some Newbery winners depicting Native Americans and African Americans are *Julie of the Wolves* (George 1972); *Walk Two Moons* (Creech 1994); and *Bud, Not Buddy* (Curtis 1999). The Boston Globe-Horn Book Award was given to the African American writer Virginia Hamilton for *M.C. Higgins, the Great* (1974) and *Sweet Whispers, Brother Rush* (1982); to Chinese American author Laurence Yep for his *Child of the Owl* (1977); and also to Mildred D. Taylor for *The Friendship* (1987). Ezra Jack Keats New Writers Award recognized Valerie Flournoy for *The Patchwork Quilt* (1985), and Faith Ringgold's *Tar Beach* (1991).

Virginia Hamilton and Paula Fox from the United States had the great honor to win in 1992 and 1978, respectively, the Hans Christian Andersen Award, a distinguished award given by the International Board for Young People to recognize an author's or an illustrator's entire body of work. Virginia Hamilton was also the recipient of the Laura Ingalls Wilder Award in 1995 for making a substantial and lasting contribution to children's literature for a period of time. *Dragonwings* by Laurence Yep (1975) and *Words by Heart* by Quida Sebestyen (1979) have won the International Reading Association Children's Book Award. The National Council of Teachers of English (NCTE) Award is given to a living

American poet in recognition of his or her entire body of work for children. Both Arnold Adoff and Eloise Greenfield have been given this award for their poetry.

The Coretta Scott King Award is presented to encourage African American authors and illustrators. It has been given annually since 1970 to a book that promotes understanding and appreciation of cultures of diverse groups. The award celebrates the life of Martin Luther King, Jr. and honors his widow, Coretta Scott King, for her strength and her continuing fight for racial equity and peace. Several outstanding African American authors have won the award more than once. They include Walter Dean Myers, Mildred D. Taylor, Virginia Hamilton, Eloise Greenfield, James Haskins, Christopher Paul Curtis, and others.

Appendix C is a brief list of outstanding authors and illustrators from four major ethnic groups. The selection of these authors or illustrators is based on the personal preference of this author and her students. The list is not intended to include every exemplary author and illustrator from the four ethnic groups. Omission from the list does not imply a lack of literary merit or aesthetic value of authors or illustrators, but rather a limitation of space.

CONCLUSION

As the population of our nation and schools becomes more diverse, the need for multicultural resources is becoming critical. Although most students are from families who have lived in the United States for generations, others may be from immigrant families totally new to this land. In spite of the difference, all students have their own distinctive cultural heritages and ethnic backgrounds that must be understood, respected, and appreciated. Multicultural resources are important vehicles to promote and encourage mutual understanding and respect in schools. As global trade increases and the world economy reduces the distance between countries, we are truly becoming a people living in a global village. Some degree of interaction with people from other cultural groups is not only inevitable but also highly desirable. To that effect, mutual understanding and respect is first nurtured and extended to schoolmates, then to fellow Americans, and finally to people worldwide. As educators, media specialists have the duty and responsibility to enhance mutual understanding and respect through provision of quality library resources and services.

Building a library media collection reflecting multiple perspectives is not only necessary for school curriculum but also practical to enhance each student's sense of belonging and self-worth. As media specialists, we also have duties to select and purchase multicultural books that reflect students' ethnic and cultural backgrounds. Authenticity, sensitivity, and individuality are the essential elements of quality multicultural resources. Multicultural books span the gamut of all genres, including folklore, legends, poetry, realistic fiction, historical fiction, informational books, and biographies. Each genre is important for students so that they may understand better their own origin, as well as others outside their ethnic or cultural groups. Finally, collaboration between teachers and media specialists is the key to helping students gain information literacy in using library resources and literary skills in reading and appreciating multicultural literature.

The United States is one land with many peoples living together. This land belongs to everyone who claims this place as home. Media specialists can make a difference in this great land by encouraging mutual understanding and respect through providing quality library resources and services to culturally and linguistically diverse students.

REFERENCES

American Association of School Librarians. (1998). *Information power: Building partnerships for learning.* Chicago: American Library Association.

The American Heritage College Dictionary (3d ed.). (1993). Boston: Houghton Mifflin.

American Library Association. (1986). *Access to resources and services in the school library media program: An interpretation of the library bill of rights.* Chicago.

————. (2000a). *Diversity.* [Brochure]. Chicago.

————. (2000b). *Recommendations: Congress for professional education.* [Online]. Available: http://www.ala.org/congress/recommendation. (Accessed May 8, 2000).

Bannerman, H. (1951). *The story of Little Black Sambo.* Philadelphia: Lippincott.

Beilke, P., and Sciara, F. J. (1986). *Selecting materials for and about Hispanic and East Asian children and young people.* Hamden, CT: Library Publications.

Bishop, C. H., and Wiese, K. (1938). *The five Chinese brothers.* New York: Coward-McCann.

Blumberg, R. (1985). *Commodore Perry in the land of the shogun.* New York: Lothrop.

Booth, W. (1998, March). Diversity and division: America's new wave of immigration is changing its "melting pot" image. *The Washington Post National Weekly Edition,* 6–8.

Bowie, M. M. (1992). Understanding and appreciating the unique needs of African Americans. In K. H. Latrobe and M. K. Laughlin (eds.), *Multicultural aspects of library media programs.* Englewood, CO: Libraries Unlimited.

Brown, C. D., Snedeker, C. C., and Sykes, B. eds. (1997). *Conflict and diversity.* Cresskill, NJ: Hampton Press.

Campbell, D. E. (2000). *Choosing democracy: A practical guide to multicultural education* (2d ed.). Upper Saddle River, NJ: Prentice Hall.

Carter, E., Kepner, E., Shaw, M., and Woodson, W. B. (1982). The effective management of diversity. *SAM Advanced Management Journal* 47:4, 49–53.

Creech, S. (1994). *Walk two moons.* New York: HarperCollins.

Curtis, C. P. (1999). *Bud, not Buddy.* New York: Delacorte.

Dame, M. A. (1993). *Serving linguistically and culturally diverse students: Strategies for the school library media specialist.* New York: Neal-Schuman.

Flournoy, V. (1985). *The patchwork quilt.* New York: Dial.

Gale, E. (2001, January 10). Latinos now schools' biggest ethnic group. *Los Angeles Times.* [Online]. Available: http://neptune.libs.uga.edu/WebZ/html/galileo/homeframe.html. (Accessed May 24, 2001).

George, J. C. (1972). *Julie of the wolves.* New York: Harper & Row.

Hamilton, V. (1974). *M. C. Higgins, the great.* New York: Macmillan.

————. (1982). *Sweet whispers, Brother Rush.* New York: Philomel.

Larrick, N. (1965, September 11). The all white world of children's books. *Saturday Review,* 63–65.

Latimer, B. I. (1976). Telegraphing messages to children about minorities. *The Reading Teacher* 30:2, 151–156.

Martinez, E. (1997). Diversity: The 21st-century spectrum. *American Libraries,* 28:3, 32.

A melting pot for the 21st century. (1999, September 27). *Newsweek,* 134, 37.

Myers, W. D. (1988). *Scorpions.* New York: Harper-Collins.

National Center for Education Statistics. (2001a). *The condition of education 2000 in brief* (NCES 2001-045). Washington, DC: U.S. Government Printing Office.

————. (2001b). *Statistics in brief* (NCES 2001-326). Washington, DC: U.S. Government Printing Office.

Nilsen, A. L., and Donelson, K. L. (2001). *Literature for today's young adult* (6th ed.). New York: Longman.

Norton, D. E. (1998). Teaching multicultural literature in the reading curriculum. In M. F. Opitz (ed.), *Literacy instruction for culturally and linguistically diverse students.* Newark, NJ: International Reading Association.

————. (2001). *Multicultural children's literature: Through the eyes of many children.* Upper Saddle River, NJ: Prentice-Hall.

Pang, V. O., Colvin, C., Tran, M., and Barba, R. (1998). Beyond chopsticks and dragons: Selecting Asian American literature for children. In M. F. Opitz (ed.), *Literacy instruction for culturally and linguistically diverse Students.* Newark, DE: International Reading Association.

Pollar, O., and Gonzalez, R. (1994). *Dynamics of diversity.* Menlo Park, CA: Crisp.

Ringgold, F. (1991). *Tar beach.* New York: Crown.

Say, A. (1993). *Grandfather's journey.* Boston: Houghton Mifflin.

Sebestyen, Q. (1979). *Words by heart.* Boston: Little, Brown.

Sharp, P. T. (1992). Collection development in a multicultural world. In K. H. Latrobe and M. K. Laughlin (eds.), *Multicultural aspects of library media programs.* Englewood, CO: Libraries Unlimited.

Snyder, D. (1992). Access and intellectual freedom. In K. H. Latrobe and M. K. Laughlin (eds.), *Multicultural aspects of library media programs.* Englewood, CO: Libraries Unlimited.

Steptoe, J. (1987). *Mufaro's beautiful daughters: An African tale.* New York: Lothrop, Lee & Shepherd.

Taylor, M. D. (1976). *Roll of thunder, hear my cry.* New York: Dial.

————. (1987). *The friendship.* New York: Dial.

Temple, C., Martinez, M., Yokota, J., and Naylor, A. (1998). *Children's books in children's hands: An introduction to their literature.* Boston: Allyn & Bacon.

Totten, H. L., Garner, C., and Brown, R. W. (1996). *Culturally diverse library collections for youth.* New York: Neal-Schuman.

U.S. Bureau of Census. (2001). *An analysis of state and county population changes by characteristics: 1990–1999.* [Online]. Available: http://www.census.gov/population. (Accessed February 4, 2001).

U.S. Department of Education. (2001). *Population projections of young people.* [Online]. Available: http://www.ed.gov/pubs/YouthIndicators. (Accessed May 11, 2001).

Van Orden, P. J. (1995). *The collection program in schools* (2d ed.). Englewood, CO: Libraries Unlimited.

————. (2000). *Selecting books for the elementary school library media center.* New York: Neal-Schuman.

Yep, L. (1975). *Dragonwings.* New York: HarperCollins.

————. (1977). *Child of the owl.* New York: Harper & Row.

Yokota, J. (1993). Issues in selecting multicultural children's literature. *Language Arts,* 70:3, 156–167.

Young, E. (1989). *Lon Po Po: A Red-Riding Hood story from China.* New York: Philomel.

APPENDIX A

Selection Aids for Multicultural Literature

Books

Bishop, R. S., ed. (1994). *Kaleidoscope: A multicultural booklist for grades K–8* (2d ed.). Urbana, IL: National Council of Teachers of English.
An annotated list of 400 titles published during 1990–1992. Covers poetry, biographies, picture books, and folktales, with emphasis on people of diversity.

Hayden, C. D. (1992). *Venture into culture: A resource book of multicultural materials and programs.* Chicago: American Library Association.
Recommends books for K–8 students about African American, Arabic, Asian, Hispanic, Jewish, Native American, and Persian cultures.

Helbig, A., and Perkins, A. R. (2001). *Many peoples, one land: A guide to new multicultural literature for children and young adults.* Westport, CT: Greenwood.
The annotated list, a successor to *This Land Is Our Land,* includes 541 titles, published 1994–1999, on African, Asian, Native American, and Hispanic cultures within the United States. Intended to be used by librarians, teachers, and parents.

Helbig, A., and Perkins, A. R. (1994). *This land is our land.* Westport, CT: Greenwood.
Covers more than 1,100 books of multicultural literature for young readers, published 1985–1993.

Kuipers, B. J. (1991). *American Indian reference books for children and young adults.* Englewood, CO: Libraries Unlimited.
Suggests 200 titles for grades 3–12. Describes the strength and weakness of each title and its use in the curriculum. Includes selection criteria.

Miller-Lackmann, L. (1992). *Our family, our friends, our world: An annotated guide to significant multicultural books for children and teenagers.* New Providence, NJ: Bowker.
Annotated lists of fiction and nonfiction about ethnic and cultural groups in the United States and Canada and also about cultures in other parts of the world.

Norton, D. E. (2001). *Multicultural children's literature: Through the eyes of many children.* Upper Saddle River, NJ: Prentice-Hall.
Intended for adults in evaluating, selecting, and sharing multicultural literature of children and young adults, the book covers outstanding literature in the following areas: African American, Native American, Latino, Asian, Jewish, and Middle Eastern.

Rochma, H. (1993). *Against borders: Promoting books for a multicultural world.* Chicago: American Library Association.
Annotated book lists on specific ethnic groups and issues. Gives suggestions on teaching themes such as outsiders, friends, family, and racial oppression for grades 6–12. Features literature of the major ethnic groups.

Schon, I. (1993). *Books in Spanish for children and young adults: An annotated guide.* Metuchen, NJ: Scarecrow Press.
The bilingual book lists titles representing diverse Hispanic cultures in Central and South American countries.

———. (1995). *A Latino heritage: A guide to juvenile books about Latino peoples and Cultures.* Lanham, MD: Scarecrow Press.
An annotated bibliography for K–12 about Latino peoples and cultures in the United States.

Thomas, R. L. (1996). *Connecting cultures: A guide to multicultural literature for children.* New Providence, NJ: Bowker.
The annotated list covers children's fiction, poetry, songs, and music on diverse cultural groups.

Totten, H. L., and Brown, R. S. (1994). *Culturally diverse library collections for children.* New York: Neal Schuman.
An annotated bibliography of multicultural resources for elementary children.

Totten, H. L., Garner, C., and Brown, R. W. (1996). *Culturally diverse library collections for youth.* New York: Neal Schuman.
Contains resources about African Americans, Native Americans, Hispanic Americans, Asian Americans, and multiethnic materials. Includes various genres: biographies, folklore, literature, poetry, fiction, reference sources, scholarly works, and informational books.

Williams, H. E. (1991). *Books by African-American authors and illustrators for children and young adults.* Chicago: American Library Association.
Features books written with an African American perspective.

Woodward, M., and Woodward, G. (1985). *The Black American in books for children: Reading in racism* (2d ed.). New York: Scarecrow Press.
An annotated list of books about the black experience in the United States and other parts of the world.

Journals

Alan Review (Assembly on Literature for Adolescents)
Reviews of young adult books mostly by secondary school teachers or librarians.

Bookbird, Journal of the International Institute for Children's Literature
Includes articles and reviews.

Booklist
Reviews current books, videos, and software in all areas. Features a foreign language bibliography in each issue.

Horn Book Magazine
Evaluates hardback and paperback books including multicultural literature.

Interracial Books for Children Bulletin
Published by the Council on Interracial Books for Children, the journal includes articles and book reviews related to race and cultural issues.

Multicultural Review
Includes articles and reviews of books for juvenile and adults.

School Library Journal
Reviews print, nonprint, and electronic resources in all areas, including multicultural resources.

USBBY Newsletter (United States Board on Books for Young People)
USBBY is an affiliate of IBBY (International Board on Books for Young People). Its newsletter talks about juvenile titles in the United States and abroad.

VOYA (Voice of Youth Advocates)
Features reviews of new books and articles on current trends in literature.

APPENDIX B

Multicultural Literature Web Sites

The African-American Mosaic
http://lcweb.lob.gov/exhibits/african/intro.html
A Library of Congress resource guide for studying black history and culture. Discusses colonization, abolition, migration, and other topics.

Black History Hotlist
http://sln.fi.edu/tfi/hotlists/blackhistory.html
Links to numerous good sites for curriculum use. Contains 120 trivia questions about African Americans in science.

Don Mabry's Historical Text Archive
http://www.geocities.com/djmabry/afro/afro.html
Features articles, books, documents, and photos on historical events in the world. Includes sites related to black history and culture.

Hall of Multiculturalism
Site of Texas Education Network (TENET)
http://www.tenet.edu/academia/multi.html
An extensive collection of resources on major ethnic groups and their countries of origin. Includes
African/African American, Latino/Chicano/Hispanic/Mexican, Asian/Asian American, indigenous
people, and Native American resources, as well as cross category multicultural resources.

K–12: A Webbliography of Multicultural Resources
http://members.home.net/borek/homepage/multic.htm#/Literature
Contains resources that will be of interest to librarians or teachers working with children
from many diverse cultures. Includes electronic journals and multicultural research.

Multicultural
Maintained by Edmonds School District, Lynnwood, WA 98036
http://dent.edmonds.wednet.edu/IMD/Multicultural.html
Features sites for the K–12 community on children's resources, children's perception of race and
class, calendar of ethnic and cultural events, and *Edge, The-E-Journal of Intercultural Relations.*

Multicultural Children's Literature
http://members.home.net/borek/homepage/MULTLIT.HTM
Links to children's multicultural resources, multicultural Web links for K–12 educators,
and information about writing multicultural children's books.

Multicultural Pavilion: Teacher's Corner
http://curry.edschool.virginia.edu/go/multicultural/teachers.html
Includes projects, lesson plans, and many resources for educators, students, and activists.

Multicultural Resources for Children
http://falcon.jmu.edu/~ramseyil/multipub.htm
This excellent site includes extensive multicultural bibliographies on ethnic and diverse groups.
For young adults it provides history and literature resources and author sites.

Vandergrift's Children's Literature Page
http://www.scils.rutgers.edu/special/kay/afro.html
Contains separate lists of picture books about African Americans, Asian Americans, Latino Americans, Native Americans, and other ethnic groups. Also provides tips for librarians and teachers on
evaluating illustrations in multicultural literature for children.

APPENDIX C

Multicultural Literature

African American

Aardema, V. (1978). *Why mosquitoes buzz in people's ears: A West African tale.* Illustrated by Leo
   Dillon and Diane Dillon. New York: Dial. (Interest level: ages P–8)

Aardema, V. (1989). Rabbit makes a monkey of lion: A Swahili tale. Illustrated by Jerry Pinkney. New
   York: Dial. (Interest level: ages P–7)

Adoff, A. (1982). *All the colors of the race.* Illustrated by John Steptoe. New York: Lothrop, Lee &
   Sheperd. (Interest level: ages 8–11)

Baldwin, J. (1974). *If Beale Street could talk.* New York: Dial. (Interest level: age 19)

Bryan, A. (1980). *Beat the story-drum, pum-pum.* New York: Atheneum. (Interest level: ages 7–10)

Brooks, B. (1984). *The moves make the man.* New York: HarperCollins. (Interest level: young teens)

Childress, A. (1973). *A hero ain't nothin' but a sandwich.* New York: Coward McCann. (Interest level:
   early teens)

Curtis, C. P. (1999). *Bud, not Buddy.* New York: Delacorte. (Interest level: ages 10–YA).

Flournoy, V. (1985). *The patchwork quilt*. Illustrated by Jerry Pinkney. New York: Dial. (Interest level: ages 6–9)

Fox, P. (1973). *The slave dancer*. Scarsdale, NY: Bradbury. (Interest level: ages 10–13)

Giovanni, N. (1985). *Spin a soft black song*. Illustrated by George Martins. New York: Harper-Collins. (Interest level: ages 6–10)

Greenfield, E. (1978). *Honey, I love and other love poems*. Illustrated by Diane Dillon and Leo Dillon. New York: Harper. (Interest level: ages 7–9)

Grimes, N. (1994). *Meet Danitra Brown*. Illustrated by Floyd Cooper. New York: Lothrop, Lee, and Shepherd. (Interest level: ages P–8)

Hamilton, V. (1968). *The House of Dies Drear*. Illustrated by Eros Keith. New York: Simon & Schuster. (Interest level: ages 10–YA)

———. (1974). *M. C. Higgins, the great*. New York: Macmillan. (Interest level: ages 10–YA)

———. (1982). *Sweet whispers, Brother Rush*. New York: Philomel. (Interest level: ages 10–YA)

Haskins, J. (1999). *Bound for America: The forced migration of Africans to the New World*. New York: Lothrop, Lee & Shepherd. (Interest level: ages 6–9)

Lester, J. (1996). *Sam and tigers*. Illustrated by Jerry Pinkney. New York: Dial. (Interest level: ages 6–9)

Mathis, S. B. (1975). *The hundred penny box*. Illustrated by Leo and Diane Dillon. New York: Puffin. (Interest level: ages 8–10)

Myers, W. D. (1988). *Scorpions*. New York: Harper-Collins. (Interest level: ages YA)

———. (1994). *The glory field*. New York: Scholastic. (Interest level: ages YA)

Nelson, V. M. (1993). *Mayfield crossing*. Illustrated by Leonard Jenkins. New York: Putnam. (Interest level: ages 9–12)

Pinkney, A. D. (1993). *Seven candles for Kwanzaa*. Illustrated by Brian Pinkney. New York: Dial. (Interest level: ages 6–9)

Ringgold, F. (1991). *Tar beach*. New York: Crown. (Interest level: ages 6–9)

Sebestyen, Q. (1979). *Words by heart*. Boston: Little, Brown. (Interest level: ages 9–12)

Steptoe, J. (1987). *Mufaro's beautiful daughters*: An African tale. New York: Lothrop, Lee & Shepherd. (Interest level: ages P–7)

Taylor, M. D. (1976). *Roll of thunder, hear my cry*. Illustrated by Jerry Pinkney. New York: Dial. (Interest level: ages 11–13)

———. (1987). *The friendship*. New York: Dial. (Interest level: ages 8–11)

Walter, M. P. (1992). *Justin and the best biscuit in the world*. Illustrated by Catherine Stock. New York: Lothrop, Lee, and Shepherd. (Interest level: ages 9–11)

Williams, S. A. (1992). *Working cotton*. Illustrated by Carole Byard. San Diego, CA: Harcourt. (Interest level: ages P–8)

Willian-Garcia, R. (1991). *Like sisters on the homefront*. New York: Lodestar/Dutton. (Interest level: ages YA).

Woolff, V. E. (1933). *Make lemonade*. New York: Holt. (Interest level: ages 14–17)

Woodson, J. (1992). *Last summer with Maizon*. New York: Delacorte. (Interest level: ages 11–YA).

Asian American

Aruego, J., and Aruego, A. (1972). *A Crocodile's tale: A Philippine folk story*. New York: Scribner's. (Interest level: ages P–7)

Carlson, Lori M., ed. (1994). *American eyes: New Asian-American short stories for young adults*. New York: Holt. (Interest level: ages YA)

Choi, S. N. (1991). Year of impossible goodbyes. Boston: Houghton Mifflin. (Interest level: ages 11–YA)

Coerr, E. (1993). *Sadako and the thousand paper cranes*. Illustrated by Ed Young. New York: Putnam. (Interest level: ages 9–12)

Demi. (1990). *The empty pot*. New York: Holt. (Interest level: ages 6–9)

Garland, S. (1993). *Shadow of the dragon*. New York: Harcourt. (Interest level: ages 12–YA)

Hamanaka, S. (1993). *Screen of frogs*. New York: Orchard. (Interest level: ages 6–9)

Ho, M. (1991). *The clay marble*. New York: Farrar. (Interest level: ages 12–YA)

Ishii, M. (1987). *The tongue-cut sparrow*. Illustrated by Suekichi Akaba. Translated by Katherine Paterson. New York: Dutton. (Interest level: ages 6–9)

Mahy, M. (1993). *The seven Chinese brothers*. Illustrated by Jean and Mou-sien Tseng. New York: Scholastic. (Interest level: ages 6–9)

Mochizuki, K. (1993). *Baseball saved us*. Illutrated by Dom Lee. New York: Lee & Low. (Interest level: ages 6–9)

Perkins, M. (1993). *The Sunita experiment*. Boston: Little, Brown. (Interest level: ages 11–YA)

Salisbury, G. (1994). *Under the blood-red sun*. New York: Delacorte. (Interest level: ages 10–YA)

Say, A. (1993). *Grandfather's journey*. Boston: Houghton Mifflin. (Interest level: ages 6–9)

Shea, P. D. (1995). *The Whispering cloth: A refugee's story*. Illustrated by Anita Riggio. Honesdale, PA: Boyds Mills. (Interest level: ages 7–10)

Snyder, D. (1988). *The boy of the three-year nap*. Illustrated by Allen Say. Boston: Houghton Mifflin. (Interest level: ages 6–9)

So, M. (1992). *The emperor and the nightingale*. New York: Bradbury. (Interest level: ages 6–9)

Uchida, Y. (1984). *Journey to Topaz*. Illustrated by Donald Carick. Berkeley: CA: Creative Arts. (Interest level: ages 9–12)

Vuong, L. D. (1993). *The golden carp and other tales from Vietnam*. Illustrated by Manabu Saito. New York: Lothrop, Lee & Shepherd. (Interest level: ages 8–11)

Yep, L. (1975). *Dragonwings*. New York: HarperCollins. (Interest level: ages 10–12)

——— . (1977). *Child of the owl*. New York: Harper & Row. (Interest level: ages YA)

Young, E. (1989). *Lon Po Po: A Red-Riding Hood story from China*. New York: Philomel. (Interest level: ages 7–10)

Latin American

Ada, A. F. (1991). *The gold coin*. New York: Macmillan. (Interest level: ages 9–11)

——— . (1993). *My name Is Maria Isabel*. New York: Atheneum. (Interest level: ages 8–11)

Buss, F. L., and Cubias, D. (1991). *Journey of the sparrows*. New York: Dutton/Lodestar. (Interest level: ages 9–12)

Cisneros, S. (1983). *The house on Mango Street*. Houston: Arte Publico. (Interest level: ages 10–13)

Cofer, J. O. (1995). *An island like you: Stories if the barrio*. New York: Orchard. (Interest level: ages YA)

Cowley, J. (1996). *Gracias: The Thanksgiving turkey*. Illustrated by Joe Cepeda. New York: Scholastic. (Interest level: ages 6–9)

Delacre, L. (1996). *Golden tales: Myths, legends and folktales from Latin America*. New York: Scholastic. (Interest level: ages 9–12)

Emberley, R. (1990). *My house/Mi casa*: A book in two languages. Boston: Little, Brown. (Interest level: ages P–7)

Mohr, N. (1990). *Felita*. New York: Bantam. (Interest level: ages 9–12)

Santiago, D. (1983). *Famous all over town*. New York: Simon & Schuster. (Interest level: ages YA)

Soto, G. (1990). *Baseball in April and other stories*. New York: Harcourt. (Interest level: ages 9–12)

———. (1991). *Taking sides*. New York: Harcourt. (Interest level: ages 10–12)

Native American

Begay, S. (1995). *Navajo visions and voices across the Mesa*. New York: Scholastic. (Interest level: ages 7–12)

Borland, H. (1963). *When the legends die*. New York: HarperCollins. (Interest level: ages YA)

Bruchac, J. (1993). *The first strawberries: A Cherokee story*. Illustrated by Anna Vojtech. New York: Dial. (Interest level: ages P–8)

———. (1995). *The boy who lived with the bears and other Iroquois stories*. Illustrated by Murv Jacob. New York: HarperCollins. (Interest level: ages 8–11)

De Paola, T. (1983). *The legend of the bluebonnet*. New York: Putnam. (Interest level: ages 6–9)

Goble, P. (1978). *The girl who loved wild horses*. New York: Macmillan. (Interest level: ages 6–8)

———. (1987). *Death of the iron horse*. New York: Bradbury. (Interest level: ages 8–10)

Hobbs, W. (1989). *Bearstone*. New York: Atheneum. (Interest level: ages 9–12)

Lipsyte, R. (1991). *The brave*. New York: HarperCollins. (Interest level: age 18)

Martin, R. (1993). *The boy who lived with the seals*. Illustrated by David Shannon. New York: Putnam. (Interest level: ages 6–9)

Steptoe, J. (1984). *The story of jumping mouse: A Native American legend*. New York: Lothrop, Lee & Shepherd. (Interest level: ages 9–13)

Welch, J. (1974). *Winter in the blood*. New York: Penguin. (Interest level: ages 10–YA)

Yolen, J. (1992). *Encounter*. Illustrated by David Shannon. San Diego, CA: Harcourt. (Interest level: ages 7–11)

Image-Text Relationships
in Web Pages

Emily Marsh
University of Maryland College Park

ABSTRACT

The functions that illustrations perform within text documents have been analyzed from a variety of different viewpoints, most of them anecdotal and speculative rather than systematic and theoretical. This chapter describes the framework of a systematic examination of image-text relationship of home pages on the World Wide Web. Its conceptual framework is skewed more toward humanistic and qualitative methodology than more traditional content analysis. A quota-based sample of 45 home pages was taken from the educational, retail, and newspaper categories of a popular Web ranking service. The three-tiered method for the study started with a reader response-based examination of illustration functions using a specific theory-based approach. The second stage was a qualitative content analysis using an original typology of illustration functions, identification of relevance relationships, and identification of pictorial figures such as puns. The last stage was a more traditional quantitative content analysis of the physical characteristics of images and their text-based counterparts. The results of the study promise value for those information designers and educators who aspire to create illustrated documents with images that enrich, rather than simply decorate or distract from, the text.

INTRODUCTION

Few communication tools developed in recent history compare to the World Wide Web's capacity for storing and delivering illustrated documents. As this tool becomes more sophisticated, its users are moving beyond simple browsing behavior (i.e., surfing) to more demanding types of research, with an attendant need for information that fulfills specific needs thoughtfully and efficiently. This shift to a preference for Web-based information with "depth, breadth, and integrity" (Lynch and Horton 1999, ix) means that it is not just desirable but necessary that Web-based documents meet the same high standards for content and design that discriminating users apply to printed sources.

Given the large number of designers who focus on the mechanical elements of Web architecture (i.e., HTML techniques) to the exclusion of content (Powell 1998; Sammons 1999; Vitanza 1998), it is easy to forget that Web documents are not simply collections of formatted text, images, and tags. They are complex tools created to communicate messages to readers, like any other type of document.

Another element that adds to the inherent complexity of many Web pages is the characteristic of illustration. One of the main attractions of the World Wide Web is its ability to display complex documents with richly formatted text and engaging graphics. However, this mix of rhetorical elements makes it difficult to predict or determine with any certainty why or how a given Web page will be useful for a given reader. This dynamic will affect Web designers and Web users. How can Web designers use and combine elements to achieve a given end? How can Web users go about deconstructing this collection of elements to determine meaning and usefulness? For obvious reasons, these questions become especially critical when placed within the context of illustrated educational media. Its audience and authors are bound together by highly specific ends (what students need to learn) and the techniques necessary to reach them (how the writer needs to design the text for learning to take place). Before a set of guidelines can be proposed, however, it would be useful to study the current state of affairs on the Web to see just what types of text-image combinations commonly occur. That is the focus for the dissertation described in this chapter.

FUNCTIONS OF ILLUSTRATION

The best way to start such a study is to determine first how others have addressed the larger question of illustration as a generic rhetorical device, independent of medium. Researchers in the disciplines of education, advertising, journalism, and information design have produced analyses of varying sophistication and usefulness to explain and predict the ways that images work with text. A review of these literatures will produce a list of image-text relationships that can serve as the raw material for a tentative typology. This typology can then be applied to actual images to discover the ways illustration is used on the Web to achieve different editorial ends.

It is clearly beyond the scope of this chapter to provide a complete literature review of illustration. Instead of attempting to summarize a large body of literature in a limited space, only the final typology of image functions is presented in Figure 1, pages 190–95, especially because it was distilled primarily from education studies.

Soergel's (1985) method for index language construction was used to create this typology of text-image relationship types. First, every item cited as common or valuable by the authors consulted was systematically reviewed and recorded. Next, these elements were classed into equivalent concept groups. For example, the closely synonymous terms "achieve redundancy," "repeat," "reinforce," "reiterate," and "transcribe" were collected into a single concept group: "Reiterate." This word was selected as the group's official descriptor for its clarity and efficiency; the other related terms were designed as lead-in terms for this descriptor. This process continued until every study was reviewed. Once all terms were collected a distinct pattern emerged. Each concept group could be ordered roughly along a single conceptual facet: the degree to which an image relates to the meaning in a text. Once this facet was identified, the concept groups, descriptors, and lead-in terms were further reorganized and refined.

STUDY METHODOLOGY

The typology will be applied to a survey of randomly selected illustrated home pages. This will serve two functions: (1) it will test the accuracy and power of the typology to classify Web illustrations, and (2) it will help to reveal ways that images are linked to text that heretofore have been overlooked by the published literature on illustration.

This inquiry will rely on the quota method of sampling wherein a range of data types is identified as being theoretically important and "large enough to make meaningful comparisons" (Mason 1996, 98). Because the fields of education, retail business (signified by advertising), and newspapers (represented by journalism) have the richest histories of illustration studies, they will serve as the basis for a theoretical, quota sample of three groups of 15 Web pages each. These 45 home pages were drawn from listings compiled by the popular Web ranking service 100hot.[1] A quota sample was made by drawing 15 pages randomly from each of the following 100hot groups: "Education—Kids," "News—Newspapers," and "Shopping—Shopping Sites" as listed on the 100hot Web site July 28, 2000. To maintain consistency, each page was loaded on the same personal computer (IBM Aptiva, model E84, type 2137) attached to the same monitor (IBM model 2124; 13.6-inch viewable size; display resolution = 800 X 600). Internet Explorer (Version 5) was the browser used to load the files because of its flexibility in archiving Web page content in a variety of formats.

Figure 1. Typology of Rhetorical Image Functions Arranged by Degree of Relation to the Text.

A. Functions with little relation to the text

DESCRIPTOR	LEAD-IN TERM(S)	SOURCES
A.1. Decorate make the text more attractive without aiming to produce any real effects on the reader's understanding or memory		Berinstein 1997; Bodner 1992; Duchastel 1980; Levin 1981; Woodward 1993.
A.1.1 Change Pace interrupt continuity by shifting to a different activity	**Novel Stimulus** provide something new or unusual	Brody 1984
A.1.2 Match Style image and text match along same stylistic dimension		Bodner 1992; Stamm 1988
A.2. Elicit Emotion encourage emotional response from reader through display of content or style that is especially arresting or disturbing	**Tone or Mood-inducing** create a specific emotional atmosphere designed to engage the reader	Berinstein 1997; Bodner 1992; Fang 1996; Stamm 1988
A.2.1 Alienate create tension between image and text through contrast in style or mood (for content-based differences use B.3.2 Contrast)		Schwarcz 1982
A.2.2 Humanize represent elements within the text in human form, thereby making it more accessible		Stamm 1988
A.2.3 Express Poetically suggest the spiritual qualities or effects of the object depicted		Stamm 1988
A.3. Control exercise restraining or directing influence	**Direct** regulate activities or course	Brody 1984; Duchastel 1978
A.3.1 Engage hold the attention of the reader (if method of engagement is primarily emotional, then use A.2. Elicit Emotion)	**Gain attention**	Tanner and Larsen 1994
A.3.2 Motivate encourage some response from reader (if desired response is emotional in nature, then use A.2. Elicit Emotion)		Brody 1984

B. Functions with close relation to the text

DESCRIPTOR	LEAD-IN TERM(S)	SOURCES
B.1. Reiterate restate with minimal change or interpretation	**Achieve Redundancy**	Brody 1984; Schriver 1997
	Reinforce one source provides a visual or textual restatement of another	Fang 1996; Stamm 1988
	Repeat **Transcribe**	Stamm, 1988
B.1.1 Concretize make explicit	**Make the Unseen Visible** "concretize" a textual reference to an abstract concept	Berinstein 1997; Levin and Mayer 1993; Stamm 1988
B.1.2 Common Referent text and image share same symbolic source of meaning		Brody 1984
B.1.3 Describe represent or give an account	**Discuss** present in detail for examination or consideration	Stamm 1988
	Convey Ideas impart or communicate by statement, suggestion, gesture, or appearance	Tanner and Larsen 1994
B.1.4 Translate convert from one form to another	**Represent** reinforce by repeating written content in visual form	Levin 1981
B.1.5 Graph translate numeric data into a visual representation		Berinstein 1997
B.1.6 Exemplify present a paragon that captures the essential meaning of a concept		Brody 1984; Stamm 1988
B.2. Organize form into a coherent unity or functioning whole; includes Advance Organizers	**Make Coherent** organize or structure text	Brody 1984; Levin and Mayer 1993
B.2.1 Isolate select from among others		Brody 1984
B.2.2.Contain keep within limits		Stamm 1988
B.2.3 Locate to set or establish in a time or place	**Establish Setting** indicate time, place, historical era	Berinstein 1997; Fang1996

(Figure 1 continues on page 192.)

Fig. 1—*Continued*

DESCRIPTOR	LEAD-IN TERM(S)	SOURCES
	Stage-Setting images or text introduces or sets the scene for the other	Schriver 1997
B.2.4 Induce Perspective capacity to view things in their true relations or relative importance (more complex than B.2.3 Locate)		Peeck 1994
B.3 Relate (these terms refer to processes intended to bring out concepts contained wholly *within* text; functions classed under C.2.1 Analogize & C.2.2 Contrast use concepts *outside* of text to explain and interpret)		
B.3.1 Compare make explicit intended elements of comparison between objects depicted in text		Brody 1984; Stamm 1988
B.3.2 Contrast make explicit intended elements of contrast between objects depicted in text		
B.4 Condense reduce to essential elements	**Simplify** reduce to basic essentials	Brody 1984
B.4.1 Concentrate bring the most critical information to the reader's attention (reduces text more than B.4.2 Compact)	**Reduce** some aspects of the text are ignored in order to emphasize others	Schwarcz 1982; Levin and Mayer 1993
B.4.2 Compact represent succinctly (reduces text less than B.4.1 Concentrate)	**Summarize** tell or reduce to an abstract, abridgment, or compendium	Levin and Mayer 1993
	Make Concise	Levin and Mayer 1993
B.5 Explain make plain or understandable (use only when original text is followed closely; if external constructs are used to explain by means of comparison or contrast, use terms under C.2.1 Analogize or C.2.2 Contrast)		Bodner 1992; Duchastel 1978; Stamm 1988
B.5.1 Define determine or identify essential qualities or meaning	**Comprehensible** **Explicate**	Bodner 1992; Duchastel 1978; Fang 1996; Levin and Mayer 1993; Stamm 1988

DESCRIPTOR	LEAD-IN TERM(S)	SOURCES
B.5.2 Complement one mode helps the other convey the message		Schriver 1997

C. Functions that go beyond the text

DESCRIPTOR	LEAD-IN TERM(S)	SOURCES
C.1 Interpret provide illustrations of complex ideas in concrete form (provides a lesser degree of interpretation than C.3.2 Model)		Bodner 1992; Levin 1981
C.1.1 Emphasize provide force or intensity of expression that gives impressiveness or importance to something	**Underscore** make evident	Brody 1984; Stamm 1988
C.1.2 Correspond provide links between reader's preexisting knowledge and new ideas within text		Levin and Mayer 1993
C.1.3 Instruct provide authoritative information or advice	**Document** provide factual or substantial support	Berinstein 1997; Brody 1984; Levin, Anglin, and Carney 1987
C.2 Develop set forth or make clear by degrees or in detail	**Amplify** expand (as a statement) by the use of detail or illustration or by closer analysis	Bodner 1992; Fang 1996; Schwarcz 1982; Stamm 1988
	Elaborate expand something in detail	Bodner 1992; Fang 1996; Schwarcz 1982
	Expand express at length or in greater detail	Bodner 1992; Fang 1996; Schwarcz 1982
	Extend provide additional details	Brody 1984; Fang 1996; Schwarcz 1982
	Specify bring out information about the story embedded in the text	Schwarcz 1982
	Supplement	Schriver 1997

(Figure 1 continues on page 194.)

Fig. 1—*Continued*

DESCRIPTOR	LEAD-IN TERM(S)	SOURCES
C.2.1 Analogize create a resemblance in some particulars between things otherwise unlike (unlike B.3.1 Compare: the point of reference rests outside the original meaning of the text)		Brody 1984
C.2.2 Contrast (unlike B.3 Relate: the point of reference rests outside the original meaning of the text)	**Counterpoint** add new information creating a wholly different narrative thrust	Schwarcz 1982
	Different Viewpoint differing as to a position from which something is considered or evaluated	Fang 1996
	Oppose add new information providing depth or insight	Schwarcz 1982
	Juxtapose	Schriver 1997
C.3 Transform recode into concrete form; relate components to each other; provide organization to facilitate recall (introduces more interpretation than C.1 Interpret, C.2.1 Analogize, or C.2.2 Contrast)	**Code** perform a mnemonic function and make the text more readily available for processing into memory	Duchastel 1978; Levin 1981; Levin and Mayer 1993
C.3.1 Alternate progress text and illustrations "take turns" in progressing the story		Schwarcz, 1982
C.3.2 Model provide a description or analogy used to help visualize something that cannot be directly observed (provides a greater degree of interpretation than C.1 Interpret)		
C.3.2.1 Model Cognitive Process visual representation of abstract process		Brody 1984
C.3.2.2 Model Physical Process visual representation of material or mechanical process		

DESCRIPTOR	LEAD-IN TERM(S)	SOURCES
C.3.3 Inspire using the text as a starting point, the illustration veers away to introduce new content; the new content adheres to the spirit of the original story		Schwarcz 1982

In addition to being a proving ground for this new index language of image functions, the sample was part of a larger mixed qualitative and quantitative study design. The conceptual framework for this study is laid out in Figure 2.

Figure 2. Conceptual Framework.

A. Themes for a *Reader Response Theory- Based Literary Analysis* (Critical Study)		B. Categories for a *Qualitative Content Analysis* (Rhetorical Study)		C. Variables for a *Quantitative Content Analysis* (Media Study)	
A1.	Identification of **blanks** (conceptual links between images and text)	B1.	Illustration **functions**	C1.	Image **type**: style, color, medium
A2.	Identification of **gaps** (conceptual frames necessary for reader to understand images)	B2.	**Relevance relationships** between images and text	C2.	Image **frequency** (per relevant text segment)
A3.	Identification of **repertoires** (conceptual frames at a higher level of abstraction)	B3.	**Rhetorical figures** embodied within images (*e.g.*, schemes, tropes, metaphors)	C3.	Image **size** (as displayed on screen, in pixels)
				C4.	**Distance** of image from relevant text (in pixels)
				C5.	Text **length** (in characters)

Each component of this framework will be described briefly before presenting some examples of the methodology in action.

Part A: Reader Response Theory-Based Literary Analysis (Critical Study)

Reader response criticism is a designation for a diffuse group of literary theories that seeks to understand texts as artifacts of human communication. Reader response theory (RRT) argues that it is impossible to derive a complete understanding of a text without looking at the networks of shared meaning that surround it as it is read by a socially situated audience. So its analytical emphasis is placed not so much on identifying the contents of the text as it is on understanding the processes that go into reading and understanding the text. These processes necessarily depend and draw on extratextual elements including, but not limited to, the mindset and motives of the reader and the larger world of socially created constructs.

Wolfgang Iser, a leading figure in RRT, writes, "it is presumed that the literary work is a form of communication, for it impinges upon the world, upon prevailing social structures, and upon existing literature" (1978, ix). In terms of the present study, the classification of image-text relationships in Web pages must be grounded in a methodology that is flexible enough to capture the sorts of complex associations that exist between these media and clear enough for the coding to be understood (for the sake of validity). Given that this study will adopt the tenets of reader response theory, the question now turns on which form of RRT to use and how best to translate that theory into a comprehensible methodology.

Iser (1978) sets out a program that will fulfill these conditions. Three constructs form the center of his theory: blanks, gaps, and repertoires. Blanks are what Iser calls "the unseen joints in the text" that link the constituent pieces of a text together into a whole, thematically coherent composition. In this case, a blank is the bridge between a given Web image and the portion(s) of text deemed relevant to its function. Gaps link an image-word pair to an archetype closely related to the text that somehow informs and explains the rhetorical operation at work. In essence, it clarifies the meaning of the image-word pair (something that is presumed to be new to the reader) by referring to a cultural archetype outside of the text (something that is presumed to be familiar). Repertoires are even more generic mental models that organize the component textual elements and then merge them into a broader social context.

Part B: Image Functions and Relevance Relationships

The typology of image functions leads off Part B of the framework. After assigning the number of functions that apply to each image in relation to its relevant text, two further classifications will be made. The second assignment identifies the way in which each image shares a relevance relationship with its textual counterpart. Relevance is a complex construct with a long history in information studies. In essence it can be operationally defined as, "the relationship of [a] text to a user need that it helps resolve" (Green and Bean 1995, 654). The most common type of relevance relationship is that of topical matching: text A is relevant to user need B because they both address topic C.

As Green and Bean point out, however, this is not the only type of relevance relationship possible. Broadly conceived, relevance is best seen as a kind of relationship that can fall within one of three categories: topicality, conceptual hierarchical relationships (e.g., broader/narrower concept networks), and conceptual structural relationships. This last category includes those types of conceptual frames built on commonly understood, everyday knowledge. For example, the complex frame "college class" includes, teacher, students, classroom, subject, and syllabus, among many others. This qualifies as a conceptual frame for two reasons: It has a fixed structure with predetermined slots, and, more important, it is immediately, universally understood by most every person competent in western culture, whether they have ever actually set foot in a college classroom. Frames are a very efficient way to convey a great deal of information in a very compact linguistic space.

Part B: Pictorial Figures

The final element in Part B is an investigation of pictorial rhetorical figures. McQuarrie and Mick's (1996, 1999) work in advertising advances the idea that one of the most common features of this genre is its reliance on complex pictorial figures such as metaphors, puns, schemes, and tropes. McQuarrie and Mick's assertion that rhetorical figures are often embodied as pictures will be tested by recording and classifying any such expressions in the Web images captured by this study.

Quantitative Content Analysis

The last group of variables falls under the rubric of what is often called content analysis. The unstated assumption implicit in this phrase is that the content being analyzed is quantitative (or at least easily quantifiable) in nature. Examples of such content categories are image type, frequency, size, distance from text, and length. This type of methodology has become quite popular in recent studies of Web content (Bauer and Scharl 2000; Bucy et al. 1999; Cohen and Still 1999; Haas and Grams 2000). It seemed logical to include these variables because this analytic approach has become the de facto standard of Web research.

APPLICATION OF METHODOLOGY

At this point, an example of this study's three-part methodology in action will be useful. The picture–text combination in Figure 3 was captured from the home page for Macy's, a retailer, on April 25, 2000.[2] The phrase "What's the Perfect Gift that Mom is Wishing for?" is the caption for a drawing of a wistful young woman as she imagines different personal items, seen in thought bubbles above her head.

Figure 3. An Image Taken from Macy's Web Site (Macy's, Inc. 2000).

Part A: (A1) One *blank* exists between the mom in the text and the woman in the image. One understands instantly and intuitively that the illustrated woman is a mom. More specifically, she is designed as a stand-in for the reader's mom, so she is not just *any* mom; she could be *your* mom. A second blank connects the gifts in the caption and the images of items being imagined by the woman. (A2) The *gap* links the caption, the image of the young woman, and the surrounding images of potential gifts to a larger idealized model: the Mother's Day frame. This idealized model links desired objects (perfume, jewelry, a robe, or sweater) for sale at a store (Macy's) to a buyer (the reader of the Web page) for a prospective recipient (the mom in the image, or, more specifically, the mom of the person looking at the Web page), based on highly personal preferences (what is "wished for," what would be "perfect"), in honor of a particular occasion (Mother's Day). (A3) Last, the more generic, gift-giving schema wherein one shops for a personal, desired gift at a store and then gives that gift to commemorate an occasion and please the recipient acts as the organizing *repertoire* of this small text.

Part B: (B1) The illustration *functions* in three capacities:

1. **A.2. Elicit Emotion**: The image tries to encourage an emotional reaction from the reader (i.e., the reader should want to please Mom by giving her a "perfect" gift; guilt might also be an intended response);

2. **A.3.2 Motivate**: It also tries to encourage a behavioral response from the reader (i.e., to shop for that gift at Macy's); and

3. **C.3.2 Model**: It provides a description to help visualize something that cannot be directly observed: wishing for a gift.

(B2) The image shares a Conceptual Structural *relevance relationship* with the text, whereby the abstract frame (Mother's Day) is called on with all its attendant slots: gift, giver/receiver, shopper/seller, wish made/desire fulfilled, and so on. (B3) Rhetorical figure: none.

Part C: The image-text pair has the following morphological characteristics. (C1) Image type: *style*: realistic; *color*: full color; *medium*: drawing. (C2) Image *frequency* (per relevant text segment): 1 (C3) Image *size* (as displayed on screen, in pixels): area = 112014. (C4) *Distance* of image from relevant text (in pixels): 38. (C5) *Text length*: 48 characters.

Two further examples help illustrate the methodology in a bit more depth (see Figure 4, page 199, and Figure 5, page 200). Because the variables measured in Part C are fairly straightforward, the last two examples will cover Parts A and B of the framework only.

**Figure 4. Example of Image-Text Relationship from an
Educational Web Page (http://www.studyweb.com).**

Image	(1) a stylized drawing of an insect with multiple arms holding an apple, a book, and two pencils
	(2) a stylized drawing of a spider's web
Relevant Text	(1) "Study Buddy" & (2) "Study Web"
A1. Blank	(1) between the insect image and "Study Buddy"
	(2) between the Web site itself and "Study Web"
A2. Gap	(1) The spiderlike "Study Buddy" is a native of the "Study Web" (because spiders live in webs) and can therefore be a guide for the reader. The apple—a common metaphor for schools and teachers—pencils, and book signify the spider's teaching credentials
	(2) the reader is enclosed in a metaphorical web of learning
A3. Repertoire	(1) Web navigation can be facilitated by a knowledgeable guide.
	(2) Content stored on the internet is organized in an interconnected Web.
B1. Illustration Function	(1) A.1. Decorate; A.2.2 Humanize; A.3.2 Motivate; C.3.2 Model
	(2) C.3.2 Model
B2. Relevance Type	(1) Conceptual Structure: Metaphor—spider is a Web guide.
	(2) Conceptual Structure: Metaphor—Web is an interconnected learning environment.
B3. Rhetorical Figure	(1) Metaphor: A spider can be an Internet expert because it lives in the [World Wide] "Web."
	(2) Metaphor: Web content is connected like a spider's web.

**Figure 5. Example of Image-Text Relationship from an
Educational Web Page (General Mills 1998).**

Image	Boy in sunglasses and T-shirt holds aloft two halves of a broken, oversized pencil.
Relevant Text	"Commercial Break"
A1. Blank	between the broken pencil and the commercial "Break"
A2. Gap	The boy holding the broken pencil links the reader to a virtual school where the students are stylish (hence, the sunglasses) and in control (it is they who determine when learning will happen and when a Web site advertisement will be read).
A3. Repertoire	Learning takes place in schools that are normally not controlled by students; a school that can be controlled by students (a "You Rule" school) is open to independent action and possible interruptions.
B1. Illustration Function	A.1. Decorate; A.2. Elicit Emotion; C.2.1. Analogize
B2. Relevance Type	Conceptual Structure: Metaphor—A pencil represents orderly learning that can be interrupted by student action.
B3. Rhetorical Figure	**Puns** break = break pencil break = interrupt content for advertisement **Metaphor** The pencil stands in for the educational activities of the "You Rule School" that are interrupted ("broken") by the advertisements (commercial "breaks") on the Web site.

SPECULATIONS AND EXPECTATIONS

The methodology and examples above provide a glimpse into the kind of data set the study will produce. The methods of pattern detection, constant comparison, and iterative analysis used in qualitative research (Mason 1996) should help to fashion a good starting point from which to ask and address, though certainly not definitively answer, questions such as the following:

- What rhetorical functions do pictures serve? Are they similar to those types identified with previous studies of different document types or does the Web encourage atypical image use?

- What types of elements are at work within the reader response analytical framework?

- Is this a useful means for understanding Web illustration?

- Is it easy or difficult to discern relevance between images and text?

- Do Green and Bean's (1995) relevance relationship types apply to Web illustrations and text?

- What kinds of conceptual schemes are used within Web illustration?

- Are rhetorical figures a common feature of Web-based images?

- What patterns can be discerned over these three Web page types regarding image type, frequency, and size?

- Are images placed close to relevant text?

- Are images paired with short or long text segments?

- Do Web pages with a nominal focus on education show patterns different from those designed with different rhetorical goals in mind?

The first and last questions will probably hold the most interest for designers and users of educational media. It is hoped that this study will answer them with some compelling evidence and convincing analyses.

NOTES

1. http://www.100hot.com/help/fact_sheet.html

2. http://www.macys.com

REFERENCES

100hot.com. (n.d.) *100hot.com Fact Sheet.* [Online]. Available: http://www.100hot.com/help/fact_sheet .html. (Accessed July 28, 2000).

Bauer, C., and Scharl, A. (2000). Quantitative evaluation of web site content and structure. *Internet Research,* 10:1, 31–43.

Berinstein, P. (1997). Moving multimedia: The information value in images. *Searcher,* 5:8, 40–46,48–49.

Bodner, G. R. (1992). Approaching the illustrated text. In G. E. Sadler (ed.), *Teaching Children's Literature: Issues, Pedagogy, Resources.* New York: The Modern Language Association of America.

Brody, P. J. (1984). In search of instructional utility: A function-based approach to pictorial research. *Instructional Science,* 13, 47–61.

Bucy, E. P., Lang, A., Potter, R. F., and Grabe, M. E. (1999). Formal features of cyberspace: Relationships between Web page complexity and site traffic. *Journal of the American Society for Information Science,* 50:13, 1246–1256.

Cohen, L. B., and Still, J. M. (1999). A comparison of research university and two-year college library web sites: Content, functionality, and form. *College and Research Libraries,* 60:3, 275–289.

Duchastel, P. C. (1978). Illustrating instructional texts. *Educational Technology,* 18:11, 36–39.

———. (1980). *Research on illustrations in text: Issues and perspectives. Educational Communication and Technology Journal,* 28:4, 283–287.

Fang, Z. (1996). Illustrations, text, and the child reader: What are pictures in children's storybooks for? *Reading Horizons,* 37:2, 130–142.

General Mills. (1998). [Online]. Available: http://www.youruleschool.com/sidebar/commercial.html. (Accessed March 10, 2001).

Green, R., and Bean, C. A. (1995). Topical relevance relationships. 2. An exploratory study and preliminary topology. *Journal of the American Society for Information Science,* 46:9, 654–662.

Haas, S. W., and Grams, E. S. (2000). Readers, authors, and page structure: A discussion of four questions arising from a content analysis of Web pages. *Journal of the American Society for Information Science,* 51:2, 181–192.

Iser, W. (1978). *The act of reading: A theory of aesthetic response.* Baltimore, MD: Johns Hopkins University Press.

Levin, J. R. (1981). On functions of pictures in prose. In F. J. Pirozzolo and M. C. Wittrick (eds.), *Neuropsychological and cognitive processes in reading.* New York: Academic Press.

Levin, J. R., Anglin, G. J., and Carney, R. N. (1987). On empirically validating functions of pictures in prose. In D. M. Willows and H. A. Houghton (eds.), *The Psychology of illustration. Volume 1: Basic research.* New York: Springer-Verlag.

Levin, J. R., and Mayer, R. E. (1993). Understanding illustrations in text. In B. K. Britton, A. Woodward, and M. Binkley (eds.), *Learning from textbooks: Theory and practice.* Hillsdale, NJ: Lawrence Erlbaum.

Lightspan, Inc. (n.d.) Lightspan StudyWeb: Links for learning. [Online]. Available http://www.studyweb.com. (Accessed March 10, 2001).

Lynch, P. J., and Horton, S. (1999). *Web style guide: Basic design principles for creating Web sites.* New Haven, CT: Yale University Press.

Macy's, Inc. (n.d.). Macy's home page. [Online]. Available: http://www.macys.com. (Accessed April 25, 2000).

Mason, J. (1996). *Qualitative researching.* Thousand Oaks, CA: Sage.

McQuarrie, E. F., and Mick, D. G. (1996). Figures of rhetoric in advertising language. *Journal of Consumer Research,* 22, 424–438.

———. (1999). Visual rhetoric in advertising: Text-interpretive, experimental, and reader-response analyses. *Journal of Consumer Research,* 26, 37–54.

Peeck, J. (1994). The perspective-inducing function of text illustrations. In H. van Oostendorp and R. A. Zwaan (eds.), *Naturalistic text comprehension.* Norwood, NJ: Ablex.

Powell, T. C. (1998). *Web site engineering: Beyond Web page design.* Upper Saddle River, NJ: Prentice Hall.

Sammons, M. C. (1999). *The Internet writer's handbook.* Boston: Allyn & Bacon.

Schriver, K. A. (1997). *Dynamics in document design.* New York: Wiley.

Schwarcz, J. H. (1982). *Ways of the illustrator: Visual communication in children's literature.* Chicago: American Library Association.

Soergel, D. (1985). *Organizing information.* San Diego: Academic Press.

Stamm, D. C. (1988). Art historians and their use of illustrated texts. In *Scholarly Resources in art history: Issues in preservation*. Washington, DC: Commission on Preservation and Access. [Online]. Available: http://www.clir.org/cpa/reports/cpaarth/cpaarth.html. (Accessed February 2000).

Tanner, B., and Larson, P. (1994). "Worth a Thousand Words": Choosing and using illustrations for technical communication. *Technical Communication,* 41:1, 150–153.

Vitanza, V. J. (1998). *Writing for the World Wide Web*. Boston: Allyn & Bacon.

Woodward, A. (1993). Do illustrations serve a purpose in U.S. textbooks? In B. K. Britton, A. Woodward, and M. Binkley (eds.), *Learning from textbooks: Theory and practice*. Hillsdale, NJ: Lawrence Erlbaum.

Aiming for Effective Student Learning in Web-Based Courses
Insights from Student Experiences

Joi L. Moore, Kyung-Sun Kim, and Linda R. Esser
School of Information Science and Learning Technologies
University of Missouri–Columbia

With the rapid advancement of Internet technology and the popularity of distance education programs, many colleges and universities are transitioning courses from traditional, face-to-face (FTF) classroom settings to Web-based learning environments. Higher education institutions are reaching out to attract students who are place-bound or those who live in geographically remote locations. In 1996, Barron reported that approximately 800 off-campus courses were offered by accredited library and information science schools in North America (Barron 1996). Although the off-campus courses are delivered through a variety of different delivery vehicles, such as instructors with mobility, asynchronous audio/video recordings, and synchronous audio/video conferencing, many of these courses are being offered through the Internet (Barreau 2000).

Because Web-based courses (i.e., courses offered or delivered entirely through the World Wide Web) are becoming more popular, many researchers are conducting studies to compare the effectiveness of traditional FTF learning and Web-based learning. Most of the research studies suggest that Web-based courses are as effective as conventional FTF courses in that the two different types of delivery methods showed no difference in students' learning outcomes (Capper and Fletcher 1996; Carter 1996; Moore and Thompson 1997). According to Lockee (2001), however, researchers should focus not only on learning outcomes but also on students' attitudes, which can influence their satisfaction with Web-based courses. Although some studies have reported that learners were very satisfied with their online courses (Wayland, Swift, and Wilson 1994; Wegner, Holloway, and Garton 1999), other studies describe less satisfying student experiences with the Web-based learning environments because of technical problems, limited and slow feedback, and ambiguous instructions (Hara and Kling 1999). Anecdotal data gathered while teaching Web-based courses led us to question whether students' dissatisfaction might be related to their perceptions or mental models of Web-based courses.

Many of the learning theories that have emerged from research regarding FTF learning environments can be applied to Web-based learning environments. Adult learning theory is essential for understanding student experiences in Web-based environments. Adults have been described as learning in a separate or connected manner (Belenky et al. 1986; MacKeracher 1994). A separate manner is associated with autonomy, separation, certainty, control, and abstraction. A connected manner, which is empathetic in nature, emphasizes relationships and stresses cooperation rather than competition.

As designers and implementers of Web-based courses, we must determine how to create effective learning environments so students will have an enriching experience as well as intellectual development. To meet this challenge, it is imperative to understand students who are taking Web-based courses. Why do students take Web-based courses? What are the characteristics of students enrolled in these courses? What do they expect from Web-based courses? How do they perceive and experience the courses? How satisfied are they with Web-based courses? This study is an attempt to gain insight into these questions.

DESCRIPTION OF STUDY

An exploratory study was conducted to understand what attracts students to Web-based courses, how students experience learning in a Web-based course, and what aspects should be considered to improve their learning experience. Thirty-eight individuals participated in this study. All of the participants were graduate students, taking at least one Web-based course from the School of Information Science and Learning Technologies, University of Missouri–Columbia.

A questionnaire, made available on the Web, was used to gather information from the participants. Through the questionnaire, we collected demographic and other information, such as experience with different technologies and Web-based courses.

The composition of participants was rather nontraditional in terms of age. One-third of the participants (32 percent) were in their 20s. The remainder of the participants were in their 30s (21 percent), 40s (26 percent), and 50s (31 percent). The majority of the participants were female (85 percent). Most of the students (approximately 90 percent) considered themselves as intermediate or advanced users of the Web and Internet, and 10 percent were novices. Approximately three-fourths of the students (74 percent) had previous experience with Web-based courses.

RESULTS

Initial Perceptions

The data suggest that students' initial perceptions regarding the degree of difficulty of Web-based courses can affect their overall satisfaction with the course, if it is different from the learning experience that was expected. As the number of courses taken increased, the level of difficulty students experienced decreased. This may indicate that participants are becoming more accustomed to the look and feel of Web-based learning environments and more adept at the strategies necessary to be successful in online classrooms.

Students enroll in Web-based courses for a variety of reasons, including distance and time constraints, conflicts with personal schedules and family responsibilities, and the lack of availability of a course in a FTF classroom setting (Fredericksen et al. 2000). Participants in the study paralleled these reasons: required course (20 percent), distance from campus (20 percent), conflicts with schedule (13 percent), course not offered off-line (10 percent), and family responsibilities (11 percent). Other reasons reported were interest in technologies, the Internet, or both (26 percent).

Many students have significant misconceptions concerning Web-based courses, such as correspondence courses with little or no interactivity. The students assume that they will set their own schedules, work individually, and only turn in assignments by the end of the course. Experienced instructors and students of Web-based learning environments are aware that a perception of no or little interaction with other students is inaccurate. The majority (70 percent) of the students without previous experience in Web-based courses were surprised that there was much more interaction with other students and the instructor than expected. Interaction occurs frequently with group work and discussion boards, which are typical components in Web-based courses.

Another misconception appears to be that Web-based courses require less work than FTF courses. However, students quickly learn that there is at least the same amount of work, if not more, for both students and instructors. The time required for success in an online course is increased because of the nature of electronic communications (i.e., e-mail, discussion boards, chat rooms). Composing e-mail or posting to a discussion board tends to be more time intensive than expressing thoughts verbally. In written communication, students usually want to make sure they are appropriately and clearly communicating their ideas. Furthermore, it takes longer to discuss a topic online because students do not have immediate responses available, as they do in face-to-face class settings. For example, an in-class discussion that takes 10 minutes could easily expand to four or five days because of the nature of online communication and because of the structure of asynchronous discussion forums.

Learning Preferences

We asked two questions relating to learning preferences: (1) Do you prefer to work alone or in groups and (2) In what type of learning environment do you learn best: lecture, seminar, or independent study. The majority of the students (80 percent) preferred to work alone. This may be related to some students being solo performers, preferring to work independently. Or it may be attributed to students' prior experiences with group work, which is often frustrating. In addition, even positive experiences with group work may be exacerbated in online environments because of problems created by electronic communication media (Barreau 2000).

The majority of the students (79 percent) preferred an environment in which they actively control their learning rather than having the control in the hands of the instructor. This finding correlates with the work of Wegner, Holloway, and Garton (1999), who found that students in Web-based courses assume control of constructing meanings from course material rather than relying on the instructor to interpret the content for them. Web-based courses require students to be more proactive, which can be difficult for those students who prefer passive learning environments (i.e., students as receptacles of knowledge transmitted by an instructor). In an online learning environment, the instructor acts as the facilitator or coach who guides the student through learning experiences.

Perceptions of Satisfaction in a Web-Based Course

The majority of the participants (87 percent) were satisfied with their learning experience in the course. However, there were a few students who were not satisfied with the Web-based learning experience. One person did not like the required interaction with other students via the discussion board and group work. This person preferred independent learning and preferred to work alone. Another student complained that there was more work than in FTF courses; the student assumed that teachers create busy work to replace the activities that occur in a FTF setting. In Web-based environments, the instructor and student do not have the typical visual cues, which can assist with the immediate exchange of negotiated meanings. Many students fail to realize that Web-based learning requires more written communication (e.g., e-mail, discussion forums, and assignments) for the instructor to assess learning.

In our study, student satisfaction with Web-based courses could be explained by a combination of two variables. One variable was the number of Web-based courses taken before the current course. The higher the number of Web-based courses students have taken, the lower the level of student satisfaction. We speculate that as students become more experienced with Web-based courses as well as the online instructional design, they become more critical of the learning environment and its influence on their learning. The other variable was the level of interaction with classmates. The more students interacted with other students, the greater their level of satisfaction with the course.

Approximately 38 percent of the participants, most of whom were experienced computer users, perceived Web-based courses as more effective than FTF courses. Over half of the participants (52 percent) indicated that Web-based learning was almost the same as the learning in FTF, and 10 percent indicated that Web-based learning was less effective. Negative perceptions were influenced by the following factors: (1) initial perception that the course would be difficult, (2) preference to work alone, (3) first experience in a Web-based course, and (4) resentment that the same course is not offered in a FTF setting. The first two factors influenced the negative attitude toward Web-based learning. Inexperience in a Web-based learning environment, the third factor, must be addressed regardless of learning preferences. For novices, there must be an appropriate orientation to the Web-based environment, which is especially important for adult learners returning to school and who may have relatively little experience using the computer and the Internet. An introductory course or seminar that orients novices to Web-based learning could dramatically affect their learning experiences. The fourth factor (unavailability of the course off-line) can be an administrative and political issue that is not within the control of the instructor. An alternative would be to offer each Web-based course as a FTF course once a year. However, this strategy may cause a department to trade significant numbers of online students for a limited environment of local students.

WHAT HAVE WE LEARNED?

We found that the main reasons for taking Web-based courses tend to be external ones, which implies that the level of students' motivation toward learning through the Web is not likely to be high. Instructors of the Web courses should take this into account and might need to put extra efforts on providing students with rewarding experience that can motivate students and change their rather neutral or negative attitude toward the Web-based course.

It seems that students' previous experience plays an important role in their perception of Web-based learning. Students' experience with computers and Web-based courses influence their expectation and appreciation of the courses, which seems logical. In Web-based courses, almost all instructions are delivered through the computer and the Internet. Students in Web-based courses must deal with computer and other information technologies on a regular basis, and they must be able to successfully use them. Their experience with these technologies would definitely help lower their technology anxiety. Because not all students would come with computer competencies of desired level, it is important to provide orientation sessions to students before the course begins so that students would not be doubly burdened (i.e., new content and technology).

It was interesting to find the relation between the level of interaction with classmates and satisfaction with the Web-based course. Apparently, many students perceive a Web-based course as an independent study or correspondence course that allows students to learn at their own individual pace, with little or no interaction with other students. They also tend to think that Web-based courses are easier than traditional FTF courses. We believe that it is essential to inform students that Web-based courses are designed more like a traditional FTF course without the simultaneous FTF meeting/communication components. Different from independent study or correspondence courses, Web-based courses require a great deal of interaction with the instructor and students. We should also let students know that they should be focused, organized, and proactive. Instructors should assist and scaffold students to become autonomous learners who take responsibility for their learning, understand their own learning habits, set realistic goals and adjust their goals in light of feedback (Linn 1996). A student's mental model of Web-based courses can greatly affect their learning behavior and experience. We strongly suggest that a short course or an orientation should be given before students take Web-based courses so that they can be prepared for the demands of online learning environments. Suggested topics for an orientation include the following:

- How Web-based and FTF courses are similar and dissimilar.
- How to learn in a Web-based course.
- How to be proactive and self motivated.
- How to manage time and tasks.

- How to prepare your computer for Web-based courses.

- How to use the Web-based course management tools (e.g., Blackboard, WebCT, FirstClass).

- How to communicate effectively through discussion boards, e-mail, chat rooms, and so on.

Educators must ensure that students in Web-based courses have enriching, successful learning experiences. This means preparing both instructors and students for this rapidly changing and innovative instructional delivery medium. Although our tendency has been to tout the successes and strengths of Web-based learning, we also need to explore the weaknesses and the critical issues that relate to students' affective and cognitive learning experiences.

REFERENCES

Barreau, D. (2000). Distance learning: Beyond content. *Journal of Education for Library and Information Science*, 41:2, 79–93.

Barron, D. D. (1996). Distance education in North American library and information science education: applications of technology and commitment. *Journal of the American Society for Information Science*, 47:11, 805–810.

Belenky, M. F., Clinchy, B. M., Goldberger, N. R., and Tarule, J. M. (1986). *Women's ways of knowing: The development of self, voice, and mind*. New York: Basic Books.

Capper, J., and Fletcher, D. (1996). *Effectiveness and cost-effectiveness of print-based correspondence study*. A paper presented for the Institute for Defense Analysis, Alexandria, VA.

Carter, V. (1996). Do media influence learning? Revisiting the debate in the context of distance education. *Open Learning*, 11:1, 31–40.

Fredericksen, E., Pickett, A., Shea, P., Pelz, W. and Swan, K. (2000). Student satisfaction and perceived learning with on-line courses: Principles and examples from the SUNY learning network. *Journal of Asynchronous Learning* 4:2, 1–26. [Online]. Available: http://www.aln.org/alnweb/journal. (Accessed March 2, 2001).

Hara, N., and Kling, R. (1999). Students' frustrations with a Web-based distance education course. *Firstmonday*, 4:12. [Online]. Available: http://www.firstmonday.org. (Accessed March 2, 2001).

Linn, M. C. (1996). Cognition and distance learning. *Journal of the American Society for Information Science*, 47:11, 826–842.

Lockee, B. B. (2001) What matters in judging distance teaching? Not how much it's like a classroom course. *The Chronicle of Higher Education*. [Online]. (Accessed March 2, 2001).

MacKeracher, D. (1994). Women as learners. In T. Barer-Stein and J. A. Draper (eds.), *The craft of teaching adults*. Malabar, FL: Krieger Publishing Company.

Moore, M. G., and Thompson, M. M. (1997). The effects of distance learning: Revised edition. *ACSDE Research Monograph*, 15.

Wayland, J. P., Swift, C. O., and Wilson, J. W. (1994). Student attitudes toward distance learning. In B. Engelland and A. J. Bush (eds.), *Marketing: Advances in theory and thought*. New Orleans, LA: Southern Marketing Association.

Wegner, S. B., Holloway, K. C., and Garton, E. M. (1999). The effects of Internet-based instruction on student learning. *Journal of Asynchronous Learning Networks*, 3:2, 98–106.

Part Four
Leadership Profiles

Introduction

This section profiles individuals who have made significant contributions to the field of instructional technology. There is no formal survey or popularity contest to determine the persons for whom the profiles are written, but those selected are usually emeritus faculty that may or may not be active in the field.

Leaders profiled in the *Yearbook* have either held prominent offices, written important works, or made significant contributions that have in some way influenced the contemporary vision of the field. Often, they have been directly responsible for mentoring individuals who have themselves become recognized for their contributions. The following are those previously profiled in earlier volumes of the *Yearbook*:

James D. Finn	Paul Saettler
James W. Brown	Donald P. Ely
Wilbur Schramm	James Okey
Robert E. De Kieffer	Constance Dorothea Weinman
Jean E. Lowrie	Castelle (Cass) G. Gentry
Robert Morris	Thomas F. Gilbert
William Travers	Wesley Joseph McJulien
Robert Mills Gagné	Stanley A. Huffman
Robert Heinich	John C. Belland
Charles Francis Schuller	Robert M. Diamond
Harry Alleyn Johnson	Paul Robert Wendt
Robert M. Morgan	Don Carl Smellie

There are special reasons to feature people of national and international renown, and the editors of this volume of the *Educational Media and Technology Yearbook* believe we have selected four outstanding leaders in our field for this issue. I have had the privilege of meeting each of these gentlemen, and each has contributed tremendously to the field of instructional technology worldwide. Those people we have chosen to profile this year are

Bob Casey

Kent Gustafson

Tjeerd Plomp

Walter Dick

You are welcome to nominate individuals to be featured in this section. Your nomination of someone to be profiled in this section must also be accompanied by the name of the person who would agree to compose the leadership profile. Please direct any comments, questions, and suggestions about the selection process to the senior editor.

Michael Orey

Robert J. Casey, Jr.
Professor, Humanitarian, Tinkerer

Ann Kwinn, Ph.D.
MOHR Learning

A "junkyard mind" was attributed to a particular eclectic individual by some of the people who shared with him the wild ride that was his life. Robert Casey did spend time in junkyards, coal mines, nightclubs, high schools, bazaars, police stations, Air Force bases, and just about every place in between. His influence spanned from Massachusetts to the California coast, Europe to the Middle East. Although it's true that creating educational programs can take you to strange places, Casey's restless creative energy stood out. He sold weather information to donut shops, created a head gasket out of aluminum foil, and hunted eels. About most forces of nature, there is no point explaining more, except in this case to say, "That's Casey."

Of Irish heritage, Casey was born in Weymouth, Massachusetts, in 1927 as Robert James Casey, Jr. But to those of us who hung out with him in the media lab in the basement of the University of Southern California's (USC) Education building, he was simply "Casey." He is remembered in the Instructional Technology department for many contributions, including his "Casey-isms," such as Number 5, "You can teach a pig to sing, but it takes a long time and annoys the pig," or Number 12, "That's just the sort of thing for people who like that sort of thing." His boundless fascination with technology as a means of communication may have been genetic. Casey's father, Robert Senior, worked for the telephone company for many years and was granted three patents.

During World War II, while still in high school, Casey entered the Massachusetts Maritime Academy, where at one time he was confined to the barracks for failing to meet the standards of military neatness. He was allowed off the base once a week to direct a band and play trumpet for a national radio program intended to recruit new students. (Casey-ism Number 14: "The most proficient staff they had was their brochure writers.") He also played a lot of trumpet—big band and jazz. In fact, the musical thread in his life led him to the acquaintance of a vocalist, Rhoda Lintz, his partner in a marriage that began in 1954 and lasted for 42 years.

Because of a lack of swimming ability, Casey resigned from the Maritime Academy and enlisted in the Army Air Corps, where science saved his military career. His favorite teacher in high school had taught him meteorology, which enabled him to serve as weather station chief at Alamogordo, New Mexico, where he met Robert Oppenheimer, Director of the Los Alamos laboratory, where the first atomic bomb was developed. After the bomb was detonated at Alamogordo in 1945, Casey participated in Oppenheimer's Sunday meetings on the moral implication of what the Los Alamos group had unleashed.

Casey attended many colleges. A listing of his courses of study resembles a college catalog itself. Of note, he earned bachelor's and master's degrees in education from Massachusetts State College in Bridgewater in 1952 and 1960, respectively, and a Doctor of Education from the University of Southern California in 1971.

To his students' luck, Casey spent 38 years in education. He taught math and music to elementary school students in Massachusetts and also in France for the Department of Defense before becoming a professor of instructional technology at the postgraduate level. For being president of the first American Federation of Teachers union on Long Island, he was blackballed along the entire eastern seaboard. (Casey-ism Number 27: "I don't see any place in teaching for objectiveness;" and Number 10: "Reading is moral.") Lack of work in the East prompted the family's move to California in 1961, where Casey taught and then became the Secondary Curriculum Consultant for the Covina Valley Unified School District. After earning his doctorate, he became assistant professor in 1971, vice chair in 1974, and then chairman of USC's Department of Instructional Technology in 1978.

Many projects wove through Casey's life before, during, and after his professorship. He served as principal investigator on contracts for the U.S. Bureau of Mines, the U.S. Army Training and Doctrine Command, the Association of Educational Communications and Technology, the U.S. Office of Education, and the National Iranian Radio/Television, where, working for the Shah, he had to haggle at the Iranian bazaars for cables and connectors to make operable a warehouse full of unconnected equipment. He also conducted research for Canyon Research Group and Vreuls Research, Inc.

After serving as media consultant for the National Teacher's Corps and as staffing consultant for National Training Systems, Casey became director of development for McGraw-Hill/TRATEC Division. He cofounded an instructional design company called FLI, for Frozen Leopard, Incorporated, a reference to one of Casey's favorite short stories, Ernest Hemingway's "The Snows of Kilmanjaro." The FLI business model, unique at the time, was that of a "virtual corporation," in which employees were allowed and encouraged to work from home. Casey's next, similar company was called Beammus (short for "Beam Me Up, Scotty"). In addition, Casey carried out development projects for Video Systems Network, Newcraft Panasonic, and United Airlines Services Corporation.

While on the board of directors of the University Consortium for Instructional Design and Technology, which created the Instructional Development Institute (IDI) curriculum, Casey served as national coordinator of the IDI. The UCIDT also established the PIST (Professors of Instructional Systems Technology) Conference (pun intended), which took place in Bloomington, Indiana, and was attended by an elite force of instructional design professors. Casey received three fellowships from the National Defense Education Act. (Casey-ism Number 31: "It is generally not a good idea to give a person with an I.Q. of 38 a 38-caliber gun. The caliber should at least be below the I.Q.") And in 1993, he was the recipient of the Special Award for Exceptional Practice in the Field of Instructional Design and Technology, given by the Association for Educational Communication and Technology.

Casey was the author and coauthor of numerous articles and reports, and delivered papers and acted as producer on major productions for the U.S. Air Force, the Los Angeles Police Academy, the National Reading Association Convention, American Medical International, and Video Systems Network—documenting the past, instilling skills, spreading literacy, and saving lives. Other projects were self-initiated, including "The Change Game," which simulates an organization's ability to adopt technical innovation; "ROXO-ROO," based on Campbell and Stanley's hazards to internal and external validity; and "Which Way to the Ph.D.," an early interactive videodisc. The production team for the latter included teaching assistants, and the program featured a good actor who also happened to work as a bartender at USC's Faculty Center.

As a professor, Casey loved trying out new technology and managed to get funding for his experiments. Thanks to Casey, USC was a beta test site for software tools such as Icon Author version 1.0, and Casey and his students were regulars at video-production and disc-mastering facilities in Hollywood. Casey was the recipient of IBM Educational Systems' Secondary Courseware College Grant Program, through which he received numerous PCs and software programs, free of charge, for classroom use. (Casey-ism Number 3: "The more money you pay, the less reliable the equipment will be.") He encouraged a "learn by doing" approach. (Number 26: "Go ahead and press the button. If it breaks, we'll fix it.")

At USC, Casey chaired more than 65 doctoral dissertation committees. This very yearbook last year cited Casey as one of the top 25 chairs of the last 20 years. Despite his publication record, Casey's main priority was, according to one friend, "publishing students"—preparing them for the real world. (Casey-ism Number 20: "I have two bases for giving grades: Whether I liked the person and whether I felt guilty about the grade I wanted to give him.")

He helped students get work through his own or his company's projects or through former student, university, and professional connections. At times, he and Rhoda even lent Casey's more impoverished students money or let them stay at their house.

As his last doctoral student, I saw how Casey held research-planning meetings to make sure we completed our dissertations and graduated. He was not the inaccessible kind of professor. He took all of the teaching assistants to lunch at the Faculty Center every week. (The Irishman preferred the chile relleno.) He let his students take qualifying exams on the computer versus on paper, gave a student a desk in the lab when he said it would be more convenient, and held wine and cheese screenings for the Educational Video courses, showing up in a tuxedo and beret.

Each Thanksgiving, Casey and Rhoda took into their home by the sea their extended family of students, colleagues, and the other interesting persons collected throughout their lives. Casey's retirement party in 1990 and memorial celebration in the aftermath of his death in 1995 drew former students from all over the country and from every era of his tenure. Two former students named their children Casey in his memory.

A rare combination of compassion, competence, and resourcefulness, Casey was the ultimate professor. When he was overcome by cancer, many felt lost at his passing. Buried at sea on Saint Patrick's Day, he is survived by his wife, Rhoda, also a professor, as well as his son, Sean, and two grandchildren. It is with gratitude and fondness that I memorialize this impish leprechaun, technical wizard, and decent man. (Casey-ism Number 39: "Why I was spending a weekend in a junkyard in Lake Charles, Louisiana, is another story.")

AUTHOR NOTE

The author thanks Rhoda Lintz Casey for her contribution to this article.

Tribute to Kent L. Gustafson
Professor of Instructional Technology, The University of Georgia

Thomas C. Reeves
Professor of Instructional Technology
The University of Georgia

Professor Kent L. Gustafson officially "retires" in the autumn of 2001 after a long and distinguished career in the field of instructional technology, primarily at two large research universities, Michigan State University (11 years) and The University of Georgia (20 years). But anyone who knows Professor Gustafson ("Gus" or "Kent," as he is known to his family, friends, and colleagues and "Dr. Gus" to generations of students) expects that he'll be active for many years to come as a professor emeritus and internationally recognized scholar of instructional design and technology.

Born and raised in a small town in central Massachusetts, Kent graduated from Worcester State College in 1961 and then served as a high school math teacher and part-time audiovisual director for the Narragansett Regional School District in Templeton, Massachusetts, for five years. He reportedly drove a fast Corvette in those days, and given his height, he must have cut a dashing figure up and down the highways of the Commonwealth.

Advanced degrees are essential for any ambitious educator, and it wasn't long before Kent enrolled in graduate school at The University of Massachusetts. While there, he met his future wife, Elaine, and they were married in 1965. That same year, Kent completed his Master of Education degree, an accomplishment that obviously whet his appetite for more education because in 1966 he and Elaine moved to East Lansing, Michigan, so that Kent could enter a doctoral program at Michigan State University (MSU). When he completed his Ph.D. in 1969, the MSU faculty recognized that they had a scholar they could not afford to lose, and so he was offered a faculty position there. Subsequently, he became an assistant, associate, and later a full professor in instructional development and technology, serving there from 1969 to 1981. In addition to teaching, research, and advisement roles, Kent provided instructional development consulting to faculty as part of a campus-wide effort to improve instruction under the auspices of MSU's Instructional Media Services unit.

Kent's years at Michigan State coincided with what many view as the most formative years of the field. He played a role in several large-scale initiatives, including the Instructional Systems Development project. Led by Professor John Barson, the project was the first large-scale attempt to apply systematic instructional design processes to improve courses in higher education. The first education-oriented instructional design (ID) model, as well as the term "instructional development," are generally considered to have emanated from this effort.

The ID expertise developed by Kent and his contemporaries was later extended to public education by the Instructional Development Institute, a five-day professional development package, and several related projects that yielded an extensive collection of training materials for public school personnel on the topic of instructional development. These materials were used by more than 20,000 teachers in the mid-1970s, as well as by many of the higher education institutions preparing instructional designers and developers. Kent managed this project for the University Consortium of Instructional Design and Technology under the direction of Professor Charlie Schuller, and he even starred in a series of five films that depicted the design/development process being carried out by a school curriculum committee. Later, that same consortium conducted a multiyear project to train instructional designers and developers in Iran to prepare educational programming for National Iranian Radio and Television, an innovative project that was halted by the tumultuous political events in Iran in the late 1970s.

Kent came to The University of Georgia in 1981 when the Instructional Technology department there was called Educational Media and Librarianship. Under his leadership, the department changed its name and its size, from a small, regionally focused graduate program to one with a large, international focus. It also changed its academic reputation from good to one that is widely recognized as one of the top five programs of its kind around the globe. For all of its existence, the Department of Instructional Technology at Georgia has benefited from the strong and forward-thinking leadership that is perhaps Kent's greatest strength. He has especially encouraged faculty and students to take an international perspective on our field, and he has led the effort to establish relationships between the Georgia program and similar programs around the globe. Most recently, he helped establish a fund to support instructional technology students who want to spend a semester abroad during their graduate studies at The University of Georgia, and he signed a collaborative agreement between The University of Georgia and the University of Twente in The Netherlands.

After Kent and Elaine moved their family to Athens, Georgia, in 1981, they quickly adapted to the southern climes, switching their avid sports allegiance from the Spartans to the Bulldogs. Elaine, who has a doctorate in education from The University of Georgia, recently retired from the Northeast Georgia Regional Education Services Agency (RESA), after a distinguished career as a middle school teacher and a professional development expert. Kent and Elaine plan to spend their retirement time between their rural home nestled in 100 acres of woodlands in Olgethorpe County, Georgia, and their summer house on the shores of Lake Burton in the North Georgia mountains. They will especially treasure more quality time with their daughter, Kara, and her husband, Bucky, both teachers in Bartow County, Georgia, and their two energetic grandchildren, Jackson and William. Undoubtedly, Kent will spend a lot more time driving his truck, tractor, and boat. He is an outdoorsman in the best sense, enjoying sports such as hunting and boating, but always with a genuine concern for the environment.

It is difficult to sum up the accomplishments of a scholar of Kent's stature in the few words allowed for this tribute. For starters, he has been both a major proponent of and an important critic of instructional systems design (ISD). Books that he has written or edited with colleagues, such as *Instructional Design: Principles and Applications*, and *Survey of Instructional Development Models,* are ISD classics. And yet, Kent has never hesitated to step out in new directions by pointing others toward instructional design innovations or developing them himself. For example, he was the leader of an initiative in the late 1980s that created the first electronic performance support system for instructional designers called *ID*

Library, and he even was co-awarded a U.S. Patent Award (# 5,655,O86) for a configurable electronic performance support system for total quality management in 1997. As a scholar, he has also authored scores of book chapters and journal articles and has guided numerous doctoral students through the doctoral dissertation process.

With respect to service, Kent has served in numerous professional leadership roles, most notably as president of the Association for Educational Communications and Technology (AECT) in 1994–1995. He has received several important awards from AECT, including the coveted Special Achievement Award for Lifetime Contribution to the Profession in 1996.

Despite an often heavy administrative load, Kent has always been a committed teacher of graduate courses in areas as diverse as instructional design, research methodology, project management, and diffusion of innovations. He has been a frequent international speaker in places as widespread as Australia, Austria, Iran, Malaysia, The Netherlands, Norway, Switzerland, Taiwan, and other countries. His colleagues suspect that his passport will see even more activity in retirement, as universities, corporations, and other agencies around the globe seek to tap into his strong expertise in instructional systems design, project management, and related subjects.

In terms of accomplishments, none may be more important than Kent's mentoring of numerous graduate students and new faculty members (myself included) into the field of instructional technology. To them, he'll always be known fondly as Dr. Gus, a man whose door was never closed. To sum up Kent's career in one word, the consensus at The University of Georgia would be "generous"—generous in mind, body, and spirit.

Tjeerd Plomp
A Citizen of the World

Donald P. Ely
Professor Emeritus, Syracuse University

Since the leadership profile series began, not one professional from outside the United States has been featured. This oversight, although not deliberate, reflects a type of ethnocentrism that characterizes professionals from North America who often neglect outstanding professionals from other parts of the world. This leadership profile reaches out beyond U.S. borders to The Netherlands, where one professional colleague has led the development of educational technology worldwide for the past 25 years.

I first met Tjeerd Plomp in 1978 when he was on the Planning Committee for the Faculty of Educational Science and Technology at the University of Twente. The University was about to launch an undergraduate curriculum in educational technology. He was visiting programs in the United States, and Syracuse University was on his list. Little did I realize at the time that we would become professional collaborators, coauthors, and good friends.

Tjeerd Plomp was appointed Lecturer in Mathematics at the University of Twente in 1964 after completing his bachelor's and master's degrees in the Faculty of Mathematics and Science at the University of Amsterdam. His Ph.D. is in the social sciences. As a result of his research on instructional problems and the development and evaluation of individualized instruction in higher education, he became a member of the Planning Committee to create the Faculty of Educational Science and Technology in 1976. He was awarded his professorship in 1981 (a special honor in The Netherlands, where the person's title becomes Professor Doctor), and soon after was appointed dean of the faculty. After a three-year deanship, he was appointed director of the Institute for Applied Educational Research. He was awarded an honorary doctorate in psychology and pedagogy by the University of Ghent (Belgium) in 1996.

During his tenure in the Faculty of Educational Science and Technology he facilitated the creation of a new curriculum, taught a variety of courses, and mentored 23 Ph.D. candidates to the successful completion of their degrees. He organized and chaired the Master of Science program in Education and Training System Design, which is now offered on campus and at a distance using English as the language of instruction. The program attracts individuals from around the world. All of these new ventures broke new ground but did not deter the leader who was behind them all. He epitomized the Dutch phrase, "Kalmpjes aan, dan breekt het lijntje niet" (Take risks, but never be reckless).

Not satisfied with the confines of a relatively small country, Tjeerd Plomp was a visiting professor at Syracuse University in 1987. He was elected chair of the prestigious International Association for the Evaluation of Educational Achievement (IEA) and has also served as chair of the steering committee for the well-known Third International Mathematics and Science Study (TIMSS) since 1991. These appointments, in addition to his continuing concern for information communication and technology, took him to many parts of the world, including Botswana, China, Japan, Hong Kong, Indonesia, Mozambique, Russia, Singapore, South Africa, and almost every European country. His tasks in each country included, among other things, consulting, organizing, teaching, and other facilitative activities. He actively participates every year in the annual meeting of the American Educational Research Association.

With such an exhausting agenda, it might seem that his academic publications would be curtailed. Not at all! His list of books, scientific articles, and research reports is 12 pages long. On a personal note, the ones I know best are Plomp and Ely, the *International Encyclopedia of Educational Technology,* 2nd edition, and Ely and Plomp, *Classic Writings on Instructional Technology,* Volumes 1 and 2. One interesting aspect of his publications list is that almost every document is coauthored with a colleague, Ph.D. student, or staff associate.

Beyond all the facts and figures of Tjeerd Plomp's contributions to our field, he helps to "grow people." In almost every professional endeavor he involves others in his effort to study and report on emerging areas of concern that are worthy of further exploration or development. As an example, one of the most recent books with his name as a coeditor is *Design Approaches and Tools in Education and Training.* One of his coeditors is a colleague from the University of Twente, one is a recent Ph.D. graduate, and two are colleagues from The University of Georgia in the United States. His ideas are sought for programs, projects, and publications worldwide. In his quiet and thoughtful manner, he provides special insights by contributing questions and information that others can use in addressing a wide variety of challenging situations. He is a problem solver, a substantive contributor, and a wise counselor. Always the eager learner, Professor Plomp seems to delight in exploring new places, meeting new people, and "trying on" new ideas. Those who know him personally know that his work ethic is extremely strong, and his energy level is legendary.

The foundations of this international leader began with his family and their values. His father was a Dutch Reformed minister whose family was imprisoned in Indonesia by the Japanese during World War II. His young son, Tjeerd, was imprisoned with his family for two and one-half years. Later, after the family returned to The Netherlands, Tjeerd developed a passion for music. (He still plays the carillon on the Twente campus and in nearby communities.) His boat is docked at a summer home in the north of Holland, where he is captain of the ship when his grandchildren are aboard. His three grown children live in different parts of the country. There are regular family gatherings when Tjeerd is in the country. He is spending a little more time at home these days, since "retiring" from the Faculty of Educational Science and Technology in June 2000, but he still maintains an office in the department. We probably have not seen or heard the last from this great scholar and warm human being. Colleagues and friends look forward to seeing and hearing more from this genial, facilitative, and productive scholar.

In a recent interview, Tjeerd was asked about his personal philosophy of life. He replied, "I strongly believe in the good aspects of human beings. People are basically good and one should teach others to be critical, but flexible, communicative and easy going." This is the way Tjeerd Plomp has lived his life and all who know him are the beneficiaries of his contributions, both personal and professional.

Allow Me to Introduce
Walter Dick

James D. Russell
Purdue University

Most of you have heard of the Dick and Carey model for instructional design. I want to help you get to know the man behind the model. Let me tell you about him, both professionally and personally. His undergraduate advisor became his respected colleague. His major professor in graduate school became a working associate years later. His advice to students, "Stay flexible and apply what you have learned in an ever-changing environment."

Walt grew up in Brookville, Pennsylvania. His childhood ambitions were to be a professional baseball player and a disc jockey. Walt enjoyed playing football, basketball, and baseball in high school and really was a disc jockey at the local radio station. He also worked in a brick and tile plant. While on a hot assembly line, Walt decided he wanted to go to college. He attended Princeton University and majored in psychology. Walt is living testimony to "When some doors close, a window usually flies open!" After he was unable to schedule a meeting with his assigned advisor, the department chair recommended that he go down the hall to see if the new faculty member would work with him. Fortunately, the faculty member agreed to advise Walt. His name—Robert Gagné!

Two of Walt's early heroes were B. F. Skinner and Robert Gagné. Because of Walt's interest in Skinnerian psychology and programmed instruction, he became Gagné's research assistant. Walt remembers how Gagné mentored him by being enthusiastically dedicated to research and totally committed to the field. While Walt was working with him, Gagné was editing a book and advised Walt to "never edit a book . . . write one." Thank goodness for that well-taken advice.

Following his graduation from Princeton, Walt entered the master's program in psychology at Penn State. He received a lucrative scholarship, but soon after he arrived the program split into pure psychologists and educational psychologists. Because of Walt's interest in human learning and his desire not to be a "rat watcher," he opted for educational psychology—the only student to do so. Bob Lathrop was his major professor at Penn State. Bob later was dean of education and Walt's colleague at Florida State. In 1965, Walt became the first educational psychology doctoral graduate from Penn State. Other interests began to emerge at this time as well, namely, computer programming and electronic scoring machines.

While many of his peers in graduate school took positions in higher education, Walt sought the challenge of business and industry. With doctorate in hand, he went to work for HRB Singer Company in State College, Pennsylvania. At Singer he developed programmed instruction and applied his growing interest in computers to computer-assisted instruction.

In 1966, Duncan Hansen, from Stanford University, and Walt were invited to join the faculty at Florida State University. Duncan was setting up a computer-assisted instruction center and needed help. Duncan told Walt that Florida State was an "up and coming" institution. Having lived all his life in western Pennsylvania, Walt thought he would take this position to get a start in academia, and, after a couple of years, he would go back north and "get a real job." That was more than 30 years ago, and Walt is still on the faculty at Florida State.

Walt's research blossomed at Florida State. He received a grant from the U. S. Office of Education to train graduate students to use computers in instruction. He and his colleagues began offering courses on how to develop programmed instruction, how to develop computer-assisted instruction, and technology in the classroom. However, he soon realized that he was a faculty member in an educational research department that had little direction.

That changed in 1968 when Bob Morgan was hired as department chair. Bob got permission from the school administration "to build the top instructional design program in the country." And Bob did just that. He already had Walt on the faculty. His next hire—Walt's undergraduate mentor, Robert Gagné.

Later, Morgan hired Les Briggs, Bob Branson, Roger Kaufman, and Bob Reiser. They were all recruited because of their research interests. The program was then called Instructional Design and Development. Walt and the rest of his colleagues were psychologists with an interest in human learning. Later, the name of the program was changed to Instructional Systems to denote a broader scope.

Because of Walt's interest in programmed instruction as a graduate student, he was tapped by his colleagues to teach the programmed instruction course at Florida State. He did not use a textbook, just a collection of readings. One day a student came into his office and strongly suggested that he write a book for the course. She even volunteered to help. Her name—Lou Carey.

Together, Walt and Lou developed the well-known Dick and Carey model. They constructed the model to facilitate designing programmed instruction and later modular instruction (short learning units). Remembering Gagné's earlier admonition, the first edition of their textbook was published in 1977. The fifth edition of *The Systematic Design of Instruction* is scheduled to come off the presses this fall with a new third author, Jim Carey, another Florida State doctoral graduate and Lou's husband.

In 1989, Walt collaborated with his Florida State colleague, Bob Reiser, to coauthor a book on systematic planning for teachers. The book, *Planning Effective Instruction*, is now in its second edition and has been retitled *Instructional Planning: A Guide for Teachers.* This book was written to help teachers benefit from the ideas of the field of instructional design.

During a sabbatical with Motorola in the Chicago area, Walt was given the responsibility to work with the National Productivity Board of Singapore to develop a curriculum to train instructional designers in Singapore. Under the auspices of Motorola, he spent time in Singapore developing and implementing the successful curriculum. He was able to culturally adapt the instructional design process to work in that country.

Even though Walt has a Skinnerian psychology background, he understands and promotes, when appropriate, the use of constructivism. He believes that, as human performance technologists, we must use the strengths of each faction and balance the two. Further Walt asserts that we should focus on results—not the psychological means of getting there. In other words, be flexible and use what works.

Walt has had a profound impact on the instructional design field. As he considers other fields closely related to instructional design, he believes that performance technology is an important set of competencies that instructional designers should possess. The proper integration of instructional design and performance technology is necessary. One without the other will not get the job done.

Likewise, instructional technology will continue to receive "more and more emphasis," according to Walt. The hardware will improve, networks will expand, and the Internet will continue to grow, possibly at the expense of the instructional design process. He points out that the field is instructional technology, and it must continue to incorporate instructional design with the use of technology.

Reflecting on his career, which spans more than a third of a century, Walt believes that his biggest professional satisfaction has been his contribution to the very successful Instructional Systems program at Florida State. Some, including this author, would say that it is the top program in the country. Walt reflects with great joy, and a smile, when he describes his many former and current colleagues in the program. He has directed many doctoral students and has served on hundreds of graduate student committees. Students who sat at his feet number in the thousands. In addition, we can only speculate as to the number students and professionals who have read and learned from his writings.

If you only know Walt through his writings, you know part of this accomplished individual. He is the father of three children, one of whom has followed him into the instructional design field. He is also the proud grandfather of five. He and his wife, Donna, share interests in physical fitness and spectator sports, especially football. His mother lived to be 100, and even though Walt is more than halfway there himself, he has completed 10 marathons and still competes regularly in local 5K and 10K races. He confesses that ideas for papers and speeches have often originated during long-distance runs. He looks forward to spending more time on the sunny beaches of Florida following his retirement at the end of 2001. He plans to continue teaching and consulting on a part-time basis.

In spite of his incredible accomplishments, Walt is a shy, soft-spoken, humble, and gentle individual with a remarkable wit. His dry, unassuming sense of humor causes colleagues and students to smile with appreciative respect.

Part Five
Organizations and Associations

Introduction

Part Five includes annotated entries for associations and organizations, most of which are headquartered in North America, whose interests are in some manner significant to the fields of instructional technology and educational media. For the most part, these organizations are associations of professionals in the field or agencies that offer services to the educational media community. Entries are separated into sections for the United States and Canada. The U.S. section begins with a classified list designed to facilitate location of organizations by their specialized interests or services. (The Canadian section is small enough not to need such a list.) In addition, one organization based in Cape Town, South Africa, is named.

This year the section editor used a new method for contacting organization representatives. Brooke Price, the section editor for 2001, helped develop a new database mechanism through which we receive updates. The 2002 editing team benefited from her contribution to the research and development of this new information retrieval process. Dr. Michael Orey created the Web form used for retrieving updated information for the 2002 edition. Dr. Orey designed the Web form so that organization respondents could edit only their own entry. His work made the updating process more efficient, while maintaining the integrity of the information gathered.

Information for this section was obtained by e-mail directing each organization to an individual Web form through which the updated information could be submitted electronically. Although the section editor made every effort to contact and follow up with organization representatives, it is up to the organization representatives to respond to the annual request for an update. The editing team would like to thank those respondents who helped ensure the currency and accuracy of this section by responding to the request for an update. Organizations from which we did not receive updated information are marked by an asterisk, and their entries contain information from the 2001 edition. Two new organizations are listed in this edition. Readers are encouraged to contact the editors with names of unlisted media-related organizations for investigation and possible inclusion in the 2003 edition.

Figures quoted as dues refer to annual amounts, unless stated otherwise. Where dues, membership, and meeting information are not applicable, such information is omitted.

Leslie Cole

United States

Education—General
American Society of Educators (ASE)
Association for Childhood Education International (ACEI)
Association for Experiential Education (AEE)
Council for Basic Education
Education Development Center, Inc.
ERIC Clearinghouse for Science, Mathematics, and Environmental Education (SE)
ERIC Clearinghouse for Social Studies/Social Science Education (ERIC/ChESS)
ERIC Clearinghouse on Counseling and Student Services (CG)
ERIC Clearinghouse on Disabilities and Gifted Education (EC)
ERIC Clearinghouse on Educational Management (EA)
ERIC Clearinghouse on Elementary and Early Childhood Education (PS)
ERIC Clearinghouse on Rural Education and Small Schools (RC)
ERIC Clearinghouse on Teaching and Teacher Education (SP)
ERIC Clearinghouse on Urban Education (UD)
Institute for Development of Educational Activities, Inc. (|I|D|E|A|)
Minorities in Media (MIM)
National Association of State Textbook Administrators (NASTA)
National Clearinghouse for Bilingual Education
National Council for Accreditation of Teacher Education (NCATE)
National School Boards Association (NSBA)
Institute for the Transfer of Technology to Education (ITTE)
The Learning Team (TLT)

Education—Higher
American Association of Community Colleges (AACC)
American Association of State Colleges and Universities
Association for Continuing Higher Education (ACHE)
Association for Library and Information Science Education (ALISE)
Community College Association for Instruction and Technology (CCAIT)
Consortium of College and University Media Centers (CCUMC)
ERIC Clearinghouse for Community Colleges (JC)
ERIC Clearinghouse on Higher Education (HE)
Multimedia Education Group (MEG)
Northwest College and University Council for the Management of Educational Technology
PBS Adult Learning Service

University Continuing Education Association (UCEA)

Equipment
Association for Childhood Education International (ACEI)
Educational Products Information Exchange (EPIE Institute)
ERIC Clearinghouse on Assessment and Evaluation (TM)
ITA
Library and Information Technology Association (LITA)
National School Supply and Equipment Association (NSSEA)
Society of Cable Telecommunications Engineers (SCTE)

ERIC
ACCESS ERIC
Adjunct ERIC Clearinghouse for Art Education (ADJ/AR)
Adjunct ERIC Clearinghouse for ESL Literacy Education (ADJ/LE)
Adjunct ERIC Clearinghouse for United States-Japan Studies (ADJ/JS)
Adjunct ERIC Clearinghouse on Clinical Schools (ADJ/CL)
Adjunct ERIC Clearinghouse on Consumer Education (ADJ/CN)
ERIC (Educational Resources Information Center)
ERIC Clearinghouse on Adult, Career, and Vocational Education (CE)
ERIC Clearinghouse on Assessment and Evaluation (TM)
ERIC Clearinghouse for Community Colleges (JC)
ERIC Clearinghouse on Counseling and Student Services (CG)
ERIC Clearinghouse on Educational Management (EA)
ERIC Clearinghouse on Elementary and Early Childhood Education (PS)
ERIC Clearinghouse on Disabilities and Gifted Education (EC)
ERIC Clearinghouse on Higher Education (HE)
ERIC Clearinghouse on Information & Technology (IR)
ERIC Clearinghouse on Languages and Linguistics (FL)
ERIC Clearinghouse on Reading, English, and Communication Skills (CS)
ERIC Clearinghouse on Rural Education and Small Schools (RC)
ERIC Clearinghouse for Science, Mathematics, and Environmental Education (SE)
ERIC Clearinghouse for Social Studies/Social Science Education (SO)

ERIC Clearinghouse on Teaching and Teacher
Education (SP)
ERIC Clearinghouse on Urban Education (UD)
ERIC Document Reproduction Service (EDRS)
ERIC Processing and Reference Facility

Film and Video
Academy of Motion Picture Arts and Sciences
(AMPAS)
(AECT) Division of Telecommunications
(DOT)
(AECT) Industrial Training and Education
Division (ITED)
Agency for Instructional Technology (AIT)
American Society of Cinematographers
Anthropology Film Center (AFC)
Association for Educational Communications
and Technology (AECT)
Association of Independent Video and Film-
makers/Foundation for Independent
Video and Film (AIVF/FIVF)
Cable in the Classroom
Central Educational Network (CEN)
Children's Television International, Inc.
Close Up Foundation
Community College Satellite Network
Council on International Non-theatrical Events
(CINE)
Film Advisory Board
Film Arts Foundation (FAF)
Film/Video Arts, Inc.
Great Plains National ITV Library (GPN)
Hollywood Film Archive
International Teleconferencing Association
(ITCA)
International Television Association (ITVA)
ITA
National Aeronautics and Space Administration
(NASA)
National Alliance for Media Arts and Culture
(NAMAC)
National Association of Broadcasters (NAB)
National Education Telecommunications Orga-
nization & Education Satellite Company
(NETO/EDSAT)
National Endowment for the Humanities (NEH)
National Film Board of Canada (NFBC)
National Film Information Service (offered by
AMPAS)
National Information Center for Educational
Media (NICEM)
National ITFS Association (NIA/ITFS)
National Telemedia Council, Inc. (NTC)
The New York Festivals
Pacific Film Archive (PFA)
PBS Adult Learning Service (ALS)
PBS VIDEO
Public Broadcasting Service (PBS)

Society of Cable Telecommunications
Engineers (SCTE)

Games, Toys, Play, Simulation, Puppetry
Puppeteers of America, Inc. (POA)
Society for Computer Simulation (SCS)
USA-Toy Library Association (USA-TLA)

Health-Related Organizations
Health Science Communications Association
(HeSCA)
Lister Hill National Center for Biomedical
Communications
Medical Library Association (MLA)
National Association for Visually Handicapped
(NAVH)
Network for Continuing Medical Education
(NCME)

Information Science
Association for Library and Information
Science Education (ALISE)
ERIC Clearinghouse on Information and
Technology (IR)
Freedom of Information Center
International Information Management
Congress (IMC)
Library and Information Technology Associa-
tion (LITA)
Lister Hill National Center for Biomedical
Communications
National Commission on Libraries and Informa-
tion Science (NCLIS)

Innovation
Institute for Development of Educational
Activities, Inc. (|I|D|E|A|)
Institute for the Future (IFTF)
World Future Society (WFS)

**Instructional Technology, Design, and
Development**
(AECT) Division of Educational Media
Management (DEMM)
(AECT) Division of Instructional Development
(DID)
Agency for Instructional Technology (AIT)
Association for Educational Communications
and Technology (AECT)
Community College Association for Instruction
and Technology (CCAIT)
ERIC Clearinghouse on Information &
Technology (IR)
International Society for Performance and
Instruction (ISPI)
Professors of Instructional Design and
Technology (PIDT)

Society for Applied Learning Technology
 (SALT)
The Learning Team (TLT)
Multimedia Education Group, University of
 Cape Town (MEG)

International Education
Adjunct ERIC Clearinghouse for US-Japan
 Studies (ADJ/JS)
(AECT) International Division (INTL)
East-West Center
International Association for Learning Labora-
 tories, Inc. (IALL)
International Visual Literacy Association, Inc.
 (IVLA)
National Clearinghouse for Bilingual Education
 (NCBE)

Language
ERIC Clearinghouse on Languages and
 Linguistics (FL)
ERIC Clearinghouse on Reading, English, and
 Communication (CS)
International Association for Learning Labora-
 tories, Inc. (IALL)
National Clearinghouse for Bilingual Education
 (NCBE)

Libraries—Academic, Research
American Library Association (ALA)
Association of College and Research Libraries
 (ACRL)
ERIC Clearinghouse on Information & Tech-
 nology (IR)

Libraries—Public
American Library Association (ALA)
Association for Library Service to Children
 (ALSC)
ERIC Clearinghouse on Information & Tech-
 nology (IR)
Library Administration and Management Asso-
 ciation (LAMA)
Library and Information Technology Associa-
 tion (LITA)
Public Library Association (PLA)
Young Adult Library Services Association
 (YALSA)

Libraries and Media Centers—School
(AECT) Division of School Media Specialists
 (DSMS)
(ALA Round Table) Continuing Library Educa-
 tion Network and Exchange (CLENERT)
American Association of School Librarians
 (AASL)
American Library Association (ALA)
American Library Trustee Association (ALTA)

Association for Educational Communications
 and Technology (AECT)
Association for Library Collections and Techni-
 cal Services (ALCTS)
Association for Library Service to Children
 (ALSC)
Catholic Library Association (CLA)
Consortium of College and University Media
 Centers
ERIC Clearinghouse on Information &
 Technology (IR)
International Association of School Librarian-
 ship (IASL)
Library of Congress
National Alliance for Media Arts and Culture
 (NAMAC)
National Association of Regional Media
 Centers (NARMC)
National Commission on Libraries and
 Information Science (NCLIS)
National Council of Teachers of English
 (NCTE), Commission on Media
On-Line Audiovisual Catalogers (OLAC)
Southeastern Regional Media Leadership
 Council (SRMLC)

Libraries—Special
American Library Association (ALA)
Association for Library Service to Children
 (ALSC)
Association of Specialized and Cooperative
 Library Agencies (ASCLA)
ERIC Clearinghouse on Information &
 Technology (IR)
Medical Library Association (MLA)
Special Libraries Association
Theater Library Association
USA Toy Library Association (USA-TLA)

Media Production
(AECT) Media Design and Production Division
 (MDPD)
American Society of Cinematographers (ASC)
Association for Educational Communications
 and Technology (AECT)
Association of Independent Video and Film-
 makers/Foundation for Independent
 Video and Film (AIVF/FIVF)
Film Arts Foundation (FAF)
International Graphics Arts Education
 Association (IGAEA)

Museums and Archives
(AECT) Archives
Association of Systematics Collections
George Eastman House
Hollywood Film Archive
Library of Congress

Museum Computer Network (MCN)
Museum of Modern Art (MoMA)
National Gallery of Art (NGA)
National Public Broadcasting Archives (NPBA)
Pacific Film Archive (PFA)
Smithsonian Institution

Photography
Electronic Camera Repair, C&C Associates
George Eastman House
International Center of Photography (ICP)
National Press Photographers Association, Inc.
   (NPPA)
Photographic Society of America (PSA)
Society for Photographic Education (SPE)
Society of Photo Technologists (SPT)

Publishing
Graphic Arts Technical Foundation (GATF)
International Graphics Arts Education Associa-
   tion (IGAEA)
Magazine Publishers of America (MPA)
National Association of State Textbook
   Administrators (NASTA)

Radio
(AECT) Division of Telecommunications
   (DOT)
American Women in Radio and Television
   (AWRT)
Corporation for Public Broadcasting (CPB)
National Endowment for the Humanities (NEH)
National Federation of Community Broad-
   casters (NFCB)
National Public Broadcasting Archives (NPBA)
National Religious Broadcasters (NRB)
Western Public Radio (WPR)

Religious Education
Catholic Library Association (CLA)
National Council of the Churches of Christ in
   the USA
National Religious Broadcasters (NRB)

Research
(AECT) Research and Theory Division (RTD)
American Educational Research Association
   (AERA)
Appalachia Educational Laboratory, Inc. (AEL)
ECT Foundation
Education Development Center, Inc.
ERIC Clearinghouses
HOPE Reports
Mid-continent Regional Educational Laboratory
   (McREL)
Multimedia Education Group, University of
   Cape Town (MEG)

National Center for Improving Science
   Education
National Education Knowledge Industry Asso-
   ciation (NEKIA)
National Endowment for the Humanities (NEH)
National Science Foundation (NSF)
The NETWORK
North Central Regional Educational Laboratory
   (NCREL)
Northwest Regional Educational Laboratory
   (NWREL)
Pacific Regional Educational Laboratory
   (PREL)
Research for Better Schools, Inc. (RBS)
SouthEastern Regional Vision for Education
   (SERVE)
Southwest Educational Development Labora-
   tory (SEDL)
WestEd

Special Education
Adaptech Research Project
American Foundation for the Blind (AFB)
Association for Experiential Education (AEE)
Association of Specialized and Cooperative
   Library Agencies (ASCLA)
Council for Exceptional Children (CEC)
ERIC Clearinghouse on Adult, Career, and
   Vocational Education (CE)
ERIC Clearinghouse on Disabilities and Gifted
   Education (EC)
National Association for Visually Handicapped
   (NAVH)
National Center to Improve Practice (NCIP)
Recording for the Blind and Dyslexic (RFB&D)

Telecommunications
(AECT) Division of Telecommunications
   (DOT)
Association for the Advancement of Computing
   in Education (AACE)
Association of Independent Video and Film-
   makers/Foundation for Independent
   Video and Film (AIVF/FIVF)
Community College Satellite Network (CCSN)
ERIC Clearinghouse on Information &
   Technology (IR)
Instructional Telecommunications Council
   (ITC)
International Telecommunications Satellite
   Organization (INTELSAT)
International Teleconferencing Association
   (ITCA)
Library and Information Technology Associa-
   tion (LITA)
National Education Telecommunications
   Organization & Education Satellite
   Company (NETO/EDSAT)

Research for Better Schools, Inc. (RBS)
Teachers and Writers Collaborative (T&W)

Television
American Women in Radio and Television
(AWRT)
Central Educational Network (CEN)
Children's Television International, Inc. (CTI)
Corporation for Public Broadcasting (CPB)
International Television Association (ITVA)
National Cable Television Institute (NCTI)
National Federation of Community Broad-
casters (NFCB)
Society of Cable Telecommunications
Engineers (SCTE)

Training
(AECT) Industrial Training and Education
Division (ITED)
American Management Association (AMA)
American Society for Training and Develop-
ment (ASTD)
Association for Educational Communications
and Technology (AECT)
ERIC Clearinghouse on Adult, Career, and
Vocational Education (CE)
Federal Educational Technology Association
(FETA)
International Society for Performance Improve-
ment (ISPI)

ALPHABETICAL LIST

All dues are annual fees, unless stated otherwise.

*Academy of Motion Picture Arts and Sciences (AMPAS). 8949 Wilshire Blvd., Beverly Hills, CA 90211-1972. (310)247-3000. Fax (310)859-9351. E-mail answers@oscars.org. Web site http://www.oscars.org. Bruce Davis, Exec. Dir. An honorary organization composed of outstanding individuals in all phases of motion pictures. Seeks to advance the arts and sciences of motion picture technology and artistry. Presents annual film awards; offers artist-in-residence programs; operates reference library and National Film Information Service. *Membership:* 6,000. *Publications:* Annual Index to Motion Picture Credits; Academy Players Directory.

*Agency for Instructional Technology (AIT). Box A, Bloomington, IN 47402-0120. (812)339-2203. Fax (812)333-4218. E-mail ait@ait.net. Web site http://www.ait.net. Michael F. Sullivan, Exec. Dir. AIT is a nonprofit educational organization established in 1962 to develop, acquire, and distribute quality technology-based resources, providing leadership to the educational technology policy community. AIT fulfills this mission by being the largest single provider of instructional television programs and is a major player in the development of curriculum products. AIT has established a national model for contextual learning materials. AIT's strength lies in sound instructional design, early and continual involvement of classroom practitioners, formative evaluation, and creative production of video, Web services videodisc, software, and print resources. AIT products have won many national and international awards, including the only Emmy and Peabody awards given to classroom television programs. Since 1970, 37 major curriculum packages have been developed by AIT through a process it pioneered. U.S. state and Canadian provincial agencies have cooperatively funded and widely used these learning resources. Funding for other product development comes from state, provincial, and local departments of education, federal and private institutions, corporations and private sponsors, and AIT's own resources. Currently, AIT offers 130 learning resource products, containing nearly 2,500 separate titles. Programming addresses pre-kindergarten through adult learners covering traditional curricular areas plus career development, early childhood, guidance, mental health, staff development, and vocational education. AIT programs account for 40 percent of the National Instructional Satellite Service (NISS) schedule, which is broadcast to K–12 classrooms across the country. AIT learning resources are used on six continents and teach nearly 34 million students in North America each year via electronic distribution and audio visual use. *Publications:* TECHNOS: Quarterly for Education & Technology, a forum for the discussion of ideas about the use of technology in education with a focus on reform ($28/yr, 4 issues). AIT is also the home of TECHNOS Press, publisher of *Final Exam* by Gerald W. Bracey.

American Association of Community Colleges (AACC). One Dupont Cir. NW, Suite 410, Washington, DC 20036-1176. (202)728-0200, ext. 209. Fax (202)833-9390. E-mail nkent@aacc.nche.edu. Web site http://www.aacc.nche.edu. George R. Boggs, Pres. AACC is a national organization representing the nations more than 1,100 community, junior, and technical colleges. Headquartered in Washington, D.C., AACC serves as a national voice for the colleges and provides key services in the areas of advocacy, research, information, and professional development. The nation's community colleges serve more than 10 million students annually, almost half (44%) of all U.S. undergraduates. *Membership:* 1,151 institutions, 31 corporations, 15 international associates, 79 educational associates, 4 foundations. *Dues:* vary by category. *Meetings:* Annual Convention, April of each year; 2002: April 20-23, Seattle, Wash. *Publications:* Community College Journal (bi-mo.); Community College Times (bi-weekly newspaper); College Times; Community College Press (books, research and program briefs, and monographs).

American Association of School Librarians (AASL). 50 E. Huron St., Chicago, IL 60611-2795. (312)280-4386. (800)545-2433, ext. 4386. Fax (312)664-7459. E-mail aasl@ala.org. Web site http://www.ala.org/aasl. Julie A. Walker, Exec. Dir. A division of the American Library Association, AASL is interested in the general improvement and extension of school library media services for children and youth. Activities and projects of the association are divided among 30 committees and 3 sections. *Membership:* 8,800. *Dues:* Personal membership in ALA (1st yr., $50; 2nd yr., $75; 3rd and subsequent yrs., $100) plus $40 for personal membership in AASL. Inactive, student, retired, unemployed, and reduced-salary memberships are available. *Meetings:* National conference every two years; next national conference to be held in 2003. *Publications:* School Library Media Research (electronic research journal, http://www.ala.org/aasl/SLMR/). Knowledge Quest (print journal; online companion at http://www.ala.org/aasl/kqweb/) Non-serial publications (http://www.ala.org/aasl/pubs_menu.html)

*American Association of State Colleges and Universities (AASCU). One Dupont Cir. NW, Suite 700, Washington, DC 20036-1192. (202)293-7070. Fax (202)296-5819. E-mail currisc.aascu.org. James B. Appleberry, Pres. Membership is open to regionally accredited institutions of higher education (and those in the process of securing accreditation) that offer programs leading to the degree of Bachelor, Master, or Doctor, and that are wholly or partially state-supported and state-controlled. Organized and operated exclusively for educational, scientific, and literary purposes, its particular purposes are to improve higher education within its member institutions through cooperative planning, studies, and research on common educational problems and the development of a more unified program of action among its members; and to provide other needed and worthwhile educational services to the colleges and universities it may represent. *Membership:* 393 institutions (university), 28 systems, and 10 associates. *Dues:* based on current student enrollment at institution. *Publications:* MEMO: To the President; The Center Associate; Office of Federal Program Reports; Office of Federal Program Deadlines. (Catalogs of books and other publications available upon request.)

American Educational Research Association (AERA). 1230 17th St. NW, Washington, DC 20036-3078. (202)223-9485. Fax (202)775-1824. E-mail outreach@aera.net. Web site http://www.aera.net. William J. Russell, Exec. Dir. AERA is an international professional organization with the primary goal of advancing educational research and its practical application. Its members include educators and administrators; directors of research, testing, or evaluation in federal, state, and local agencies; counselors; evaluators; graduate students; and behavioral scientists. The broad range of disciplines represented includes education, psychology, statistics, sociology, history, economics, philosophy, anthropology, and political science. AERA has more than 140 Special Interest Groups including Advanced Technologies for Learning, Computer Applications in Education, Electronic Networking, Instructional Systems and Intelligent Tutors, Instructional Technology, and Text, Technology and Learning Strategies. *Membership:* 23,000. *Dues:* vary by category, ranging from $20 for students to $45 for voting members, for one year. *Meetings:* 2002 Annual Meeting, April 1-5, New Orleans; 2003 Annual Meeting, April 21-25, Chicago. *Publications:* Educational Researcher; American Educational Research Journal; Journal of Educational Statistics; Educational Evaluation and Policy Analysis; Review of Research in Education; Review of Educational Research.

*American Foundation for the Blind (AFB). 11 Penn Plaza, Suite 300, New York, NY 10001. (212)502-7600, (800)AFB-LINE (232-5463). Fax (212)502-7777. E-mail afbinfo@afb.org. Web site http://www.afb.org. Carl R. Augusto, Pres.; Liz Greco, Vice Pres. of Communications. AFB is a leading national resource for people who are blind or visually impaired, the organizations that serve them, and the general public. A nonprofit organization founded in 1921 and recognized as Helen Keller's cause in the United States, AFB's mission is to enable people who are blind or visually impaired to achieve equality of access and opportunity that will ensure freedom of choice in their lives. AFB is headquartered in New York City with offices in Atlanta, Chicago, Dallas, and San Francisco. A governmental relations office in AFB is headquartered in New York City with offices in Atlanta, Chicago, Dallas, San Francisco, and Washington, DC. *Publications: AFB News* (free); *Journal of Visual Impairment & Blindness; AFB Press Catalog of Publications* (free).

American Library Association (ALA). 50 E. Huron St., Chicago, IL 60611. (800) 545-2433. (312)440-9374. E-mail ala@ala.org. Web site http://www.ala.org. William R. Gordon, Exec. Dir. The ALA is the oldest and largest national library association. Its 61,100 members represent all types of libraries: state, public, school, and academic, as well as special libraries serving persons in government, commerce, the armed services, hospitals, prisons, and other institutions. The ALA is the chief advocate of achievement and maintenance of high-quality library information services through protection of the right to read, educating librarians, improving services, and making information widely accessible. See separate entries for the following affiliated and subordinate organizations: American Association of School Librarians, American Library Trustee Association, Association for Library Collections and Technical Services, Association for Library Service to Children, Association of College and Research Libraries, Association of Specialized and Cooperative Library Agencies, Library Administration and Management Association, Library and Information Technology Association, Public Library Association, Reference and User Services Association, Young Adult Library Services Association, and Continuing Library Education Network and Exchange Round Table. *Membership:* 61,100 members at present; everyone who cares about libraries is allowed to join the American Library Association. *Dues:* Professional rate: $50, first year; $75, second year; third year & renewing, $100, Student members: $25, Retirees: $35, International librarians: $60, Trustees: $45, Associate members (those not in the library field): $45. *Meetings:* 2002: Midwinter Meeting Jan 18-23, New Orleans; Annual Conference, June 13-19, Atlanta. 2003: Midwinter Meeting, Jan 24-29, Philadelphia; Annual Conference, June 19-25, Toronto. *Publications: American Libraries; Booklist; Choice; Book Links.*

*American Library Trustee Association (ALTA). 50 E. Huron St., Chicago, IL 60611. (312)280-2161. Fax (312)280-3257. E-mail kward@ala.org. Web site http://www.ala.org/alta. Susan Roman, Exec. Dir. A division of the American Library Association, ALTA is interested in the development of effective library service for people in all types of communities and libraries. Members, as policymakers, are concerned with organizational patterns of service, the development of competent personnel, the provision of adequate financing, the passage of suitable legislation, and the encouragement of citizen support for libraries. *Membership:* 1,710. *Dues:* $50 plus membership in ALA. *Meetings:* Held in conjunction with ALA. *Publications: Trustee Voice* (q. newsletter); professional monographs and pamphlets.

*American Management Association International (AMA). 1601 Broadway, New York, NY 10019-7420. (212)586-8100. Fax (212)903-8168. E-mail cust_serv@amanet.org. Web site http://www.amanet.org. Barbara M. Barrett, Pres. and CEO. Founded in 1923, AMA provides educational forums worldwide where members and their colleagues learn superior, practical business skills and explore best practices of world-class organizations through interaction with each other and expert faculty practitioners. AMA's publishing program provides tools individuals use to extend learning beyond the classroom in a process of life-long professional growth and development through education. AMA operates management centers and offices in Atlanta, Boston (Watertown), Chicago, Hamilton (NY), Kansas City (Leawood), New York, San Francisco, Saranac Lake (NY), and Washington, DC, and through AMA/International, in Brussels, Tokyo, Shanghai, Islamabad, and Buenos Aires. In addition, it has affiliated centers in Toronto, Mexico City, Sao Paulo, Taipei, Istanbul, Singapore, Jakarta, and Dubai. AMA offers conferences, seminars, and membership briefings where there is an interchange of information, ideas, and experience in a wide variety of management topics. *Membership:* over 75,000. *Dues:* corporate, $595–1645; growing company, $525–1845; indiv., $165 plus $40 per additional newsletter. *Publications: Management Review* (membership); *Compensation & Benefits Review; Organizational Dynamics; HR Focus; President; Getting Results,* and *The Take-Charge Assistant.* Also 70 business-related books per year, as well as numerous surveys and management briefings. Other services offered by AMA include FYI Video; Extension Institute (self-study programs in both print and audio formats); AMA Interactive Series (self-paced learning on CD-ROM); Operation Enterprise (young adult program); AMA On-Site (videoconferences); the Information Resource Center (for AMA members only), a management information and library service; and six bookstores.

American Montessori Society (AMS). 281 Park Ave. S, New York, NY 10010. (212)358-1250. Fax (212)358-1256. E-mail mimi@amshq.org. Web site http://www.amshq.org. Michael N. Eanes, Natl. Dir. Dedicated to promoting better education for all children through teaching strategies consistent with the Montessori system. Membership is composed of schools in the private and public sectors employing this method, as well as individuals. It serves as a resource center and clearinghouse for information and data on Montessori affiliates, trains teachers in different parts of the country, and conducts a consultation service and accreditation program for school members. The mission of the American Montessori Society is to promote high quality Montessori education for all children by providing service to parents, teachers and schools. *Membership:* Membership includes schools, teachers, parents, school heads, and friends of Montessori. This total is approximately 11,000. *Dues:* Dues vary based on membership. Membership is available for Certified Montessori Teachers, Montessori School, and General Members (includes those who are not Certified Montessori Teachers, parents, friends of AMS). *Meetings:* three regional and four professional development symposia under the auspices of the AMS Teachers' Section. 42nd Annual Conference, Apr 25-28, 2002, Crystal City, VA; Regional Conferences, August 11-13, 2001, Breckenridge, CO; October 19-21, Atlanta, GA. *Publications: AMS Montessori LIFE* (q); *Schoolheads (*newsletter); *Montessori in Contemporary American Culture,* Margaret Loeffler, Editor; *Authentic American Montessori School; AMS The Montessori School Management Guide;* AMS position papers; and the following AMS *Publications: Montessori Teaching a Growth Profession; The Elemenary School Years 6-12; Your Child Is in an Accredited School; Some Considerations in Starting a Montessori School; Montessori Education Q&A; The Early Childhood Years, 3-6; Attracting and Preparing Montessori Teacher for the 21st Century; Adolescent Programs; The Kindergarten Experience; Some Comparisons of Montessori Education with Traditional Education; Helping Children Become All They Can Become; The Montessori Family: A Parent Brochure; Tuition and Salary Surveys.*

American Society for Training and Development (ASTD). 1640 King St., Box 1443, Alexandria, VA 22313. (703)683-8100. Fax (703)683-8103. E-mail customercare@astd.org. Web site http://www.astd.org. Tina Sung Pres. and CEO. Founded in 1944, ASTD is the worlds premiere professional association in the field of workplace learning and performance. ASTD's membership includes more than 70,000 people in organizations from every level of the field of workplace performance in more than 100 countries. Its leadership and members work in more than 15,000 multinational corporations, small and medium-sized businesses, government agencies, colleges, and universities. ASTD is the leading resource on workplace learning and performance issues, providing information, research, analysis, and practical information derived from its own research, the knowledge and experience of its members, its conferences and publications, and the coalitions and partnerships it has built through research and policy work. *Membership:* 70,000 national and chapter members. *Dues:* The Classic Membership ($150.00) is the foundation of ASTD member benefits. Publications, newsletters, research reports, discounts and services and much more, are all designed to help you do your job better. Heres what you have to look forward to when you join: *Training and Development*—Monthly publication of the industry. Stay informed on trends, successful practices, public policy, ASTD news, case studies and more. *Performance in Practice*—Quarterly newsletter offers articles written by members for members. *Hot Topics*—ASTDs online reading list gets you up to speed on leading-edge issues in the training and performance industry. *Database and Archive Access*—FREE on-linc access to Trainlit, ASTDs searchable database, featuring products reviews, book and article summaries, and archived articles. *Learning Circuits*—Monthly Webzine features articles, departments, and columns that examine new technologies and how they're being applied to workplace learning. *Human Resource Development Quarterly*—In-depth studies and reports on human resource theory and practice give you a scholarly look at the training profession. HRDQ is available ONLY online with archives dating back to 1998. *ASTD News Briefs*—Weekly news briefs relating to the training and performance industry. *Special Reports and Research*—Trends Report, State of the Industry, Learning Outcomes and International Comparison Report. *Training Data Book*—An annual publication, now on-line, draws on ASTD research and highlights the nature and magnitude of corporate investment in employer-provided training. *Research Assistance*—ASTD provides an information center that can provide you with the research you're looking for while you're on the phone. You can also send your research request through the Web site. Just provide your member number. *Membership Directory*—Online directory and searchable by a variety of criteria. Access to the Membership Directory is for members only and is being enhanced for future networking capabilities. *Buyers Guide & Consultants Directory*—A one stop resource for information on over 600 suppliers of training and performance products and services. Segments that can be added on to the Classic Membership: Membership Plus: Choice of 12 info lines or four prechosen ASTD books, $79.00. Training Professionals: Includes an annual subscription to *Info-lines, Pfeiffers Best of Training, and the ASTD Training and Performance Yearbook,* $130.00. Organizational Development/Leadership Professionals: Includes *Pfeiffers Consulting Annual, Leader to Leader and Leadership in Action,* $200.00. Consulting: Includes annual subscription to *C2M* (quarterly journal) and *Pfeiffers Consulting Annual,* $75.00. E-Learning: Includes Training Media Review Online (database and newsletter that evaluates audio, video, software, and online products 6/year e-mail newsletters) and ASTD Distance Learning Yearbook, $175.00. *Meetings:* International Conferences, June 1-7 2001, Orlando, Florida; Techknowledge Conference, October 9-12, Charlotte, North Carolina; International Conference 2002, New Orleans, Louisiana, May 31-June 6; International Conference 2003, San Diego,CA, May 17-22. *Publications: Training & Development Magazine; Info-Line; The American Mosaic: An In-depth Report of Diversity on the Future of Diversity at Work; ASTD Directory of Academic Programs in T&D/HRD; Training and Development Handbook; Quarterly publications: Performance in Practice; National Report on Human Resources; Washington Policy Report.* ASTD also has recognized professional forums, most of which produce newsletters.

*American Society of Cinematographers (ASC). 1782 N. Orange Dr., Hollywood, CA 90028. (213)969-4333. Fax (213)876-4973, (213)882-6391. E-mail suzanne.lezotte @creativeplanet.com. Victor Kemper, Pres. ASC is an educational, cultural, and professional organization. *Membership:* 336. Membership is by invitation to those who are actively engaged as directors of photography and have demonstrated outstanding ability. Classifications are Active, Active Retired, Associates, and Honorary. *Meetings:* Book Bazaar (Open House); Awards Open House; Annual ASC Awards. *Publications: American Cinematographer Video Manual; Light on Her Face;* and *American Cinematographers Magazine.*

*American Society of Educators (ASE). 1429 Walnut St., Philadelphia, PA 19102. (215)563-6005. Fax (215)587-9706. E-mail michelesok@aol.com. Web site http://www.media -methods.com. Michele Sokolof, Publisher & Editorial Dir. ASE services the information needs of K–12 teachers, librarians, media specialists, curriculum directors, and administrators in evaluating the practical applications of today's multimedia and technology resources for teaching and learning purposes. ASE delivers timely information on technology integration in K–12 schools, classrooms, and labs. *Publications:* bimonthly yearly subscription: cost, $33.50.

*American Women in Radio and Television (AWRT). 1650 Tyson Blvd., Suite 200, McLean, VA 22102-3915. (703)506-3290. Fax (703)506-3266. E-mail info@awrt.org. Jacci Duncan, Exec. Dir. Organization of professionals in the electronic media, including owners, managers, administrators, and those in creative positions in broadcasting, satellite, cable, advertising, and public relations. AWRT's objectives are to work worldwide to improve the quality of radio and television; to promote the entry, development, and advancement of women in the electronic media and allied fields; to serve as a medium of communication and idea exchange; and to become involved in community concerns. Organized in 1951. *Membership:* 40 chapters. Student memberships available. *Dues:* $125. *Publications*: *News and Views; Resource Directory; Careers in the Electronic Media; Sexual Harassment;* Mentoring Brochure (pamphlet).

Anthropology Film Center (AFC). 1626 Upper Canyon Rd., Santa Fe, NM 87501-6138. (505)983-4127. E-mail info@anthrofilm.org. Web site http://www.anthrofilm.org. Carroll Williams, Dir. Offers the Ethnographic/Documentary Film Program, a 30-week full-time course in 16mm film in CD and DVD production and theory. Summer workshops are offered as well. AFC also provides consultation, research facilities, and a specialized library. Workshops in visual anthropology are offered. *Membership:* We have no memberships. *Meetings:* None scheduled until 2002. *Publications:* A filmography for American Indian Education.

AEL, Inc. (AEL). P.O. Box 1348, Charleston, WV 25325-1348. (304)347-0400, (800)624-9120. Fax (304)347-0487. E-mail aelinfo@ael.org. Web site http://www.ael.org. Allen D. Arnold, President and CEO. AEL is a catalyst for schools and communities to build lifelong learning systems that harness resources, research, and practical wisdom. To contribute knowledge that assists low-performing schools to move toward continuous improvement, AEL conducts research, development, evaluation, and dissemination activities that inform policy, affect educational practice, and contribute to the theoretical and procedural knowledge bases on effective teaching, learning, and schooling. Strategies build on research and reflect a commitment to empowering individuals and building local capacity. AEL serves Kentucky, Tennessee, Virginia, and West Virginia.

*Association for Childhood Education International (ACEI). 17904 Georgia Ave., Suite 215, Olney, MD 20832. (301)570-2111. Fax (301)570-2212. E-mail ACEIHQ@aol.com. Web site http://www.udel.edu/bateman/acei. Anne W. Bauer, Ed. and Dir. ACEI publications reflect careful research, broad-based views, and consideration of a wide range of issues affecting children from infancy through early adolescence. Many are media related in nature. The journal (*Childhood Education*) is essential for teachers, teachers-in-training, teacher educators, day-care workers, administrators, and parents. Articles focus on child development and emphasize practical application. Regular departments include book reviews (child and adult), film reviews, pamphlets, software, research, and classroom idea-sparkers. Six issues are published yearly, including a theme issue devoted to critical concerns. *Membership:* 12,000. *Dues:* $45, professional; $26, student; $23, retired; $80, institutional. *Meetings:* 1999 Annual International Conference and Exhibition, Apr 7-11, San Antonio; 2000, Baltimore. *Publications: Childhood Education* (official journal) with *ACEI Exchange* (insert newsletter); *Journal of Research in Childhood Education;* professional division newsletters (*Focus on Infants and Toddlers, Focus on Pre-K and K, Focus on Elementary,* and *Focus on Middle School*); *Celebrating Family Literacy Through Intergenerational Programming; Selecting Educational Equipment for School and Home; Developmental Continuity Across Preschool and Primary Grades; Implications for Teachers; Developmentally Appropriate Middle Level Schools; Common Bonds: Antibias Teaching in a Diverse Society; Childhood 1892–1992; Infants and Toddlers with Special Needs and Their Families* (position paper); and pamphlets.

*Association for Computers and the Humanities. c/o Elli Mylonas, Exec. Secretary, Box 1885-C15, Brown University, Providence, RI 02912. E-mail ach@stg.brown.edu. Web site http://www.ach.org. Elli Mylonas, Exec. Secretary. The Association for Computers and the Humanities is a forum for humanists who incorporate computing into their teaching and research. *Membership:* 300. *Dues:* $75. *Meetings:* Annual meetings held with the Association for Literary and Linguistic Computing. *Publications: Journal for Computers and the Humanities.*

*Association for Continuing Higher Education (ACHE). Continuing Education, Trident Technical College, P.O. Box 118067, CE-P, Charleston, SC 29423-8067. (803)574-6658. Fax (803)574-6470. E-mail zpbarrineavi@trident.tec.sc.us. Web site http://www.charleston.net /organization/ACHE/. Wayne Whelan, Exec. Vice Pres. ACHE is an institution-based organization of colleges, universities, and individuals dedicated to the promotion of lifelong learning and excellence in continuing higher education. ACHE encourages professional networks, research, and exchange of information for its members and advocates continuing higher education as a means of enhancing and improving society. *Membership:* 1,622 individuals in 674 institutions. *Dues:* $60, professional; $240, institutional. *Meetings:* 1999 Annual Meeting, Nov 7-9, Cincinnati. 2000 Oct 14-17, Myrtle Beach, SC. *Publications: Journal of Continuing Higher Education* (3/yr.); *Five Minutes with ACHE* (newsletter, 10/yr.); Proceedings (annual).

Association for Educational Communications and Technology (AECT). 1800 N Stonelake Dr., Suite 2, Bloomington, IN 47404. (812) 335-7675. Fax (812)335-7678. E-mail aect@aect.org. Web site http://www.aect.org. Phillip Harris, Executive Director; Charlie White, President. AECT is an international professional association concerned with the improvement of learning and instruction through media and technology. It serves as a central clearinghouse and communications center for its members, who include instructional technologists, library media specialists, religious educators, government media personnel, school administrators and specialists, and training media producers. AECT members also work in the armed forces, public libraries, museums, and other information agencies of many different kinds, including those related to the emerging fields of computer technology. Affiliated organizations include the Association for Media and Technology in Education in Canada (AMTEC), Community College Association for Instructional and Technology (CCAIT), Consortium of College and University Media Centers (CCUMC), International Association for Learning Laboratories (IALL), International Visual Literacy Association (IVLA), Minorities in Media (MIM), National Association of Regional Media Centers (NARMC), New England Educational Media Association (NEEMA), and the Southeastern Regional Media Leadership Council (SRMLC). Each of these affiliated organizations has its own listing in the Yearbook. The ECT Foundation is also related to the Association for Educational Communications and Technology and has an independent listings. Divisions are listed below. *Membership:* 3,000 members in good standing from K–12, college and university and private sector/government training. Anyone interested can join. There are different memberships available for students, retirees, corporations, and international parties. *Dues:* $85.00 standard membership; discounts are available for students and retirees. Additional fees apply to corporate memberships or international memberships. *Meetings:* Summer Leadership Institute held each July. In 2002 it will be in Chicago, IL. Annual Conference each year in conjunction with the NSBA Technology Conference in early November. In 2002 it will be held in Dallas. *Publications: TechTrends* (6/yr., free with membership; $55 nonmembers); *Educational Technology Research and Development* (q., $35 members; $75 nonmembers); *Quarterly Review of Distance Education* (q., $40 members); many books; videotapes.

Association for Educational Communications and Technology (AECT) Divisions:

*(AECT) Division of Educational Media Management (DEMM). 1025 Vermont Ave. NW, Suite 820, Washington, DC 20005-3516. (202)347-7834. Fax (202)347-7839. E-mail aect@aect.org;mcfarlin@ksu.edu. Web site http://www.aect.org /Divisions/aectdiv.html and http://teams.lacoe.edu/demm/demm.html. Nancy McFarlin, Pres. As leaders in the field of educational media, members of DEMM are actively involved in the design, production, and instructional applications of new and emerging multimedia technologies. DEMM members are proactive media managers who provide solutions, share information on common problems, and support the development of model media programs. *Membership:* 438. *Dues:* One division membership included in the basic AECT membership; additional division memberships $10. *Meetings:* DEMM meets in conjunction with the annual AECT National Convention. *Publications: DEMM Perspective* (newsletter, q.).

*(AECT) Division of Instructional Development (DID). 1025 Vermont Ave. NW, Suite 820, Washington, DC 20005. (202)347-7834. E-mail rodney-earle@byu.edu. Rodney Earle, Pres. DID is composed of individuals from business, government, and academic settings concerned with the systematic design of instruction and the development of solutions to performance problems. Members' interests include the study, evaluation, and refinement of design processes; the creation of new models of instructional development; the invention and improvement of techniques for managing the development of instruction; the development and application of professional ID competencies; the promotion of academic programs for preparation of ID professionals; and the dissemination of research and development work in ID. *Membership:* 726. *Dues:* One division membership included in the basic AECT membership; additional division memberships $10. *Meetings:* held in conjunction with the annual AECT Convention.. *Publications:* DID Newsletter; occasional papers.

*(AECT) Division of Interactive Systems and Computers (DISC). 1025 Vermont Ave. NW, Suite 820, Washington, DC 20005. (202)347-7834. E-mail garya@sprynet.com. Web site http://www.aect.org/Divisions/disc.html. Gary Addison, Pres. Concerned with the generation, access, organization, storage, and delivery of all forms of information used in the processes of education and training. DISC promotes the networking of its members to facilitate sharing of expertise and interests. *Membership:* 686. *Dues:* One division membership included in the basic AECT membership; additional division memberships $10. *Meetings:* held in conjunction with the annual AECT Convention. *Publications:* Newsletter; listserv at DISC-L@vm.cc.purdue.edu (to subscribe, send the message "subscribe DISC-L firstname lastname").

*(AECT) Division of Learning and Performance Environments (DLPE). 1025 Vermont Ave. NW, Suite 820, Washington, DC 20005. (202)347-7834. E-mail eggersre@emporia.edu. Web site http://dlpe.base.org. Renee Eggers, Pres. Supports human learning and performance through the use of computer-based technology; design, development, evaluation, assessment, and implementation of learning environments and performance systems for adults. *Dues:* One division membership included in the basic AECT membership; additional division memberships $10. *Meetings:* held in conjunction with the annual AECT Convention.

*(AECT) Division of School Media and Technology (DSMT). 1025 Vermont Ave. NW, Suite 820, Washington, DC 20005. (202)347-7834. E-mail freibergs@po.atlantic.county.lib.nj.us. Sherry Freiberg, Pres. DSMS strives to improve instruction and promotes excellence in student learning in the K–12 setting by developing, implementing, and evaluating media programs and by planning and integrating technology in the classroom. *Membership:* 902. *Dues:* One division membership included in the basic AECT membership; additional division memberships $10. *Meetings:* held in conjunction with the annual AECT Convention. *Publications:* Newsletter.

*(AECT) Division of Telecommunications (DOT). 1025 Vermont Ave. NW, Suite 820, Washington, DC 20005. (202)347-7834. E-mail mitchell@wneo.org. Steve Mitchell, Pres. DOT represents those members with an interest in a broad range of telecommunications as a means of addressing the educational needs of students, the educational community, and the general public. *Membership:* 607. *Dues:* One division membership included in the basic AECT membership; additional division memberships $10. *Meetings:* held in conjunction with annual AECT Convention. *Publications:* Newsletter.

*(AECT) Industrial Training and Education Division (ITED). 1025 Vermont Ave. NW, Suite 820, Washington, DC 20005. (202)347-7834. E-mail rpearson@passport.ca. Rob Pearson, Pres. ITED is involved with designing, planning, evaluating, and managing training and performance programs, and promoting appropriate uses of educational techniques and media. *Membership:* 273. *Dues:* One division membership included in the basic AECT membership; additional division memberships $10. *Meetings:* held in conjunction with annual AECT Convention. *Publications: ITED Newsletter.* Back issues of the *Newsletter* are indexed in the ERIC database (ED 409 883).

*(AECT) International Division (INTL). 1025 Vermont Ave. NW, Suite 820, Washington, DC 20005. (202)347-7834. E-mail khanb@gwis2.circ.gwu.edu. Badrul Khan, Pres. INTL encourages practice and research in educational communication and distance education for social and economic development across national and cultural lines, promotes international exchange and sharing of information, and enhances relationships among international leaders. *Membership:* 295. *Dues:* one division membership included in the basic AECT membership; additional division memberships $10. *Meetings:* held in conjunction with the annual AECT Convention. *Publications:* Newsletter.

*(AECT) Media Design and Production Division (MDPD). 1025 Vermont Ave. NW, Suite 820, Washington, DC 20005. (202)347-7834. E-mail chuck@cc.usu.edu. Chuck Stoddard, Pres. MDPD provides an international network that focuses on enhancing the quality and effectiveness of mediated communication, in all media formats, in educational, governmental, hospital, and corporate settings through the interaction of instructional designers, trainers, researchers, and evaluators with media designers and production team specialists who utilize state-of-the-art production skills. *Membership:* 318. *Dues:* one division membership included in the basic AECT membership; additional division memberships $10. *Meetings:* held in conjunction with annual AECT Convention. *Publications:* Newsletter.

*(AECT) Research and Theory Division (RTD). 1025 Vermont Ave. NW, Suite 820, Washington, DC 20005. (202)347-7834. E-mail lowther.deborah@coe.memphis.edu. Deborah Lowther, Pres. Seeks to improve the design, execution, utilization, and evaluation of educational technology research; to improve the qualifications and effectiveness of personnel engaged in educational technology research; to advise the educational practitioner as to the use of the research results; to improve research design, techniques, evaluation, and dissemination; to promote both applied and theoretical research on the systematic use of educational technology in the improvement of instruction; and to encourage the use of multiple research paradigms in examining issues related to technology in education. *Membership:* 452. *Dues:* one division membership included in the basic AECT membership; additional division memberships $10. *Meetings:* held in conjunction with annual AECT Convention. *Publications:* Newsletter.

*(AECT) Systemic Change in Education Division (CHANGE). 1025 Vermont Ave. NW, Suite 820, Washington, DC 20005. (202)347-7834. E-mail mch002@alph.morningside.edu. Mary Herring Pres. CHANGE advocates fundamental changes in educational settings to improve the quality of education and to enable technology to achieve its potential. *Dues:* one division membership included in the basic AECT membership; additional division memberships $10. *Meetings:* held in conjunction with annual AECT Convention. *Publications:* Newsletter.

*AECT Archives. University of Maryland, Hornbake Library, College Park, MD 20742. (301)405-9255. Fax (301)314-2634. E-mail tc65@umail.umd.edu. Web site http://www.library.umd.edu/UMCP/NPBA/npba.html. Thomas Connors, Archivist, National Public Broadcasting Archives. A collection of media, manuscripts, and related materials representing important developments in visual and audiovisual education and in instructional technology. The collection is housed as part of the National Public Broadcasting Archives. Maintained by the University of Maryland in cooperation with AECT. Open to researchers and scholars.

*Association for Experiential Education (AEE). 2305 Canyon Blvd., Suite 100, Boulder, CO 80302-5651. (303)440-8844 ext. 10. Fax (303)440-9581. E-mail citin@rochester.rr.com. Web site http://www.aee.org. Sharon Heinlen, Exec. Dir. AEE is a nonprofit, international, professional organization with roots in adventure education, committed to the development, practice, and evaluation of experiential learning in all settings. AEE's vision is to be a leading international organization for the development and application of experiential education principles and methodologies with the intent to create a just and compassionate world by transforming education and promoting positive social change. *Membership:* more than 2,500 members in more than 30 countries, including individuals and organizations with affiliations in education, recreation, outdoor adventure programming, mental health, youth service, physical education, management development training, corrections, programming for people with disabilities, and environmental education. *Dues:* $55-$95, indiv. (depending on annual income); $110-$125, family; $200-$500, organizations and corporations. *Meetings:* Annual AEE International Conference, fall. Regional Conferences held in the Northwest, Heartland, Southeast, Mid-South, Mid-Atlantic, Northeast, West, and Rocky Mountains. *Publications: Jobs Clearinghouse* (m.); *The Journal of Experiential Education* (3/yr.); *Experience and the Curriculum; Adventure Education; Adventure Therapy; Therapeutic Applications of Adventure Programming; Manual of Accreditation Standards for Adventure Programs; The Theory of Experiential Education, Third Edition; Experiential Learning in Schools and Higher Education; Ethical Issues in Experiential Education, Second Edition; The K.E.Y. (Keep Exploring Yourself) Group: An Experiential Personal Growth Group Manual; Book of Metaphors, Volume II; Women's Voices in Experiential Education;* bibliographies, directories of programs, and membership directory. New publications since last year: *Exploring the Boundaries of Adventure Therapy; A Guide to Women's Studies in the Outdoors; Administrative Practices of Accredited Adventure Programs; Fundamentals of Experience-Based Training; Wild Adventures: A Guidebook of Activities for Building Connections with Others and the Earth; Truth Zone: An Experimental Approach to Organizational Development.*

The Association for Information and Image Management (AIIM). 1100 Wayne Avenue, Suite 1100, Silver Spring, MD 20910. 301-587-8202. Fax 301-587-2711. E-mail drowe@aiim.org. Web site http://www.aiim.org/. John Mancini, President. AIIM International is the industry's leading global organization. We believe that at the center of an effective business infrastructure in the digital age is the ability to capture, create, customize, deliver, and manage enterprise content to support business processes. The requisite technologies to establish this infrastructure are an extension of AIIMs core document and content technologies. These enterprise content management (ECM) technologies are key enablers of e-business and include content/document management, business process management, enterprise portals, knowledge management, image management, warehousing, and data mining. AIIM is a neutral and unbiased source of information. We produce educational, solution-oriented events and conferences, provides up-to-the-minute industry information through publications and our online Knowledge Center, and is an ANSI/ISO-accredited standards developer. *Membership:* Full Trade Membership; Associate Trade Membership; Corporate Membership; Institutional Membership; Individual Membership; Student Membership. *Dues:* Varies by membership level. *Meetings:* Future exhibitions planned for Dubai, UAE, and Singapore (please contact IMC for more information). *Publications: e-doc Magazine; DOC.1 Weekly Newsletter.*

*Association for Library and Information Science Education (ALISE). P.O. Box 7640, Arlington, VA 22207. (703)522-1899. Fax (703)243-4551. E-mail sroger7@ibm.net. Web site http://www.alise.org. Sharon J. Rogers, Exec. Dir. Seeks to advance education for library and information science and produces annual *Library and Information Science Education Statistical Report.* Open to professional schools offering graduate programs in library and information science; personal memberships open to educators employed in such institutions; other memberships available to interested individuals. *Membership:* 500 individuals, 73 institutions. *Dues:* institutional, sliding scale, $325-$600; $200 associate; $125 international; personal, $90 full-time; $50 part-time, $40 student, $50 retired. *Meetings:* 1999, Jan 26-29, Philadelphia; 2000, Jan 11-14, San Antonio; 2001, Jan 9-12, Washington, DC. *Publications: Journal of Education for Library and Information Science; ALISE Directory and Handbook; Library and Information Science Education Statistical Report.*

*Association for Library Collections &Technical Services (ALCTS). 50 E. Huron St., Chicago, IL 60611. (312)944-6780. Fax (312)280-5033. E-mail alcts@ala.org. Karen Muller, Exec. Dir; Sheila S. Intner, Pres. A division of the American Library Association, ALCTS is dedicated to acquisition, identification, cataloging, classification, and preservation of library materials; the development and coordination of the country's library resources; and aspects of selection and evaluation involved in acquiring and developing library materials and resources. Sections include Acquisitions, Cataloging and Classification, Collection Management and Development, Preservation and Reformatting, and Serials. *Membership:* 4,984. *Dues:* $45 plus membership in ALA. *Meetings:* 2000, Chicago, Jul 6-12; 2001, San Francisco, Jun 14-20; 2002, Atlanta, June 13-19; ALA Midwinter Meeting; 2000, San Antonio, Jan 14-19; 2001, Washington, Jan 12-17; 2002, New Orleans, Jan 18-23. *Publications: Library Resources & Technical Services* (q.); *ALCTS Newsletter* (6/yr.); *ALCTS Network News* (AN2), electronic newsletter issued irregularly.

Association for Library Service to Children (ALSC). 50 E. Huron St., Chicago, IL 60611. (312)280-2163. Fax (312)944-7671. E-mail alsc@ala.org. Web site http://www.ala.org /alsc. Stephanie Anton, Interim Executive Director. The Association for Library Service to Children develops and supports the profession of childrens librarianship by enabling and encouraging its practitioners to provide the best library service to our nations children. The Association for Library Service to Children is interested in the improvement and extension of library services to children in all types of libraries. It is responsible for the evaluation and selection of book and nonbook library materials and for the improvement of techniques of library service to children from preschool through the eighth grade or junior high school age, when such materials and techniques are intended for use in more than one type of library. Committee membership is open to ALSC members. *Membership:* 3,600. *Dues:* $45 plus membership in ALA. *Meetings:* Annual Conference and Midwinter Meeting with ALA National Institutes, next is October 2002, site to be announced. *Publications: Journal of Youth Services in Libraries* (q.); *ALSC Newsletter* (q.).

*Association for the Advancement of Computing in Education (AACE). P.O. Box 2966, Charlottesville, VA 22902. (804)973-3987. Fax (804)978-7449. E-mail aace@virginia.edu. Web site http://www.aace.org.. Gary Marks, Exec. Dir; April Ballard, contact person. AACE is an international, educational, and professional organization dedicated to the advancement of learning and teaching at all levels with information technology. AACE publishes major journals, books, and CD-ROMs on the subject and organizes major conferences. AACE's membership includes researchers, developers, and practitioners in schools, colleges, and universities; administrators, policy decision makers, trainers, adult educators, and other specialists in education, industry, and the government with an interest in advancing knowledge and learning with information technology in education. *Membership:* 6,500. *Dues:* basic membership of $75 includes one journal subscription and *Educational Technology Review* subscription. *Meetings:* SITE '99 and M/SET 99, Feb 28-Mar 4, San Antonio. Ed-Media/Ed-Telecom 99, June, New Orleans. Web Net 99, Nov, Hawaii. SITE 2000, March, Phoenix.*Publications*: Educational Technology Review (ED-TECH Review) (2 or 3 times yearly); *Journal of Computers in Mathematics and Science Teaching* (JCMST); *Journal of Computing in Childhood Education* (JCCE); *Journal of Educational Multimedia and Hypermedia* (JEMH); *Journal of Interactive Learning Research* (JILR) (formerly *Journal of Artificial Intelligence in Education*); *Journal of Technology and Teacher Education* (JTATE); *International Journal of Educational Telecommunications* (IJET). A catalog of books and CD-ROMs is available on request or by visiting http://www.aace.organize/conf/pubs.

Association of American Publishers (AAP). 50 F Street, NW, Suite 400, Washington, DC 20001. (202)347-3375. Fax (202)347-3690. E-mail jplatt@publishers.org. Web site http://www.publishers.org. Patricia S. Schroeder, Pres. and CEO (DC); Judith Platt, Dir. of Communications/Public Affairs. The Association of American Publishers is the national trade association of the U.S. book publishing industry. AAP was created in 1970 through the merger of the American Book Publishers Council, a trade publishing group, and the American Textbook Publishers Institute, a group of educational publishers. AAPs approximately 200 members include most of the major commercial book publishers in the United States, as well as smaller and nonprofit publishers, university presses, and scholarly societies. AAP members publish hardcover and paperback books in every field and a range of educational materials for the elementary, secondary, postsecondary, and professional markets. Members of the Association also produce computer software and electronic products and services, such as online databases and CD-ROMs. AAP's primary concerns are the protection of intellectual property rights in all media, the defense of free expression and freedom to publish at home and abroad, the management of new technologies, development of education markets and funding for instructional materials, and the development of national and global markets for its members products. *Membership:* Regular Membership in the Association is open to all U.S. companies actively engaged in the publication of books, journals, looseleaf services, computer software, audiovisual materials, databases and other electronic products such as CD-ROM and CD-I, and similar products for educational, business and personal use. This includes producers, packagers, and copublishers who coordinate or manage most of the publishing process involved in creating copyrightable educational materials for distribution by another organization. "Actively engaged" means that the candidate must give evidence of conducting an ongoing publishing business with a significant investment in the business.

Each Regular Member firm has one vote, which is cast by an official representative or alternate designated by the member company. Associate Membership (nonvoting) is available to U.S. not-for-profit organizations that otherwise meet the qualifications for regular membership. A special category of associate membership is open to nonprofit university presses. Affiliate Membership is a nonvoting membership open to paper manufacturers, suppliers, consultants, and other nonpublishers directly involved in the industry. *Dues:* Dues are assessed on the basis of annual sales revenue from the print and electronic products listed above (under Regular Membership) but not from services or equipment. To maintain confidentiality, data is reported to an independent agent. *Meetings:* Annual

Meeting (February), Small and Independent Publishers Meeting (February), School Division Annual Meeting (January), PSP Annual Meeting (February). *Publications: AAP Monthly Report*

Association of College and Research Libraries (ACRL). 50 E. Huron St., Chicago, IL 60611-2795. (312)280-3248. Fax (312)280-2520. E-mail ajenkins@ala.org. Web site http://www.ala.org/acrl.html. Althea H. Jenkins, Exec. Dir. An affiliate of the American Library Association, ACRL provides leadership for development, promotion, and improvement of academic and research library resources and services to facilitate learning, research, and the scholarly communications process. It provides access to library standards for colleges, universities, and two-year institutions, and publishes statistics on academic libraries. Committees include Academic or Research Librarian of the Year Award, Appointments, Hugh C. Atkinson Memorial Award, Budget and Finance, Colleagues, Committee on the Status of Academic Librarians, Constitution and Bylaws, Copyright, Council of Liaisons, Doctoral Dissertation Fellowship, Government Relations, Intellectual Freedom, International Relations, Samuel Lazerow Fellowship, Media Resources, Membership, Nominations, Orientation, Professional Development, Professional Enhancement, Publications, Racial and Ethnic Diversity, Research, K. G. Saur Award for the Best C&RL Article, Standards and Accreditation, Statistics. The association administers 15 different awards in three categories: Achievement and Distinguished Service Awards, Research Awards/Grants, and Publications. *Membership:* over 11,000. *Dues:* $35 (in addition to ALA membership). *Meetings:* 2003 ACRL National Conference, Apr 10-13, Charlotte. *Publications: College & Research Libraries* (6/yr.); *College & Research Libraries News* (11/yr.); *Rare Books and Manuscripts Librarianship* (semi-annual); *CHOICE Magazine: Current Review for Academic Libraries* (11/yr.). *CLIP Notes* (current issues are nos. 16, 17, 20-26). Recent titles include: *Literature in English; The Collaborative Imperative; Library Web Site Policies; Academic Library Trends and Statistics;* and *Proceedings of the 10th ACRL National Conference.* A free list of materials is available. ACRL also sponsors an open discussion listserv, ACRL-FRM@ALA.ORG.

Association of Independent Video and Filmmakers/Foundation for Independent Video and Film (AIVF/FIVF). 304 Hudson St., 6th Floor, New York, NY 10013. (212)807-1400. Fax (212)463-8519. E-mail info@aivf.org. Web site http://www.aivf.org. Elizabeth Peters, Exec., Dir. Michelle Coe, Program & Information Services Dir. AIVF is the national trade association for independent video and filmmakers, representing their needs and goals to industry, government, and the public. Programs include screenings and seminars, insurance for members and groups, and information and referral services. Recent activities include seminars in filmmaking technology, a screening series with mid-career artists, and or monthly forum with industry professionals. AIVF also advocates public funding of the arts, public access to new telecommunications systems, and monitoring censorship issues. *Membership:* membership includes annual subscription to the independent magazine; AIVF trade discounts; online and phone information service; Web members-only area; discounted admission to events, etc. *Dues:* $55, indiv.; $75, library; $100, non-profit organization; $150, business/industry; $35, student. *Meetings:* annual membership meeting. *Publications: The Independent Film and Video Monthly; The AIVF Guide to International Film and Video Festivals; The AIVF Guide to Film and Video Distributors; The Next Step: Distributing Independent Films and Videos;* the AIVF Self Distribution Toolkit & the AIVF Film & Video Exhibitors Guide.

*Association of Specialized and Cooperative Library Agencies (ASCLA). 50 E. Huron St., Chicago, IL 60611. (800)545-2433, ext. 4398. Fax (312)944-8085. E-mail ascla@ala.org. Web site http://www.ala.org/ascla. Cathleen Bourdon, Exec. Dir. An affiliate of the American Library Association, ASCLA represents state library agencies, multitype library cooperatives, independent libraries and libraries serving special clienteles to promote the development of coordinated library services with equal access to information and material for all persons. The activities and programs of the association are carried out by 21 committees,

4 sections, and various discussion groups. *Membership:* 1,300. *Dues:* (in addition to ALA membership) $40, personal; $50, organization; $500, state library agency. *Meetings:* 1999 Conference, Jun 24-Jul 1, New Orleans. 2000, Jul 6-13, Chicago. *Publications*: Interface (q.); *The Americans with Disabilities Act: Its Impact on Libraries; Deafness: An Annotated Bibliography and Guide to Basic Materials; Library Standards for Adult Correctional Institutions 1992.* Write for free checklist of materials.

*Association of Systematics Collections (ASC). 1725 K St. NW, Suite 601, Washington, DC 20006. (202)835-9050. E-mail asc@ascoll.org. Web site http://www.ascoll.org. Fosters the care, management, and improvement of biological collections and promotes their utilization. Institutional members include free-standing museums, botanical gardens, college and university museums, and public institutions, including state biological surveys and agricultural research centers. ASC also represents affiliate societies, keeps members informed about funding and legislative issues, and provides technical consulting about collection care and taxonomy. *Membership:* 79 institutions, 25 societies, 1,200 newsletter subscribers. Dues: depend on the size of collections. *Publications: ASC Newsletter* (for members and nonmember subscribers, bi-mo.); *Guidelines for Institutional Policies and Planning in Natural History Collections; Access to Genetic Resources; Collections of Frozen Tissues; Guidelines for Institutional Database Policies.*

*Cable in the Classroom. 1900 N. Beauregard St., Suite 108, Alexandria, VA 22311. (703)845-1400. Fax (703)845-1409. E-mail cicofc@aol.com. Web site http://www.ciconline.org. Megan Hookey, Managing Dir. Cable in the Classroom is the cable industry's $420 million public service initiative to enrich education. It provides free cable connections to more than 77,000 public and private K–12 schools, reaching more than 82 percent of all U.S. students with commercial-free, quality educational programming. It also provides curriculum-related support materials for its programming and conducts Teacher Training and Media Literacy workshops throughout the country. *Membership:* Cable in the Classroom is a consortium of more than 8,500 local cable companies and 38 national cable programming networks. *Meetings:* Cable in the Classroom exhibits at 15 major education conferences each year. *Publications: Delivering the Future: Cable and Education Partnerships for the Information Age* (Dr. Bobbi Kamil); *Cable in the Classroom Magazine* (mo.); *Taking Charge of Your TV: A Guide to Critical Viewing for Parents and Children* (booklet, available on request).

*Catholic Library Association (CLA). 100 North Street, Suite 224, Pittsfield, MA 01201-5109. (413)443-2CLA. Fax (413)442-2CLA. E-mail cla@vgernet.net. Jean R. Bostley, SSJ, Exec. Dir. Provides educational programs, services, and publications for Catholic libraries and librarians. *Membership:* approx. 1,000. Dues: $45, indiv.; special rates for students and retirees. *Meetings:* Meetings are held in conjunction with the National Catholic Educational Association: 2001, Apr 17-20, Milwaukee; 2002, Apr 2-5, Atlantic City; 2003, Apr 22-25, St. Louis. *Publications: Catholic Library World* (q.); *Catholic Periodical and Literature Index* (q. with annual cumulations).

*C&C Associates. 11112 S. Spotted Rd, Cheney, WA 99004. (888)662-7678 or (509)624-9621. Fax (509)323-4811 or (509)624-5320. E-mail cc@iea.com. C&C Associates has the only Electronic Camera Repair Home Study course in the world. It has more than two centuries' experience with educating camera repair technicians. The only college certified camera repair instructor in the world teaches the 18-lesson course. C&C also publishes repair guides for cameras and also writes technical repair guides for several manufactures.

*Central Educational Network (CEN). 1400 E. Touhy, Suite 260, Des Plaines, IL 60018-3305. (847)390-8700. Fax (847)390-9435. E-mail ceninfo@mcs.net. James A. Fellows, Pres. The Central Educational Network is a not-for-profit, public television membership organization dedicated to leading, supporting, and serving the needs and interests of community, university, and state organizations that are educating and enriching their citizens through public telecommunications services. CEN is associated with the American Telecommunications Group. ATG includes the American Center for Children and Media, Making Children's Television and Media Experiences Better, The Benton Academy for Public Telecommunications Continuing Professional Development, The Center for Education Initiatives, Extending and Improving Educational Opportunities, Continental Program Marketing Acquiring and Placing Quality Programming, Higher Education Telecommunication Consortium, Building on the Distinctive Resources of Colleges and Universities, and the Hartford Gunn Institute, Planning for a Productive and Effective Second Generation of Public Broadcasting. *Membership:* Membership in the CEN component of ATG is available to public television and telecommunications organizations and agencies.

*Children's Television International (CTI)/GLAD Productions, Inc. (CTI/GLAD). Planting Field Drive, South Riding, VA 20152. (800)CTI-GLAD (284-4523). Fax (703)327-6470. Ray Gladfelter, Pres. and Dir. of Customer Services. An educational organization that develops, produces, and distributes a wide variety of color television and video programming and related publications as a resource to aid the social, cultural, and intellectual development of children and young adults. Programs cover language arts, science, social studies, history, and art for home, school, and college viewing. *Publications:* Teacher guides for instructional series; *The History Game: A Teacher's Guide;* complimentary catalog for educational videos.

*Close Up Foundation. 44 Canal Center Plaza, Alexandria, VA 22314. (703)706-3300. Fax (703)706-0000. E-mail alumni@closeup.org. Web site http://www.closeup.org. Stephen A. Janger, CEO. A nonprofit, nonpartisan civic education organization promoting informed citizen participation in public policy and community service. Programs reach more than a million participants each year. Close Up brings 25,000 secondary and middle school students and teachers and older Americans each year to Washington for week-long government studies programs and produces television programs on the C-SPAN cable network for secondary school and home audiences. *Membership:* 25,000 participants. *Meetings:* Meetings are scheduled most weeks during the academic year in Washington, DC, all with a government, history, or current issues focus. *Publications: Current Issues; The Bill of Rights: A User's Guide; Perspectives; International Relations; The American Economy;* documentary videotapes on domestic and foreign policy issues.

*Community College Association for Instruction and Technology (CCAIT). New Mexico Military Institute, 101 W. College Blvd., Roswell, NM 88201-5173. (505)624-8382. Fax (505)624-8390. E-mail klopfer@yogi.nmmi.cc.nm.us. Jerry Klopfer, Pres. A national association of community and junior college educators interested in the discovery and dissemination of information relevant to instruction and media technology in the community environment. Facilitates member exchange of data, reports, proceedings, and other information pertinent to instructional technology and the teaching-learning process; sponsors AECT convention sessions, an annual video competition, and social activities. *Membership:* 250. *Dues:* $20. *Meetings:* 1998, AECT National Convention, St. Louis, Feb 18-22. *Publications:* Regular newsletter; irregular topical papers.

*(AACC) Community College Satellite Network (CCSN). One Dupont Cir. NW, Suite 410, Washington, DC 20036. (202)728-0200. Fax (202)833-2467. E-mail CCSN@AACC.NCHE.EDU. Web site http://www.aacc.nche.edu. Monica W. Pilkey, Dir. An office of the American Association of Community Colleges (AACC), CCSN provides leadership and facilitates distance education, teleconferencing, and satellite training to the nation's community colleges. CCSN offers satellite training, discounted teleconferences, free program resources, and general informational assistance in telecommunications to the nation's community colleges. CCSN meets with its members at various industry trade shows and is very active in the AACC annual convention held each spring. CCSN produces a directory of community college satellite downlink and videoconference facilities. *Membership:* 150. *Dues:* $400 for AACC members; $800 for non-AACC members. *Publications: Schedule of Programming* (2/yr.; contains listings of live and taped teleconferences for training and staff development); *CCSN Fall & Spring Program Schedule* (listing of live and taped teleconferences for training, community and staff development, business and industry training, and more); *Teleconferencing at U.S. Community Colleges* (directory of contacts for community college satellite downlink facilities and videoconference capabilities). A free catalog is available.

Computer Assisted Language Instruction Consortium (CALICO). 214 Centennial Hall, Southwest Texas State University, 601 University Dr., San Marcos, TX 78666. (512)245-1417. Fax (512)245-9089. E-mail info@calico.org. Web site http://www.calico.org. Robert Fischer, Exec. Dir. CALICO is devoted to the dissemination of information on the application of technology to language teaching and language learning. *Membership:* 1,000 members from United States and 20 foreign countries. Anyone interested in the development and use of technology in the teaching/learning of foreign languages is invited to join. *Dues:* $50, indiv. *Meetings:* 2001, University of Central Florida, Orlando, FL. *Publications: CALICO Journal* (three times a year), *CALICO Monograph Series.*

*Computer Learning Foundation. P.O. Box 60007, Palo Alto, CA 94306-0007. (408)720-8898. Fax (408) 720-8777. Web site http://www.ComputerLearning.org. Sally Bowman Alden, Exec. Dir. The Computer Learning Foundation is in international nonprofit educational foundation dedicated to the improvement of education and preparation of youth for the workplace through the use of technology. Foundation programs provide parents and educators with the information, resources, and assistance they need to use technology effectively with children. The Computer Learning Foundation is the official host each October of Computer Learning Month, a month-long focus on the important role technology plays in our lives and a major national grassroots educational effort. During Computer Learning Month, the Computer Learning Foundation announces new materials and projects and hosts North American annual competitions for children, adults, community groups, and schools. Thousands of dollars in technology products are awarded to winners and their schools. The Computer Learning Foundation is endorsed by and collaborates with 56 U.S. state departments and Canadian ministries of education and 26 national nonprofit organizations; however, the Foundation is funded by corporate and individual donations. *Publications: Computer Learning,* annual publication.

*Computer-Using Educators, Inc. (CUE). 1210 Marina Village Parkway, Suite 100, Alameda, CA 94501. (510)814-6630. Fax (510)814-0195. E-mail cueinc@cue.org. Web site http://www.cue.org. Bob Walczak, Exec, Dir. CUE, a California nonprofit corporation, was founded in 1976 by a group of teachers interested in exploring the use of technology to improve learning in their classrooms. The organization has never lost sight of this mission. Today, CUE has an active membership of 11,000 professionals worldwide in schools, community colleges, and universities. CUE's 23 affiliates in California provide members with local year-round support through meetings, grants, events, and miniconferences. Special interest groups (SIGs) support members interested in a variety of special topics. CUE's annual conferences, newsletter, advocacy, Web site, and other programs help the technology-using educator connect with other professionals. *Membership:* 11,000 individual, corporate, and institutional members. *Dues:* $30. *Meetings:* 1999 Spring CUE Conference, May 6-8, Palm Springs, CA; Fall CUE Conference, Oct. 28-30, Sacramento; 2000, May 11-13, Palm Springs, Nov 9-11, Sacramento. *Publications: CUE NewsLetter.*

Consortium of College and University Media Centers (CCUMC). 1200 Communications Bldg.-ITC, Iowa State University, Ames, IA 50011-3243. (515)294-1811. Fax (515)294-8089. E-mail ccumc@ccumc.org. Web site www.ccumc.org. Don Rieck, Exec. Dir. CCUMC is a professional group of higher education media personnel whose purpose is to improve education and training through the effective use of educational media. Assists educational and training users in making films, video, and educational media more accessible. Fosters cooperative planning among university media centers. Gathers and disseminates information on improved procedures and new developments in instructional technology and media center management. *Membership:* 650. Institutional Memberships—Individuals within an institution of higher eduucation who are associated with the support of instruction and presentation technologies in a media center and/or technology support service; Corporate Memberships—Individuals within a corporation, firm, foundation, or other commercial or philanthrophic whose business or activity is in support of the purposes and objectives of CCUMC; Associate Membershsips—Individuals from a public library, religious, governmental, or other organization not otherwise eligible for other categories of membership; Student Memberships—Any student in an institution of higher education who is not eligible for an institutional membership. *Dues:* $195, institutional; $195, corporate; $25, student; $175, associate. *Meetings:* 2001, New Orleans, Nov.1-5; 2002, Wichita, KS, Oct. 24-29. *Publications: Media Review* (journal), *Leader* (newsletter).

*Continuing Library Education Network and Exchange Round Table (CLENERT).
50 E. Huron St., Chicago, IL 60611. (800)545-2433. E-mail wramsey@cml.lib.oh.us. Web site http://www.ala.org. Wendy Ramsey. An affiliate of the American Library Association, CLENERT seeks to provide access to quality continuing education opportunities for librarians and information scientists and to create an awareness of the need for such education in helping individuals in the field to respond to societal and technological changes. *Membership:* 350. *Dues:* open to all. ALA members; $15, indiv.; $50, organization. *Publications: CLENExchange* (q.), available to nonmembers by subscription at $20.

*Copyright Clearance Center, Inc. (CCC). 222 Rosewood Dr., Danvers, MA 01923. (978)750-8400. Fax (978)750-4470. E-mail ihinds@copyright.com. Web site http://www.copyright .com/. Joseph S. Alen, Pres. CCC, the largest licenser of photocopy reproduction rights in the world, was formed in 1978 to facilitate compliance with U.S. copyright law. CCC provides licensing systems involving the reproduction and distribution of copyrighted materials throughout the world. CCC currently manages rights relating to over 1.75 million works and represents more than 9,600 publishers and hundreds of thousands of authors and other creators, directly or through their representatives. CCC licensed customers in the United States number over 9,000 corporations and subsidiaries (including 90 of the Fortune 100 companies), as well as thousands of government agencies, law firms, document suppliers, libraries, academic institutions, copy shops, and bookstores in the United States. CCC is a member of the International Federation Rights Organizations (IFRRO) and has bilateral agreements with RROs in 11 countries worldwide, under which it repatriates fees for overseas use of U.S. works.

*Corporation for Public Broadcasting (CPB). 901 E Street, NW, Washington, DC 20004-2037. (202)879-9600. Fax (202)783-1039. E-mail info@cpb.org. Web site http://www.cpb.org. Robert T. Coonrod, Pres. and CEO. A private, nonprofit corporation created by Congress in 1967 to develop noncommercial television, radio and online services for the American people. CPB created the Public Broadcasting Service (PBS) in 1969 and National Public Radio (NPR) in 1970. CPB distributes grants to over 1,000 local public television and radio stations that reach virtually every household in the country. The Corporation is the industry's largest single source of funds for national public television and radio program development and production. In addition to quality educational and informational programming, CPB and local public stations make important contributions in the areas of education, training, community service, and application of emerging technologies. *Publications: Annual Report; CPB Public Broadcasting Directory* ($15).

Council for Basic Education (CBE). 1319 F St. NW, Suite 900, Washington, DC 20004-1152. (202)347-4171. Fax 202-347-5047. E-mail info@c-b-e.org. Web site http://www .c-b-e.org. Christopher T. Cross, Pres., Maxine P. Frost, Chair of Board of Directors. CBE's mission is to strengthen teaching and learning of the core subjects (mathematics,

English, language arts, history, government, geography, the sciences, foreign languages, and the arts) to develop the capacity for lifelong learning and foster responsible citizenship. As an independent, critical voice for education reform, CBE champions the philosophy that all children can learn and that the job of schools is to achieve this goal. CBE advocates this goal by publishing analytical periodicals and administering practical programs as examples to strengthen content in curriculum and teaching. CBE is completing a kit of Standards for Excellence in Education, which includes a CD-ROM; guides for teachers, parents, and principals, and a book of standards in the core subjects. *Publications: BE.*

*Council for Exceptional Children (CEC). 1920 Association Dr., Reston, VA 20191-1589. (703)620-3660. TTY: (703)264-9446. Fax (703)264-9494. E-mail cec@cec.sped .org. Web site http://www.cec.sped.org. Nancy Safer, Exec. Dir. CEC is the largest international professional organization dedicated to improving educational outcomes for individuals with exceptionalities (students with disabilities and the gifted). CEC advocates appropriate governmental policies, sets professional standards, provides professional development, advocates for newly and historically underserved individuals with exceptionalities, and helps professionals obtain conditions and resources necessary for effective professional practice. Services include professional development opportunities and resources, 17 divisions for specialized information, public policy advocacy and information, conferences, and standards for the preparation and certification of special educators and professional practice. CEC has expanded its professional development activities to include distance learning activities such as satellite broadcasts and Internet-based study groups. The CEC annual convention features the most current educational technology as well as adaptive and assistive technology in formats ranging from full-day workshops to hands-on demonstrations. In collaboration with another agency, CEC is involved in a research project that examines teachers' use of technology to promote literacy in children with exceptionalities. *Membership:* teachers, administrators, students, parents, related support service providers. *Publications:* Journals and newsletters with information on new research findings, classroom practices that work, and special education publications. (See also the ERIC Clearinghouse on Disabilities and Gifted Education.)

*(CEC) Technology and Media Division (TAM). 1920 Association Dr., Reston, VA 20191-1589. (703)620-3660. TTY: (703)264-9446. Fax (703)264-9494. E-mail cec@cec.sped.org. Web site http://www.cec.sped.org. Council for Exceptional Children. The Technology and Media Division (TAM) of The Council for Exceptional Children (CEC) encourages the development of new applications, technologies, and media for use as daily living tools by special populations. This information is disseminated through professional meetings, training programs, and publications. TAM members receive four issues annually of the *Journal of Special Education Technology,* containing articles on specific technology programs and applications, and five issues of the TAM newsletter, providing news of current research, developments, products, conferences, and special programs information. *Membership:* 1,700. *Dues:* $10 in addition to CEC membership.

*Council on International Non-Theatrical Events (CINE). 1001 Connecticut Ave. NW, Suite 625, Washington, DC 20036. (202)785-1136. Fax (202)785-4114. E-mail info@cine.org. Web site http://www.cine.org. Donna Tschiffely, Exec. Dir. Coordinates the selection and placement of U.S. documentary, television, short subject, and didactic films in more than 100 overseas film festivals annually. A Golden Eagle Certificate is awarded to each professional film considered most suitable to represent the United States in international competition and to winning films made by adults, amateurs, youths, and university students. Prizes and certificates won at overseas festivals are presented at an annual awards ceremony. CINE receives approximately 1,300 entries annually for the competition. Deadlines for receipt of entry forms are Feb 1 and Aug 1. *Meetings:* CINE Showcase and Awards held annually in Washington, DC. *Publications: CINE Annual Yearbook of Film and Video Awards; Worldwide Directory of Film and Video Festivals and Events.*

*East-West Center. 1601 East-West Rd., Honolulu, HI 96848-1601. (808)944-7111. Fax (808)944-7376. E-mail ewcinfo@ewc.hawaii.edu. Web site http://www.ewc.hawaii.edu. Dr. Charles E. Morrison, Pres. The U.S. Congress established the East-West Center in 1960 with a mandate to foster mutual understanding and cooperation among the governments and peoples of Asia, the Pacific, and the United States. Officially known as the Center for Cultural and Technical Interchange Between East and West, it is a public, nonprofit institution with an international board of governors. Funding for the center comes from the U.S. government, with additional support provided by private agencies, individuals, and corporations, and several Asian and Pacific governments, private agencies, individuals, and corporations. The center, through research, education, dialog, and outreach, provides a neutral meeting ground where people with a wide range of perspectives exchange views on topics of regional concern. Scholars, government and business leaders, educators, journalists, and other professionals from throughout the region annually work with Center staff to address issues of contemporary significance in such areas as international economics and politics, the environment, population, energy, the media, and Pacific islands development.

*Educational Communications. P.O. Box 351419, Los Angeles, CA 90035. (310)559-9160. Fax (310)559-9160. E-mail ECNP@aol.com. Web site http://home.earthlink.net/~dragonflight /ecoprojects.htm. Nancy Pearlman, CEO. Educational Communications is dedicated to enhancing the quality of life on this planet and provides radio and television programs about the environment. Serves as a clearinghouse on ecological issues. Programming is available on 100 stations in 25 states. *Publications: Compendium Newsletter* (bi-monthly); *Directory of Environmental Organizations.*

ECT Foundation (ECT). c/o AECT, 1800 N. Stone Lake Drive, Bloominbgton, IN 47404. 812-335-7675. E-mail aect@aect.org. Web site www.aect.org. Hans-Erik Wennberg, Pres. The ECT Foundation is a nonprofit organization whose purposes are charitable and educational in nature. Its operation is based on the conviction that improvement of instruction can be accomplished, in part, by the continued investigation and application of new systems for learning and by periodic assessment of current techniques for the communication of information. In addition to awarding scholarships, internships, and fellowships, the foundation develops and conducts leadership training programs for emerging professional leaders. Its operations are closely allied to AECT program goals, and the two organizations operate in close conjunction with each other.

*Education Development Center, Inc. 55 Chapel St., Newton, MA 02158-1060. (617)969-7100. Fax (617)969-5979. Web site http://www.edc.org. Janet Whitla, Pres. Seeks to improve education at all levels, in the United States and abroad, through curriculum development, institutional development, and services to the school and the community. Produces videocassettes, primarily in connection with curriculum development and teacher training. *Publications: Annual Report.*

*Educational Products Information Exchange (EPIE Institute). 103 W. Montauk Highway, Hampton Bays, NY 11946. (516)728-9100. Fax (516)728-9228. E-mail komoski@aurora.lionet.edu. Web site http://www.epie.org. P. Kenneth Komoski, Exec. Dir. Assesses educational materials and provides consumer information, product descriptions, and citations for virtually all educational software and curriculum-related Web sites. All of EPIE's services are available to schools and state agencies as well as parents and individuals. Online access is restricted to states with membership in the States Consortium for Improving Software Selection (SCISS). *Publications: The Educational Software Selector Database* (TESS), available to anyone. All publication material now available on CD-ROM.

*Educational Resources Information Center (ERIC). National Library of Education (NLE), Office of Educational Research and Improvement (OERI), 555 New Jersey Ave. NW, Washington, DC 20208-5720. (202)219-2289. Fax (202)219-1817. E-mail eric@inet

.ed.gov. Keith Stubbs, Dir. ERIC is a federally funded, nationwide information network that provides access to the English-language education literature. The ERIC system consists of clearinghouses, adjunct clearinghouses, and system support components, including ACCESS ERIC, the ERIC Document Reproduction Service (EDRS), and the ERIC Processing and Reference Facility. ERIC actively solicits papers, conference proceedings, literature reviews, and curriculum materials from researchers, practitioners, educational associations and institutions, and federal, state, and local agencies. These materials, along with articles from nearly 800 different journals, are indexed and abstracted for entry into the ERIC database. The ERIC database (the largest education database in the world) now contains more than 850,000 records of documents and journal articles. Users can access the ERIC database online, on CD-ROM, or through print and microfiche indexes. ERIC microfiche collections, which contain the full text of most ERIC documents, are available for public use at more than 1,000 locations worldwide. Reprints of ERIC documents, on microfiche or in paper copy, can also be ordered from EDRS. Copies of journal articles can be found in library periodical collections, through interlibrary loan, or from article reprint services. A list of the ERIC Clearinghouses, together with addresses, telephone numbers, and brief domain descriptions, follows here. *Publications: Resources in Education* (U.S. Government Printing Office); *Current Index to Journals in Education* (Oryx Press).

*ACCESS ERIC. Aspen Systems Corp., 2277 Research Blvd., Mailstop 6L, Rockville, MD 20850. 1-800-LET-ERIC [538-3742]. Fax 301)519-6760. E-mail accesseric@accessiceric.org. ACCESS ERIC coordinates ERIC's outreach and systemwide dissemination activities, develops new ERIC publications, and provides general reference and referral services. Its publications include several reference directories designed to help the public understand and use ERIC as well as provide information about current education-related issues, research, and practice. *Publications: A Pocket Guide to ERIC; All About ERIC; The ERIC Review;* the *Parent Brochure* series; *Catalog of ERIC Clearinghouse Publications; ERIC Calendar of Education-Related Conferences; ERIC Directory of Education-Related Information Centers; ERIC User's Interchange; Directory of ERIC Resource Collections. Databases:* ERIC Digests Online (EDO); Education-Related Information Centers; ERIC Resource Collections; ERIC Calendar of Education-Related Conferences. (The databases are available through the Internet: http://www.accesseric.org.)

*ERIC Clearinghouse for Community Colleges (JC). University of California at Los Angeles (UCLA), 3051 Moore Hall, P.O. Box 951521, Los Angeles, CA 90025-1521. (310)825-3931, (800)832-8256. Fax (310)206-8095. E-mail ericcc@ucla .edu. Web site http://www.gseis.ucla.edu/ERIC/eric.html. Arthur M. Cohen, Dir. Selects, synthesizes, and distributes reports and other documents about two-year public and private community and junior colleges, technical institutes, and two-year branch university programs, and outcomes of these institutions; linkages between two-year colleges and business, industrial, and community organizations; and articulation between two-year colleges and secondary and four-year postsecondary institutions.

ERIC Clearinghouse for Social Studies/Social Science Education (SO). Indiana University, Social Studies Development Center, 2805 East 10th St., Suite 120, Bloomington, IN 47408-2698. (812)855-3838, (800)266-3815. Fax (812)855-0455. E-mail ericso@indiana.edu. Web site http://ericso.indiana.edu/. John Patrick, Director. All levels of social studies, social science, art, and music education; the contributions of history, geography, and other social science disciplines; applications of theory and research to social science education; education as a social science; comparative education (K–12); content and curriculum materials on social topics such as law-related education, ethnic studies, bias and discrimination, aging, and womens equity. Includes input from the Adjunct Clearinghouses for U.S.-Japan Studies, for

Service Learning, and for International Civics. *Publications:* Listed in ERIC/ChESS catalog; contact to obtain a free copy.

*Adjunct ERIC Clearinghouse for Art Education. Indiana University, Social Studies Development Center, 2805 East 10th St., Suite 120, Bloomington, IN 47408-2698. (812)855-3838, (800)266-3815. Fax (812)855-0455. E-mail clarkgil@indiana.edu; zimmerm@ucs.indiana.edu. Enid Zimmerman, Director. Adjunct to the ERIC Clearinghouse on Social Studies/Social Science Education.

*Adjunct ERIC Clearinghouse for Law-Related Education (ADJ/LR). Indiana University, Social Studies Development Center, 2805 East 10th St., Suite 120, Bloomington, IN 47408-2698. (812)855-3838, (800)266-3815. Fax (812)855-0455. E-mail patrick@indiana.edu, tvontz@indiana.edu. Web site http://www.indiana.edu/~ssdc/iplre.html. John Patrick and Robert Leming, Co-Directors. Adjunct to the ERIC Clearinghouse on Social Studies/Social Sciences Education.

National Clearinghouse for United States-Japan Studies (NCUSJS). 2805 E. 10th St., Suite 120, Bloomington, IN 47408-2698. (812)855-3838, (800)266-3815. Fax (812)855-0455. E-mail japan@indiana.edu. Web site http://www.indiana.edu/~japan. Nicole Restrick, Assoc. Dir. Provides educational information on topics concerning Japan and U.S.-Japan relations. Adjunct to the ERIC Clearinghouse for Social Studies/Social Science Education. *Membership:* Anyone interested in teaching or learning about Japan may contact the Clearinghouse for information. *Publications: Guide to Teaching Materials on Japan; Teaching About Japan: Lessons and Resources; The Constitution and Individual Rights in Japan: Lessons for Middle and High School Students; Internationalizing the U.S. Classroom: Japan as a Model; Tora no Maki II: Lessons for Teaching About Contemporary Japan; The Japan Digest Series* (complimentary, concise discussions of various Japan-related topics): *Fiction About Japan in the Elementary Curriculum; Daily Life in Japanese High Schools; Rice: It's More Than Food in Japan; Ideas for Integrating Japan into the Curriculum; Japanese Popular Culture in the Classroom; An Introduction to Kabuki; Building a Japanese Language Program from the Bottom Up; Teaching Primary Children about Japan through Art; The History and Artistry of Haiku; Learning from the Japanese Economy; Teaching about Japanese-American Internment; Shinbun* (project newsletter).

ERIC Clearinghouse on Adult, Career, and Vocational Education (ERIC/ACVE). The Ohio State University, Center on Education and Training for Employment, 1900 Kenny Rd., Columbus, OH 43210-1090. (614)292-7069, (800)848-4815, ext. 2-7069. Fax (614)292-1260. E-mail ericacve@postbox.acs .ohio-state.edu. Web site http://ericacve.org. Susan Imel, Dir. Judy Wagner, Assoc. Dir. All levels and settings of adult and continuing, career, and vocational/technical education. Adult education, from basic literacy training through professional skill upgrading. Career awareness, career decision making, career development, career change, and experience-based education. Vocational and technical education, including new subprofessional fields, industrial arts, corrections education, employment and training programs, youth employment, work experience programs, education and business partnerships, entrepreneurship, adult retraining, and vocational rehabilitation for individuals with disabilities. Includes input from the Adjunct ERIC Clearinghouse on Consumer Education. *Publications:* ERIC Digests; *Trends* *and Issues Alerts; Practice Application Briefs; Myths and Realities; ERIC File* (newsletter); *Practitioner File;* major publications.

*Adjunct ERIC Clearinghouse for Consumer Education (ADJ/CN). National Institute for Consumer Education, 207 Rackham Bldg., Eastern Michigan University, Ypsilanti, MI 48197-2237. (313)487-2292. Fax (313)487-7153. E-mail nice@emuvax.emich.edu; NICE@online.emich.edu. Web site http://www.emich.edu/public/coe/nice. Rosella Bannister, Dir. Adjunct to the ERIC Clearinghouse on Adult, Career, and Vocational Education.

*ERIC Clearinghouse on Assessment and Evaluation. The University of Maryland, 1129 Shriver Lab, College Park, MD 20742-5701. (301)405-7449, (800)464-3742. Fax (301)405-8134. E-mail ericae@.net. Web site http://ericae.net. Lawrence M. Rudner, Dir. Tests and other measurement devices; methodology of measurement and evaluation; application of tests, measurement, or evaluation in educational projects and programs; research design and methodology in the area of assessment and evaluation; and learning theory. Includes input from the Adjunct Test Collection Clearinghouse.

*ERIC Clearinghouse on Counseling and Student Services. University of North Carolina at Greensboro, School of Education, 201 Ferguson Building, P.O. Box 26171, Greensboro, NC 27402-6171. (336)334-4114, (336)334-4116, (800)414-9769. E-mail ericcass@uncg.edu. Web site http://www.uncg.edu/~ericcass2. Garry R. Walz, Dir. Preparation, practice, and supervision of counselors and therapists at all educational levels and in all settings; theoretical development of counseling and student services; assessment and diagnosis procedures, such as testing and interviewing and the analysis and dissemination of the resultant information; outcomes analysis of counseling interventions; groups and case work; nature of pupil, student, and adult characteristics; identification and implementation of strategies that foster student learning and achievement; personnel workers and their relation to career planning, family consultations, and student services activities; identification of effective strategies for enhancing parental effectiveness; and continuing preparation of counselors and therapists in the use of new technologies for professional renewal and the implications of such technologies for service provision. *Meetings:* Annual Assessment Conference. *Publications: Career Transitions in Turbulent Times; Exemplary Career Development Programs & Practices; Career Development; Counseling Employment Bound Youth; Internationalizing Career Planning; Saving the Native Son; Cultural and Diversity Issues in Counseling; Safe Schools, Safe Students;* many others. Call for catalog.

ERIC Clearinghouse on Disabilities and Gifted Education (EC). 1110 N. Glebe Rd., Arlington, VA 22201-5704. (703)264-9474, (800)328-0272. Fax (703) 620-2521. E-mail ericec@cec.sped.org. Web site http://ericec.org. Information specialist. ERIC EC is part of the U.S. Department of Education's information network. ERIC EC collects the professional literature on disabilities and gifted education for inclusion in the ERIC database. ERIC EC also responds to requests for information on disabilities and gifted education; serves as a resource and referral center for the general public; conducts general information searches; and publishes and disseminates free or low-cost materials on disability and gifted education research, programs, and practices. *Publications:* Please visit the Web site for a complete list of publications.

*ERIC Clearinghouse on Educational Management (EA). University of Oregon (Dept. 5207), 1787 Agate St., Eugene, OR 97403-5207. (541)346-5043, (800)438-8841. Fax (541)346-2334. E-mail ppiele@oregon.uoregon.edu. Philip K.

Piele, Dir. The governance, leadership, management, and structure of K–12 public and private education organizations; local, state, and federal education law and policy making; practice and theory of administration; preservice and inservice preparation of administrators; tasks and processes of administration; methods and varieties of organization and organizational change; and the social context of education organizations.

ERIC Clearinghouse on Elementary and Early Childhood Education (PS/NPIN). University of Illinois, Children's Research Center, 51 Gerty Dr., Champaign, IL 61820. (217)333-1386, (800)583-4135. Fax (217)333-3767. E-mail ericeece@uiuc.edu. Web site http://ericps.crc.uiuc.edu/ericeece.html. Lilian G. Katz, Dir. The ERIC Clearinghouse on Elementary and Early Childhood (ERIC/EECE) provides information and resources in the areas of child development, the education and care of children from birth through early adolescence, the teaching of young children, and parenting and family life. These resources relate to the physical, cognitive, social, educational, and cultural development of children from birth through early adolescence; prenatal factors; parents, parenting, and family relationships that impinge on education; learning theory research and practice related to the development of young children, including the preparation of teachers for this educational level; interdisciplinary curriculum and mixed-age teaching and learning; educational, social, and cultural programs and services for children; the child in the context of the family and the family in the context of society; theoretical and philosophical issues pertaining to childrens development and education. *Membership:* not applicable. *Publications:* ERIC/EECE publishes ERIC Digests, books and monographs, newsletters, *Early Childhood Research & Practice,* a scholarly peer-reviewed Internet journal, *Parent News,* an online parenting magazine. For details see: http://ericeece.org/eecepub.html.

*Adjunct ERIC Clearinghouse for Child Care (ADJ/CC). National Child Care Information Center, 301 Maple Ave., Suite 602, Vienna, VA 22180. (703)938-6555, (800)516-2242. Fax (800)716-2242. E-mail agoldstein@acf .dhhs.gov. Web site http://ericps.crc.uiuc.edu/nccic/nccichome.html. Anne Goldstein, Proj. Dir. Adjunct to the ERIC Clearinghouse on Elementary and Early Childhood Education. Works with Bureau, Administration for Children and Families (ACF) of DHHS, to complement, enhance, and promote child care linkages and to serve as a mechanism for supporting quality, comprehensive services for children and families. NCCIS's activities include: dissemination of child care information in response to requests from states, territories and tribe, other policy makers, child care organizations, providers, business communities, parents, and the general public; outreach to ACF child care grantees and the boarder child care community; publication of the child care bulletin and development and dissemination of other publications on key child care issues; and coordination of National Leadership Forums, which provide an opportunity for experts from across the country to participate in one-day conferences on critical issues affecting children and families. Working closely with ACF regional offices, the NCCIC also provides technical assistance to states through a network of state technical assistance specialists. Many materials produced and distributed by NCCIC are available in Spanish. NCCIC is the Adjunct ERIC Clearinghouse for Child Care.

ERIC Clearinghouse on Higher Education (ERIC-HE). George Washington University, One Dupont Circle, NW, Suite 630, Washington, DC 20036-1183. (202)296-2597, (800)773-3742. Fax (202)452-1844. E-mail eric-he@eric-he.edu. Web site http://www.eriche.org. Adrianna Kezar, Dir. Topics relating to college and university conditions, problems, programs, and students. Curricular and instructional programs, and institutional research at the college or university level. Federal programs, professional education (medicine, law, etc.), professional continuing education, collegiate computer-assisted learning and management, graduate education, university extension programs, teaching and learning, legal issues and legislation, planning, governance, finance, evaluation, interinstitutional arrangements, management of institutions of higher education, and business or industry educational programs leading to a degree. *Membership:* Free government-funded service. *Meetings:* Annual Advisory Board Meeting, Spring. *Publications: Higher Education Leadership: Analyzing the Gender Gap; The Virtual Campus: Technology and Reform in Higher Education; Early Intervention Programs: Opening the Door to Higher Education; Enriching College with Constructive Controversy; A Culture for Academic Excellence: Implementing the Quality Principles in Higher Education; From Discipline to Development: Rethinking Student Conduct in Higher Education; Proclaiming and Sustaining Excellence: Assessment as a Faculty Role; The Application of Customer Satisfaction Principles to Universities; Saving the Other Two-Thirds: Practices and Strategies for Improving the Retention and Graduation of African American Students in Predominately White Institutions; Enrollment Management: Change for the 21st Century; Faculty Workload: States; Perspectives.* NEW ASHE-ERIC REPORTS: Walvoord, B. et al. (2000) Academic departments: How they work, how they change. ASHE-ERIC Higher Education Report, (Volume 27, No.8). San Francisco: Jossey-Bass Publishers; Wolverton, M. et al. (2001) The changing nature of the academic deanship. ASHE-ERIC Higher Education Report (Volume 28, No.1), San Francisco: Jossey-Bass Publishers; Sutton, T. & Bergerson, P. Faculty, *Compensation Systems: Impact on the Quality of Higher Education.* ASHE-ERIC Higher Education Report, (Volume 28, No.2). San Francisco: Jossey-Bass Publishers.

ERIC Clearinghouse on Information & Technology (IR). Syracuse University, 621 Skytop Rd., Suite 160, Syracuse, NY 13244-4100. (315)443-3640, (800)464-9107. Fax (315)443-5448. E-mail eric@ericir.syr.edu;askeric@ericir.syr.edu. Web site www.ericit.org. R. David Lankes, Dir. Educational technology and library and information science at all levels. Instructional design, development, and evaluation within educational technology, along with the media of educational communication: computers and microcomputers, telecommunications, audio and video recordings, film, and other audiovisual materials as they pertain to teaching and learning. The focus is on the operation and management of information services for education-related organizations. Includes all aspects of information technology related to education.

ERIC Clearinghouse on Languages and Linguistics (ERIC/CLL). Center for Applied Linguistics, 4646-403 St., NW, Washington, DC 20016-1859. (202)362-0700. Fax (202)362-3740, (202)659-5641. E-mail eric@cal.org. Web site http://www.cal.org/ericcll. Joy Peyton, Dir.; Dr. Craig Packard, User Services Coordinator, contact person. Languages and language sciences. All aspects of second language instruction and learning in all commonly and uncommonly taught languages, including English as a second language. Bilingualism and bilingual education. Cultural education in the context of second language learning, including intercultural communication, study abroad, and international education exchange. All areas of linguistics, including theoretical and applied linguistics, socio-linguistics, and psycholinguistics. Includes input from the National Clearinghouse for ESL Literacy Education (NCLE).

*Adjunct ERIC Clearinghouse for ESL Literacy Education (ADJ/LE). National Clearinghouse for ESL Literacy Education, Center for Applied Linguistics (CAL), 4646-403 St., NW, Washington, DC 20016-1859.

(202)362-0700, Ext. 200. Fax (202)362-3740. E-mail ncle@cal.org. Web site http://www.cal.org/ncle/. Joy Kreeft Peyton, Dir. Adjunct to the ERIC Clearinghouse on Languages and Linguistics. NCLE is the national clearinghouse focusing on the education of adults learning English as a second or additional language. NCLE collects, analyzes, synthesizes, and disseminates information on literacy education for adults and out-of-school youth. NCLE publishes books (available from Delta Systems in McHenry, IL), free ERIC digests and annotated bibliographies on a wide range of topics, and *NCLE Notes,* a newsletter. *Publications: Literacy and Language Diversity in the United States,* by Terrence Wiley (1996; McHenry, IL: Delta Systems)

*ERIC Clearinghouse on Reading, English, and Communication (CS). Indiana University, Smith Research Center, Suite 150, 2805 E. 10th St., Bloomington, IN 47408-2698. (812)855-5847, (800)759-4723. Fax (812)855-4220. E-mail ericcs@indiana.edu. Web site http://www.indiana.edu/~eric_rec. Carl B. Smith, Dir. Reading, English, and communication (verbal and nonverbal), preschool through college; research and instructional development in reading, writing, speaking, and listening; identification, diagnosis, and remediation of reading problems; speech communication (including forensics), mass communication; interpersonal and small group interaction; interpretation; rhetorical and communication theory; speech sciences; and theater. Preparation of instructional staff and related personnel. All aspects of reading behavior with emphasis on physiology, psychology, sociology, and teaching; instructional materials, curricula, tests and measurement, and methodology at all levels of reading; the role of libraries and other agencies in fostering and guiding reading; diagnostics and remedial reading services in schools and clinical settings. Preparation of reading teachers and specialists. The Web site makes available a wealth of information pertaining to the full gamut of language arts topics enumerated above.

*ERIC Clearinghouse on Rural Education and Small Schools (RC). Appalachia Educational Laboratory (AEL), 1031 Quarrier St., P.O. Box 1348, Charleston, WV 25325-1348. (304)347-0465, (800)624-9120. Fax (304)347-0487. E-mail lanhamb@ael .org. Web site http://www.ael.org/erichp.htm. Hobart Harmon, Acting Dir. Economic, cultural, social, or other factors related to educational programs and practices for rural residents; American Indians and Alaska Natives, Mexican Americans, and migrants; educational practices and programs in all small schools; and outdoor education. Check Web site to subscribe to print newsletter, or call toll-free.

ERIC Clearinghouse on Science, Mathematics, and Environmental Education (SE). The Ohio State University, 1929 Kenny Road, Columbus, OH 43210-1080. (614)292-6717, (800)276-0462. Fax (614)292-0263. E-mail ericse@osu.edu. Web site http://www.ericse.org. David L. Haury, Director; Linda A. Milbourne, Associate Director. Science, mathematics, and environmental education at all levels, and within these three broad subject areas, the following topics: development of curriculum and instructional materials; teachers and teacher education; learning theory and outcomes (including the impact of parameters such as interest level, intelligence, values, and concept development upon learning in these fields); educational programs; research and evaluative studies; media applications; computer applications. *Meetings:* Attend various meetings throughout the year: NCTM, NSTA, etc. *Publications: CSMEE Horizon* newsletter. Various other publications: *Proceedings of Annual Meetings for the North American Chapter of the International Group for the Psychology of Mathematics Education; Developing Teacher Leaders (Professional Development in Science and Mathematics); Elementary Teachers Do Science (Guidelines for Teacher Preparation Programs); Rethinking Portfolio Assessment (Documenting the Intellectual Work of Learners in Science and Mathematics); Creative*

Childhood Experiences in Mathematics and Science; Trends in Science Education Research.

ERIC Clearinghouse on Teaching and Teacher Education (ERIC-SP). American Association of Colleges for Teacher Education (AACTE), 1307 New York Avenue, N.W., Suite 300, Washington, DC 20005. (202)293-2450, (800)822-9229. Fax 202)457-8095. E-mail query@aacte.org. Web site http://www.ericsp.org. Mary E. Dilworth, Dir. An information clearinghouse funded by the Department of Education, Office of Educational Research and Information. The Clearinghouse serves school personnel at all levels. The scope area covers teacher recruitment, selection, licensing, certification, training, preservice and inservice preparation, evaluation, retention, and retirement. The theory, philosophy, and practice of teaching. Curricula and general education not specifically covered by other clearinghouses. Organization, administration, finance, and legal issues relating to teacher education programs and institutions. All aspects of health, physical, recreation, and dance education. *Publications:* Monographs, digests, information cards.

> ***Adjunct ERIC Clearinghouse on Clinical Schools (ADJ/CL).** American Association of Colleges for Teacher Education, One Dupont Cir. NW, Suite 610, Washington, DC 20036-1186. (202)293-2450, (800)822-9229. Fax (202)457-8095. E-mail iabdalha@inet.ed.gov. Web site http://www.aacte.org /menu2.html. Ismat Abdal-Haqq, Coord. Adjunct to the ERIC Clearinghouse on Teaching and Teacher Education.

*ERIC Clearinghouse on Urban Education. Teachers College, Columbia University, Institute for Urban and Minority Education, Main Hall, Rm. 303, Box 40, 525 W. 120th St., New York, NY 10027-6696. (212)678-3433, (800)601-4868. Fax (212)678-4012. E-mail eric-cue@columbia.edu. Web site http://eric-web.tc.columbia .edu. Erwin Flaxman, Dir. Programs and practices in public, parochial, and private schools in urban areas and the education of particular ethnic minority children and youth in various settings; the theory and practice of educational equity; urban and minority experiences; and urban and minority social institutions and services.

*ERIC Document Reproduction Service (EDRS). 7420 Fullerton Rd., Suite 110, Springfield, VA 22153-2852. (703)440-1400, (800)443-ERIC (3742). Fax (703)440-1408. E-mail service@edrs.com. Web site http://edrs.com. Peter M. Dagutis, Dir. Provides subscription services for ERIC document collections in electronic format (from 1996 forward) and on microfiche (from 1966 forward). On-demand delivery of ERIC documents is also available in formats including paper, electronic PDF image, fax, and microfiche. Delivery methods include shipment of hardcopy documents and microfiche, document fax-back, and online delivery. Back collections of ERIC documents, annual subscriptions, cumulative indexes, and other ERIC-related materials are also available. ERIC documents can be ordered by toll-free phone call, fax, mail, or online through the EDRS Web site. Document ordering also available from DIALOG and OCLC.

ERIC Processing and Reference Facility (ERIC). 4483-A Forbes Blvd., Lanham, MD 20706. (301)552-4200, (800)799-ERIC(3742). Fax (301)552-4700. E-mail ericfac@inet.ed.gov. Web site http://www.ericfacility.org. Donald Frank, Dir. A central editorial and quality control office that coordinates document processing and database building activities for ERIC, the U.S. Department of Educations database on education research; performs acquisition, lexicographic, and reference functions; and maintains systemwide quality control standards. *Publications:* The ERIC Facility also prepares *Resources in Education* (RIE); *Current Index to Journals in*

Education (CIJE); the *ERIC Processing Manual*; *Thesaurus of ERIC Descriptors*; *Identifier Authority List* (IAL); *ERIC Ready References;* and other products.

*Educational Videos and CD-ROM. Penn State Media Sales, 118 Wagner Building, University Park, PA 16802. (800)770-2111, (814)863-3102. Fax (814)865-3172. E-mail mediasales@cde.psu.edu. Web site http://www.cde.psu.edu/MediaSales. Sue Oram, Media Sales Coordinator. Makes available to professionals videos in the behavioral sciences judged to be useful for university teaching and research. Also distributes training videos to business and industry. A catalog of the videos in the collection is available online. Special topics and individual brochures available. The online catalog now contains videos in the behavioral sciences (psychology, psychiatry, anthropology), animal behavior, sociology, teaching and learning, folklife and agriculture, business, education, biological sciences, and Pennsylvania topics. Videos and CD-ROMs may be submitted for international distribution. Stock footage available also.

*Eisenhower National Clearinghouse for Mathematics and Science Education. 1929 Kenny Road, Columbus, OH 43210-1079. (800)621-5785, (614)292-7784. Fax (614)292-2066. E-mail info@enc.org. Web site http://www.enc.org. Dr. Len Simutis, Dir. The Eisenhower National Clearinghouse for Mathematics and Science Education (ENC) is located at The Ohio State University and funded by the U.S. Department of Education's Office of Educational Research and Improvement (OERI). ENC provides K–12 teachers and other educators with a central source of information on mathematics and science curriculum materials, particularly those that support education reform. Among ENC's products and services are ENC Online, which is available through a toll-free number and the Internet; 12 demonstration sites located throughout the nation; and a variety of publications, including the *Guidebook of Federal Resources for K–12 Mathematics and Science,* which lists federal resources in mathematics and science education. In 1998 ENC produced CD-ROMs on topics such as equity and professional development, including curriculum resources and the ENC Resource Finder, which is the same searchable catalog of curriculum resources as the ENC Online. STET users include K–12 teachers, other educators, policy makers, and parents. *Publications: ENC Update* (newsletter); *ENC Focus* (a magazine on selected topics); *Ideas That Work: Mathematics Professional Development* and *Ideas That Work: Science Professional Development* (two booklets on professional development); *Guidebook of Federal Resources for K–12 Mathematics and Science* (federal programs in mathematics and science education). ENC Online is available online (http://www.enc.org) or toll-free at (800)362-4448.

*Federal Communications Commission (FCC). 445 12th St. S.W., Washington, DC 20554. (202)418-0190. Fax (202)418-1232. E-mail mpowell@fcc.gov or fccinfo@fcc.gov. Web site http://www.fcc.gov. William Kennard, Chairman. The FCC regulates the telecommunications industry in the United States.

*Federal Educational Technology Association (FETA). FETA Membership, Sara Shick, P.O. Box 3412, McLean, VA 22103-3412. (703)406-3040. Fax (703)406-4318. E-mail feta@clearspringinc.com. Web site http://www.feta.org. Beth Borko, Board Chair. An affiliate of AECT, FETA is dedicated to the improvement of education and training through research, communication, and practice. It encourages and welcomes members from all government agencies, federal, state, and local; from business and industry; and from all educational institutions and organizations. FETA encourages interaction among members to improve the quality of education and training in any arena, but with specific emphasis on government-related applications. *Membership:* 150. *Dues:* $20. *Meetings:* meets in conjunction with AECT InCITE, concurrently with SALT's Washington meeting in August, and periodically throughout the year in Washington, DC. *Publications:* Newsletter (occasional).

Film Arts Foundation (FAF). 346 9th St., 2nd Floor, San Francisco, CA 94103. (415)552-8760. Fax (415)552-0882. E-mail info@filmarts.org. Web site http://www.filmarts .org. Gail Silva, Director. Service organization that supports and promotes independent film and video production. Services include low-cost 16mm, Super-8, and AVID equipment rental; on and off-line editing including AVID, Final Cut, 16mm flatbeds, VHS and S-VHS, as well as a Pro Tools sound room and Optical Printer; resource library; group legal and production insurance plans; monthly magazine; seminars; grants program; annual film and video festival; nonprofit sponsorship; exhibition program; and advocacy and significant discounts on film- and video-related products and services. *Membership:* 3,500+. *Dues:* $45 for "supporter" level benefits including monthly magazine, discounts on goods and services, including equipment rental and film processing, access to libraries and online databases; $65 for full "filmmaker" benefits including above plus access to equipment and postproduction facilities, discounts on seminars, nonprofit fiscal sponsorship, group legal and production insurance plans. *Meetings:* Annual Festival, biannual membership meetings, various and sundry other events. *Publications: Release Print* (magazine).

*Film/Video Arts (F/VA). 817 Broadway, 2nd Floor, New York, NY 10003. (212)673-9361. Fax (212)475-3467. E-mail education@fva.com. Frank Millspaugh, Exec. Dir. Film/Video Arts is the largest nonprofit media arts center in the New York region. Dedicated to the advancement of emerging and established media artists of diverse backgrounds, F/VA is unique in providing a fertile environment where aspiring producers can obtain training, rent equipment, and edit their projects all under one roof. Every year more than 2,500 individuals participate in F/VA's programs. More than 50 courses are offered each semester, covering topics such as rudimentary technical training in 16mm filmmaking and video production, advanced editing courses in online systems, history, cultural analysis, installation art, fundraising, grant writing, and distribution. F/VA is supported by the New York State Council on the Arts, the National Endowment for the Arts, and numerous foundations and corporations, and is therefore able to offer courses and production services at the lowest possible rates. Artists who got their start at F/VA include Jim Jarmusch, Mira Nair, Leslie Harris, Kevin Smith, and Cheryl Dunye. F/VA takes pride in meeting the needs of a broad range of filmmakers, working on features, documentaries, shorts, experimental pieces, industrials, cable shows, music videos, and more by offering affordable services essential to the creation of their work and development of their careers. *Dues:* $40, indiv.; $70, organization.

Freedom of Information Center (FOI Center). 127 Neff Annex, University of Missouri, Columbia, MO 65211-0012. (573)882-4856. Fax (573)882-9002. E-mail FOI@missouri.edu. Web site http://www.missouri.edu/~foiwww. Dr. Charles N. Davis, Director; Kathleen Edwards, Manager; Robert W. Anderson, Web Manager. Located in the Missouri School of Journalism, the Freedom of Information Center is an academic research facility specializing in educational advocacy. The collection focuses on the centrality of open government to its role in fostering democracy. The Center staff assists the public with requests or questions about freedom of information with the help of an extensive archive of materials dating from the FOI movements inception. The Centers operating hours are Monday through Friday, 8:00 A.M. to 5:00 P.M., excluding University holidays. *Membership:* The FOI Center does not offer memberships. The Center serves approximately 23,000 researchers annually through its Web page and through individual contacts. *Dues:* No dues charged. Minimal fees may be charged for research. *Meetings:* The FOI Center meets annually with the National Freedom of Information Coalition. *Publications: Access to Public Information: A Resource Guide to Government in Columbia and Boone County, Missouri,* a directory of public records, and the *FOI Advocate,* a periodic electronic newsletter. Both publications are linked to the Center's Web page. Some older publications are available for sale by contacting the Center.

*George Eastman House. 900 East Ave., Rochester, NY 14607. (716)271-3361. Fax (716)271-3970. E-mail tbannon@geh.org. Web site http://www.eastman.org. Anthony

Bannon, Dir. World-renowned museum of photography and cinematography established to preserve, collect, and exhibit photographic art and technology, film materials, and related literature, and to serve as a memorial to George Eastman. Services include archives, traveling exhibitions, research library, school of film preservation, center for the conservation of photographic materials, and photographic print service. Educational programs, exhibitions, films, symposia, music events, tours, and internship stipends offered. Eastman's turn-of-the-century mansion and gardens have been restored to their original grandeur. *Membership:* 4,000. *Dues:* $40, library; $50, family; $40, indiv.; $36, student; $30, senior citizen; $75, Contributor; $125, Sustainer; $250, Patron; $500, Benefactor; $1,000, George Eastman Society. *Publications: IMAGE; Microfiche Index to Collections; Newsletter; Annual Report: The George Eastman House and Gardens; Masterpieces of Photography from the George Eastman House Collections;* and exhibition catalogs.

*The George Lucas Educational Foundation. P.O. Box 3494, San Rafael, CA 94912. (415)662-1600. Fax (415)662-1605. E-mail edutopia@glef.org. Web site http://glef.org. Dr. Milton Chen, Exec. Dir. The Foundation promotes innovative efforts to improve education, especially those that integrate technology with teaching and learning, so all students will be prepared to learn and live in an increasingly complex world. Projects include a documentary film and resource book, a Web site, and bi-annual newsletter, all of which feature compelling education programs from around the country. The target audience is community and opinion leaders, parents, educators, media, corporate executives, and elected officials. The Foundation works to give these stakeholders useful tools to develop, make, and sustain changes in teaching and learning. The George Lucas Educational Foundation is a private operating foundation, not a grantmaking organization. *Publications: EDUTOPIA* (bi-annual newsletter).

Graphic Arts Technical Foundation (GATF). 200 Deer Run Road, Sewickley, PA 15143-2600. (412)741-6860. Fax (412)741-2311. E-mail info@gatf.org. Web site http://www.gatf.org. George Ryan, Pres. GATF is a member-supported, nonprofit, scientific, technical, and educational organization dedicated to the advancement of graphic communications industries worldwide. For 77 years GATF has developed leading-edge technologies and practices for printing, and each year the Foundation develops new products, services, and training programs to meet the evolving needs of the industry. GATF consolidated its operations with the Printing Industries of America (PIA) in 1999. *Membership:* 14,000 corporate members, 520 teachers, 100 students. *Dues:* $45, teachers; $30, students; corporations pay dues to regional printing organizations affiliated with GATF/PIA. *Meetings:* Annual GATF/PIA Joint Fall Conference. *Publications:* GATF publishes books relating to graphic communications. GATFs 2001 Publications Catalogs promotes 320 books, 100 of which are published by GATF. Recent publications include *Customer Service in the Printing Industry, What the Printer Should Know About Ink, Total Production Maintenance, Managing Mavericks: The Official Printing Industry Guide to Effective Sales Management, Print Production Scheduling Primer, Paper Buying Primer,* and *Print Production Management Primer.*

Great Plains National ITV Library (GPN). P.O. Box 80669, Lincoln, NE 68501-0669. (402)472-2007, (800)228-4630. Fax (800)306-2330. E-mail gpn@unl.edu. Web site http://gpn.unl.edu. Stephen C. Lenzen, Executive Director. Produces and distributes educational media, video, CD-ROMs and DVDs, prints and Internet courses. Available for purchase for audiovisual or lease for broadcast use. *Membership:* This is a national distributor of educational programming that is available to the K–12 and the college/adult audience. Membership is not required to receive promotional and catalog materials or to purchase the videos, CD-ROMs, and DVDs. *Meetings:* There are no meetings. Organization members do attend subject specific conventions to promote products. *Publications:* GPN Educational Video Catalogs by curriculum areas; periodic brochures. Complete listing of GPN's product line is available via the Internet along with online purchasing. Free previews available.

Health Sciences Communications Association (HeSCA). One Wedgewood Dr., Suite 27, Jewett City, CT 06351-2428. (203)376-5915. Fax (203)376-6621. E-mail HeSCAOne@aol.com. Web site http://www.hesca.hesca.org. Ronald Sokolowski, Exec. Dir. An affiliate of AECT, HeSCA is a nonprofit organization dedicated to the sharing of ideas, skills, resources, and techniques to enhance communications and educational technology in the health sciences. It seeks to nurture the professional growth of its members; serve as a professional focal point for those engaged in health sciences communications; and convey the concerns, issues, and concepts of health sciences communications to other organizations that influence and are affected by the profession. International in scope and diverse in membership, HeSCA is supported by medical and veterinary schools, hospitals, medical associations, and businesses where media are used to create and disseminate health information. *Membership:* 150. *Dues:* $150, indiv.; $195, institutional ($150 additional institutional dues); $60, retiree; $75, student; $1,000, sustaining. All include subscriptions to the journal and newsletter. *Meetings:* Annual meetings, May-June. *Publications: Journal of Biocommunications; Feedback* (newsletter).

*Hollywood Film Archive. 8391 Beverly Blvd., #321, Hollywood, CA 90048. (213)933-3345. E-mail cabaret66@aol.com. D. Richard Baer, Dir. Archival organization for information about feature films produced worldwide, from the early silents to the present. *Publications:* Comprehensive movie reference works for sale, including *Variety Film Reviews* (1907–1996) and the *American Film Institute Catalogs* (1893–1910, 1911–1920, 1921–1930, 1931–1940, 1941–1950, 1961–1970), as well as the *Film Superlist* (1894–1939, 1940–1949, 1950–1959) volumes, which provide information both on copyrights and on motion pictures in the public domain; *Harrison's Reports and Film Reviews* (1919–1962).

*HOPE Reports, Inc. 58 Carverdale Dr., Rochester, NY 14618-4004. (716)442-1310. Fax (716)442-1725. E-mail hopereport@aol.com. Thomas W. Hope, Chairman and CEO; Mabeth S. Hope, Vice Pres. Supplies statistics, marketing information, trends, forecasts, and salary and media studies to the visual communications industries through printed reports, custom studies, consulting, and by telephone. Clients and users in the United States and abroad include manufacturers, dealers, producers, and media users in business, government, health sciences, religion, education, and community agencies. *Publications: Hope Reports Presentation Media Events Calendar* (annual); *Video Post-Production; Media Market Trends; Educational Media Trends through the 1990's; LCD Panels and Projectors; Overhead Projection System; Presentation Slides; Producer & Video Post Wages & Salaries; Noncommercial AV Wages & Salaries; Corporate Media Salaries; Digital Photography: Pictures of Tomorrow; Hope Reports Top 100 Contract Producers; Contract Production II; Executive Compensation; Media Production; Outsource or Insource.*

*Institute for Development of Educational Activities, Inc. (|I|D|E|A|). 259 Regency Ridge, Dayton, OH 45459. (937)434-6969. Fax (937)434-5203. E-mail IDEADayton@aol.com. Web site http://www.idea.org. Dr. Steven R. Thompson, Pres. I|D|E|A| is an action-oriented research and development organization originating from the Charles F. Kettering Foundation. It was established in 1965 to assist the educational community in bridging the gap that separates research and innovation from actual practice in the schools. Its goal is to design and test new responses to improve education and to create arrangements that support local application. Activities include developing new and improved processes, systems, and materials; training local facilitators to use the change processes; and providing information and services about improved methods and materials. |I|D|E|A| sponsors an annual fellowship program for administrators and conducts seminars for school administrators and teachers.

*Institute for the Future (IFTF). 2744 Sand Hill Rd., Menlo Park, CA 94025-7020. (650)854-6322. Fax (650)854-7850. E-mail info@iftf.org. Web site http://www.iftf.org. Robert Johansen, Pres. The cross-disciplinary professionals at IFTF have been providing global and domestic businesses and organizations with research-based forecasts and action-oriented tools for strategic decision making since 1968. IFTF is a nonprofit, applied research and consulting firm dedicated to understanding technological, economic, and societal changes and their long-range domestic and global consequences. Its work falls into four main areas: Strategic Planning, Emerging Technologies, Health Care Horizons, and Public Sector Initiatives. IFTF works with clients to think systematically about the future, identify socioeconomic trends and evaluate their long-term implications, identify potential leading-edge markets around the world, understand the global marketplace, track the implications of emerging technologies for business and society, leverage expert judgment and data resources, offer an independent view of the big picture, and facilitate strategic planning processes.

Instructional Telecommunications Council (ITC). One Dupont Cir., NW, Suite 410, Washington, DC 20036-1176. (202)293-3110. Fax (202)833-2467. E-mail cdalziel@aacc .nche.edu. Web site http://www.itcnetwork.org. Christine Dalziel, Executive Director. ITC represents over 500 educational institutions from the United States and Canada that are involved in higher educational instructional telecommunications and distance learning. ITC holds annual professional development meetings, tracks national legislation, supports research, and provides members with a forum to share expertise and materials. *Membership:* 504. *Dues:* $450, Institutional; $125, Individual; $750, Corporate. *Meetings:* 2001Telelearning Conference.*Publications: New Connections: A Guide to Distance Education* (2d ed.); *New Connections: A College Presidents Guide to Distance Education; Quality Enhancing Practices in Distance Education: Teaching and Learning; Digital Video: A Handbook for Educators; Faculty Compensation and Support Issues in Distance Education; ITC News* (monthly publication/newsletter); ITC listserv.

International Association for Language Learning Technology (IALL). 618 Van Hise Hall, 1220 Linden Drive, Madison, WI 53706. (608)262-4066. Fax (608)265-3892. E-mail business@iall.net. Web site http://iall.net. David Pankratz, President; Lauren Rosen, Business Manager. IALL is a professional organization working for the improvement of second language learning through technology in learning centers and classrooms. *Membership:* 400. *Dues:* $40, regular; $15, student; $40, library; $55 commercial. *Meetings:* Biennial IALL conferences treat the entire range of topics related to technology in language learning as well as management and planning. IALL also sponsors sessions at conferences of organizations with related interests, including CALICO. *Publications: IALL Journal of Language Learning Technologies* (2 times annually); materials for labs, teaching, and technology.

*International Association of Business Communicators (IABC). One Hallidie Plaza, Suite 600, San Francisco, CA 94102. (415)544-4700. Fax (415)544-4747. E-mail service_centre @iabc.com. Web site http://www.iabc.com. Elizabeth Allan, Pres. and CEO. IABC is the worldwide association for the communication and public relations profession. It is founded on the principle that the better an organization communicates with all its audiences, the more successful and effective it will be in meeting its objectives. IABC is dedicated to fostering communication excellence, contributing more effectively to organizations' goals worldwide, and being a model of communication effectiveness. *Membership:* 13,500 plus. *Dues:* $175 in addition to local and regional dues. *Meetings:* 1999, June 20-23, Washington, DC; 2000, June 25-28, Vancouver. *Publications: Communication World.*

*International Association of School Librarianship (IASL). Box 34069, Dept. 300, Seattle, WA 98124-1069. (604)925-0266. Fax (604)925-0566. E-mail iasl@rockland.com. Web site http://www.rhi.hi.is/~anne/iasl.html. Dr. Ken Haycock, Exec. Dir. Seeks to encourage development of school libraries and library programs throughout the world; promote professional preparation and continuing education of school librarians; achieve collaboration among school libraries of the world; foster relationships between school librarians and other professionals connected with children and youth and to coordinate activities, conferences, and other projects in the field of school librarianship. *Membership:*

900 plus. *Dues:* $50, personal and institution for North America, Western Europe, Japan, and Australia; $15 for all other countries. *Meetings:* 1999, Birmingham, AL, November. *Publications: IASL Newsletter* (q.); *School Libraries Worldwide* (semi-annual); *Conference Professionals and Research Papers* (annual); *Connections: School Library Associations and Contact People Worldwide; Sustaining the Vision: A Collection of Articles and Papers on Research in School Librarianship; School Librarianship: International Issues and Perspectives; Information Rich but Knowledge Poor? Issues for Schools and Libraries Worldwide: Selected Papers from the 26th Annual Conferences of the IASL.*

*International Center of Photography (ICP). 1130 Fifth Ave., New York, NY 10128. (212)860-1777. Fax (212)360-6490. E-mail education@icp.org. Web site http://www.icp.org. Willis Hartshorn, Dir.; Phyllis Levine, Dir. of Public Information. A comprehensive photographic institution whose exhibitions, publications, collections, and educational programs embrace all aspects of photography from aesthetics to technique; from the nineteenth century to the present; from master photographers to newly emerging talents; from photojournalism to the avant garde. Changing exhibitions, lectures, seminars, workshops, museum shops, and screening rooms make ICP a complete photographic resource. ICP offers a two-year NYU-ICP Master of Arts in Studio Art with Studies in Photography and one-year certificate programs in Documentary Photography and Photojournalism and General Studies in Photography. *Membership:* 6,500. *Dues:* $50, indiv.; $60, double; $125, Supporting Patron; $250, Photography Circle; $500, Silver Card Patron; $1,000, Gold Card Patron; $2,500 Benefactor; corporate memberships available. *Meetings:* ICP Infinity Awards. *Publications: Reflections in a Glass Eye; Images from the Machine Age: Selections from the Daniel Cowin Collection; Library of Photography; A Singular Elegance: The Photographs of Baron Adolph de Meyer; Talking Pictures: People Speak about the Photographs That Speak to Them; Encyclopedia of Photography: Master Photographs from PFA Collection; Man Ray in Fashion; Quarterly Program Guide; Quarterly Exhibition Schedule.*

*International Council for Educational Media (ICEM). University of Central Florida, Education Room 310, Orlando, FL 32816-0992. (407)823-2053. Fax (407)823-5135. E-mail cornell@pegasus.cc.ucf.edu. Web site http://pegasus.cc.ucf.edu/~cornell/icem-usa. Richard Cornell, Pres. and U.S. member. The objectives of ICEM are to provide a channel for the international exchange of information and experience in the field of educational technology, with particular reference to preschool, primary, and secondary education, technical and vocational training, and teacher and continuing education; encourage organizations with a professional responsibility for the design, production, promotion, distribution, and use of educational media in member countries; promote an understanding of the concept of educational technology on the part of both educators and those involved in their training; contribute to the pool of countries by the sponsorship of practical projects involving international cooperation and co-production; advise manufacturers of hardware and software on the needs of an information service on developments in educational technology; provide consultancy for the benefit of member countries; and cooperate with other international organizations in promoting the concept of educational technology. ICEM has established official relations with UNESCO.

International Graphics Arts Education Association (IGAEA). 200 Deer Run Road, Sewickley, PA 15143-2328. (412)741-6860. Fax (412)741-2311. E-mail dw.dailey@eku.edu. Web site http://www.igaea.org. David W. Dailey, Ed.D., President. IGAEA is an association of educators in partnership with industry, dedicated to sharing theories, principles, techniques, and processes relating to graphic communications and imaging technology. Teachers network to share and improve teaching and learning opportunities in fields related to graphic arts, imaging technology, graphic design, graphic communications, journalism, photography, and other areas related to the large and rapidly changing fields in the printing, publishing, packaging, and allied industries. *Membership:* approx. 600. *Dues:* $20, regular; $12, associate (retired); $5, student; $10, library; $50-$200, sustaining membership based on number of employees. *Meetings:* 2001, College of DuPage, Chicago, Jul 29-Aug 2; 2002, Graphic Arts Technical Foundation, Pittsburgh, PA, Jul 28-Aug 1. *Publications: The Communicator; Visual Communications Journal* (annual).

International Society for Technology in Education (ISTE). 480 Charnelton Street, Eugene, OR 97401. 800.336.5191 (U.S. & Canada), 541.302.3777 (Intl.). Fax 541.302.3778. E-mail iste@oregon.uoregon.edu. Web site http://www.iste.org. Leslie Concery, Interim CEO; Cheryl Williams, President. As the leading organization for educational technology professionals, the International Society for Technology in Education is a professional organization that supports a community of members through research, publications, workshops, symposia, and inclusion in national policy making through ISTE-DC. Home of the National Center for Preparing Tomorrows Teachers to Use Technology (NCPT3), ISTE works in conjunction with the U.S. Department of Education and various private entities to create and distribute solutions for technology integration. ISTE's National Educational Technology Standards (NETS) for students and teachers have been adopted by hundreds of districts nationwide. *Membership:* ISTE members are leaders. ISTE members contribute to the field of educational technology as classroom teachers, lab teachers, technology coordinators, school administrators, teacher educators, and consultants. As of May 2001, ISTE had more than 10,000 individual members, 30 international affiliates, six special interest groups, and more than 50 corporate sponsors members, through the ISTE 100 program. ISTE provides leadership and professional development opportunities for its members. In addition to other benefits, ISTE members can participate in ISTE-sponsored invitational events at the National Educational Computer Conference (NECC), join one of ISTE's many special interest groups (SIGs), and test and evaluate the latest in educational technology products and services through the ISTE Advocate Network. ISTE members also enjoy subscriptions to *ISTE Update* and *Learning & Leading with Technology* or the *Journal for Research on Technology in Education.* In the members areas of the ISTE Web site, ISTE members can join discussion lists and other online forums for participation, review a database of educational technology resources, network with a cadre of education professionals, and review online editions of ISTE publications. *Dues:* Annual dues for individual ISTE members are $58. Membership to SIG communities are $20 for ISTE members. Contact iste@iste.org to become a member. Annual dues for ISTE 100 members are $5,0000. Contact iste100@iste.org for more information. Group discounts are available. To see if you qualify, contact groupdiscounts@iste.org. *Meetings:* National Educational Computing Conference (NECC). *Publications:* ISTEs publications include *ISTE Update* (online member newsletter); *Learning & Leading with Technology;* the *Journal of Research on Technology in Education* (q.; formerly *Journal of Research on Computing in Education*); and books about incorporating technology in the K–16 classroom.

*International Society for Performance Improvement (ISPI). 1300 L St. NW, Suite 1250, Washington, DC 20005. (202)408-7969. Fax (202)408-7972. E-mail info@ispi.org. Web site http://www.ispi.org. Richard D. Battaglia, Exec. Dir. ISPI is an international association dedicated to increasing productivity in the workplace through the application of performance and instructional technologies. Founded in 1962, its members are located throughout the United States, Canada, and 45 other countries. The society offers an awards program recognizing excellence in the field. *Membership:* 5,500. *Dues:* $125, active members; $40, students and retirees. *Meetings:* Annual Conference and Expo, spring; Human Performance Technology Institute (HPTI), late spring and fall. Annual Conference & Expo held in Cincinnati OH, April 10-14, 2000. *Publications: Performance Improvement Journal* (10/yr.); *Performance Improvement Quarterly; News & Notes* (newsletter, 10/yr.); *Annual Membership Directory; ISPI Book Program and Catalog.*

International Telecommunications Satellite Organization (INTELSAT). 3400 International Dr. NW, Washington, DC 20008. (202)944-7500. Fax (202)944-7890. Web site http://www.intelsat.int. Conng L. Kullman, Dir. Gen. and CEO; Tony A. Trujillo, Dir., Corporate Communications. INTELSAT owns and operates a global communications satellite system providing capacity for voice, video, corporate/private networks, and Internet in more than 200 countries and territories. In addition, the INTELSAT system provides educational and medical programming via satellite for selected participants around the world.

*International Teleconferencing Association (ITCA). 100 Four Falls Corporate Center, Suite 105, West Conshohocken, PA 19428. (610)941-2015. Fax (610)941-2015. E-mail Staff@itca.org and president@itca.org. Web site http://www.itca.org. Henry S. Grove III, Pres.; Eileen Hering, Manager, Member Services; Rosalie DiStasio, Asst. Manager, Member Services. ITCA, an international nonprofit association, is dedicated to the growth and development of teleconferencing as a profession and an industry. ITCA provides programs and services that foster the professional development of its members, champions teleconferencing and related technology as communications tools, recognizes and promotes broader applications and the development of teleconferencing and related technologies, and serves as the authoritative resource for information and research on teleconferencing and related technologies. *Membership:* ITCA represents over 1,000 teleconferencing professionals throughout the world. ITCA members use teleconferencing services to advise customers and vendors, conduct research, teach courses via teleconference, and teach about teleconferencing. They represent such diverse industry segments as health care, aerospace, government, pharmaceutical, education, insurance, finance and banking, telecommunications, and manufacturing. *Dues:* $6,250, Platinum Sustaining; $2,500, Gold Sustaining; $1,250, Sustaining; $625, Organizational; $325, small business; $125, indiv.; and $35, student. *Meetings:* spring and fall MultimediaCom Shows; spring show in San Jose, fall show in Boston, August 30-September 2. *Publications: Forum* newsletter; *Member Directories; White Paper; Teleconferencing Success Stories.*

Media Communications Association—International (MCA-I). 9202 North Meridian Street, Suite 200, Indianapolis, IN 46260. 317-816-6269. Fax 317-571-5603. E-mail info@mca-i.org. Web site http://www.mca-i.org. Glenna Alibegovic, Director of Operations. Formerly the International Television Association. Founded in 1968, MCA-I's mission is to advance the video profession, serve the needs and interests of its members, and promote the growth and quality of video and related media. Association members are video, multimedia, and film professionals working in or serving the corporate, governmental, institutional, or educational markets. MCA-I provides professional development opportunities through local and national workshops, video festivals, networking, and publications. MCA-I welcomes anyone who is interested in professional video and who is seeking to widen horizons either through career development or networking. MCA-I offers its members discounts on major medical, production, and liability insurance; hotel, car rental, and long distance telephone discounts; and a MasterCard program. *Membership:* 6,000; 50 commercial member companies. *Dues:* $160, indiv.; $455, organizational; $950 Commercial Level Bronze, $1,900 Commercial Level Silver, $4,750 Commercial Level Gold, $6,500 Commercial Level Platinum. *Meetings:* Annual International Conference. *Publications* : *MCA-I Member2Member E-News* (6/yr.); *Membership Directory* (annual).

*International Visual Literacy Association, Inc. (ILVA). Gonzaga University, E. 502 Boone AD 25, Spokane, WA 99258-0001. (509)328-4220 ext. 3478. Fax (509)324-5812. E-mail bclark@soe.gonzaga.edu. Richard Couch, Pres. Dr. Barbara I. Clark, Exec. Treas. IVLA provides a multidisciplinary forum for the exploration, presentation, and discussion of all aspects of visual learning, thinking, communication, and expression. It also serves as a communication link bonding professionals from many disciplines who are creating and sustaining the study of the nature of visual experiences and literacy. It promotes and evaluates research, programs, and projects intended to increase effective use of visual communication in education, business, the arts, and commerce. IVLA was founded in 1968 to promote the concept of visual literacy and is an affiliate of AECT. *Dues:* $40, regular; $20, student and retired; $45 outside United States. *Meetings:* Meets in conjunction with annual

AECT Convention. *Publications: Journal of Visual Literacy; Readings from Annual Conferences.*

The International Recording Media Association (IRMA). 182 Nassau St., Princeton, NJ 08542-7005. (609)279-1700. Fax (609)279-1999. E-mail info@recordingmedia.org. Web site http://www.recordingmedia.org. Charles Van Horn, President; Phil Russo, Exec. Director. IRMA is the advocate for the growth and development of all recording media and is the industry forum for the exchange of information regarding global trends and innovations. Members include recording media manufacturers, rights holders to video programs, recording and playback equipment manufacturers, and audio and video replicators. For more than 30 years, the Association has provided vital information and educational services throughout the magnetic and optical recording media industries. By promoting a greater awareness of marketing, merchandising, and technical developments, the association serves all areas of the entertainment, information, and delivery systems industries. *Membership:* 450 corporations. Corporate membership includes benefits to all employees. *Dues:* Corporate membership dues based on sales volume. *Meetings:* 30th Annual Conference (IRMA Executive Forum) LaQuita Resort, LaQuita, CA. March 15-19, 2000. Mar 10-14, 1999, Amelia Island, FL; REPLItech North America, June 8-10 1999, San Francisco. *Publications: Membership Quarterly Magazine; Seminar Proceedings; 2001 International Source Directory, Marketing Statistics.*

*Library Administration and Management Association (LAMA). 50 E. Huron St., Chicago, IL 60611. (312)280-5038. Fax (312)280-5033. E-mail lama@ala.org. Web site http://www.ala.org/lama. Karen Muller, Exec. Dir.; Thomas L. Wilding, Pres.; Carol L. Anderson, Pres. Elect. A division of the American Library Association, LAMA provides an organizational framework for encouraging the study of administrative theory, improving the practice of administration in libraries, and identifying and fostering administrative skills. Toward these ends, the association is responsible for all elements of general administration that are common to more than one type of library. Sections include Buildings and Equipment Section (BES); Fundraising & Financial Development Section (FRFDS); Library Organization & Management Section (LOMS); Personnel Administration Section (PAS); Public Relation Section (PRS); Systems & Services Section (SASS); and Statistics Section (SS). *Membership:* 4,996. *Dues:* $45 (in addition to ALA membership); $15, library school students. *Meetings:* 1999 ALA Annual Conference, New Orleans, Jun 24-Jun 30; 2000, Chicago, Jul 6-12; ALA Midwinter Meeting, 1999; 2000, San Antonio, Jan 14-19; 2001, Washington, DC, Jan 12-17. *Publications: Library Administration & Management* (q); *LEADS from LAMA* (electronic newsletter, irregular).

*Library and Information Technology Association (LITA). 50 E. Huron St, Chicago, IL 60611. (312)280-4270, (800)545-2433, ext. 4270. Fax (312)280-3257. E-mail lita@ala.org. Web site http://www.lita.org. Jacqueline Mundell, Exec. Dir. An affiliate of the American Library Association, LITA is concerned with library automation; the information sciences; and the design, development, and implementation of automated systems in those fields, including systems development, electronic data processing, mechanized information retrieval, operations research, standards development, telecommunications, video communications, networks and collaborative efforts, management techniques, information technology, optical technology, artificial intelligence and expert systems, and other related aspects of audiovisual activities and hardware applications. *Membership:* 5,400. *Dues:* $45 plus membership in ALA; $25, library school students; $35, first year. *Meetings:* National Forum, fall. *Publications: Information Technology and Libraries; LITA Newsletter* (electronic only; see Web site).

*Library of Congress. James Madison Bldg., 101 Independence Ave. SE, Washington, DC 20540. (202)707-5000. Fax (202)707-1389. E-mail lcweb@loc.gov. Web site http://www.loc.gov. The Library of Congress is the major source of research and information for the Congress. In its role as the national library, it catalogs and classifies library materials in some 460 languages, distributes the data in both printed and electronic form, and makes its vast collections available through interlibrary loan and on-site to anyone over high school age. The Library is the largest library in the world, with more than 115 million items on 532 miles of bookshelves. The collections include more than 17 million cataloged books, 2 million recordings, 12 million photographs, 4 million maps, and 49 million manuscripts. It contains the world's largest television and film archive, acquiring materials through gift, purchase, and copyright deposit. In 1998, the materials produced by the Library in Braille and recorded formats for persons who are blind or physically challenged were circulated to a readership of 769,000. The collections of the Motion Picture, Broadcasting and Recorded Sound Division include more than 770,000 moving images. The Library's public catalog, as well as other files containing copyright and legislative information, are available over the Internet.

*Lister Hill National Center for Biomedical Communications. National Library of Medicine, 8600 Rockville Pike, Bethesda, MD 20894. (301)496-4441. Fax (301)402-0118. Web site http://www.nlm.nih.gov. Alexa McCray, Ph.D., Dir. The center conducts research and development programs in three major categories: Computer and Information Science; Biomedical Image and Communications Engineering; and Educational Technology Development. Major efforts of the center include its involvement with the Unified Medical Language System (UMLS) project; research and development in the use of expert systems to embody the factual and procedural knowledge of human experts; research in the use of electronic technologies to distribute biomedical information not represented in text and in the storage and transmission of x-ray images over the Internet; and the development and demonstration of new educational technologies, including the use of microcomputer technology with videodisc-based images, for training health care professionals. A Learning Center for Interactive Technology serves as a focus for displaying new and effective applications of educational technologies to faculties and staff of health sciences, educational institutions, and other visitors, and health professions educators are assisted in the use of such technologies through training, demonstrations, and consultations.

*Magazine Publishers of America (MPA). 919 Third Ave., 22nd Floor, New York, NY 10022. (212)872-3700. Fax (212)888-4217. E-mail infocenter@magazine.org. Web site http://www.magazine.org. Donald D. Kummerfeld, Pres. MPA is the trade association of the consumer magazine industry. MPA promotes the greater and more effective use of magazine advertising, with ad campaigns in the trade press and in member magazines, presentations to advertisers and their ad agencies, and magazine days in cities around the United States. MPA runs educational seminars, conducts surveys of its members on a variety of topics, represents the magazine industry in Washington, DC, and maintains an extensive library on magazine publishing. *Membership:* 230 publishers representing more than 1,200 magazines. *Meetings:* 1999 American Magazine Conference, Boca Resort & Country Club, Boca Raton, FL, Oct 28-31; 2000, Southampton Princess, Bermuda, Oct 22-25. *Publications: Newsletter of Consumer Marketing; Newsletter of Research; Newsletter of International Publishing; Magazine; Washington Newsletter.*

Medical Library Association (MLA). 65 E. Wacker Pl., Ste. 1900, Chicago, IL 60601-7298. (312)419-9094. Fax (312)419-8950. E-mail info@mlahq.org. Web site http://www.mlanet.org. Carla J. Funk, MLS, MBA, CAE, Executive Director. MLA is an educational organization of more than 1,100 institutions and 3,800 individual members in the health sciences information field. MLA members serve society by developing new health information delivery systems, fostering educational and research programs for health sciences information professionals, and encouraging an enhanced public awareness of health care issues. *Membership:* MLA fosters excellence in the professional achievement and leadership of health sciences library and information professionals to enhance the quality of health care, education, and research. Membership categories: Regular Membership, Institutional Membership, International Membership, Affiliate Membership, Student Membership. *Dues:* $135, regular; $210-$495, institutional, based on number of paid periodical subscriptions; $90, international; $80, affiliate; $30, student. *Meetings:* National annual meeting held every May; chapter meetings are held in the fall. *Publications: MLA News* (newsletter, 10/yr.); *Journal of the Medical Library Association* (quarterly scholarly publication.); *MLA DocKit series,* collections of representative, unedited library documents from a variety of institutions that illustrate the range of approaches to health sciences library management topics); *MLA BibKits,* selective, annotated bibliographies of discrete subject areas inthe health sciences literature; standards, surveys, and copublished monographs.

Mid-continent Research for Education and Learning (McREL). 2550 S. Parker Rd., Suite 500, Aurora, CO 80014. (303)337-0990. Fax (303)337-3005. E-mail info@mcrel.org. Web site http://www.mcrel.org. J. Timothy Waters, Exec. Dir. McREL is a private, nonprofit organization whose purpose is to improve education through applied research and development. McREL provides products and services, primarily for K–12 educators, to promote the best instructional practices in the classroom. McREL houses one of 10 Office of Educational Research and Improvement (OERI)regional educational laboratories designed to help educators and policymakers work toward excellence in education for all students. It also houses one of 10 Eisenhower Regional Consortia for Mathematics and Science Education. McREL has particular expertise in standards-based education systems, leadership for school improvement, teacher quality, mathematics and science education improvement, early literacy development, and education outreach programs. *Meetings:* annual conference. *Publications: Changing Schools* (q. newsletter); *Noteworthy* (annual monograph on topics of current interest in education reform). Numerous technical reports and other publications. Check Web site for current listings.

*Minorities in Media (MIM). Wayne State University, College of Education, Instructional Technology, Detroit, MI 48202. (313)577-5139. Fax (313)577-1693. E-mail GPOWELL@CMS.CC.WAYNE.EDU. Dr. Gary C. Powell, Pres. MIM is a special interest group of AECT that responds to the challenge of preparing students of color for an ever-changing international marketplace and recognizes the unique educational needs of today's diverse learners. It promotes the effective use of educational communications and technology in the learning process. MIM seeks to facilitate changes in instructional design and development, traditional pedagogy, and instructional delivery systems by responding to and meeting the significant challenge of educating diverse individuals to take their place in an ever-changing international marketplace. MIM encourages all of AECT's body of members to creatively develop curricula, instructional treatments, instructional strategies, and instructional materials that promote an acceptance and appreciation of racial and cultural diversity. Doing so will make learning for all more effective, relevant, meaningful, motivating, and enjoyable. MIM actively supports the Wes McJulien Minority Scholarship, and selects the winner. *Membership:* contact MIM president. *Dues:* $20, student; $30, nonstudent. *Publications:* Newsletter is forthcoming online. The MIM listserv is a membership benefit.

Museum Computer Network (MCN). 1550 S. Coast Hwy, Suite 201, Laguna Beach, CA 92651. (877) 626-3800. Fax (949) 376-3456. E-mail membership@mcn.edu. Web site http://www.mcn.edu. Susan Patterson, Pres. 2000–2001; Leonard Steinbach, Pres. 2001–2002; Fred Droz, Admin. MCN is a nonprofit organization of professionals dedicated to fostering the cultural aims of museums through the use of computer technologies. We serve individuals and institutions wishing to improve their means of developing, managing and conveying museum information through the use of automation. We support cooperative efforts that enable museums to be more efficient at creating and disseminating cultural and scientific knowledge as represented by their collections and related documentation. MCN members are interested in building databases complete with images and multimedia components for their collections, in using automated systems to tract membership, manage events and design exhibits, in discovering how multimedia systems can increase the effectiveness of educational programs, and in developing professional standards to ensure the investment that information represents. *Membership:* MCNs membership includes a wide range of museum professionals representing more than 600 major cultural institutions throughout the world. The primary job duties of our membership include 33 percent Registrar/Collection Managers; 33 percent IT professionals; and the remaining third comprised of administrator, curators, and education professionals. Our membership comes from all sorts of cultural heritage organizations, including art, historical and natural history museums and academia. Each member receives a complimentary issue of *Spectra* (published three times a year), a discount on conference fees, can subscribe to MCN-L, the online discussion list, and can join, at no additional cost, any of our Special Interest Groups which focus on such topics as intellectual property, controlled vocabulary, digital imaging, IT managers, and data standards. *Dues:* $300, corporate; $200, institution; $60, individual. *Meetings:* Annual Conference, held in the fall; educational workshops. *Publications: Spectra* (newsletter), published three times a year. Subscription to *Spectra* is available to libraries only for $75 plus $10 surcharge for delivery. *eSpectra* is a monthly electronic magazine featuring online links to information of interest to the museum computing community, job openings, and a calendar of museum-related events, such as workshops, conferences, or seminars.

Museum of Modern Art, Circulating Film and Video Library (MoMA). 11 W. 53rd St., New York, NY 10019. (212)708-9530. Fax (212)708-9531. E-mail circfilm@moma.org. Web site http://www.moma.org. William Sloan, Libr. Provides film and video rentals and sales of over 1,300 titles covering the history of film from the 1890s to the present. It also includes an important collection of work by leading video artists. The Circulating Film and Video Library continues to add to its holdings of early silents, contemporary documentaries, animation, avant-garde, independents and video and to make these available to viewers who otherwise would not have the opportunity to see them. The Circulating Film and Video Library has 16mm prints available for rental, sale, and lease. A few of the 16mm titles are available on videocassette. The classic film collection is not. The video collection is available in all formats for rental and sale. The Library also has available a limited number of titles on 35mm, including rare early titles preserved by the Library of Congress. *Publications:* Information on titles may be found in the free *Price List,* the *Documentaries on the Arts* brochure and the *Films of Andy Warhol* brochure, all available from the *Library. Circulating Film and Video Catalog Vols. 1 and 2,* a major source book on film and history, is available from the Museum's Mail Order Dept. (To purchase by mail order, a form is included in the Price List.)

National Aeronautics and Space Administration (NASA). NASA Headquarters, Code FE, Washington, DC 20546. (202)358-1110. Fax (202)358-3048. E-mail malcom.phelps@hq .nasa.gov. Web site http://www.nasa.gov. Dr. Malcom V. Phelps, Asst. Dir.; Frank C. Owens, Dir., Education Division. From elementary through postgraduate school, NASA's educational programs are designed to capture students interest in science, mathematics, and technology at an early age; to channel more students into science, engineering, and technology career paths; and to enhance the knowledge, skills, and experiences of teachers and university faculty. NASAs educational programs include NASA Spacelink (an electronic information system); videoconferences (60-minute interactive staff development videoconferences to be delivered to schools via satellite); and NASA Television (informational and educational television programming). Additional information is available from the Education Division at NASA Headquarters and counterpart offices at the nine NASA field centers. Over 200,000 educators make copies of Teacher Resource Center Network materials each year, and thousands of teachers participate in interactive video teleconferencing, use Spacelink, and watch NASA Television. Additional information may be obtained from the NASA Education home page www.education.nasa.gov, or Spacelink http://spacelink.nasa.gov. *Publications:* see http://spacelink.nasa.gov.

National Alliance for Media Arts and Culture (NAMAC). 346 9th St., San Francisco, CA 94103. (415)431-1391. Fax (415)431-1392. E-mail namac@namac.org. Web site http://www.namac.org. Helen DeMichel, National Dir. NAMAC is a nonprofit organization dedicated to increasing public understanding of and support for the field of media arts in the United States. Members include media centers, cable access centers, universities, and media artists, as well as other individuals and organizations providing services for production, education, exhibition, distribution, and preservation of video, film, audio, and intermedia. NAMACs information services are available to the general public, arts and non-arts organizations, businesses, corporations, foundations, government agencies, schools, and universities. *Membership:* 200 organizations, 150 individuals. *Dues:* $75-$450, institutional (depending on annual budget); $75, indiv. *Meetings:* Annual Conference. *Publications: Media Arts Information Network; The National Media Education Directory,* annual anthology of case-studies *A Closer Look,* periodic white paper reports, *Digital Directions: Convergence Planning for the Media Arts.*

National Association for the Education of Young Children (NAEYC). 1509 16th St., Washington, DC 20036-1426. (202)232-8777, (800)424-2460. Fax (202)328-1846. E-mail naeyc@naeyc.org. Web site http://www.naeyc.org. Mark R. Ginsberg, Ph.D., Exec. Dir.; Alan Simpson, contact person. Dedicated to improving the quality of care and education provided to young children (birth-8 years). *Membership:* over 100,000 members. *Dues:* $45, independent member. *Meetings:* 2001 Annual Conference, Anaheim, CA; 2002 Annual Conference, New York, NY. *Publications: Young Children* (journal); more than 100 books, posters, videos, and brochures.

National Association for Visually Handicapped (NAVH). 22 W. 21st St., 6th Floor, New York, NY 10010. (212)889-3141. Fax (212)727-2931. staff@navh.org. Web site http://www.navn .org. Lorraine H. Marchi, Founder/CEO. Dir.; Eva Cohen, Asst. to CEO. Dir., 3201 Balboa St., San Francisco, CA 94121. (415)221-3201. Serves the partially sighted (not totally blind). Offers informational literature for the layperson and the professional, most in large print. Maintains a loan library of large-print books. Provides counseling and guidance for the visually impaired and their families and the professionals and paraprofessionals who work with them. *Membership:* 15,000. *Dues:* $50 indiv.; free for those unable to afford membership. *Meetings:* Seniors support group 2 times a month. *Publications:* Newsletter updated quarterly, distributed free throughout the English-speaking world; *NAVH Update* (quarterly); *Visual Aids and Informational Material Catalog; Large Print Loan Library;* informational pamphlets on topics ranging from Diseases of the Macula to knitting and crochet instructions.

National Association of Regional Media Centers (NARMC). NARMC, Education Service Center, Region 20, 1314 Hines Ave., San Antonio, TX 78208. (210)270-9256. Fax (210)224-3130. E-mail jtaylor@tenet.edu. Web site http://esu3.k12.ne.us/prof/narmc. Larry Vice, Pres.; James H. Taylor, Treasurer. An affiliate of AECT, NARMC is committed to promoting leadership among its membership through networking, advocacy, and support activities that will enhance the equitable access to media, technology, and information services to educational communities. The purpose of NARMC is to foster the exchange of ideas and information among educational communications specialists whose responsibilities relate to the administration of regional media centers and large district media centers. *Membership:* 285 regional centers (institutions), 70 corporations. *Dues:* $55, institutions; $250, corporations. *Meetings:* held annually with AECT/Incite. Regional meetings are held throughout the United States annually. *Publications:* Membership newsletter is *'ETIN.* NARMC Press was established in 1996 to provide members with publications related to the field of media and technology. These publications are available for purchase through this publication outlet. Publications are solicited and submitted from the NARMC membership. Current publications include *An Anthology of Internet Acceptable Use Policies* and *Basic MAC/Windows Internet.* In addition, there is the *Annual Membership Report* and the *Bi-annual Survey Report of Regional Media Centers.*

National Association of State Textbook Administrators (NASTA). E-mail president@nasta.org. Web site http://www.nasta.org. William Lohman, Pres. NASTA's purposes are to (1) foster a spirit of mutual helpfulness in adoption, purchase, and distribution of instructional materials; (2) arrange for study and review of textbook specifications; (3) authorize special surveys, tests, and studies; and (4) initiate action leading to better quality instructional materials. Services provided include a working knowledge of text construction, monitoring lowest prices, sharing adoption information, identifying trouble spots, and discussions in the industry. The members of NASTA meet to discuss the textbook adoption process and to improve the quality of the instructional materials used in the elementary, middle, and high schools. NASTA is not affiliated with any parent organization and has no permanent address. *Membership:* Textbook administrators from each of the 23 states that adopt textbooks at the state level. *Dues:* $25, indiv. *Publications:* conducted with the American Association of Publishers and the Book Manufacturers' Institute.

The National Cable Television Institute (NCTI). 801 W. Mineral Ave., Littleton, CO 80120. (303)797-9393. Fax (303)797-9394. E-mail info@ncti.com. Web site http://www.ncti.com. Tom Brooksher, COO; Alan Babcock, VP Learning & Development. NCTI is the largest independent provider of broadband technology training in the world. More than 200,000 students have graduated from these courses since 1968. NCTI partners with companies by providing self-paced study, classroom and Web-based courses to be complemented by company hands-on experiences. NCTI administers lessons and final examinations and issues the Certificate of Graduation, which is recognized throughout the industry as a symbol of competence and technical achievement.

*The National Center for Improving Science Education. 1726 M Street, NW, #704, Washington, DC 20036. (202)467-0652. Fax (202)467-0659. E-mail info@ncise.org. Web site www.wested.org. Senta A. Raizen, Dir. A division of WestEd (see separate listing) that works to promote changes in state and local policies and practices in science curriculum, teaching, and assessment through research and development, evaluation, technical assistance, and dissemination. *Publications: Science and Technology Education for the Elementary Years: Frameworks for Curriculum and Instruction; Developing and Supporting Teachers for Elementary School Science Education; Assessment in Elementary School Science Education; Getting Started in Science: A Blueprint for Elementary School Science Education; Elementary School Science for the 90s; Building Scientific Literacy: Blueprint for the Middle Years; Science and Technology Education for the Middle Years: Frameworks for Curriculum and Instruction; Assessment in Science Education: The Middle Years; Developing and Supporting Teachers for Science Education in the Middle Years; The High Stakes of High School Science; Future of Science in Elementary Schools: Educating Prospective Teachers; Technology Education in the Classroom: Understanding the Designed World; What College-Bound Students Abroad Are Expected to Know About Biology (with AFT); Examining the Examinations: A Comparison of Science and Mathematics Examinations for College-Bound Students in Seven Countries. Bold Ventures series: Vol. 1: Patterns of U.S. Innovations in Science and Mathematics Education; Vol. 2: Case Studies of U.S. Innovations in Science Education; Vol. 3: Case Studies of U.S. Innovations in Mathematics.* A publications catalog and project summaries are available on request.

*National Center to Improve Practice (NCIP). Education Development Center, Inc., 55 Chapel St., Newton, MA 02158-1060. (617)969-7100 ext. 2387TTY (617)969-4529. Fax (617)969-3440. E-mail ncip@edc.org. Web site http://www.edc.org/FSC/NCIP. Judith Zorfass, Project Dir.; Lucy Lorin, information. NCIP, a project funded by the U.S. Department of Education's Office for Special Education Programs (OSEP), promotes the effective use of technology to enhance educational outcomes for students (preschool to grade 12) with sensory, cognitive, physical, social, and emotional disabilities. NCIP's award-winning Web site offers users online discussions (topical discussions and special events) about technology and students with disabilities, an expansive library of resources (text, pictures, and video clips), online workshops, "guided tours" of exemplary classrooms, "spotlights" on new technology, and links to more than 100 sites dealing with technology and/or students with disabilities. NCIP also produces a series of videos illustrating how students with disabilities use a range of assistive and instructional technologies to improve their learning. *Meetings:* NCIP presents sessions at various educational conferences around the country. *Publications: Video Profile Series: Multimedia and More: Help for Students with Learning Disabilities; Jeff with Expression: Writing in the Word Prediction Software; "Write" Tools for Angie: Technology for Students Who Are Visually Impaired; Telling Tales in ASL and English: Reading, Writing and Videotapes; Welcome to My Preschool: Communicating with Technology.* Excellent for use in training, workshops, and courses, videos may be purchased individually or as a set of five by calling (800)793-5076. A new video to be released this year focuses on standards, curriculum, and assessment in science.

National Clearinghouse for Bilingual Education (NCBE). The George Washington University, 2121 K Street NW, Suite 260, Washington, DC 20037. (800) 321-NCBE, (202)467-0867. Fax (800)531-9347, (202)467-4283. E-mail askncbe@ncbe.gwu.edu. Web site http://www.ncbe.gwu.edu. Dr. Minerva Gorena, Director. NCBE is funded by the U.S. Department of Educations Office of Bilingual Education and Minority Languages Affairs (OBEMLA) to collect, analyze, synthesize, and disseminate information relating to the education of linguistically and culturally diverse students in the United States. NCBE is operated by The George Washington University Graduate School of Education and Human Development, Center for the Study of Language and Education in Washington, DC. Online services include the NCBE Web site containing an online library of hundreds of cover-to-cover documents, resources for teachers and administrators, and library of links to related Internet sites; an e-mail-based, weekly news bulletin, *Newsline;* an electronic discussion group, NCBE Roundtable; and an e-mail-based question answering service, AskNCBE. *Membership:* Funded by the Department of Education, therefore our services are free. *Publications:* short monographs, syntheses, and reports. Request a publications catalog for prices. The catalog and some publications are available at no cost from the NCBE and other Web sites.

*National Commission on Libraries and Information Science (NCLIS). 1110 Vermont Ave. NW, Suite 820, Washington, DC 20005-3552. (202)606-9200. Fax (202)606-9203. E-mail info@nclis.gov. Web site http://www.nclis.gov. Robert S. Willard, Acting Exec. Dir. A permanent independent agency of the U.S. government charged with advising the executive and legislative branches on national library and information policies and plans. The Commission reports directly to the president and Congress on the implementation of national policy; conducts studies, surveys, and analyses of the nation's library and information needs; appraises the inadequacies of current resources and services; promotes research and development activities; conducts hearings and issues publications as appropriate; and develops overall plans for meeting national library and information needs and for the coordination of activities at the federal, state, and local levels. The Commission provides general policy advice to the Institute of Museum and Library Services (IMLS) director relating to library services included in the Library Services and Technology Act (LSTA). *Membership:* 16 commissioners (14 appointed by the president and confirmed by the Senate, the Librarian of Congress, and the Director of the IMLS). *Publications: Annual Report.*

*National Communication Association (NCA). 5105 Backlick Rd., Bldg. E, Annandale, VA 22003. (703)750-0533. Fax (703)914-9471. E-mail jguardino@natcom.org. Web site http://www.natcom.org. James L. Gaudino, Exec. Dir. A voluntary society organized to promote study, criticism, research, teaching, and application of principles of communication, particularly of speech communication. *Membership:* 7,000. *Meetings:* 1999 Annual Meeting, Nov 4-7, Chicago.*Publications: Spectra Newsletter* (mo.); *Quarterly Journal of Speech; Communication Monographs; Communication Education; Critical Studies in Mass Communication; Journal of Applied Communication Research; Text and Performance Quarterly; Communication Teacher; Index to Journals in Communication Studies through 1995; National Communication Directory of NCA and the Regional Speech*

Communication Organizations (CSSA, ECA, SSCA, WSCA). For additional publications, request brochure.

*National Council for Accreditation of Teacher Education (NCATE). 2010 Massachusetts Ave. NW, Suite 500, Washington, DC 20036. (202)466-7496. Fax (202)296-6620. E-mail ncate@ncate.org. Web site http://www.ncate.org. Arthur E. Wise, Pres. NCATE is a consortium of professional organizations that establishes standards of quality and accredits professional education units in schools, colleges, and departments of education, and is interested in the self-regulation and improvement of standards in the field of teacher education. *Membership:* Over 500 colleges and universities, over 30 educational organizations. *Publications: Standards, Procedures and Policies for the Accreditation of Professional Education Units; A Guide to College programs in Teacher Preparation Quality Teaching* (newsletter, 2/yr.).

National Council of Teachers of English: Commission on Media, Committee on Instructional Technology, Assembly on Media Arts (NCTE). 1111 W. Kenyon Rd., Urbana, IL 61801-1096. (217)328-3870. Fax (217)328-0977. E-mail public_info@ncte.org. Web site http://www.ncte.org. Andrew Garrison, Commission Director; Trevor Owen, Committee Chair; Alan Teasley, Assembly Chair. The NCTE Commission on Media is a deliberative and advisory body which each year identifies and reports to the NCTE Executive Committee on key issues in the teaching of media; reviews what the Council has done concerning media during the year; recommends new projects and persons who might undertake them. The commission monitors current and projected NCTE publications (other than journals), suggests topics for future NCTE publications on media, and performs a similar role of review and recommendation for the NCTE Annual Convention program. Occasionally, the commission undertakes further tasks and projects as approved by the Executive Committee. The NCTE Committee on Instructional Technology studies emerging technologies and their integration into English and language arts curricula and teacher education programs; identifies the effects of such technologies on teachers, students, and educational settings, with attention to people of color, handicapped, and other students not well served in current programs; explores means of disseminating information about such technologies to the NCTE membership; serves as liaison between NCTE and other groups interested in computer-based education in English and language arts; and maintains liaison with the NCTE Commission on Media and other Council groups concerned with instructional technology. The NCTE Assembly on Media Arts promotes communication and cooperation among all individuals who have a special interest in media in the English language arts; presents programs and special projects on this subject; encourages the development of research, experimentation, and investigation in the judicious uses of media in the teaching of English; promotes the extensive writing of articles and publications devoted to this subject; and integrates the efforts of those with an interest in this subject. *Membership:* The National Council of Teachers of English, with 77,000 individual and institutional members worldwide, is dedicated to improving the teaching and learning of English and the language arts at all levels of education. Members include elementary, middle, and high school teachers, supervisors of English programs, college and university faculty, teacher educators, local and state agency English specialists, and professionals in related fields. The members of the NCTE Commission on Media and Committee on Instructional Technology are NCTE members appointed by the director and chair of the groups. Membership in the Assembly on Media Arts is open to members and nonmembers of NCTE. *Dues:* Membership in NCTE is $40 a year; adding subscriptions to our various journals add additional fees. Membership in the Assembly on Media Arts is $10 a year. *Meetings:* 91st NCTE Annual Convention, November 15-20, 2001, Baltimore, Maryland; 92nd NCTE Annual Convention, November 21-26, 2002, Atlanta, Georgia. *Publications:* NCTE publishes approximately 20 books a year. NCTEs journals include *Language Arts; English Journal; College English; College Composition and Communication; English Education; Research in the Teaching of English; Teaching English in the Two-Year College; Voices from the Middle; Primary Voices, K-6; Talking Points; Classroom Notes Plus; English*

Leadership Quarterly; The Council Chronicle (included in NCTE membership). The Commission on Media and Committee on Instructional Technology do not have their own publications. The Assembly on Media Arts publishes *Media Matters*, a newsletter highlighting issues, viewpoints, materials, and events related to the study of media. Assembly members receive this publication.

National Council of the Churches of Christ in the USA (NCC). Communication Commission, 475 Riverside Dr., New York, NY 10115. (212)870-2574. Fax (212)870-2030. E-mail dpomeroy@ncccusa.org. Web site http://www.ncccusa.org. Wesley "Pat" Pattillo, Dir. Ecumenical arena for cooperative work of Protestant and Orthodox denominations and agencies in broadcasting, film, cable, and print media. Offers advocacy to government and industry structures on media services. Services provided include liaison to network television and radio programming; film sales and rentals; distribution of information about syndicated religious programming; syndication of some programming; cable television and emerging technologies information services; and news and information regarding work of the National Council of Churches, related denominations, and agencies. Works closely with other faith groups in the Interfaith Broadcasting Commission. Online communication via Ecunet/NCCLink. *Membership:* 36 denominations. *Publications: EcuLink.*

National Education Knowledge Industry Association (NEKIA). 1718 Connecticut Avenue, NW, Suite 700, Washington, DC 20009-1162. (202)518-0847. Fax (202)785-3849. E-mail info@nekia.org. Web site http://www.nekia.org. C. Todd Jones, Pres. The National Education Knowledge Industry Association (NEKIA) is the only national trade association for organizations dedicated to educational research and development. The mission of NEKIA is to serve the nations common schools by making cost-effective education innovation and expertise available to all communities. Members of NEKIA include the nation's foremost research and development institutions devoted to using research-based products and services to enhance the quality of education for the common good. NEKIA serves as a national voice for its members, making sure knowledge from research, development, and practical experience is part of the national discussion on education. NEKIA also ensures that educational research and development institutions are able to maintain neutrality and objectivity in reporting findings, and ensures a field-based, decentralized system of setting priorities. *Membership:* 15. *Meetings:* Annual Legislative and Policy Conference; job fairs; annual meeting. *Publications: Checking Up on Early Childhood Care and Education; What We Know About Reading, Teaching and Learning; Plugging In: Choosing and Using Educational Technology; Probe: Designing School Facilities for Learning; Education Productivity; Technology Infrastructure in Schools.*

*National Education Telecommunications Organization & EDSAT Institute (NETO/EDSAT). 1899 L Street NW, Suite 600, Washington, DC 20036. (202)293-4211. Fax (202)293-4210. E-mail neto-edsat@mindspring.com. Web site http://www.netoedsat.org. Shelly Weinstein, Pres. and CEO. NETO/EDSAT is a nonprofit organization bringing together U.S. and non-U.S. users and providers of telecommunications to deliver education, instruction, health care, and training in classrooms, colleges, workplaces, health centers, and other distance education centers. NETO/EDSAT facilitates and collaborates with key stakeholders in the education and telecommunications fields. Programs and services include research and education, outreach, seminars and conferences, and newsletters. The NETO/EDSAT mission is to help create an integrated multitechnology infrastructure, a dedicated satellite that links space and existing secondary access roads (telephone and cable) over which teaching and education resources are delivered and shared in a user-friendly format with students, teachers, workers, and individuals. NETO/EDSAT seeks to create a modern-day "learning place" for rural, urban, migrant, suburban, disadvantaged, and at-risk students that provides equal and affordable access to and utilization of educational resources. *Membership:* Members include more than 60 U.S. and non-U.S. school districts, colleges, universities, state agencies, public and private educational consortia, libraries, and other distance education providers. *Publications:*

NETO/EDSAT "UPDATE" (newsletter, q.); *Analysis of a Proposal for an Education Satellite, EDSAT Institute, 1991; Global Summit on Distance Education Final Report, Oct 1996; International Report of the NETO/EDSAT Working Group on the Education and Health Care Requirements for Global/Regional Dedicated Networks, June 1998.*

*National Endowment for the Humanities (NEH). Division of Public Programs, Media Program, 1100 Pennsylvania Ave., NW, Room 426, Washington, DC 20506. (202)606-8269. Fax (202)606-8557. E-mail info@neh.gov. Web site http://www.neh.gov. Jim Vore, Mgr. of Media/Special Projects. The NEH is an independent federal grant-making agency that supports research, educational, and public programs grounded in the disciplines of the humanities. The Media Program supports film and radio programs in the humanities for public audiences, including children and adults. *Publications: Overview of Endowment Programs; Humanities Projects in Media* (for application forms and guidelines).

*National Federation of Community Broadcasters (NFCB). Ft. Mason Center, Bldg. D, San Francisco, CA 94123. Fax (415)771-1160. E-mail nfcb@aol.com. Web site http://www.nfcb.org. Lynn Chadwick, Pres. NFCB represents noncommercial, community-based radio stations in public policy development at the national level and provides a wide range of practical services, including technical assistance. *Membership:* 200. *Dues:* range from $150 to $2,500 for participant and associate members. *Meetings:* 1999, San Francisco. *Publications: Legal Handbook; Audio Craft; Community Radio News.*

*National Film Board of Canada (NFBC). 350 Fifth Ave., Suite 4820, New York, NY 10118. (212)629-8890. Fax (212)629-8502. E-mail j.sirabella@nfb.ca. John Sirabella, U.S. Marketing Mgr./Nontheatrical Rep. Established in 1939, the NFBC's main objective is to produce and distribute high-quality audiovisual materials for educational, cultural, and social purposes.

*National Film Information Service. Center for Motion Picture Study, 333 S. La Cienega Blvd., Beverly Hills, CA 90211. (310)247-3000.

National Gallery of Art (NGA). Department of Education Resources: Art Information and Extension Programs, Washington, DC 20565. (202)842-6273. Fax (202)842-6935. E-mail extprog@nga.gov. Web site http://www.hga.gov. Leo J. Kasun, Education Resources Supervisory Specialist. This department of NGA is responsible for the production and distribution of educational audiovisual programs, including interactive technologies. Materials available (all loaned free to schools, community organizations, and individuals) range from films, videocassettes, and color slide programs to videodiscs and CD-ROMs. A free catalog of programs is available upon request. Two videodiscs on the gallerys collection are available for long-term loan. *Publications: Extension Programs Catalogue.*

*National Information Center for Educational Media (NICEM). P.O. Box 8640, Albuquerque, NM 87198-8640. (505)265-3591, (800)926-8328. Fax (505)256-1080. E-mail nicem@nicem.com. Web site http://www.nicem.com. Roy Morgan, Exec. Dir.; Marjorie M. K. Hlava, Pres., Access Innovations, Inc. The National Information Center for Educational Media maintains an international database of information about educational nonprint materials for all age levels and subject areas in all media types. NICEM editors collect, catalog, and index information about media that is provided by producers and distributors. This information is entered into an electronic masterfile. Anyone who is looking for information about educational media materials can search the database by a wide variety of criteria to locate existing and archival materials. Producer and distributor information in each record then leads the searcher to the source of the educational media materials needed. NICEM makes the information from the database available in several forms and through several vendors. CD-ROM editions are available from NICEM, SilverPlatter, and BiblioFile. Online access to the database is available through NICEM, EBSCO,

SilverPlatter, and The Library Corporation. NICEM also conducts custom searches and prepares custom catalogs. NICEM is used by college and university media centers, public school libraries and media centers, public libraries, corporate training centers, students, media producers and distributors, and researchers. *Membership:* NICEM is a nonmembership organization. There is no charge for submitting information to be entered into the database. Corporate member of AECT, AIME, NAMTC, CCUMC. *Publications: A-V Online on SilverPlatter; NICEM A-V MARC by BiblioFile; NICEM Reference CD-ROM; NICEM MARC CD-ROM; NICEM Producer & CD-ROM.*

National ITFS Association (NIA). 77 W. Canfield, Detroit, MI 48201. (313) 577-2085. Fax (313) 577-5577. E-mail p.gossman@wayne.edu. Web site http://www.itfs.org. Patrick Gossman, Chair, Bd. of Dirs.; Don MacCullough, Exec. Dir. Established in 1978, NIA is a nonprofit, professional organization of Instructional Television Fixed Service (ITFS) licensees, applicants, and others interested in ITFS broadcasting. The goals of the association are to gather and exchange information about ITFS, gather data on utilization of ITFS, act as a conduit for those seeking ITFS information, and assist migration from video broadcast to wireless, broadband Internet services using ITFS channels. The NIA represents ITFS interests to the FCC, technical consultants, and equipment manufacturers. The association uses its Web site and listserv list to provide information to its members in areas such as technology, programming content, FCC regulations, excess capacity leasing and license and application data. *Membership:* ITFS licensees and other educational institutions. *Dues:* We have two main types of memberships: Voting memberships for ITFS licensees only, and nonvoting memberships for other educational institutions and sponsors. See the Web site http://www.itfs.org for details. *Meetings:* Annual Member Conference, January/February. *Publications:* http://www.itfs.org.

National PTA (PTA or PTSA). 330 N. Wabash, Suite 2100, Chicago, IL 60611. (312)670-6782. Fax (312)670-6783. E-mail info@pta.org. Web site http://www.pta.org. Ginny Markell, Pres. (term ends July 2001); Shirley Igo, President-elect (2001–03); Pam Grotz, Executive Director. Advocates the education, health, safety, and well-being of children and teens. Provides parenting education and leadership training to PTA volunteers. The National PTA continues to be very active in presenting Family and Television Critical TV Viewing workshops across the country in cooperation with the National Cable Television Association. The workshops teach parents and educators how to evaluate programming so they can make informed decisions about what to allow their children to see. The National PTA in 1997 convinced the television industry to add content information to the TV rating system. *Membership:* 6.5 million Membership open to all interested in the health, welfare, and education of children and support the PTA mission—http://www.pta.org/apta /mission.htm. *Dues:* vary by local unit—national dues portion is $1.25 per member annually. *Meetings:* National convention, held annually in June in different regions of the country, is open to PTA members; convention information available on the Web site. *Publications: Our Children* (magazine). In addition, information can be downloaded from the Web site.

*National Press Photographers Association, Inc. (NPPA). 3200 Croasdaile Dr., Suite 306, Durham, NC 27705. (919)383-7246. Fax (919)383-7261. E-mail nppa@mindspring.com. Web site http://www.nppa.org. Bradley Wilson, Dir. An organization of professional news photographers who participate in and promote photojournalism in publications and through television and film. Sponsors workshops, seminars, and contests; maintains an audiovisual library of subjects of media interest. *Membership:* 9,000. *Dues:* $75, domestic; $105, international; $40, student. *Meetings:* Annual convention and education days. An extensive array of other conferences, seminars, and workshops are held throughout the year. *Publications: News Photographer* (magazine, mo.); *The Best of Photojournalism* (annual book).

*National Public Broadcasting Archives (NPBA). Hornbake Library, University of Maryland, College Park, MD 20742. (301)405-9255. Fax (301)314-2634. E-mail tc65@umail.umd.edu. Web site http://www.library.umd.edu/UMCP/NPBA/npba.html. Thomas Connors, Archivist. NPBA brings together the archival record of the major entities of noncommercial broadcasting in the United States. NPBA's collections include the archives of the Corporation for Public Broadcasting (CPB), the Public Broadcasting Service (PBS), and National Public Radio (NPR). Other organizations represented include the Midwest Program for Airborne Television Instruction (MPATI), the Public Service Satellite Consortium (PSSC), America's Public Television Stations (APTS), Children's Television Workshop (CTW), and the Joint Council for Educational Telecommunications (JCET). NPBA also makes available the personal papers of many individuals who have made significant contributions to public broadcasting, and its reference library contains basic studies of the broadcasting industry, rare pamphlets, and journals on relevant topics. NPBA also collects and maintains a selected audio and video program record of public broadcasting's national production and support centers and of local stations. Oral history tapes and transcripts from the NPR Oral History Project and the Televisionaries National History Project are also available at the archives. The archives are open to the public from 9 A.M. to 5 P.M., Monday through Friday. Research in NPBA collections should be arranged by prior appointment. For further information, call (301)405-9988.

*National Religious Broadcasters (NRB). 7839 Ashton Ave., Manassas, VA 20109. (703)330-7000. Fax (703)330-7100. E-mail ssmith@nrb.organization. Web site http://www.nrb.org. Wayne A. Pederson, Chairman ; Michael Glenn, Executive Vice President. NRB essentially has two goals: (1) to ensure that religious broadcasters have access to the radio and television airwaves and (2) to encourage broadcasters to observe a high standard of excellence in their programming and station management for the clear presentation of the gospel. Holds national and regional conventions. *Membership:* 1,400 organizational stations, program producers, agencies, and individuals. *Dues:* based on income. *Meetings:* 59th Annual NRB Convention and Exhibition, Feb. 16-20, 2002, Nashville, TN. *Publications: Religious Broadcasting Magazine* (mo.); *Annual Directory of Religious Media; Religious Broadcasting Inside NRB Broadcast Fax* (members only).

*National School Boards Association/Institute for the Transfer of Technology to Education (NSBA/ITTE). 1680 Duke St, Alexandria, VA 22314. (800)838-6722. Fax (703)683-7590. E-mail itte@nsba.org. Web site http://www.nsba.org/itte. Cheryl S. Williams, Dir. ITTE was created to help advance the wise uses of technology in public education. ITTE renders several services to state school board associations, sponsors conferences, publishes, and engages in special projects. The Technology Leadership Network, the membership component of ITTE, is designed to engage school districts nationwide in a dialogue about technology in education. This dialogue is carried out via newsletters, meetings, special reports, projects, and online communications. The experience of the Network is shared more broadly through the state associations' communications with all school districts. *Membership:* over 400 school districts in 44 states, Canada, and the United Kingdom. *Dues:* based on the school district's student enrollment. *Meetings:* 1999, Technology & Learning Conference, Nov 10-12, Dallas; Oct 28-30; Nov 15-17, Denver. *Publications: Investing in School Technology: Strategies to Meet the Funding Challenge/School Leader's Version; Technology for Students with Disabilities: A Decision Maker's Resource Guide; Leadership and Technology: What School Board Members Need to Know; Plans and Policies for Technology in Education: A Compendium; Telecommunications and Education: Surfing and the Art of Change; Multimedia and Learning: A School Leader's Guide; Electronic School: Technology Leadership News: Legal Issues and Education Technology: A School Leader's Guide; Models of Success: Case Study of Technology in Schools; Technology & School Design: Creating Spaces for Learning; Leader's Guide to Education Technology; Teachers and Technology: Staff Development for Tomorrow's Schools; Education Leadership Toolkit: A Desktop Companion* (q.)

*National School Supply and Equipment Association (NSSEA). 8300 Colesville Rd., Suite 250, Silver Spring, MD 20910. (301)495-0240. Fax (301)495-3330. E-mail nssea@aol.com. Web site http://www.nssea.org. Tim Holt, Pres. A service organization of more than 1,600 manufacturers, distributors, retailers, and independent manufacturers' representatives of school supplies, equipment, and instructional materials. Seeks to maintain open communications between manufacturers and dealers in the school market and to encourage the development of new ideas and products for educational progress. *Meetings:* 2000, School Equipment Show, Tampa, FL, March 2-4; 2000, Ed Expo '00, Dallas, TX, March 9-11; Fall Trade Show & Education Conference, Kansas City, MO, Oct 26-28. *Publications: Tidings; Annual Membership Directory.*

*National Science Foundation (NSF). 4201 Wilson Blvd., Arlington, VA 22230. (703)306-1070. E-mail lboutchy@nsf.gov. Mary Hanson, Chief, Media Relations and Public Affairs. Linda Boutchyard, contact person. NSF is an independent federal agency responsible for fundamental research in all fields of science and engineering, with an annual budget of about $3 billion. NSF funds reach all 50 states, through grants to more than 2,000 universities and institutions nationwide. NSF receives more than 50,000 requests for funding annually, including at least 30,000 new proposals. Applicants should refer to the NSF Guide to Programs. Scientific material and media reviews are available to help the public learn about NSF-supported programs. NSF news releases and tipsheets are available electronically via NSFnews. To subscribe, send an e-mail message to listmanager@nsf.gov; in the body of the message, type "subscribe nsfnews" and then type your name. Also see NSF news products at http://www.nsf.gov/od/lpa/news/start.htm, http://www.eurekalert.org/ and http://www.ari.net/newswise. In addition, NSF has developed a Web site that offers information about NSF directorates, offices, programs, and publications at http://nsf.gov.

*National Telemedia Council Inc. (NTC). 120 E. Wilson St., Madison, WI 53703. (608)257-7712. Fax (608)257-7714. E-mail NTelemedia@aol.com. Web site http://danenet .wicip.org/NTC. Rev. Stephen Umhoefer, Interim Pres.; Marieli Rowe, Exec. Dir. The NTC is a national, nonprofit professional organization dedicated to promoting media literacy, or critical media viewing skills. This is done primarily through work with teachers, parents, and caregivers. NTC activities include publishing *Telemedium: The Journal of Media Literacy,* the *Teacher Idea Exchange (T.I.E.),* the Jessie McCanse Award for individual contribution to media literacy, assistance to media literacy educators and professionals. *Dues:* $30, basic; $50, contributing; $100, patron. *Publications: Telemedium; The Journal of Media Literacy* (q. newsletter).

*Native American Public Telecommunications (NAPT). 1800 North 33rd St., P.O. Box 83111, Lincoln, NE 68501-3111. (402)472-3522. Fax (402)472-8675. E-mail native@unl .edu. Web site http://nativetelecomn.org. Frank Blythe, Exec. Dir. The mission of NAPT is to inform, educate, and encourage the awareness of tribal histories, cultures, languages, opportunities, and aspirations through the fullest participation of America Indians and Alaska Natives in creating and employing all forms of educational and public telecommunications programs and services, thereby supporting tribal sovereignty. *Publications: The Vision Maker* (newsletter).

*Network for Continuing Medical Education (NCME). One Harmon Plaza, 6th Floor, Secaucus, NJ 07094. (201)867-3550. Produces and distributes videocassettes, CD-ROMs and Web-based programs to hospitals for physicians' continuing education. Programs are developed for physicians in the practice of general medicine, anesthesiology, emergency medicine, gastroenterology, and surgery. Physicians who view all the programs can earn up to 25 hours of Category 1 (AMA) credit and up to 10 hours of Prescribed (AAFP) credit each year. *Membership:* More than 1,000 hospitals provide NCME programs to their physicians. *Dues:* subscription fees: VHS-$2,160/yr. Sixty-minute videocassettes and CD-ROMs are distributed to hospital subscribers every 18 days.

*The NETWORK, Inc. 136 Fenno Drive, Rowley, MA 01969. (978)948-7764. Fax (978)948-7836. E-mail davidc@network.org. David Crandall, contact person. A nonprofit research and service organization providing training, research and evaluation, technical assistance, and materials for a fee to schools, educational organizations, and private sector firms with educational interests. The NETWORK has been helping professionals manage and learn about change since 1969. A Facilitator's Institute is held at least annually for trainers and staff developers who use the simulations. *Publications: An Action Guide for School Improvement; Making Change for School Improvement: A Simulation Game; Systems Thinking/Systems Changing: A Simulation Game; People, Policies, and Practices: Examining the Chain of School Improvement; Systemic Thinking: Solving Complex Problems; Benchmarking: A Guide for Educators.*

*New England Educational Media Association (NEEMA). c/o Jean Keilly, 58 South Mammoth Road, Manchester, NH 03109. (603)622-9626. Fax (603)424-6229. E-mail nadeau@ccsu.edu. An affiliate of AECT, NEEMA is a regional professional association dedicated to the improvement of instruction through the effective utilization of school library media services, media, and technology applications. For over 75 years, it has represented school library media professionals through activities and networking efforts to develop and polish the leadership skills, professional representation, and informational awareness of the membership. The Board of Directors consists of departments of education as well as professional leaders of the region. An annual conference program and a Leadership Program are offered in conjunction with the various regional state association conferences.

*The New York Festivals. 780 King St., Chappaqua, NY 10514. (914)238-4481. Fax (914)236-5040. E-mail info@nyfests.com. Web site http://www.nyfests.com. Bilha Goldberg, Vice Pres. The New York Festivals sponsors the International Non-Broadcast Awards, which are annual competitive festivals for industrial and educational film and video productions, filmstrips and slide programs, multi-image business theater and interactive multimedia presentations, and television programs. Entry fees begin at $125. First entry deadline is Aug 3 for U.S. entrants and Sept 15 for overseas entrants. The Non-Broadcast competition honors a wide variety of categories, including Education Media. As one of the largest competitions in the world, achieving finalist status is a notable credit to any company's awards roster. Winners are announced each year at a gala awards show in New York City and published on the World Wide Web.

North Central Regional Educational Laboratory (NCREL). 1120 E. Diehl Road Suite 200, Naperville, IL 60563-1486. (630)649-6500, (800)356-2735. Fax (630)649-6700. E-mail info@ncrel.org. Web site http://www.ncrel.org. Gina Burkhardt, Executive Director. NCRELs work is guided by a focus on comprehensive and systemic school restructuring that is research-based and learner-centered. One of 10 Office of Educational Research and Improvement (OERI) regional educational laboratories, NCREL disseminates information about effective programs, develops educational products, holds conferences, provides technical assistance, and conducts research and evaluation. A special focus is on technology and learning. In addition to conventional print publications, NCREL uses computer networks, videoconferencing via satellite, and video and audio formats to reach its diverse audiences. NCREL's Web site includes the acclaimed Pathways to School Improvement. NCREL operates the Midwest Consortium for Mathematics and Science Education, which works to advance systemic change in mathematics and science education. Persons living in Illinois, Indiana, Iowa, Michigan, Minnesota, Ohio, and Wisconsin are encouraged to call the NCREL Resource Center with any education-related questions. NCREL also hosts the North Central Regional Technology in Education Consortium that helps states and local educational agencies successfully integrate advanced technologies into K–12 classrooms, library media centers, and other educational settings. *Membership:* staff of 100, region covers Michigan, Minnesota, Wisconsin, Illinois, Ohio, Indiana, and Iowa. *Meetings:* annual conference in the fall. *Publications*: *Learning Point* (q).

Northwest College and University Council for the Management of Educational Technology (NW/MET). c/o WITS, Willamette University, 900 State St., Salem, OR 97301. (503)370-6650. Fax (503)375-5456. E-mail mmorandi@willamette.edu. Web site http://www.nw-met.org. Kees Hof, Director.; Marti Morandi, Membership Chair. NW/MET was the first regional group representing institutions of higher education in Alberta, Alaska, British Columbia, Idaho, Montana, Oregon, Saskatchewan, and Washington to receive affiliate status in AECT. *Membership:* Restricted to information technology managers with campus-wide responsibilities for information technology services in the membership region. Corresponding membership is available to those who work outside the membership region. Current issues under consideration include managing emerging technologies, distance education, adaptive technologies, staff evaluation, course management, faculty development, copyright, and other management/administration issues. Organizational goals include identifying the unique status problems of media managers in higher education. Membership: approx. 75. *Dues:* $35. *Meetings:* An annual conference and business meeting are held each year, rotating through the region. *Publications:* An annual newsletter and *NW/MET Journal.*

*Northwest Regional Educational Laboratory (NWREL). 101 SW Main St., Suite 500, Portland, OR 97204. (503)275-9500. Fax (503)275-0448. E-mail info@nwrel.org. Web site http://www.nwrel.org. Dr. Ethel Simon-McWilliams, Exec. Dir. One of 10 Office of Educational Research and Improvement (OERI) regional educational laboratories, NWREL works with schools and communities to improve educational outcomes for children, youth, and adults. NWREL provides leadership, expertise, and services based on the results of research and development. The specialty area of NWREL is school change processes. It serves Alaska, Idaho, Oregon, Montana, and Washington. *Membership:* 817. *Publications*: *Northwest Report* (newsletter).

*On-line Audiovisual Catalogers (OLAC). E-mail karend@selway.emt.edu. Formed as an outgrowth of the ALA conference, OLAC seeks to permit members to exchange ideas and information, and to interact with other agencies that influence audiovisual cataloging practices. *Membership:* 700. *Dues:* available for single or multiple years; $10-$27, indiv.; $16-$45, institution. *Meetings:* bi-annual. *Publications: OLAC Newsletter.*

*Online Computer Library Center, Inc. (OCLC). 6565 Frantz Rd., Dublin, OH 43017-3395. (614)764-6000. Fax (614)764-6096. E-mail oclc@oclc.org. Web site http://www.oclc.org. Jay Jordan, Pres. and CEO; Nita Dean, Mgr., Public Relations. A non-profit membeship organization that engages in computer library service and research and makes available computer-based processes, products, and services for libraries, other educational organizations, and library users. From its facility in Dublin, Ohio, OCLC operates an international computer network that libraries use to catalog books, order custom-printed catalog cards and machine-readable records for local catalogs, arrange interlibrary loans, and maintain location information on library materials. OCLC also provides online reference products and services for the electronic delivery of information. More than 34,000 libraries contribute to and/or use information in WorldCat (the OCLC Online Union Catalog). OCLC FOREST PRESS, a division of OCLC since 1988, publishes the Dewey Decimal Classification. Reservation Resources, a division of OCLC since 1994, provides preservation reformatting services worldwide. *Publications: OCLC Newsletter* (6/yr.); *OCLC Reference News* (4/yr.); *Annual Report.*

*Pacific Film Archive (PFA). University of California, Berkeley Art Museum, 2625 Durant Ave., Berkeley, CA 94720-2250. (510)642-1437 (library); (510)642-1412 (general). Fax (510)642-4889. E-mail pfalibrary@uclink.berkeley.edu. Web site http://www .bampfa.berkeley.edu. Edith Kramer, Dir. and Curator of Film; Nancy Goldman, Head, PFA Library and Film Study Center. Sponsors the exhibition, study, and preservation of classic, international, documentary, animated, and avant-garde films. Provides on-site research screenings of films in its collection of over 7,000 titles. Provides access to its collections of books, periodicals, stills, and posters (all materials are noncirculating). Offers BAM/PFA members and University of California, Berkeley, affiliates reference and research services to locate film and video distributors, credits, stock footage, and so forth. Library hours are 1 P.M. to 5 P.M. Mon.-Thurs. *Membership:* through parent organization, the Berkeley Art Museum. *Dues:* $40 indiv. and nonprofit departments of institutions. *Publications: BAM/PFA Calendar* (6/yr.).

*Pacific Resources for Education and Learning (PREL). 828 Fort Street Mall Suite 500, Honolulu, HI 96813-4321. (808)533-6000. Fax (808)533-7599. E-mail askprel@prel.hawaii .edu. Web site http://prel.hawaii.edu. John W. Kofel, Exec. Dir. One of 10 regional educational laboratories designed to help educators and policymakers solve educational problems in their schools. Using the best available information and the expertise of professionals, PREL furnishes research results, provides training to teachers and administrators, and helps to implement new approaches in education. The PREL Star program, funded by a U.S. Department of Education Star Schools Grant, utilizes telecommunications technology to provide distance learning opportunities to the Pacific region. PREL serves American Samoa, Commonwealth of the Northern Mariana Islands, Federated States of Micronesia, Guam, Hawaii, Republic of the Marshall Islands, and Republic of Palau.

*Photographic Society of America (PSA). 3000 United Founders Blvd., Suite 103, Oklahoma City, OK 73112. (405)843-1437. Fax (405)843-1438. Web site http://www .psa-photo.org. Jacque Noel, Operations Mgr. A nonprofit organization for the development of the arts and sciences of photography and for the furtherance of public appreciation of photographic skills. Its members, largely advanced amateurs, consist of individuals, camera clubs, and other photographic organizations. Divisions include electronic imaging, color slide, video motion picture, nature, photojournalism, travel, pictorial print, stereo, and techniques. Sponsors national, regional, and local meetings, clinics, and contests. *Membership:* 7,000. *Dues:* $40, North America; $45 elsewhere. *Meetings:* 1999 International Conference of Photography, Aug 30-Sep 4, Toronto, Delta Meadowvale Hotel. *Publications: PSA Journal.*

*Professors of Instructional Design and Technology (PIDT). Instructional Technology Dept., 220 War Memorial Hall, Virginia Tech, Blacksburg, VA 24061-0341. (540)231-5587. Fax (540)231-9075. E-mail moorem@VT.EDU. Dr. Mike Moore, contact person. An informal organization designed to encourage and facilitate the exchange of information among members of the instructional design and technology academic and corporate communities. Also serves to promote excellence in academic programs in instructional design and technology and to encourage research and inquiry that will benefit the field while providing leadership in the public and private sectors in its application and practice. *Membership:* 300 faculty employed in higher education institutions whose primary responsibilities are teaching and research in this area, their corporate counterparts, and other persons interested in the goals and activities of the PIDT. *Meetings:* Annual conference; see above e-mail address for information and registration.

*Public Broadcasting Service (PBS). 1320 Braddock Pl., Alexandria, VA 22314. Web site http://www.pbs.org. Ervin S. Duggan, CEO and Pres. National distributor of public television programming, obtaining all programs from member stations, independent producers, and sources around the world. PBS services include program acquisition, distribution, and scheduling; development and fundraising support; engineering and technical development; and educational resources and services. Through the PBS National Program Service, PBS uses the power of noncommercial television, the Internet, and other media to enrich the lives of all Americans through quality programs and education services that inform and inspire. Subsidiaries of PBS include PBS Adult Learning Service, and PBS Video, which are described below. PBS is owned and operated by local public television organizations through annual membership fees and governed by a board of directors elected by PBS members for three-year terms.

*PBS Adult Learning Service (ALS). 1320 Braddock Pl, Alexandria, VA 22314-1698. (800)257-2578. Fax (703)739-8471. E-mail als@pbs.org. Web site http://www.pbs.org/als/college. Will Philipp, Senior Dir. The mission of ALS is to help colleges, universities, and public television stations increase learning opportunities for distance learners; enrich classroom instruction; update faculty; train administrators, management, and staff; and provide other educational services for local communities. A pioneer in the widespread use of video and print packages incorporated into curricula and offered for credit by local colleges, ALS began broadcasting telecourses in 1981. Since that time, over 3 million students have earned college credit through telecourses offered in partnership with more than two-thirds of the nation's colleges and universities. In 1988, ALS established the Adult Learning Satellite Service (ALSS) to provide colleges, universities, and other organizations with a broad range of educational programming via direct satellite. Since 1994, ALS has facilitated the capability for colleges nationwide to offer full two-year degrees at a distance through the popular Going the Distance® project. Over 170 colleges are currently participating in 37 states. In 1998, ALS launched the first teleWEBcourse^{SM}, Internet Literacy, an online credit offering available through the PBS Web site. *Membership:* 700-plus colleges, universities, hospitals, and government agencies are now ALSS Associates. Organizations that are not Associates can still acquire ALS programming, but at higher fees. *Dues:* $1,500; multisite and consortia rates are available. *Publications: ALSS Programming Line-Up* (catalog of available programming, 3/yr.); *The Agenda* (news magazine about issues of interest to distance learning and adult learning administrators); *Changing the Face of Higher Education* (an overview of ALS services); *Teaching Telecourses: Opportunities and Options; Ideas for Increasing Telecourse Enrollment; Going the Distance® Handbook* (case studies for offering distance learning degrees).

*PBS VIDEO. 1320 Braddock Pl., Alexandria, VA 22314. (703)739-5380; (800)344-3337. Fax (703)739-5269. Web site http://shop2.org/pbsvideo/. Jon Cecil, Dir. PBS VIDEO Marketing. Markets and distributes PBS television programs for sale on videocassette or videodisc to colleges, public libraries, schools, governments, and other organizations and institutions. *Publications: PBS VIDEO Catalogs of New and Popular Video* (6/yrs). Web site: PBS VIDEO Online Catalog at http://shop2.org/pbsvideo/.

*Public Library Association (PLA). 50 E. Huron St., Chicago, IL 60611. (312)280-5PLA. Fax (312)280-5029. E-mail pla@ala.org. Greta Southard, Exec. Dir. An affiliate of the American Library Association, PLA is concerned with the development, effectiveness, and financial support of public libraries. It speaks for the profession and seeks to enrich the professional competence and opportunities of public librarians. Sections include Adult Lifelong Learning, Community Information, Metropolitan Libraries, Public Library Systems, Small and Medium-sized Libraries, Public Policy for Public Libraries, Planning, Measurement and Evaluation, and Marketing of Public Library Services. *Membership:* 8,500. *Dues:* $50, open to all ALA members. *Meetings:* 1999 PLA Spring Symposium, Mar 25-28; 2000 PLA National Conference, Mar 28-Apr 1, "Public Libraries: Vital, Valuable, Virtual." *Publications: Public Libraries* (bi-monthly).

*Audiovisual Committee (of the Public Library Association). 50 E. Huron St., Chicago, IL 60611. (312)280-5752. James E. Massey, Chair. Promotes use of audiovisual materials in public libraries.

*Technology in Public Libraries Committee. 50 E. Huron St., Chicago, IL 60611. (312)280-5752. William Ptacek, Chair. Collects and disseminates information on technology applications in public libraries.

Puppeteers of America, Inc. (POA). PO Box 29417, Parma, OH 44129-0417. (888)568-6235. Fax (440)843-7867. E-mail PofAjoin@aol.com. Web site http://www .puppeteers.org. Joyce and Chuck Berty, Membership Officers. Formed in 1937, POA holds festivals for puppetry across the country, supports local guilds, presents awards, sponsors innovative puppetry works, provides consulting, and provides research materials through the Audio-Visual Library. A National Festival is held in the odd number years and Regional Festivals are held in the even number years at various locations around the United States. The group supports a National Day of Puppetry on the last Saturday in April. Local celebrations of the Art of Puppetry are held throughout the United States. The Puppetry Store is an invaluable source of books and miscellaneous printed materials for puppeteers or anyone interested in puppetry. *The Puppetry Journal* is the magazine published quarterly for the members of the organization and *Playboard* is the bi-monthly newletter. *Membership:* over 2,200. *Dues:* $40, single adult; $50, couple; $20, youth (6-17); $25 full-time student; $25 senior (65 and over, $60, family; $70 company or business; $35, journal subscription available to libraries. *Meetings:* National Festival, Tampa Florida, July 8-14, 2001. *Publications: The Puppetry Journal* (q); *Playboard* (bi-monthly).

*Recording for the Blind and Dyslexic (RFB&D). 20 Roszel Road, Princeton, NJ 08540. (609)452-0606. Customer Service (800)221-4792. Fax (609)987-8116. E-mail information @rfbd.org. Web site http://www.rfbd.org. Richard Scribner, Pres. RFB&D is a national nonprofit organization that provides educational and professional books in accessible format to people with visual impairments, learning disabilities, or other physical disabilities that prevent them from reading normal printed material. This includes students from kindergarten to graduate school and people who no longer attend school but who use educational books to pursue careers or personal interests. RFB&D's 78,000-volume collection of audio titles is the largest educational resource of its kind in the world. RFB&D provides a wide range of library services as well as "E-Text" books on computer disk, including dictionaries, computer manuals, and other reference books. For an additional fee, a custom recording service is also available, to make other publications accessible. Potential individual members must complete an application form, which contains a "disability verification" section. *Membership:* 39,139 individuals, 275 institutions. *Dues:* for qualified individuals, $50 registration, $25 annual. Institutional Memberships also available (contact Customer Service).

*Recording Industry Association of America, Inc. (RIAA). 1330 Connecticut Ave. NW #300, Washington, DC 20036. (202)775-0101. Fax (202)775-7253. Web site http://www.riaa.com/. Hilary Rosen, Pres. and CEO. Founded in 1952, RIAA's mission is to promote the mutual interests of recording companies, as well as the betterment of the industry overall through successful government relations (both federal and state), intellectual property protection, and international activities; evaluating all aspects of emerging technologies and technology-related issues; and promoting an innovative and secure online marketplace. RIAA represents the recording industry, whose members create and/or distribute approximately 90 percent of all legitimate sound recordings produced and sold in the United States. RIAA is the official certification agency for gold, platinum, and multi-platinum record awards. *Membership:* Over 250 recording companies. *Publications: Annual Report; Fact Book.*

*Reference and User Services Association (RUSA). 50 E. Huron St., Chicago, IL 60611. (800)545-2433, ext. 4398. Fax (312)944-8085. E-mail cbourdon@ala.org. Cathleen Bourdon, Exec. Dir. A division of the American Library Association, RUSA is responsible for stimulating and supporting in every type of library the delivery of reference information services to all groups and of general library services and materials to adults. *Membership:* 5,500. *Dues:* $45 plus membership in ALA. *Publications: RUSQ* (q.); *RUSA Update.*

Research for Better Schools, Inc. (RBS). 444 North Third St., Philadelphia, PA 19123-4107. (215)574-9300. Fax (215)574-0133. E-mail info@rbs.org. Web site http://www .rbs.org/. Keith M. Kershner & Louis Maguire, Co-Executive Directors. RBS is a nonprofit educational R&D firm that has been serving educators since 1966. Our mission is to help students achieve by supporting improvement efforts in schools and other education programs. RBS currently operates the Mid-Atlantic Eisenhower Consortium for Mathematics and Science Education, has programs in Technology Development and Applications, Program Evaluation, Improvement Program Planning and Implementation, and Curriculum and Instruction in Mathematics and Science. RBS also operates an educational publications division. *Membership:* There is no membership in Research for Better Schools. The Mid-Atlantic Eisenhower Consortium, however, does encourage regional educators to become members (information available online at http://www.rbs.org /eisenhower). *Meetings:* The Mid-Atlantic Eisenhower Consortium sponsors an annual regional conference and state team meetings throughout the year. *Publications:* RBS publishes the *Currents* newsletter, available in print, online, and delivered via e-mail (http://www.rbs.org/ec.nsf/Currents?OpenView). The Consortium also publishes the electronic newsletter *Riptides* (http://www.rbs.org/ec.nsf/pages/Riptides). The catalog for the RBS Publications program is online (visit our homepage at http://www.rbs.org).

*Smithsonian Institution. 1000 Jefferson Drive SW, Washington, DC 20560. (202)357-2700. Fax (202)786-2515. E-mail info@info.si.edu. Web site http://www.si.edu. I. Michael Heyman, Sec. An independent trust instrumentality of the United States that conducts scientific, cultural, and scholarly research; administers the national collections; and performs other educational public service functions, all supported by Congress, trusts, gifts, and grants. Includes 16 museums, including the National Museum of Natural History, the National Museum of American History, the National Air and Space Museum, and the National Zoological Park. Museums are free and open daily except December 25. The Smithsonian Institution Traveling Exhibition Service (SITES) organizes exhibitions on art, history, and science and circulates them across the country and abroad. *Membership:* Smithsonian Associates. *Dues:* $24-$45. *Meetings:* n/a. *Publications: Smithsonian; Air & Space/Smithsonian; The Torch* (staff newsletter, mo.); *Research Reports* (semitechnical, q.); Smithsonian Institution Press Publications, 470 L'Enfant Plaza, Suite 7100, Washington, DC 20560.

Society for Applied Learning Technology (SALT). 50 Culpeper St., Warrenton, VA 20186. (540)347-0055. Fax (540)349-3169. E-mail info@lti.org. Web site http://www.salt.org. Raymond G. Fox, Pres. The society is a nonprofit, professional membership organization that was founded in 1972. Membership in the society is oriented to professionals whose work requires knowledge and communication in the field of instructional technology. The society provides members with a means to enhance their knowledge and job performance by participation in society-sponsored meetings, subscription to society-sponsored publications, association with other professionals at conferences sponsored by the society, and membership in special interest groups and special society-sponsored initiatives. In addition, the society offers member discounts on society-sponsored journals, conferences, and publications. *Membership:* 1,000. *Dues:* $55. *Meetings:* Orlando Multimedia. '99, Kissimmee, FL; Interactive Multimedia '99, Arlington, VA.. *Publications: Journal of Educational Technology Systems; Journal of Instruction Delivery Systems; Journal of Interactive Instruction Development.* Send for list of books.

*Society for Computer Simulation (SCS). P.O. Box 17900, San Diego, CA 92177-7900. (619)277-3888. Fax (619)277-3930. E-mail info@scs.org. Web site http://www.scs.org. Bill Gallagher, Exec. Dir. Founded in 1952, SCS is a professional-level technical society devoted to the art and science of modeling and simulation. Its purpose is to advance the understanding, appreciation, and use of all types of computer models for studying the behavior of actual or hypothesized systems of all kinds and to sponsor standards. Additional office in Ghent, Belgium. *Membership:* 1,900. *Dues:* $75 (includes journal subscription).

Meetings: local, regional, and national technical meetings and conferences. *Publications: Simulation* (mo.); *Simulation series* (q.); *Transactions of SCS* (q.).

*Society for Photographic Education (SPE). P.O. Box 2811, Daytona Beach, FL 32120-2811. (904)255-8131, ext. 3944. Fax (904)255-3044. E-mail SocPhotoEd@aol.com or SPENews@aol.com. Web site http://www.spenational.org. James J. Murphy, Exec. Dir. An association of college and university teachers of photography, museum photographic curators, writers, and publishers. Promotes discourse in photography education, culture, and art. *Membership:* 1,700. *Dues:* $55. *Meetings:* 1999, Mar 11-14, Tucson; 2000, Mar 16-19, Cleveland. *Publications: Exposure* (newsletter).

Society of Cable Telecommunications Engineers (SCTE). 140 Philips Rd., Exton, PA 19341-1319. (610)363-6888. Fax (610)363-5898. E-mail info@scte.org. Web site http://www.scte.org. John Clark, Pres. and CEO. SCTE is dedicated to the technical training and further education of members. A nonprofit membership organization for persons engaged in engineering, construction, installation, technical direction, management, or administration of cable television and broadband communications technologies. Also eligible for membership are students in communications, educators, government and regulatory agency employees, and affiliated trade associations. SCTE provides technical training and certification, and is an American National Standards Institute (ANSI)-approved Standards Development Organization for the cable telecommunications industry. *Membership:* 17,500 U.S. and international. *Dues:* $48 North America; $72 international. *Meetings:* Conference on Emerging Technologies: San Jose, CA, Jan 8-10, 2002; Cable-Tec Expo, San Antonio, TX, June 5-8, 2002. *Publications: Interval*; technical documents, standards, training materials, and videotapes (some available in Spanish).

*Society of Photo Technologists (SPT). 11112 S. Spotted Rd., Cheney, WA 99004. (888)662-7678 or (509)624-9621. Fax (509)323-4811 or (509)624-5320. E-mail ccspt@concentric.net. An organization of photographic equipment repair technicians, which improves and maintains communications between manufacturers and independent repair technicians. *Membership:* 1,000. *Dues:* $80-$360. *Publications: SPT Journal; SPT Parts and Services Directory; SPT Newsletter; SPT Manuals—Training and Manufacturer's Tours.*

*Southeastern Regional Media Leadership Council (SRMLC). Dr. Vykuntapathi Thota, Director, Virginia State University, P.O. Box 9198, Petersburg, VA 23806. (804)524-5937. Fax (804)524-5757. An affiliate of AECT, the purpose of the SRMLC is to strengthen the role of the individual state AECT affiliates within the Southeastern region; to seek positive change in the nature and status of instructional technology as it exists within the Southeast; to provide opportunities for the training and development of leadership for both the region and the individual affiliates; and to provide opportunities for the exchange of information and experience among those who attend the annual conference.

*SouthEastern Regional Vision for Education (SERVE). SERVE Tallahassee Office, 1203 Governor's Square Blvd., Suite 400, Tallahassee, FL 32301. (800)352-6001, (904)671-6000. Fax (904)671-6020. E-mail bfry@SERVE.org. Mr. Don Holznagel, Exec. Dir. Betty Fry, contact person. SERVE is a regional educational research and development laboratory funded by the U.S. Department of Education to help educators, policy makers, and communities improve schools so that all students achieve their full potential. The laboratory offers the following services: field-based models and strategies for comprehensive school improvement; publications on hot topics in education, successful implementation efforts, applied research projects, and policy issues; database searches and information search training; a regional bulletin board service that provides educators electronic communication and Internet access; information and assistance for state and local policy development; and services to support the coordination and improvement of assistance for young children and their families. The Eisenhower Mathematics and Science Consortium at

SERVE promotes improvement of education in these targeted areas by coordinating regional resources, disseminating exemplary instructional materials, and offering technical assistance for implementation of effective teaching methods and assessment tools. *Meetings:* For dates and topics of conferences and workshops, contact Betty Fry, (800)352-6001. *Publications: Reengineering High Schools for Student Success; Schools for the 21st Century: New Roles for Teachers and Principals* (rev. ed.); *Designing Teacher Evaluation Systems That Promote Professional Growth; Learning by Serving: 2,000 Ideas for Service-Learning Projects; Sharing Success: Promising Service-Learning Programs; Future Plans* (videotape, discussion guide, and pamphlet); *Future Plans Planning Guides.*

Southwest Educational Development Laboratory (SEDL). 211 East Seventh St., Austin, TX 78701. (512)476-6861. Fax (512)476-2286. E-mail info@sedl.org. Web site http://www.sedl.org/. Dr. Wesley A. Hoover, Pres. and CEO; Dr. Joyce Pollard, Dir., Institutional Communications & Policy Services. The Southwest Educational Development Laboratory (SEDL) is a private, not-for-profit education research and development corporation based in Austin, Texas. SEDLs heritage of education R&D, which spans more than 30 years, began when SEDL investigated early English language learning and developed multimedia curriculum materials for use in teaching English to Spanish-speaking children. SEDLs recent research and development activities in constructivist teaching supported by technologies has resulted in the production of Active Learning with Technology, a multimedia training program for teachers. Using the modules, videotapes, CD, teachers can learn and see how to apply student-centered, problem-based learning theory to their instructional strategies that are supported by technologies. Copies of Active Learning can be ordered from SEDLs Publications Department. SEDL also operates the SouthCentral Regional Technology in Education Consortium (SouthCentral RTEC), which seeks to support educational systems in Arkansas, Louisiana, New Mexico, Oklahoma, and Texas using technology to foster student success in achieving state content standards, particularly in schools serving high populations of disadvantaged students. The RTEC delivers research-based professional development and information resources to teachers, college faculty, district and state level staff developers, as well as local and state decision makers. *Meetings:* Not applicable. *Publications: SEDLETTER* for free general distribution; a range of topic-specific publications related to educational change, education policy, mathematics, language arts, science, and disability research.

*Special Libraries Association. 1700 Eighteenth St., NW, Washington, DC 20009-2514. (202)234-4700. Fax (202)265-9317. E-mail sla@sla.org. Web site http://www.sla.org. Dr. David R. Bender, Exec. Dir. The Special Libraries Association is an international association representing the interests of nearly 15,000 information professionals in 60 countries. Special librarians are information and resource experts who collect, analyze, evaluate, package, and disseminate information to facilitate accurate decision making in corporate, academic, and government settings. The association offers myriad programs and services designed to help its members serve their customers more effectively and succeed in an increasingly challenging environment of information management and technology. These services include career and employment services, and professional development opportunities. *Membership:* 14,500. *Dues:* $105, indiv.; $25, student. *Meetings:* 1999, Jan 21-23, San Francisco; Jun 5-10, Minneapolis; 2000, Jan 20-22, St. Louis; Jun 10-15, Philadelphia; Oct 16-19, Brighton, United Kingdom. *Publications: Information Outlook* (monthly glossy magazine that accepts advertising). Special Libraries Association also has an active book publishing program.

Teachers and Writers Collaborative (T&W). 5 Union Square W., New York, NY 10003-3306. (212)691-6590. Toll-free (888)266-5789. Fax (212)675-0171. E-mail info@twc.org. Web site http://www.twc.org and http://www.writenet.org. Nancy Larson Shapiro, Dir. Teachers & Writers Collaborative (T&W) provides a link between New York City's rich literary community and the public schools, where the needs for effective ways to teach writing and for programs that support innovative teaching are greater than ever. T&W

not only places professional writers and artists into schools and other community settings, but also publishes books on teaching writing—books that provide sound theory and practical curriculum ideas for the classroom. In our welcoming Center for Imaginative Writing on Union Square, writers and educators come together for workshops, readings, and seminars, and through our Youth Speaks program we hold free after-school writing workshops for students. The National Endowment for the Arts has called T&W the nation's group that is "most familiar with creative writing/literature in primary and secondary schools." *Membership:* T&W has over 1,000 members across the country. The basic membership is $35; patron membership is $75; and benefactor membership is $150 or more. Members receive a free book or T-shirt; discounts on publications; and a free one-year subscription to *Teachers & Writers* magazine. (Please see http://www.twc.org/member.htm.) *Dues:* T&W is seeking general operating support for all of our programs and program support for specific projects, including: 1) T&W writing residencies in New York City area schools; 2) T&W publications, books and a bimonthly magazine, which we distribute across the country; 3) Youth Speaks, T&Ws free after-school writing and performance workshops for teens; and 4) WriteNet, T&Ws Internet programs for teachers, writers, and students. Grants to T&Ws Endowment support the stability of the organization and help to guarantee the continuation of specific programs. *Meetings:* T&W offers year-round public events in our Center for Imaginative Writing in New York City. For a list of events, please see http://www.twc.org/events.htm. *Publications:* T&W has published over 60 books on the teaching of imaginative writing, including *The T&W Handbook of Poetic Forms; The Dictonary of Wordplay; The Story in History; Personal Fiction Writing; Luna, Luna: Creative Writing from Spanish and Latino Literature; The Nearness of You: Students and Teachers Writing On-Line.* To request a free publications catalog, please send E-mail to info@twc.org or call 888-BOOKS-TW (see http://www.twc.org/tpubs.htm).

The Learning Team (TLT). Suite 307 84 Business Park Drive, Armonk, NY 10504. 914-273-2226. Fax 914-273-2227. E-mail NMcLaren@LearningTeam.org. Web site http://www.learningteam.org. Executive Driector, Tom Laster. The Learning Team is a not-for-profit company that is focused on publishing inquiry-based, supplementary, technology resources for science education. The multimedia resources include science, mathematics, and utilities software and videos. Science subjects include physics, physical sciences, biology, earth sciences (geosciences), environmental sciences, general science, chemistry, energy use, and culture and technology. Software includes inquiry-based student resources, teacher resources, and professional development. Resources available include High School Geography Product (HSGP), Intermediate Science Curriculum Study (ISCS), Man: A Course of Study (MACOS), and Human Sciences Project (HSP). Most of the resources come from National Science Foundation (NSF)funding and have been done in conjunction with institutions such as the American Association of Physics Teachers (AAPT), the American Institute of Physics (AIP), American Geological Institute (AGI). *Membership:* Although the term membership does not apply specifically to our organization, it loosely applies to the range of licensors, collaborators, and colleagues that cooperate with us and are active in the area of science education. *Publications: Physics InfoMall;CPU; Constructing Physics Understanding; Exploring the Nardoo; Investigating Lake Iluka; The Dynamic Rainforests; Insects; Little Creatures in a Big World; Culture & Technology; Enhanced Science Helper; Enhanced Science Helper Video; The Green Home&;The Sun;s Joules;Whelmers;EarthView Explorer; GETIT; Geosciences Education Through Interactive Technology; Crossword Wizard; Cloze word Wizard; Maths Worksheet Wizard.*

*Theatre Library Association (TLA). 149 W. 45th St., New York, NY 10036. (212)944-3895. Fax (212)944-4139. E-mail kwinkler@nypl.org. Web site http://www.brown.edu /Facilities/University_Library/beyond/TLA/TLA.html. Maryann Chach, Exec. Sec. Seeks to further the interests of collecting, preserving, and using theater, cinema, and performing arts materials in libraries, museums, and private collections. *Membership:* 500. *Dues:* $30, indiv.; $30, institutional; $20, students and retirees. *Publications: Performing Arts Resources* (membership annual, Vol. 20, Denishawn Collections).

USA Toy Library Association (USA-TLA). 1213 Wilmette Ave., Ste. 201, Wilmette, IL 60091. (847)920-9030. Fax (847)920-9032. E-mail usatla@aol.com. Web site http://usatla .deltacollege.org. Judith Q. Iacuzzi, Exec. Dir. The mission of the USA-TLA is to provide a networking system answering to all those interested in play and play materials to provide a national resource to toy libraries, family centers, resource and referrals, public libraries, schools, institutions serving families of special need, and other groups and individuals involved with children; to support and expand the number of toy libraries; and to advocate for children and the importance of their play in healthy development. Individuals can find closest toy libraries by sending an e-mail or written inquiry in a self-addressed stamped envelope. *Membership:* 80 institutions, 150 individuals. *Dues:* $165, comprehensive; $55, basic; $15, student. *Meetings:* regional workshops in the spring and fall. *Publications: Childs Play* (q. newsletter); *How to Start and Operate a Toy Library; Play Is a Child's Work* (videotapes); other books on quality toys and play.

*University Continuing Education Association (UCEA). One Dupont Cir. NW, Suite 615, Washington, DC 20036. (202)659-3130. Fax (202)785-0374. E-mail postmaster@nucea .edu. Web site http://www.nucea.edu. Tom Kowalik, Pres. 1999–2000. Kay J. Kohl, Exec. Dir.; Susan Goewey, Dir. of Pubs; Philip Robinson, Dir. of Govt. Relations & Public Affairs; Joelle Brink, Dir. of Information Services. UCEA is an association of public and private higher education institutions concerned with making continuing education available to all population segments and to promoting excellence in continuing higher education. Many institutional members offer university and college courses via electronic instruction. *Membership:* 425 institutions, 2,000 professionals. *Dues:* vary according to membership category. *Meetings:* UCEA has an annual national conference and several professional development seminars throughout the year. *Publications:* monthly newsletter; quarterly; occasional papers; scholarly journal, *Continuing Higher Education Review; Independent Study Catalog.* With Peterson's, *The Guide to Distance Learning; Guide to Certificate Programs at American Colleges and Universities; UCEA-ACE/Oryx Continuing Higher Education* book series; *Lifelong Learning Trends* (a statistical factbook on continuing higher education); organizational issues series; membership directory.

WestEd (WestEd). 730 Harrison St., San Francisco, CA 94107-1242. (415)565-3000. Fax (415)565-3012. E-mail dtorres@wested.org. Web site http://www.WestEd.org. Glen Harvey, CEO. WestEd is a nonprofit research, development, and service agency dedicated to improving education and other opportunities for children, youth, and adults. Drawing on the best from research and practice, WestEd works with practitioners and policymakers to address critical issues in education and other related areas, including early childhood intervention; curriculum, instruction and assessment; the use of technology; career and technical preparation; teacher and administrator professional development; science and mathematics education; and safe schools and communities. WestEd was created in 1995 to unite and enhance the capacity of Far West Laboratory and Southwest Regional Laboratory, two of the nation's original education laboratories. In addition to its work across the nation, WestEd serves as the regional education laboratory for Arizona, California, Nevada, and Utah. A publications catalog is available. *Meetings:* various, relating to our work, plus quarterly board meetings. *Publications:* See Resources at www.wested.org.

*Western Public Radio (WPR). Ft. Mason Center, Bldg. D, San Francisco, CA 94123. (415)771-1160. Fax (415)771-4343. E-mail wprsf@aol.com. Karolyn van Putten, Ph.D., Pres./CEO; Lynn Chadwick, Vice Pres./COO. WPR provides analog and digital audio production training, public radio program proposal consultation, and studio facilities for rent. WPR also sponsors a continuing education resource for audio producers, www.radiocollege.org.

*World Future Society (WFS). 7910 Woodmont Ave., Suite 450, Bethesda, MD 20814. (301)656-8274. Fax (301)951-0394. E-mail wfsinfo@wfs.org. Web site http://www.wfs.org. Edward Cornish, Pres. Organization of individuals interested in the study of future trends and possibilities. Its purpose is to provide information on trends and scenarios so that individuals and organizations can better plan their future. *Membership:* 30,000. *Dues:* \$39, general; \$95, professional; call Society for details on all membership levels and benefits. *Meetings:* 1999, Ninth General Assembly, July 29-Aug 1, Washington; 2000, Annual Conference, July 23-25, Houston. *Publications: The Futurist: A Journal of Forecasts, Trends and Ideas About the Future; Futures Research Quarterly; Future Survey.* The society's bookstore offers audiotapes and videotapes, books, and other items.

*Young Adult Library Services Association (YALSA). 50 E. Huron St., Chicago, IL 60611. (312)280-4390. Fax (312)664-7459. E-mail yalsa@ala.org. Web site http://www.ala .organization/yalsa. Julie A. Walker, Exec. Dir.; Linda Waddle, Deputy Exec. Dir.; Joel Shoemaker, Pres. An affiliate of the American Library Association, YALSA seeks to advocate, promote, and strengthen service to young adults as part of the continuum of total library services, and assumes responsibility within the ALA to evaluate and select books and nonbook media and to interpret and make recommendations regarding their use with young adults. Committees include Best Books for Young Adults, Popular Paperbacks, Recommended Books for the Reluctant Young Adult Reader, Media Selection and Usage, Publishers' Liaison, and Selected Films for Young Adults. *Membership:* 2,223. *Dues:* \$40 (in addition to ALA membership); \$15, students. *Publications: Journal of Youth Services in Libraries* (q.).

Canada/International

This section includes information on eleven organizations whose principal interests lie in the general fields of educational media, instructional technology, and library and information science.

*ACCESS NETWORK. 3720-76 Ave., Edmonton, AB T6B 2N9. (403)440-7777. Fax (403)440-8899. E-mail promo@ccinet.ab.ca. Dr. Ronald Keast, Pres.; John Verburgt, Creative Services Manager. The ACCESS Network (Alberta Educational Communications Corporation) was purchased by Learning and Skills Television of Alberta in 1995. The newly privatized network works with Alberta's educators to provide all Albertans with a progressive and diverse television-based educational and training resource to support their learning and skills development needs using cost-effective methods and innovative techniques, and to introduce a new private sector model for financing and efficient operation of educational television in the province.

Adaptech Research Project. Dawson College, 3040 Sherbrooke St. West, Montreal, QC H3Z 1A4. (514) 931-8731 #1546. Fax (514) 931-3567 Attn: Catherine Fichten. E-mail catherine.fichten@mcgill.ca. Web site http://www.adaptech.org. Dr. Catherine Fichten & Maria Barile, Research co-Investigators; Jennison Asuncion, Project Coordinator. Based out of Dawson College (Montreal), we are a Canada-wide, grant-funded team, conducting bilingual empirical research into the use of computer, instructional and adaptive technologies by postsecondary students with disabilities. One of our primary interests lies in issues around ensuring that newly emerging educational media is accessible to learners with disabilities. *Membership:* Our research team is composed of academics, practitioners, consumers, and others interested in the issues of access to technology by students with disabilities in postsecondary education. *Publications:* 2001 Fossey, M.E., Fichten, C.S., Barile, M., and Asuncion, J.V. *Computer technologies for postsecondary students with disabilities.* ISBN 2-9803316-6-X. Montréal: Adaptech Project, Dawson College. Available on the World Wide Web: http://www.omega.dawsoncollege.qc.ca/adaptech/booklete.htm and http://www.omega.dawsoncollege.qc.ca/adaptech/booklete.pdf (see Web site for a complete listing of all publications).

Association for Media and Technology in Education in Canada (AMTEC). 3-1750 The Queensway, Suite 1318, Etobicoke, ON M9C 5H5. (403)220-3721. Fax (403)282-4497. E-mail wstephen@ucalgary.ca. Web site http://www.amtec.ca. Maureen Baron, Pres.; Dr. Len Proctor, Past Pres.; Wendy Stephens, Sec./Treas. AMTEC is Canada's national association for educational media and technology professionals. The organization provides national leadership through annual conferences, publications, workshops, media festivals, and awards. It responds to media and technology issues at the international, national, provincial, and local levels, and maintains linkages with other organizations with similar interests. *Membership:* AMTEC members represent all sectors of the educational media and technology fields. *Dues:* $101.65, Canadian regular; $53.50, student and retiree. *Meetings:* Annual conferences take place in late May or early June. 1999, Ottawa; 2000, Vancouver. *Publications: Canadian Journal of Educational Communication* (q.); *Media News* (3/yr.); *Membership Directory* (with membership).

*Canadian Broadcasting Corporation /Société Radio-Canada (CBC/SRC). P.O. Box 500, Station A, Toronto, ON. E-mail fortinj@toronto.cbc.ca. Web site http://www.cbc.ca. The CBC is a publicly owned corporation established in 1936 by an Act of the Canadian Parliament to provide a national broadcasting service in Canada in the two official languages. CBC services include English and French television networks; English and French AM mono and FM stereo radio networks virtually free of commercial advertising; CBC North, which serves Canada's North by providing radio and television programs in English,

French, and eight native languages; Newsworld and its French counterpart, Le Réseau de l'information (RDI), 24-hour national satellites to cable English-language and French-language news and information service respectively, both funded entirely by cable subscription and commercial advertising revenues; and Radio Canada International, a shortwave radio service that broadcasts in seven languages and is managed by CBC and financed by External Affairs. The CBC is financed mainly by public funds voted annually by Parliament.

*Canadian Education Association/Association canadienne d'éducation (CEA). 252 Bloor St. W., Suite 8-200, Toronto, ON M5S 1V5. (416)924-7721. Fax (416)924-3188. E-mail cea-ace@acea.ca. Web site http://www.acea.ca. Penny Milton, Exec. Dir.; Suzanne Tanguay, Dir. of Communication Services. The Canadian equivalent of the U.S. National Education Association, CEA has one central objective: to promote the improvement of education. It is the only national, bilingual organization whose function is to inform, assist, and bring together all sectors of the educational community. *Membership:* all 12 provincial and territorial departments of education, the federal government, 400 individuals, 120 organizations, 100 school boards. *Dues:* $120, indiv.; $320, organization; $500, businesses; 10 cents per pupil, school boards. *Meetings:* Annual CEA Convention. *Publications: Promoting Achievement in School: What Works; CEA Handbook; Education Canada* (q.); *CEA Newsletter* (8/yr.); *Education in Canada: An Overview; Class Size, Academic Achievement and Public Policy; Disruptive Behaviour in Today's Classroom; Financing Canadian Education; Secondary Schools in Canada: The National Report of the Exemplary Schools Project; Making Sense of the Canadian Charter of Rights and Freedom: A Handbook for Administrators and Teachers; The School Calendar.*

*Canadian Library Association. 200 Elgin St., Suite 602, Ottawa, ON K2P IL5. (613)232-9625. Fax (613)563-9895. E-mail ai075@freenet.carleton.ca. Web site http://www.cla.amlibs.ca. Vicki Whitmell, Exec. Dir. The mission of the Canadian Library Association is to provide leadership in the promotion, development, and support of library and information services in Canada for the benefit of Association members, the profession, and Canadian society. In the spirit of this mission, CLA aims to engage the active, creative participation of library staff, trustees, and governing bodies in the development and management of high quality Canadian library service; to assert and support the right of all Canadians to the freedom to read and to free universal access to a wide variety of library materials and services; to promote librarianship and to enlighten all levels of government as to the significant role that libraries play in educating and socializing the Canadian people; and to link libraries, librarians, trustees, and others across the country for the purpose of providing a unified nationwide voice in matters of critical concern. *Membership:* 2,300 individuals, 700 institutions, 100 Associates and Trustees. *Dues:* $50-$300. *Meetings:* 1999 Annual Conference, Jun 18-22, Toronto; 2000, Edmonton, June. *Publications: Feliciter* (membership magazine, 10/yr.).

*Canadian Museums Association/Association des musées canadiens (CMA/AMC). 280 Metcalfe St., Suite 400, Ottawa, ON K2P 1R7. (613)567-0099. Fax (613)233-5438. E-mail info@museums.ca. Web site http://www.museums.ca. John G. McAvity, Exec. Dir. The Canadian Museums Association is a nonprofit corporation and registered charity dedicated to advancing public museums and museum works in Canada, promoting the welfare and better administration of museums, and fostering a continuing improvement in the qualifications and practices of museum professionals. *Membership:* 2,000. *Meetings:* CMA Annual Conference, spring. *Publications: Museogramme* (bi-mo. newsletter); *Muse* (q. journal, Canada's only national, bilingual, scholarly magazine devoted to museums, it contains museum-based photography, feature articles, commentary, and practical information*); The Official Directory of Canadian Museums and Related Institutions* (1997–99 edition) lists all museums in Canada plus information on government departments, agencies, and provincial and regional museum associations.

Canadian Publishers' Council (CPC). 250 Merton St., Suite 203, Toronto, ON M4S 1B1. (416)322-7011. Fax (416)322-6999. E-mail pubadmin@pubcouncil.ca. Web site http://www.pubcouncil.ca. Jacqueline Hushion, Exec. Dir. CPC members publish and distribute an extensive list of Canadian and imported learning materials in a complete range of formats from traditional textbook and ancillary materials to CDs and interactive video. The primary markets for CPC members are schools, universities and colleges, bookstores, and libraries. CPC also provides exhibits throughout the year and works through a number of subcommittees and groups within the organization to promote effective book publishing. CPC was founded in 1910. *Membership:* 27 companies, educational institutions, or government agencies that publish books as an important facet of their work. *Dues:* assessed when a membership application form is submitted for consideration. *Meetings:* TBA. *Publications:* Please visit the CPC Web site at www.pubcouncil.ca for various publications.

National Film Board of Canada (NFBC). 350 Fifth Ave., Suite 4820, New York, NY 10118. (212)629-8890. Fax (212)629-8502. E-mail NewYork@onf.ca. Web site www.nfb.ca. John Sirabella, U.S. Marketing Mgr./Nontheatrical Rep. Established in 1939, the NFBCs main objective is to produce and distribute high-quality audiovisual materials for educational, cultural, and social purposes.

*Ontario Film Association, Inc. (also known as the Association for the Advancement of Visual Media/L'association pour l'avancement des médias visuels). 100 Lombard St. 303, Toronto, ON M5C 1M3. (416)363-3388. 1-800-387-1181. E-mail info@accessola.com. Web site www.accessola.org. Lawrence A. Moore, Exec. Dir. A membership organization of buyers, and users of media whose objectives are to promote the sharing of ideas and information about visual media through education, publications, and advocacy. *Membership:* 112. *Dues:* $120, personal membership; $215, associate membership. *Meetings:* OFA Media Showcase, spring.

Multimedia Education Group, University of Cape Town. (MEG). Hlanganani Building, Upper Campus, University of Cape Town, Rondebosche, Cape Town, 7700 South Africa. Tel 27 21 650 3841. Fax 27 21 650 3841. E-mail lcz@its.uct.ac.za. Web site http://www.meg.uct.ac.za. Laura Czerniewicz, Coordinator; Martin Hall, Director. MEG aims to research and harness the potential of interactive computer-based technologies and approaches (ICBTA) to support effective learning and teaching. Organization focuses on meeting the needs of South African students from diverse backgrounds, particularly those at the University of Cape Town. *Membership:* researchers and developers with strong educational interests in diversity, redress, and access are welcome.

Part Six
Graduate Programs

Introduction

This directory describes graduate programs in Instructional Technology, Educational Media and Communications, School Library Media, and closely allied programs in the United States. This year's list includes four new programs, one of which is based in Malaysia. One institution indicated that their program had been discontinued, and that program was deleted from the listings. Master's, specialist, and doctoral degrees are combined into one unified list.

Entries provide as much of the following information as furnished by respondents: (1) name and address of the institution; (2) chairperson or other individual in charge of the program; (3) types of degrees offered and specialization, emphases, or tracks, including information on careers for which candidates are prepared; (4) special features of the degree program; (5) admission requirements; (6) degree requirements; (7) number of full-time and part-time faculty; (8) number of full-time and part-time students; (9) types of financial assistance available; and (10) the number of degrees awarded by type in 2000. All grade-point averages (GPAs), test scores, and degree requirements are minimums, unless stated otherwise. The Graduate Record Examination (GRE), Miller Analogies Test (MAT), National Teacher's Examination NTE), and other standardized tests are referred to by their acronyms. The Test of English as a Foreign Language (TOEFL) appears in many of the Admission Requirements, and in most cases this test is required only for international students. Although some entries explicitly state application fees, most do not. Prospective students should assume that most institutions require a completed application, transcripts of all previous collegiate work, and a nonrefundable application fee.

Directors of advanced professional programs for instructional technology or media specialists should find this degree program information useful as a means of comparing their own offerings and requirements with those of institutions offering comparable programs. This listing, along with the Classified List, should also assist individuals in locating institutions that best suit their interests and requirements. In addition, a comparison of degree programs across several years may help scholars with historical interests trace trends and issues in the field over time.

This year the section editor used a new method for contacting graduate program representatives. Brooke Price, the section editor for 2001, helped develop a new database mechanism through which we receive updates. The 2002 editing team benefited from her contribution to the research and development of this new information retrieval process. Dr. Michael Orey created the Web form used for retrieving updated information for the 2002 edition. Dr. Orey designed the Web form so that program respondents could edit only their own entry. His work made the updating process more efficient while maintaining the integrity of the information gathered.

Information in this section can be considered current as of late 2001 for most programs. Information for this section was obtained by e-mail directing each organization to an individual Web form through which the updated information could be submitted electronically. Although the section editor made every effort to contact and follow up with program representatives, it is up to the program representatives to respond to the annual request for

289

an update. The editing team would like to thank those respondents who helped ensure the currency and accuracy of this section by responding to the request for an update. Programs from which we did not receive updated information are marked by an asterisk, and their entries contain information from the 2001 edition.

Additional information on the programs listed, including admission procedure instructions, may be obtained by contacting individual program coordinators. General or graduate catalogs and specific program information usually are furnished for a minimal charge. In addition, most graduate programs now have e-mail contact addresses and Web sites that provide a wealth of descriptive information.

Again, we are greatly indebted to those individuals who responded to our requests for information. Although the editors expended considerable effort to ensure currency and completeness of the listings, there may be institutions within the United States that now have programs of which we are unaware. Readers are encouraged to furnish new information to the publisher who, in turn, will contact the program for inclusion in the next edition of *EMTY*.

Leslie Cole

Graduate Programs in Instructional Technology [IT]

Computer Applications

California State University-San Bernardino [M.A.]

State University of New York at Stony Brook [Master's: Technological Systems Management/Educational Computing]

Temple University. Instructional and Learning Technology (ILT)/ Educational Psychology Program [Ed.M., Ph.D.]

University of Iowa [M.A.]

Valdosta State University [M.Ed. in IT/Technology Applications]

Computer Education

Appalachian State University [M.A.: Educational Media and Technology/ Computers]

Arizona State University, Dept. of Educational Media and Computers [M.A., Ph.D.: Educational Media and Computers]

Arkansas Tech University [Master's]

Buffalo State College [M.S.: Education/ Educational Computing]

California State University-Dominguez Hills [M.A., Certificate: Computer-Based Education]

California State University-Los Angeles [M.A. in Education/Computer Education]

California State University-San Bernardino [Advanced Certificate Program: Educational Computing]

Central Connecticut State University [M.S.: Educational Technology/Computer Technologies]

Concordia University [M.A.: Computer Science Education]

East Carolina University [M.A.: Education/IT Computers]

Eastern Washington University [M.Ed.: Computer Education]

Emporia State University. School of Library and Information Management

Fairfield University [M.A.: Media/Educational Technology with Computers in Education]

Florida Institute of Technology [Master's, Ph.D.: Computer Education]

Fontbonne College [M.S.]

George Mason University [M.Ed.: Special Education Technology, Computer Science Educator]

Iowa State University [M.S., M.Ed., Ph.D.: Curriculum and IT/Instructional Computing]

Jacksonville University [Master's: Computer Education]

Kansas State University [M.S. in Secondary Education/Educational Computing; Ed.D., Ph.D.: Curriculum and Instruction/ Educational Computing]

Kent State University [M.A., M.Ed.: Instructional Computing]

Minot State University [M.Ed., M.S.: Math and Computer Science]

New York Institute of Technology [Specialist Certificate: Computers in Education]

North Carolina State University [M.S., M.Ed.: IT-Computers]

Northern Illinois University [M.S.Ed., Ed.D.: IT/Educational Computing]

Northwest Missouri State University [M.S.: School Computer Studies; M.S.Ed.: Educational Uses of Computers]

Nova Southeastern University [M.S., Ed.S.: Computer Science Education]

Ohio University [M.Ed.: Computer Education and Technology]

Pace University [M.S.E.: Curriculum and Instruction/Computers]

San Diego State University [Master's in Educational Technology/Computers in Education]

San Francisco State University [Master's: Instructional Computing]

San Jose State University [Master's: Computers and Interactive Technologies]

State University of New York at Stony Brook [Master's: Technological Systems Management/Educational Computing]

State University College of Arts and Sciences at Potsdam [M.S.Ed.: IT and Media Management/Educational Computing]

Syracuse University [M.S., Ed.D., Ph.D., Advanced Certificate: Media Production]

Texas A&M University-Commerce [Master's: Learning Technology and Information Systems/Educational Micro Computing]

Texas Tech University [M.Ed.: IT/Educational Computing]

University of Georgia [M.Ed., Ed.S.: Computer-Based Education]

University of Illinois at Urbana-Champaign [M.A., M.S., Ed.M.: Educational Computing; Ph.D.: Education Psychology/ Educational Computing]

University of Memphis. Instruction and Curriculum Leadership/Instructional Design & Technology [M.S., Ed.D]

University of North Texas [M.S.: Computer Education and Instructional Systems]

The University of Oklahoma [Master's: Computer Applications]

University of Toledo [Master's, Ed.S., D.Ed.: Instructional Computing]

University of Washington [Master's, Ed.D., Ph.D.]

Virginia Polytechnic Institute and State University [M.A., Ed.D., Ph.D.: IT]

Wright State University [M.Ed.: Computer Education; M.A.: Computer Education]

Distance Education

Emporia State University. School of Library and Information Management [Ph.D.: Library and Information Management]

Fairfield University [M.A.: Media/Educational Technology with Satellite Communications]

Iowa State University [M.S., M.Ed., Ph.D.: Curriculum and IT]

New York Institute of Technology [Specialist certificate]

Nova Southeastern University [M.S., Ed.D.: IT]

San Jose State University [Master's: Telecommunications & online courses via Internet]

Texas A&M University [Ph.D.: EDCI]

Texas Tech University [M.Ed.: IT]

University of Missouri-Columbia. College of Education [Masters: Technology in Schools, Networked Learning Systems, or Training and Development]

University of Northern Colorado [Ph.D.: Educational Technology]

Western Illinois University [Master's]

Educational Leadership

Auburn University [Ed.D.]

Barry University [Ph.D.: Educational Technology Leadership]

George Washington University [M.A.: Education and Human Development/ Educational Technology Leadership]

United States International University [Master's, Ed.D.: Technology Leadership for Learning]

University of Colorado at Denver [Ph.D.: Educational Leadership and Innovation/ Curriculum, Learning, and Technology]

Valdosta State University [M.Ed., Ed.S.: IT/Technology Leadership]

Human Performance

Boise State University [M.S.: IT and Performance Technology]

Governors State University [M.A.: Communication with Human Performance and Technology]

Temple University. Instructional and Learning Technology (ILT)/ Educational Psychology Program [Ed.M., Ph.D.]

University of Southern California [Ed.D.: Human Performance Technology]

University of Toledo [Master's, Ed.S., Ed.D.: Human Resources Development]

Information Studies

Drexel University [M.S., M.S.I.S.]

Emporia State University [Ph.D.: Library and Information Management]

Rutgers [M.L.S.: Information Retrieval; Ph.D.: Communication (Information Systems)]

Simmons College [M.S.: Information Science/Systems]

Southern Connecticut State University [Sixth Year Professional Diploma: Library-Information Studies/IT]

St. Cloud State University [Master's, Ed.S.: Information Technologies]

Texas A&M-Commerce [Master's: Learning Technology and Information Systems/ Library and Information Science]

University of Alabama [Ph.D.]

University of Arizona [M.A.: Information Resources and Library Science]

University of Central Arkansas [M.S.: Information Science/Media Information Studies]

University of Florida. School of Teaching and Learning. [M.S., Ed.S., Ed.D., Ph.D.]

University of Maryland [Doctorate: Library and Information Services]

University of Missouri-Columbia [Ph.D.: Information and Learning Technologies]

The University of Oklahoma [Dual Master's: Educational Technology and Library and Information Systems]

The University of Rhode Island [M.L.I.S.]

University of Washington [Master's, Ed.D., Ph.D.]

Western Oregon State College [MS: Information Technology]

Innovation

Pennsylvania State University [M.Ed., M.S., Ed.D., Ph.D.: Instructional Systems/Emerging Technologies]

University of Colorado at Denver [Ph.D.: Educational Leadership and Innovation]

Walden University [M.S., Ph.D.: Educational Change and Technology Innovation]

Instructional Design and Development

Auburn University [M.Ed., M.S.]

Bloomsburg University [M.S.: IT]

Brigham Young University [M.S., Ph.D.]

Clarion University of Pennsylvania [M.S.: Communication/Training and Development]

Fairfield University [Certificate of Advanced Studies: Media/Educational Technology: Instructional Development]

George Mason University [M.Ed.: IT/Instructional Design and Development]

Governors State University [M.A.: Communication with Human Performance and Training/Instructional Design]

Indiana University [Ph.D., Ed.D.: Instructional Analysis, Design, and Development]

Iowa State University [M.S., M.Ed., Ph.D.: Curriculum and IT/Instruction Design]

Ithaca College [M.S.: Corporate Communications]

Lehigh University [Master's]

Michigan State University [M.A.: Educational Technology and Instructional Design]

North Carolina Central University [M.S.: Instructional Development/Design]

Northern Illinois University [M.S.Ed., Ed.D.: IT/Instructional Design]

Pennsylvania State University [M.Ed., M.S., D.Ed., Ph.D.: Instructional Systems/ Systems Design]

Purdue University [Master's, Specialist, Ph.D.: Instructional Development]

San Francisco State University [Master's Training and Designing Development]

San Jose State University [M.S.: Instructional Design and Development]

Southern Illinois University at Carbondale [M.S.: Education/Instructional Design]

State University of New York at Albany [M.Ed., Ph.D.: Curriculum and Instruction/Instructional Design and Technology]

State University of New York at Stony Brook [Master's: Technological Systems Management/Educational Computing]

Syracuse University [M.S., Ed.D., Ph.D., Advanced Certificate: Instructional Design; Educational Evaluation; Instructional Development]

Temple University. Instructional and Learning Technology (ILT)/ Educational Psychology Program [Ed.M., Ph.D.]

Towson State University [M.S.: Instructional Development]

University of Cincinnati [M.A., Ed.D.: Curriculum and Instruction/Instructional Design and Technology]

University of Colorado at Denver [Master's, Ph.D.: Instructional Design]

University of Florida. School of Teaching and Learning. [M.S., Ed.S., Ed.D., Ph.D.]

University of Houston at Clear Lake [Instructional Design]

University of Illinois at Urbana-Champaign [M.A., M.S., Ed.M.; Ph.D. in Educational Psychology/Instructional Design]

University of Iowa [M.A., Ph.D.: Training and Human Resources Development]

University of Massachusetts-Boston [M.Ed.]

University of Memphis. Instruction and Curriculum Leadership/Instructional Design & Technology [M. S., Ed.D]

University of Missouri-Columbia [Master's, Ed.S., Ph.D.]

University of Northern Colorado [Ph.D. In Educational Technology/Instructional Development and Design]

The University of Oklahoma [Master's]

University of Toledo [Master's, Specialist, doctorate: Instructional Development]

University of Washington [Master's, Ed.D., Ph.D.]

Utah State University [M.S., Ed.S.: Instructional Development]

Virginia Polytechnic Institute and State University [Master's, Ed.D., Ph.D.: IT]

Instructional Technology [IT]

Appalachian State University [M.A.: Educational Media and Technology]

Arizona State University, Learning and IT Dept. [M.Ed., Ph.D.]

Azusa Pacific University [M.Ed.]

Barry University [M.S., Ed.S.: Educational Technology]

Bloomsburg University [M.S.: IT]

Boise State University [M.S.]

Boston University [Ed.M., Certificate of Advanced Graduate Study: Educational Media & Technology; Ed.D.: Curriculum and Teaching/Educational Media and Technology]

California State University-Los Angeles [M.A.: Education/IT]

California State University-San Bernardino [Advanced Certificate in Educational Technology]

Central Connecticut State University [M.S.:
Educational Technology]
Clarke College [M.A.: Technology and
Education]
East Carolina University [M.A.: Education/
IT Computers]
East Tennessee State [M.Ed.]
Eastern Michigan University [M.A.:
Educational Psychology/Educational
Technology]
Edgewood College [M.A.: Education/IT]
Fairfield University [M.A., Certificate of
Advanced Study: Media/Educational
Technology]
Fitchburg State College [M.S.: Communications
Media/IT]
Florida Institute of Technology [Master's,
Ph.D.]
George Mason University [M.Ed., Ph.D.]
George Washington University [M.A.: Educa-
tion and Human Development/
Educational Technology Leadership]
Georgia Southern University [M.Ed., Ed.S.: IT;
Ed.D.: Curriculum Studies/IT]
Georgia State University [M.S., Ph.D.]
Harvard University [M.Ed.: Technology in
Education]
Indiana State University [Master's, Ed.S.]
Indiana University [M.S., Ed.S., Ed.D., Ph.D.]
Iowa State University [M.S., M.Ed., Ph.D.:
Curriculum and IT]
Jacksonville University [Master's: Educational
Technology and Integrated Learning]
Johns Hopkins University [M.S. in Educational
Technology for Educators]
Kent State University [M.Ed., M.A; Ph.D.:
Educational Psychology/IT]
Lehigh University [Master's; Ed.D.: Educa-
tional Technology]
Lesley College [M.Ed., Certificate of Advanced
Graduate Study: Technology Education;
Ph.D.: Education/Technology Education]
Mankato State University [M.S.: Educational
Technology]
Michigan State University [M.A.: Educational
Technology]
Montclair State College [certification]
New York Institute of Technology [Master's]
New York University [M.A., Certificate of
Advanced Study in Education, Ed.D.,
Ph.D.]
North Carolina Central University [M.A.:
Educational Technology]
North Carolina State University [M.Ed., M.S.:
IT—Computers; Ph.D.: Curriculum and
Instruction/IT]
Northern Illinois University [M.S.Ed., Ed.D.]
Nova Southeastern University [Ed.S., M.S.: Ed-
ucational Technology; M.S., Ed.D.: IT]

Ohio University [M.Ed.: Computer Education
and Technology]
Purdue University [Master's, Specialist, Ph.D.:
Educational Technology]
Radford University [M.S.: Education/
Educational Media/Technology]
Rosemont College [M.Ed.: Technology in
Education; Certificate in Professional
Study in Technology in Education]
San Diego State University [Master's: Educa-
tional Technology]
Southern Connecticut State University [M.S.]
Southern Illinois University at Carbondale
[M.S.: Education; Ph.D.: Education/IT]
State University College of Arts and Sciences at
Potsdam [M.S.: Education/IT]
State University of New York at Albany
[M.Ed., Ph.D.: Curriculum and Instruc-
tion/Instructional Theory, Design, and
Technology]
State University of West Georgia [M.Ed., Ed.S.]
Temple University. Instructional and Learning
Technology (ILT)/ Educational Psychol-
ogy Program [Ed.M., Ph.D.]
Texas A&M University [M.Ed.: Educational
Technology; Ph.D.: EDCI/Educational
Technology; Ph.D.: Educational
Psychology Foundations/Learning and
Technology]
Texas Tech University [M.Ed.; Ed.D.]
Texas A&M University-Commerce [Master's:
Learning Technology and Information
Systems/Educational Media and Tech-
nology]
United States International University [Ed.D.:
Technology and Learning]
University of Central Florida [M.A.: IT/
Instructional Systems, IT/Educational
Media; Doctorate: Curriculum and
Instruction/IT]
University of Cincinnati [M.A., Ed.D.:
Curriculum and Instruction/Instructional
Design and Technology]
University of Colorado at Denver [Master's,
Ph.D.: Learning Technologies]
University of Connecticut [Master's, Ph.D.:
Educational Technology]
University of Florida. School of Teaching and
Learning. [M.S., Ed.S., Ed.D., Ph.D.]
University of Georgia [M.Ed., Ed.S., Ph.D.]
University of Hawaii-Manoa [M.Ed.: Educa-
tional Technology]
University of Houston. Department of Curricu-
lum and Instruction. [M.Ed.]
University of Louisville [M.Ed.: Occupational
Education/IT]
University of Maryland [Ph.D.: Library Science
and Educational Technology/Instruc-
tional Communication]

University of Massachusetts-Lowell [M.Ed., Ed.D., Certificate of Advanced Graduate Study: Educational Technology]

University of Michigan [Master's, Ph.D.: IT]

University of Missouri-Columbia [Master's, Ed.S., Ph.D.]

University of Nebraska at Kearney [M.S.]

University of Nevada [M.S., Ph.D.]

University of Northern Colorado [M.A., Ph.D.: Educational Technology]

University of Northern Iowa [M.A.: Educational Technology]

The University of Oklahoma [Master's: Educational Technology Generalist; Educational Technology; Teaching with Technology; dual Master's: Educational Technology and Library and Information Systems; Doctorate: Instructional Psychology and Technology]

University of South Alabama [M.S., Ph.D.]

University of South Carolina [Master's]

University of Southern California [M.A., Ed.D., Ph.D.]

University of Tennessee-Knoxville [M.S.: Education, Ed.S., Ed.D., Ph.D.]

The University of Texas [Master's, Ph.D.]

University of Toledo [Master's, Specialist, Doctorate]

University of Virginia [M.Ed., Ed.S., Ed.D., Ph.D.]

University of Washington [Master's, Ed.D., Ph.D.]

University of Wisconsin-Madison [M.S., Ph.D.]

Universiti Sains Malaysia. Centre for Instructional Technology and Multimedia Centre for Instructional Tech and Multimedia [M.Ed. Instructional Technology, Ph.D. Instructional Technology]

Utah State University [M.S., Ed.S., Ph.D.]

Virginia Polytechnic Institute and State University [M.A., Ed.D., Ph.D.: IT]

Virginia State University [M.S., M.Ed.: Educational Technology]

Wayne State University [Master's, Ed.D., Ph.D., Ed.S.]

Webster University [Master's]

Western Illinois University [Master's]

Western Washington University [M.Ed.: IT in Adult Education; Elementary Education; IT in Secondary Education]

Wright State University [Specialist: Curriculum and Instruction/Educational Technology; Higher Education/Educational Technology]

Integration

Bloomsburg University [M.S.: IT]

George Mason University [M.Ed.: IT/Integration of Technology in Schools]

Jacksonville University [Master's: Educational Technology and Integrated Learning]

University of Northern Colorado [Ph.D.: Educational Technology/Technology Integration]

Management

Bloomsburg University [M.S.: IT]

Central Connecticut State University [M.S.: Educational Technology/Media Management]

Drexel University [M.S., M.S.I.S.]

Emporia State University [Ph.D.: Library and Information Management]

Fairfield University [Certificate of Advanced Studies: Media/Educational Technology with Media Management]

Fitchburg State College [M.S.: Communications Media/Management]

Indiana University [Ed.D., Ph.D.: Implementation and Management]

Minot State University [M.S.: Management]

Northern Illinois University [M.S.Ed., Ed.D.: IT/Media Administration]

Rutgers [M.L.S.: Management and Policy Issues]

Simmons College [M.L.S.: History (Archives Management); Doctor of Arts: Administration; Media Management]

State University College of Arts and Science [M.S.: Education/IT and Media Management]

State University of New York at Stony Brook [Master's: Technological Systems Management]

Syracuse University [M.S., Ed.D., Ph.D., Advanced Certificate]

Temple University. Instructional and Learning Technology (ILT)/ Educational Psychology Program [Ed.M., Ph.D.]

University of Tennessee-Knoxville [Certification: Instructional Media Supervisor]

Virginia Polytechnic Institute and State University [M.A., Ed.D., Ph.D.: IT]

Wright State University [M.Ed.: Media Supervisor; Computer Coord.]

Media

Appalachian State University [M.A.: Educational Media and Technology/Media Management]

Arizona State University, Dept. of Educational Media and Computers [M.A., Ph.D.: Educational Media and Computers]

Boston University [Ed.M., Certificate of Advanced Graduate Study: Educational Media and Technology; Ed.D.: Curriculum and Teaching/Educational Media and Technology]

Central Connecticut State University [M.S.: Educational Technology/Materials Production]
Fitchburg State College [M.S.: Communications Media]
Indiana State University [Ph.D.: Curriculum and Instruction/Media Technology]
Indiana University [Ed.D., Ph.D.: Instructional Development and Production]
Jacksonville State University [M.S.: Education/Instructional Media]
Montclair State College [certification]
Radford University [M.S.: Education/ Educational Media/Technology]
San Jose State University [Master's.: Media Design and Development/Media Services Management]
Simmons College [Master's: Media Management]
St. Cloud State University [Master's, Ed.S.: Educational Media]
State University College of Arts and Science at Potsdam [M.S.: Education/IT and Media Management]
Syracuse University [M.S., Ed.D., Ph.D., Advanced Certificate: Media Production]
Texas A&M University-Commerce [Master's: Learning Technology and Information Systems/Educational Media and Technology]
University of Central Florida [M.Ed.: IT/ Educational Media]
University of Florida. School of Teaching and Learning. [M.S., Ed.S., Ed.D., Ph.D.]
University of Iowa [M.A.: Media Design and Production]
University of Memphis. Instruction and Curriculum Leadership/Instructional Design & Technology [M. S. and Ed. D]
University of Nebraska at Kearney [M.S., Ed.S.: Educational Media]
University of Nebraska-Omaha [M.S.: Education/Educational Media; M.A.: Education/Educational Media]
University of South Alabama [M.A., Ed.S.]
University of Tennessee-Knoxville [Ph.D.: Instructional Media and Technology; Ed.D.: Curriculum and Instruction/ Instructional Media and Technology]
University of Virginia [M.Ed., Ed.S., Ed.D., Ph.D.: Media Production]
Virginia Polytechnic Institute and State University [M.A., Ed.D., Ph.D.: IT]
Wright State University [M.Ed.: Educational Media; Media Supervision; M.A.: Educational Media]

Multimedia

Bloomsburg University [M.S.: IT]
Brigham Young University [M.S.: Multimedia Production]
Fairfield University [M.A.: Media/Educational Technology with Multimedia]
Ithaca College [M.S.: Corporate Communications]
Jacksonville University [Master's: Educational Technology and Integration Learning]
Johns Hopkins University [Graduate Certificate]
Lehigh University [Master's]
New York Institute of Technology [Specialist Certificate]
San Francisco State University [Master's: Instructional Multimedia Design]
State University of New York at Stony Brook [Master's: Technological Systems Management/Educational Computing]
Syracuse University [M.S., Ed.D., Ph.D., Advanced Certificate: Media Production]
Temple University. Instructional and Learning Technology (ILT)/ Educational Psychology Program [Ed.M., Ph.D.]
Texas A&M University [M.Ed.: Educational Technology]
University of Northern Colorado [Ph.D.: Educational Technology/Interactive Technology]
University of Virginia [M.Ed., Ed.S., Ed.D., Ph.D.: Interactive Multimedia]
University of Washington [Master's, Ed.D., Ph.D.]
University of Memphis. Instruction and Curriculum Leadership/Instructional Design & Technology [M. S. and Ed. D]
Utah State University [M.S., Ed.S.]
Wayne State University [Master's: Interactive Technologies]
Western Illinois University [Master's: Interactive Technologies]

Research

Brigham Young University [M.S., Ph.D.: Research and Evaluation]
Drexel University [M.S., M.S.I.S.]
Iowa State University [Ph.D.: Educational/Technology Research]
Syracuse University [M.S., Ed.D., Ph.D., Advanced Certificate: Educational Research and Theory]
University of Washington [Master's, Ed.D., Ph.D.]

School Library Media

Alabama State University [Master's, Ed.S., Ph.D.]
Arkansas Tech University [Master's]
Auburn University [M.Ed., Ed.S.]
Bloomsburg University [M.S.]
Boston University [Massachusetts certification]
Bridgewater State College [M.Ed.]
Central Connecticut State University [M.S.: Educational Technology/Librarianship]
Chicago State University [Master's]
East Carolina University [M.L.S., Certificate of Advanced Study]
East Tennessee State [M.Ed.: Instructional Media]
Emporia State University [Ph.D.: Library and Information Management; M.L.S.; School Library certification]
Kent State University
Louisiana State University [M.L.I.S., C.L.I.S. (post-Master's certificate), Louisiana School Library certification]
Mankato State University [M.S.]
Northern Illinois University [M.S.Ed. Instructional Technology with Illinois state certification]
Nova Southeastern University [Ed.S, M.S.: Educational Media]
Radford University [M.S.: Education/ Educational Media; licensure]
Rutgers [M.L.S., Ed.S.]
Simmons College [M.L.S.: Education]
Southern Illinois University at Edwardsville [M.S. in Education: Library/Media]
Southwestern Oklahoma State University [M.Ed.: Library/Media Education]
St. Cloud State University [Master's, Ed.S.]
St. John's University [M.L.S.]
State University of West Georgia [M.Ed., Ed.S.: Media]
Towson State University [M.S.]
University of Alabama [Master's, Ed.S.]
University of Central Arkansas [M.S.]
University of Florida. School of Teaching and Learning. [M.S., Ed.S., Ed.D., Ph.D.]
University of Georgia [M.Ed., Ed.S]
University of Maryland [M.L.S.]
University of Montana [Master's, Ed.S.]
University of North Carolina [M.S.]
University of Northern Colorado [M.A.: Educational Media]
University of South Florida [Master's]
University of Toledo
University of Wisconsin-La Crosse [M.S.: Professional Development/Initial Instructional Library Specialist; Instructional Library Media Specialist]
Utah State University [M.S., Ed.S.]

Valdosta State University [M.Ed., Ed.S.: Instructional Technology/Library/Media]
Webster University
Western Maryland College [M.S.]
William Paterson College [M.Ed., Ed.S., Associate]

Special Education

George Mason University [M.Ed.: IT/Assistive/ Special Education Technology; M.Ed.: Special Education Technology; Ph.D.: Special Education Technology]
Johns Hopkins University [M.S. in Special Education/Technology in Special Education]
Minot State University [M.S.: Early Childhood Special Education; Severe Multiple Handicaps; Communication Disorders]
Western Washington University [M.Ed.: IT in Special Education]

Systems

Bloomsburg University [M.S.: IT]
Drexel University [M.S., M.S.I.S.]
Florida State University [M.S., Ed.S., Ph.D.: Instructional Systems]
Pennsylvania State University [M.Ed., M.S., D.Ed., Ph.D.: Instructional Systems]
Simmons College [Master's: Information Science/Systems]
Southern Illinois University at Edwardsville [M.S.: Education/Instructional Systems Design]
State University of New York at Stony Brook [Master's: Technological Systems Management]
Texas A&M University-Commerce [Master's: Learning Technology and Information Systems]
University of Central Florida [M.A.: IT/ Instructional Systems]
University of Maryland, Baltimore County [Master's: School Instructional Systems]
University of North Texas [M.S.: Computer Education and Instructional Systems]
The University of Oklahoma [Dual Master's: Educational Technology and Library and Information Systems]

Technology Design

Governors State University [M.A.: Design Logistics]
Kansas State University [Ed.D., Ph.D.: Curriculum and Instruction/Educational Computing, Design, and Telecommunications]
United States International University [Master's, Ed.D.: Designing Technology for Learning]

University of Colorado at Denver [Master's, Ph.D.: Design of Learning Technologies]

Telecommunications

Appalachian State University [M.A.: Educational Media and Technology/Telecommunications]

Johns Hopkins University [Graduate Certificate]

Kansas State University [Ed.D., Ph.D.: Curriculum and Instruction/Educational Computing, Design, and Telecommunications]

San Jose State University [Telecommunications and Distance Learning]

Western Illinois University [Masters: Telecommunications]

Training

Clarion University of Pennsylvania [M.S.: Communication/Training and Development]

Pennsylvania State University [M.Ed., M.S., D.Ed., Ph.D.: Instructional Systems/Corporate Training]

St. Cloud State University [Master's, Ed.S.: Human Resources Development/Training]

Syracuse University [M.S., Ed.D., Ph.D., Advanced Certificate]

University of Maryland, Baltimore County [Master's: Training in Business and Industry]

University of Northern Iowa [M.A.: Communications and Training Technology]

Wayne State University [Master's: Business and Human Services Training]

Video Production

California State University-San Bernardino [M.A.]

Fairfield University [Certificate of Advanced Study: Media/Educational Technology with TV Production]

ALPHABETICAL LIST

Institutions in this section are listed alphabetically by state.

ALABAMA

Alabama State University. Department of Instructional Support Programs. P.O. Box 271, Montgomery, AL 36101-0271. (334)229-5138. Fax (334)229-4961. E-mail dvertrees@asunet .alasu.edu. Web site http://www.alasu.edu. Dr. Agnes Bellel, Coord. Instructional Technology and Media. *Specializations:* School media specialist preparation (K–12) only; Master's and Specialist degrees. *Admission Requirements:* Master's: undergraduate degree with teacher certification, two years classroom experience. Specialist: Master's degree in library/media education. *Degree Requirements:* Master's: 33 semester hours with 300 clock-hour internship. Specialist: 36 semester hours in 600-level courses. *Faculty:* 3 full-time. *Students:* Master's, 50 part-time; Specialist, 8 part-time. *Financial Assistance:* student loans and scholarships. *Degrees awarded 2000:* 15 M.Ed.; 1 Ed.S.

*Auburn University. Educational Foundations, Leadership, and Technology. 3402 Haley Center, Auburn, AL 36849-5216. (334)844-4291. Fax (334)844-4292. E-mail bannosh@mail.auburn.edu. Susan H. Bannon, Coord., Educational Media and Technology. *Specializations:* M.Ed. (non-thesis) and Ed.S. for Library Media certification; M.Ed. (non-thesis) for instructional design specialists who want to work in business, industry, and the military. Ed.D. in Educational Leadership with emphasis on curriculum and new instructional technologies. *Features:* All programs emphasize interactive technologies and computers. *Admission Requirements:* all programs: recent GRE test scores, three letters of recommendation, bachelor's degree from accredited institution, teacher certification (for library media program only). *Degree Requirements:* Library Media Master's: 52 qtr. hours. Instructional Design: 48 qtr. hours. Specialist: 48 qtr. hours. Ed.D.: 120 qtr. hours beyond B.S. degree. *Faculty:* 3 full-time. *Students:* 2 full-time, 15 part-time. *Financial Assistance:* graduate assistantships.

*Jacksonville State University. Instructional Media Division. Jacksonville, AL 36265. (256)782-5011. E-mail mmerrill@jsucc.jsu.edu. Martha Merrill, Coord., Dept. of Educational Resources. *Specializations:* M.S. in Education with emphasis on Library Media. *Admission Requirements:* Bachelor's degree in Education. *Degree Requirements:* 36–39 semester hours, including 24 in library media. *Faculty:* 2 full-time. *Students:* 20 full- and part-time.

*University of Alabama. School of Library and Information Studies. Box 870252, Tuscaloosa, AL 35487-0252. (205)348-4610. Fax (205)348-3746. E-mail GCOLEMAN@UA1VM.UA.EDU. Web site http://www.slism.slis.ua.edu. J. Gordon Coleman, Jr., Chair; Marion Paris, Ph.D., contact person. *Specializations:* M.L.I.S., Ed.S., and Ph.D. degrees in a varied program including school, public, academic, and special libraries. Ph.D. specializations in Historical Studies, Information Studies, Management, and Youth Studies; considerable flexibility in creating individual programs of study. *Admission Requirements:* M.L.I.S., Ed.S.: 3.0 GPA; 50 MAT or 1500 GRE. Doctoral: 3.0 GPA; 60 MAT or 1650 GRE. *Degree Requirements:* Master's: 36 semester hours; Specialist: 33 semester hours; Doctoral: 48 semester hours plus 24 hours dissertation research. *Faculty:* 10 full-time. *Students:* Master's, 55 full-time, 20 part-time; Specialist, 2 full-time; doctoral, 6 full-time, 6 part-time. *Financial Assistance:* assistantships, grants, student loans, scholarships, work assistance, campus work.

University of South Alabama. Department of Behavioral Studies and Educational Technology, College of Education University Commons. 3700, Mobile, AL 36688. (334)380-2861. Fax (334)380-2713. E-mail gdavidso@usamail.usouthal.edu or daughen@usamial.usouthal.edu. Web site www.coe.usouthal.edu/bset/default.htm. Gayle Davidson-Shivers, IDD Program Coor.; Richard Daughenbaugh, Ed Media Program Coor. *Specializations:* M.S. in Instructional

Design and Development(IDD), Ph.D. in IDD., M.Ed. in Educational Media (Ed Media). An online master's degree in either ED Media or IDD is available for qualified students. For information about online master's degree programs visit http://usaonline.southalabama.edu. *Features:* The IDD master's and doctoral programs emphasize an extensive education and training in the instructional design process, human performance technology and multi-media- and online-based training. The IDD doctoral program has an additional emphasis in research design and statistical analyses. The Ed Media master's program prepares students in planning, designing, and administering library/media centers at most levels of education, including higher education. *Admission Requirements:* For the ED-Media & IDD Master's: undergraduate degree in appropriate academic field from an accredited university or college; admission to Graduate School; satisfactory score on the MAT or GRE. The IDD master's program also requires applicants take GRE writing exam. For IDD Ph.D.: Master's degree, all undergraduate and graduate transcripts, three letters of recommendations, written statement of the applicants purpose(s) for pursuing Ph.D. in IDD, satisfactory score on GRE. *Degree Requirements:* Ed Media masters: satisfactorily complete program requirements (minimum 33 semester hours), 3.0 or better GPA, satisfactory score on comprehensive exam. IDD masters: satisfactorily complete program requirements (minimum 39 semester hours), 3.0 or better GPA, satisfactory comprehensive exam. Ph.D.: satisfactory complete program requirements (minimum 82 semester hours of approved graduate coures), one-year residency, satisfactory score on examinations (research and statistical, ed media and computing portfolio, and comprehensive), approved dissertation completed. Any additional requirements will be determined by students doctoral advisory committee. *Faculty:* 18 full-time in department; 8 part-time faculty. *Students:* IDD Master's, 40; Ph.D., 76; Ed Media Masters 30. *Financial Assistance:* 10 graduate assistantships. *Degrees awarded 2000:* 8 Ed Media master's; 6 IDD master's; 5 IDD doctoral.

ARIZONA

Arizona State University, Educational Technology program. Division of Psychology in Education. Box 870611, Tempe, AZ 85287-0611. (480)965-3384. Fax (480)965-0300. E-mail dpe@asu.edu. Web site http://seamonkey.ed.asu.edu/~gail/programs/lnt.htm. James D. Klein, Professor; Nancy Archer, Admissions Secretary. *Specializations:* The Educational Technology program at Arizona State University offers an M.Ed. degree and a Ph.D. degree, which focus on the design, development, and evaluation of instructional systems and educational technology applications to support learning. *Features:* The program offers courses in a variety of areas, such as instructional design technology, media development, technology integration, and distance education. The doctoral program emphasizes research using educational technology in applied settings. *Admission Requirements:* Requirements for admission to the M.Ed. program include a 4-year undergraduate GPA of 3.0 or above and a score of either 500 or above on verbal section of the GRE or 50 or above on the MAT. A score of 550 or above on the TOEFL is also required for students who do not speak English as their first language. Requirements for admission to the Ph.D. program include a 4-year undergraduate GPA of 3.20 or above and a combined score of 1800 or above on the verbal, quantitative, and analytic sections of the GRE. A score of 600 or above on the TOEFL is also required for students who do not speak English as their first language. *Degree Requirements:* The M.Ed. degree requires completion of a minimum of 30 credit hours including 18 credit hours of required course work and a minimum of 12 credit hours of electives. M.Ed. students also must complete an internship and a comprehensive examination. The Ph.D. degree requires a minimum of 84 semester hours beyond the bachelor's degree. At least 54 of these hours must be taken at ASU after admission to the program. Ph.D. students must fulfill a residence requirement and are required to be continuously enrolled in the program. Students also take a comprehensive examination and must satisfy a publication requirement prior to beginning work on their dissertation. *Faculty:* The Educational Technology program at ASU has 7 full-time faculty. *Students:* 60 M.Ed. and 30 Ph.D. students are enrolled in the program. *Financial Assistance:* Financial assistance, such as scholarships, fellowships, graduate assistantships, loans, and professional work opportunities, are available to qualified applicants. *Degrees awarded 2000:* 15 M.Ed.; 3 Ph.D.

*Arizona State University, Department of Educational Media and Computers. Box 870111, Tempe, AZ 85287-0111. (602)965-7192. Fax (602)965-7193. E-mail bitter@asu.edu. Dr. Gary G. Bitter, Coord. *Specializations:* M.A. and Ph.D. in Educational Media and Computers. *Features:* A three semester-hour course in Instructional Media Design is offered via CD-ROM or World Wide Web. *Admission Requirements:* M.A.: Bachelor's degree, 550 TOEFL, 500 GRE, 45 MAT. *Degree Requirements:* M.A.: 36 semester hours (24 hours in educational media and computers, 9 hours education, 3 hours outside education); internship; comprehensive exam; practicum; thesis not required. Ph.D.: 93 semester hours (24 hours in educational media and computers, 57 hours in education, 12 hours outside education); thesis; internship; practicum. *Faculty:* 6 full-time. *Financial Assistance:* Assistantships, grants, student loans, and scholarships.

*University of Arizona. School of Information Resources and Library Science. 1515 E. First St., Tucson, AZ 85719. (520)621-3565. Fax (520)621-3279. sirls@u.arizona.edu. Web site http://www.sir.arizona.edu. *Specializations:* The School of Information Resources and Library Science offers courses focusing on the study of information and its impact as a social phenomenon. *Features:* The School offers a virtual education program via the Internet. Between two and three courses are offered per semester. *Admission Requirements:* Very competitive for both degrees. Minimum criteria include: undergraduate GPA of 3.0 or better; competitive GRE scores; two letters of recommendation reflecting the writer's opinion of the applicant's potential as a graduate student; a resume of work and educational experience; written statement of intent. The School receives a large number of applications and accepts the best qualified students. Admission to the doctoral program may require a personal interview and a faculty member must indicate willingness to work with the student. *Degree Requirements:* M.A.: a minimum of 36 units of graduate credit. Students may elect the thesis option replacing 6 units of course work. Ph.D.: at least 48 hours of course work in the major, a substantial number of hours in a minor subject supporting the major, dissertation. The University has a 12-unit residency requirement which may be completed in the summer or in a regular semester. More detailed descriptions of the program are available at the School's Web site. *Faculty:* 5 full-time. *Students:* 220 total; M.A.: 51 full-time; Ph.D.: 12 full-time.

ARKANSAS

Arkansas Tech University. Curriculum and Instruction. 308 Crabaugh, Russellville, AR 72801-2222. (501)968-0434. Fax (501)964-0811. E-mail Connie.Zimmer@mail.atu.edu. Web site http://education.atu.edu/people/czimmer. Connie Zimmer, Asst. Professor of Secondary Education, Coord. *Specializations:* Master of Education in Instructional Technology with specializations in library media education, computer education, general program of study, and training education. NCATE accredited institution. *Features:* A standards based program meeting the requirements of the Arkansas State Department of Educations licensure requirements for school library media specialist. Classrooms have the latest technology available. *Admission Requirements:* GRE or MAT, 2.5 undergraduate GPA, bachelor's degree. Teaching licensure required for the school library media specialization. *Degree Requirements:* 36 semester hours, B average in major hours, action research project. *Faculty:* 2 full-time, 1 part-time. *Students:* 16 full-time, 71 part-time. *Financial Assistance:* graduate assistantships, grants, student loans. *Degrees awarded 2000:* 32.

University of Central Arkansas. Educational Media/Library Science Campus. Box 4918, Conway, AR 72035. (501)450-5463. Fax (501)450-5680. E-mail selvinr@mail.uca.edu. Web site http://www.coe.uca.edu/aboutaat.htm. Selvin W. Royal, Prof., Chair, Academic Technologies and Educational Leadership. *Specializations:* M.S. in Educational Media/

Library Science and Information Science; tracks: School Library Media, Public Information Agencies, Media Information Studies. *Features:* Specialization in school library media. *Admission Requirements:* Transcripts, GRE scores, two letters of recommendation, personal interview, written rationale for entering the profession. *Degree Requirements:* 36 semester hours, optional thesis, practicum (for School Library Media), professional research paper. *Faculty:* 5 full-time, 2 part-time. *Students:* 6 full-time, 51 part-time. *Financial Assistance:* 3 to 4 graduate assistantships each year. *Degrees awarded 2000:* 35.

CALIFORNIA

*Azusa Pacific University. 901 E. Alosta, Azusa, CA 91702. (626)815-5376. Fax (626)815-5416. E-mail arnold@apu.edu. Brian Arnold, contact person. *Specializations:* M.Ed. with emphasis in Technology. *Admission Requirements:* Undergraduate degree from accredited institution, 3.0 GPA, ownership of a designated laptop computer and software. *Faculty:* 2 full-time, 16 part-time. *Students:* 180 part-time. *Financial Assistance:* Student loans.

*California State University-Dominguez Hills. 1000 E. Victoria St., Carson, CA 90747. (310)243-3524. Fax (310)243-3518. E-mail pdesberg@dhvx20.csudh.edu. Web site http://www.csudh.soe.edu. Peter Desberg, Prof., Coord., Computer-Based Education Program. *Specializations:* M.A. and Certificate in Computer-Based Education. *Admission Requirements:* 2.75 GPA. *Degree Requirements:* M.A.: 30 semester hours including project; certificate: 15 hours. *Faculty:* 2 full-time, 2 part-time. *Students:* 50 full-time, 40 part-time.

*California State University-Los Angeles. Division of Educational Foundations and Interdivisional Studies. 5151 State University Drive, Los Angeles, CA 90032. (323)343-4330. Fax (323)343-5336. E-mail efis@calstatela.edu. Web site http://web.calstatela.edu/academic/found/efis/index.html. Dr. Fernando A. Hernandez, Division Chairperson. *Specializations:* M.A. degree in Education, option in New Media Design and Production; Computer Education and Leadership. *Degree Requirements:* 2.75 GPA in last 90 qtr. units, 45 qtr. units, comprehensive written exam or thesis or project. Must also pass Writing Proficiency Examination (WPE), a California State University-Los Angeles requirement. *Faculty:* 7 full-time.

*California State University-San Bernardino. 5500 University Parkway, San Bernardino, CA 92407. (909)880-5600, (909)880-5610. Fax (909)880-7010. E-mail monaghan@wiley.csusb.edu. Web site http://soe.csusb.edu/soe/programs/eyec/. Jim Monaghan, Program Coord. *Specializations:* M.A. with two emphases: Video Production and Computer Applications. *Admission Requirements:* Bachelor's degree, appropriate work experience, 3.0 GPA, completion of introductory computer course and expository writing course. *Degree Requirements:* 48 units including a master's project (33 units completed in residence); 3.0 GPA; grades of C or better in all courses. *Faculty:* 5 full-time, 1 part-time. *Students:* 106. *Financial Assistance:* Contact Office of Graduate Studies.

San Diego State University. Educational Technology. 5500 Campanile Dr., San Diego, CA 92182-1182. (619)594-6718. Fax (619)594-6376. E-mail dritchie@mail.sdsu.edu. Web site http://edweb.sdsu.edu. Dr. Donn Ritchie, Prof., Chair. *Specializations:* Master's degree in Educational Technology with specializations in Computers in Education, Workforce Education, and Lifelong Learning. The Educational Technology Department participates in a College of Education joint doctoral program with The Claremont Graduate School and a joint doctoral program with University of San Diego. *Features:* Combining theory and practice in relevant, real-world experiences. *Admission Requirements:* Please refer to SDSU Graduate bulletin at http://libweb.sdsu.edu/bulletin/. Requirements include 950 GRE (verbal + quantitative) and GRE Writing Assessment Exam with score of 4.5 or better. *Degree Requirements:* 36 semester hours for the master's (including 6 prerequisite hours) 15-18 semester hours for the certificates. *Faculty:* 9 full-time, 8 part-time. *Students:* 120. *Financial Assistance:* Graduate assistantships. *Degrees awarded 2000:* 50.

*San Francisco State University. College of Education, Department of Instructional Technology. 1600 Holloway Ave., San Francisco, CA 94132. (415)338-1509. Fax (415)338-0510. E-mail michaels@sfsu.edu. Dr. Eugene Michaels, Chair; Mimi Kasner, Office Coord. *Specializations:* Master's degree with emphasis on Instructional Multimedia Design, Training and Designing Development, and Instructional Computing. The school also offers an 18-unit Graduate Certificate in Training Systems Development, which can be incorporated into the master's degree. *Features:* This program emphasizes the instructional systems approach, cognitivist principles of learning design, practical design experience, and project-based courses. *Admission Requirements:* Bachelor's degree, appropriate work experience, 2.5 GPA, interview with the department chair. *Degree Requirements:* 30 semester hours, field study project, or thesis. *Faculty:* 1 full-time, 16 part-time. *Students:* 250-300. *Financial Assistance:* Contact Office of Financial Aid.

*San Jose State University. One Washington Square, San Jose, CA 95192-0076. (408)924-3618. Fax (408)3713. E-mail office@wahoo.sjsu.edu. Web site http://www.sjsu.edu.depts /it/Home.html. Dr. Roberta Barba, Program Chair. *Specializations:* Master's degree. *Admission Requirements:* Baccalaureate degree from approved university, appropriate work experience, minimum GPA of 2.5, and minimum score of 550 on TOEFL (Test of English as a Foreign Language). 36 semester hours (which includes 6 prerequisite hours). *Faculty:* 4 full-time, 12 part-time. *Students:* 10 full-time master's students, 260 part-time. *Financial Assistance:* Assistantships, grants, student loans, and scholarships.

*United States International University. School of Education. 10455 Pomerado Rd., San Diego, CA 92131-1799. (619)635-4715. Fax (619)635-4714. E-mail feifer@sanac.usiu.edu. Richard Feifer, contact person. *Specializations:* Master's in Designing Technology for Learning, Planning Technology for Learning, and Technology Leadership for Learning. Ed.D. in Technology and Learning offers three specializations: Designing Technology for Learning, Planning Technology for Learning, and Technology Leadership for Learning. *Features:* Interactive multimedia, cognitive approach to integrating technology and learning. *Admission Requirements:* Master's: English proficiency, interview, 3.0 GPA with 1900 GRE or 2.0 GPA with satisfactory MAT score. *Degree Requirements:* Ed.D.: 88 graduate qtr. units, dissertation. *Faculty:* 2 full-time, 4 part-time. *Students:* Master's, 32 full-time, 12 part-time; doctoral, 6 full-time, 1 part-time. *Financial Assistance:* Internships, graduate assistantships, grants, student loans, scholarships.

University of Southern California. Instructional Technology, Division of Learning and Instruction. 702C W.P.H., Rossiee School of Education, Los Angeles, CA 90089-0031. (213)740-3288. Fax (213)740-3889. E-mail kazlausk@usc.edu. Web site http://www.usc.edu /department/education/. Dr. Richard Clark, Prof., Doctoral programs; Dr. Edward J. Kazlauskas, Prof., Program Chair, Masters programs in Instructional Technology. *Specializations:* M.A., Ed.D., Ph.D. to prepare individuals to teach instructional technology; manage educational media and training programs in business, industry, research and development organizations, schools, and higher educational institutions; perform research in instructional technology and media; and deal with computer-driven technology. *Features:* Special emphasis on instructional design, human performance at work, systems analysis, and computer-based training. *Admission Requirements:* Bachelor's degree, 1000 GRE. *Degree Requirements:* M.A.: 28 semester hours, thesis optional. Doctoral: 67 units, 20 of which can be transferred from a previous master's degree. Requirements for degree completion vary according to type of degree and individual interest. Ph.D. requires an outside field in addition to course work in instructional technology and education, more methodology and statistics work, and course work in an outside field. *Faculty:* 3 full-time, 4 part-time. *Students:* M.A., 5 full-time, 15 part-time; doctoral, 5 full-time, 20 part-time. *Financial Assistance:* Part-time, instructional technology-related work available in the Los

Angeles area and on campus; some scholarship monies available. *Degrees awarded 2000:* 28.

COLORADO

University of Colorado at Denver. School of Education. Campus Box 106, P.O. Box 173364, Denver, CO 80217-3364. (303)556-6022. Fax (303)556-4479. Web site http://cudenver.edu/ilt or http://soe.cudenver.edu. E-mail brent.wilson@cudenver.edu. Brent Wilson, Program Chair, Information and Learning Technologies, Division of Technology and Special Services. *Specializations:* M.A in Information and Learning Technologies; Ph.D. in Educational Leadership and Innovation with emphasis in Instructional Design and Technology Design and use of learning technologies; instructional design. *Features:* Design and use of learning technologies; instructional design. Ph.D. students complete 10 semester hours of doctoral labs (small groups collaborating with faculty on difficult problems of practice). Throughout the program, students complete a product portfolio of research, design, teaching, and applied projects. The program is cross-disciplinary, drawing on expertise in technology, adult learning, systemic change, research methods, reflective practice, and cultural studies. *Admission Requirements:* M.A. and Ph.D.: satisfactory GPA, GRE, writing sample, letters of recommendation, transcripts. *Degree Requirements:* M.A.: 36 semester hours including 27 hours of core courses and studio/project work; portfolio; practicum and additional requirements for state certification in library media. Ph.D.: 40 semester hours of course work and labs, plus 30 dissertation hours; portfolio; dissertation. *Faculty:* 5 full-time, 3 part-time. *Students:* M.A., 25 full-time, 120 part-time; Ph.D., 4 full-time, 18 part-time. *Financial Assistance:* Assistantships, internships. *Degrees awarded 2000:* 56.

University of Northern Colorado. Educational Technology College of Education. Greeley, CO 80639. (970)351-2816. Fax (970)351-1622. E-mail persi@unco.edu. Web site http://www.coe.unco.edu/edtech/index.html. Kay Persichitte, Assoc. Prof., Chair, Educational Technology. *Specializations:* M.A. in Educational Technology; M.A. in Educational Media; nondegree endorsement for school library media specialists; Ph.D. in Educational Technology with emphases in Distance Education, Instructional Development/Design, Interactive Technology, and Technology Integration. *Features:* Graduates are prepared for careers as instructional technologists, course designers, trainers, instructional developers, media specialists, and human resource managers. *Admission Requirements:* M.A.: Bachelors degree, 3.0 undergraduate GPA, 1500 GRE, three letters of recommendation, statement of career goals. Endorsement: Same as M.A. but no GRE. Ph.D.: 3.2 GPA, three letters of recommendation, congruency between applicants statement of career goals and program goals, 1650 GRE, interview with faculty. *Degree Requirements:* M.A.-Ed Tech: 30 semester hours (min); M.A.-Ed Media: 36-39 semester hours (min); Endorsement: 30-33 semester hours (min); Ph.D: 67 semester hours (min). *Faculty:* 7 full-time, 1 part-time. *Students:* M.A., 15 full-time, 85 part-time; Ph.D., 18 full-time, 25 part-time. *Financial Assistance:* Assistantships, grant development, student loans, fellowships, scholarships. *Degrees awarded 2000:* 40 M.A.; 6 Ph.D.

CONNECTICUT

*Central Connecticut State University. 1615 Stanley St., New Britain, CT 06050. (860)832-2130. Fax (860)832-2109. E-mail abedf@ccsu.ctstateu.edu. Web site http://www.ccsu.edu. Farough Abed, Coord., Educational Technology Program. *Specializations:* M.S. in Educational Technology. Curriculum emphases include instructional technology, instructional design, message design, and computer technologies. *Features:* The program supports the Center for Innovation in Teaching and Technology to link students with client-based projects. *Admission Requirements:* Bachelor's degree, 2.7 undergraduate GPA. *Degree Requirements:* 33 semester hours, optional thesis or master's final project (3 credits). *Faculty:* 2 full-time, 4 part-time. *Students:* 45. *Financial Assistance:* Graduate assistant position.

*Fairfield University. N. Benson Road, Fairfield, CT 06430. (203)254-4000. Fax (203)254-4047. E-mail imhefzallah@fair1.fairfield.edu.;jahnn@fair.fairfield.edu. Dr. Ibrahim M. Hefzallah, Prof., Dir., Educational Technology Department; Dr. Justin Ahnn, Assistant Professor of Educational Technology. *Specializations:* M.A. and a certificate of Advanced Studies in Educational Technology in one of four areas of concentrations: Computers-in-Education, Instructional Development, School Media Specialist, and Television Production; customized course of study also available. *Features:* Emphasis on theory, practice, and new instructional developments in computers in education, multimedia, and satellite communications. *Admission Requirements:* Bachelor's degree from accredited institution with 2.67 GPA. *Degree Requirements:* 33 credits. *Faculty:* 2 full-time, 8 part-time. *Students:* 4 full-time, 110 part-time. *Financial Assistance:* Assistantships, student loans.

*Southern Connecticut State University. Department of Library Science and Instructional Technology. 501 Crescent St., New Haven, CT 06515. (203)392-5781. Fax (203)392-5780. E-mail libscienceit@scsu.ctstateu.edu. Web site http://scsu.ctstateu.edu. Nancy Disbrow, Chair. *Specializations:* M.S. in Instructional Technology; Sixth-Year Professional Diploma Library-Information Studies (student may select area of specialization in Instructional Technology). *Degree Requirements:* For Instructional Technology only, 36 semester hours. For sixth-year degree: 30 credit hours with 6 credit hours of core requirements, 9-15 credit hours in specialization. *Faculty:* 1 full-time. *Students:* 3 full-time and 38 part-time in M.S./IT program. *Financial Assistance:* Graduate assistantship (salary $1,800 per semester; assistants pay tuition and a general university fee sufficient to defray cost of student accident insurance).

*University of Connecticut. U-64, Storrs, CT 06269-2064. (860)486-0181. Fax (860)486-0180. E-mail sbrown@UConnvm.UConn.edu or myoung@UConnvm.UConn.edu. Web site http://www.ucc.uconn.edu/~wwwepsy/. Scott W. Brown, Chair; Michael Young, contact person. *Specializations:* M.A. and Ph.D. degrees with an emphasis in Educational Technology as a specialization within the Program of Cognition and Instruction, in the Department of Educational Psychology. *Features:* The emphasis in Educational Technology is a unique program at UConn. It is co-sponsored by the Department of Educational Psychology in the School of Education and the Psychology Department in the College of Liberal Arts and Sciences. The emphasis in Educational Technology within the Cognition and Instruction Program seeks to provide students with knowledge of theory and applications regarding the use of advanced technology to enhance learning and thinking. This program provides suggested courses and opportunities for internships and independent study experiences that are directed toward an understanding of both the effects of technology on cognition and instruction, and the enhancement of thinking and learning with technology. Facilities include the UCEML computer lab featuring Mac and IBM networks upgraded for 1998 and a multimedia development center. The School of Education also features a multimedia classroom and auditorium. Faculty research interests include interactive videodisc for anchored instruction and situated learning, telecommunications for cognitive apprenticeship, technology-mediated interactivity for generative learning, and in cooperation with the National Research Center for Gifted and Talented, research on the use of technology to enhance cooperative learning and the development of gifted performance in all students. *Admission Requirements:* Admission to the graduate school at UConn, GRE scores (or other evidence of success at the graduate level). Previous experience in a related area of technology, education, or training is a plus. *Faculty:* The program in Cognition and Instruction has 7 full-time faculty; 3 full-time faculty administer the emphasis in Educational Technology. *Students:* M.A., 4, Ph.D., 18. *Financial Assistance:* Graduate assistantships, research fellowships, teaching assistantships, and federal and minority scholarships are available competitively.

DISTRICT OF COLUMBIA

*George Washington University. School of Education and Human Development. Washington, District of Columbia 20052. (202)994-1701. Fax (202)994-2145. E-mail unirel@www.gwu.edu. Web site http://www.gwu.edu/~etl. Dr. William Lynch, Educational Technology Leadership Program. Program is offered through Jones Education Company (JEC). Contact student advisors at (800)777-MIND. *Specializations:* M.A. in Education and Human Development with a major in Educational Technology Leadership. *Admission Requirements:* Application fee, transcripts, GRE or MAT scores (50th percentile), two letters of recommendation from academic professionals, computer access, undergraduate degree with 2.75 GPA. *Degree Requirements:* 36 credit hours (including 24 required hours). Required courses include computer application management, media and technology application, software implementation and design, public education policy, and quantitative research methods. *Faculty:* Courses are taught by GWU faculty. *Financial Assistance:* For information, contact the Office of Student Financial Assistance, GWU. Some cable systems that carry JEC offer local scholarships.

FLORIDA

*Barry University. Department of Educational Computing and Technology, School of Education. 11300 N.E. Second Ave., Miami Shores, Florida 33161. (305)899-3608. Fax (305)899-3718. E-mail jlevine@bu4090.barry.edu. Joel S. Levine, Dir. *Specializations:* M.S. and Ed.S. in Educational Technology, Ph.D. in Educational Technology Leadership. *Features:* Majority of the courses (30/36) in M.S. and Ed.S. programs are in the field of Educational Technology. *Admission Requirements:* GRE scores, letters of recommendation, GPA, interview, achievements. *Degree Requirements:* M.S. or Ed. S.: 36 semester credit hours. Ph.D.: 54 credits beyond the master's including dissertation credits. *Faculty:* 7 full-time, 10 part-time. *Students:* M.S., 8 full-time, 181 part-time; Ed.S., 5 full-time, 44 part-time; Ph.D., 3 full-time, 15 part-time. *Financial Assistance:* Assistantships, student loans.

Florida Institute of Technology. Science Education Department. 150 University Blvd., Melbourne, FL 32901-6988. (321)674-8126. Fax (321)674-7598. E-mail fronk@fit.edu. Web site http://www.fit.edu/AcadRes/sci-ed/degree.html#comp-tech-ed. Dr. Robert Fronk, Dept. Head. *Specializations:* Master's degree options in Computer Education and Instructional Technology; Ph.D. degree options in Computer Education and Instructional Technology. *Features:* Flexible program depending on student experience. *Admission Requirements:* 3.0 GPA for regular admission; 2.75 for provisional admission. *Degree Requirements:* Master's: 33 semester hours (15 in computer or and technology education, 9 in education, 9 electives); practicum; no thesis or internship required. Ph.D.: 48 semester hours (12 in computer and technology education, 12 in education, 24 dissertation and research). *Faculty:* 5 full-time. *Students:* 11 full-time, 10 part-time. *Financial Assistance:* Graduate student assistantships (full tuition plus stipend) available. *Degrees awarded 2000:* 6.

*Florida State University. Instructional Systems Program, Department of Educational Research. College of Education 305 Stone Bldg., Tallahassee, FL 32306. (904)644-4592. Fax (904)644-8776. E-mail laseur@mail.coe.fsu.edu. Web site http://www.fsu.edu/~edres/. *Specializations:* M.S., Ed.S., Ph.D. in Instructional Systems with specializations for persons planning to work in academia, business, industry, government, or military. *Features:* Core courses include systems and materials development, development of multimedia, project management, psychological foundations, current trends in instructional design, and research and statistics. Internships are recommended. *Admission Requirements:* M.S.: 3.2 GPA in last two years of undergraduate program, 1000 GRE (verbal plus quantitative), 550 TOEFL (for international applicants). Ph.D.: 1100 GRE (V + Q), 3.5 GPA in last two years; international students, 550 TOEFL. *Degree Requirements:* M.S.: 36 semester hours, 2-4 hour internship, written comprehensive exam. *Faculty:* 5 full-time, 5 part-time. *Students:* M.S., 55; Ph.D., 50. *Financial Assistance:* Some graduate research assistantships on faculty grants and contracts, university fellowships.

*Jacksonville University. Division of Education. 2800 University Boulevard North, Jacksonville, FL 32211. (904)745-7132. Fax (904)745-7159. E-mail mjanz@mail.ju.edu. Dr. Margaret Janz, Interim Dir., School of Education, or Dr. June Main, Coordinator of MAT in Integrated Learning with Educational Technology. *Specializations:* The Master's in Educational Technology and Integrated Learning is an innovative program designed to guide certified teachers in the use and application of educational technologies in the classroom. It is based on emerging views of how we learn, of our growing understanding of multiple intelligences, and of the many ways to incorporate technology in teaching and learning. Activity-based classes emphasize instructional design for a multimedia environment to reach all students. M.A.T. degrees in Computer Education and in Integrated Learning with Educational Technology. The M.A.T. in Computer Education is for teachers who are already certified in an area of education, for those who wish to be certified in Computer Education, kindergarten through community college level. *Degree Requirements:* M.A.T. in Computer Education and in Integrated Learning with Educational Technology: 36 semester hours, including 9-12 hours in core education graduate courses and the rest in computer education with comprehensive exam in last semester of program. Master's in Educational Technology and Integrated Learning: 36 semester hours, including 9 in core graduate education courses, 6 in integrated learning, and the rest in educational technology. Comprehensive exam is to develop a practical group of multimedia applications. *Financial Assistance:* Student loans and discounts to graduate education students. *Students:* Computer Education, 8; Integrated Learning with Educational Technology, 20.

*Nova Southeastern University. Fischler Center for the Advancement of Education. 3301 College Ave., Fort Lauderdale, FL 33314. (954)475-7440,. (800)986-3223, ext. 8563. Fax (954)262-3905. E-mail simsmich@fcae.nova.edu. Michael Simonson, Program Professor, Instructional Technology and Distance Education. *Specializations:* M.S. and Ed.D. in Instructional Technology and distance Education. *Admission Requirements:* M.S.: three letters of recommendation, completed application and transcripts. Ed.D.: Three letters of recommendation, completed application, transcripts, and completed master's degree in Instructional Technology or Distance Education, or related area. *Degree Requirements:* 21 months and 30 semester credits. Ed.D. 3 years and 66 semester credits. *Faculty:* 6 full-time and 20 adjuncts. *Students:* 250 full-time.

University of Central Florida. College of Education. 4000 Central Florida Blvd., Orlando, FL 32816-1250. (407)823-6139. Fax 407)823-5144. E-mail cornell@pegasus.cc.ucf.edu; jlee@pegasus.cc.ucf.edu; ggunter@pegasus.cc.ucf.edu. Web site http://pegasus.cc.ucf.edu /~edmedia and http://pegasus.cc.ucf.edu/~edtech. Richard Cornell, Instructional Systems; Judy Lee, Educational Media; Glenda Gunter, Educational Technology. *Specializations:* M.A. in Instructional Technology/Instructional Systems; M.Ed. in Instructional Technology/Educational Media; M.A. in Instructional Technology/Educational Technology. A doctorate in Curriculum and Instruction with an emphasis on Instructional Technology is offered. *Admission Requirements:* Interviews for Educational Media and Educational Technology programs.GRE scores and letters of recommendation. *Degree Requirements:* M.A. in Instructional Technology/Instructional Systems, 39-42 semester hours; M.Ed. in Instructional Technology/Educational Media, 39-45 semester hours; M.A. in Instructional Technology/Educational Technology, 36-45 semester hours. Practicum required in all three programs; thesis, research project, or substitute additional course work. *Faculty:* 4 full-time, 6 part-time. *Students:* Instructional Systems, 70; Educational Media, 35; Educational Technology, 50. Full-time, 120; part-time, 35. *Financial Assistance:* Competitive graduate assistantships in department and college, numerous paid internships, limited number of doctoral fellowships. *Degrees awarded 2000:* 65.

University of Florida. School of Teaching and Learning. 2403 Norman Hall, Gainesville, FL 32611-7048. 352-392-9191 X261. Fax 352-392-9193. E-mail cswain@coe.ufl.edu. Web site http://www.coe.ufl.edu/Courses/EdTech/ET.html. Colleen Swain. *Specializations:* Educational technology students may earn M.S., Ed.S., Ed.D. or Ph.D. degrees and have an opportunity to specialize in one of four tracks: (1) Teaching and teacher education, (2) Production, (3) Instructional design, or (4) Information/media specialist. Teacher education students and students in other degree programs may also elect to specialize in Educational Technology. *Admission Requirements:* Please see the Educational Technology Web site for the most up-to-date information. Current admission requirements are as follows: (1) Obtain a GRE score of 1000 or more on the verbal and quantitative components of the GRE. Applicants must have a score of 450 or higher for each component (verbal and quantitative). (2) Submit a written document outlining career goals and the track in which you wish to specialize in the Educational Technology program. *Degree Requirements:* Please see the Educational Technology Web site for the most up-to-date information. Program and college requirements must be met but there is considerable flexibility for doctoral students to plan an appropriate program with their advisors. *Faculty:* 5 full-time faculty members; number of adjunct instructors is dependent on the semester. *Students:* Approximately 80 students are enrolled in our Educational Technology. *Financial Assistance:* A limited number of graduate assistantships are available. Interested students should submit an assistantship application with their admissions application. Students should also check the Web site for information about available assistantships.

*University of South Florida. Instructional Technology Program, Secondary Education Department, College of Education. 4202 Fowler Ave. East, EDU 208B, Tampa, FL 33620. (813)974-1632 (M.Ed.); (813)974-1629 (doctoral). Fax (813)974-3837. E-mail breit@tempest.coedu.usf.edu (M.Ed.), jwhite@typhoon.coedu.usf.edu (doctoral). Web site http://www.coedu.usf.edu/institute_tech/. Dr. Frank Breit, master's program, Dr. James A. White, doctoral program. *Specializations:* M.Ed. in Curriculum and Instruction with emphasis in Instructional Technology; Ph.D. in Curriculum and Instruction with emphasis in Instructional Technology. *Features:* Student gain practical experience in the Florida Center for Instructional Technology (FCIT), which provides services to the Department of Education and other grants and contracts, and the Virtual Instructional Team for the Advancement of Learning (VITAL), which provides USF faculty with course development services. The College of Education is one of the largest in the United States in terms of enrollment and facilities. As of Fall 1997, a new, technically state-of-the-art building was put into service. *Admission Requirements:* M.Ed.: 3.0 undergraduate GPA, at least half of undergraduate degree earned from accredited institution, and 800 GRE (V + Q), or 2.5 undergraduate GPA in last half of undergraduate degree from accredited institution and 1000 GRE, or a prior graduate degree from an accredited institution and 800 GRE. Applicants must also have a minimum of two years of relevant educational or professional experience as judged by the program faculty. Ph.D.: contact Dr. White for full details; include 3.0 undergraduate GPA in last half of course work or 3.5 GPA at master's level and 1000 GRE, a master's degree from an accredited institution, three letters of recommendation, and favorable recommendations from program faculty. *Degree Requirements:* M.Ed.: 36-38 semester hours, comprehensive exam. Ph.D.: 77-79 hours, two research tools, two semesters of residency, qualifying examination, and dissertation. *Faculty:* 3 full-time, 2 part-time. *Students:* M.Ed.: 100 full-time, 100 part-time (approx.); Ph.D.: 2 full-time, 14 part-time. *Financial Assistance:* Assistantships, grants, loans, scholarships, and fellowships.

GEORGIA

*Georgia Southern University. College of Education, Statesboro, GA 30460-8131. (912)681-5307. Fax (912)681-5093. E-mail rcarlson@gasou.edu. Kenneth F. Clark, Assoc. Prof., Dept. of Leadership, Technology, and Human Development. *Specializations:* M.Ed. The school also offers a six-year specialist degree program (Ed.S.), and an Instructional Technology strand is available in the Ed.D. program in Curriculum Studies. *Features:*

Strong emphasis on technology. *Degree Requirements:* 36 semester hours, including a varying number of hours of media for individual students. *Financial Assistance:* See graduate catalog for general financial aid information.

*Georgia State University. Middle-Secondary Education and Instructional Technology University Plaza, Atlanta, GA 30303. (404)651-2510. Fax (404)651-2546. E-mail swharmon@gsu.edu. Web site http://www.gsu.edu/~wwwmst/. Dr. Stephen W. Harmon, contact person. *Specializations:* M.S., Ed.S., and Ph.D. in Instructional Technology or Library Media. *Features:* Focus on research and practical application of instructional technology in educational and corporate settings. *Admission Requirements:* M.S.: Bachelor's degree, 2.5 undergraduate GPA, 44 MAT or 800 GRE, 550 TOEFL. Ed.S.: Master's degree, teaching certificate, 3.25 graduate GPA, 48 MAT or 900 GRE. Ph.D.: Master's degree, 3.30 graduate GPA, 53 MAT or 500 verbal plus 500 quantitative GRE or 500 analytical GRE. *Degree Requirements:* M.S.: 36 sem. hours, internship, portfolio, comprehensive examination. Ed.S.: 30 sem. hours, internship, and scholarly project. Ph.D.: 66 sem. hours, internship, dissertation. *Faculty:* 6 full-time, 3 part-time. *Students:* 200 M.S., 30 Ph.D. *Financial Assistance:* Assistantships, grants, student loans.

State University of West Georgia. Department of Media and Instructional Technology. 137 Education Annex, Carrollton, GA 30118. (770)836-6558. Fax (770)838-3088. E-mail mwaugh@westga.edu. Web site http://coe.westga.edu/mit/index.html. Dr. Michael Waugh, Prof., Chair. *Specializations:* M.Ed. with specializations in Media and Instructional Technology and add-on certification for students with master's degrees in other disciplines. The Department also offers an Ed.S. program in Media with two options, Media Specialist or Instructional Technology. The program strongly emphasizes technology in the schools. *Features:* Master's degree students and initial certification students are required to complete a practicum. *Admission Requirements:* M.Ed.: 800 GRE, 44 MAT, 550 NTE Core, 2.5 undergraduate GPA. Ed.S.: 900 GRE, 48 MAT, or 575 NTE and 3.25 graduate GPA. *Degree Requirements:* 36 semester hours for M.Ed. 27 semester hours for Ed.S. *Faculty:* 7 full-time in Media/Technology; 1 full-time instructor in Instructional Technology; 2 part-time in Media/Instructional Technology. *Students:* Approximately 300, part-time. *Financial Assistance:* Three graduate research assistantships for the department. *Degrees awarded 2000:* Approximately 50 across both levels.

University of Georgia. Department of Instructional Technology, College of Education. 604 Aderhold Hall, Athens, GA 30602-7144. (706)542-3810. Fax (706)542-4032. E-mail rbranch@coe.uga.edu. Web site http://it.coe.uga.edu. Robert Maribe Branch, Prof. and Chair. *Specializations:* M.Ed. and Ed.S. in Instructional Technology; Ph.D. for leadership positions as specialists in instructional design and development and college faculty. The program offers advanced study for individuals with previous preparation in instructional media and technology, as well as a preparation for personnel in other professional fields requiring a specialty in instructional systems or instructional technology. Representative career fields for graduates include designing new courses, tutorial programs, and instructional materials in the military, industry, medical professional schools, allied health agencies, teacher education, staff development, state and local school systems, higher education, research, and in instructional products development. *Features:* Minor areas of study available in a variety of other departments. Personalized programs are planned around a common core of courses and include practica, internships, or clinical experiences. Research activities include special assignments, applied projects, and task forces, as well as thesis and dissertation studies. *Admission Requirements:* All degrees: application to graduate school, satisfactory GRE score, other criteria as outlined in Graduate School Bulletin. *Degree Requirements:* M.Ed.: 36 semester hours with 3.0 GPA, portfolio with oral exam. Ed.S.: 30 semester hours with 3.0 GPA and portfolio exam. Ph.D.: three full years of study beyond the master's degree, two consecutive semesters full-time residency, comprehensive exam with oral defense, internship, dissertation with oral defense. *Faculty:* 10 full-time, 3 part-time. *Students:* M.Ed and Ed.S., 18 full-time, 53 part-time; Ph.D., 24 full-time, 10 part-time. *Financial Assistance:* Graduate assistantships available. *Degrees awarded 2000:* 32.

*Valdosta State University. College of Education. 1500 N. Patterson St., Valdosta, GA 31698. (912)333-5927. Fax (912)333-7167. *Specializations:* M.Ed. in Instructional Technology with three tracks: Library/Media, Technology Leadership, or Technology Applications; Ed.S. in Instructional Technology; Ed.D. in Curriculum and Instruction. *Features:* The program has a strong emphasis on technology in M.Ed., Ed.S., and Ed.D.; strong emphasis on applied research in Ed.S. and Ed.D. *Admission Requirements:* M.Ed.: 2.5 GPA, 750 GRE. Ed.S.: Master's in Instructional Technology or related area, 3.0 GPA, 850 GRE. Ed.D.: Master's degree, 3 years of experience, 3.50 GPA, 1000 GRE. *Degree Requirements:* M.Ed.: 33 semester hours. Ed.S.: 27 semester hours. *Faculty:* 7 full-time, 3 part-time. *Students:* 15 full-time, 90 part-time. *Financial Assistance:* Graduate assistantships, student loans, scholarships.

HAWAII

University of Hawaii-Manoa. Department of Educational Technology. 1776 University Ave, Honolulu, Hawaii 96822-2463. (808) 956-7671. Fax (808)956-3905. E-mail edtech-dept@hawaii.edu. Web site http://www2.hawaii.edu/edtech. Geoffrey Z. Kucera, Prof., Chair. *Specializations:* M.Ed. in Educational Technology. *Features:* Min. 39 semester hours, including 3 in practicum, 3 in internship; thesis and nonthesis available. *Admission Requirements:* Bachelor's degree in any field, B average (3.0 GPA). *Degree Requirements:* 39 sem. hours (plus 6 sem.hrs of prerequisites if needed). *Faculty:* 5 full-time, 2 part-time. *Students:* 20 full-time, 29 part-time students. *Financial Assistance:* Consideration given to meritorious second-year students for tuition waivers and scholarship applications. *Degrees awarded 2000:* 11.

IDAHO

*Boise State University. IPT. 1910 University Drive, Boise, ID 83725. (208)385-4457; (800)824-7017 ext. 4457. Fax (208)342-7203. E-mail bsu-ipt@micron.net. Web site http://www.cot.idbsu.edu/~ipt/. Dr. David Cox, IPT Program Dir.; Jo Ann Fenner, IPT Program Developer and distance program contact person. *Specializations:* M.S. in Instructional & Performance Technology available in a traditional campus setting or via computer conferencing to students located anywhere on the North American continent. The program is fully accredited by the Northwest Association of Schools and Colleges and is the recipient of an NUCEA award for Outstanding Credit Program offered by distance education methods. *Features:* Leading experts in learning styles, evaluation, and leadership principles serve as adjunct faculty in the program via computer and modem from their various remote locations. *Admission Requirements:* Undergraduate degree with 3.0 GPA, one to two page essay describing why you want to pursue this program and how it will contribute to your personal and professional development, and a resume of personal qualifications and work experience. *Degree Requirements:* 36 semester hours in instructional and performance technology and related course work; project or thesis available for on-campus program and an oral comprehensive exam required for distance program (included in 36 credit hours). *Faculty:* 3 full-time, 7 part-time. *Students:* 140 part-time. *Financial Assistance:* DANTES funding for some military personnel, low-interest loans to eligible students, graduate assistantships for on-campus enrollees.

ILLINOIS

*Chicago State University. Department of Library Science and Communications Media. Chicago, IL 60628. (312)995-2278; (312)995-2503. Fax (312)995-2473. E-mail l-robinson @csu.edu. Janice Bolt, Prof., Chair, Dept. of Library Science and Communications Media.

Specializations: Master's degree in School Media. Program has been approved by NCATE: AECT/AASL through accreditation of University College of Education; State of Illinois Entitlement Program. *Admission Requirements:* Teacher's certification or bachelor's in education; any B.A. or B.S. *Degree Requirements*: 36 semester hours; thesis optional. *Faculty:* 2 full-time, 5 part-time. *Students:* 88 part-time. *Financial Assistance:* Assistantships, grants, student loans.

*Governors State University. College of Arts and Sciences. University Park, IL 60466. (708)534-4082. Fax (708)534-7895. E-mail m-stelni@govst.edu. Michael Stelnicki, Prof., Human Performance and Training. *Specializations:* M.A. in Communication with HP&T major. *Features:* Emphasizes three professional areas: Instructional Design, Performance Analysis, and Design Logistics. *Admission Requirements:* Undergraduate degree in any field. *Degree Requirements:* 36 credit hours (trimester), all in instructional and performance technology; internship or advanced field project required. Metropolitan Chicago-area based. *Faculty:* 2 full-time. *Students:* 32 part-time.

*Northern Illinois University. Leadership and Educational Policy Studies Department College of Education. DeKalb, IL 60115-2896. (815)753-0464. Fax (815)753-9371. E-mail LSTOTT@NIU.EDU. Web site http://coe.cedu.niu.edu. Dr. Peggy Bailey, Chair, Instructional Technology. *Specializations:* M.S.Ed. in Instructional Technology with concentrations in Instructional Design, Distance Education, Educational Computing, and Media Administration; Ed.D. in Instructional Technology, emphasizing instructional design and development, computer education, media administration, and preparation for careers in business, industry, and higher education. In addition, Illinois state certification in school library media is offered in conjunction with either degree or alone. *Features:* Considerable flexibility in course selection, including advanced seminars, numerous practicum and internship opportunities, individual study, and research. Program is highly individualized. More than 60 courses offered by several departments or faculties, including communications, radio/television/film, art, journalism, educational psychology, computer science, and research and evaluation. Facilities include well-equipped computer labs. Students are encouraged to create individualized Web pages. Master's program started in 1968, doctorate in 1970. *Admission Requirements:* M.S.: 2.75 undergraduate GPA, GRE verbal and quantitative scores, two references. Ed.D.: 3.5 M.S. GPA, GRE verbal and quantitative scores (waiver possible), writing sample, three references. *Degree Requirements:* M.S.: 39 hours, including 30 in instructional technology; no thesis. Ed.D.: 63 hours beyond master's, including 15 hours for dissertation. *Faculty:* 8 full-time, 12 part-time. *Students:* M.S., 135 part-time; Ed.D., 115 part-time. *Financial Assistance:* Assistantships available at times in various departments, scholarships, minority assistance.

*Southern Illinois University at Carbonda. Department of Curriculum and Instruction. Carbondale, IL 62901-4610. (618)536-2441. Fax (618)453-4244. E-mail sashrock@siu.edu. Web site http://www.siu.edu/~currinst/index.html. Sharon Shrock, Coord., Instructional Technology/Development. *Specializations:* M.S. in Education with specializations in Instructional Development and Instructional Technology; Ph.D. in Education including specialization in Instructional Technology. *Features:* All specializations are oriented to multiple education settings. The ID program emphasizes nonschool (primarily corporate) learning environments. *Admission Requirements:* M.S.: Bachelor's degree, 2.7 undergraduate GPA, transcripts. Ph.D.: Master's degree, 3.25 GPA, MAT or GRE scores, letters of recommendation, transcripts, writing sample. *Degree Requirements:* M.S., 32 credit hours with thesis; 36 credit hours without thesis; Ph.D., 40 credit hours beyond the master's degree in courses, 24 credit hours for the dissertation. *Faculty:* 5 full-time, 2 part-time. *Students:* M.S., 35 full-time, 45 part-time; Ph.D., 8 full-time, 19 part-time. *Financial Assistance:* Some graduate assistantships and scholarships available to qualified students.

*Southern Illinois University at Edwardsville. Instructional Technology Program, School of Education. Edwardsville, IL 62026-1125. (618)692-3277. Fax (618)692-3359. E-mail cnelson@siue.edu. Web site http://www.siue.edu. Dr. Charles E. Nelson, Dir., Dept. of Educational Leadership. *Specializations:* M.S. in Education with concentrations in (1) Instructional Design and (2) Teaching, Learning, and Technology. *Features:* Evening classes only. *Degree Requirements:* 36 semester hours; thesis optional. *Faculty:* 6 part-time. *Students:* 125.

*University of Illinois at Urbana-Champaign. Department of Educational Psychology. 210 Education Bldg.1310 S. 6th St., Champaign, IL 61820. (217)333-2245. Fax (217)244-7620. E-mail c-west@uiuc.edu. Charles K. West, Prof., Div. of Learning and Instruction, Dept. of Educational Psychology. *Specializations:* M.A., M.S., and Ed.M. with emphasis in Instructional Design and Educational Computing. Ph.D. in Educational Psychology with emphasis in Instructional Design and Educational Computing. *Features:* Ph.D. program is individually tailored and strongly research-oriented with emphasis on applications of cognitive science to instruction. *Admission Requirements:* Excellent academic record, high GRE scores, and strong letters of recommendation. *Degree Requirements:* 8 units for Ed.M., 6 units and thesis for M.A. or M.S. Ph.D.: 8 units course work, approx. 4 units of research methods courses, minimum 8 hours of written qualifying exams, 8 units thesis credits. *Faculty:* 8 full-time, 5 part-time. *Students:* 31 full-time, 7 part-time. *Financial Assistance:* Scholarships, research assistantships, and teaching assistantships available; fellowships for very highly academically talented; some tuition waivers.

*Western Illinois University. Instructional Technology and Telecommunications. 37 Harrabin Hall, Macomb, IL 61455. (309)298-1952. Fax (309)298-2978. E-mail mh-hassan@wiu.edu. Web site http://www.wiu.edu/users/miitt/. M.H. Hassan, Chair. *Specialization:* Master's degree. *Features:* New program approved by Illinois Board of Higher Education in January 1996 with emphases in Instructional Technology, Telecommunications, Interactive Technologies, and Distance Education. Selected courses delivered via satellite TV and compressed video. *Admission Requirements:* Bachelor's degree, 3.0/4.0 GRE score. *Degree Requirements:* 32 semester hours, thesis or applied project, or 35 semester hours with portfolio. Certificate Program in Instructional Technology Specialization. Graphic applications, training development, video production. Each track option is made of five courses or a total of 15 semester hours. *Faculty:* 8 full-time. *Students:* 35 full-time, 150 part-time. *Financial Assistance:* Graduate and research assistantships, internships, residence hall assistants, veterans' benefits, loans, and part-time employment.

INDIANA

*Indiana State University. Dept. of Curriculum, Instruction, and Media Technology. Terre Haute, IN 47809. (812)237-2937. Fax (812)237-4348. E-mail efthomp@befac.indstate .edu. Dr. James E. Thompson, Program Coord. *Specializations:* Master's degree in Instructional Technology with education focus or with noneducation focus; Specialist Degree program in Instructional Technology; Ph.D. in Curriculum, Instruction with specialization in Media Technology. *Degree Requirements:* Master's: 32 semester hours, including 18 in media, thesis optional; Ed.S.: 60 semester hours beyond bachelor's degree; Ph.D., approximately 100 hours beyond bachelor's degree. *Faculty:* 5 full-time. *Students:* 17 full-time, 13 part-time. *Financial Assistance:* 7 assistantships.

*Indiana University. School of Education. W. W. Wright Education Bldg., Rm. 2276, 201 N. Rose Ave., Bloomington, IN 47405-1006. (812)856-8451 (information), (812)856-8239 (admissions). Fax (812)856-8239. E-mail rteh@indiana.edu. Thomas Schwen, Chair, Dept. of Instructional Systems Technology. *Specializations:* M.S. and Ed.S. degrees designed for individuals seeking to be practitioners in the field of Instructional Technology. Offers Ph.D. and Ed.D. degrees with four program focus areas: Foundations; Instructional Analysis, Design, and Development; Instructional Development and Production; and

Implementation and Management. *Features:* Requires computer skills as a prerequisite and makes technology utilization an integral part of the curriculum; eliminates separation of various media formats; and establishes a series of courses of increasing complexity integrating production and development. The latest in technical capabilities have been incorporated in the new Center for Excellence in Education, including teaching, photographic, computer, and science laboratories, a 14-station multimedia laboratory, and television studios. *Admission Requirements:* M.S.: Bachelor's degree from an accredited institution, 1350 GRE (3 tests required), 2.65 undergraduate GPA; Ed.D and Ph.D.: 1550 GRE (3 tests required), 3.5 graduate GPA. *Degree Requirements:* M.S.: 40 credit hours (including 16 credits in required courses); colloquia; an instructional product or Master's thesis; and 12 credits in outside electives. Ed.D.: 60 hours in addition to previous Master's degree, thesis. Ph.D.: 90 hours, thesis. *Faculty:* 6 full-time, 5 part-time. *Financial Assistance:* Assistantships, scholarships.

Purdue University. School of Education, Department of Curriculum and Instruction. 1442 LAEB, W. Lafayette, IN 47907-1442. (765)494-5669. Fax (765)496-1622. E-mail edtech@soe.purdue.edu. Web site http://www.edci.purdue.edu/et/. Dr. James D. Lehman, Prof. of Educational Technology. *Specializations:* Master's degree, Educational Specialist, and Ph.D. in Educational Technology. Master's program started in 1982, Specialist and Ph.D. in 1985. *Features:* Vision Statement: The Educational Technology Program at Purdue University nurtures graduates who are effective designers of learning experiences and environments that incorporate technology to engage learners and improve learning. *Admission Requirements:* Master's, Ed.S., and Ph.D: 3.0 GPA, three letters of recommendation, statement of personal goals. A score of 550 (paper-based) or 213 (computer-based) or above on the Test of English as a Foreign Language (TOEFL) for individuals whose first language is not English. Ph.D. Additional Requirement: 1000 GRE (V + Q); Verbal score of at least 500 preferred. *Degree Requirements:* Master's: 33 semester hours (15 in educational technology, 9 in education, 12 unspecified); thesis optional. Specialist: 60-65 semester hours (15-18 in educational technology, 30-35 in education); thesis, internship, practicum (currently revising degree requirements to be competency based). Ph.D: 60 semester hours beyond the master's degree (15-18 in educational technology, 27-30 in education and supporting areas; 15 dissertation research hours). *Faculty:* 5 full-time; 2 part-time. *Students:* M.S., 48; Ed.S., 1; Ph.D., 40. *Financial Assistance:* Assistantships and fellowships. *Degrees awarded 2000:* 17.

IOWA

*Clarke College. Graduate Studies. 1550 Clarke Drive, Dubuque, IA 52001. (319)588-6331. Fax (319)588-6789. E-mail RADAMS@KELLER.CLARKE.EDU. Web site http://www.clarke.edu. Robert Adams. *Specializations:* M.A. in Technology and Education. *Admission Requirements:* 2.5 GPA, GRE (verbal + quantitative) or MAT, $25 application fee, two letters of recommendation. *Degree Requirements:* 25 semester hours in computer courses, 12 hours in education. *Faculty:* 1 full-time, 1-2 part-time. *Students:* 20 part-time. *Financial Assistance:* Scholarships, student loans.

*Iowa State University. College of Education. Ames, IA 50011. (515)294-6840. Fax (515)294-9284. E-mail lspask@lsu.edu. Gary Downs, Professor and Department Head. *Specializations:* M.S., M.Ed., and Ph.D. in Curriculum and Instructional Technology with specializations in Instructional Computing; Ph.D. in Education with emphasis in Instructional Computing, Technology Research. *Features:* Practicum experiences related to professional objectives, supervised study and research projects tied to long-term studies within the program, development and implementation of new techniques, teaching strategies, and operational procedures in instructional resources centers and computer labs, program emphasis on technologies for teachers. *Admission Requirements:* M.S. and M.Ed.: three letters, top half of undergraduate class, autobiography. Ph.D.: three letters, top half of undergraduate class, autobiography, GRE scores. *Degree Requirements:* Master's: 30

semester hours, thesis, no internship or practicum. Ph.D.: 78 semester hours, thesis, no internship or practicum. *Faculty:* 4 full-time, 6 part-time. *Students:* Master's, 40 full-time, 40 part-time; Ph.D., 30 full-time, 20 part-time. *Financial Assistance:* 10 assistantships.

*University of Iowa. Division of Psychological and Quantitative Foundations College of Education. Iowa City, IA 52242. (319)335-5519. Fax (319)335-5386. E-mail provost-office @uiowa.edu. Web site http://www.uiowa.edu/~coe2/facstaff/salessi.htm. Stephen Alessi, 361 Lindquist Center. *Specializations:* M.A. and Ph.D. with specializations in Training and Human Resources Development, Computer Applications, and Media Design and Production (M.A. only). *Features:* Flexibility in planning to fit individual needs, backgrounds, and career goals. The program is interdisciplinary, involving courses within divisions of the College of Education, as well as in the schools of Business, Library Science, Radio and Television, Linguistics, and Psychology. *Admission Requirements:* M.A.: 2.8 undergraduate GPA, 500 GRE (V + Q), personal letter of interest. Ph.D.: Master's degree, 1000 GRE (V + Q), 3.2 GPA on all previous graduate work for regular admission. Conditional admission may be granted. Teaching or relevant experience may be helpful. *Degree Requirements:* M.A.: 35 semester hours, 3.0 GPA, final project or thesis, comprehensive exam. Ph.D.: 90 semester hours, comprehensive exams, dissertation. *Faculty:* 4 full-time, 3 part-time. *Financial Assistance:* Assistantships, grants, student loans, and scholarships.

*University of Northern Iowa. Educational Technology Program. Cedar Falls, IA 50614-0606. (319)273-3250. Fax (319)273-5886. E-mail SmaldinoS@UNI.edu. Web site www.uni.edu/edtech. Sharon E. Smaldino. *Specializations:* M.A. in Educational Technology, M.A. in Communications and Training Technology. *Admission Requirements:* Bachelor's degree, 3.0 undergraduate GPA, 500 TOEFL. *Degree Requirements:* 38 semester credits, optional thesis worth 6 credits or alternative research paper of project, comprehensive exam. *Faculty:* 3 full-time, 6 part-time. *Students:* 120. *Financial Assistance:* Assistantships, grants, student loans, scholarships, student employment.

KANSAS

Emporia State University. School of Library and Information Management. 1200 Commercial, P.O. Box 4025, Emporia, KS 66801. 800/552-4770. Fax 620/341-5233. E-mail sliminfo@emporia.edu. Web site http://slim.emporia.edu. Daniel Roland, Director of Communications. *Specializations:* Master of Library Science (ALA accredited program); School Library Certification program, which includes 30 hours of the M.L.S. program; Ph.D. in Library and Information Management; B.S. in Information Resource Studies; Information Management Certificate—18 hours of MLS curriculum; Library Services Certificates—five separate 12-hour programs of undergraduate work available for credit or noncredit. *Features:* The M.L.S. program is also available in Colorado, Oregon, Utah. Audio/Video delivery via ISDN to Idaho begins Fall 2001. *Admission Requirements:* Undergraduate GPA of 3.0 or better, GRE score of 1,000 points combined in Verbal and Analytical sections. GRE can be waived for students already holding a graduate degree in which they earned a 3.75 GPA or better; admission interview. *Degree Requirements:* M.L.S.: 42 semester hours, comprehensive exam. Ph.D.: total of 83-97 semester hours, depending on the number of hours received for an M.L.S. *Faculty:* 10 full-time, 35 part-time. *Students:* M.L.S.: 64 full-time, 305 part-time; Ph.D.: 23 part-time. *Financial Assistance:* Assistantships, grants, student loans, scholarships. *Degrees awarded 2000:* 120 M.L.S.; 2 Ph.D.

*Kansas State University. Educational Computing, Design, and Telecommunications. 363 Bluemont Hall, Manhattan, KS 66506. (913)532-7686. Fax (913)532-7304. E-mail dmcgrath@coe.educ.ksu.edu. Web site http://www2.educ.ksu.edu/Faculty/McGrathD /ECDT/ECDTProg.htm. Dr. Diane McGrath. *Specializations:* M.S. in Secondary Education with an emphasis in Educational Computing, Design, and Telecommunications; Ph.D. and Ed.D. in Curriculum and Instruction with an emphasis in Educational Computing,

Design, and Telecommunications. Master's program started in 1982; doctoral in 1987. *Admission Requirements:* M.S.: B average in undergraduate work, one programming language, 590 TOEFL. Ed.D. and Ph.D.: B average in undergraduate and graduate work, one programming language, GRE or MAT, three letters of recommendation, experience or course in educational computing. *Degree Requirements:* M.S.: 30 semester hours (minimum of 12 in Educational Computing); thesis, internship, or practicum not required, but all three are possible. Ed.D.: 94 semester hours (minimum of 18 hours in Educational Computing or related area approved by committee, 16 hours dissertation research, 12 hours internship); thesis. Ph.D.: 90 semester hours (minimum of 21 hours in Educational Computing, Design, and Telecommunications or related area approved by committee, 30 hours for dissertation research); thesis; internship or practicum not required but available. *Faculty:* 2 full-time, 1 part-time. *Students:* M.S., 10 full-time, 27 part-time; doctoral, 16 full-time, 14 part-time. *Financial Assistance:* Four assistantships directly associated with the program; other assistantships sometimes available in other departments.

University of Louisville. College of Education and Human Development Belknap Campus. Louisville, KY 40292. (502)852-6667. Fax (502)852-4563. E-mail cparkins@louisville .edu. Web site http://www.louisville.edu/edu. Carolyn Rude-Parkins, Chair of Leadership, Foundations, Human Resource Education. *Specializations:* Master's in Instructional Technology (appropriate for K–12 teacher and for trainers/adult educators), Post Master's/Rank 1 in Instructional Technology (K–12 teachers). *Features:* Appropriate for business or school audiences. Program is based on ISTE and ASTD standards. *Admission Requirements:* 2.75 GPA, 800 GRE, two letters of recommendation, application fee. *Degree Requirements:* 30 semester hours, internship. *Faculty:* 2 full-time, 3 part-time. *Students:* 50 part-time students. *Financial Assistance:* Graduate assistantships. *Degrees awarded 2000:* 10 M.Ed.

*Louisiana State University. School of Library and Information Science. Baton Rouge, LA 70803. (225)388-3158. Fax (225)388-4581. E-mail gradadmin@lsu.edu. Web site http://adam.slis.lsu.edu. Bert R. Boyce, Dean, Prof., School of Library and Information Science. *Specializations:* M.L.I.S., C.L.I.S. (post-Master's certificate), Louisiana School Library Certification. An advanced certificate program is available. *Degree Requirements:* M.L.I.S.: 40 hours, comprehensive exam, one semester full-time residence, completion of degree program in five years. *Faculty:* 10 full-time. *Students:* 84 full-time, 86 part-time. *Financial Assistance:* A large number of graduate assistantships are available to qualified students.

MARYLAND

*The Johns Hopkins University. Graduate Division of Education, Technology for Educators Program. Columbia Gateway Park 6740 Alexander Bell Drive, Columbia, MD 21046. (410)309-9537. Fax (410)290-0467. E-mail tsantis@jhu.edu. Web site http://www.jhu.edu. Dr. Jacqueline A. Nunn, Department Chair; Dr. Linda Tsantis, Program Coordinator. *Specializations:* The Department of Technology for Education offers programs leading to the M.S. degree in Education, the M.S. in Special Education, and three specialized advanced Graduate Certificates: Technology for Multimedia and Internet-Based Instruction; Teaching with Technology for School to Career Transition; and Assistive Technology for Communication and Social Interaction. *Features:* Focuses on training educators to become decision makers and leaders in the use of technology, with competencies in the design, development, and application of emerging technologies for teaching and learning. Incorporates basic elements that take into account the needs of adult learners, the constantly changing nature of technology, and the need for schools and universities to work together for schoolwide change. The Center for Technology in Education is a partnership project linking research and teaching of the University with the leadership and policy direction of the Maryland State Department of Education. The Center is directed by Dr. Nunn (2500 E. Northern Parkway, Baltimore, MD 21214-1113, 254-8466, jnunn@jhuniz.hcf.jhu.edu).

Admission Requirements: Bachelor's degree with strong background in teaching, curriculum and instruction, special education, or a related service field. *Faculty:* 2 full-time, 30 part-time. *Students:* 201 part-time. *Financial Assistance:* Grants, student loans, scholarships.

*Towson State University. College of Education. Hawkins Hall, Rm. 103B, Towson, MD 21252. (410)830-6268. Fax (410)830-2733. E-mail wiser@toe.towson.edu. Web site http://www.towson.edu/~coe/istc.html. Dr. David R. Wiser, Assistant Professor. Dept.: Reading, Special Education, and Instructional Development; School Library Media and Education Technology. Prof., General Education Dept. *Specializations:* M.S. degrees in Instructional Development and School Library Media. *Admission Requirements:* Bachelor's degree from accredited institution with 3.0 GPA. (Conditional admission granted for many applicants with a GPA over 2.75). *Degree Requirements:* 36 graduate semester hours without thesis. *Faculty:* 7 full-time, 5 adjunct. *Students:* 150. *Financial Assistance:* Graduate assistantships, work study, scholarships.

*University of Maryland. College of Library and Information Services. 4105 Hornbake Library Bldg., South Wing, College Park, MD 20742-4345. (301)405-2038. Fax (301)314-9145. E-mail ap57@umail.umd.edu. Ann Prentice, Dean and Program Chair. *Specializations:* Master of Library Science, including specialization in School Library Media; doctorate in Library and Information Services including specialization in Educational Technology/Instructional Communication. *Features:* Program is broadly conceived and interdisciplinary in nature, using the resources of the entire campus. The student and the advisor design a program of study and research to fit the student's background, interests, and professional objectives. Students prepare for careers in teaching and research in information science and librarianship and elect concentrations including Educational Technology and Instructional Communication. *Admission Requirements:* Doctoral: Bachelor's degree (the majority of doctoral students enter with master's degrees in Library Science, Educational Technology, or other relevant disciplines), GRE general tests, three letters of recommendation, statement of purpose. Interviews required when feasible for doctoral applicants. *Degree Requirements:* M.L.S.: 36 semester hours; thesis optional. *Faculty:* 15 full-time, 8 part-time. *Students:* Master's, 106 full-time, 149 part-time; doctoral, 5 full-time, 11 part-time. *Financial Assistance:* Assistantships, grants, student loans, scholarships, fellowships.

*University of Maryland Baltimore County (UMBC). Department of Education. 1000 Hilltop Circle, Baltimore, MD 21250. (410)455-2310. Fax (410)455-3986. E-mail gist@umbc.edu. Web site http://www.research.umbc.edu/~eholly/ceduc/isd/. Dr. William R. Johnson, Dir., Graduate Programs in Education. *Specializations:* M.A. degrees in School Instructional Systems, Post-Baccalaureate Teacher Certification, Training in Business and Industry. *Admission Requirements:* 3.0 undergraduate GPA, GRE scores. *Degree Requirements:* 36 semester hours (including 18 in systems development for each program); internship. *Faculty:* 18 full-time, 25 part-time. *Students:* 59 full-time, 254 part-time. *Financial Assistance:* Assistantships, scholarships.

*Western Maryland College. Department of Education. Main St, Westminster, MD 21157. (410)857-2507. Fax (410)857-2515. E-mail rkerby@wmdc.edu. Dr. Ramona N.Kerby, Coord., School Library Media Program, Dept. of Education. *Specializations:* M.S. in School Library Media. *Degree Requirements:* 33 credit hours (including 19 in media and 6 in education), comprehensive exam. *Faculty:* 1 full-time, 7 part-time. *Students:* 140, most part-time.

MASSACHUSETTS

Boston University. School of Education. 605 Commonwealth Ave., Boston, MA 02215-1605. (617)353-3181. Fax (617)353-3924. E-mail whittier@bu.edu. Web site http://web.bu.edu/EDUCATION. David B. Whittier, Asst. Professor and Coord., Program in Educational Media and Technology. *Specializations:* Ed.M., C.A.G.S. (Certificate of Advanced Graduate Study) in Educational Media and Technology; Ed.D. in Curriculum and Teaching, Specializing in Educational Media and Technology; preparation for Massachusetts public school certificates as Instructional Technology Specialist. *Features:* The Master's Program prepares graduates for professional careers as educators, instructional designers, developers of educational materials, and managers of the human and technology-based resources necessary to support education and training with technology. Graduates are employed in K–12 schools, higher education, industry, medicine, government, and publishing. Students come to the program from many different backgrounds and with a wide range of professional goals. The doctoral program sets the study of Educational Media & Technology within the context of education and educational research in general, and curriculum and teaching in particular. In addition to advanced work in the field of Educational Media and Technology, students examine and conduct research and study the history of educational thought and practice relating to teaching and learning. Graduates make careers in education as professors and researchers, technology directors and managers, and as developers of technology-based materials and systems. Graduates also make careers in medicine, government, business, and industry as instructional designers, program developers, project managers, and training directors. Graduates who work in both educational and noneducational organizations are often responsible for managing the human and technological resources required to create learning experiences that include the development and delivery of technology-based materials and distance education. *Admission Requirements:* Ed.M.: recommendations, minimum 2.7 undergraduate GPA, graduate test scores are required and either the GRE or MAT must be completed within past five years. C.A.G.S.: Ed.M., recommendations, 2.7 undergraduate GPA, graduate test scores are required and either the GRE or MAT must be completed within past five years. Ed.D.: three letters of recommendation, MAT or GRE scores, transcripts, writing samples, statement of goals and qualifications, analytical essay, minimum 2.7 GPA. *Degree Requirements:* Ed.M.: 36 credit hours (including 24 hours from required core curriculum, 12 from electives). C.A.G.S.: 32 credits beyond Ed.M., one of which must be a curriculum and teaching course and a minicomprehensive exam. Ed.D.: 60 credit hours of courses in Educational Media and Technology, curriculum and teaching, and educational thought and practice with comprehensive exams; course work and apprenticeship in research; dissertation. *Faculty:* 1 full-time, 1 half-time, 10 part-time. *Students:* 25 full-time, 25 part-time. *Financial Assistance:* U.S. government sponsored work study, assistantships, grants, student loans, scholarships. *Degrees awarded 2000:* 18 Ed.M.; 1 C.A.G.S.

*Bridgewater State College. Library Media Program. Hart Hall, Rm. 219, Bridgewater, MA 02325. (508)697-1320. Fax (508)697-1771. E-mail fzilonis@bridgew.edu. Web site http://www.bridgew.edu. Mary Frances Zilonis, Coord., Library Media Program. Specialization: M.Ed. in Library Media Studies. *Features:* This program heavily emphasizes teaching and technology. *Degree Requirements:* 39 semester hours; comprehensive exam. *Faculty:* 2 full-time, 6 part-time. *Students:* 58 in degree program, 30 nondegree. *Financial Assistance:* Graduate assistantships, graduate internships.

*Fitchburg State College. Division of Graduate and Continuing Education. 160 Pearl St., Fitchburg, MA 01420. (978)665-3181. Fax (978)665-3658. E-mail dgce@fsc.edu. Web site http://www.fsc.edu. Dr. Lee DeNike, Chair. *Specializations:* M.S. in Communications Media with specializations in Management, Technical and Professional Writing, Instructional Technology, and Library Media. *Features:* Collaborating with professionals working in the field both for organizations and as independent producers, Fitchburg offers a unique M.S. program. The objective of the Master of Science in Communications/Media Degree Programs is to develop in candidates the knowledge and skills for the effective implementation of communication within business, industry, government, not-for-profit agencies, health services, and education. *Admission Requirements:* MAT or GRE scores, official transcript(s) of a baccalaureate degree, two or more years of experience in communications or media, department interview and portfolio presentation, three letters of recommendation. *Degree Requirements:* 36 semester credit hours. Faculty: 1 full-time, 7 part-time. Students: 84 part-time. *Financial Assistance:* Assistantships, student loans, scholarships.

*Harvard University. Appian Way, Cambridge, MA 02138. (617)495-3541. Fax (617)495-3626. E-mail Admit@hugse2.harvard.edu. Web site http://GSEWeb.harvard.edu /TIEHome.html. David Perkins, Interim Dir. of Technology in Education Program. *Specializations:* M.Ed. in Technology in Education; an advanced certificate program is available. *Admission Requirements:* Bachelor's degree, MAT or GRE scores, 600 TOEFL, three recommendations. Students interested in print information about the TIE Program should e-mail a request to the address above. *Degree Requirements:* 32 semester credits. *Faculty:* 1 full-time, 9 part-time. *Students:* approx. 50: 39 full-time, 11 part-time. *Financial Assistance:* Within the school's policy.

*Lesley College. 29 Everett St., Cambridge, MA 02138-2790. (617)349-8419. Fax (617)349-8169. E-mail nroberts@mail.lesley.edu. Web site http://www.lesley.edu/soe /tech-in-ed/techined.html. Dr. Nancy Roberts, Prof. of Education. *Specializations:* M.Ed. in Technology Education; C.A.G.S. (Certificate of Advanced Graduate Study) in Technology Education; Ph.D. in Education with a Technology Education major. *Features:* M.Ed. program is offered off campus at 65 sites in 16 states; contact Professional Outreach Associates, (800)843-4808, for information. The degree is also offered online. Contact Maureen Yoder, myoder@mail.lesley.edu, or (617)348-8421 for information. *Degree Requirements:* M.Ed.: 33 semester hours in technology, integrative final project in lieu of thesis, no internship or practicum. C.A.G.S.: 36 semester hours. Ph.D. requirements available on request. *Faculty:* 9 full-time, 122 part-time on the Master's and C.A.G.S. levels. *Students:* 1,200 part-time.

*Simmons College. Graduate School of Library and Information Science. 300 The Fenway, Boston, MA 02115-5898. (617)521-2800. Fax (617)521-3192. E-mail jbaughman@simmons.edu. Web site http://www.simmons.edu/gslis/. Dr. James C. Baughman, Prof. *Specializations:* M.S. dual degrees: M.L.S./M.A. in Education (for School Library Media Specialists); M.L.S./M.A. in History (Archives Management Program). A Doctor of Arts in Administration is also offered. *Features:* The program prepares individuals for a variety of careers, media technology emphasis being only one. There are special programs for School Library Media Specialist and Archives Management with strengths in Information Science/Systems, Media Management. *Admission Requirements:* B.A. or B.S. degree with 3.0 GPA, statement, three letters of reference. *Degree Requirements:* 36 semester hours. *Faculty:* 14 full-time. *Students:* 75 full-time, 415 part-time. *Financial Assistance:* Assistantships, grants, student loans, scholarships.

*University of Massachusetts-Boston. Graduate College of Education. 100 Morrissey Blvd, Boston, MA 02125. (617)287-5980. Fax (617)287-7664. E-mail babcock@umbsky .cc.umb.edu. Web site http://www.umb.edu. Donald D. Babcock, Graduate Program Dir. *Specializations:* M.Ed. in Instructional Design. *Admission Requirements:* MAT or previous master's degree, goal statement, three letters of recommendation, resume, interview. *Degree Requirements:* 36 semester hours, thesis or project. *Faculty:* 1 full-time, 9 part-time. *Students:* 8 full-time, 102 part-time. *Financial Assistance:* Graduate assistantships providing tuition plus stipend.

University of Massachusetts-Lowell. Graduate School of Education. 255 Princeton Street, North Chelmsford, MA 01863. (508)934-4601. Fax (508)934-3005. E-mail John_Lebaron@uml.edu. Web site http://gse.uml.edu/. John LeBaron, Professor of Education. *Specializations:* M.Ed. and Ed.D. Educational Technology may be pursued in the context of any degree program area (Leadership, Administration and Policy; Curriculum and Instruction; Math and Science Education; Reading, Language Arts and Literacy. The M.Ed. program in Curriculum and Instruction has a specialization strand in educational technology. The Certificate of Advanced Graduate Study (C.A.G.S.), equivalent to 30 credits beyond a M.Ed., is also offered. *Features:* As part of the new state university system wide "UMass Online" initiative, a new Web-based M.Ed./state certification program in educational administration is under development for launch in 2001. The School also offers international Web-based courses in educational technology, and manages an extensive video network that links the University with other campuses in the state higher education system, and with area public schools. Technology is heavily infused into the teacher preparation and school support programs, where new initiatives have been supported by grants from several federal and non-federal agencies. *Admission Requirements:* For admission at the master's level, a bachelor's degree from an accredited institution in an academic discipline is required, along with a completed application form, recent GRE scores, a narrative statement of purpose, and three written recommendations. *Degree Requirements:* M.Ed. 30 credits beyond bachelor's; Ed.D. 60 credits beyond master's plus dissertation based on original research and demonstration of comprehensive mastery in relevant fields of inquiry. *Faculty:* One full-time faculty member to teach courses in educational technology; other faculty teach technology courses as part of their overall load. *Students:* FTE approximately 500. *Financial Assistance:* Assistantships; student loans; limited scholarships. *Degrees awarded 2000:* Approximately 75.

MICHIGAN

Eastern Michigan University. Teacher Education. 313 John W. Porter Building, Ypsilanti, MI 48197. (734)487-3260. Fax (734)487-2101. E-mail tsjones@online.emich.edu. Web site http://www.emich.edu. Toni Stokes Jones, Ph.D.-Assistant Professor/Graduate Coordinator. *Specializations:* M.A. in Educational Psychology with concentration in Educational Technology. The mission of this program is to prepare professionals who are capable of facilitating student learning in a variety of settings. The program is designed to provide students with both the knowledge base and the application skills that are required to use technology effectively in education. Focusing on the design, development, utilization, management and evaluation of instructional systems moves us toward achieving this mission. Students who complete the educational technology concentration will be able to (a) provide a rationale for using technology in the educational process; (b) identify contributions of major leaders in the field of educational media technology and instructional theory, and the impact that each leader has had on the field; (c) assess current trends in the area of educational media technology and relate the trends to past events and future implications; (d) integrate technology into instructional programs; (e) teach the operation and various uses of educational technology in instruction; (f) act as consultants/facilitators in educational media technology; (g) design and develop instructional products to meet specified needs; and (h) evaluate the effectiveness of instructional materials and systems. *Features:* Courses in our program include technology and the reflective teacher, technology and student-centered learning, technology enhanced learning environments, issues and emerging technologies, instructional design, Internet for educators, advanced technologies, psychology of the adult learning, principles of classroom learning, curriculum foundations, research seminar, and seminar in educational technology. *Admission Requirements:* Individuals seeking admission to this program must (1) comply with the Graduates School admission requirements; (2) have a combined score of 800 on the quantitative and verbal sections of the Graduate Record Examination; the GRE must have been taken within the past five years; (3) score 550 or better on the TOEFL and 5 or better on TWE, if a non-native speaker of English; (4) have a 2.75 undergraduate grade point average, or a 3.30 grade point average in 12 hours or more of work in a master's program; (5) solicit three letters of reference; and (6) submit a statement of professional goals. *Degree Requirements:* To graduate, each student is expected to (1) complete all work on an approved program of study (32 semester hours); (2) maintain a B (3.0 GPA) average or better on course work taken within the program; (3) get a recommendation from the faculty adviser; (4) fill out an application for graduation and obtain the advisers recommendation; (5) meet all other requirements for a master's degree adopted by the Graduate School of Eastern Michigan University; and (6) complete a culminating experience (thesis, internship or project) as determined by the student and faculty adviser. *Faculty:* 4 full-time; 3 part-time. *Students:* 35. *Financial Assistance:* Graduate assistantship. *Degrees awarded 2000:* 5.

*Michigan State University. College of Education. 431 Erickson, East Lansing, MI 48824. (517)355-6684. Fax (517)353-6393. E-mail yelons@pilot.msu.edu. Dr. Stephen Yelon. *Specializations:* M.A. in Educational Technology and Instructional Design. *Admission Requirements:* Bachelor's degree, 800 TOEFL, recommendations, goal statement. *Degree Requirements:* 30 semester hours, certification exam, field experience. *Faculty:* 5 full-time. *Students:* Approx. 45. *Financial Assistance:* Some assistantships for highly qualified students.

*University of Michigan. Department of Educational Studies. 610 East University, Ann Arbor, MI 48109-1259. (313)763-4668. Fax (313)763-4663. E-mail carl.berger@umich.edu. Web site http://www.soe.umich.edu. Carl F. Berger, Chair. *Specializations:* M.Ed.; Ph.D. in Instructional Technology with concentrations in Science, Math, or Literacy. *Features:* Programs are individually designed. *Admission Requirements:* GRE, B.A. for M.Ed., Master's for Ph.D. *Degree Requirements:* M.Ed.: 30 hours beyond B.A. Ph.D.: 60 hours beyond B.A. or 30 hours beyond master's plus comprehensive exams and dissertation. *Faculty:* 3 full-time, 6 part-time. *Students:* 35 full-time, 7 part-time. *Financial Assistance:* Assistantships, grants, student loans, scholarships, internships.

*Wayne State University. 381 Education, Detroit, MI 48202. (313)577-1728. Fax (313)577-1693. E-mail rrichey@coe.wayne.edu. Web site http://www.coe.wayne.edu /InstructionalTechnology. Rita C. Richey, Prof., Program Coord., Instructional Technology Programs, Div. of Administrative and Organizational Studies, College of Education. *Specializations:* M.Ed. degrees in Performance Improvement and Training, K–12 Educational Technology, and Interactive Technologies. Ed.D. and Ph.D. programs to prepare individuals for leadership in business, industry, health care, and the K–12 school setting as instructional design and development specialists; media or learning resources managers or consultants; specialists in instructional video; and computer-assisted instruction and multimedia specialists. The school also offers a six-year specialist degree program in Instructional Technology. *Features:* Guided experiences in instructional design and development activities in business and industry are available. *Admission Requirements:* Ph.D.: Master's degree, 3.5 GPA, GRE, MAT, strong professional recommendations, interview. *Degree Requirements:* M.Ed.: 36 semester hours, including required project; internship recommended. *Faculty:* 6 full-time, 5 part-time. *Students:* M.Ed., 525; doctoral, 95, most part-time. *Financial Assistance:* Student loans, scholarships, and paid internships.

MINNESOTA

*Mankato State University. MSU Box 20, P.O. Box 8400, Mankato, MN 56001-8400. (507)389-1965. Fax (507)389-5751. E-mail pengelly@mankato.msus.edu. Web site http://lme.mankato.msus.edu. Frank R. Birmingham Ph.D., Dept. of Library Media Education. *Specializations:* M.S. in Educational Technology with three tracks. *Admission Requirements:* Bachelor's degree, 2.75/4.0 for last two years of undergraduate work. *Degree Requirements:* 32 semester hour credits, comprehensive exam. *Faculty:* 4 full-time.

*St. Cloud State University. College of Education. St. Cloud, MN 56301-4498. (612)255-2022. Fax (612)255-4778. E-mail jberling@tigger.stcloud.msus.edu. John G. Berling, Prof., Dir., Center for Information Media. *Specializations:* Master's degrees in Information Technologies, Educational Media, and Human Resources Development/Training. A Specialist degree is also offered. *Admission Requirements:* acceptance to Graduate School, written preliminary examination, interview. *Degree Requirements:* Master's: 51 qtr. hours with thesis; 54 qtr. hours, Plan B; 57 qtr. hours, portfolio; 200-hour practicum is required for media generalist licensure. Course work applies to Educational

Media Master's program. *Faculty:* 7 full-time. *Students:* 15 full-time, 150 part-time. *Financial Assistance:* Assistantships, scholarships.

*****Walden University.** 155 5th Avenue South, Minneapolis, MN 55401. (800)444-6795. E-mail www@waldenu.edu or info@waldenu.edu. Web site http://www.waldenu.edu; http://www.waldenu.edu/ecti/ecti.html. Dr. Gwen Hillesheim, Chair. *Specializations:* M.S. in Educational Change and Technology Innovation. Ph.D. in Education in Learning and Teaching with specialization in Educational Technology. In 1998 a specialization in Distance Learning will be added. In addition, there is a generalist Ph.D. in Education in which students may choose and design their own areas of specialization. *Features:* Delivered primarily online. *Admission Requirements:* Accredited bachelor's. Ph.D.: accredited master's, goal statement, letters of recommendation. *Degree Requirements:* Master's: 45 credit curriculum, two brief residencies, master's project. *Faculty:* 18 part-time. *Students:* 50 full-time, 53 part-time in master's program. *Financial Assistance:* Student loans, 3 fellowships with annual review.

MISSOURI

Fontbonne College. 6800 Wydown Blvd., St. Louis, MO 63105. (314)889-1497. Fax (314)889-1451. E-mail mabkemei@fontbonne.edu. Dr. Mary K. Abkemeier, Chair. *Specializations:* M.S. in Computer Education. Features: small classes and course work immediately applicable to the classroom. *Features: Admission Requirements:* 2.5 undergraduate GPA, three letters of recommendation. *Degree Requirements:* 33 semester hours, 3.0 GPA. *Faculty:* 2 full-time, 12 part-time. *Students:* 4 full-time, 90 part-time. *Financial Assistance:* Grants.

Northwest Missouri State University. Department of Computer Science/Information Systems. 800 University Ave., Maryville, MO 64468. (660)562-1600. Fax (660)-562-1963. E-mail pheeler@mail.nwmissouri.edu. Web site http://www.nwmissouri .edu/~csis. Dr. Phillip Heeler, Chairperson. *Specializations:* M.S. in School Computer Studies; M.S.Ed. in Instructional Technology. *Features:* These degrees are designed for computer educators at the elementary, middle school, high school, and junior college level. *Admission Requirements:* 3.0 undergraduate GPA, 700 GRE (V + Q). *Degree Requirements:* 32 semester hours of graduate courses in computer science education and instructional technology courses. *Faculty:* 12 full-time, 4 part-time. *Students:* 5 full-time, 20 part-time. *Financial Assistance:* Assistantships, grants, student loans, and scholarships. *Degrees awarded 2000:* 10.

Southwest Missouri State University. School of Teacher Education. Hill Hall 207, 901 S. National, Springfield, MO 65804. (417)836-6769. Fax (417)836-6252. E-mail RogerTipling@smsu.edu Dr. Roger Tipling, Graduate Coord. Instructional Media Technology. *Specializations*: M.S. in Education with areas of emphasis in Instructional Technology, Library Media Specialist, Building Level Technology Specialist, Technology Coordinator, Master Teacher and occupations outside of schools such as medical, business and industrial. *Features:* Foundations of Instructional Design, Administration/Management, Production with different course options for the different tracks or professional goals. *Admission Requirements:* Admission to Graduate College (http://www.smsu.edu/grad/catalog), three letters of recommendation, comprehensive autobiography. *Degree Requirements:* Minimum of 33 semester hours. *Faculty:* Two full-time. *Students:* 5 full-time, 60 part-time. *Financial Assistance:* Graduate assistantships.

University of Missouri-Columbia. College of Education. 303 Townsend Hall, Columbia, MO 65211. (573)882-4546. Fax 573-884-2917. E-mail wedmanj@missouri.edu. Web site http:www.coe.missouri.edu/sis. John Wedman. *Specializations:* The Educational Technology emphasis area prepares educators and technologists for excellence and leadership in the design, development and implementation of technology in education, training and performance support. The program offers three tracks: Technology in Schools, Networked Learning Systems, and Training and Development. Each track has its own set of competencies, course work, and processes. *Features:* The Technology in Schools track is completely available online. Students from around the world participate in this track. The Networked Learning Systems track offers a truly challenging and innovative set of technical learning experiences. Students have the opportunities to work on large-scale software development projects, acquiring valuable experience and a broadened skill set. *Admission Requirements:* Bachelor's degree with a 3.0 in last 60 credit hours of course work, 1500 combined on GRE, TOEFL of 540 (270 Computer based test), three letters of reference. *Degree Requirements:* Master's: 32 credit hours; 15 hours at 400 level. Specific course requirements vary by track. *Faculty:* 8 full-time, 20 part-time. *Students:* 30 full-time,150 part-time. *Financial Assistance:* Assistantships, grants, student loans, scholarships. Assistantships include a stipend and tuition waiver. *Degrees Awarded 2000*: 35.

Webster University. Instructional Technology. St. Louis, MO 63119. (314)968-7490. Fax (314)968-7118. E-mail steinmpe@websteruniv.edu. Web site http://www.websteruniv.edu. Paul Steinmann, Assoc. Dean and Dir., Graduate Studies and Instructional Technology. *Specializations:* Master's degree (M.A.T.); State Certification in Media Technology is a program option. *Admission Requirements:* Bachelor's degree with 2.5 GPA. *Degree Requirements:* 33 semester hours (including 24 in media); internship required. *Faculty:* 5. *Students:* 7 full-time, 28 part-time. *Financial Assistance:* Partial scholarships, minority scholarships, government loans, and limited state aid.

MONTANA

*University of Montana. School of Education. Missoula, MT 59812. (406)243-5785. Fax (406)243-4908. E-mail cjlott@selway.umt.edu. Dr. Carolyn Lott, Assoc. Prof. of Library/Media. *Specializations:* M.Ed. and Specialist degrees; K–12 School Library Media specialization with School Library Media Certification endorsement. *Features: Admission Requirements:* Both degrees: GRE, letters of recommendation, 2.5 GPA. *Degree Requirements:* M.Ed.: 37 semester credit hours (18 overlap with library media endorsement); Specialist: 28 semester hours (18 overlap). *Faculty:* 2 full-time. *Students:* 5 full-time, 20 part-time. *Financial Assistance:* Assistantships; contact the University of Montana Financial Aid Office.

NEBRASKA

*University of Nebraska at Kearney. Kearney, NE 68849-1260. (308)865-8833. Fax (308)865-8097. E-mail fredrickson@unk.edu. Web site http://www.unk.edu/departments/pte. Dr. Scott Fredrickson, Dir. of Instructional Technology. *Specializations:* M.S. in Instructional Technology, M.S. in Educational Media, Specialist in Educational Media. *Admission Requirements:* M.S. and Specialist: GRE, acceptance into graduate school, approval of Instructional Technology Committee. *Degree Requirements:* M.S.: 36 credit hours, master's comprehensive exam or field study. Specialist: 39 credit hours, field study. *Faculty:* 5 full-time, 10 part-time. *Students:* 62 full-time. *Financial Assistance:* Assistantships, grants, student loans.

*University of Nebraska-Omaha. Department of Teacher Education College of Education. Kayser Hall 208D, Omaha, NE 68182. (402)5543790. Fax (402)554-3491. E-mail langan@unomaha.edu. John Langan, Teacher Education. *Specializations:* M.S. in Education, M.A. in Education, both with Educational Media concentration. *Degree Requirements:* 36 semester hours (including 24 in media), practicum; thesis optional. *Faculty:* 2 full-time, 4 part-time. *Students:* 10 full-time, 62 part-time. *Financial Assistance:* Contact Financial Aid Office.

NEVADA

*University of Nevada. Counseling and Educational Psychology Dept. College of Educatio. Reno, NV 89557. (702)784-6327. Fax (702)784-1990. E-mail ljohnson@unr.edu. Web site http://www.unr.edu/unr/colleges/educ/cep/cepindex.html. Dr. LaMont Johnson, Program Coord., Information Technology in Education. Marlowe Smaby, Dept. Chair. *Specializations:* M.S. and Ph.D. *Admission Requirements:* Bachelor's degree, 2.75 undergraduate GPA, 750 GRE (V + Q). *Degree Requirements:* 36 semester credits, optional thesis worth 6 credits, comprehensive exam. *Faculty:* 2 full-time, 1 part-time. *Students:* M.S., 15; Ph.D., 10.

NEW JERSEY

*Montclair State University. Department of Reading and Educational Media. Upper Montclair, NJ 07043. (973)655-7040. Fax (973)655-5310. E-mail pauld@mail.montclair.edu. Web site http://www.monclair.edu. Robert R. Ruezinsky, Dir. of Academic Technology. *Specializations:* No degree program exists. Two certification programs, A.M.S. and E.M.S, exist on the graduate level. *Degree Requirements:* Certification requirements:18-21 semester hours of media and technology are required for the A.M.S. program and 30-33 hours for the E.M.S. program. *Faculty:* 7 part-time.

*Rutgers-The State University of New Jersey. Ph.D. Program in Communication, Information, and Library Studies. The Graduate School, New Brunswick, NJ 08901-1071. (732)932-7447. Fax (732)932-6916. E-mail chabrak@sclis.rutgers.edu. Dr. Lea P. Stewart, Director, Master's Program, Dept. of Library and Information Studies, School of Communication, Information and Library Studies. (732)932-9717. Fax (732)932-2644. Dr.Carol Kuhlthan, Chair. *Specializations:* M.L.S. degree with specializations in Information Retrieval, Technical and Automated Services, Reference, School Media Services, Youth Services, Management and Policy Issues, and Generalist Studies. Ph.D. programs in Communication; Media Studies; Information Systems, Structures, and Users; Information and Communication Policy and Technology; and Library and Information Services. The school also offers a six-year specialist certificate program. *Features:* Ph.D. Program provides doctoral-level course work for students seeking theoretical and research skills for scholarly and professional leadership in the information and communication fields. A course on multimedia structure, organization, access, and production is offered. *Admission Requirements:* Ph.D.: Master's degree in Information Studies, Communication, Library Science, or related field; 3.0 undergraduate GPA; GRE scores; TOEFL (for applicants whose native language is not English). *Degree Requirements:* M.L.S.: 36 semester hours, in which the hours for media vary for individual students; practicum of 150 hours. *Faculty:* M.L.S., 15 full-time, 12 adjunct; Ph.D., 43. *Students:* M.L.S., 97 full-time, 199 part-time; Ph.D., 104. *Financial Assistance:* M.L.S.: scholarships, fellowships, and graduate assistantships; Ph.D.: assistantships.

*William Paterson University. College of Education. 300 Pompton Rd., Wayne, NJ 07470. (973)720-2140. Fax (973)720-2585. E-mail kaplan@wpunj.edu. Web site http://pwcweb.wilpaterson.edu/wpcpages/library/default.htp. Dr. Amy G. Job, Librarian, Assoc. Prof., Coord., Program in Library/Media, Curriculum and Instruction Dept. *Specializations:* M.Ed. for Educational Media Specialist, Associate Media Specialist, Ed.S. *Admission Requirements:* Teaching certificate, 2.75 GPA, MAT or GRE scores, one year teaching experience. Ed.S.: certificate, 2.75 GPA. *Degree Requirements:* M.Ed.: 33 semester hours, including research projects and practicum. Ed.S.: 18 sem. hours. *Faculty:* 6 full-time, 2 part-time. *Students:* 30 part-time.

NEW YORK

*Buffalo State College. 1300 Elmwood Ave., Buffalo, NY 14222-1095. (716)878-4923. Fax (716)878-6677. E-mail nowakoaj@buffalostate.edu. Dr. Anthony J. Nowakowski, Program Coord. *Specializations:* M.S. in Education in Educational Computing. *Admission Requirements:* Bachelor's degree from accredited institution, 3.0 GPA in last 60 hours, three letters of recommendation. *Degree Requirements:* 33 semester hours (15 hours in computers, 12-15 hours in education, 3-6 electives); thesis or project (see: www.buffalostate.edu/edc). *Faculty:* 5 part-time. *Students:* 3 full-time, 98 part-time.

*Fordham University. Rose Hill Campus, 441 E. Fordham Rd., Bronx, NY 10458. (718)817-4860. Fax (718)817-4868. E-mail pcom@murray.fordham.edu. Web site http://www.fordham.edu. Robin Andersen, Department Chair, James Capo, Director of Graduate Studies. *Specializations:* M.A. in Public Communications. *Features:* Internship or thesis option; full-time students can complete program in 12 months. *Admission Requirements:* 3.0 undergraduate GPA. *Degree Requirements:* 10 courses plus internship or thesis. *Faculty:* 8 full-time, 2 part-time. *Students:* 8 full-time, 22 part-time. *Financial Assistance:* Assistantships, student loans, scholarships.

Ithaca College. School of Communications. Park Hall, Ithaca, NY 14850. (607)274-1025. Fax (607)274-7076. E-mail herndon@ithaca.edu. Web site http://www.ithaca.edu/ocld. Sandra L. Herndon, Professor, Chair, Graduate Program in Communications; Roy H. Park, School of Communications. *Specializations:* M.S. in Communications. Students in this program find employment in such areas as instructional design, multimedia, public relations and marketing, and employee communication. The program can be tailored to individual career goals. *Features:* Program is interdisciplinary, incorporating organizational communication, instructional design, and technology. *Admission Requirements:* 3.0 GPA, TOEFL 550, or 213 computer-scored (where applicable). *Degree Requirements:* 36 semester hours including capstone seminar. *Faculty:* 8 full-time. *Students:* approx. 25 full-time, 10 part-time. *Financial Assistance:* Graduate assistantships. *Degrees awarded 2000:* 15.

*New York Institute of Technology. Dept. of Instructional Technology. Tower House, Old Westbury, NY 11568. (516)686-7777. Fax (516)686-7655. E-mail dplumer460@aol.com. Web site http://www.nyit.edu. Davenport Plumer, Chair, Depts. of Instructional Technology and Elementary Education—pre-service and in-service. *Specializations:* M.S. in Instructional Technology; M.S. in Elementary Education; Specialist Certificates in Computers in Education, Distance Learning, and Multimedia (not degrees, but are earned after the first 18 credits of the master's degree). *Features:* Computer integration in virtually all courses; online courses; evening, weekend, and summer courses. *Admission Requirements:* Bachelor's degree from accredited college with 3.0 cumulative average. *Degree Requirements:* 36 credits with 3.0 GPA for M.S., 18 credits with 3.0 GPA for certificates. *Faculty:* 11 full-time, 42 part-time. *Students:* 112 full-time, 720 part-time. *Financial Assistance:* Graduate assistantships, institutional and alumni scholarships, student loans.

New York University. Educational Communication and Technology Program. School of Education 239 Greene St., Suite 300, New York, NY 10003. (212)998-5520. Fax (212)995-4041. E-mail ectprogram@nyu.edu. Web site http://www.nyu.edu/education/alt /ectprogram. Francine Shuchat-Shaw, Assoc. Prof. (MA Advisor), Dir.; Michael Reed, Assoc. Prof., (Doctoral Advisor). *Specializations:* M.A., Ed.D., and Ph.D. in Education—for the preparation of individuals as instructional media designers, developers, media producers, and/or researchers in education, business and industry, health and medicine, community services, government, museums and other cultural institutions; and to teach or become involved in administration in educational communications and instructional technology programs in higher education, including instructional television, microcomputers, multi-media, Internet and telecommunications. The program also offers a post-M.A. 30-point Certificate of Advanced Study in Education. *Features:* Emphasizes theoretical foundations, especially a cognitive science perspective of learning and instruction, and their implications for designing media-based learning environments and materials. All efforts focus on video, multimedia, instructional television, Web-based technology and telecommunications; participation in special research and production projects and field internships. *Admission Requirements:* M.A.: 3.0 undergraduate GPA, responses to essay questions, interview related to academic and professional goals. Ph.D.: 3.0 GPA, 1000 GRE, responses to essay questions, interview related to academic or professional preparation and career goals. For international students, 600 TOEFL and TWE. *Degree Requirements:* M.A.: 36 semester hours including specialization, elective courses, thesis, English Essay Examination. Ph.D.: 57 semester hours including specialization, foundations, research, content seminar, and elective course work; candidacy papers; dissertation; English Essay Examination. *Faculty:* 2 full-time, 10 part-time. *Students:* M.A.: 40 full-time, 35 part-time. Ph.D.: 14 full-time, 20 part-time. *Financial Assistance:* Graduate and research assistantships, student loans, scholarships, and work assistance programs. *Degrees awarded 2000:* M.A., Ph.D., and Ed.D.

Pace University. Westchester Dept, School of Education Bedford Road, Pleasantville, NY 10570. (914)773-3829, (914)773-3979. Fax (914)773-3521. E-mail sflank@pace.edu. Web site http://www.pace.edu. Dr. Sandra Flank, Co-Chair. *Specializations:* M.Ed. in Instructional Technology. *Features:* Results in New York State Educational Technology Specialist Certification (2/2004). Program is individualized to meet the needs of two distinct populations: those with an education background or those with a technology background. Some courses are delivered through a distance learning platform. *Admission Requirements:* GPA 3.0, transcript review, interview. *Degree Requirements:* 33-36 semester hours. *Faculty:* 8 full-time, 50 part-time. *Students:* 60-70 part-time. *Financial Assistance:* Assistantships, internships, scholarships. *Degrees awarded 2000:* Program is new and is being implemented as of 9/01.

St. Johns University. Division of Library and Information Science. 8000 Utopia Parkway, Jamaica, NY 11439. (718)990-6200. Fax (718)990-2071. E-mail libis@stjohns.edu. Web site http://www.stjohns.edu/gsas/dlis/. Elizabeth B. Pollicino, Associate Director. *Specializations:* M.L.S. with specialization in School Media. The school also offers a 24-credit Advanced Certificate program in which students may also take School Media and Technology courses. *Features:* Small class size, personal advisement, student lounge and computer lab, high-tech classrooms. *Admission Requirements:* 3.0 GPA, two letters of reference, statement of professional goals. GRE (General) required for assistantships. *Degree Requirements:* 36 semester hours, comprehensive exam, practicum. *Faculty:* 6 full-time, 10 part-time. *Students:* 15 full-time, 83 part-time. *Financial Assistance:* 4 assistantships in DLIS; others available in University Library. *Degrees awarded 2000:* 28.

State University College of Arts and Science at Potsdam. School of Education. 116 Satterlee Hall, Potsdam, NY 13676. (315)267-2535. Fax (315)267-4895. E-mail mlynarhc@potsdam.edu. Web site http://www.potsdam.edu/educ/it/index.html. Dr. Charles Mlynarczyk, Chair, Information and Communications Technology. *Specializations:* M.S. in Education in Instructional Technology with concentrations in General K–12, Educational Communications Specialist, and Training and Development. *Features:* A progressive, forward-looking program. *Admission Requirements:* (1) Submission of an official transcript of an earned baccalaureate degree from an accredited institution. (2) A minimum GPA of 2.75 (4.0 scale) in the most recent 60 credit hours of course work. (3) Submission of the Application for Graduate Study (w/$50 nonrefundable fee). (4) For students seeking the Education Communications Specialist Certification, a valid NYS Teaching Certificate is required. *Degree Requirements:* 33 semester hours, including internship or practicum; culminating project required. *Faculty:* 3 full-time, 2 part-time. *Students:* 26 full-time, 85 part-time. *Financial Assistance:* Student loans, student assistantships. *Degrees awarded 2000:* 32.

*State University of New York at Albany. School of Education. 1400 Washington Ave., Albany, NY 12222. (518)442-5032. Fax (518)442-5008. E-mail swan@cnsunix.albany.edu. Karen Swan (ED114A), contact person. *Specializations:* M.Ed. and Ph.D. in Curriculum and Instruction with specializations in Instructional Theory, Design, and Technology. M.Ed. offered entirely online over the Internet. *Admission Requirements:* Bachelor's degree, GPA close to 3.0, transcript, three letters of recommendation. Students desiring New York State permanent teaching certification should possess preliminary certification. *Degree Requirements:* M.Ed.: 30 semester hours with 15-18 credits in specialization. Ph.D.: 78 semester hours, internship, portfolio certification, thesis. *Faculty:* 13 full-time, 7 part-time. *Students:* 100 full-time, 350 part-time. *Financial Assistance:* Fellowships, assistantships, grants, student loans, minority fellowships.

*State University of New York at Stony Brook. Technology & Society College of Engineering & Applied Sciences. SUNY at Stony Brook, Stony Brook, NY 11794-2250. (516)632-8763, (516)632-7809. E-mail dferguson@dts.tns.sunysb.edu. Web site http://www.ceas.sunysb.edu/DTS/. Prof. David L. Ferguson, contact person. *Specializations:* Master's degree in Technological Systems Management with concentration in Educational Computing. *Features:* Emphasis on courseware design, multimedia and modeling, applications, and problem solving. *Admission Requirements:* bachelor's degree in engineering, natural sciences, social sciences, mathematics, or closely related area; 3.0 undergraduate GPA; experience with computer applications or computer applications or use of computers in teaching. *Degree Requirements:* 30 semester credits, including two general technology core courses, five required educational computing courses, and three eligible electives. *Faculty:* 5 full-time, 3 part-time. *Students:* 10 full-time, 15 part-time. *Financial Assistance:* Assistantships, grants, student loans.

*Syracuse University. Instructional Design, Development, and Evaluation Program, School of Education. 330 Huntington Hall, Syracuse, NY 13244-2340. (315)443-3703. Fax (315)443-9218. E-mail lltucker@sued.syr.edu. Web site http://www.idde.syr.edu. Philip L. Doughty, Prof., Chair. *Specializations:* M.S., Ed.D., and Ph.D. degree programs for Instructional Design of programs and materials, Educational Evaluation, Human Issues in Instructional Development, Media Production (including computers and multimedia), and Educational Research and Theory (learning theory, application of theory, and educational media research). Graduates are prepared to serve as curriculum developers, instructional developers, program and product evaluators, researchers, resource center administrators, communications coordinators, trainers in human resource development, and higher education instructors. The school also offers an advanced certificate program. *Features:* Field work and internships, special topics and special issues seminar, student- and faculty-initiated minicourses, seminars and guest lecturers, faculty-student formulation of department policies, and multiple international perspectives. *Admission Requirements:* M.S.: undergraduate transcripts, recommendations, personal statement, interview recommended; TOEFL for international applicants; GRE recommended. Doctoral: Relevant master's degree from accredited institution, GRE (three tests required) scores, recommendations, personal statement, TOEFL for international applicants; interview recommended. *Degree Requirements:* M.S.: 36 semester hours, comprehensive exam and portfolio required. *Faculty:* 2 full-time, 4 part-time. *Students:* M.S., 22 full-time, 23 part-time; doctoral, 25 full-time, 30 part-time. *Financial Assistance:* Fellowships, scholarships, and graduate assistantships entailing either research or administrative duties in instructional technology.

NORTH CAROLINA

*Appalachian State University. Department of Leadership and Educational Studies. Boone, NC 28608. (704)262-2243. Fax (704)262-2128. E-mail Webbbh@appstate.edu. Web site http://www.ced.appstate.edu/ltl.html. John H. Tashner, Prof., Coord. *Specializations:* M.A. in Educational Media and Technology with three areas of concentration: Computers, Telecommunications, and Media Production. *Features:* IMPACT NC (business, university, and public school) partnership offers unusual opportunities. *Degree Requirements:* 36 semester hours (including 15 in Computer Education), internship; thesis optional. *Faculty:* 2 full-time, 1 part-time. *Students:* 10 full-time, 60 part-time. *Financial Assistance:* Assistantships, grants, student loans.

East Carolina University. Department of Librarianship, Educational Technology, and Distance Instruction. 102 Joyner East, Greenville, NC 27858-4353. (252)328-6621. Fax (252)328-4368. E-mail kesterd@mail.ecu.edu. Web site www.soe.ecu.edu/ltdi. Dr. Diane D. Kester, Assoc. Prof., Chair. *Specializations:* Master of Library Science; Certificate of Advanced Study (Library Science); Master of Arts in Education (North Carolina Instructional Technology—Specialist licensure); Master of Science in Instructional Technology; Certificate of Tele-learning;Certificate of Virtual Reality in Education and Training. *Features:* M.L.S. graduates are eligible for North Carolina School Media Coord. certification; C.A.S. graduates are eligible for North Carolina School Media Supervisor certification; M.A.Ed. graduates are eligible for North Carolina Instructional Technology-Computers certification. *Admission Requirements:* Master's: bachelor's degree; C.A.S.: M.L.S. or equivalent degree. *Degree Requirements:* M.L.S.: 39 semester hours; M.A.Ed.: 39 semester hours; M.S.: 39 semester hours; C.A.S.: 30 semester hours. *Faculty:* 8 full-time. *Students:* 7 full-time, 150 part-time. *Financial Assistance:* Graduate assistantships. *Degrees awarded 2000:* 20 MLS; 19 MAED.

*North Carolina Central University. School of Education. 1801 Fayetteville St., Durham, NC 27707. (919)560-6692. Fax (919)560-5279. E-mail bwebb@nccu.edu. Dr. James N. Colt, Assoc. Prof., Coordinator., Graduate Program in Educational Technology. *Specializations:* M.A. with special emphasis on Instructional Development/Design. *Features:* Graduates are prepared to implement and utilize a variety of technologies applicable to many professional ventures, including institutions of higher education (college resource centers), business, industry, and professional schools such as medicine, law, dentistry, and nursing. *Admission Requirements:* Undergraduate degree, GRE. *Degree Requirements:* 33 semester hours (including thesis). *Faculty:* 2 full-time, 2 part-time. *Students:* 19 full-time, 18 part-time. *Financial Assistance:* Assistantships, grants, student loans.

North Carolina State University. Department of Curriculum and Instruction. P.O. Box 7801, Raleigh, NC 27695-7801. (919)515-1779. Fax (919)515-6978. E-mail Ellen_Vasu @ncsu.edu. Web site http://www2.ncsu.edu/ncsu/cep/ci/it2000/index.html. Dr. Ellen Vasu, Professor. *Specializations:* M.Ed. and M.S. in Instructional Technology-Computers (program track within one Master's in Curriculum and Instruction). Ph.D. in Curriculum and Instruction with focus on Instructional Technology as well as other areas. *Admission Requirements:* Master's: undergraduate degree from an accredited institution, 3.0 GPA in major or in latest graduate degree program; transcripts; GRE or MAT scores; three references; goal statement. Ph.D.: undergraduate degree from accredited institution, 3.0 GPA in major or latest graduate program; transcripts; recent GRE scores, writing sample, interview, three references, vita, goal statement (see http://www2.acs.ncsu.edu/grad/admision .htm). *Degree Requirements:* Master's: 36 semester hours, practicum, thesis optional; Ph.D.: 72 hours beyond bachelors (minimum 33 in Curriculum and Instruction core, 27 in Research); other information available upon request. *Faculty:* 3 full-time. *Students:* Master's, 41 part-time; Ph.D., 11 part-time, 1 full-time. *Financial Assistance:* Some assistantships available on a limited basis. *Degrees awarded 2000:* 3 master's degrees.

University of North Carolina. School of Information and Library Science. CB#3360, Chapel Hill, NC 27599-3360. (919)962-8062, 962-8366. Fax (919)962-8071. E-mail daniel@ils.unc.edu. Web site http://www.ils.unc.edu/. Evelyn H. Daniel, Prof., Coord., School Media Program. *Specializations:* Master of Science Degree in Library Science (M.S.L.S.) with specialization in school library media work. *Features:* Rigorous academic program plus teaching practicum requirement; excellent placement record. *Admission Requirements:* Competitive admission based on all three GRE components (quantitative, qualitative, analytical), undergraduate GPA (plus graduate work if any), letters of recommendation, and student statement of career interest and school choice. *Degree Requirements:* 48 semester hours, practicum, comprehensive exam, master's paper. *Faculty:* 18 full-time, 10 part-time. *Students:* 30 full-time, 20 part-time. *Financial Assistance:* Grants, assistantships, student loans. *Degrees awarded 2000:* 120 degrees awarded, 12 for school library media certification.

NORTH DAKOTA

Minot State University. Graduate School. 500 University Ave. W., Minot, ND 58707. (701)858-3250. Fax (701)839-6933. E-mail butler@misu.nodak.edu. Web site www.minotstateu.edu. Dr. Jack L. Rasmussen, Dean of the Graduate School. *Specializations:* M.S. in Elementary Education (including work in educational computing); M.S. in Special Education with Specialization in Severe Multiple-Handicaps, Early Childhood Special Education, Education of the Deaf, and Learning Disabilities; M.S. in Communication Disorders, Specializations in Audiology and Speech Language Pathology. *Features:* All programs include involvement in computer applications appropriate to the area of study, including assistive technologies for persons with disabilities. Computer laboratories are available for student use in the library and various departments. Some courses are offered through the Interactive Video Network, which connects all universities in North Dakota. All programs have a rural focus and are designed to offer a multitude of practical experiences. *Admission Requirements:* $30 fee, three letters of recommendation, 300-word autobiography, transcripts, GRE in Communication Disorders or GMAT for M.S. in Management. *Degree Requirements:* 30 semester hours (hours in computers, education, and outside education vary according to program); written comprehensive exams; oral exams; thesis or project. *Faculty:* 10 full-time. *Students:* 61 full-time, 63 part-time. *Financial Assistance:* Loans, assistantships, scholarships. *Degrees awarded 2000:* 60.

OHIO

Kent State University. Instructional Technology. 405 White Hall, Kent, OH 44242. (330)672-2294. Fax (330)672-2512. E-mail ddalton@kent.edu. Web site http://itec.educ.kent.edu. Dr. David Dalton, Coord., Instructional Technology Program. *Specializations:* M.Ed. or M.A. in Instructional Technology, Instructional Computing, and Library/Media Specialist; Ph.D. in Educational Psychology with emphasis in Instructional Technology. *Features:* Programs are planned individually to prepare students for careers in elementary, secondary, or higher education, business, industry, government agencies, or health facilities. Students may take advantage of independent research, individual study, practica, and internships. *Admission Requirements:* Master's: bachelor's degree with 2.75 undergraduate GPA. *Degree Requirements:* Master's: 37 semester hours. *Faculty:* 4 full-time, 7 part-time. *Students:* 39. *Financial Assistance:* 6 graduate assistantships, John Mitchell and Marie McMahan Awards, 4 teaching fellowships. *Degrees awarded 2000:* 15.

*Ohio University. School of Curriculum and Instruction. 248 McCracken Hall, Athens, OH 45701-2979. (740)593-9826. Fax (740)593-0177. E-mail turners@ohiou.edu. Sandra Turner, Chair. *Specializations:* M.Ed. in Computer Education and Technology; Ph.D. in Curriculum and Instruction with emphasis in Technology also available; call for details. *Admission Requirements:* Bachelor's degree, 2.5 undergraduate GPA, 35 MAT, 420 GRE (verbal), 400 GRE (quantitative), 550 TOEFL, three letters of recommendation. *Degree Requirements:* 54 qtr. credits, optional thesis worth 2-10 credits or alternative seminar and paper. Students may earn two graduate degrees simultaneously in education and in any other field. *Faculty:* 2 full-time, 1 part-time. *Students:* M.Ed.: 60. *Financial Assistance:* Assistantships.

University of Cincinnati. College of Education. 401 Teachers College, ML002, Cincinnati, OH 45221-0002. (513)556-3579. Fax (513)556-1001. E-mail Janet.Bohren@uc.edu. Web site http://uc.edu/. Janet L. Bohren, Division of Teacher Education. *Specializations:* M.Ed. or Ed.D. in Curriculum and Instruction with an emphasis on Instructional Design and Technology; Educational Technology degree programs for current professional, technical, critical, and personal knowledge. *Features:* Contact division for features. *Admission Requirements:* Bachelor's degree from accredited institution, 2.8 undergraduate GPA; GRE 1500 or better. *Degree Requirements:* 54 qtr. hours, written exam, thesis or research project (12-15 credit hours college core; 12-15 C & I; 18-27 credit hours specialization; 3-6 credit hours thesis or project). *Faculty:* 3 full-time. *Students:* In C & I there are 75 doctoral students and 10 master's students. *Financial Assistance:* Scholarships, assistantships, grants. *Degrees awarded 2000:* C & I degrees, 32 M.Ed. and 8 Ed.D.

*University of Toledo. Area of Education. 2801 West Bancroft, Toledo, OH 43606. (419)530-6176. Fax (419)530-7719. E-mail APATTER@UTNET.UTOLEDO.EDU. Web site http://carver.carver.utoledo. Dr. Lester J. Elsie, Dir. *Specializations:* Master's (M.Ed. and M.S.Ed.), Ed.S., doctorate (Ed.D., Ph.D.) degrees in Instructional Development, Library/Media Education, Instructional Computing, and Human Resources Development. *Admission Requirements:* Master's: 3.0 undergraduate GPA, GRE, recommendations; Ed.S.: master's degree, GRE, recommendations; doctorate: master's degree, GRE, TOEFL, recommendations, entrance writing sample, and interview. *Degree Requirements:* Master's: 36 semester hours, master's project; Ed.S.: 32 semester hours, internship; doctorate: 84 semester hours, dissertation. *Faculty:* 5 full-time, 1 part-time. *Students:* Master's, 10 full-time, 72 part-time; Ed.S., 2 full-time, 21 part-time; doctoral, 9 full-time, 56 part-time. *Financial Assistance:* Assistantships, student loans, scholarships, work assistance program.

*Wright State University. College of Education and Human Services, Dept. of Educational Leadership. 228 Millett Hall, Dayton, OH 45435. (937)775-2509 or (937)775-2182. Fax (937)775-4485. E-mail bonnie.mathies@wright.edu. Web site http://www.ed.wright.edu. Dr. Bonnie K. Mathies, Asst. Dean Communication and Technology. *Specializations:* M.Ed. in or for Media Supervisor or Computer Coord.; M.A. in Educational Media or Computer Education; Specialist degree in Curriculum and Instruction with a focus on Educational Technology; Specialist degree in Higher Education with a focus on Educational Technology. *Admission Requirements:* Completed application with nonrefundable application fee, bachelor's degree from accredited institution, official transcripts, 2.7 overall GPA for regular status (conditional acceptance possible), statement of purpose, satisfactory scores on MAT or GRE. *Degree Requirements:* M.Ed. requires a comprehensive exam that includes a portfolio with videotaped presentation to the faculty. M.A. requires a 6-hour thesis. *Faculty:* 2 full-time, 12 part-time, including other university full-time faculty and staff. *Students:* Approx. 3 full-time, approx. 200 part-time. *Financial Assistance:* 3 graduate assistantships in the College's Educational Resource Center; plus graduate fellowship for full-time students available limited number of small graduate scholarships.

OKLAHOMA

*Southwestern Oklahoma State University. School of Education. 100 Campus Drive, Weatherford, OK 73096. (405)774-3140. Fax (405)774-7043. E-mail mossg@swosu.edu. Web site http://www.swosu.edu. Gregory Moss, Asst. Prof., Chair, Dept of School Service Programs. *Specializations:* M.Ed. in Library/Media Education. *Admission Requirements:* 2.5 GPA, GRE or GMAT scores, letter of recommendation, GPA x 150 + GRE = 1100. *Degree Requirements:* 32 semester hours (including 24 in library media). *Faculty:* 1 full-time, 4 part-time. *Students:* 17 part-time.

*The University of Oklahoma. Instructional Psychology and Technology, Department of Educational Psychology. 321 Collings Hall, Norman, OK 73019. (405)325-2882. Fax (405)325-6655. E-mail psmith@ou.edu. Web site http://www.uoknor.edu/education/iptwww/. Dr. Patricia L. Smith, Chair. *Specializations:* Master's degree with emphases in Educational Technology Generalist, Educational Technology, Computer Application, Instructional Design, Teaching with Technology; Dual Master's Educational Technology and Library and Information Systems. Doctoral degree in Instructional Psychology and Technology. *Features:* Strong interweaving of principles of instructional psychology with design and development of Instructional Technology. Application of IP&T in K–12, vocational education, higher education, business and industry, and governmental agencies. *Admission Requirements:* Master's: acceptance by IPT program and Graduate College based on minimum 3.0 GPA for last 60 hours of undergraduate work or last 12 hours of graduate work; written statement that indicates goals and interests compatible with program goals. Doctoral: 3.0 in last 60 hours undergraduate, 3.25 GPA, GRE scores, written statement of background and goals. *Degree Requirements:* Master's: approx. 39 hours course work (specific number of hours dependent on emphasis) with 3.0 GPA; successful completion of thesis or comprehensive exam. Doctorate: see program description from institution or http://www.ou.education.iptwww. *Faculty:* 10 full-time. *Students:* Master's, 10 full-time, 200 part-time; doctoral, 10 full-time, 50 part-time. *Financial Assistance:* Assistantships, grants, student loans, scholarships.

OREGON

*Western Oregon State College. 345 N. Monmouth Ave., Monmouth, OR 97361. (503)838-8471. Fax (503)838-8228. E-mail engler@fsa.wosc.osshe.edu. Dr. Randall Engle, Chair. *Specializations:* M.S. in Information Technology. *Features:* Offers advanced courses in library management, instructional development, multimedia, and computer technology. Additional course offerings in distance delivery of instruction and computer-interactive video instruction. *Admission Requirements:* 3.0 GPA, GRE or MAT. *Degree Requirements:* 45 qtr. hours; thesis optional. *Faculty:* 3 full-time, 6 part-time. *Students:* 6 full-time, 131 part-time. *Financial Assistance:* Assistantships, grants, student loans, scholarship, work assistance.

PENNSYLVANIA

*Bloomsburg University. Institute for Interactive Technologies. 1210 McCormick Bldg., Bloomsburg, PA 17815. (717)389-4506. Fax (717)389-4943. E-mail tphillip@bloomu.edu. Web site http://iit.bloomu.edu. Dr. Timothy L. Phillips, contact person. *Specializations:* M.S. in Instructional Technology with emphasis on preparing for careers as interactive media specialists. The program is closely associated with the Institute for Interactive Technologies. *Features:* Instructional design, authoring languages and systems, media integration, managing multimedia projects. *Admission Requirements:* Bachelor's degree. *Degree Requirements:* 33 semester credits (27 credits + 6 credit thesis, or 30 credits + 3 credit internship). *Faculty:* 4 full-time. *Students:* 53 full-time, 50 part-time. *Financial Assistance:* Assistantships, grants, student loans.

*Clarion University of Pennsylvania. Becker Hall, Clarion, PA 16214. (814)226-2245. Fax (814)226-2186. E-mail reed@clarion.edu. Carmen S. Felicetti, Chair, Dept. of Communications. *Specializations:* M.S. in Communication with specialization in Training and Development. The curriculum is process and application oriented with basic courses in television and computer applications, Internet, Web, and HTML authoring. Major projects are team and client oriented with an emphasis on multimedia presentations. *Admission Requirements:* Bachelor's degree, 2.75 undergraduate GPA, MAT score. *Degree Requirements:* 36 semester credits (including 27 specific to Training and Development) with 3.0 GPA, optional thesis worth 6 credits. *Faculty:* 9 full-time. *Financial Assistance:* Ten 1/4 time or five 20-hour graduate assistantships.

Drexel University. College of Information Science and Technology 3142 Chestnut Street, Philadelphia, PA 19104. (215)895-2474. Fax (215)895-2494. E-mail info@cis.drexel.edu. Web site http://www.cis.drexel.edu. David E. Fenske, Prof. and Dean. *Specializations:* M.S. in Library and Information Science; M.S.I.S. in Information Systems; M.S.S.E in Software Engineering. *Features:* On-campus and online degree programs. *Admission Requirements:* GRE scores; applicants with a minimum 3.2 GPA in last half of undergraduate credits may be eligible for admission without GRE scores. *Degree Requirements:* 60 credits. *Faculty:* 23 full-time, 47 adjunct. *Students:* M.S., 20 full-time, 161 part-time; M.S.I.S., 261 full-time, 302 part-time. *Financial Assistance:* Some financial assistance is available. *Degrees awarded 2000:* 245 graduate degrees.

*Lehigh University. College of Education. Bethlehem, PA 18015. (610)758-3231. Fax (610)758-6223. E-mail WMC0@LEHIGH.EDU. Web site http://www.lehigh.edu. Leroy Tuscher, Coord., Educational Technology Program. *Specializations:* M.S. degree with emphasis on design and development of interactive multimedia (both stand-alone and on the Web) for teaching and learning; Ed.D. in Educational Technology. *Admission Requirements:* M.S.: competitive; 2.75 undergraduate GPA or 3.0 graduate GPA, GRE recommended, transcripts, at least two letters of recommendation, statement of personal and professional goals, application fee. Ed.D.: 3.5 graduate GPA, GRE required. Deadlines are July 15 for fall admission, Dec. 1 for spring admission, April 30 for summer admission. *Degree Requirements:* M.S.: 33 semester hours (including 8 in media); thesis option. Ed.D.: 48 hours past the master's plus dissertation. *Faculty:* 3 full-time, 2 part-time. *Students:* M.S.: 13 full-time, 34 part-time; Ed.D.: 6 full-time, 32 part-time. *Financial Assistance:* University graduate and research assistantships, graduate student support as participants in R&D projects, employment opportunities in local businesses and schools doing design and development.

Pennsylvania State University. Instructional Systems. 314 Keller Bldg., University Park, PA 16802. (814)865-0473. Fax (814)865-0128. E-mail aac3@psu.edu. Web site http://www.ed.psu.edu/insys/. A.Carr-Chellman, Prof. in Charge. *Specializations:* M.Ed., M.S., D.Ed., and Ph.D. in Instructional Systems. Current teaching emphases are on Corporate Training, Interactive Learning Technologies, and Educational Systems Design. Research interests include multimedia, visual learning, educational reform, emerging technologies, constructivist learning, open-ended learning environments, scaffolding, technology integration in classrooms, technology in higher education, change and diffusion of innovations. *Features:* A common thread throughout all programs is that candidates have basic competencies in the understanding of human learning; instructional design, development, and evaluation; and research procedures. Practical experience is available in mediated independent learning, research, instructional development, computer-based education, and dissemination projects. Exceptional opportunities for collaboration with faculty (30%+ of publications and presentations are collaborative between faculty and students). *Admission Requirements:* D.Ed., Ph.D.: GRE, TOEFL, transcript, three letters of recommendation, writing sample, vita or resume, and letter of application detailing rationale for interest in the degree, match with interests of faculty. *Degree Requirements:* M.Ed.: 33 semester hours; M.S.: 36 hours, including either a thesis or project paper; doctoral: candidacy exam, courses, residency, comprehensives, dissertation. *Faculty:* 9 full-time, 1 joint appointment in Information Sciences, 4 affiliate and 1 adjunct. *Students:* Master's, approx. 46; doctoral, 103. *Financial Assistance:* Assistantships, graduate fellowships, student aid loans, internships; assistantships on grants, contracts, and projects. *Degrees awarded 2000:* Ph.D., D.Ed., M.S., M.Ed.

*Rosemont College. Graduate Studies in Education. 1400 Montgomery Ave., Rosemont, PA 19010-1699. (610)526-2982; (800)531-9431. Fax (610)526-2964. E-mail roscolgrad @rosemont.edu. Web site http://techincd.roscmont.cdu/CSTE/info.html. Dr. Richard Donagher, Dir. *Specializations:* M.Ed. in Technology in Education, Certificate in Professional Study in Technology in Education. *Admission Requirements:* GRE or MAT scores.

Degree Requirements: Completion of 12 units (36 credits) and comprehensive exam. *Faculty:* 7 full-time, 10 part-time. *Students:* 110 full- and part-time. *Financial Assistance:* Graduate student grants, assistantships, Federal Stafford Loan Program.

Temple University. Instructional and Learning Technology (ILT)/ Educational Psychology Program. 1301 Cecil B. Moore Avenue, Philadelphia, PA 19122. (215) 204-4497. Fax (215) 204-6013. E-mail susan.miller@temple.edu. Web site www.temple.edu/education/pse/ILT. Susan Miller, Ph.D. *Specializations:* Instructional Design, Organization and Management of Instructional Technology programs. *Features:* Issues related to Instructional Design address psychology of the learner, cognitive processes, instructional theories, human development, individual differences, psychological and educational characteristics of technology resources, and identification of strengths and weaknesses of instructional technology resources. Application of Technology focuses on clarification of instructional objectives, identification of resources to facilitate learning, operation and application of current and emergent technologies, facility using graphic design, multimedia, video, distributed learning resources, WWW and print publishing. Management, Consultation, and Problem Solving competence is structured around defining instructional needs, monitoring progress, and evaluating outcomes, designing technology delivery systems, preparing policy statements, budgets, and facility design criteria, managing skill assessment and training, understanding legal and ethical issues, and managing and maintaining facilities. *Admission Requirements:* Bachelors degree from an accredited institution,GRE Aptitude Test Score or MAT scores (or other evidence of scholarly potential), two letters of recommendation, transcripts from each institution of higher leanring attended, (undergraduate and graduate), goal statement. *Degree Requirements:* Course work (33 hours: 5 core courses, 3 technology electives, 3 cognate area courses), practicum in students area of interest, comprehensive exam, Portfolio of Certification Competencies (for students interested in PA Dept. of Ed Certification as Instructional Technology Specialist). *Faculty:* 7 full-time, 5 part-time. *Students:* 34 full-time, 135 part-time. *Financial Assistance:* Presidential, Russell Conwell, and University Fellowships, Graduate School Tuition and Fellowship Funds, Graduate Teaching Assistantships and Assistantships in Administrative Offices, CASHE (College Aid Sources for Higher Education National comput). *Degrees awarded 2000:* 0.

RHODE ISLAND

*The University of Rhode Island. Graduate School of Library and Information Studies. Rodman Hall, Kingston, RI 02881-0815. (401)874-2947. Fax (401)874-4964. E-mail gslis@etal.uri.edu. Web site http://www.uri.edu/artsci/lsc. W. Michael Novener, Assoc. Prof. and Dir. *Specializations:* M.L.I.S. degree with specialties in Archives, Law, Health Sciences, Rare Books, and Youth Services Librarianship. *Degree Requirements:* 42 semester-credit program offered in Rhode Island and regionally in Boston and Amherst, MA, and Durham, NH. *Faculty:* 7 full-time, 24 part-time. *Students:* 48 full-time, 196 part-time. *Financial Assistance:* Graduate assistantships, some scholarship aid, student loans.

SOUTH CAROLINA

*University of South Carolina. Educational Psychology Department. Columbia, SC 29208. (803)777-6609. E-mail vmorton@gwm.sc.edu. Dr. Margaret Gredler, Prof., Chair. *Specializations:* Master's degree. *Degree Requirements:* 33 semester hours, including instructional theory, computer design, and integrated media. *Faculty:* 3. *Students:* 10.

TENNESSEE

*East Tennessee State University. College of Education, Dept. of Curriculum and Instruction. Box 70684, Johnson City, TN 37614-0684. (423)439-4186. Fax (423)439-8362.

E-mail danielsh@etsu.edu. Harold Lee Daniels, contact person. *Specializations:* M Ed. in Instructional Media (Library), M.Ed. in Instructional Technology. *Admission Requirements:* Bachelor's degree from accredited institution, transcripts, personal essay; in some cases, GRE and/or interview. *Degree Requirements:* 39 semester hours, including 18 hours in instructional technology. *Faculty:* 2 full-time, 4 part-time. *Students:* 9 full-time, 40 part-time. *Financial Assistance:* Scholarships, assistantships, aid for the disabled.

University of Memphis. Instruction and Curriculum Leadership/Instructional Design & Technology. 406 Ball Hall, Memphis, TN 38152. 901-678-3921. Fax 901-678-3881. E-mail rvaneck@memphis.edu. Web site http://www.people.memphis.edu/~coe_icl/idt /index.html. Dr. Richard Van Eck, contact person. *Specializations:* Instructional Design, Web-based instruction, Computer-based instruction, Digital Video. *Features:* K–12 and Corporate training areas of emphasis, Advanced Instructional Media (AIM) lab for developing technology-assisted instruction (Dreamweaver, Flash, Authorware, WebCT, DV cameras, DV editing, DVD authoring, etc.), residency in the FedEx Emerging Technology Center, and excellent internship and job placement opportunities locally. *Admission Requirements:* Minimum standards which identify a pool of master's-level applicants from which each department selects students to be admitted: An official transcript showing a bachelor's degree awarded by an accredited college or university with a minimum GPA of 2.0 on a 4.0 scale, competitive MAT or GRE scores, GRE writing test, two letters of recommendation, graduate school and departmental application. Doctoral students must also be interviewed by at least two members of the program. *Degree Requirements:* M.S.: 36 hours, internship, master's project or thesis, 3.0 GPA. Ed.D: 54 hours, 45 in major, 9 in research; residency project; comprehensive exams; dissertation. *Faculty:* 3 full-time, 7 part-time. *Students:* 10 full-time, 50 part-time. *Financial Assistance:* Teaching assistantships (two classes, full tuition waiver plus stipend); graduate assistantships (20 hours per week, full tuition plus stipend). *Degrees awarded 2000:* 20.

*University of Tennessee-Knoxville. College of Education, Education in the Sciences, Mathematics, Research, and Technology. Unit 319 Claxton Addition, Knoxville, TN 37996-3400. (423)974-4222 or (423)974-3103. E-mail mlw@utk.edu. Dr. Al Grant, Coord., Instructional Media and Technology Program. *Specializations:* M.S. in Ed., Ed.S., and Ed.D. under Education in Sciences, Mathematics, Research, and Technology; Ed.D. in Curriculum and Instruction, concentration in Instructional Media and Technology; Ph.D. under the College of Education, concentration in Instructional Media and Technology. *Features:* Course work in media management, advanced software production, utilization, research, theory, psychology, instructional computing, television, and instructional development. Course work will also meet the requirements for state certification as Instructional Materials Supervisor in the public schools of Tennessee. *Admission Requirements:* Send for Graduate Catalog, The University of Tennessee. *Degree Requirements:* M.S.: 33 semester hours; thesis optional. *Faculty:* 1 full-time, with additional assistance from Ed SMRT Unit, College of Ed. and university faculty. *Students:* M.S., 2 part-time; Ed.S., 2 part-time.

TEXAS

Texas A&M University. Educational Technology Program, Dept. of Educational psychology College of Education. College Station, TX 77843-4225. (979)845-7276. Fax (979)862-1256. E-mail zellner@tamu.edu. Web site http://educ.coe.tamu.edu/~edtc/edtc /prog/edtcintro.html. Ronald D. Zellner, Assoc. Prof., Coord. *Specializations:* M.Ed. in Educational Technology; EDCI Ph.D. program with specializations in Educational Technology and in Distance Education; Ph.D. in Educational Psychology Foundations: Learning and Technology. The purpose of the Educational Technology Program is to prepare educators with the competencies required to improve the quality and effectiveness of instructional programs at all levels. A major emphasis is placed on multimedia instructional materials development and techniques for effective distance education and communication. Teacher preparation with a focus on field-based instruction and school to university collaboration is also a major component. The program goal is to prepare graduates with a wide range of skills to work as professionals and leaders in a variety of settings, including education, business, industry, and the military. *Features:* Program facilities include laboratories for teaching, resource development, and production. Computer, video, and multimedia development are supported in a number of facilities. The college and university also maintain facilities for distance education materials development and fully equipped classrooms for course delivery to nearby collaborative school districts and sites throughout the state. *Admission Requirements:* M.Ed.: Bachelor's degree, 400 GRE Verbal, 550 (213 computer version) TOEFL; Ph.D.: 3.0 GPA, 450 GRE Verbal. Composite score from GRE verbal and quantitative and GPA, letters of recommendation, general background, and student goal statement. *Degree Requirements:* M.Ed.: 39 semester credits, oral exam; Ph.D.: course work varies with student goals—degree is a Ph.D. in Educational Psychology Foundations with specialization in educational technology. *Faculty:* 4 full-time, 1 lecturer; several associated faculty from related programs in EPSY. *Students:* M.Ed., 25 full-time, 15 part-time; Ph.D., 8 full-time, 14 part-time. *Financial Assistance:* Several graduate assistantships and teaching assistantships. *Degrees awarded 2000:* M.Ed., 12.

Texas A&M University-Commerce. Department of Secondary and Higher Education. PO Box 3011, Commerce, TX 75429-3011. (903)886-5607. Fax (903)886-5603. E-mail Sue_Espinoza@tamu-commerce.edu. Web site http://www.tamu-commerce.edu/. Dr. Sue Espinoza, Associate Professor, Program Coordinator. *Specializations:* M.S. or M.Ed. degree in Learning Technology and Information Systems with emphases in Educational Computing, Educational Media and Technology, and Library and Information Science. Certifications offered—School Librarian, and Technology Applications, both approved by the Texas State Board for Educator Certification. *Features:* Courses are offered in a variety of formats, including traditional classroom/lab based, and distance ed, via video teleconferencing and/or online. Most courses are taught in only one of these, but some include multiple delivery methods. *Admission Requirements:* 700 GRE (combined). *Degree Requirements:* 36 hours for each master's degree; Educational Computing includes 30 hours of required courses and 6 hours of electives; Media and Technology includes 21 hours of required courses and 15 hours of electives, selected in consultation with advisor; Library includes courses in Library, Educational Technology, and Education. *Faculty:* 3 full-time, 5 part-time. *Students:* 30 full-time, 150 part-time. *Financial Assistance:* Graduate assistantships in teaching and research, scholarships, federal aid program. *Degrees awarded 2000:* 15.

*Texas Tech University. College of Education. Box 41071, TTU, Lubbock, TX 79409. (806)742-1997, ext. 299. Fax (806)742-2179. E-mail gradschool@ttu.edu. Web site http://www.educ.ttu.edu. Dr. Robert Price, Dir., Instructional Technology. *Specializations:* M.Ed. in Instructional Technology (Educational Computing and Distance Education emphasis); Ed.D. in Instructional Technology. *Features:* Program is NCATE accredited and follows ISTE and AECT guidelines. *Admission Requirements:* Holistic evaluation based on GRE scores, GPA, student goals, and writing samples. *Degree Requirements:* M.Ed.: 39 hours (24 hours in educational technology, 15 hours in education or outside education); practicum. Ed.D.: 87 hours (45 hours in educational technology, 18 hours in education, 15 hours in resource area or minor); practicum. *Faculty:* 5 full-time. *Students:* M.Ed., 10 full-time, 20 part-time; Ed.D., 15 full-time, 15 part-time. *Financial Assistance:* Teaching and research assistantships available ($8,500 for 9 months); small scholarships.

University of Houston. Department of Curriculum and Instruction. 256 Farish, Houston, TX 77204. (713)743-4950. Fax (713)743-4990. E-mail Brobin@uh.edu. Bernard Robin, Program Area Director. Web site http://www.it.coe.uh.edu. *Specializations:* Urban community partnerships enhanced by technology, integration of Technology in teaching visual representation of information, collaborative design teams, innovative uses of technology in instruction. Features: The IT program at the University of Houston can be distinguished from other IT programs through a unique philosophy based on a strong commitment to the representations of community to the individual, and the collaboration that strengthens the two. *Admission Requirements:* Information for graduate programs: http://www.it.coe.uh.edu. Master's program: 3.0 GPA for unconditional admission. *Degree Requirements:* Master's program: Students with backgrounds in education technology can complete the master's program in 36 hours of course work. This typically involves 9 hours of core courses required by the College of Education and an additional 18 hours. *Faculty:* 5 full-time, 5 part-time. *Students*: 20 full-time, 120 part-time. *Financial Assistance*: 20 hour/wk graduate assistantships; University and College Scholarships. *Degrees Awarded in 2000*: approximately 30.

*University of North Texas. College of Education. Box 311337, Denton, TX 76203-1337. (940)565-2057. Fax (940)565-2185. E-mail coeinfo@coefs.coe.unt.edu. Web site http://www.cecs.unt.edu. Dr. Terry Holcomb, Program Coord., Computer Education and Cognitive Systems. Dr. Jon Young, Chair, Dept. of Technology and Cognition. *Specializations:* M.S. in Computer Education and Instructional Systems. *Admission Requirements:* 1000 GRE (400 verbal and 400 quantitative minimums). *Degree Requirements:* 36 semester hours (including 27 in Instructional Technology and Computer Education), comprehensive exam. *Faculty:* 7 full-time, 1 part-time. *Students:* 90 + 500 service/ minor students, approx. half full-time.

The University of Texas at Austin. Curriculum & Instruction. 406 Sanchez Building, Austin, TX 78712-1294. (512)471-5211. Fax (512)471-8460. E-mail judi.harris@mail.utexas.edu. Web site http://www.edb.utexas.edu/coe/depts/ci/it/it.html. Judi Harris, Ph.D., Associate Professor and Area Coordinator, Instructional Technology. *Specializations:* Master's degrees (M.A. and M.Ed.) in Instructional Technology at U.T.-Austin focus on the processes of systematic planning, design, and development of instruction. Because IT requires more than skill in the production of instructional materials and use of machines, the instructional technologist emerging from our program uses knowledge of learning theory, curriculum development, instructional systems, communications theory, and evaluation to support appropriate uses of instructional resources. The doctoral programs in Instructional Technology at U.T.-Austin are comprehensive and research oriented, providing knowledge and skills in areas such as instructional systems design, learning and instructional theories, instructional materials development, and design of learning environments using various technology-based systems and tools. Graduates assume academic, administrative, and other leadership positions such as instructional designers and evaluators, managers of instructional systems, and professors and researchers of instructional design and performance technology. *Features:* The program is interdisciplinary in nature, although certain competencies are required of all students. Programs of study and dissertation research are based on individual needs and career goals. Learning resources include a model Learning Technology Center, computer labs and classrooms, a television studio, and interactive multimedia lab. Many courses are offered cooperatively by other departments, including Radio-TV Film, Computer Science, and Educational Psychology. *Admission Requirements:* Master's: 3.5 GPA; 450 GRE Verbal, 1150 GRE Verbal + Quantitative; statement of study goals that can be satisfied with existing program offerings and resources. Doctoral: 3.5 GPA; 500 GRE Verbal, 1250 GRE Verbal + Quantitative; statement of study goals that can be satisfied with existing program offerings and resources. *Degree Requirements:* Masters: 36 semester hours minimum. Ph.D.: 54 semester hours + a 6 dissertation hours minimum, including 9-hour area of special expertise related to dissertation research; first-year and midprogram reviews; 9 hours of directed research completed before dissertation proposal; written comprehensive and specialization exam with oral defense; dissertation with proposal defense and oral defense. *Faculty:* 4 full-time, 1 part-time. *Students:* 12 master's (9 part-time; 3 full-time), 36 doctoral (15 part-time; 21 full-time). *Financial Assistance:* Assistantships are often available to develop instructional materials, assist in undergraduate teaching methods courses, and assist with research/service projects. There are also several paid internships. *Degrees awarded 2000:* (in 2000–2001:) 3 master's; 4 doctoral.

UTAH

*Brigham Young University. Department of Instructional Psychology and Technology. 201 MCKB, BYU, Provo, UT 84602. (801)378-5097. Fax (801)378-8672. E-mail paul_merrill@byu.edu. Web site http://www.byu.edu/acd1/ed/InSci/InSci.html. Paul F. Merrill, Prof., Chair. *Specializations:* M.S. degrees in Instructional Design, Research and Evaluation, and Multimedia Production. Ph.D. degrees in Instructional Design, and Research and Evaluation. *Features:* Course offerings include principles of learning, instructional design, assessing learning outcomes, evaluation in education, empirical inquiry in education, project management, quantitative reasoning, microcomputer materials production, multimedia production, naturalistic inquiry, and more. Students participate in internships and projects related to development, evaluation, measurement, and research. *Admission Requirements:* Both degrees: transcript, three letters of recommendation, letter of intent, GRE scores. Apply by Feb. 1. Students agree to live by the BYU Honor Code as a condition for admission. *Degree Requirements:* Master's: 38 semester hours, including prerequisite (3 hours), core courses (14 hours), specialization (12 hours), internship (3 hours), thesis or project (6 hours) with oral defense. Ph.D.: 94 semester hours beyond the bachelor's degree, including prerequisite and skill requirements (21 hours), core course (16 hours), specialization (18 hours), internship (12 hours), projects (9 hours), and dissertation (18 hours). The dissertation must be orally defended. Also, at least two consecutive 6-hour semesters must be completed in residence. *Faculty:* 9 full-time, 2 half-time. *Students:* Master's, 25 full-time, 2 part-time; Ph.D., 47 full-time, 3 part-time. *Financial Assistance:* Internships, tuition scholarships, loans, and travel to present papers.

Utah State University. Department of Instructional Technology, College of Education. 2830 Old Main Hill, Logan, UT 84322-2830. (435)797-2694. Fax (435)797-2693. E-mail bburnham@coe.usu.edu. Web site http://www.coe.usu:edu/it/. Dr. Byron R. Burnham, Prof., Chair. *Specializations:* M.S. and Ed.S. with concentrations in the areas of Instructional Development, Multimedia, Educational Technology, and Information Technology/School Library Media Administration. Ph.D. in Instructional Technology is offered for individuals seeking to become professionally involved in instructional development in corporate education, public schools, community colleges, and universities. Teaching and research in higher education is another career avenue for graduates of the program. *Features:* M.S. and Ed.S. programs in Information Technology/School Library Media Administration and Educational Technology are also delivered via an electronic distance education system. The doctoral program is built on a strong master's and specialists program in Instructional Technology. All doctoral students complete a core with the remainder of the course selection individualized, based upon career goals. *Admission Requirements:* M.S. and Ed.S.: 3.0 GPA, a verbal and quantitative score at the 40th percentile on the GRE or 43 MAT, three written recommendations. Ph.D.: Master's degree in Instructional Technology, 3.0 GPA, verbal and quantitative score at the 40th percentile on the GRE, three written recommendations. *Degree Requirements:* M.S.: 39 sem. hours; thesis or project option. Ed.S.: 30 sem. hours if M.S. is in the field, 40 hours if not. Ph.D.: 62 total hours, dissertation, 3-sem. residency, and comprehensive examination. *Faculty:* 9 full-time, 7 part-time. *Students:* M.S., 70 full-time, 85 part-time; Ed.S., 6 full-time, 9 part-time; Ph.D., 15 full-time, 14 part-time. *Financial Assistance:* Approx. 18 to 26 assistantships (apply by April 1). *Degrees awarded 2000:* 32 M.S.; 7 M.Ed.; 4 Ed.S.; 3 Ph.D.

VIRGINIA

*George Mason University. Instructional Technology Programs. Mail Stop 4B3, 4400 University Dr., Fairfax, VA 22030-4444. (703)993-2051. Fax (703)993-2013. E-mail mbehrman@wpgate.gmu.edu. Web site http://gse.gmu.edu/programs/it/index.htm. Dr. Michael Behrmann, Coord. of Instructional Technology Academic Programs. *Specializations:* M.Ed. in Curriculum and Instruction with tracks in Instructional Design and Development, Integration of Technology in Schools, and Assistive/Special Education

Technology; M.Ed. in Special Education; Ph.D. with specialization in Instructional Technology or Special Education Technology. Certificate Programs (12-15 cr.) in Integration of Technology in Schools; Multimedia Development; Assitive Technology. *Features:* Master's program started in 1983 and doctoral in 1984. Integration of Technology in Schools is a cohort program in which students are admitted in the spring semester only. ID & D full-time immersion admits students in summer. All other tracks admit throughout the year. *Admission Requirements:* Teaching or training experience, introductory programming course or equivalent; introductory course in educational technology or equivalent. *Degree Requirements:* M.Ed. in Curriculum and Instruction: 36 hours; practicum, internship, or project. M.Ed. in Special Education: 36-42 hours. Ph.D.: 56-62 hours beyond master's degree for either specialization. Certificate programs: 12-15 hours. *Faculty:* 6 full-time, 5 part-time. *Students:* M.Ed. in Curriculum and Instruction: 5 part-time, 125 part-time. M.Ed. in Special Education: 10 full-time, 8 part-time. Ph.D.: 19 part-time, 10 full time. ITS certificate, 250; MM Certificate, 30; At Certificate, 45. *Financial Assistance:* Assistantships and tuition waivers available for full-time graduate students.

*Radford University. Educational Studies Department, College of Education and Human Development. P.O. Box 6959, Radford, VA 24142. (540)831-5302. Fax (540)831-5059. E-mail ljwilson@runet.edu. Web site http://www.radford.edu. Dr. Linda J. Wilson. *Specializations:* M.S. in Education with Educational Media/Technology emphasis. *Features:* School Library Media Specialist licensure. *Admission Requirements:* Bachelor's degree, 2.7 undergraduate GPA. *Degree Requirements:* 33 semester hours, practicum; thesis optional. *Faculty:* 2 full-time, 3 part-time. *Students:* 2 full-time, 23 part-time. *Financial Assistance:* Assistantships, grants, student loans, scholarships.

*University of Virginia. Department of Leadership, Foundations, and Policy, Curry School of Education. Ruffner Hall, Charlottesville, VA 22903. (804)924-7471. Fax (804)924-0747. E-mail jbbunch@virginia.edu. Web site http://curry.edschool.virginia.edu /curry/dept/edlf/instrtech/. John B. Bunch, Assoc. Prof., Coord., Instructional Technology Program, Dept. of Leadership, Foundations and Policy Studies. *Specializations:* M.Ed., Ed.S., Ed.D, and Ph.D. degrees with focal areas in Media Production, Interactive Multimedia, and K–12 Educational Technologies. *Admission Requirements:* Undergraduate degree from accredited institution in any field, undergraduate GPA 3.0, 1000 GRE (V + Q), 600 TOEFL. Admission application deadline is March 1 of each year for the fall semester for both master's and doctoral degrees. *Degree Requirements:* M.Ed.: 36 semester hours, comprehensive examination. Ed.S.: 60 semester hours beyond undergraduate degree. Ed.D.: 54 semester hours, dissertation, at least one conference presentation or juried publication, comprehensive examination, residency; Ph.D.: same as Ed.S. with the addition of 18 semester hours. For specific degree requirements, see Web site, write to the address above, or refer to the UVA. *Faculty:* 4 full-time, 1 part-time. *Students:* M.Ed., 24; Ed.D., 3; Ph.D., 15. *Financial Assistance:* Some graduate assistantships and scholarships are available on a competitive basis.

*Virginia Polytechnic Institute and State University. College of Human Resources and Education. 220 War Memorial Hall, Blacksburg, VA 24061-0341. (540)231-5587. Fax (540)231-9075. E-mail moorem@vt.edu. Web site http://www.chre.vt.edu/Admin/IT/. David M. (Mike) Moore, Program Area Leader, Instructional Technology, Dept. of Teaching and Learning. *Specializations:* M.A., Ed.D., and Ph.D. in Instructional Technology. Preparation for education, higher education, faculty development, business, and industry. *Features:* Areas of emphasis are Instructional Design, Educational Computing, Evaluation, and Media Management and Development. Facilities include two computer labs (70 PC and Macintosh computers), plus interactive video, speech synthesis, telecommunication labs, distance education classroom, and computer graphics production areas. *Admission Requirements:* Ed.D. and Ph.D.: 3.3 GPA from master's degree, GRE scores, interview, writing samples, three letters of recommendation, transcripts. MA.: 3.0 GPA undergraduate. *Degree Requirements:* Ph.D.: 96 hrs above B.S., 2 year residency, 12 hrs.

research classes, 30 hrs. dissertation; Ed.D.: 90 hrs. above B.S., 1 year residency, 12 hrs. research classes; M.A.: 30 hrs. above B.S. *Faculty:* 7 full-time, 5 part-time. *Students:* 35 full-time and 10 part-time at the doctoral level. 10 full-time and 15 part-time at the master's level. *Financial Assistance:* 10 assistantships, limited tuition scholarships.

*Virginia State University. School of Liberal Arts & Education, Petersburg, VA 23806. (804)524-6886. E-mail tjeter@vsu.edu. Vykuntapathi Thota, Chair, Dept. of Education. *Specializations:* M.S., M.Ed. in Educational Technology. *Features:* Video Conferencing Center and PLATO Laboratory, internship in ABC and NBC channels. *Degree Requirements:* 30 semester hours plus thesis for M.S.; 33 semester hours plus project for M.Ed.; comprehensive exam. *Faculty:* 1 full-time, 2 part-time. *Students:* 8 full-time, 50 part-time. *Financial Assistance:* Scholarships through the School of Graduate Studies.

WASHINGTON

*Eastern Washington University. Department of Computer Science. Cheney, WA 99004-2431. (509)359-7093. Fax (509)359-2215. E-mail LKieffer@ewu.edu. Dr. Linda M. Kieffer, Assoc. Prof. of Computer Science. *Specializations:* M.Ed. in Computer and Technology Supported Education; M.S. in Computer Education (Interdisciplinary). Master's program started in 1983. *Features:* Many projects involve the use of high-level authoring systems to develop educational products, technology driven curriculum, and Web projects. *Admission Requirements:* 3.0 GPA for last 90 qtr. credits. *Degree Requirements:* M.S.: 52 qtr. hours (30 hours in computers, 15 hours outside education; the hours do not total to 52 because of freedom to choose where Methods of Research is taken, where 12 credits of supporting courses are taken, and where additional electives are taken); research project with formal report. M.Ed.: 52 qtr. hours (28 hours in computer education, 16 hours in education, 8 hours outside education). *Faculty:* 3 full-time. *Students:* approx. 35. *Financial Assistance:* Some research and teaching fellowships.

*University of Washington. College of Education. 115 Miller Hall, Box 353600, Seattle, WA 98195-3600. (206)543-1847. Fax (206)543-8439. E-mail stkerr@u.washington.edu. Web site http://www.educ.washington.edu/COE/c-and-i/c_and_i_med_ed_tech.htm. Stephen T. Kerr, Prof. of Education. *Specializations:* M.Ed., Ed.D, and Ph.D. for individuals in business, industry, higher education, public schools, and organizations concerned with education or communication (broadly defined). *Features:* Emphasis on instructional design as a process of making decisions about the shape of instruction; additional focus on research and development in such areas as message design (especially graphics and diagrams); electronic information systems; interactive instruction via videodisc, multimedia, and computers. *Admission Requirements:* M.Ed.: goal statement (2-3pp.), writing sample, 1000 GRE (verbal plus quantitative), undergraduate GPA indicating potential to successfully accomplish graduate work. Doctoral: GRE scores, letters of reference, transcripts, personal statement, master's degree or equivalent in field appropriate to the specialization with 3.5 GPA, two years of successful professional experience and/or experience related to program goals. *Degree Requirements:* M.Ed.: 45 qtr. hours (including 24 in media); thesis or project optional. Ed.D.: see www.educ.washington.edu/COE/admissions/DoctorOfEducationProgram .htm. Ph.D.: see www.educ.washington.edu/COE/admissions/DoctorOfPhilosophyDegree .htm. *Faculty:* 2 full-time, 3 part-time. *Students:* 12 full-time, 32 part-time; 26 M.Ed., 18 doctoral. *Financial Assistance:* Assistantships awarded competitively and on basis of program needs; other assistantships available depending on grant activity in any given year.

*Western Washington University. Woodring College of Education, Instructional Technology. MS 9087, Bellingham, WA 98225-9087. (360)650-3387. Fax (360)650-6526. E-mail Les.Blackwell@wwu.edu. Web site http://www.wce.wwu.edu/depts/IT. Dr. Les Blackwell, Prof., Deparment Chair. *Specializations:* M.Ed. with emphasis in Instructional Technology in Adult Education, Special Education, Elementary Education, and Secondary Education. *Admission Requirements:* 3.0 GPA in last 45 qtr. credit hours, GRE or MAT scores, three letters of recommendation, and, in some cases, three years of teaching experience. *Degree Requirements:* 48-52 qtr. hours (24-28 hours in instructional technology; 24 hours in education-related courses, thesis required; internship and practicum possible). *Faculty:* 6 full-time, 8 part-time. *Students:* 5 full-time, 10 part-time. *Financial Assistance:* Assistantships, student loans, scholarships.

WISCONSIN

*Edgewood College. Department of Education. 855 Woodrow St, Madison, WI 53711-1997. (608)257-4861, ext. 2293. Fax (608)259-6727. E-mail schmied@edgewood.edu. Web site http://www.edgewood.edu. Dr. Joseph E. Schmiedicke, Chair, Dept. of Education. *Specializations:* M.A. in Education with emphasis on Instructional Technology. Master's program started in 1987. *Features:* Classes conducted in laboratory setting with emphasis on applications and software. *Admission Requirements:* 2.75 GPA. *Degree Requirements:* 36 semester hours. *Faculty:* 2 full-time, 3 part-time. *Students:* 5 full-time, 135 part-time. *Financial Assistance:* Grants, student loans.

*University of Wisconsin-La Crosse. Educational Media Program. Rm. 235C, Morris Hall, La Crosse, WI 54601. (608)785-8121. Fax (608)785-8128. E-mail Phill.rm@mail.uwlax .edu. Dr. Russell Phillips, Dir. *Specializations:* M.S. in Professional Development with specializations in Initial Instructional Library Specialist, License 901; Instructional Library Media Specialist, License 902 (39 credits). *Degree Requirements:* 30 semester hours, including 15 in media; no thesis. *Faculty:* 2 full-time, 4 part-time. *Students:* 21. *Financial Assistance:* Guaranteed student loans, graduate assistantships.

*University of Wisconsin-Madison. Dept. of Curriculum and Instruction, School of Education. 225 N. Mills St, Madison, WI 53706. (608)263-4672. Fax (608)263-9992. E-mail adevaney@facstaff.wisc.edu. Ann De Vaney, Prof. *Specializations:* M.S. degree and State Instructional Technology License; Ph.D. programs to prepare college and university faculty. *Features:* The program is coordinated with media operations of the university. Traditional instructional technology courses are processed through a social, cultural, and historical frame of reference. Current curriculum emphasizes communication and cognitive theories, critical cultural studies, and theories of textual analysis and instructional development. Course offered in the evening. *Admission Requirements:* Master's and Ph.D.: previous experience in Instructional Technology preferred, previous teaching experience, 3.0 GPA on last 60 undergraduate credits, acceptable scores on GRE, 3.0 GPA on all graduate work. *Degree Requirements:* M.S.: 24 credits plus thesis and exam; Ph.D.: 3 years of residency beyond the bachelor's (master's degree counts for one year; one year must be full-time), major, minor, and research requirements, preliminary exam, dissertation, and oral exam. *Faculty:* 3 full-time, 1 part-time. *Students:* M.S., 33; Ph.D., 21. Most master's candidates are part-time; half of Ph.D. students are full-time. *Financial Assistance:* Several stipends of approx. $1,000 per month for 20 hours of work per week; other media jobs are also available.

Universiti Sains Malaysia. Centre for Instructional Technology and Multimedia Centre for Instructional Tech and Multimedia. Universiti Sains Malaysia, Minden, Pg 11800. 604-8603222. Fax 604-6576749. E-mail ina@usm.my. Web site http://www.ptpm.usm.my. Zarina Samsudin, Deputy Director. *Specializations:* Instructional Design, Web/Internet Instruction and learning, Educational Training/Resource Management, Instructional Training Technology/Evaluation, Instructional System Development, Design and Development of Multimeida/Video/Training materials, Instructional and Training Technology, Constructivism in Instructional Technology. *Features:* Teaching Programs—postgraduate programs and research. Consultancy—services on the application of educational technology in teaching learning. Training and Diffusion—diploma in Multimedia, Certificate in Training Technology & Continuing Education. Academic Support Services—services to support research, teaching and learning activities, and centres within the University. *Admission Requirements:* Bachelor's and master's degree from accredited institution. *Degree Requirements:* Part-time, full-time. *Faculty:* 12. *Students:* 30 full-time; 40 part-time. *Degrees awarded 2000:* Ph.D. in Instructional Technology and M.Ed. in Instructional Technology.

Part Seven
Mediagraphy

Print and Nonprint Resources

Introduction

CONTENTS

This resource lists media-related journals, books, ERIC documents, journal articles, and nonprint media resources of interest to practitioners, researchers, students, and others concerned with educational technology and educational media. This section lists current publications in the field. The majority of materials cited here were published in 2000 or early 2001. Media-related journals include those listed in past issues of *EMTY* and new entries in the field. Brooke Price, section editor for the 2001 edition, established a thorough list of journals in the educational technology field. This list of journals has been modified and updated for the 2002 edition.

It is not the intention of the authors for this chapter to serve as a specific resource location tool, although it may be used for that purpose in the absence of database access. Rather, readers can peruse the categories of interest in this chapter to gain an idea of recent developments within the field. For archival purposes, this chapter serves as a snapshot of the field in 2002. Readers must bear in mind that technological developments occur well in advance of publication and should take that fact into consideration when judging the timeliness of resources listed in this chapter.

SELECTION

Items were selected for the Mediagraphy in several ways. The ERIC (Educational Resources Information Center) Database was the source for most ERIC document and journal article citations. Others were reviewed directly by the editors. Items were chosen for this list when they met one or more of the following criteria: reputable publisher, broad circulation, coverage by indexing services, peer review, and coverage of a gap in the literature. The editors chose items on subjects that seem to reflect the Instructional Technology field as it is today. Because of the increasing tendency for media producers to package their products in more than one format and for single titles to contain mixed media, titles are no longer separated by media type. The editors make no claims as to the comprehensiveness of this list. It is, instead, intended to be representative.

OBTAINING RESOURCES

Media-Related Periodicals and Books. Publisher, price, and ordering/subscription address are listed wherever available.

ERIC Documents. ERIC documents can be read and often copied from their microfiche form at any library holding an ERIC microfiche collection. The identification number beginning with ED (for example, ED 332 677) locates the document in the collection. Copies of most ERIC documents can also be ordered from the ERIC Document Reproduction Service. Prices charged depend upon format chosen (microfiche or paper copy), length of the document, and method of shipping. Online orders, fax orders, and expedited delivery are available.

To find the closest library with an ERIC microfiche collection, contact:

ACCESS ERIC
1600 Research Blvd.
Rockville, MD 20850-3172
1 (800) LET-ERIC (538-3742)
E-mail: acceric@inet.ed.gov

To order ERIC documents, contact:

ERIC Document Reproduction Service (EDRS)
7420 Fullerton Rd., Suite 110
Springfield, VA 22153-2852
voice: 1 (800) 443-ERIC (443-3742), (703) 440-1400
fax: (703) 440-1408
E-mail: service@edrs.com.

Journal Articles. Photocopies of journal articles can be obtained in one of the following ways: (1) from a library subscribing to the title; (2) through interlibrary loan; (3) through the purchase of a back issue from the journal publisher; or (4) from an article reprint service such as UMI.

UMI Information Store
500 Sansome St., Suite 400
San Francisco, CA 94111
1 (800 248-0360 (toll-free in U.S. and Canada)
(415) 433-5500 (outside U.S. and Canada)
E-mail: orders@infostore.com

Journal articles can also be obtained through the Institute for Scientific Information (ISI).

ISI Document Solution
P.O. Box 7649
Philadelphia, PA 19104-3389
(215) 386-4399
Fax (215) 222-0840 or (215) 386-4343
E-mail: ids@isinet.com

ARRANGEMENT

Mediagraphy entries are classified according to major subject emphasis under the following headings:

- Artificial Intelligence, Robotics, and Electronic Performance Support Systems
- Computer-Assisted Instruction
- Distance Education
- Educational Research
- Educational Technology
- Information Science and Technology
- Innovation
- Instructional Design and Development
- Interactive Multimedia
- Libraries and Media Centers
- Media Technologies
- Professional Development
- Simulation, Gaming, and Virtual Reality
- Special Education and Disabilities
- Telecommunications and Networking

Leslie Cole

Mediagraphy

ARTIFICIAL INTELLIGENCE, ROBOTICS, AND ELECTRONIC PERFORMANCE SUPPORT SYSTEMS

Artificial Intelligence Review. Kluwer Academic Publishers, 101 Philip Drive, Norwell, MA 02061. [6 issues/yr, $182 indiv., $364 inst.]. Serves as a forum for the work of researchers and application developers from Artificial Intelligence, Cognitive Science, and related disciplines.

Baylor, A. (1999). Intelligent Agents as cognitive tools for education. **Educational Technology, 39**(2), 36–40. Examines the educational potential for intelligent agents as cognitive tools. Discusses the role of intelligent agents: managing large amounts of information, serving as a pedagogical expert, and creating programming environments for the learner.

Bopry, J. (1999). The warrant for constructivist practice within educational technology. **Educational Technology Research and Development, 47** (4), 5–26. Discusses educational technology as a form of technical rationality and considers the conflict between practitioners' epistemological position as constructivists and technical rationality. Topics include cybernetics; autonomous systems theory; enactive constructivism; representation versus effective action; mind and memory; enaction in artificial intelligence; and design of social systems. Contains 54 references.

Berners-Lee, T. (1999). Realising the full potential of the Web. **Technical Communication: Journal of the Society for Technical Communication, 46** (1), 79–82. Argues that the first phase of the Web is communication through shared knowledge. Predicts that the second side to the Web, yet to emerge, is that of machine-understandable information, with humans providing the inspiration and the intuition.

Brown, A. (1999). Simulated classrooms and artificial students: The potential effects of new technologies on teacher education. **Journal of Research on Computing in Education, 32**(2), 307–318. Describes and discusses how simulation activities can be used in teacher education to augment the traditional field-experience approach, focusing on artificial intelligence, virtual reality, and intelligent tutoring systems. Includes an overview of simulation as a teaching and learning strategy and specific examples of high-technology simulations in development and in use.

Chen, C., Czerwinski, M. & Macredie, R. (2000). Individual differences in virtual environments—Introduction and overview. **Journal of the American Society for Information Science, 51**(6), 499–507. Presents a brief historical overview of research in individual differences in the context of virtual environments. Highlights the notion of structure in the perception of individual users of an information system and the role of individuals' abilities to recognize and use such structures to perform various information-intensive tasks.

Deal, W. F. III. (2000). XBOT: Programmed to move. Resources in technology. **Technology Teacher, 59**(5), 25–31. This learning activity describes how a robot moves and the systems that power robots. Provides detailed information about XBOT, which uses modified servomotors to power its wheels.

Ely, D. (1999). Toward a philosophy of instructional technology: Thirty years on. **British Journal of Educational Technology, 30** (4), 305–310. Makes a current assessment of the philosophy of instructional technology using a 1970 *British Journal of Educational Technology* (BJET) article as the basis of comparison. Discusses the influence of distance education, public acceptance of media and technology, and training by artificial intelligence in business and industry.

Gustafson, K. (2000). Designing technology-based performance support. **Educational Technology, 40**(1), 38–44. Describes electronic performance support systems (EPSSs) that can enhance performance and reduce training times and costs. Provides examples of EPSSs; explains why instructional designers and trainers should be interested in EPSSs; and discusses design considerations, including part task/whole task support, embedded versus linked, and user controlled versus system controlled.

International Journal of Robotics Research. Sage Science, (805) 499-0721. [Mo., $122 indiv., $686 inst.]. Interdisciplinary approach to the study of robotics for researchers, scientists, and students.

Journal of Robotic and Intelligent Systems. Kluwer Academic Publishers, 101 Philip Drive, Norwell, MA 02061. [Mo., $850]. The main objective is to provide a forum for the fruitful interaction of ideas and techniques that combine systems and control science with artificial intelligence—and other related computer science—concepts.

Knowledge-Based Systems. Elsevier Science Inc., 655 Avenue of the Americas, New York, NY 10010-5107. [Q., $730]. Interdisciplinary applications-oriented journal on fifth-generation computing, expert systems, and knowledge-based methods in system design.

McKenzie, J. (2000). Making a difference in student performance. **American School Board Journal, 187**(3), suppl., 20–23. Students and teachers benefit from emphasizing literacy and professional development, not technology itself. Districts must also put learning first, build support, consider alternative delivery systems, provide adequate resources, use assessments to steer programs, shed the ineffectual, remember past lessons, heed research, and ask good questions.

Miglino, O., Henrik H., &Cardaci, M. (1999). Robotics as an educational tool. **Journal of Interactive Learning Research, 10**(1), 25–47. Explores a new educational application of Piaget's theories of cognitive development: the use, as a teaching tool, of physical robots conceived as artificial organisms. Reviews educational projects using real robots. Shows that the use of intelligent systems to enlarge the view of biological reality could become an integral part of curricula in science, technology, psychology, and biology.

Minds and Machines. Kluwer Academic Publishers, 101 Philip Drive, Norwell, MA 02061. [Q., $379, American inst.]. Discusses issues concerning machines and mentality, artificial intelligence, epistemology, simulation, and modeling.

Rehg, James A. (2000). **Introduction to robotics in CIM systems** (4th ed.). [Book, 440p., $126.50]. Prentice Hall, www.prenticehall.com.

Wagner, S. (1999). Robotics and children: Science achievement and problem solving. **Information Technology in Childhood Education Annual,** 101–145. Compares the impact of robotics (computer-powered manipulative) to a battery-powered manipulative (novelty control) and traditionally taught science class on science achievement and problem solving of fourth through sixth graders. Found that the robotics group had higher scores on programming logic-problem solving than did the novelty control group. Both experimental groups scored better than the traditionally taught class.

Wild, M. (2000). Designing and evaluating an educational performance support system. **British Journal of Educational Technology, 31**(1), 5–20. Provides an account of the design of the Lesson Planning System, a hypermedia performance support system (PSS) predicated on task performance to support novice teacher-education students in lesson planning. Reports on an initial research study to investigate the effectiveness of the software and discusses the role of PSSs in teacher education

Wright, J. R., Jr., Jung, S., Steplight, S., Wright, J. R., Sr., & Das, A. (2000). Employing omni-directional visual control for mobile robotics. **Technology Teacher, 59**(5), 32–38. Compared the impact of robotics (computer-powered manipulative) to a battery-powered manipulative (novelty control) and traditionally taught science class on science achievement and problem solving of fourth through sixth graders. Found that the robotics group had higher scores on programming logic-problem solving than did the novelty control group. Both experimental groups scored better than the traditionally taught class.

COMPUTER-ASSISTED INSTRUCTION

Aggarwal, A. (2000). **Web-based learning and teaching technologies: Opportunities and challenges.** [Book, 384 p., $69.95]. Idea Group Publishing, www.idea-groupp.com. Addresses trends and issues facing academic institutions in managing Web-based teaching and learning technologies.

Australian Educational Computing. Australian Council for Computers in Education. P.O. Box 1255, Belonnen, ACT 2616, Australia. Available online at http://www.acce.edu.au /journal/journal.html Ed. Hjeremy Pagram, [online]. Educational computer issues forum.

Brett, P. P. (2000). Integrating multimedia into the business English curriculum: A case study. **English for Specific Purposes, 19**(3), 269–290. Reports on a study designed to investigate the viability of the formal integration of multimedia business English software into an undergraduate curriculum. The study showed clear areas of success in attempts to integrate multimedia with the curriculum but suggests that some aspects of such a deployment will need reconsideration.

Bulla Gymnasia Virtuals. CyberCorp., Inc. info@cybercoro.net, http://www.cybercorp.net /gymv/bulla/ Ed. Robert N. Higgins. [Q., free of charge]. Online journal devoted to online training and education.

Bybee, R. W., & Loucks-Horsley, S. (2000). Standards as a catalyst for change in technology education. **Technology Teacher, 59**(5), 14–16. Suggests that technology education standards will initiate changes and are a first step in guiding the improvement of educational programs and classroom practices.

CALICO Journal. Computer Assisted Language Instruction Consortium, Southwest Texas State University, 116 Centennial Hall, San Marcos, TX 78666, info@calico.org, www.calico.org. [Q.; $50 indiv., $90 inst., $140 corporations]. Provides information on the applications of technology in teaching and learning languages.

Children's Software Review. Active Learning Associates, Inc., 44 Main St., Flemington, NJ 08822, www.childrenssoftware.com. [6/yr., $24]. Provides reviews and other information about software to help parents and educators more effectively use computers with children.

Computer Assisted Composition Journal. Human Technology Interface, Inc. Press 163 Wood Wedge Way, Sandford, NC 27330. (919)499-9216. Ed. Lynn Veach Sadler. [3/yr., $15]. Publishes essays pertaining to computer applications in writing.

Computer Book Review. Bookwire, P.O. Box 61067, Honolulu, HI 96839. www.bookwire.com/cbr [Q., $20 ($30, outside North America)]. Provides critical reviews of books on computers and computer-related subjects.

Computer Education, Staffordshire University, Computer Education Group, c/o CEG Treasurer, Beacoinside, Staffs, ST18 0AD, United Kingdom, Ed. I Selwood. [3/yr., 24 GBP to US]. Covers Educational Computer application for students 11–18 years of age.

Computer Education. K. K. Roy, Ltd., 55 Gariahat Road, P.O. Box 10210, Calcutta, West Bengal 700 019, India, Ed. K.K. Roy. Tel. 91-33-475-4872. [Bi. $35 US]. Discusses how schools and universities are using educational software. Profiles and reviews new educational software on the market in content areas such as science, social science, and the humanities.

Computer Learning. Computer Learning Foundation, P.O. Box 60007, Palo Alto, CA 94306-0007, clf@computerlearning.org, http://www.computerlearning.org. Newsletter dedicated to informing teachers and parents about current educational technology trends.

Computer Studies: Computers In Education. Dushkin-McGraw-Hill, Sluice Dock, Gyulliford, CT 06437-9989 Eds. Dwight Bishop, John Hirschbuhl, [Annual, $12.25]. Features articles on computer-based education applications, specifically logistics surrounding the use of computers in education.

Computers and Composition. Ablex Publishing Corp., 100 Prospect Street, P.O. Box 811, Stamford, CT 06904-0811, (203)323-9606, fax (203)357-8446. www.jaipress.com. [3/yr., $55 indiv.]. International journal for teachers of writing focuses on the use of computers in writing instruction and related research and dialogue.

Computers & Education. Elsevier Science Inc., 655 Avenue of the Americas, New York, NY 10010-5107. [8/yr., $1,078]. Presents technical papers covering a broad range of subjects for users of analog, digital, and hybrid computers in all aspects of higher education.

Computers and the Humanities. Kluwer Academic Publishers, 101 Philip Drive, Norwell, MA 02061. [Q., $317 US inst.]. Contains papers on computer-aided studies, applications, automation, and computer-assisted instruction.

Computers In Education Journal. American Society for Engineering Education, Computers in Education Decision, P.O. Box 68, Por Royal Sq, Port Royal, VA 22535, Ed. W.W. Everett, Jr. [Q., $45 US, $65 foreign]. Discusses and presents scholarly papers, application articles, and teaching notes relating to computers in education.

Computers in Human Behavior. Pergamon Press, 660 White Plains Road, Tarrytown, NY 10591-5153. [6/yr., $845]. Addresses the psychological impact of computer use on individuals, groups, and society.

Computers in the Schools. Haworth Press, 10 Alice Street, Binghamton, NY 13904-1580, (800)HAWORTH, fax (800)895-0582, getinfo@haworthpressinc.com, www.haworthpress .com. [Q., $60 indiv., $90 inst., $300 libraries]. Features articles that combine theory and practical applications of small computers in schools for educators and school administrators.

Connections. **Online-Offline,** 4(5), 2–25. Provides an annotated list of resources dealing with the theme of various types of connections. Includes Web sites, CD-ROMs/software, videos, books, and additional resources with appropriate grade levels and subject disciplines indicated in most cases. Sidebars include toys that connect, connecting with nature, it's a small world-satellites, connecting with the past-through our senses. Offers suggestions for classroom activities.

Converge. Imagine Media, Inc. 150 North Hill Drive, Brisbane, CA 94005, cz@cinvergemag.com, http://www.convergemag.com. Ed. Olga Amador. Discusses technology applications in all grade levels.

Crane, B. (2000). **Teaching with the Internet: Strategies and models for the K–12 curricula.** [Book, 277p., $45]. Neal-Schuman, orders@neal-schuman.com. Offers creative teaching solutions for using the Internet as an instructional tool.

CUE Newsletter. Computer Using Educators, Inc. 1210 Marina Village Parkway, Ste 100, Alameda CA 94501-0195, cueinc@cue.org, http://www.cue.org. Ed. F. Robert Walczak. [Bi-m., $30 domestic, $50 foreign]. Contains articles, news items and trade advertisements addressing computer-based education.

Curriculum-Technology Quarterly. Association for Supervision and Curriculum Development, Education & Technology Resource Center, 1703 N Beauregard Street, Alexandria, VA 22314, (800)933-2723, member@ascd.org, http://www.ascd.org. Ed. Larry Mann.

[Q.]. Discusses strategies for integrating technology into education. Also contains book and software reviews.

Dr. Dobb's Journal. Miller Freeman Inc., 600 Harrison Street, San Francisco, CA 94107, 1(800)456-1215. www.djj.com/djj. [Mo., $25 US, $45 Mexico and Canada, $70 elsewhere]. Articles on the latest in operating systems, programming languages, algorithms, hardware design and architecture, data structures, and telecommunications; in-depth hardware and software reviews.

Education Technology News. Businss Publishers, Inc. 8737 Colesville Road, Suite 11, Silver Spring, MD 20910-3928, (800)274-6737, bpinews@bpinews.com, http://www.bpinews .com. Ed. Rasheda Childress. [bi-w., $337 domestic, 356 out of North America]. Features articles discussing educational applications of computer technologies.

Educational Software Review. Growh Systems, Inc. 855 Normandy Road, Encinitas, CA 92024, Ed. Stewart Walton. [M., $33.75].

Educational Technology and Society. International Forum of Educational Technology and Society. IEEE Computer Society, Learning Technology Task Force, kinshuk@ieee.org, http://ifets.gmd.de/periodical. Ed., Dr. Kinshuk. [Q., no cost]. Explores issues concerning educational software developers and educators.

Educational Technology Review. Association for the Advancement of Computing in Education, P.O. Box 2966, Charlottesville, VA 22902-2966, info@aace.org, http://www.aace.org. Ed. Gary H Marks. [Q., $40 domestic to nonmembers, $50 to nonmembers]. Publishes articles dealing with the issues in instructional technology application.

Electronic Education Report. SIMBA Information, 11 Riverbend Drive S, Box 4234, Stamford, CT 06907-0234, (800)307-2529, info@simbanet.com, http://www.simbanet.com. Ed. Kathleen Martucci. [bi-w., $479 North America, $529 elsewhere]. Newsletter discussing software and multimedia educational technologies.

Electronic School. National School Boards Association, 1680 Duke Street, Alexandria VA 22314; electronic-school@nsba.org, http://www.electronic-school.com/. [Q.]. Trade publication that discusses trends and strategies for integrating technology into primary and secondary education.

Extended Studies E-zine. California State University at San Marcos, (800)500-9377, jubran@mailhost1.csusm.edu, http://www.csusm.edu/es/ezine. Online newsletter dedicated to the topic of distance learning.

Fredericks, A. (2000). **Science discoveries on the net: An integrated approach.** [Book, 312p., $27.50]. Libraries Unlimited, www.lu.com. Internet-based research lessons based on science concepts. Each section includes a list of follow-up discussion questions and related literature and Web site suggestions.

Fredericks, A. (2000). **Social studies discoveries on the net: An integrated approach.** [Book, 275p., $26]. Libraries Unlimited, www.lu.com. Contains 75 lessons integrating Internet researching skills and social science concepts.

Going Online in Your Classroom. (2000). [Video, 57 min., $129]. Films for the Humanities & Sciences, www.films.com. Explains how to maximize the potential of Internet access in the classroom through collaborative communication, videoconferences, e-mail, virtual field trips, and online publishing capabilities.

Grabe, M., & Grabe, C. (2001). **Integrating technology for meaningful learning.** (3d Ed.). Houghton Mifflin. www.college.hmco.com. This media package contains updated information on the Internet, voice recognition technology, and digital camera applications as well as several example student projects. The CD-ROM contains demos of instructional software and provides the user with Internet links corresponding to each chapter in the book.

Groves, M., & Zemel P. (2000). Instructional technology adoption in higher education: An action research case study. **International Journal of Instructional Media, 27**(1). Describes an action research study of faculty and graduate teaching assistants at the University of Tennessee that was conducted to assess technology use by faculty, including their perceived barriers to and needs for technology adoption and use. Discusses the development of a Web-based resource in response to these needs.

Higher Education Technology News. Business Publishers, Inc., 8737 Colesville Road, Suite 1100, Silver Spring, MD 20910-3928. 1(800)274-6737, bpinews@bpinews.com, http://www.bpinews.com. [Bi-w., $298, $314 out of North America]. For teachers and those interested in educational uses of computers in the classroom. Features articles on applications and educational software.

Holahan, P., Jurkat, P., & Friedman, E. (2000). Evaluation of a mentor teacher model for enhancing mathematics instruction through the use of computers. **Journal of Research on Computing in Education, 32**(3), 336–350. Describes the development of the Mentor Teacher Model that trained middle school and high school mathematics teachers in New Jersey as mentor teachers in the effective use of computer-based technologies for teaching mathematics. Highlights include student-centered teaching methods; cooperative learning; problem-solving activities; and technology diffusion and institutionalization.

Home Office Computing. Box 51344, Boulder, CO 80321-1344. [Mo., $19.97, foreign $27.97]. For professionals who use computers and conduct business at home.

Hung, D., &Wong, A. Activity theory as a framework for project work in learning environments. **Educational Technology, 2001, 40**(2) 33–37. Proposes activity theory as a framework for student project work that is a form of open-ended contextual activity-based learning emphasizing problem solving as a collaborative effort. Topics include project work from a Vygotskian perspective of activity theory and the design of a prototype for Web-based project work.

Information Technology in Childhood Education. Association for the Advancement for Computing in Education, P.O. Box 2966, Charlottesville, VA 22902-2966. infor@aace.org, http://www.aace.org. [Q., $75 domestic, $85 domestic to institutions, $85 foreign to individuals, $95 foreign to institutions]. Scholarly trade publication reporting on research and investigations into the applications of instructional technology.

InfoWorld. InfoWorld Publishing, 155 Bovet Road, Suite 800, San Mateo, CA 94402, (650)572-7341. [W., $155]. News and reviews of PC hardware, software, peripherals, and networking.

Instructor. Scholastic Inc., 555 Broadway, New York, NY 10012, (212)505-4900. [8/yr., $19.95; 2 yr.'s, $29.90]. Features articles on applications and advances of technology in education for K–12 and college educators and administrators.

Integrated Learning: Technologize Your Lesson. (2000). [Video, 55 min, $129]. Films for the Humanities & Sciences, www.films.com. Profiles three applications of technology in the middle and high schools setting, including a virtual trip for geography class, a slide show presentation program that teaches environmentalism, and a simulated corporate level office for business education.

INTERACTIVE. Question Publishing Company, Ltd., 27 Frederick Street, Hockley, Birmingham, Warks, B1 3HH, United Kingdom, Tel 44-121-212-0919, FAX 44-121-212-1959. [9/yr., GBP 18 outside Europe, GBP 22 in Europe]. Gives primary and secondary educators information pertaining to information technology use in the classroom.

Interactive Learning Environments. Swets and Zeitlinger, P.O. Box 582 Downingtown, PA 19335-998. orders@swets.nl, http://www.swets.nl/sps/journals/ile1.html. [3/yr., $79 indiv., $205 inst. with online]. Explores the implications of the Internet and multimedia presentation software in education and training environments.

Journal of Computer Assisted Learning. Blackwell Scientific Ltd., Journal Subscriptions, journals.cs@blacksci.co.uk, www.blackwell-science.com. [Q., $98.50 indiv., $424.50 inst.]. Articles and research on the use of computer-assisted learning.

Journal of Educational Computing Research. Baywood Publishing Co., 26 Austin Avenue, P.O. Box 337, Amityville, NY 11701. [8/yr. $104 indiv., $250 inst.]. Presents original research papers, critical analyses, reports on research in progress, design and development studies, article reviews, and grant award listings.

Journal of Research on Computing in Education. ISTE, University of Oregon, 1787 Agate St., Eugene, OR 97403-1923, (800)336-5191, cust_svc@ccmail.uoregon.edu, www.iste.org. [Q., $38,1 year; $73, 2 years; $108, 3 years]. Contains articles reporting on the latest research findings related to classroom and administrative uses of technology, including system and project evaluations.

Koller, C. A., Frankenfield, J. J., & Sarley, C. A. (2000). Twelve tips for developing educational multimedia in a community-based teaching hospital. **Medical Teacher, 22**(1), 7–10. Discusses proper planning and project management techniques. Suggests tips for selecting a first project and instructional design based on constructivism and introducing computer-based training into the curriculum.

Kozlowski, S. C. (2000). Better learning with technology? **School Administrator, 56**(4), 24–26, 28, 30. As one Illinois district found, using educational technology cannot guarantee that students will learn any better. Educators must first change the classroom/school ambience, work within the new high-tech environment, apply appropriate tools for using technology effectively, and connect student achievement and technology usage.

Learning and Leading with Technology: Serving Teachers in the Classroom. ISTE, University of Oregon, 1787 Agate St., Eugene, OR 97403-1923, (800)336-5191, cust_svc@ccmail.uoregon.edu, www.iste.org. [8/yr, $38, 1 year; $73, 2 years; $108, 3 years]. Focuses on the use of technology, coordination, and leadership; written by educators for educators. Appropriate for classroom teachers, lab teachers, technology coordinators, and teacher educators.

Logo Exchange. ISTE, University of Oregon, 1787 Agate Street, Eugene, OR 97403-1923, (800)336-5191, cust_svc@ccmail.uoregon.edu, www.iste.org. [Q., $29, $44 intl., $34 intl. air]. Brings ideas from Logo educators throughout the world, with current information on Logo research, resources, and methods.

MacWorld. MacWorld Communications, Box 54529, Boulder, CO 80322-4529. [Mo., $19.97]. Describes hardware, software, tutorials, and applications for users of the Macintosh microcomputer.

McKenzie, J. (2000). **The Internet: A tool for research and communication.** [Video, 1 hour 40 min., $179]. Canter, www.caner.net. This video is a part of a five-module series that aims to show teachers how to use technology to bring relevant knowledge and skills to the classroom.

McKinnon, D., Nolan, C. J., & Sinclair, K. (2000). A longitudinal study of student attitudes toward computers: Resolving an attitude decay paradox. **Journal of Research on Computing in Education, 32**(3), 325–335. Describes results of an integrated curriculum project in New Zealand that generated paradoxical results regarding student motivation and attitudes toward computer use during junior high school, where attitudes became less positive. Examines implications for the design and implementation of curriculum projects involving student use of computer applications.

Microcomputer Abstracts. Information Today, 143 Old Marlton Pike, Medford, NJ 08055, (800)300-9868. [4/yr., $199 US; $208 Canada/Mexico; $214 elsewhere]. Abstracts literature on the use of microcomputers in business, education, and the home, covering over 175 publications.

Miller, E. (2000). **The Internet resource directory for k–12 teachers and librarians: 2000/2001 edition.** [Book, 462 p., $27.50]. Libraries Unlimited, www.lu.com. Describes approximately 1,500 of the most useful educational Web sites for educators. Organized by subject area and thoroughly indexed.

Mitra, A., & Steffensmeier, T. (2000). Changes in student attitudes and student computer use in a computer-enriched environment. **Journal of Research on Computing in Education, 32**(3), 417–433. Examines the pedagogic usefulness of the computer by focusing on changes in student attitudes and use of computers in a computer-enriched environment using data from a longitudinal study at Wake Forest University. Results indicate that a networked institution where students have easy access can foster positive attitudes.

Montgomery, N. (2000). Technology and authority: How the collaborative paradigm shifts in a networked writing environment. **Composition Forum, 10**(2), 31–51. Discusses the redistribution of power and authority invited by networked computers. Examines the changing roles of teachers and tutors as they set up and monitor occasions for writing to take advantage of the increased participation and involvement when students write with computers. Discusses how this valuable experience can be most effectively brought into the writing center.

November, A. (2000). **Technology, the learning process and a vision for the future.** [Video, 1 hour 40 min., $179]. Canter, www.caner.net. This video is a part of a five-module series, which shows teachers how to use technology to bring relevant knowledge and skills to the classroom.

The one-computer classroom. [Video, 36 min., $129]. Films for the Humanities & Sciences, www.films.com. Explores how a single computer in the classroom can be used as a workstation, a presentation device, and a tool used for interactive learning.

Online learning: Students and teachers as researchers. (2000). [Video, 39 min, $129]. Films for the Humanities & Sciences, www.films.com. Demonstrates how students and teachers of all grade levels use the Internet for dynamic research projects.

Overy, M. (2000). Integrating the Internet into the classroom by removing "Technology" barriers. **Education in Science,** (186), 25. Describes three Web sites that feature resources for science teachers, students, and department heads. The first allows teachers to design their own online worksheets, the second contains a collection of science-related images, and the third focuses on issues related to the running, organization, and management of science departments.

PC Magazine: The Independent Guide to IBM-Standard Personal Computing. Ziff-Davis Publishing Co., Box 54093, Boulder, CO 80322. [22 issues, $22.97]. Comparative reviews of computer hardware and general business software programs.

PC Week. Ziff-Davis Publishing Co., 1 Park Avenue, New York, 10016. [W., $195, Canada and Mexico $250, free to qualified personnel]. Provides current information on the IBM PC, including hardware, software, industry news, business strategies, and reviews of hardware and software.

PC World. PC World Communications, Inc., Box 55029, Boulder, CO 80322-5029. [Mo., $19.97 US, $34.97 Mexico, $65.97 elsewhere]. Presents articles on applications and columns containing news, systems information, product announcements, and hardware updates.

Penn, J., Nedeff, V., & Gozdzik, G. (2000). Organic chemistry and the Internet: A Web-based approach to homework and testing using the WE_LEARN System. **Journal of Chemical Education, 77**(2), 227–231. Describes the development and implementation of a Web-based software engine that selects from a database of questions for students to answer and provides immediate feedback for students and instructor. Discusses the results of using this technology in an organic chemistry section.

RECALL. European Association for Computer Assisted Language Learning. (EUROCALL), Cambridge University Press, Edinburgh Building, Sharftesbury Road, Cambridge CB2 2RU, United Kingdom, http://www.cupp.cam.ac.uk. Ed. June Thompson. [Semi-annual, $104 US, $65 Great Britain]. Contains articles on research and development in the area of computer-assisted language learning.

Social Science Computer Review. Sage Publications Inc., 2455 Teller Road, Thousand Oaks, CA 91320, order@sagepub.com, www.sagepub.com. [Q., $63 indiv., $274 inst.]. Features include software reviews, new product announcements, and tutorials for beginners.

Software Magazine. Sentry Publishing Co., Inc., 1 Research Drive, Suite 400B, Westborough, MA 01581-3907. [6 issues/yr., $42 US, $58 Canada, $140 elsewhere, free to qualified personnel]. Provides information on software and industry developments for business and professional users and announces new software packages.

Students as multimedia authors. (2000). [Video, 49 min., $129]. Films for the Humanities & Sciences, www.films.com. Demonstrates 2nd to 12th grade students using multimedia programs collaboratively.

Swanson, N. (2000). **Project-based learning and technology.** [Video, 1 hour, 10 min., $ 179]. Canter, www.canter.net. This video is a part of a five-module series, which shows teachers how to use technology to bring relevant knowledge and skills to the classroom.

Technology and Learning. Miller Freeman, Inc. 600 Harrison Street, San Francisco, CA 94107, (415)905-2200, http://www.teachlearning.com. [8/yr., $29.95 US, $39.95 Can and Mexico, $69.95 elsewhere]. Discusses and features new innovations in educational hardware and software.

Thronburg, D. (2001). **Managing change with new technologies.** [Video, 1 hour, 20 min., $179]. Canter, www.canter.net. This video is a part of a five-module series, which shows teachers how to use technology to bring relevant knowledge and skills to the classroom.

Thronburg, D. (2001). **Campfires in cyberspace.** [Book, 163 p., $ 24.95]. Canter, www.canter.net. Techniques to help K–12 teachers integrate the Internet into the class as an effective learning tool.

Wissick, C., & Gardner, J. (2000). Multimedia or not to multimedia? **Teaching Exceptional Children, 32**(4), 34–43. This article presents instructional factors that teachers should consider when selecting multimedia materials appropriate for students with learning disabilities. Specific programs and Web sites that use design features effectively are discussed, and problematic features in multimedia software packages are described, along with strategies that make appropriate accommodations.

DISTANCE EDUCATION

Adams, C., & Cross, T. (2000). Distance learning opportunities for academically gifted students. **Journal of Secondary Gifted Education, 11**(2), 88–96. This article provides background information about distance learning, the rationale for it, descriptions of three distance learning programs designed specifically for gifted students, and the pros and cons of providing instruction using this method of delivery. The ability of distance learning to provide access to higher level coursework is stressed.

American Journal of Distance Education. American Center for the Study of Distance Education, Pennsylvania State University, 110 Rackley Building, University Park, PA 16802-3202, www.cde.psu.edu/ACSDE/. [3/yr.; $45 indiv.; $75 inst.]. Created to disseminate information and act as a forum for criticism and debate about research in and practice of politics, and administration of distance education.

Barker, B. O. (2000). Anytime, anyplace learning. **FORUM for Applied Research and Public Policy, 15**(1), 88–92. Describes trends and innovations involving use of the World Wide Web in distance learning. Discusses Choice 2000, the first totally online public (charter) high school; Web information resources for more conventional schools; student access to the Internet; virtual learning communities; Web-based learning strategies; and skills involved in technological literacy. Lists 13 noteworthy educational Web sites.

Belanger, F., & Jordan, D. (2000). **Evaluation and implementation of distance learning: Technologies, tools, and techniques.** [Book, 256 p., $69.95]. IDEA Group, www.idea-group.com. Addresses the processes, techniques, and tools of this emerging teaching and learning environment.

Carswell, L., Thomas, P., Petre, M., Price, B., & Richards, M. (2000). Distance education via the Internet: The student experience. **British Journal of Educational Technology, 31**(1), 29–46. Compares the experiences of a group of Internet students to those of conventional distance learning students in the same Computer Science course at the Open University (United Kingdom). Discusses learning styles; background questionnaires that included computer use, e-mail experience, programming, education, and attitudes; learning outcomes; gender; performance; and interaction.

Cifuentes, L., & Murphy, K. L. (2000). Promoting multicultural understanding and positive self-concept through a distance learning community: Cultural connections. **Educational Technology Research and Development, 48**(1), 69–83. Explores the effectiveness of distance learning and multimedia technologies in facilitating an expanded learning community between geographically separated elementary and secondary schools with Hispanic students in Texas. Highlights include the Cultural Connections program; teacher collaboration; curricular activities; identity-forming multicultural activities; interactive videoconferencing; multicultural understanding; and students' positive self-concept.

DEOS News. (Distance Education Online Symposium). Penn State University, College of Education, American Center for the Study of Distance Education, 110 Rackley Building, University Park, PA 16802-3202. acsde@psuvm.psu.edu, http://www.ed.psu.edu/acsde /deosnews.htm/. [Online]. Posts information on distance education research and practice.

Distance Education Report. Magna Publications, Inc., 2718 Dryden Drive, Madison, WI 53704. [Mo., $399]. Digests periodical, Internet, and conference information into monthly reports.

Goodson, C. (2001). **Providing library services for distance education students: A how to do it manual.** [Book, 200p., $59.95]. Neal–Schuman. This manual gives comprehensive instructions on how to plan and implement a distance learning program.

Green, A., Esperat, C., Seale, D., Chalambaga, M., Smith, S., Walker, G., Ellison, P., Berg, B., & Robinson, S. (2000). The evolution of a distance education initiative into a major telehealth project. **Nursing and Health Care Perspectives, 21**(2), 66–70. Three Texas nursing schools collaborated in establishing a telehealth clinic to provide services for chronically ill children. Expanded into public schools, the project provides distance learning and telehealth services to school nurses, teachers, administrators, and families involved in the care of these children.

Grimes, S. (2000). Rural areas in the information society: Diminishing distance or increasing learning capacity? **Journal of Rural Studies, 16**(1), 13–21. Examines prospects for rural areas within the Information Society, referring particularly to the European Union.

Discusses effects of diminished distance from core markets, increased learning capacity through improved access to information, public policy emphasis on building infrastructure, disappointing outcomes for telecommunications initiatives and rural telework, and the potential of rural areas to exploit new technologies.

Javid, M. (2000). A suggested model for a working cyberschool. **Educational Technology, 40**(1), 61–63. Suggests a model for a working cyberschool based on a case study of Kamiak Cyberschool (Washington), a technology-driven public high school. Topics include flexible hours; one-to-one interaction with teachers; a supportive school environment; use of computers, interactive media, and online resources; and self-paced, project-based learning.

Journal of Distance Education. Canadian Association for Distance Education, Secretariat, One Stewart St., Suite 205, Ottawa, ON K1N 6H7, Canada. (Text in English and French.) [2/yr., $40, add $5 outside Canada]. Aims to promote and encourage scholarly work of empirical and theoretical nature relating to distance education in Canada and throughout the world.

Journal of Library and Information Services for Distance Learning. 2710 University Drive, Richland, WA, 99352-1671, (509)372-7204, Haworth Information Press, www.HaworthPress.com. [Q., $36 indiv., $75 inst., $75 libraries]. Contains peer-reviewed articles, essays, narratives, current events, and letters from distance learning and information science experts.

Journal of Online Learning. International Society for Technology in Education. SIG, 1787 Agate St., Eugene, OR, 97403-1923. (541)346-4414, FAX (541)346-5890, Ed. Terresa Gibry. [Q., $29 domestic to nonmembers, $39 foreign to nonmembers, $20 domestic to members, $30 foreign to members, $12 domestic to students, $22 foreign to students]. Presents communications technology, projects, research findings, publication references, and international contact information in instructional technology.

Koehler, A. G. (2000). Teaching on television. **Research and Teaching in Developmental Education, 16**(2), 97–108. Describes experiences in teaching with Interactive TV (ITV) network and the mindsets and goals educators encounter in utilizing this technology. Presents four basic principles of teaching well on TV: Television technology is a brand new member of the class, every student is present in class with you, our goal is not "good TV" but a good class, and "good TV" can only help.

Lau, L. (2000). **Distance learning technologies: Issues, trends and opportunities.** [Book, 264 p., $69.95]. IDEA Group, www.idea-group.com. Follows the evolution of distance learning from early beginnings to the present.

MacDonald, L., & Caverly, D. (2000). Techtalk: Synchronous distance developmental education. **Journal of Developmental Education, 23**(3), 38–39. Discusses the third generation (G3) model of online education named synchronous online education. Reviews terminology, hardware, different stages of G3, software, and implications of G3 for the future.

Mottet, T. P. (2000). Interactive television instructors' perceptions of students' nonverbal responsiveness and their influence on distance teaching. **Communication Education, 49**(2), 146–164. Finds that interactive television instructors' perceptions of students' nonverbal responses are positively related to their impressions of students, their perceptions of teaching effectiveness and satisfaction, perceptions of teacher-student interpersonal relationships, and preference for teaching in the interactive television classroom; these perceptions are significantly higher in the traditional face-to-face classroom; and two-way audio/video delivery systems increase positive perceptions.

New Review of Virtual Universities. Taylor Graham Publishing, 500 Chesham House, Chesham House, 150 Regent Street, London W1R 5FA, United Kingdom, http://www .taylorgraham.com, Eds. Mark Chamers & Peter Roberts. [Annual, GBP 70, $130].

Offir, B. (2000). Map for decision making in operating distance learning system—Research results. **Educational Media International, 37**(1), 9–15. Examines decision-making aspects of the introduction of distance learning into university instruction and learning based on experiences in Israel. Discusses the introduction of information technology into the classroom; examines teacher/student interactions; and suggests a model for introducing distance learning that focuses on the role of the teacher in decision making.

Open Learning. Pitman Professional, Subscriptions Dept., P.O. Box 77, Harlow, Essex CM19 5BQ, England. [3/yr., £68 UK, £73 Europe, $78 elsewhere]. Academic, scholarly publication on aspects of open and distance learning anywhere in the world. Includes issues for debate and research notes.

Open Praxis. International Centre for Distance Education, National Extension College, 18 Brooklands Avenue, Cambridge CB2 2HN, England. [2/yr., $70 indiv., $55 libraries]. Reports on activities and programs of the ICDE.

Passey, D. (2000). Developing teaching strategies for distance (out-of-school) learning in primary and secondary schools. **Educational Media International, 37**(1), 45–57. Discussion of distance education in the United Kingdom focuses on how teachers in primary and secondary schools can develop teaching strategies to adopt and implement distance learning practices. Topics include lifelong learning; social support; the use of technology; homework activities; teacher access to computers; and learning strategies.

Schifter, C. (2000). Faculty motivators and inhibitors for participation in distance education. **Educational Technology, 40**(2) 43–46. Discussion of distance education for higher education and the use of interactive computer-mediated communication systems focuses on the results of a survey of faculty and administrators that examined motivating factors for participation in distance education and inhibiting factors, including technical support, faculty workload, and concerns about course quality.

Sharma, S. (2000). Interactive distance education for in-service teachers in India. **Educational Media International, 37**(1), 68–72. Discusses interactive television technologies that are under development and experimentation in India for in-service teacher education at the Indira Gandhi National Open University. Describes the VSAT (Very Small Aperture Terminal) system and ISDN (Integrated Services Digital Network) that are used for video technology in distance education.

SIGCUE Outlook. (Special Interest Group on Computer Uses in Education). Association for Computing Machinery, Special Interest Group on Computer Uses in Education, 1515 Broadway, 17th Floor, New York, NY 10036-5701. (212)869-7440, http://www.acm.org, Ed. John Impagliazzo. [Q., #36 to non-members, $19 to members]. Discusses educational computer systems, hardware, and software applications.

SIGTC Connections. International Society for Technology in Education, Special Interest Group for Technology Coordinators, 1787 Agate Street, Eugene, OR 97403-1923. (541)346-4414, FAX (541)346-5890, Ed. Gordon Dahl. [Q., $29 domestic to nonmembers, $39 foreign to non-members, $20 domestic to members, $30 to members]. Provides a forum for sharing information on issues affecting technology coordinator professionals.

Squires, D. (2000). The impact of ICT use on the role of the learner. **Lifelong Learning in Europe, 5**(1), 55–60. Information and communications technologies used in interactive learning environments and networked communities have led to new constructivist roles for the learner: explorer, constructor, researcher, collaborator, judge, reflective practitioner, and problem solver.

St-Pierre, A. (2000). A proposal for an instructional technology and media center for distance educators. **International Journal of Instructional Media, 27**(1), 29–35. Presents a proposal describing the characteristics that a modern ITMC (Instructional Technology and Media Center) for distance educators who teach in the Office of Continuing Education, via the World Wide Web, should have. Highlights include a mission statement; goals and objectives; staff needs; and public relations.

Swalec, J., & Regnier, J. (2000). Doing our "home-work." **Community College Journal, 70**(3), 42–46. Summarizes the steps taken by Waubonsee Community College (Illinois) in offering courses using multiple technologies to serve their diverse "market" of students. Describes the creation and development of a pilot distance learning paradigm that would expand upon the existing networks by using television access and computers to send video classes to students' homes.

Tuovinen, J. E. (2000). Multimedia distance education interactions. **Educational Media International, 37**(1), 16–24. Discusses multimedia interactions in distance education synthesizes approaches based on distance education theory, cognition research, and multimedia development. Proposes a composite framework for discussion of multimedia and multimodal interactions in a distance education context, which is based on interactions between the instructor, students, and content.

Wheeler, S. (2000). User reaction to videoconferencing. Which students cope best? **Educational Media International, 37**(1), 31–38. Reviews a study conducted at the University of Plymouth (United Kingdom) to establish the psychological basis for user responses to digital videoconferencing. Discusses possible predictor variables, including left and right brain laterality and factors of age and gender; measurement of behavioral and affective responses in distance learners; self-consciousness; and anxiety level.

White, Ken W., & Weight, Bob H., Eds. (2000). **The online teaching guide: A handbook of attitudes, strategies, and techniques for the virtual classroom**. [Book, 192p., $29]. Allyn & Bacon, 160 Gould Street, Needham Heights, MA 02494-2310. Presents 14 papers that offer guidance to college teachers venturing into online instruction. It is based on the experiences and ideas of faculty at the University of Phoenix (Arizona) online campus, which has been offering online courses since 1989.

Windelborn, A. (2000). Telepresent teaching. **Physics Teacher, 38**(1), 16–17. Discusses possibilities for the application of telepresence to physics and teaching. Telepresence allows a computer user to effectively be present at some other location through the use of remote cameras, sensors, and controls.

EDUCATIONAL RESEARCH

American Educational Research Journal. American Educational Research Association, 1230 17th Street, NW, Washington, DC 20036-3078. [Q., $41 indiv., $56 inst.]. Reports original research, both empirical and theoretical, and brief synopses of research.

Cates, W., & Bruce, R. (2000). Conceptualizing learner support space. **Educational Technology Research and Development, 48**(1), 85–98. Discussion of computer-based online help systems for instructional software focuses on three types of learner support: for optimizing use of a computer program; for learning content; and for monitoring and enhancing learning. Proposes a multidimensional model of learner-support space defined by the intrusiveness of the delivery methods and recommends future research topics.

Clark, S., Lehaney, B. (2000). **Human centered methods in information systems: Current research and practice**. [Book, 250p., $69.95]. IDEA Group, www.idea-group.com. Discusses the dynamics of human computer interaction, organizational issues, and technology.

Current Index to Journals in Education (CIJE). Oryx Press, 4041 N. Central at Indian School Road, Phoenix, AZ 85012-3397, [Mo., $245 ($280 outside North America); semi-ann. cumulations $250 ($285 foreign); combination $475]. A guide to articles published in some 830 education and education-related journals. Includes complete bibliographic information, annotations, and indexes. Semiannual cumulations available. Contents are produced by the ERIC (Educational Resources Information Center) system, Office of Educational Research and Improvement, and the U.S. Department of Education.

Education Index. H. W. Wilson, 950 University Avenue, Bronx, NY 10452. [Mo., except July and August; $1,295 for CD-ROM, including accumulations]. Author-subject index to educational publications in the English language. Cumulated quarterly and annually.

Educational Research. Routledge, 11 Fetter Lane, London EC4P 4EE, England. [3/yr., £40 indiv. ($68 US and Canada)]. Reports on current educational research, evaluation, and applications.

Educational Researcher. American Educational Research Association, 1230 17th Street, NW, Washington, DC 20036-3078. [9/yr., $44 indiv., $61 inst.]. Contains news and features of general significance in educational research.

Ely, D., & Plomp, T. (2000). **Classic writings in instructional technology** (Vol. 2). [Book, 268 p., $60]. Libraries Unlimited, www.lu.com. Collected essays outlining the foundations and principles of instructional technology written by experts in the field.

Journal of Interactive Learning Research. Association for the Advancement of Computing in Education, P.O. Box 2966, Charlottesville, VA 22902-2966, info@aace.org, http://www.aace.org. Ed. Tom Reeves. [Q., $75 domestic indiv., $85 foreign indiv., $95 domestic inst., $105 foreign inst.]. Publishes articles pertaining to theory, implementation, and overall impact of interactive learning environments in education.

Learning Technology. IEEE Computer Society, Learning Technology Task Force, Private Bag 11-222, Massey University, Palmerston North, New Zealand. http://lttf.ieee.org /learn_tech. Ed. Dr. Kinshuk. [Q., online]. Reports developments, projects, conferences, and findings of the Learning Technology Task Force.

Logo Exchange. International Society for Technology in Education, Special Interest Group for Logo-Using Educators, 1787 Agate St., Eugene, OR 97403-1923, Ed. Gary Stager. [Q., $34 domestic to nonmembers, $44 foreign to members, $24 domestic to members, $34 foreign to members, $14.40 domestic to students, $24.40 foreign to students]. Provides current information on research, lesson plans, and methods related to LOGO.

LTRREPORT. Node Learning Technologies Network, 410 Dufferin Avenue, London, ON N6B 1Z6, Canada, http://thenode.org/ltreport/. Ed. Erin Bale. [Semiannual, online, $90]. Provides practical information for the use of technology in education and training.

MERIDIAN (RALEIGH). C/O Edwin Gerler, College of Education and Psychology, North Carolina State University, Box 7801, Raleigh, NC 27695-7801. Meridian@poe .coe.ncsu.edu, http://www.ncsu.edu/meridian. Ed. Cheryl Mason. [semi-annual, online]. Online journal dedicated to research in middle school educational technology use.

Research in Science & Technological Education. Taylor & Francis Group, 11 New Fetter Lane, London EC4P 4EE, www.tandf.co.uk. [2/yr., $104 indiv., $578 inst.]. Publication of original research in the science and technological fields. Includes articles on psychological, sociological, economic, and organizational aspects of technological education.

Resources in Education (RIE). Superintendent of Documents, U.S. Government Printing Office, P.O. Box 371954, Pittsburgh, PA 15250-7954, www.access.gpo.gov. [Mo., $78 US, $97.50 elsewhere]. Announcement of research reports and other documents in education, including abstracts and indexes by subject, author, and institution. Contents produced by the ERIC (Educational Resources Information Center) system, Office of Educational Research and Improvement, and the U.S. Department of Education.

Ronis, Diane. (2000). **Brain compatible assessments. K–college**. [Book, 162p., $38.95]. Skylight Professional Development, 2626 S. Clearbrook Drive, Arlington Heights, IL 60005-5310, (800)348-4474. This guide uses current brain research to show that some traditional instructional and assessment methods may actually work against the brain's natural way of learning. The guide shows how to enhance traditional methods of assessment using techniques derived from recent research on the brain. Practical approaches to assessment are illustrated with lesson plans that include opportunities for assessment.

Software and Networks for Learning, Shrewsbury Publishing, P.O. Box 3894, Santa Barbara, CA, 93130, Ed. Urban Streitz. [9/yr., $65, online full text]. Newsletter.

TESS (The Educational Software Selector). Educational Products Information Exchange (EPIE) Institute, 103 3 W. Montauk Highway, 3, Hampton, NY, 11946-4006, (516)728-9100, FAX (516)728-9228. [Annual, $82.50 base volume (1996), $ 32.50 for update]. A guide listing annotated references to educational software for preschool through postgraduate education.

Willis, J., Mukta, J., & Nilakanta. (2001). **Qualitative research methods for education and instructional technology.** Informational Age Publishing, Inc. Infoage@infoagepub .com. [Book, $29.95]. Discusses trends in positivism, interpretivism, and critical theory. Outlines data collection and analysis approaches.

EDUCATIONAL TECHNOLOGY

Appropriate Technology. Intermediate Technology Publications, Ltd., 103-105 Southampton Row, London, WC1B 4HH, England, journals.edit@itpubs.org.uk. [Q., $28 indiv., $37 inst.]. Articles on less technologically advanced, but more environmentally sustainable, solutions to problems in developing countries.

British Journal of Educational Technology. National Council for Educational Technology, Millburn Hill Road, Science Park, Coventry CV4 7JJ, England. [Q., $101 indiv., $230 inst.]. Published by the National Council for Educational Technology, this journal includes articles on education and training, especially theory, applications, and development of educational technology and communications.

CÆLL Journal. ISTE, University of Oregon, 1787 Agate Street, Eugene, OR 97403-1923, (800)336-5191, cust_svc@ccmail.uoregon.edu, www.iste.org. [Q., $29; $39 intl., $42 intl. air]. Focuses on current issues facing computer-using language teachers; covers trends, products, applications, research, and program evaluation.

Canadian Journal of Educational Communication. Association for Media and Technology in Education in Canada, 3-1750 The Queensway, Suite 1318, Etobicoke, ON M9C 5H5, Canada. [3/yr., $75]. Concerned with all aspects of educational systems and technology.

Duhaney, D. (2000). Technology and the educational process: Transforming classroom activities. **International Journal of Instructional Media, 27**(1), 67–72. Explores the integration of technology into the education process and some of the changes they have generated in classroom activities. Topics include technology in teaching and learning activities; computer-assisted instruction; the Internet; telecommunications technologies; the classroom environment; and interchange among teachers and students.

Educational Technology. Educational Technology Publications, Inc., 700 Palisade Avenue, Englewood Cliffs, NJ 07632-0564, (800)952-BOOK. [Bi-mo., $119 US, $139 elsewhere]. Covers telecommunications, computer-aided instruction, information retrieval, educational television, and electronic media in the classroom.

Educational Technology Abstracts. Taylor & Francis Group, 11 New Fetter Lane, London EC4P 4EE, www.tandf.co.uk. [6/yr., $292 indiv., $791 inst.]. An international publication of abstracts of recently published material in the field of educational and training technology.

Educational Technology Research and Development. AECT, ETR&D Subscription Dept., 1800 N. Stonelake Drive, Suite 2, Bloomington, IN 47404, www. aect.org. [Q., $55 US, $63 foreign]. Focuses on research, instructional development, and applied theory in the field of educational technology; peer-reviewed.

International Journal of Educational Technology. University of Western Australia, Department of Education, Nedlands, W.A. 6907 Australia, rhacker@ecel.uwa.edu.au, http://www.outreach.uluc.edu/ijet/, Ed. Roger Hacker. [Semiannual, online full text]. Posts information about computer-based educational technologies.

International Journal of Technology and Design Education. Kluwer Academic Publishers, 101 Philip Drive, Norwell, MA 02061, (617)871-6600, fax (617)871-6528, kluwer@wkap.com. [3/yr., $104 individual, $172 institution]. Publishes research reports and scholarly writing about aspects of technology and design education.

Januszewski, A. (2001). **Educational technology: The development of a concept.** [Book, 180p., $48.00]. Libraries Unlimited, www.lu.com. Outlines the evolution of educational technology from its beginnings in the fields of audiovisual education, science, and engineering from the 1960s to the present.

Javid, M. (2000). A suggested model for a working cyberschool. **Educational Technology, 40**(1), 61–63. Suggests a model for a working cyberschool based on a case study of Kamiak Cyberschool (Washington), a technology-driven public high school. Topics include flexible hours; one-to-one interaction with teachers; a supportive school environment; use of computers, interactive media, and online resources; and self-paced, project-based learning.

Journal of Computing in Higher Education. Norris Poublishers, *Journal of Computing in Higher Education,* Box 2593, Amherst, MA 01004-2593. cmacknight@oit.umass.edu, http://www-unix.oit.umass.edu/~carolm/jche/, Ed. Carol B MacKinght. [Semi-annual, $35 US indiv., $65 foreign indiv., $65 domestic to inst., $75 in Canada to inst., $80 foreign to inst.]. Publishes scholarly essays, case studies, and research that discuss instructional technologies.

Journal of Educational Technology Systems. Society for Applied Learning Technology, Baywood Publishing Co., Inc., 26 Austin Avenue Box 337, Amityville, NY 11701, Baywood@baywood.com, http://baywood.com. [Q., $175 US]. Discusses educational hardware and software.

Journal of Interactive Media In Education. Open University, Knowledge Media Institute, Milton Keynes, MK7 6AA United Kingdom, Eds. Simon Buckingham Shum, Tamara Sumner. [online, full text]. A multidisciplinary forum for debate and idea sharing concerning the practical aspects of interactive media and instructional technology.

Journal of Science Education and Technology. Kluwer Academic/Plenum Publishers, 233 Spring Street, New York, NY 10013-1578, (781)871-6600, info@plenum.com, www.plenum.com. [Q., $68 individual, $325 institution]. Publishes studies aimed at improving science education at all levels in the United States.

Kozma, R. (2000). Reflections on the state of educational technology research and development. **Educational Technology Research and Development, 48**(1), 5–15. Addresses the importance of research and development in the field of educational technology, based on reflections of previous articles and a symposium. Highlights include the centrality of design; the enabling capabilities of technology; collaboration; scaling up of projects; the use of alternative research methodologies; and instructional systems design (ISD) technology programs.

Multimedia Schools. Information Today, Inc., 213 Danbury Road, Wilton, CT 06897-4006, custserv@info today.com, http://www.infotoday.com/MMSchools/, Ed. Ferdi Serim. [online, full-text]. Reviews and evaluates hardware and software. Presents information pertaining to basic trouble-shooting skills.

Rankin, W. (2000). A survey of course Web sites and online syllabi. **Educational Technology, 40**(2), 38–42. Reports the results of a survey of course Web sites and online syllabi used by students and faculty at higher education institutions across the country and offers suggestions for ways of incorporating relevant and often overlooked links to other sites. Discusses e-mail, course topic links, administrative links, and disability support.

Richey, R. (2000). Reflections on the state of educational technology research and development: A response to Kozma. **Educational Technology Research and Development, 48**(1), 16–18. Offers a response to Kozma's article and his views on educational technology. Maintains that Kozma focuses too much on technology-driven instruction and learning and overemphasizes the role of media research. Discusses the role of technology and considers the future of academic programs in the field, particularly doctoral programs.

Science Communication (formerly **Knowledge: Creation, Diffusion, Utilization**). Sage Publications Inc., 2455 Teller Road, Thousand Oaks, CA 91320, order@sagepub.com, www.sagepub.com. [Q., $85 indiv., $363 inst.]. An international, interdisciplinary journal examining the nature of expertise and the translation of knowledge into practice and policy.

Shotsberger, P. (2000). The human touch: Synchronous communication in Web-based learning. **Educational Technology, 40**(1), 53–56. Discusses synchronous communication in learning via the World Wide Web and considers arguments for advantages of asynchronous approaches. Describes a synchronous Web-based professional development program for mathematics teachers in North Carolina and discusses the nature of online communication.

Shyu, H. (2000). Using video-based anchored instruction to enhance learning: Taiwan's experience. **British Journal of Educational Technology, 31**(1), 57–69. Describes a study that investigated the effects of computer-assisted videodisc-based anchored instruction on attitudes toward mathematics and instruction as well as problem-solving skills among Taiwanese elementary students. Findings suggest that video-based anchored instruction provided a more motivating environment that enhanced students' problem-solving skills.

SIGTC Connections. ISTE, University of Oregon, 1787 Agate Street, Eugene, OR 97403-1923, (800)336-5191, cust_svc@ccmail.uoregon.edu, www.iste.org. [Q., $29, $39 intl., $42 intl. air]. Provides forum to identify problems and solutions and to share information on issues facing technology coordinators.

Social Science Computer Review. North Carolina State University, Social Science Research and Instructional Computing Lab, Sage Publications, Inc., 2455 Teller Road, Thousand Oaks, CA, 91320 info@sagepub.com, http:/hcl.chass.ncsu.edu/sscore/toc16n1.txt, Ed. David Garson. [Q., GBP 46, $65 indiv., GBP 203, $310 inst., GBP 13, $17 newsstand]. Presents research and practical applications of instructional technology in social science.

TECHNOS. Agency for Instructional Technology, Box A, 1800 North Stonelake Drive, Bloomington, IN 47402-0120. [Q., $26 indiv., $24 libr., $30 foreign]. A forum for discussion of ideas about the use of technology in education, with a focus on reform.

TechTrends. AECT, 1800 N Stonelake Drive, Suite 2, Bloomington, IN 47404, www.aect.org. [6/yr., $40 US, $44 elsewhere, $6 single copy]. Targeted at leaders in education and training; features authoritative, practical articles about technology and its integration into the learning environment.

T.H.E. Journal (Technological Horizons in Education). T.H.E., 150 El Camino Real, Suite 112, Tustin, CA 92680-3670. [11/yr., $29 US, $95 elsewhere]. For educators of all levels. Focuses on a specific topic for each issue, as well as technological innovations as they apply to education.

INFORMATION SCIENCE AND TECHNOLOGY

Benson, C. (2001). **Neal-Schuman complete Internet companion for librarians** (2d ed.). [Book, 600p., $79.95]. Neal-Scuman, orders@neal-schuman.com. Comprehensive reference for librarians.

Canadian Journal of Information and Library Science/Revue canadienne des sciences de l'information et de bibliothèconomie. CAIS, University of Toronto Press, Journals Dept., 5201 Dufferin Street, Downsview, ON M3H 5T8, Canada. [Q., $65 indiv., $95 inst., orders outside Canada +$15]. Published by the Canadian Association for Information Science to contribute to the advancement of library and information science in Canada.

CD-ROM Databases. Worldwide Videotex, Box 3273, Boynton Beach, FL 33424-3273. [Mo., $150 US, $190 elsewhere]. Descriptive listing of all databases being marketed on CD-ROM with vendor and system information.

Chen, H. (2000). Introduction to the special topic issue, in this issue. **Journal of the American Society for Information Science, 51**(4), 311–312. Discusses four major trends that have been encouraging the transition to a global digital library: (1) economics of the Internet, including inflation, multimedia, collaboration, timeliness, and scholarly communication; (2) improved service; (3) new digital library technologies, including network technology, data compression, full-text indexing, and object-oriented techniques; and (4) internationally acceptable standards.

Clyde, L. (2000). **Managing infotech in school library media centers.** [Book, 290p., $35]. Libraries Unlimited, www.lu.com. Offers a broad overview of managing electronic information resources including such issues as hardware selection, facilities, staffing, and curriculum consideration.

Econtent (formerly *Database*). Online, Inc. 462 Danbury Road, Wilton, CT 06897. [Bi-mo., $55 US, $65 Canada, $90 intl. airmail]. Features articles on topics of interest to on-line database users; includes database search aids.

Fletcher, P., & Bertot, J. (2000). **World libraries on the information superhighway: Preparing for the challenges of the new millennium.** IDEA Group, www.idea-groupp.com. [Book, 288p., $64.95]. Provides case study examples of library successes in delivering information to patrons through Internet-based systems.

Gale Directory of Databases (in two vols: Vol. 1, **Online Databases**; Vol 2, **CD-ROM, Diskette, Magnetic Tape Batch Access, and Handheld Database Products**). The Gale Group, P.O. Box 9187, Farmington Hills, MI 48333-9187. [Annual plus semiannual update $280; Vol. 1, $199; Vol. 2, $119]. Contains information on database selection and database descriptions, including producers and their addresses.

Gregory, V. (2000). **Selecting and managing electronic resources.** [Book, 115p., $55]. Neal-Schuman, www.neal-schuman.com. Discusses selection policies in light of new developments in electronic resource availability.

Hjorland, B. (2000). Library and information science: Practice, theory, and philosophical basis. **Information Processing & Management, 36**(3), 501–503. Presents different aspects of library and information science (LIS) from a theoretical and philosophical perspective. Topics include attitudes toward LIS; knowledge production versus knowledge utilization; specialists versus generalists; institutional affiliations; technology-driven paradigms; theoretical models; related disciplines; and research methods.

Horner, K. C. (2000). Today's media centers/libraries: Changing roles, changing spaces. **School Planning and Management, 39**(2), 48–49. Explains how school media centers and libraries are transforming into bustling workrooms and why they deserve serious consideration during the design process. The main factors to consider in the planning phase of a media center are reviewed.

Information Management. IDEA Group, www.idea-group.com, 1331 E. Chocolate Avenue, Hershey, PA, 17033-1117, 1(800)345-4332. [Semiannual, $40 indiv., $65 inst.]. This semiannual newsletter includes essays on current topics in information science, expert reviews of information management products, and updates on professional conferences and events.

Information Processing and Management. Pergamon Press, 660 White Plains Road, Tarrytown, NY 10591-5153. [Bi-mo., $152 indiv. whose inst. subscribes, $811 inst.]. International journal covering data processing, database building, and retrieval.

Information Retrieval and Library Automation. Lomond Publications, Inc., Box 88, Mt. Airy, MD 21771. [Mo., $66 US, foreign $79.50]. News, articles, and announcements on new techniques, equipment, and software in information services.

Information Services & Use. I.O.S. Press, Box 10558, Burke, VA 22009-0558. [4/yr., $254]. An international journal for those in the information management field. Includes online and offline systems, library automation, micrographics, videotex, and telecommunications.

The Information Society. Taylor & Francis Group, 11 New Fetter Lane, London EC4P 4EE, www.tandf.co.uk Taylor and Francis, 47 Runway Road, Suite G, Levittown, PA 19057, tisj@indiana.edu. [Q., $82 indiv.; $178 inst.]. Provides a forum for discussion of the world of information, including transborder data flow, regulatory issues, and the impact of the information industry.

Information Technology and Libraries. American Library Association, ALA Editions, 50 East Huron Street, Chicago, IL 60611-2795, (800)545-2433, fax (312)836-9958. [Q., $50 US, $55 Canada, Mexico; $60 elsewhere]. Articles on library automation, communication technology, cable systems, computerized information processing, and video technologies.

Information Technology Newsletter. IDEA Group, www.idea-group.com, 1331 E. Chocolate Avenue, Hershey, PA, 17033-1117, 1(800)345-4332. [Biannual, $20 indiv., $35 inst.]. Designed for library information specialists, this biannual newsletter presents current issues and trends in information science presented by and for specialists in the field.

Information Today. Information Today, 143 Old Marlton Pike, Medford, NJ 08055, (800)300-9868. [11/yr., $59.95; Canada and Mexico, $78; outside North America, $85]. Newspaper for users and producers of electronic information services. Articles and news about the industry, calendar of events, and product information

Internet Reference Service Quarterly. 223 Capen Hall, University at Buffalo, Buffalo, NY 14260, (716)645-2756, Haworth Information Press, www.HaworthPress.com. [Q., $36 indiv., $48 inst., $48 libraries.] Discusses multidisciplinary aspects of incorporating the Internet as a tool for reference service.

Jacsó, P. (2001). **Content evaluation of textual CD-ROM and Web databases.** [Book, 175p., $37.00]. Libraries Unlimited, www.lu.com. Guidebook for sorting, abstracting, indexing text and page-image databases from CD-ROM format using online services. Cites evaluation models for some of the most widely used databases as examples.

Jakobs, K. (2000). **Information technology standards and standardization: A global perspective.** [Book, 272p., $69.95]. IDEA Group, www.idea-group.com. Manual serving as a foundation for research and development as well as implementation of information technology standards.

Journal of Access Services. SUNY Albany, Science Library, Room 142, 1400 Washington Avenue, Albany, NY 12222, (518)437-3951, Haworth Information Press, www.HaworthPress.com. [Q., $48 indiv., $120 inst., $120 libraries]. Peer-reviewed journal containing feature columns, essays, articles, reviews, and conference reports on a large scope of information resource issues.

Journal of the American Society for Information Science. American Society for Information Science, 8720 Georgia Avenue, Suite 501, Silver Spring, Maryland 20910-3602, (301)495-0900, www.asis.org. [14/yr., inst. rate: $1,259 US, $1,399 Canada/Mexico, $1,518 Outside N. America]. Provides an overall forum for new research in information transfer and communication processes, with particular attention paid to the context of recorded knowledge.

Journal of Bibliographic Instruction for Electronic Resources. 207 Hillman Library, Pittsburg, PA, 15260, (412)648-7732, Haworth Information Press, www.HaworthPress.com. [Q., $36 indiv., $48 inst., $48 libraries]. Peer-reviewed journal covering emerging trends in electronic resources.

Journal of Database Management. Idea Group Publishing, 4811 Jonestown Road, Suite 230, Harrisburg, PA 17109-1751. [Q., $85 indiv., $195 inst.]. Provides state-of-the-art research to those who design, develop, and administer DBMS-based information systems.

Journal of Documentation. Aslib, The Association for Information Management, Staple Hall, Stone House Court, London EC3A 7PB, +44 (0) 20 7903 0000, aslib@aslib.com. [6/yr.; £176 ($275) members, £220 ($345) nonmembers]. Describes how technical, scientific, and other specialized knowledge is recorded, organized, and disseminated.

Journal of Electronic Resources. 128 Owsley Avenue, Lexington, KY, 40502-1526, (606)257-0500, ext. 2120, Haworth Information Press, www.HaworthPress.com. [Q., $48 indiv., $75 inst., $75 libraries]. Devoted to issues related to selecting, budgeting, and assessing effectiveness of electronic resources for the academic, special and public library setting.

Journal of Internet Cataloging. 121 Pikemont Drive, Wexford, PA, 15090-8447, (724)940-4192, Haworth Information Press, www.HaworthPress.com. [Q., $40 indiv., $85 inst., $85 libraries]. Gives library cataloging experts a system for managing Internet reference resources in the library catalog.

Kaplan, N. R., & Nelson, M. L. Determining the publication impact of a digital library. **Journal of the American Society for Information Science, 2000, 51**(4), 324–339. Assesses the publication impact of a digital library of aerospace scientific and technical information through usage statistics and citation analysis. Examines the Langley Technical Report Server available on the World Wide Web, compares usage with the hardcopy distribution center, and suggests retrieval analysis as a complementary metric to citation analysis.

Katz, B. (2000). **New technologies and reference services.** [Book, 120p., $39.95]. Hawthorne Information Press. www.HawthornePress.com. Discusses trends in information services, taking into account the ramifications of electronic resources in fostering information literacy.

Lankes, D., Collins, J., & Kasowitz, A., eds. (2000). **Digital reference service in the new millinneum: Planning, management, and evaluation.** [Book, 225p., $65]. Neal-Schuman. This handbook discusses trends in electronic reference resources.

Mieth, D. (2000). Values and morals in the information society. **Lifelong Learning in Europe, 5**(1), 49–54. Ethical and moral issues in the use of information and communication technologies include privacy, equal access, self-determination, and the notion of truth. The Information Society must use new technologies to promote human values and not allow the instrumentalization of human beings.

Miller, E. (2000). **The Internet resource directory for k–12 teachers and librarians: 2000/2001 edition.** [Book, 462 p., $27.50]. Libraries Unlimited, www.lu.com. Describes 1,500 of the most useful, current and reliable Internet-based resources available. Organized by subject.

Miller, W. & Laurence, H. (2000). **Academic research on the Internet.** [Book, 425p., $79.95]. Hawthorne Information Press. www.HawthornePress.com. Provides a subject indexed guide to academically relevant Internet resources.

Oborne, D. J., & Arnold, K. M. (2000). Organizational change in the information society: Impact on skills and training. **Industry and Higher Education, 14** (2), 125-133. The Information Society is affecting organizations and the people who work in them. European projects resulted in a change model emphasizing the role of communication structures within organizations and the ways in which information and communications technologies interact with them.

Resource Sharing & Information Networks. Haworth Press, 10 Alice Street, Binghamton, NY 13904-1580, (800)HAWORTH, fax (800)895-0582, getinfo@haworth.com, www.haworthpress.com. [2/yr., $42 indiv., $200 inst. and libraries]. A forum for ideas on the basic theoretical and practical problems faced by planners, practitioners, and users of network services.

Shuman, B. (2001). **Issues for libraries and information science in the Internet age.** [Book, 170p., $45]. Libraries Unlimited, www.lu.com. Addresses censorship, information overload, archiving, and other challenges posed by Internet integration in public libraries.

Thomas, A., & Shearer, J. (2000). **Internet searching and indexing.** [Book, 217p., $24.95]. Hawthorne Information Press. www.HawthornePress.com. Provides information on searching and categorizing Internet resources for cataloging.

Ward, S., Fong, Y., & Nickleson, D. (2000). **Information delivery in the 21st century.** [Book, 115p., $39.95]. Haworth Information Press, www.HaworthPres.com. Discusses issues pertaining to fee-based information delivery services.

Web Feet. Rock Hill Press, 14 Rock Hill Road, Bala Cynwyd, PA 19004, (888)ROCK HILL, fax (610)667-2291, www.rockhillpress.com. [12/yr., $165]. Indexes Web sites for general interest, classroom use, and research; reviews Web sites for quality, curricular relevance, timeliness, and interest.

INNOVATION

Donlevy, J. (2000). Teachers, technology, and training: Closing the digital divide: ELITE schools—transforming special education in public and private settings. **International Journal of Instructional Media, 27**(1), 1–20. Proposes ELITE (Everyone Learning with Information Technology) Schools as one remedy to transform schooling for children in special education, particularly institutionally placed foster-care children, many of whom are minority youths. Compares ELITE Schools with other school reform models and discusses technological, psychological, ideological, and sociological perspectives.

Tobias, S. (2000). From innovation to change: Forging a physics education reform agenda for the 21st century. **Journal of Science Education and Technology, 9**(1), 1–5. Argues that education reform cannot be limited to what goes on in the classroom. Contends that innovation does not inevitably lead to change until and unless the innovators take back control over factors exogenous to the classroom, factors such as precollege selection, outside testing, accreditation requirements, and class size.

Van Buren, C. (2000). Multimedia learning at "the school that business built": Students' perceptions of education at New Technology High School. **Journal of Curriculum and Supervision, 15**(3), 236–254. Summarizes a study evaluating California's first digital magnet school, designed to emulate a Silicon-Valley high-tech start-up company. A survey of 159 junior and seniors revealed positive perceptions of the school's program and business atmosphere and very high expectations for achieving college and career success.

Warschauer, M. (2000). Technology & school reform: A View from both sides of the tracks. **Education Policy Analysis Archives, 8**(4). Explored the relationships among technology, reform, and equality through quantitative studies at an elite private school and an impoverished public school. Although reforms appeared similar, underlying differences in resources and expectations reinforced patterns by which the two schools channel students into different futures.

INSTRUCTIONAL DESIGN AND DEVELOPMENT

Ahern, T., & El-Hindi, A. (2000). Improving the instructional congruency of a computer-mediated small-group discussion: A case study in design and delivery. **Journal of Research on Computing in Education, 32**(3), 385–400. Presents an exploratory case study with preservice teacher education students of an experience in collaborative discourse mediated through an educationally designed network-based application. Topics include computer-mediated communication; text-based communication; small group discussion; and software design, including the design of IdeaWeb that allows messages to be linked to multiple messages.

Chen, Q. (2001). **Human computer interaction: Issues and challenges.** [Book, 300p., $74.95]. IDEA Group, www.idea-group.com. Guides researchers, designers, analysts, and managers through the most up-to-date issues regarding human computer interaction.

Gibson, R. (2000). **Object oriented technologies: Opportunities and challenges.** [Book, 250p., $69.95]. IDEA Group, www.idea-grou..com. Discusses software development testing, reengineering with object-oriented (OO) technology, and design techniques associated with OO technologies.

Harrison, N., & Bergen, C. (2000). Some design strategies for developing an online course. **Educational Technology, 40**(1), 57–60. Provides general design suggestions for developing a Web-based online course for distance education in higher education. Highlights include faculty training and preparation; course structure; course outline for students; weekly modules; fostering a community of learners; required papers; and testing.

Human-Computer Interaction. Lawrence Erlbaum Associates, 365 Broadway, Hillsdale, NJ 07642. [Q., $50 indiv. US and Canada, $80 elsewhere, $320 inst., $350 elsewhere]. A journal of theoretical, empirical, and methodological issues of user science and of system design.

Instructional Science. Kluwer Academic Publishers, 101 Philip Drive, Norwell, MA 02061, (617)871-6600, fax(617) 871-6528, kluwer@wkap.com. [Bi-mo., $374 inst.]. Promotes a deeper understanding of the nature, theory, and practice of the instructional process and the learning resulting from this process.

Journal of Educational Technology Systems. Baywood Publishing Co., 26 Austin Avenue, Box 337, Amityville, NY 11701. [Q., $175]. In-depth articles on completed and ongoing research in all phases of educational technology and its application and future within the teaching profession; enhancing instruction and facilitation of learning in the typical classroom; design and implementation of telecommunication networks and Web sites; contributions of librarians to Web-based teaching.

Journal of Interactive Instruction Development. Learning Technology Institute, Society for Applied Learning Technology, 50 Culpeper Street, Warrenton, VA 22186. [Q., $40 member, $60 nonmember; add $18 postage outside N. America]. A showcase of successful programs that will heighten awareness of innovative, creative, and effective approaches to courseware development for interactive technology.

Journal of Technical Writing and Communication. Baywood Publishing Co., 26 Austin Avenue, Box 337, Amityville, NY 11701. [Q., $48 indiv., $170 inst.]. Essays on oral and written communication, for purposes ranging from pure research to needs of business and industry.

Journal of Visual Literacy. International Visual Literacy Association, c/o John C. Belland, 122 Ramseyer Hall, 29 West Woodruff Avenue, Ohio State University, Columbus, OH 43210. [Biann., $40]. Interdisciplinary forum on all aspects of visual/verbal languaging.

Lohr, L. (2000). Three principles of perception for instructional interface design. **Educational Technology, 40**(1), 45–52. Discusses graphical user interfaces used for instructional purposes in educational environments, which promote learning goals, and in support environments, which promote performance goals. Explains three key principles of perception and gives guidelines for their use, including the figure/ground principle, the hierarchy principle, and the gestalt principle.

Mizukoshi, T., Kim, Y., & Lee, J. Y. (2000). Instructional technology in Asia: Focus on Japan and Korea. **Educational Technology Research and Development, 48**(1), 101–112. Discussion of information technology in Japan includes historical background, government-initiated movements for school reform backed by computer networks, and the introduction of an information technology course in senior high schools. Describes a nationwide open education project in Korea and the state of cyber universities supported by the Korean government.

Moonen, J. (2000). A three-space design strategy for digital learning material. **Educational Technology, 40**(2), 26–32. Discusses the change in learning materials to digital formats and considers whether current design and production methods for educational software are still appropriate or if there is a need for a new design and production strategy.

Performance Improvement. International Society for Performance Improvement, 1300 L St. NW, Suite 1250, Washington, DC 20005. [10/yr., $69]. Journal of ISPI; promotes performance science and technology. Contains articles, research, and case studies relating to improving human performance.

Performance Improvement Quarterly. International Society for Performance Improvement, 1300 L Street NW, Suite 1250, Washington, DC 20005. [Q., $50]. Presents the cutting edge in research and theory in performance technology.

Training. Lakewood Publications, Inc., 50 S. Ninth, Minneapolis, MN 55402. [Mo., $78 US, $88 Canada, $99 elsewhere]. Covers all aspects of training, management, and organizational development, motivation, and performance improvement.

INTERACTIVE MULTIMEDIA

Brown, J. V. (2000). Technology integration in a high school study skills program. **Journal of Adolescent & Adult Literacy, 43**(7), 634–637. Describes a high school study skills program that uses technology as a tool for learning to teach skills and help students produce quality work for their subject area assignments. Describes how computer resources and software are integrated into study skills courses to teach writing and presentation skills, research skills, basic skills, thinking skills, and strategies for success.

Donlevy, J. G., & Donlevy, T.R. (2000). Instructional media initiatives focusing on the educational resources center at Thirteen/WNET. What's up in factories? Introducing teachers and students to the dynamic world of modern manufacturing. **International Journal of Instructional Media, 27**(1), 21–24. Describes "What's Up in Factories?," an experimental curriculum developed by WNET television that combines video and a variety of interactive activities, including field trips to manufacturing facilities. Discusses goals that include an appreciation of manufacturing, learning about current trends and innovations, and discovering and exploring career possibilities.

Journal of Educational Multimedia and Hypermedia. Association for the Advancement of Computing in Education, Box 2966, Charlottesville, VA 22902-2966, aace@virginia.edu, www.aace.org. [Q., $40 indiv., $50 foreign]. A multidisciplinary information source presenting research about and applications for multimedia and hypermedia tools.

Journal of Hypermedia and Multimedia Studies. ISTE, University of Oregon, 1787 Agate Street, Eugene, OR 97403-1923, (800)336-5191, cust_svc@ccmail.uoregon.edu, www.iste.org. [Q., $29; $39 intl., $42 intl. air]. Features articles on projects, lesson plans, and theoretical issues, as well as reviews of products, software, and books.

Journal of Interactive Learning Research. Association for Advancement of Computing in Education, Box 2966, Charlottesville, VA 22902-2966, aace@virginia.edu, www.aace.org. [Q.; $40 indiv., $50 foreign]. International journal publishes articles on how intelligent computer technologies can be used in education to enhance learning and teaching. Reports on research and developments, integration, and applications of artificial intelligence in education.

Katz, Yaacov J. (2000). The comparative suitability of three ICT distance learning methodologies for college level instruction. **Educational Media International, 37**(1), 25–30. Describes a study that compared Israeli university students' satisfaction with three different distance learning methods: one an interactive video system, one an Internet-based system, and one that allowed synchronous communication between teacher and students. Discusses information and communication technology (ICT) and examines student achievement.

Rowley, James B., & Hart, Patricia M. (2000). **High-performance mentoring: A multimedia program for training mentor teachers. Facilitator's guide**. Corwin Press, Inc., A Sage Publications Company, 2455 Teller Road, Thousand Oaks, CA 91320, order@corwinpress .com. [Book, 224p., $39.95]. Designed to be used with a training workshop that helps veteran teachers be effective mentors to beginning teachers, provides instructions on how to facilitate a successful workshop. The book offers six chapters that include strategies and materials to help readers learn how to plan and promote a workshop; facilitate a successful workshop; select, match, and support mentor teachers; and assess the mentor teacher program.

Squire, K. D., & Johnson, C. B. (2000). Supporting distributed communities of practice with interactive television. **Educational Technology Research and Development, 48**(1), 23–43. Examines three distance learning programs conducted over Vision Athena, an interactive television distance learning system. Emphasis in each project was on using interactive television to engage secondary school students in communities of practice in designed, or intentional, learning environments. Discusses the changing role of teachers, students, and experts.

Tuovinen, J. E. (2000). Multimedia distance education interactions. **Educational Media International, 37**(1), 16–24. Discussion of multimedia interactions in distance education synthesizes approaches based on distance education theory, cognition research, and multimedia development. Proposes a composite framework for discussion of multimedia and multimodal interactions in a distance education context, which is based on interactions between the instructor, students, and content.

Wang, P., Hawk, W. B., & Tenopir, C. (2000). Users' interaction with World Wide Web resources: An exploratory study using a holistic approach. **Information Processing & Management, 36**(2), 229–251. Presents results of a study that explores factors of user-Web interaction in finding factual information, develops a conceptual framework for studying user-Web interaction, and applies a process-tracing method for conducting holistic user-Web studies. Describes measurement techniques and proposes a model consisting of the user, interface, and the World Wide Web.

LIBRARIES AND MEDIA CENTERS

Barclay, D. (2000). **Managing public access computers: A how-to-do-it manual for librarians.** [Book, 240p., $59.95]. Neal-Schumann. Discusses technical and service aspects of how to manage public access computer terminals in the library setting.

Barry, J. (2001). Automated system marketplace 2001: Closing in on content. **Library Journal 126**(6), 46–58. Discusses innovations in public library automated systems and compares automation systems by vendor share of the marketplace. Also discusses vendor mergers and acquisitions and includes vendor profiles.

Baule, S. (2001). **Technology planning for effective teaching and learning.** (2d ed.) Linworth, www.linworth.com. [Book, 160p., $39.95]. Presents guidelines for creating an effective information technology integration plan, taking into account the various administrative policies and specifications.

Book Report. Linworth Publishing, 480 E. Wilson Bridge Road, Suite L., Worthington, OH 43085-2372, (800)786-5017, fax (614)436-9490, orders@linworth.com, linworth.com. [5/school yr., $44 US, $9 single copy]. Journal for junior and senior high school librarians provides articles, tips, and ideas for day-to-day school library management, as well as reviews of audiovisuals and software, all written by school librarians.

Cohn, J., Kelsey, A., & Fields, M. (2000). **Writing and updating technology plans: A guidebook with sample plans on CD-ROM.** [Book + CD-ROM, 101p., $99.95]. Neal-Schuman. This guide provides information on how to write a technology plan, maintain it, and use the plan as leverage for writing grant proposals. The CD-ROM provides technology plan templates in HTML format, usable on IBM and Macintosh computer systems.

Collection Building. M.C.B. University Press Ltd., 60-62 Toller Lane, Bradford, W. Yorks. BD8 9BY, England, www.mcb.co.uk. [Q., $599]. Focuses on all aspects of collection building, ranging from microcomputers to business collections to popular topics and censorship.

Computers in Libraries. Information Today, 143 Old Marlton Pike, Medford, NJ 08055, (800)300-9868. [10/yr., $89.95 US; $99.95 Canada, Mexico; $59.95 outside North America]. Covers practical applications of microcomputers to library situations and recent news items.

Curry, A., & Haycock, K. Filtered or unfiltered? **School Library Journal 47**(1), 43–47. Discusses the controversy of filtering Internet connections at school libraries. Explains how to select the right filter for your library as well as how filters work.

Dogget, Sandra L. (2000). **Beyond the book: Technology integration into the secondary school library media curriculum.** [Book, 177p., $29.50]. Libraries Unlimited, (800)237-6124, lu-books@lu.com, www.lu.com.

The Electronic Library. Information Today, 143 Old Marlton Pike, Medford, NJ 08055, (800) 300-9868. [Bi-mo., $127 US; $137 Canada/Mexico]. International journal for minicomputer, microcomputer, and software applications in libraries; independently assesses current and forthcoming information technologies.

Gordon, M., Gordon, A, and Moore, E. (2001). New computers bring new patrons. **Library Journal 126**(3), 134–138. A University of Washington research team funded in part by the Gates Foundation found that increased public access to high-end computers with Internet access has increased the number of library users from disadvantaged backgrounds.

Government Information Quarterly. Elsevier Science/Regional Sales Office, Customer Support Department—JAI Books, P.O. Box 945, New York, NY 10159-0945. [Q., $113 indiv., $269 inst.]. International journal of resources, services, policies, and practices.

Hjorland, B. (2000). Library and information science: Practice, theory, and philosophical basis. **Information Processing & Management, 36**(3), 501–531. Presents different aspects of library and information science (LIS) from a theoretical and philosophical perspective. Topics include attitudes toward LIS; knowledge production versus knowledge utilization; specialists versus generalists; institutional affiliations; technology-driven paradigms; theoretical models; related disciplines; and research methods.

Information Outlook (formerly Special Libraries). Special Libraries Association, 1700 18th Street, NW, Washington, DC 20009-2508, www.sla.com. [Mo., $80 US; $95 elsewhere]. Discusses administration, organization, and operations. Includes reports on research, technology, and professional standards.

Information Services and Use. Elsevier Science Publishers, Box 10558, Burke, VA 22009-0558. [4/yr., $254]. Contains data on international developments in information management and its applications. Articles cover online systems, library automation, word processing, micrographics, videotex, and telecommunications.

Journal of Academic Librarianship. Elsevier Science/Regional Sales Office, Customer Support Department—JAI Books, P.O. Box 945, New York, NY 10159-0945. [6/yr., $81 indiv., $195 inst.]. Results of significant research, issues and problems facing academic libraries, book reviews, and innovations in academic libraries.

Journal of Government Information (formerly **Government Publications Review**). Elsevier Science Ltd., Journals Division, 660 White Plains Road, Tarrytown, NY 10591-5153. [6/yr., $534]. An international journal covering production, distribution, bibliographic control, accessibility, and use of government information in all formats and at all levels.

Journal of Librarianship and Information Science. Worldwide Subscription Service Ltd., Unit 4, Gibbs Reed Farm, Ticehurst, E. Sussex TN5 7HE, England. [Q., $155]. Deals with all aspects of library and information work in the United Kingdom and reviews literature from international sources.

Journal of Library Administration. Haworth Press, 10 Alice Street, Binghamton, NY 13904-1580, (800)HAWORTH, fax (800)895-0582, getinfo@haworth.com, www.haworthpress .com. [8/yr., $45 indiv., $125 inst.]. Provides information on all aspects of effective library management, with emphasis on practical applications.

Junion-Metz, G. (2000). Get plugged in with plug-ins: Five you need to know about. **School Library Journal 46**(11), 35. A list of Web sites distributing freeware plug-ins that help your Internet browser view certain forms, interactive multimedia, and animations.

Junion-Metz, G. (2000). Waking the dead: Reviving your library's technology plan. **School Library Journal 46**(12), 45. A list of Web sites designed to help the school librarian keep abreast of technology trends.

Laguardia, C., & Oka, C. (2000). **Becoming a library teacher.** [Book, 115p., $49.95]. Neal-Schuman. This concise guide provides basic instruction advice for teaching in the library setting.

Laguardia, C., & Vasi, J. (2001) **Designing, building and teaching in the electronic library classroom.** [Book, 175p., $55]. Neal-Schuman. Gives media specialists strategies for managing the electronic library classroom.

Lee, S. (2000). **Collection development in the electronic environment: Shifting priorities.** [Book, 125p., $19.95]. Haworth Information Press. www.HaworthPress.com. Discusses methods and strategies for collection development, taking into account the effects of electronic resource availability.

Library Computing (Formerly *Library Software Review*). Sage Publications Inc., 2455 Teller Road, Thousand Oaks, CA 91320, order@sagepub.com, www.sagepub.com. [Q., $59 indiv., $252 US inst.]. Emphasizes practical aspects of library computing for libraries of all types, including reviews of automated systems ranging from large-scale mainframe-based systems to microcomputer-based systems, and both library-specific and general-purpose software used in libraries.

Library and Information Science Research. Ablex Publishing Corp., 100 Prospect Street, P.O. Box 811, Stamford, CT 06904-0811, (203)323-9606, fax (203)357-8446. www.jaipress.com. [Q., $95 indiv., $245 inst.]. Research articles, dissertation reviews, and book reviews on issues concerning information resources management.

Library Hi Tech. Pierian Press, Box 1808, Ann Arbor, MI 48106, (800)678-2435, www.pierianpress.com. [Q., $169]. Concentrates on reporting on the selection, installation, maintenance, and integration of systems and hardware.

Library Hi Tech News. Pierian Press, Box 1808, Ann Arbor, MI 48106, (800)678-2435, www.pierianpress.com. [10/yr., $199]. Supplements *Library Hi Tech* and updates many of the issues addressed in depth in the journal and keeps you fully informed of the latest developments in library automation, new products, network news, new software and hardware, and people in technology.

Library Journal. 245 West 17th Street, New York, NY 10011, (212)463-6819. [20/yr., $109 US, $138.50 Canada, $188.50 elsewhere]. A professional periodical for librarians, with current issues and news, professional reading, a lengthy book review section, and classified advertisements.

Library Quarterly. University of Chicago Press, 5720 S. Woodlawn Avenue, Chicago, IL 60637. [Q., $35 indiv., $73 inst.]. Scholarly articles of interest to librarians.

Library Resources and Technical Services. Association for Library Collections and Technical Services, 50 E. Huron Street, Chicago, IL 60611-2795. [Q., $55 nonmembers]. Scholarly papers on bibliographic access and control, preservation, conservation, and reproduction of library materials.

Library Trends. University of Illinois Press, Journals Dept., 1325 S. Oak Street, Champaign, IL 61820. [Q., $60 indiv.; $85 inst.; add $7 elsewhere]. Each issue is concerned with one aspect of library and information science, analyzing current thought and practice and examining ideas that hold the greatest potential for the field.

LISA: Library and Information Science Abstracts. Bowker-Saur Ltd., Maypole House, Maypole Road, E. Grinsted, W. Sussex, RH19 1HH, England, www.bowker-saur.com. [Mo., $960 US, £545 elsewhere]. More than 500 abstracts per issue from more than 500 periodicals, reports, books, and conference proceedings.

Mangan, K. S. (2000). In revamped library schools, information trumps books. **Chronicle of Higher Education, 46**(31), A43–A44. Describes changes in many library schools' curricula to emphasize training for high-tech careers in information management rather than traditional library skills and careers. Reports on the experience of the University of Michigan, which has restructured its library school into the new School of Information Management and Systems.

Martell, C. (2000). The disembodied librarian in the digital age, Part II. **College & Research Libraries, 61**(2), 99–113. Discusses how four historical discontinuities (time and space, mind and body, real and virtual, and humans and technology) relate to new ways of being and thinking about the future of librarians and libraries. Topics include computers and books; entertainment industry growth; information uses; global economy effects; and future library possibilities.

Minkel, W. (2001). Add Web sites to your materials selection policy. **School Library Journal, 47**(3), 39. Explains the reasons why every school library that has cataloged Web sites should include justification for including those sites in the collection.

Minkel, W. (2000). Copycat. **School Library Journal 46**(8), 48–50. Describes the various models, capabilities, and prices of scanners on the market. Also includes online resources that present reviews of computer hardware.

Minkel, W. (2001). E-book anxieties: The coming of electronic books has left librarians dazed and confused. **School Library Journal, 47**(2), 29. Explains how the unique nature of electronic books poses challenges for acquisitions and circulation of this new book format.

Minkel, W. (2001). Great Expectations: Will yourhomework.com make librarians dreams come true? **School Library Journal, 47**(4), 39. Discusses how a start-up dot com company may help improve communication between parents, teachers, students, and public librarians.

Minkel, W. (2000). Seeing the big picture: With a media retrieval system, video can be viewed wherever you need it. **School Library Journal 46**(11), 33. Explains how a television network can help school librarians simultaneously distribute a number of video and television programs throughout the school.

Minkel, W. (2000). Thin is in. **School Library Journal, 46**(10), 41. Explains the benefits of using thin-client networks as an alternative to bulky PC-based labs. Explains how the thin-network labs work and names some vendors supplying this new technology.

Murphy-Walters, A. (2000). The creatures from the black room. **School Library Journal, 46**(12), 58–61. Often librarians choose to keep nonbook materials such as equipment and audiovisual media outside the automated system. To avoid cataloging problems, the school librarian keeps these materials on a manual checkout system. This article details a plan for integrating such nonbook materials into the existing automated catalog system.

Oder, N. (2001). The shape of e-reference. **Library Journal, 126**(2), 46–50. Discusses the e-reference trend. Describes the Library of Congress Q&A style dot com reference service as a model for other library systems.

Prestbank, J., & Wightman, K. (2000). Losing our drawers. **School Library Journal, 46**(10), 66–73. Sites the finding of a survey asking school librarians to rate their automation system. Reports satisfaction levels and market share by vendor. This article also gives helpful tips on what to consider when purchasing an automated system.

The Public-Access Computer Systems Review. An electronic journal published on an irregular basis by the University Libraries, University of Houston, Houston, TX 77204-2091, LThompson@uh.edu. Free to libraries. Contains articles about all types of computer systems that libraries make available to their patrons and technologies to implement these systems.

Public Libraries. Public Library Association, American Library Association, ALA Editions, 50 East Huron Street, Chicago, IL 60611-2795, (800)545-2433, fax (312)836-9958. [Bi-mo., $50 US nonmembers, $60 elsewhere, $10 single copy]. News and articles of interest to public librarians.

Public Library Quarterly. Haworth Press, 10 Alice Street, Binghamton, NY 13904-1580, (800)HAWORTH, fax (800)895-0582, getinfo@haworth.com, www.haworthpress.com. [Q., $50 indiv., $165 inst.]. Addresses the major administrative challenges and opportunities that face the nation's public libraries.

372 *Mediagraphy*

Reed, S. (2000). **Making the case for your library: A how-to-do-it manual.** [Book, 200p., $45]. Neal-Schuman. Gives guidance on how to organize a library public awareness and advocacy plan to increase community support.

The Reference Librarian. Haworth Press, 10 Alice Street, Binghamton, NY 13904-1580, (800)HAWORTH, fax (800)895-0582, getinfo@haworth.com, www.haworthpress.com. [2/yr.; $60 indiv., $225 inst.]. Each issue focuses on a topic of current concern, interest, or practical value to reference librarians.

Reference Services Review. Pierian Press, Box 1808, Ann Arbor, MI 48106, (800)678-2435, www.pierianpress.com. [Q., $169.]. Dedicated to the enrichment of reference knowledge and the advancement of reference services. It prepares its readers to understand and embrace current and emerging technologies affecting reference functions and information needs of library users.

Rielding, A. (2000). **Reference skills for the school library media specialist: Tools and tips.** Linworth, www.linworth.com. [Book, 152 p., $44.95]. Textbook targeted for graduate level study of information science as it applies to the library media specialist role in schools. Includes information on terminology, research process models, and reference resource maintenance and analysis.

RQ. Reference and Adult Services Association, American Library Association, ALA Editions, 50 East Huron Street, Chicago, IL 60611-2795, (800)545-2433, fax (312)836-9958. [Q., $50 nonmembers, $55 nonmembers Canada/Mexico, $60 elsewhere, $15 single copy]. Disseminates information of interest to reference librarians, bibliographers, adult services librarians, those in collection development and selection, and others interested in public services; double-blind refereed.

Schmidt, W., & Rieck, D. (2000). **Managing media services: Theory and practice** (2nd ed.). [Book, 418p., $49]. Libraries Unlimited, www.lu.com. Textbook for graduate level study of school library media management roles such as collection maintenance, staff supervision, budgeting, managing facilities, and public relations.

School Library Journal. Box 57559, Boulder, CO 80322-7559, (800)456-9409, fax (800)824-4746. [Mo., $97.50 US, $139 Canada, $149 elsewhere]. For school and youth service librarians. Reviews about 4,000 children's books and 1,000 educational media titles annually.

School Library Media Activities Monthly. LMS Associates LLC, 17 E. Henrietta Street, Baltimore, MD 21230-3190. [10/yr., $49 US, $54 elsewhere]. A vehicle for distributing ideas for teaching library media skills and for the development and implementation of library media skills programs.

School Library Media Research. American Association of School Librarians, American Library Association. [Available online, www.ala.org/aasl/SLMR/index.html]. For library media specialists, district supervisors, and others concerned with the selection and purchase of print and nonprint media and with the development of programs and services for preschool through high school libraries.

Teacher Librarian. Box 34069, Dept. 284, Seattle, WA 98124-1069, TL@rockland.com. [Bi-mo., except July–August, $49]. "The journal for school library professionals"; previously known as *Emergency Librarian.* Articles, review columns, and critical analyses of management and programming issues for children's and young adult librarians.

Tennant, R. (2001). XML: The digital library hammer. **Library Journal 126**(5), 30–32. Explains how XML (Extensible Markup Language) works and how it can be used to facilitate digital publishing and organize digital search information more effectively.

The Unabashed Librarian. Box 2631, New York, NY 10116. [Q., $40 US, $48 elsewhere]. Down-to-earth library items: procedures, forms, programs, cataloging, booklists, software reviews.

Walter, V. (2001). The once and future library: Ten ways to create libraries that will meet the needs of tomorrow's children. **School Library Journal 47**(1), 49–53. This article gives a thorough overall library administration plan that includes a look at how technology plays a part in successful library management.

Weathers, B. (2001). Life among the Laptops: A Texas school experiences the joy of going wireless. **School Library Journal, 47**(3), 56–60. Chronicles the benefits, successes, and obstacles faced in integrating laptop technology into a Houston-area middle school curriculum.

MEDIA TECHNOLOGIES

Broadcasting and Cable. Box 6399, Torrence, CA 90504, www.broadcastingcable.com. [W., $149 US, $219 Canada, $350 elsewhere]. All-inclusive news weekly for radio, television, cable, and allied business.

Cablevision. Cahners Business Information, 245 West 17th Street, New York, NY 10011-5300, (212)645-0067, www.cvmag.com. [Semi-monthly; $75 US, $165 elsewhere]. A news magazine for the cable television industry. Covers programming, marketing, advertising, business, and other topics.

Caldwell, John Thornton, Ed. (2000). **Electronic media and technoculture.** [Book, 278p., $21.]. Rutgers University Press, 100 Joyce Kilmer Avenue, Piscataway, NJ 08854, 1(800)446-9323. Maps the intellectual terrain that has greeted the arrival of what is variously termed "new media," "digital media," and "electronic culture."

Chandler, G. E., & Hanrahan, P. (2000). Teaching using interactive video: Creating connections. **Journal of Nursing Education, 39**(2), 73–80. Using components of a work effectiveness model (information, support, resources, relationships), two elements of distance learning (technology and instruction) are described. Strategies for making interactive video invisible by managing equipment, planning ahead, and creating relationships are addressed.

Chow, J. W., Carlton, L. G., Ekkekakis, P., & Hay, J. G. (2000). A Web-based video digitizing system for the study of projectile motion. **Physics Teacher, 38**(1), 37–40 Discusses advantages of a video-based, digitized image system for the study and analysis of projectile motion in the physics laboratory. Describes the implementation of a Web-based digitized video system.

Communication Abstracts. Sage Publications Inc., 2455 Teller Road, Thousand Oaks, CA 91320, order@sagepub.com, www.sagepub.com. [Bi-mo., $175 indiv., $700 inst.]. Abstracts communication-related articles, reports, and books. Cumulated annually.

Communications News. Nelson Publishing Co., 2504 N. Tamiami Trail, Nokomis, FL 34275, www.comnews.com. [Mo.]. Up-to-date information from around the world regarding voice, video, and data communications.

Educational Media International. Routledge, 11 New Fetter Lane, London EC49.4EE, UK. [Q., $64 indiv., $248 inst.]. The official journal of the International Council for Educational Media.

Federal Communications Commission Reports. Superintendent of Documents, Government Printing Office, Box 371954, Pittsburgh, PA 15250-7954. [Irreg., price varies]. Decisions, public notices, and other documents pertaining to FCC activities.

Fielding, R. (2000). Wired vs. wireless. **School Construction News, 3**(2), 25–26. Presents a debate on which technology will be in tomorrow's classrooms and the pros and cons of wiring classrooms and using a wireless network. Concluding comments address the likelihood, and desirability, of placing computers throughout the entire educational process and what types of computers and capabilities are needed.

Harnar, M. A., Brown, S. W., & Mayall, H. J. (2000). Measuring the effect of distance education on the learning experience: Teaching accounting via PictureTel. **International Journal of Instructional Media, 27**(1), 37–49. Describes a distance education instrument developed to assess students' knowledge, attitudes, and behaviors in a college-level accounting course presented via distance education using compressed video called PictureTel. Results indicated that specific items, related to instructor characteristics, could be used to predict students' choices about taking future distance education courses.

Historical Journal of Film, Radio, and Television. Carfax Publishing Limited in association with the International Association for Media and History, 875-81 Massachusetts Avenue, Cambridge, MA 02139. [Q., $185 indiv., $532 inst.]. Articles by international experts in the field, news and notices, and book reviews concerning the impact of mass communications on political and social history of the twentieth century.

Hunter, G. (2000). **Preserving digitalk information: A how-to-do-it manual.** [Book, 185p., $59.95]. Neal-Schuman, www.neal-schuman.com. Manual covers technological aspects of digital media preservation.

International Journal of Instructional Media. Westwood Press, Inc., 116E 16th Street, New York 10003. [Q., $135 per vol., $30 single issue]. Focuses on quality research; ongoing programs in instructional media for education, distance learning, computer technology, instructional media and technology, telecommunications, interactive video, management, media research and evaluation, and utilization.

Journal of Broadcasting and Electronic Media. Broadcast Education Association, 1771 N Street, NW, Washington, DC 20036-2891. [Q., $40 US, $25 student, $50 elsewhere]. Includes articles, book reviews, research reports, and analyses. Provides a forum for research relating to telecommunications and related fields.

Journal of Educational Media (formerly *Journal of Educational Television*). Carfax Publishing Co., 875-81 Massachusetts Avenue, Cambridge, MA 02139. [3/yr., $146 indiv., $544 inst.]. This journal of the Educational Television Association serves as an international forum for discussions and reports on developments in the field of television and related media in teaching, learning, and training.

Journal of Educational Multimedia and Hypermedia. Association for the Advancement of Computing In Education, P.O. Box 2966, Charlottesville, VA 22902-2966, info @aace.org, http://www.aace.org, Ed. Gary H. Marks, R&P Sarah D Williams. [Q., $75 domestic to indiv., $85 foreign to indiv., $95 domestic to inst., $105 foreign to inst.]. Presents research and applications on multimedia and hypermedia tolls that allow one to integrate images and sound into educational software.

Journal of Popular Film and Television. Heldref Publications, 1319 Eighteenth Street, NW, Washington, DC 20036-1802, (800)365-9753. [Q., $36 indiv., $70 inst.]. Articles on film and television, book reviews, and theory. Dedicated to popular film and television in the broadest sense. Concentrates on commercial cinema and television, film and television theory or criticism, filmographies, and bibliographies. Edited at the College of Arts and Sciences of Northern Michigan University and the Department of Popular Culture, Bowling Green State University.

Lee, S. (2001). **Digital imaging: A practical handbook.** [Book, 192p., $55]. Neal-Schuman. Gives the reader information about the digitization process and technologies.

Library Talk (formerly *Technology Connection*). Linworth Publishing, 480 E. Wilson Bridge Road, Suite L., Worthington, OH 43085-2372, (800)786-5017, fax (614)436-9490, orders@linworth.com, linworth.com. [6/yr., $43 US, $7 single copy]. The only magazine published for the elementary school library media and technology specialist. A forum for K–12 educators who use technology as an educational resource, this journal includes information on what works and what does not, new product reviews, tips and pointers, and emerging technology.

Lunenfeld, Peter. (2000). **The digital dialectic: New essays on new media**. [Book, 401p., $17.95]. MIT Press, Five Cambridge Center, Cambridge, MA 02142-1493, (617)253-5646, mitpress-orders@mit.edu, www-mitpress.mit.edu. Maps out the trajectories that digital technologies have traced upon our cultural imagery.

Lunenfeld, Peter. (2000). **Snap to grid: A user's guide to digital arts, media, and cultures**. [Book, 240p., $32.95]. MIT Press, Five Cambridge Center, Cambridge, MA 02142-1493, (617)253-5646, mitpress-orders@mit.edu, www-mitpress.mit.edu. Maps out the trajectories that digital technologies have traced upon our cultural imagery.

Media and Methods: Educational Products, Technologies & Programs for Schools & Universities. American Society of Educators, 1429 Walnut Street, Philadelphia, PA 19102, http://www.media-methods.com, Ed. Christine Weiser. [5/yr., $33.50 US, %1.50 foreign]. This educational magazine offers practical information regarding instructional technologies.

Media International. Reed Business Information, Publisher. Oakfield House, Perrymount Road, W. Sussex RH16 3DH, UK. [Mo., £42 Europe, £76 elsewhere]. Contains features on the major media developments and regional news reports from the international media scene and global intelligence on media and advertising.

Multimedia Monitor (formerly *Multimedia and Videodisc Monitor*). Phillips Business Information, Inc., 1201 Seven Locks Road, Potomac, MD 20854, (301)424-3338, fax (301)309-3847, pbi@phillips.com. [Mo., $395 indiv., $425 foreign]. Describes current events in the worldwide interactive multimedia marketplace and in training and development, including regulatory and legal issues.

Multimedia Schools. Information Today, 143 Old Marlton Pike, Medford, NJ 08055, (800)300-9868. [6/yr., $39.95 US, $54 Canada/Mexico, $63 elsewhere]. Reviews new titles, evaluates hardware and software, offers technical advice and troubleshooting tips, and profiles high-tech installations.

Multimedia Systems. Springer-Verlag New York Inc., Secaucus, NJ 07096-2485, USA, 1(800)SPRINGER, custserv@springer-ny.com. [6/yr., $415 US]. Publishes original research articles and serves as a forum for stimulating and disseminating innovative research ideas, emerging technologies, state-of-the-art methods and tools in all aspects of multimedia computing, communication, storage, and applications among researchers, engineers, and practitioners.

NICEM (National Information Center for Educational Media) EZ. NICEM, P.O. Box 8640, Albuquerque, NM 87198-8640. (505)265-3591, (800)926-8328, fax (505)256-1080, nicem@nicem.com. A custom search service to help those without access to the existing NICEM products. Taps the resources of this specialized database. Fees are $50 per hour search time plus $.20 for each unit identified.

NICEM (National Information Center for Educational Media) NlightN. Contact NlightN, The Library Corp, 1807 Michael Faraday Court, Reston, VA 20190. (800)654-4486, fax (703)904-8238, help@nlightn.com, www.nlightn.com. [Subscription service]. NlightN, an Internet online service, widens the accessibility of information in the NICEM database to users of the Internet. The NICEM database of 425,000 records, updated quarterly, provides information on nonprint media for all levels of education and instruction in all academic areas.

Purcell, Lee. (2000). **CD-R/DVD: Digital recording to optical media with CD-ROM**. [Book, 500p., $49.95]. McGraw-Hill, 1221 Avenue of the Americas, New York, NY 10020, (800)352-3566. Packed with advice for selecting the right equipment and putting it to work, *CD-R/DVD* offers a wealth of practical tips and techniques, as well as insights from industry insiders.

Shyu, H. C. (2000). Using video-based anchored instruction to enhance learning: Taiwan's experience. **British Journal of Educational Technology, 31**(1), 57–69. Describes a study that investigated the effects of computer-assisted videodisc-based anchored instruction on attitudes toward mathematics and instruction as well as problem-solving skills among Taiwanese elementary students. Findings suggest that video-based anchored instruction provided a more motivating environment that enhanced students' problem-solving skills.

Telematics and Informatics. Elsevier Science Regional Sales Office, Customer Support Department, P.O. Box 945, New York, NY 10159-0945. (888)4ES-INFO, usinfo-f@elsevier .com. [3/yr., $49 indiv., $668 inst.]. Publishes research and review articles in applied telecommunications and information sciences in business, industry, government and educational establishments. Focuses on important current technologies including microelectronics, computer graphics, speech synthesis and voice recognition, database management, data encryption, satellite television, artificial intelligence, and the ongoing computer revolution. Contributors and readers include professionals in business and industry, as well as in government and academia, who need to keep abreast of current technologies and their diverse applications.

Video Systems. Intertec Publishing Corp., 9800 Metcalf, Overland Park, KS 66212-2215. [Mo., $45, free to qualified professionals]. For video professionals. Contains state-of-the-art audio and video technology reports. Official publication of the International Television Association.

Videography. Miller Freeman, PSN Publications, 2 Park Avenue, 18th Floor, New York, NY 10016. [Mo., $30]. For the video professional; covers techniques, applications, equipment, technology, and video art.

PROFESSIONAL DEVELOPMENT

Continuing Professional Development. Virtual University Press, Brookes University, School of Hotel and Restaurant Management, Gipsy Lane, Headington, Oxford, Oxon OX3 0BP, United Kingdom, Tel: 44-1642-751168, http://www.openhouse.org.uk/virtual -university-press/cpd/welcome.htm, Ed. Nigel Hammington. [Q., Great Britain $30, US $50, US $185 with online access.] Contains book reviews concerning online opportunities for continuing education.

Coutler, B. (2000). Making good: Technology choices. **Principal, 79**(3), 18–21. The push to implement classroom technology, regardless of cost or real benefit, often intrudes on making wise choices. Strong technology candidates will provide a compelling extension to ongoing classroom work, be good curriculum enhancers, offer cost-effective software and equipment options, and offer a gentle professional development learning curve.

Eberhart, George M. (2000). **The whole library handbook 3: Current data, professional advice, and curiosa about libraries and library services** (3d ed.). [Book, 569p., $40]. American Library Association. Comprehensive encyclopedia of library history combined with a humorously delivered popular wisdom.

Eisenberg, M., & Berkowitz, R. (2000). **Teaching information & technology skills: The big6™ in secondary schools.** [Book, 216p., $39.95] Linworth. Teaches educators how to teach information technology skills.

Ensor, Pat. (2000). **The cybrarian's manual 2** (2d ed.). [Book, 313p., $45]. American Library Association. This book contains articles from several experts on topics such as citing electronic resources, security, and XML.

Gorman, Michael. (2000). **Our enduring values: Librarianship in the 21st century.** [Book, 188p., $28]. American Library Association. Discusses challenges and trends to providing library service in the twenty-first century.

Hudson, S. J. (2000). "So You Had a Good Day?" Educators learn via e-mail. **Dimensions of Early Childhood, 28**(2), 17–21. Explores the use of e-mail to develop a productive mentoring relationship with a student teacher through her student teaching and first year of teaching. Finds that online discussions provide opportunities to state concerns and offer mentoring ideas in a calm environment. Also finds that both mentor and student share stories that encourage mutual learning.

Journal of Computing in Teacher Education. ISTE, University of Oregon, 1787 Agate Street, Eugene, OR 97403-1923, (800)336-5191, cust_svc@ccmail.uoregon.edu, www.iste.org. [Q., $29, $39 intl., $42 intl. air]. Contains refereed articles on preservice and in-service training, research in computer education and certification issues, and reviews of training materials and texts.

Journal of Technology and Teacher Education. Association for the Advancement of Computing in Education (AACE), P.O. Box 2966, Charlottesville, VA 22902, AACE@virginia .edu, www.aace.org. [Q., $40 US, $50 intnl.]. Serves as an international forum to report research and applications of technology in preservice, in-service, and graduate teacher education.

Kaplan, N. R., & Nelson, M. L. (2000). Determining the publication impact of a digital library. **Journal of the American Society for Information Science, 51**(4), 324–339. Assesses the publication impact of a digital library of aerospace scientific and technical information through usage statistics and citation analysis. Examines the Langley Technical Report Server available on the World Wide Web, compares usage with the hardcopy distribution center, and suggests retrieval analysis as a complementary metric to citation analysis.

Karchmer, R. A. (2000). Understanding teachers' perspectives of Internet use in the classroom: Implications for teacher education and staff development. **Reading and Writing Quarterly: Overcoming Learning Difficulties, 16**(1), 81–85. Notes that many teachers today are envisioning novel ways of integrating the Internet into their daily lessons. Examines how these teachers, experienced with the Internet, integrate the technology into their daily lessons. Suggests their stories, including their successes and failures, can inform teacher education and staff development in powerful ways.

McConnell, T., & Sprouse, H. (2000). **Video production for school library media specialists: Communication and production techniques.** [Book, 240p., $39.95]. Linworth Publishing. Addresses how the media specialist can use video to educate students about television production while also promoting the media program.

McKenzie, Jamie. (2000). **Beyond technology: Questioning, research, and the information literate school.** [Book, 180p., $20] Linworth Publishing. This book examines the potential of research in developing information literacy and improving standardized test scores.

McKenzie, Jamie. (2001). **Planning good change with technology and literacy.** [Book, 180p., $20]. Linworth Publishing. Examines ways to incorporate electronic resources and hardware into schools, making the most of networked information technologies.

Mergendoller, J. R. (2000). Technology and learning: A critical assessment. **Principal, 79**(3), 5–9. The average American school now has one instructional computer for every six students. The next hurdle is adapting educational technology to support and extend student learning. Three keys to success are technological resources, cultural commitment, and effective instructional practices. A sidebar tracks the digital divide between haves and have-nots

Peck, Robert S. (2000). **Libraries, the first amendment, and cyberspace: What you need to know.** [Book, 216p., $32]. American Library Association. Addresses the library responsibilities and rights in protecting intellectual freedom.

Schrock, Kathleen. (2000). **The technology connection: Building a successful school library media program.** [Book, 256p., $39.95]. Linworth Publishing. Addresses library media center management issues, such as funding, training, PR, and curriculum integration.

Sherman, L. (2000). Preparing to lead. **Northwest Education, 5**(3), 40–43. Training programs for principals are generally viewed to be inadequate. Various initiatives in Seattle (Washington) demonstrate that effective programs bridge the gap between theory and practice, use new kinds of delivery systems, incorporate field-based experience, and provide internships. The University of Washington's four-day workshops give state principals and superintendents a crash course in information technologies.

Shotsberger, P. G. (2000). The human touch: Synchronous communication in Web-based learning. **Educational Technology, 40**(1), 53–56. Discusses synchronous communication in learning via the World Wide Web and considers arguments for advantages of asynchronous approaches. Describes a synchronous Web-based professional development program for mathematics teachers in North Carolina and discusses the nature of online communication.

Society for Applied Learning Technology. Society for Applied Learning Technology, 50 Culpeper Street, Warrenton, VA 20186 info@salt.org, http://www.salt.org, Ed. Raymond D Fox. [Q.,]. Provides news, publication reviews, and conference updates for instructional technology professionals

Virtual University Journal. Oxford Brookes University, School of Hotel and Restaurant Management, Gipsy Lane, Headington, Oxon, OX3 0BP, United Kingdom, CR@hrm.brookes .ac.uk, http://www.openhouse.org.uk/virtual-university-press/vuj/welcome.htm, Ed. Clive Roberton. [11/yr., 40 GBP indiv.]. Presents articles related to research in the area of lifelong learning.

Vojtek, B., & Vojtek, R. O. (2000). Off and running. **Journal of Staff Development, 21**(1), 76–78. Discusses the introduction of technological innovations into schools, suggesting that rather than relying on authority-driven initiatives, leaders should initiate change by developing teachers' learning capacities, thus creating environments with widespread commitment. This ensures that the commitment to the initiative is sustained rather than dropped when the leader disappears. Strategies for teacher motivation to learn and use technology are noted.

Wash, S. L., Lovedahl, G. G., & Paige, W. D. (2000). A comparison of traditionally and alternatively certified technology education teachers' professional development and receptivity to change. **Journal of Industrial Teacher Education, 37**(2), 31–46. Survey responses from 240 technology education teachers (two thirds traditionally certified) showed no differences between alternatively and traditionally certified teachers in receptivity to change, participation in professional development, or type of development activity. Alternative certification is recommended as a way to alleviate teacher shortages.

SIMULATION, GAMING, AND VIRTUAL REALITY

Abbey, B. (2000). Instructional and cognitive impacts of Web-based education. Idea Group Publishing. [Book, 300p., $64.95]. Explores the effects of Web-based instructional tools on learning.

Akay, M. (2001). Information technologies in medicine: Medical simulation and education. [Book, 250p., $110.00]. John Wiley and Sons. Explores the use of simulations and virtual reality in medical education.

Barab, Sasha A., Hay, K. E., Squire, K., Barnett, M., Schmidt, R., Karrigan, K., Yamagata-Lynch, L., & Johnson, C. (2000). Virtual Solar System Project: Learning through a technology-rich, inquiry-based, participatory learning environment. **Journal of Science Education and Technology, 9**(1), 7–25. Describes an introductory undergraduate astronomy course in which the large-lecture format was moved to one in which students were immersed in a technologically rich, inquiry-based, participatory learning environment. Finds that virtual reality can be used effectively in regular undergraduate university courses as a tool through which students can develop rich understandings of various astronomical phenomena.

Chen, C., Czerwinski, M., & Macredie, R. (2000). Individual differences in virtual environments—Introduction and overview. **Journal of the American Society for Information Science, 51**(6), 499–507. Presents a brief historical overview of research in individual differences in the context of virtual environments. Highlights the notion of structure in the perception of individual users of an information system and the role of individuals' abilities to recognize and use such structures to perform various information-intensive tasks.

Chidambaram, L., & Zigurs, I. (2001). **Our virtual world: The transformation of work, play and life via technology.** [Book, 300p., $74.95]. IDEA Group, www.idea-group.com. Discusses socialization in virtual groups, the benefits of a virtual environment, online education, and virtual games.

Cooper, G. (2001). **New virtual field trips.** [Book, 155p., $27.50]. Libraries Unlimited.

Dibb, M., Barnes, J., & Cavanaugh, B. (2000). E-classroom extra. Bulletin boards, class newsletters, and greeting cards. **Instructor, 109**(6), 101<196>102. Presents elementary level, standards-based, technology-supported learning activities for the classroom, including: creating a virtual reality bulletin board that lets students become familiar with their computers; developing a weekly newsletter on the computer; and generating personalized greeting cards using SuperPrint 2.0.

Dillon, A. (2000). Spatial-semantics: How users derive shape from information space. **Journal of the American Society for Information Science, 51**(6), 521–528. Discussion of user problems with navigating large spaces in virtual information environments focuses on a top-down application of semantic knowledge by the user from experiences within the sociocognitive context of information production and consumption. Considers individual differences in studies of interaction; spatial and semantic cues; and cognitive and knowledge base differences.

Evans, J. G. Visual Basic science simulations. **Physics Education, 2000, 35**(1), 54–57. Explores the use of computer simulation/modeling programs for teaching a variety of science concepts.

Ford, N. (2000). Cognitive styles and virtual environments. **Journal of the American Society for Information Science, 51**(6), 543–557. Discussion of navigation through virtual information environments focuses on the need for robust user models that take into account individual differences. Considers Pask's information processing styles and strategies;

deep (transformational) and surface (reproductive) learning; field dependence/independence; divergent/convergent thinking; hypertext navigation; database searching; and problems for system development.

Hardesty, L., ed. (2000). **Books, bytes, and bridges: Libraries and computer centers in academic institutions.** [Book, $48].

Mangan, K. A. (2000). Teaching surgery without a patient. **Chronicle of Higher Education, 46**(25), A49–A50. Reports on the increasing use of virtual-reality devices at Pennsylvania State University's Milton S. Hershey Medical Center and other institutions that allow medical residents to practice their skills in simulated operations. Notes that both students and professors are enthusiastic about the simulations but that the necessary technology and devices are expensive.

Nishida, T., ed. (2000). **Dynamic knowledge interaction.** [Book, 296p., $89.95]. CRC Press. Describes an interdisciplinary approach to creating information management system technology that coincides with the cognitive processes of the human mind using artificial intelligence.

Rios, J. M., & Madhavan, S. (2000). Guide to adopting technology in the physics classroom. **Physics Teacher, 38**(2), 94–97. Presents guidelines for equipping physics labs with components from each of four technology-use categories: (1) computer interfacing; (2) modeling; (3) simulations; and (4) research-reference-presentation. Includes references to useful Web sites discussing educational technology.

Robinson, W. R. (2000). A view of the science education research literature: Scientific discovery learning with computer simulations. **Journal of Chemical Education, 77**(1), 17–18. Describes a review of research that addresses the effectiveness of simulations in promoting scientific discovery learning and the problems that learners may encounter when using discovery learning.

Simulation and Gaming. Sage Publications Inc., 2455 Teller Road, Thousand Oaks, CA 91320, order@sagepub.com, www.sagepub.com. [Q., $70 indiv., $317 inst., $19 single issue]. An international journal of theory, design, and research focusing on issues in simulation, gaming, modeling, role-play, and experiential learning.

SPECIAL EDUCATION AND DISABILITIES

Casey, J. (2000). **Early literacy: the empowerment of technology.** [Book, 198p., $27.50]. Libraries Unlimited, www.lu.com. Offers guidance on integrating technology into the elementary level language acquisition classroom through project-based learning activities.

Guptill, A. (2000). Using the Internet to improve student performance. **Teaching Exceptional Children, 32**(4), 16–20. This article discusses the benefits and outcomes of using Internet-based instruction to improve the performance of students with disabilities by developing Internet-based lessons and assessments that target the growth of higher-order thinking skills required on many state assessments. Internet resources for educators are listed.

Jordan, Dale R. (2000). **Understanding and managing learning disabilities in adults. Professional practices in adult education and human resource development series**. Krieger Publishing Company, P.O. Box 9542, Melbourne, FL 32902, (800)724-0025, info@krieger-pub.com, www.web4u.com/krieger-publishing. [Book, 137p., $22.50]. This book reviews learning disabilities (LD) in adults and makes suggestions for helping adults cope with these disabilities. Each chapter covers a type of learning disability or related syndrome or explains characteristics of the brain.

Journal of Special Education Technology. Peabody College of Vanderbilt University, Box 328, Nashville, TN 37203, (615)322-8150. [Q., $30]. The *Journal of Special Education*

Technology provides "information, research, and reports of innovative practices regarding the application of educational technology toward the education of exceptional children."

Langone, J., & Mechling, L. (2000). The effects of a computer-based instructional program with video anchors on the use of photographs for prompting augmentative communication. **Education and Training in Mental Retardation and Developmental Disabilities, 35**(1), 90–105. A study evaluated the use of computer-based video anchors to increase photograph recognition by two students with severe intellectual disabilities. A substantial increase was made in the number of photographs correctly selected with the computer program with results generalizing to selection of photographs on each participant's augmentative communication device.

Lock, R., & Carlson, D. (2000). Planning for effective, enjoyable computer lab use. **Teaching Exceptional Children, 32**(4), 4–7. This article describes how a group of elementary teachers set out to master their instructional software to turn the collection into an effective aid for enabling the success of students with and without disabilities. It discusses planning for systematic intervention and positive outcomes through the use of computer programs.

Mates, B. T., Wakefield, Doug, & Dixon, Judith M. (2000). **Adaptive technology for the Internet: Making electronic resources accessible.** [Book, 224p., $36]. ALA Editions, (800)545-2433, www.ala.org/editions. Provides advice for purchasing and managing adaptive technologies such as screen readers, Braille screens, voice recognition systems, hearing assistance devices, and HTML coding for accessibility for library settings.

Meeting the Needs of All Students with Technology. (2000). [Video, 70 min., $129]. Films for the Humanities & Sciences, www.films.com. Demonstrates how technology can be used to provide equal learning opportunities for students with learning and physical disabilities.

Mioduser, D., Lahav, O., & Nachmias, R. (2000). Using computers to teach remedial spelling to a student with low vision: A case study. **Journal of Visual Impairment & Blindness, 94**(1), 15–25. A study investigates the use of a diagnostic and remedial adaptive computer tool to help an eighth-grader with low vision decrease spelling mistakes. Results indicate a clear change in the students' performance, from phonetic writing to process writing and a gradual evolution to automation in spelling and model word retrieval.

Morgan, R. L., Ellerd, D. A., Gerity, B. P., & Blair, R. J. (2000). That's the job I want! **Teaching Exceptional Children, 32**(4), 44–49. This article describes how educators can use motion video on CD-ROM to provide more information to youth on employment and to represent the complexity of employment environments. The Youth Employment Selections program for helping students and adults with disabilities to understand critical attributes of many jobs is profiled.

Myers, M. (2000). Voice recognition software and a hand-held translation machine for second-language learning. **Computer Assisted Language Learning, 13**(1), 29–41. Presents the results of a research project subsidized by the Social Sciences and Humanities Research Council in Canada. The research constitutes one project of a number in a strategic research network, "EvNet," on the evaluation of computer technologies. The focus here is on the impact of voice recognition software on the language development of nonnative speakers.

Stahl, S. (2000). **Technology and students with special needs.** [Video, 1 hour, 5 min., $179]. Canter www.canter.net. This video is a part of a five module series which aims to show teachers how to use technology to bring relevant knowledge and skills to the classroom.

Wissick, C. A., & Gardner, J. E. (2000). Multimedia or not to multimedia? **Teaching Exceptional Children, 32**(4), 34–43. This article presents instructional factors that teachers should consider when selecting multimedia materials appropriate for students with learning disabilities. Specific programs and Web sites that use design features effectively are discussed, and problematic features in multimedia software packages are described, along with strategies that make appropriate accommodations.

TELECOMMUNICATIONS AND NETWORKING

Boardwatch. Penton Media, P.O. Box 901979, Cleveland, OH 44190-1979. [M., $72 U.S]. The Internet access industry's handbook. Each issue features the leading online editorial covering the Internet, World Wide Web, and the communications industry.

Bosak, S. (2000). Bits in the ether: Wireless LANS leave cables behind. **American School Board Journal, 187**(3) Suppl., 38–39, 41. Due to wiring limitations, network access in schools is often limited to a computer lab and a couple of classroom terminals. By exchanging cables for 500-ft. wireless connections, a South Carolina district has been able to spread network and Internet access where and when it is needed.

Canadian Journal of Educational Communication. Association for Media and Technology in Education in Canada, 3-1750 The Queensway, Suite 1318, Etobicoke, ON M9C 5H5, Canada. [3/yr., $75]. Concerned with all aspects of educational systems and technology.

Classroom Connect. Classroom Connect, 1241 East Hillsdale Boulevard, Suite 100, Foster City, CA USA 94404, (800)638-1639, fax (888)801-8299, orders@classroom.com. [9/yr., $45]. Provides pointers to sources of lesson plans for K–12 educators as well as descriptions of new Web sites, addresses for online "keypals," Internet basics for new users, classroom management tips for using the Internet, and online global projects. Each issue offers Internet adventures for every grade and subject.

Computer Communications. Elsevier Science, Inc., P.O. Box 882, Madison Square Station, New York, NY 10159-0882. [18/yr., $1,181]. Focuses on networking and distributed computing techniques, communications hardware and software, and standardization.

Duhaney, D. C. (2000). Technology and the educational process: Transforming classroom activities. **International Journal of Instructional Media, 27**(1), 67–72. Explores the integration of technology into the education process and some of the changes they have generated in classroom activities. Topics include technology in teaching and learning activities; computer-assisted instruction; the Internet; telecommunications technologies; the classroom environment; and interchange among teachers and students.

EDUCAUSE Review. EDUCAUSE, 1112 Sixteenth Street, NW, Suite 600, Washington, DC 20036-4823, (800)254-4770, info@educause.edu. [Bi-mo., $24 US/Canada/Mexico, $48 elsewhere]. Features articles on current issues and applications of computing and communications technology in higher education. Reports of EDUCAUSE consortium activities.

EMMS (Electronic Mail & Micro Systems). Telecommunications Reports, 1333 H Street NW, 11th Floor-W., Washington, DC 20005, brp.com. [Semi-mo., $765 US]. Covers technology, user, product, and legislative trends in graphic, record, and microcomputer applications.

International Journal of Educational Telecommunications. Association for the Advancement of Computing in Education, P.O. Box 2966, Charlottesville, VA 22901, (804)973-3987, fax (804)978-7449, AACE@virginia.edu, www.aace.org. [Q., $75 indiv., $95 inst., $20 single copy]. Reports on current theory, research, development, and practice of telecommunications in education at all levels.

The Internet and Higher Education. Elsevier Science/Regional Sales Office, Customer Support Department - JAI Books, P.O. Box 945, New York, NY 10159-0945. [Q., $70 indiv., $210 inst.]. Designed to reach faculty, staff, and administrators responsible for enhancing instructional practices and productivity via the use of information technology and the Internet in their institutions.

Internet Reference Services Quarterly. Haworth Press, 10 Alice Street, Binghamton, NY 13904-1580, (800)HAWORTH, fax (800)895-0582, getinfo@haworth.com, www.haworthpress .com. [Q., $36 indiv., $48 institutions, $48 libraries]. Describes innovative information practice, technologies, and practice. For librarians of all kinds.

Internet Research (previously *Electronic Networking: Research, Applications, and Policy*). MCB University Press Ltd., 60-62 Toller Lane, Bradford, W. Yorks. BD8 9BY, England. [Q., $869 US paper & electronic, $369 electronic only]. A cross-disciplinary journal presenting research findings related to electronic networks, analyses of policy issues related to networking, and descriptions of current and potential applications of electronic networking for communication, computation, and provision of information services.

Internet World. Penton Media. Internet World, P.O. Box 901979, Cleveland, OH 44190-1979, www.iw.com. [M., $160 U.S., $200 Canada, $295 elsewhere]. Analyzes developments of the Internet, electronic networking, publishing, and scholarly communication, as well as other network issues of interest to a wide range of network users.

Journal of Online Learning. ISTE, University of Oregon, 1787 Agate Street, Eugene, OR 97403-1923, (800)336-5191, cust_svc@ccmail.uoregon.edu, www.iste.org. [Q., $29, $39 intl., $42 intl. air]. Reports activities in the areas of communications, projects, research, publications, international connections, and training.

Link-Up. Information Today, 143 Old Marlton Pike, Medford, NJ 08055, (800)300-9868. [Bi-mo., $32.95 US, $40 Canada/Mexico; $60 elsewhere]. News magazine for individuals interested in small computer communications; covers hardware, software, communications services, and search methods.

Network Magazine. CMP Media INC, 600 Harrison Street, San Francisco, CA 94107, www.networkmagazine.com. [Mo., $125]. Provides users with news and analysis of changing technology for the networking of computers.

Online. Online, Inc., 213 Danbury Road, Wilton, CT 06897, www.onlineinc.com/onlinemag/. [6/yr., $55 US, half-off special]. For online information system users. Articles cover a variety of online applications for general and business use.

Online-Offline. Rock Hill Press, 14 Rock Hill Road, Bala Cynwyd, PA 19004, (888)ROCK HILL, fax (610)667-2291, www.rockhillpress.com. [9/yr., $66.50]. Examines classroom resources, linking curricular themes with Web sites and other media.

Telecommunications. (North American Edition.) Horizon House Publications, Inc., 685 Canton St., Norwood, MA 02062. [Mo., $130 US, $210 elsewhere, free to qualified individuals]. Feature articles and news for the field of telecommunications.

Weathers, B. (2001). Life among the laptops: A Texas school experiences the joys of going wireless. **School Library Journal 47**(3), 56–60. Describes the successes and challenges and adaptations made by a school that has provided each student with a wireless laptop since 1998.

Index

A+ Education Reform Bill, 163
(AACC) Community College Satellite Network
    (CCSN), 242–43
Abbey, B.
    "Instructional and cognitive impacts of
        Web-based education," 379
Academy of Motion Picture Arts and Sciences
    (AMPAS), 228
ACCESS ERIC, 247
ACCESS NETWORK, 286
Adams, C.
    "Distance learning opportunities for aca-
        demically gifted students," 352
Adaptech Research Project, 286
Administration
    Technology Standards for School Adminis-
        trators (TSSA) and, 107–8
AECT Archives, 237
(AECT) Division of Educational Media Man-
    agement (DEMM), 235
(AECT) Division of Instructional Development
    (DID), 235
(AECT) Division of Interactive Systems and
    Computers (DISC), 235
(AECT) Division of Learning and Performance
    Environment (DLPE), 235
(AECT) Division of School Media Specialists
    (DSMS), 235–36
(AECT) Division of Telecommunications
    (DOT), 236
(AECT) Industrial Training and Education
    Division (ITED), 236
(AECT) International Division (INTL), 236
(AECT) Media Design and Production Division
    (MDPD), 236
(AECT) Research and Theory Division (RTD),
    236–37
(AECT) Systemic Change in Education Divi-
    sion (CHANGE), 237
AEL, Inc., 233
Agency for Instructional Technology (AIT),
    228
Aggarwal, A.
    "Web-based learning and teaching technolo-
        gies: Opportunities and chal-
        lenges," 346
Ahern, T.
    "Improving the instructional congruency
        of a computer-mediated
        small-group discussion: A case
        study in design and delivery,"
        365

Akay, M.
    "Information technologies in medicine:
        Medical simulation and
        education," 379
Alabama
    **graduate programs in instructional tech-
        nology, 299–300**
American Association of Community Colleges
    (AACC), 228, 242–43
American Association of School Librarians
    (AASL), 229
American Association of State Colleges and
    Universities, 229
American Educational Research Association
    (AERA), 229
American Educational Research Journal, 356
American Foundation for the Blind (AFB),
    229–30
American Journal of Distance Education, 353
American Library Association (ALA), 230
    Information Power, 89
American Library Trustee Association (ALTA),
    230
American Management Association (AMA),
    230–31
American Montessori Society (AMS), 231
American Society for Training and Develop-
    ment (ASTD), 231–32
American Society of Cinematographers (ASC),
    232
American Society of Educators (ASE), 232–33
American Women in Radio and Television
    (AWRT), 233
Anglin, Gary
    "Instructional Technology: Past, Present and
        Future," 20
Anthropology Film Center (AFC), 233
Appropriate Technology, 358
Arizona
    **graduate programs in instructional tech-
        nology, 300–301**
Arkansas
    **graduate programs in instructional tech-
        nology, 301–2**
Arnold, K. M.
    "Organizational change in the information
        society: Impact on skills and
        training," 364
Artificial Intelligence Review, 344
Assessment
    of critical thinking (CT), 53–57
    of web-based courses, 206–7